Fourth Edition

MANAGEMENT SCIENCE
The Art of Modeling with Spreadsheets

Fourth Edition

MANAGEMENT SCIENCE
The Art of Modeling with Spreadsheets

STEPHEN G. POWELL

Dartmouth College

KENNETH R. BAKER

Dartmouth College

Vice President and Publisher	*George Hoffman*
Executive Editor	*Lise Johnson*
Project Editor	*Brian Baker*
Editorial Assistant	*Jacqueline Hughes*
Director of Marketing	*Amy Scholz*
Senior Marketing Manager	*Kelly Simmons*
Marketing Assistant	*Marissa Carroll*
Design Director	*Harry Nolan*
Product Designer	*Allison Morris*
Senior Production & Manufacturing Manager	*Janis Soo*
Associate Production Manager	*Joel Balbin*

This book was set in 10/12 Times Roman by Thomson Digital and printed and bound by Courier Kendallville. The cover was printed by Courier Kendallville.

This book is printed on acid free paper.

Founded in 1807, John Wiley & Sons, Inc. has been a valued source of knowledge and understanding for more than 200 years, helping people around the world meet their needs and fulfill their aspirations. Our company is built on a foundation of principles that include responsibility to the communities we serve and where we live and work. In 2008, we launched a Corporate Citizenship Initiative, a global effort to address the environmental, social, economic, and ethical challenges we face in our business. Among the issues we are addressing are carbon impact, paper specifications and procurement, ethical conduct within our business and among our vendors, and community and charitable support. For more information, please visit our website: www.wiley.com/go/citizenship.

Library of Congress Cataloging-in-Publication Data

Powell, Stephen G.
  Management science : the art of modeling with spreadsheets / Stephen G. Powell, Dartmouth College, Kenneth R. Baker, Dartmouth College. — Fourth Edition.
      pages cm
  Includes bibliographical references and index.
    ISBN 978-1-118-58269-5 (pbk. : alk. paper)   1.   Business–Computer simulation.   2.   Electronic spreadsheets.
I. Baker, Kenneth R., 1943-   II. Title.
  HF5548.2.P654 2014
  650.01′13–dc23
                                                                                                                2013031236

Printed in the United States of America
10 9 8 7 6 5 4 3 2

To Becky and Judy,
for all their encouragement and support

Brief Contents

Table of Contents

Preface

This is a book for business analysts about *modeling*. A *model* is a simplified representation of a situation or problem, and *modeling* is the process of building, refining, and analyzing that representation for greater insight and improved decision making. Some models are so common that they are thought of as routine instruments rather than models. A budget, a cash flow projection, or a business plan may have many uses, but each one is a model. In addition, many sophisticated models are embedded in software. Option pricing models, credit scoring models, or inventory models are key components of important decision-support systems. Beyond these types, we encounter many customized models, built by the millions of people who routinely use spreadsheet software to analyze business situations. This group includes consultants, venture capitalists, marketing analysts, and operations specialists. Almost anyone who uses spreadsheets in business has been involved with models and can benefit from formal training in the use of models.

Models also play a central role in management education. A short list of models that nearly every business student encounters would include cash flow models, stock price models, option pricing models, product life cycle models, market diffusion models, order quantity models, and project scheduling models. For the management student, a basic ability to model in spreadsheets can be a powerful tool for acquiring a deeper understanding of the various functional areas of business. But to fully understand the implications of these models, a student needs to appreciate what a model is and how to learn from it. Our book provides that knowledge.

For many years, modeling was performed primarily by highly trained specialists using mainframe computers. Consequently, even a simple model was costly and frequently required a long development time. The assumptions and results often seemed impenetrable to business managers because they were removed from the modeling process. This situation has changed radically with the advent of personal computers and electronic spreadsheets. Now, managers and analysts can build their own models and produce their own analyses. This new kind of modeling is known as *end-user modeling*. Now that virtually every analyst has access to a powerful computer, the out-of-pocket costs of modeling have become negligible. The major cost now is the analyst's *time*: time to define the problem, gather the data, build and debug a model, and use the model to support the decision process. For this time to be well spent, the analyst must be efficient and effective in the modeling process. This book is designed to improve modeling *efficiency* by focusing on the most important tasks and tools and by suggesting how to avoid unproductive steps in the modeling effort. This book is also designed to improve modeling *effectiveness* by introducing the most relevant analytic methods and emphasizing procedures that lead to the deepest business insights.

One of our reasons for writing this book was the conviction that many analysts were not being appropriately educated as modelers. Business students tend to receive strong training in management science but little training in practical modeling. They often receive inadequate training, as well, in using spreadsheets for modeling. In most educational programs, the emphasis is on *models*, rather than on *modeling*. That is, the curriculum covers a number of classical models that have proven useful in management education or in business. Although studying the classics may be valuable for a number of reasons (and our book covers a number of the classics), studying models does not provide the full range of skills needed to build models for new situations. We also have met many analysts who view modeling essentially as a matter of having strong spreadsheet skills. But spreadsheet skills are not sufficient. The spreadsheet is only one tool in the creative, open-ended problem-solving process we call modeling. Modeling is both a technical discipline and a *craft*. The craft aspects of the process have largely been overlooked in the education of business analysts. Our purpose is to provide both the technical knowledge and the craft skills needed to develop real expertise in business modeling. In this book, therefore, we cover the three skill areas that a business analyst needs to become an effective modeler:

- spreadsheet engineering
- management science
- modeling craft

NEW IN THE FOURTH EDITION

The major change in this latest version of our text is to our coverage of data analysis. Business analysts are increasingly expected to analyze complex datasets and employ data mining algorithms. Whereas previous editions focused on classical statistical methods, in this edition we introduce coverage of data exploration and data mining. We shift our focus from explanatory modeling to predictive modeling, and downplay the use of hypothesis tests in favor of the modern emphasis on predictive performance using validation data. We use the software XLMiner to support data exploration and data mining. XLMiner is one component of the integrated software suite Analytic Solver Platform, which we use throughout the book.

In addition to these innovations, we have revised the text in a number of ways to make it more streamlined and adaptable to different uses. We have moved the treatment of basic Excel skills and Visual Basic for Applications into separate appendices, and we have collected background material on basic probability and statistics into two other appendices. We have also updated a number of chapters to make them compatible with the latest version of Analytic Solver Platform.

TO THE READER

Modeling, like painting or singing, cannot be learned entirely from a book. However, a book can establish principles, provide examples, and offer additional practice. We suggest that the reader take an *active learning* attitude toward this book. This means working to internalize the skills taught here by tackling as many new problems as possible. It also means applying these skills to everyday situations in other classes or on the job. Modeling expertise (as opposed to modeling appreciation) can be acquired only by *doing* modeling. There is no substitute for experience.

The book is organized into four parts:

- Spreadsheet modeling in the context of problem solving (Chapters 1–4)
- Data analysis (Chapters 5–7)
- Optimization (Chapters 8–12)
- Decision analysis and simulation (Chapters 13–15)

Our table of contents provides details on the topic coverage in the various chapters, and in Chapter 1 we provide a diagram of the prerequisite logic among the chapters. Several chapters contain advanced material in sections marked with (*). Students can find spreadsheet files for all models presented in the text on the website at www.wiley.com/college/powell.

TO THE TEACHER

It is far easier to teach technical skills in Excel or in management science than it is to teach modeling. Nonetheless, modeling skills *can* be taught successfully, and a variety of effective approaches are available. Feedback from users of our book and from reviewers of previous editions suggests that there are almost as many course designs as there are instructors for this subject. Our book does not represent an idealized version of our own course; rather, it is intended to be a versatile resource that can support a selection of topics in management science, spreadsheet engineering, and modeling craft.

At the book's website, www.wiley.com/college/powell, we provide some teaching tips and describe our views on the different ways that this material can be delivered successfully in a graduate or undergraduate course. All spreadsheet files for the models in the text, as well as PowerPoint slides, can be found on the site. In addition, we provide some sample syllabi to suggest the course designs that other instructors have delivered with the help of this book. For access to the Analytic Solver Platform for Education software, contact Frontline Systems at academic@solver.com or call 775-831-0300.

SOFTWARE ACCOMPANYING THE FOURTH EDITION

Users of the Fourth Edition have access to spreadsheet files for all the models presented in the text. Users also have access to Analytic Solver Platform for Education, an integrated software platform for sensitivity analysis, optimization, decision trees, data exploration and data mining, and simulation.

Purchasers of a new text (and its electronic format) have access to Analytic Solver Platform for Education through their course instructor – see www.solver.com/student. Instructors, and purchasers not enrolled in a course, may contact Frontline Systems Inc. at academic@solver.com or 775-831-0300.

ACKNOWLEDGMENTS

A book such as this evolves over many years of teaching and research. Our ideas have been influenced by our students and by other teachers, not all of whom we can acknowledge here. Our students at Dartmouth's Tuck School of Business have participated in many of our teaching experiments and improved our courses through their invaluable feedback. Without the collaborative spirit our students bring to their education, we could not have developed our ideas as we have.

As in the first edition, we wish to mention the many excellent teachers and writers whose ideas we have adapted. We acknowledge Don Plane, Cliff Ragsdale, and Wayne Winston for their pioneering work in teaching management science with spreadsheets, and the later influence of Tom Grossman, Peter Bell, Zeger Degraeve, and Erhan Erkut on our work.

The first edition benefited from careful reviews from the following reviewers: Jerry Allison (University of Central Oklahoma), Jonathan Caulkins (Carnegie-Mellon University), Jean-Louis Goffin (McGill University), Roger Grinde (University of New Hampshire), Tom Grossman (University of Calgary), Raymond Hill (Air Force Institute of Technology), Alan Johnson (United States Military Academy), Prafulla Joglekar (LaSalle University), Tarja Joro (University of Alberta), Ron Klimberg (Saint Joseph's University), Larry Leblanc (Vanderbilt University), Jerry May (University of Pittsburgh), Jim Morris (University of Wisconsin), Jim Mote (RPI), Chuck Noon (University of Tennessee), Tava Olsen (Washington University), Fred Raafat (San Diego State University), Gary Reeves (University of South Carolina), Moshe Rosenwein (Columbia University), David Schilling (Ohio State University), Linus Schrage (University of Chicago), Donald Simmons (Ithaca College), George Steiner (McMaster University), and Stephen Thorpe (Drexel University).

Additional feedback and help on the second edition came from the following: R. Kim Craft (Southern Utah University), Joan Donohue (University of South Carolina), Steve Ford (University of the South), Phillip Fry (Boise State University), Li Guodong (Maryville University), LeRoy Honeycutt (Gardner-Webb University), Rich Kilgore (St. Louis University), Frank Krzystofiak (University at Buffalo SUNY), Shailesh Kulkarni (University of North Texas), Dale Lehman (Alaska Pacific University), Vedran Lelas (Plymouth State University), David Walter Little (High Point University), Leo Lopes (University of Arizona), Alvin J. Martinez (University of Puerto Rico, Rio Piedras), Jacquelynne McLellan (Frostburg State University), Ajay Mishra (Binghamton University SUNY), Shimon Y. Nof (Purdue University), Manuel Nunez (University of Connecticut), Alan Olinsky (Bryant University), Tava Olsen (Washington University), Susan Palocsay (James Madison University), Ganga P. Ramdas (Lincoln University), B. Madhu Rao (Bowling Green State University), Jim Robison (Sonoma State University), Christopher M. Rump (Bowling Green State University), Thomas Sandman (California State

University, Sacramento), Sergei Savin (Columbia University), Daniel Shimshak (University of Massachusetts Boston), Minghe Sun (University of Texas at San Antonio), and David Tufte (Southern Utah University).

Beth Golub of John Wiley & Sons encouraged us to write this book for years and supported us in writing a new kind of textbook. She also tapped an extensive network of contacts for feedback and helped us improve successive editions. With the Third Edition, the responsibility passed from Beth to Lisé Johnson, who has continued the supportive editorial process we have come to appreciate.

SGP
KRB

About The Authors

Steve Powell is a Professor at the Tuck School of Business at Dartmouth College. His primary research interest lies in modeling production and service processes, but he has also been active in research in energy economics, marketing, and operations. At Tuck, he has developed a variety of courses in management science, including the core Decision Science course and electives in the Art of Modeling, Collaborative Problem Solving, Business Process Redesign, and Simulation. He originated the Teacher's Forum column in *Interfaces*, and has written a number of articles on teaching modeling to practitioners. He was the Academic Director of the annual INFORMS Teaching of Management Science Workshops. In 2001 he was awarded the INFORMS Prize for the Teaching of Operations Research/Management Science Practice. Along with Ken Baker, he has directed the Spreadsheet Engineering Research Project. In 2008 he co-authored *Modeling for Insight: A Master Class for Business Analysts* with Robert J. Batt.

Ken Baker is a faculty member at Dartmouth College. He is currently Nathaniel Leverone Professor of Management at the Tuck School of Business and Adjunct Professor at the Thayer School of Engineering. At Dartmouth, he has taught courses relating to Management Science, Decision Support Systems, Manufacturing Management, and Environmental Management. Along with Steve Powell, he has directed the Spreadsheet Engineering Research Project. He is the author of two other textbooks, *Optimization Modeling with Spreadsheets* and *Principles of Sequencing and Scheduling* (with Dan Trietsch), in addition to a variety of technical articles. He has served as Tuck School's Associate Dean and as the Co-Director of the Master's Program in Engineering Management. He is an INFORMS Fellow as well as a Fellow of the Manufacturing and Service Operations Management (MSOM) Society.

1 Introduction

Modeling is the process of creating a simplified representation of reality and working with this representation in order to understand or control some aspect of the world. While this book is devoted to *mathematical* models, modeling itself is a ubiquitous human activity. In fact, it seems to be one of just a few fundamental ways in which we humans understand our environment.

As an example, a map is one of the most common models we encounter. Maps are models because they simplify reality by leaving out most geographic details in order to highlight the important features we need. A state road map, for example, shows major roads but not minor ones, gives rough locations of cities but not individual addresses, and so on. The map we choose must be appropriate for the need we have: a long trip across several states requires a regional map, while a trip across town requires a detailed street map. In the same way, a good model must be appropriate for the specific uses intended for it. A complex model of the economy is probably not appropriate for pricing an individual product. Similarly, a back-of-the-envelope calculation is likely to be inappropriate for acquiring a multibillion-dollar company.

Models take many different forms: mental, visual, physical, mathematical, and spreadsheet, to name a few. We use mental models constantly to understand the world and to predict the outcomes of our actions. Mental models are informal, but they do allow us to make a quick judgment about the desirability of a particular proposal. For example, mental models come into play in a hiring decision. One manager has a mental model that suggests that hiring older workers is not a good idea because they are slow to adopt new ways; another manager has a mental model that suggests hiring older workers is a good idea because they bring valuable experience to the job. We are often unaware of our own mental models, yet they can have a strong influence on the actions we take, especially when they are the primary basis for decision making.

While everyone uses mental models, some people routinely use other kinds of models in their professional lives. Visual models include maps, as we mentioned earlier. Organization charts are also visual models. They may represent reporting relationships, reveal the locus of authority, suggest major channels of communication, and identify responsibility for personnel decisions. Visual models are used in various sports, for instance, as when a coach sketches the playing area and represents team members and opponents as X's and O's. Most players probably don't realize that they are using a model for the purposes of understanding and communication.

Physical models are used extensively in engineering to assist in the design of airplanes, ships, and buildings. They are also used in science, as, for example, in depicting the spatial arrangement of amino acids in the DNA helix or the makeup of a chemical compound. Architects use physical models to show how a proposed building fits within its surroundings.

Mathematical models take many forms and are used throughout science, engineering, and public policy. For instance, a groundwater model helps determine where flooding is most likely to occur, population models predict the spread of infectious disease, and exposure-assessment models forecast the impact of toxic spills. In other settings, traffic-flow models predict the buildup of highway congestion, fault-tree models help reveal the causes of an accident, and reliability models suggest when equipment may need replacement. Mathematical models can be extremely powerful, especially when they give clear insights into the forces driving a particular outcome.

1.1.1 Why Study Modeling?

What are the benefits of building and using formal models, as opposed to relying on mental models or just "gut feel?" The primary purpose of modeling is to generate *insight*, by which we mean an improved understanding of the situation or problem at hand. While mathematical models consist of numbers and symbols, the real benefit of using them is to make better *decisions*. Better decisions are most often the result of improved understanding, not just the numbers themselves.

Thus, we study modeling primarily because it improves our thinking skills. Modeling is a discipline that provides a structure for problem solving. The fundamental elements of a model—such as parameters, decisions, and outcomes—are useful concepts in all problem solving. Modeling provides examples of clear and logical analysis and helps raise the level of our thinking.

Modeling also helps improve our quantitative reasoning skills. Building a model demands care with units and with orders of magnitude, and it teaches the importance of numeracy. Many people are cautious about quantitative analysis because they do not trust their own quantitative skills. In the best cases, a well-structured modeling experience can help such people overcome their fears, build solid quantitative skills, and improve their performance in a business world that demands (and rewards) these skills.

Any model is a laboratory in which we can experiment and learn. An effective modeler needs to develop an open, inquiring frame of mind to go along with the necessary technical skills. Just as a scientist uses the laboratory to test ideas, hypotheses, and theories, a business analyst can use a model to test the implications of alternative courses of action and develop not only a recommended decision but, equally important, the rationale for why that decision is preferred. The easy-to-understand rationale behind the recommendation often comes from insights the analyst has discovered while testing a model.

1.1.2 Models in Business

Given the widespread use of mathematical models in science and engineering, it is not surprising to find that they are also widely used in the business world. We refer to people who routinely build and analyze formal models in their professional lives as **business analysts**. In our years of training managers and management students, we have found that strong modeling skills are particularly important for consultants, as well as for financial analysts, marketing researchers, entrepreneurs, and others who face challenging business decisions of real economic consequence. Practicing business analysts and students intending to become business analysts are the intended audience for this book.

Just as there are many types of models in science, engineering, public policy, and other domains outside of business, many different types of models are used in business. We distinguish here four model types that exemplify different levels of interaction with, and participation by, the people who use the models:

- One-time decision models
- Decision-support models
- Models embedded in computer systems
- Models used in business education

Many of the models business analysts create are used in **one-time decision problems**. A corporate valuation model, for example, might be used intensively during merger negotiations but never thereafter. In other situations, a one-time model might be created to evaluate the profit impact of a promotion campaign, or to help select a health insurance provider, or to structure the terms of a supply contract. One-time models are usually built by decision makers themselves, frequently under time pressure. Managerial judgment is often used as a substitute for empirical data in such models, owing to time constraints and data limitations. Most importantly, this type of model involves the user intensively because the model is usually tailored to a particular decision-making need. One major benefit of studying modeling is to gain skills in building and using one-time models effectively.

Decision-support systems are computer systems that tie together models, data, analysis tools, and presentation tools into a single integrated package. These systems are intended for repeated use, either by executives themselves or by their analytic staff. Decision-support systems are used in research and development planning at pharmaceutical firms, pricing decisions at oil companies, and product-line profitability analysis at manufacturing firms, to cite just a few examples. Decision-support systems are usually built and maintained by information systems personnel, but they represent the routine use of what were once one-time decision models. After a one-time model becomes established, it can be adapted for broader and more frequent use in the organization. Thus, the models within decision-support systems may initially be developed by managers and business analysts, but later streamlined by information systems staff for a less intensive level of human interaction. An additional benefit of studying modeling is to recognize possible improvements in the design and operation of decision-support systems.

Embedded models are those contained within computer systems that perform routine, repeated tasks with little or no human involvement. Many inventory replenishment decisions are made by automated computer systems. Loan payments on auto leases or prices for stock options are also determined by automated systems. Routine real estate appraisals may also be largely automated. In these cases, the models themselves are somewhat hidden in the software. Many users of embedded models are not aware of the underlying models; they simply assume that the "system" knows how to make the right calculations. An ancillary benefit of studying modeling is to become more aware, and perhaps more questioning, of these embedded models.

1.1.3 Models in Business Education

Models are useful not only in the business world, but also in the academic world where business analysts are educated. The modern business curriculum is heavily dependent on models for delivering basic concepts as well as for providing numerical results. An introductory course in Finance might include an option-pricing model, a cash-management model, and the classic portfolio model. A basic Marketing course might include demand curves for pricing analysis, a diffusion model for new-product penetration, and clustering models for market segmentation. In Operations Management, we might encounter inventory models for stock control, allocation models for scheduling production, and newsvendor models for trading off shortage and surplus outcomes. Both micro- and macroeconomics are taught almost exclusively through models. Aggregate supply-and-demand curves are models, as are production functions.

Most of the models used in education are highly simplified, or *stylized*, in order to preserve clarity. Stylized models are frequently used to provide insight into qualitative phenomena, not necessarily to calculate precise numerical results. In this book, we frequently use models from business education as examples, so that we can combine learning about business with learning about models. In fact, the tools presented in this book can be used throughout the curriculum to better understand the various functional areas of business.

1.1.4 Benefits of Business Models

Modeling can benefit business decision making in a variety of ways.

- Modeling allows us to make inexpensive errors. Wind-tunnel tests are used in airplane design partly because if every potential wing design had to be built into a full-scale aircraft and flown by a pilot, we would lose far too many pilots. In a similar way, we can propose ideas and test them in a model, without having to suffer the consequences of bad ideas in the real world.

- Modeling allows us to explore the impossible. Many companies have policies, procedures, or habits that prevent them from making certain choices. Sometimes these habits prevent them from discovering better ways of doing business. Modeling can be used to explore these "impossible" alternatives and to help convince the skeptics to try a different approach.

- Modeling can improve business intuition. As we have said, a model is a laboratory in which we perform experiments. We can usually learn faster from laboratory experiments than from experience in the real world. With a model, we can try thousands of combinations that would take many years to test in the real world. We can also try extreme ideas that would be too risky to test in the real world. And we can learn about how the world works by simulating a hundred years of experience in just a few seconds.

- Modeling provides information in a timely manner. For example, while a survey could be used to determine the potential demand for a product, effective modeling can often give useful bounds on the likely range of demand in far less time.

- Finally, modeling can reduce costs. Data collection is often expensive and time-consuming. An effective modeler may be able to provide the same level of information at a much lower cost.

Even among those who do not build models, skill in working with models is very important. Most business students eventually find themselves on a team charged with recommending a course of action. If these teams do not build models themselves, they often work with internal or external consultants who do. Experience in building and analyzing models is, in our minds, the best training for working effectively on problem-solving teams. People who have not actually built a few models themselves often accept model results blindly or become intimidated by the modeling process. A well-trained analyst not only appreciates the power of modeling but also remains skeptical of models as panaceas.

We believe that modeling skills are useful to a very broad range of businesspeople, from junior analysts without a business degree to senior vice presidents who do their own analysis. Many recent graduates have only a superficial knowledge of these tools because their education emphasized passive consumption of other people's models rather than active model building. Thus, there is considerable potential even among master's-level graduates to improve their modeling skills so that they can become more capable of carrying out independent analyses of important decisions. The only absolute prerequisite for using this book and enhancing that skill is a desire to use logical, analytic methods to reach a higher level of understanding in the decision-making world.

1.2 THE ROLE OF SPREADSHEETS

Because spreadsheets are the principal vehicle for modeling in business, spreadsheet models are the major type we deal with in this book. Spreadsheet models are also mathematical models, but, for many people, spreadsheet mathematics is more accessible than algebra or calculus. Spreadsheet models do have limitations, of course, but they allow us to build more detailed and more complex models than traditional mathematics allows. They also have the advantage of being pervasive in business analysis. Finally, the spreadsheet format corresponds nicely to the form of accounting statements that are used for business communication; in fact, the word "spreadsheet" originates in accounting and only recently has come to mean the electronic spreadsheet.

It has been said that the spreadsheet is the *second best* way to do many kinds of analysis and is therefore the *best* way to do most modeling. In other words, for any one modeling task, a more powerful, flexible, and sophisticated software tool is almost certainly available. In this sense, the spreadsheet is the Swiss Army knife of business analysis. Most business analysts lack the time, money, and knowledge to learn and use a different software tool for each problem that arises, just as most of us cannot afford to carry around a complete toolbox to handle the occasional screw we need to tighten. The practical alternative is to use the spreadsheet (and occasionally one of its sophisticated add-ins) to perform most modeling tasks. An effective modeler will, of course, have a sense for the limitations of a spreadsheet and will know when to use a more powerful tool.

Despite its limitations, the electronic spreadsheet represents a breakthrough technology for practical modeling. Prior to the 1980s, modeling was performed only by specialists using demanding software on expensive hardware. This meant that only the most critical business problems could be analyzed using models because only these problems justified the large budgets and long time commitments required to build, debug, and apply the models of the day. This situation has changed dramatically in the past 20 years or so. First the personal computer, then the spreadsheet, and recently the arrival of add-ins for specialized analyses have put tremendous analytical power at the hands of anyone who can afford a laptop and some training. In fact, we believe the 1990s will come to be seen as the dawn of the "end-user modeling" era. End-user modelers are analysts who are not specialists in modeling, but who can create an effective spreadsheet and manipulate it for insight. The problems that end-user modelers can solve are typically not the multibillion-dollar, multiyear variety; those are still the preserve of functional-area specialists and sophisticated computer scientists. Rather, the end user can apply modeling effectively to hundreds of important but smaller-scale situations that in the past would not have benefited from this approach. We provide many illustrations throughout this book.

Spreadsheet skills themselves are now in high demand in many jobs, although experts in Excel may not be skilled modelers. In our recent survey of MBAs from the Tuck School of Business (available at http://mba.tuck.dartmouth.edu/spreadsheet/), we found that 77 percent said that spreadsheets were either "very important" or "critical" in their work. Good training in spreadsheet modeling, in what we call **spreadsheet engineering**, is valuable because it can dramatically improve both the efficiency and effectiveness with which the analyst uses spreadsheets.

1.2.1 Risks of Spreadsheet Use

Countless companies and individuals rely on spreadsheets every day. Most users assume their spreadsheet models are error-free. However, the available evidence suggests just the opposite: many, perhaps most, spreadsheets contain internal errors, and more errors are introduced as these spreadsheets are used and modified. Given this evidence, and the tremendous risks of relying on flawed spreadsheet models, it is critically important to learn how to create spreadsheets that are as close to error-free as possible and to use spreadsheets in a disciplined way to avoid mistakes.

It is rare to read press reports on problems arising from erroneous spreadsheets. Most companies do not readily admit to these kinds of mistakes. However, the few reports that have surfaced are instructive. For many years the European Spreadsheet Risks Interest Group (EUSPRIG) has maintained a website (http://www.eusprig.org/horror-stories.htm) that documents dozens of verified stories about spreadsheet errors that have had a quantifiable impact on the organization. Here is just a small sample:

- Some candidates for police officer jobs are told that they have passed the test when in fact they have failed. Reason: improper sorting of the spreadsheet.
- An energy company overcharges consumers between $200 million and $1 billion. Reason: careless naming of spreadsheet files.
- A think-tank reports that only 11 percent of a local population has at least a bachelor's degree when in fact the figure is 20 percent. Reason: a copy-and-paste error in a spreadsheet.
- Misstated earnings lead the stock price of an online retailer to fall 25 percent in a day and the CEO to resign. Reason: a single erroneous numerical input in a spreadsheet.
- A school loses £30,000 because its budget is underestimated. Reason: numbers entered as text in a spreadsheet.
- The Business Council reports that its members forecast slow growth for the coming year when their outlook is actually quite optimistic. Reason: the spreadsheet shifted, so the wrong numbers appeared in the wrong columns.
- Benefits of unbundling telecommunication services are understated by $50 million. Reason: incorrect references in a spreadsheet formula.

These cases suggest that spreadsheets can lead to costly errors in a variety of ways. But are spreadsheets themselves properly *built* in the first place? Apparently they are not, at least according to several research studies. In our own investigation of 50 spreadsheets that were being used by various organizations, fewer than 10 percent were free of errors.[1] This evidence serves notice that errors in spreadsheets may be rampant and insidious.

Despite the research evidence, very few corporations employ even the most basic design methodologies and error-detection procedures. These procedures take time and effort, whereas one of the great appeals of spreadsheet modeling is that it can be done

---

[1] S. Powell, K. Baker and B. Lawson, "Errors in Operational Spreadsheets," *Journal of End User Computing* 21, (July–September, 2009): 24–36.

quickly and easily, even by business analysts who are not professional programmers. But ease of use is a delusion if the results contain significant errors.

Briefly stated, the business world is still at an early stage of understanding how to develop error-free spreadsheets. Organizations are in need of better methods for detecting errors and more reliable procedures for preventing errors in the first place. However, the research literature on these topics has not advanced very far, and the state of the art remains somewhat primitive.

1.2.2 Challenges for Spreadsheet Users

Spreadsheets represent the ubiquitous software platform of business. Millions of spreadsheet models are used each day to make decisions involving billions of dollars, and thousands of new spreadsheets come into being each day. Given this usage pattern, we might think that spreadsheet engineering is a well-developed discipline and that expertise in spreadsheet modeling can be found in just about any company. Amazingly, the opposite is true.

What is the current state of spreadsheet use by end-user modelers? The evidence available from audits of existing spreadsheets, laboratory experiments, surveys of end users, and field visits suggests that, despite widespread use, the quality with which spreadsheets are engineered generally remains poor. There are four major problem areas:

- End-user spreadsheets frequently have bugs.
- End users are overconfident about the quality of their own spreadsheets.
- The process that end users employ to create their spreadsheets is inefficient at best and chaotic at worst.
- End users fail to employ the most productive methods for generating insights from their spreadsheets.

Our own research, conducted as part of the Spreadsheet Engineering Research Project (http://mba.tuck.dartmouth.edu/spreadsheet/), found that a substantial majority of spreadsheets in use contain at least one error. A follow-up study found that most of these errors had a substantial impact on the quantitative analysis in the spreadsheets. However, our investigation also suggested that errors in individual cells may be only a symptom. The underlying cause often seems to be a high degree of complexity in the model, even when the corresponding problem is relatively simple. Complexity arises in many ways:

- Individual cell formulas that are excessively long and involved
- Poorly designed worksheets that are difficult to navigate and understand
- Poorly organized workbooks whose underlying structure is concealed

Spreadsheets that are overly complex and difficult for anyone other than the designer to use, even if they are technically correct, may be the cause of some of the costly mistakes attributed to spreadsheets.

Laboratory experiments have uncovered another disturbing fact about spreadsheet modeling: end users appear to be overconfident about the likelihood of errors in their own spreadsheets. In these experiments, undergraduate volunteers were asked to build a spreadsheet for a well-defined problem. After they were done, the volunteers were given time to review and audit their models. Finally, they were asked to evaluate the likelihood that their model contained one or more bugs. While 18 percent of the subjects thought their models had one or more bugs, the actual proportion proved to be 80 percent. That is, 80 percent of these spreadsheets actually had bugs, but only about 18 percent of those who built them suspected they had bugs. This finding of overconfidence is consistent with the findings of other studies: people tend to underestimate the possibility that they might make mistakes. Unfortunately, this overconfidence translates directly into a casual attitude toward spreadsheet design and ultimately into a disturbingly high error rate among spreadsheets in actual use.

Our observations and research into how end users actually construct spreadsheets suggest that the process is often inefficient:

- End users typically do not plan their spreadsheets. Instead, they build them live at the keyboard. The result in many cases is extensive rework. (In our survey of MBA graduates, we found that about 20 percent sketched a spreadsheet on paper first, whereas about 50 percent started by entering data and formulas directly into the computer.)

- End users do not use a conscious prototyping approach, which involves building a series of models starting with the simplest and gradually adding complexity.

- End users rarely spend time debugging their models, unless the model performs in such a counterintuitive manner that it demands intervention.

- End users almost never subject their spreadsheets to review by another person. In general, end users appear to trust that the model they *thought* they had built is actually the model they *see* on their screens, despite the fact that spreadsheets show only numbers, not the relationships behind the numbers.

- Finally, many end users, even some who are experts in Excel, do not consistently use tools that can help generate the insights that make modeling worthwhile. Excel's Data Table and Goal Seek tools, to cite just two examples, are overlooked by the majority of end users. Without these tools, the end user either fails to ask questions that can provide telling insights, or else wastes time generating results that could be found more easily.

The evidence is strong that the existing state of spreadsheet design and use is generally inadequate. This is one reason we devote a significant portion of this book to spreadsheet engineering. Only with a solid foundation in spreadsheet engineering can the business analyst effectively generate real insights from spreadsheet models.

1.2.3 Background Knowledge for Spreadsheet Modeling

Many people new to modeling fear it because modeling reminds them of painful experiences with mathematics. We do not wish to downplay the essentially mathematical nature of modeling, even modeling using spreadsheets. However, an effective modeler does not need to know any really advanced math. Knowledge of basic algebra (including functions such as the quadratic, exponential, and logarithmic), simple logic (as expressed in an IF statement or the MAX function), and basic probability (distributions and sampling, for example) will usually suffice. When we find it necessary to use any higher math in this book, we provide explanations. But our focus here is less on the mathematical details of models than on the creative process of constructing and using models.

We assume throughout this book that the reader has a basic familiarity with Excel. This includes the ability to build a simple spreadsheet, enter and format text and data, use formulas and simple functions such as SUM, construct graphs, and so on. We do not assume the reader is an expert in Excel, nor do we assume knowledge of the advanced tools we cover, such as optimization and simulation. We have found that, in many situations, advanced Excel skills are not required for building effective models. And we believe that the main purpose of modeling is to improve the insight of the modeler. Thus, it is appropriate for a modeler with only basic Excel skills to build a model using only basic tools, and it is appropriate for a modeler with advanced skills to draw on advanced tools when needed. We have also found that too much skill in Excel can sometimes distract from the essential modeling tasks, which are almost always more about finding a simple and effective representation of the problem at hand than about finding some Excel trick.

For easy reference, we have included Appendix 1 to give an overview of Excel, from the basics of entering text and data to advanced formulas and functions. In addition, Appendix 2 covers the use of macros and an introduction to Visual Basic for Applications (VBA). We expect most readers to already know Excel to some degree, and to use these appendices as needed to hone specific skills. We believe that, by working through the examples in the book, the reader's Excel skills will improve naturally and painlessly, just as ours have improved over years of building models and teaching modeling to students whose Excel skills often exceeded ours.

1.3 THE REAL WORLD AND THE MODEL WORLD

We stated at the outset that modeling provides a structure for problem solving. It does this through a process of abstraction, in which the essence of the problem is captured in a simplified form. Because of this abstraction process, modeling does not come naturally to

FIGURE 1.1 The Real-World and the Model World

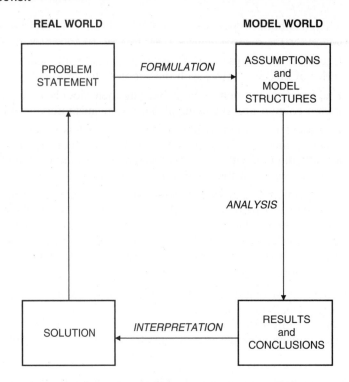

most people but must be learned. Because it does not come naturally, it can appear to be artificial and counterintuitive, causing many students of modeling to become uncomfortable with the process. This section attempts to reduce that discomfort by placing modeling in the context of problem solving in the real world.

A model is an abstraction, or simplification, of the real world. It is a laboratory—an artificial environment—in which we can experiment and test ideas without the costs and risks of experimenting with real systems and organizations. Figure 1.1 is a schematic showing how modeling creates an artificial world. We begin in the real world, usually with a messy problem to solve. If we determine that modeling is an appropriate tool, we then move across an invisible boundary into the model world.

In order to move into the model world, we abstract the essential features of the real world, leaving behind all the nonessential detail and complexity. We then construct our laboratory by combining our abstractions with specific assumptions and building a model of the essential aspects of the real world. This is the process of **model formulation**. It is an exercise in simplifying the actual situation and capturing its essence, with a specific purpose in mind. The model formulation process typically forces us to confront four features of a model:

- Decisions
- Outcomes
- Structure
- Data

Decisions refers to possible choices, or courses of action, that we might take. These would be controllable variables, such as quantities to buy, manufacture, spend, or sell. (By contrast, uncontrollable variables such as tax rates or the cost of materials are not decision variables.) **Outcomes** refers to the consequences of the decisions—the performance measures we use to evaluate the results of taking action. Examples might include profit, cost, or efficiency. **Structure** refers to the logic and the mathematics that link the elements of our model together. A simple example might be the equation $P = R - C$, in which profit is calculated as the difference between revenue and cost. Another example might be the relationship $F = I + P - S$, in which final inventory is calculated from initial inventory, production, and shipments. Finally, **data** refers to specific numerical assumptions. That may mean actual observations of the real world (often called "raw" or "empirical" data), or it may mean estimates of uncontrollable variables in the problem's environment. Examples might include the interest rate on borrowed funds, the production capacity of a manufacturing facility, or the first-quarter sales for a new product.

Once it is built, we can use the model to test ideas and evaluate solutions. This is a process of **analysis**, in which we apply logic, often with the support of software, to take us from our assumptions and abstractions to a set of derived conclusions. Unlike model formulation, which tends to be mostly an art, analysis is much more of a science. It relies on mathematics and reason in order to explore the implications of our assumptions. This exploration process leads, hopefully, to insights about the problem confronting us. Sometimes, these insights involve an understanding of why one solution is beneficial and another is not; at other times, the insights involve understanding the sources of risk in a particular solution. In another situation, the insights involve identifying the decisions that are most critical to a good result, or identifying the inputs that have the strongest influence on a particular outcome. In each instance, it is crucial to understand that these insights are derived from the *model* world and not from the *real* world. Whether they apply to the real world is another matter entirely and requires managerial judgment.

To make the model insights useful, we must first translate them into the terms of the real world and then communicate them to the actual decision makers involved. Only then do *model* insights turn into useful *managerial* insights. And only then can we begin the process of evaluating solutions in terms of their impact on the real world. This is a process of **interpretation**, and here again, the process is an art. Good modelers can move smoothly back and forth between the model world and the real world, deriving crisp insights from the model, and translating the insights, modifying them as needed, to account for real-world complexities not captured in the model world.

This schematic description of the modeling process highlights some of the reasons it can be a challenge to incorporate modeling into problem solving. Powerful in competent hands, modeling is also somewhat esoteric. It involves deliberate abstraction and simplification of a situation, which appears to many people as a counterproductive exercise. Modeling requires a willingness to temporarily set aside much of the richness of the real world and to operate in the refined and artificial world of models and model insights. It also requires confidence that whatever insights arise in the model world can be translated into useful ideas in the real world. In addition, it requires an ability to mix art with science in order to exploit the modeling process to its full potential. Until we have some experience with this process, we may be resistant and skeptical. And it is always easy to criticize a model as being too simple. Good models are as simple as they can possibly be. But this very simplicity can appear to be a fatal flaw to skeptics. Nevertheless, modeling is one of the most powerful tools in the problem solver's tool kit, simply because there is no more practical way to arrive at the insights modeling can provide.

1.4 LESSONS FROM EXPERT AND NOVICE MODELERS

Perhaps the best way to become a good modeler is to serve an apprenticeship under an expert. Unfortunately, such opportunities are rare. Moreover, experts in all fields find it difficult to express their expertise or to teach it. While narrow, **technical skills** are relatively easy to teach (e.g., how to use the NPV function in Excel), expertise consists largely of **craft skills** that are more difficult to teach (e.g., what to include and exclude from the model). In the arts, there is a tradition of studio training, where a teacher poses artistic challenges to students and then coaches them as they work through the problems on their own. This is one way for students to acquire some of the difficult-to-articulate craft skills of the master. There is no comparable tradition in the mathematical fields; in fact, there is a long-standing belief that modeling cannot be taught but must simply be acquired by experience.

One way to improve modeling skills is to understand what expert and novice modelers actually do when they build and use models. From closely observing experts, we can attempt to articulate a set of modeling best practices. From observing novices we can understand the reasons for their relatively lower level of modeling accomplishment: the blind alleys, counterproductive behaviors, misperceptions, and cognitive limitations that keep them from attaining expert performance. In this section, we summarize research studies on both expert and novice modelers.

1.4.1 Expert Modelers

An alternative to an apprenticeship under an expert is to study experts in a laboratory setting. Tom Willemain did this in a series of experiments with 12 expert modelers.

He gave each expert a short problem description as it would come from a client and observed the subject working for one hour on the problem. The subjects were asked to think out loud so that their thought processes could be recorded. Willemain's results concerning the "first hour in the life of a model" are highly suggestive of some of the ingredients of good modeling practice.[2]

Willemain was interested in determining the issues to which expert modelers devote attention as they formulate their models. He identified five topics important to modelers:

- Problem context
- Model structure
- Model realization
- Model assessment
- Model implementation

Problem context refers to the situation from which the modeler's problem arises, including the client, the client's view of the problem, and any available facts about the problem. In this activity, the modeler tries to understand the problem statement as provided by the client and to understand the messy situation out of which the problem arises.

Model structure refers to actually building the model itself, including issues such as what type of model to use, where to break the problem into subproblems, and how to choose parameters and relationships. In Figure 1.1, this would be the process of moving into the model world, making abstractions and assumptions, and creating an actual model.

Model realization refers to the more detailed activities of fitting the model to available data and calculating results. Here, the focus is on whether the general model structure can actually be implemented with the available data and whether the type of model under development will generate the hoped-for kinds of results. This topic corresponds to the analysis process in Figure 1.1.

Model assessment includes evaluating the model's correctness, feasibility, and acceptability to the client. Determining the correctness of a model involves finding whether the model assumptions correspond well enough to reality. Feasibility refers to whether the client has the resources to implement the developed model, whether sufficient data are available, and whether the model itself will perform as desired. Client acceptability refers to whether the client will understand the model and its results and whether the results will be useful to the client. In this phase, we can imagine the modeler looking from the model world back into the real world and trying to anticipate whether the model under construction will meet the needs of the client.

Finally, **model implementation** refers to working with the client to derive value from the model. This corresponds to the interpretation activity in Figure 1.1.

One of Willemain's interesting observations about his experts was that they frequently switched their attention among these five topics. That is, they did not follow a sequential problem-solving process, but rather moved quickly among the various phases—at one moment considering the problem statement, at another considering whether the necessary data would be available, and at yet another thinking through whether the client could understand and use the model. A second significant finding was that model structure, presumably the heart of a modeler's work, received a relatively small amount of attention (about 60 percent of the effort) when compared to the other four topics. Finally, it turned out that experts often alternated their attention between model structure and model assessment. That is, they would propose some element of model structure and quickly turn to evaluating its impact on model correctness, feasibility, and acceptability. Willemain suggests that the experts treat model structuring as the central task, or backbone, of their work, but they often branch off to examine related issues (data availability, client acceptance, and so on), eventually returning to the central task. In effect, model structuring becomes an organizing principle, or mental focus, around which the related activities can be arrayed.

The overall picture that emerges from this research is one in which craft skills are as essential to the effective modeler as technical skills. An effective modeler must understand the problem context, including the client, or modeling will fail. Similarly, a model that is

---

[2] T. R. Willemain, "Insights on Modeling from a Dozen Experts," *Operations Research* 42, No. 2 (1994): 213–222; "Model Formulation: What Experts Think About and When," *Operations Research* 43, No. 6 (1995): 916–932.

technically correct but does not provide information the client can use, or does not gain the trust of the client, represents only wasted effort. Experts approach modeling with a general process in mind, but they move fairly quickly among the different activities, creating, testing, and revising constantly as they go. The experts appear to be comfortable with a high degree of ambiguity as they approach the task of structuring a model. They do not rush to a solution, but patiently build tentative models and test them, always being ready to revise and improve.

1.4.2 Novice Modelers

Novices have been studied in many domains, from solving physics problems to playing golf. In general, novice problem solvers can be expected to show certain kinds of counter-productive behaviors. One is that they focus on just one approach to a problem and devote all their time to it, while experts are likely to try many different approaches. Novices also do not evaluate their performance as frequently or as critically as expert problem solvers do. Finally, novices tend to attempt to solve a problem using only the information given in that problem, while experts are more likely to draw on experience with other problems for useful analogies or tools.

In an attempt to better understand how our own students model problems, we conducted an experiment similar in most respects to Willemain's experiment with experts.[3] We audiotaped 28 MBA students while they worked through four ill-structured modeling problems. Thus, this experiment did not focus on building a spreadsheet model for a well-defined problem, as might be assigned in a course for homework, but rather on formulating an approach to an ill-structured problem of the kind that consultants typically encounter. (Some of these problems will be presented in Chapter 2.) The students were given 30 minutes to work on each problem. The task was to begin developing a model that could ultimately be used for forecasting or for analysis of a decision.

We observed five behaviors in our subjects that are not typical of experts and that limit their modeling effectiveness:

- Overreliance on given numerical data
- Use of shortcuts to an answer
- Insufficient use of abstract variables and relationships
- Ineffective self-regulation
- Overuse of brainstorming relative to structured problem solving

In the study, some of the problems included extensive tables of numerical data. In these problems, many subjects devoted their time to examining the data rather than building a general model structure. Having data at hand seemed to block these students from the abstraction process required for effective modeling. In other problems, very little data was provided, and in these cases, some students attempted to "solve" the problem by performing calculations on the given numbers. Again, the data seemed to block the abstraction process. Many subjects complained about the lack of data in problems in which little was given, seeming to believe that data alone could lead to a solution. In general, then, our subjects appear to rely more on data than do experts, who build general model structures and only tangentially ask whether data exist or could be acquired to refine or operationalize their model structures.

Another problematic behavior we observed in our subjects was taking a shortcut to an answer. Where experts would consider various aspects of a problem and try out several different approaches, some students rushed to a conclusion. Some would simply rely on intuition to decide that the proposal they were to evaluate was a good or bad idea. Others would use back-of-the-envelope calculations to come to a conclusion. Still others would claim that the answer could be found by collecting data, or performing marketing research, or asking experts in the industry. (We call this behavior "invoking a magic wand.") All of these approaches seem to avoid the assigned task, which was to structure a *model* for analyzing the problem, not to come to a conclusion.

---

[3] S.G. Powell and T.R. Willemain, "How Novices Formulate Models. Part I: Qualitative Insights and Implications for Teaching," *Journal of the Operational Research Society*, 58 (2007): 983–995; T.R. Willemain and S.G. Powell, "How Novices Formulate Models. Part II: A Quantitative Description of Behavior;" *Journal of the Operational Research Society*, 58 (2007): 1271–1283.

Expert problem solvers generally use abstract variables and relationships in the early stages of modeling a problem. We saw very little of this in our subjects, who appeared to think predominantly in concrete terms, often using specific numbers. Expert modelers tend to be well trained in formal mathematics, and they naturally think in terms of variables and relationships. Our subjects were generally less well trained in mathematics but tended to have extensive experience with spreadsheets. Their approach to spreadsheet modeling involved minimal abstraction and maximal reliance on numbers. Our subjects did not often write down variables and functions, but they fairly often sketched or talked about a spreadsheet in terms of its row and column headings.

As we noted earlier, experts pause frequently during problem solving to evaluate the approach they are taking. They are also willing to try another approach if the current one seems unproductive. By contrast, many of our subjects did little self-evaluation during the experiment. Some focused more on the problem we had given them as a business problem than a modeling problem. So the special features that a model brings to analyzing a situation seemed lost on them. Without a clear goal, a typical subject would launch into a discussion of all the factors that might conceivably influence the problem. Only rarely did we observe a subject stopping and asking whether they were making progress toward a *model*.

Finally, the predominant problem-solving strategy we observed our subjects using could be described as unstructured problem exploration. For example, they would list issues in a rambling and unstructured manner, as if they were brainstorming, without attempting to organize their thoughts in a form that would support modeling. Structured problem solving, as used by experts, seeks to impose an organized plan on the modeling process.

In general our subjects failed to think in modeling terms—that is, by deciding what the outcome of the modeling process was to be and working backwards through variables and assumptions and relationships to the beginning. Instead, they explored a variety of (usually) unrelated aspects of the problem in a discursive manner.

What can a business analyst who wants to improve modeling skills learn from this research? First, expertise takes time and practice to acquire, and the novice should not expect to perform like an expert overnight. However, some expert behaviors are worth imitating from the start. Don't look for quick answers to the problem at hand, and don't expect the data to answer the problem for you. Rather, use what you know to build a logical structure of relationships. Use whatever language you are most comfortable with (algebra, a spreadsheet, a sketch), but work to develop your ability to abstract the essential features of the situation from the details and the numbers. Keep an open mind, try different approaches, and evaluate your work often. Most important, look for opportunities to use modeling, and constantly upgrade both your technical and craft skills.

1.5   ORGANIZATION OF THE BOOK

This book is organized around the four sets of skills we believe business analysts most need in their modeling work:

- Spreadsheet engineering
- Modeling craft
- Data analysis
- Management science

Spreadsheet engineering deals with how to design, build, test, and perform analysis with a spreadsheet model. **Modeling craft** refers to the nontechnical but critical skills that an expert modeler employs, such as abstracting the essential features of a situation in a model, debugging a model effectively, and translating model results into managerial insights. **Data analysis** involves the exploration of datasets and the basic techniques used for classification and prediction. **Management science** covers optimization and simulation. A basic knowledge of these tools is important for the well-rounded analyst. Figure 1.2 provides an overview of the organization of the book.

The heart of this book is the material on building spreadsheet models and using them to analyze decisions. However, before the analyst can build spreadsheet models successfully, certain broader skills are needed. Therefore, we begin in Chapter 2 with a

FIGURE 1.2 Organization
of the Book

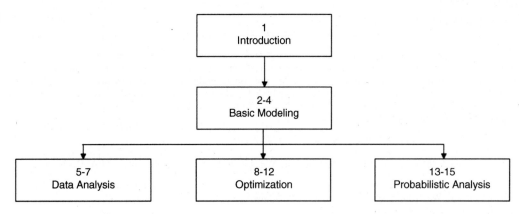

discussion of the various contexts in which modeling is carried out and the role that modeling plays in a structured problem-solving process. We also introduce in this chapter the craft aspects of modeling—the tricks of the trade that experienced and successful modelers employ. These are not Excel tricks, but rather approaches to dealing with the ambiguities of analysis using models. Chapters 3 and 4 provide the essential tools of spreadsheet engineering. Along with the earlier material, these chapters should be studied by all readers. (Appendix 1 contains a brief overview of the Excel skills needed by effective modelers, and Appendix 2 provides a glimpse of the advanced capabilities available with Visual Basic for Applications.) Chapter 3 provides guidelines for designing effective spreadsheets and workbooks, while Chapter 4 provides an overview of various tools available for analyzing spreadsheet models. Chapters 5 through 15 cover the advanced tools of the management scientist and their spreadsheet implementations. Chapters 5 through 7 deal with data exploration, basic data mining, and forecasting. Chapters 8 through 12 explore optimization, and Chapters 13 through 15 cover simulation and probability-based models. (The necessary statistical background for our coverage appears in Appendix 3.) Numerous examples throughout the text illustrate good modeling techniques, and most chapters contain exercises for practice. Many of these exercises relate to a set of case problems, which are included at the end of the book. These problems provide an opportunity to gain experience with realistic modeling problems that build on concepts in different chapters.

1.6 SUMMARY

The following statements summarize the principles on which this book is based.

• *Modeling is a necessary skill for every business analyst.*
Models are encountered frequently in business education and in the business world. Furthermore, analysts are capable of formulating their own models.

• *Spreadsheets are the modeling platform of choice.*
The wide acceptance and flexibility of the spreadsheet make it the modeling platform of choice for most business situations. Since familiarity with spreadsheets is required for almost everyone in business, the basis for learning spreadsheet-based modeling is already in place.

• *Basic spreadsheet modeling skills are an essential foundation.*
While basic knowledge about spreadsheets is usually assumed in business, spreadsheet skills and spreadsheet modeling skills are not the same. Effective education in business modeling begins with training in how to use a spreadsheet to build and analyze models.

• *End-user modeling is cost-effective.*
In an ever-growing range of situations, well-trained business analysts can build their own models without relying on consultants or experts.

• *Craft skills are essential to the effective modeler.*
Craft skills are the mark of an expert in any field. The craft skills of modeling must gradually be refined through experience, but the process can be expedited by identifying and discussing them and by providing opportunities to practice their use.

• *Analysts can learn the required modeling skills.*
Modeling skills do not involve complex mathematics or arcane concepts. Any motivated analyst can learn the basics of good modeling and apply this knowledge on the job.

• *Management science and data analysis are important advanced tools.*
Extensive knowledge of these tools is not required of most business analysts; however, solid knowledge of the fundamentals can turn an average modeler into a power modeler.

SUGGESTED READINGS

Many books are available on Excel, although most of them cover its vast array of features without isolating those of particular relevance for the business analyst. In the chapters on Excel, we provide several references to books and other materials for learning basic Excel skills. A working business analyst should probably own at least one Excel guide as a reference book. Two such references are:

Dodge, M., and C. Stinson. 2011. *Microsoft Excel 2010 Inside Out.* Redmond, WA: Microsoft Press.
Walkenbach, J. 2010. *Excel 2010 Bible*. Indianapolis: Wiley Publishing.

Several textbooks present the tools of management science using spreadsheets. We recommend these for a more detailed treatment of management science than we provide here:

Ragsdale, C. 2010. *Spreadsheet Modeling and Decision Analysis.* 6th ed. Mason, OH: South-Western.
Winston, W., and C. Albright. 2012. *Practical Management Science.* 4th ed. Mason, OH: South-Western.

The standard reference on the mathematics of management science is:

Hillier, F., and G. Lieberman. 2009. *Introduction to Operations Research*. 9th ed. Oakland, CA: McGraw-Hill.

While this text does not rely on spreadsheets, it does provide in a relatively accessible form the methods behind much of the management science we present in this book. The following two references are more narrowly focused books that apply spreadsheet modeling to specific business disciplines:

Benninga, S. 2008. *Financial Modeling*. 3d ed. Cambridge, MA: MIT Press.
Lilien, G., and A. Rangaswamy. 2006. *Marketing Engineering*. 2d ed. State College, PA: Decision Pro.

Finally, for stimulating books on modeling and problem solving, we recommend:

Casti, J. 1997. *Would-be Worlds: How Simulation Is Changing the Frontiers of Science*. New York: John Wiley & Sons.
Koomey, J. D. 2008. *Turning Numbers into Knowledge: Mastering the Art of Problem Solving*. 2d ed. Oakland, CA: Analytics Press.
Starfield, A., K. Smith, and A. Bleloch. 1994. *How to Model It.* New York: McGraw-Hill.

2 Modeling in a Problem-Solving Framework

Modeling is an approach that helps us develop a better understanding of business situations. As a result, it helps us make better decisions. Thus, we don't view modeling as an end in itself, but rather as part of the broader process of business decision making. In this chapter, we discuss how modeling contributes to that broader process. We refer to the decision-making process generically as a **problem-solving** process, although specific instances could involve making forecasts, evaluating business opportunities, or allocating resources.

Any successful problem-solving process begins with recognition of a problem and ends with implementation of a proposed solution. All the work that comes between these two points is the problem-solving process. In some cases, this process is highly structured and planned, perhaps involving a large team working over several months; in other cases, it is informal and unstructured, perhaps involving only one person for a couple of hours. Modeling is just one of many tools or strategies that can be used within problem solving. An effective problem solver knows when and how to use modeling effectively within the broader context of problem solving.

Modelers can play different roles in the problem-solving process. Primarily, these roles are:

- End user
- Team member
- Independent consultant

When the entire team consists of one person, the problem owner (or client) and modeler are one and the same. We refer to this role as the **end-user** modeler. The end user is often a small-business owner or an entrepreneur, who has no staff and no budget for consultants. In large firms, many managers are also end users at times, when there is no time to brief the staff or bring in consultants, or when the problem is too sensitive to share with anyone else. The end user carries out all of the activities in modeling: identifying a problem worthy of attention, developing a model, using the model to develop insights and practical solutions, and implementing the results. There is an enormous untapped potential for end-user modeling, because there are so many relatively small problems for which modeling can provide insight, and because there are so many end users who have (or can acquire) the spreadsheet and modeling skills necessary to develop useful models.

In addition to the end-user role, modelers are often assigned to the role of **team member** on an internal committee or task force. In many cases, the problem-solving process may have begun before the committee was formed, and the modeler may or may not have been part of that process. Although chosen for expertise in modeling, the team-member modeler's role also requires good interpersonal and communication skills. A critical part of the work is communicating with nonmodelers on the team about the assumptions that go into the model and the intuition behind the model's results. Of course, the team-member modeler must also have the necessary technical skills to apply modeling successfully, but communication skills are more important for the team-member than for the end-user modeler.

A third role for the modeler is that of **independent consultant**. This role differs from the role of team member because there is usually a client—someone who identifies the problem and ultimately manages the implementation of any solution. The role of consultant modeler also requires excellent communication and interpersonal skills. Despite being an organizational outsider, the consultant modeler must understand the client's problem deeply and translate the client's understanding of the problem into modeling terms. This role also requires the ability to translate model insights back into a language the client can understand so that the client can implement a solution.

As we build our formal modeling skills, we need to have an overall concept of the problem-solving process and where modeling fits into that process. Thus, we begin this chapter by describing a widely used problem-solving process and the role that formal modeling plays in this process.

Influence charts, which are the second topic in this chapter, help to bridge the gap between a qualitative understanding of a fuzzy problem and a formal model with numbers and equations. Influence charts help the modeler construct a logical structure within which to represent the parameters, relationships, and outcomes of a model without excessive detail or precision. They are an essential tool for both novice and expert modelers.

The final topic of the chapter is the craft of modeling. The technical side of modeling concerns the specific and well-defined tasks necessary to build a model, such as how to use an IF statement. The craft side of modeling, on the other hand, represents the artistry that experts bring to bear. Craft skills are harder to learn than technical skills, but they are just as important for successful modeling. We describe some of the most important craft skills and discuss the role these skills play in modeling. The modeling cases that appear later in the book provide opportunities to practice these skills in ill-structured problem situations.

2.2 THE PROBLEM-SOLVING PROCESS

While problem solving is an almost universal aspect of life, very few individuals follow a structured approach to it. This could indicate that effective problem solving is instinctive and intuitive and that the only way to improve in this area is through experience. We do not, however, subscribe to this point of view. In our experience, some degree of conscious attention to the process pays off in improved results and efficiency, even for experienced modelers and managers. This is especially true for problem-solving teams, where intuitive methods often fail because what is intuitive to one member makes no sense to another. While the end-user modeler can perhaps get by with shortcuts, team members and independent consultants are more effective when they carefully manage the problem-solving process.

The problem-solving process is often described as a sequential, step-by-step procedure. While this makes for easy description, there is, in fact, no simple plan that represents the universal problem-solving process. Moreover, when people look back on their own problem-solving activities, they tend to remember more structure than was really there. Thus, a sequential description of problem solving should not be taken literally. As we described in the previous chapter, even modeling experts appear to jump around from one aspect of a problem to another as they attempt to formulate models. Any process must be flexible enough to accommodate different work styles, unexpected discoveries and disappointments, and inevitable fluctuations in effort and creativity. The process we discuss later in this chapter helps focus attention on some of the critical aspects of effective problem solving, without providing a straitjacket that will cramp a problem solver's style. Our description comes from what experts tell us, from what we observe in our students, and from what we have experienced in our own problem solving.

2.2.1 Some Key Terms

We begin by making an important distinction between a **problem** and a **mess**. On the one hand, a mess is a morass of unsettling symptoms, causes, data, pressures, shortfalls, and opportunities. A problem, on the other hand, is a well-defined situation that is capable of resolution. Why is the concept of a mess important in problem solving? Simply because problems do not come to us fully defined and labeled. Rather, we operate in a world full of confusion: causes and effects are muddled, data exist but there is little relevant information, problematic shortfalls or inadequacies appear alongside attractive opportunities, and so on. Where are the problems in this mess? Identifying a problem in the mess is itself a creative act that will do much to determine the quality of any solutions we propose. In most situations, a number of problems could be extracted from a given mess. Which one we choose depends on our understanding of the situation and on our insight into where analysis and action could be most effective. Our first piece of advice on problem solving, then, is to recognize that defining the problem to be solved is a critical step in the process— one that deserves considerable attention.

One way to focus attention on the problem definition is to use a problem statement of this form: "In what ways might. . . . ?" Imagine the situation facing a manufacturing company whose costs are rising sharply due to increasing wages. Here are some possible problem statements the company could use:

- In what ways might we increase the productivity of our workforce?
- In what ways might we reduce the labor content of our products?
- In what ways might we shift our manufacturing to lower-cost regions?
- In what ways might we increase revenues to keep pace with costs?
- In what ways might we change our product line to maintain profit margins?

This is just a sample of the problem statements that could apply to a given situation. It should be obvious that the approach taken to resolving the "problem" will be very different depending on which of these statements is adopted. Our advice is to pay close attention to the problem definition, take any problem definition as tentative, and prepare to alter it if evidence suggests that a different problem statement would be more effective.

The appropriate problem-solving approach depends, of course, on the problem at hand. Some problems are simple and require only a rudimentary approach, while others are complex and require a much more elaborate and thought-out process. It is useful to distinguish **well-structured** from **ill-structured problems**.

Well-structured problems have the following characteristics:

- The objectives of the analysis are clear.
- The assumptions that must be made are obvious.
- All the necessary data are readily available.
- The logical structure behind the analysis is well understood.

Algebra problems are typically well-structured problems. Consider solving the following system of equations for X and Y:

$$
\begin{aligned}
3X + 4Y &= 18 \\
9X + Y &= 21
\end{aligned}
$$

The solution to this problem consists of the values $X = 2$, $Y = 3$. Not only can we easily demonstrate that these values actually do solve the problem, but we can also prove that this is the only solution to the problem. Once we have found these values for X and Y, there is nothing more to be said about the problem.

By contrast, in a typical ill-structured problem, to varying degrees, the objectives, assumptions, data, and structure of the problem are all unclear. Here are several examples of ill-structured problems:

- Should the Red Cross institute a policy of paying for blood donations?
- Should Boeing's next major commercial airliner be a small supersonic jet or a slower jumbo jet?
- Should an advertiser spend more money on the creative aspects of an ad campaign or on the delivery of the ad?
- How much should a midcareer executive save out of current income toward retirement?

Unlike well-structured problems, ill-structured problems require *exploration* more than *solution*. Exploring a problem involves formulating hypotheses, making assumptions, building simple models, and deriving tentative conclusions, all with an inquiring mind and in a spirit of discovery. Problem exploration is a more creative and open-ended process than problem solving. It often reveals aspects of the problem that are not obvious at first glance. These discoveries can become useful insights.

At any stage in the problem-solving process, there are two quite different styles of thinking: **divergent** and **convergent**. Divergent thinking stresses generating ideas over evaluating ideas. It involves thinking in different directions or searching for a variety of answers to questions that may have many right answers. Brainstorming, in which the evaluation process is strictly prohibited, promotes divergent thinking and allows many ideas to flourish at the same time, even ideas that contradict each other. Convergent thinking, on the other hand, is directed toward achieving a goal, a single solution, answer, or result. It involves trying to find the one best answer. In convergent thinking, the emphasis shifts from idea generation to evaluation: Which of these ideas leads to the best outcomes? In many cases, this evaluation is carried out using a model.

Why is this distinction between divergent and convergent thinking useful? One reason is that some individuals naturally prefer, enjoy, or are skilled at one or the other type of thinking. When working as end users, these individuals should be conscious of their preference or skill and take steps to ensure that they devote sufficient time and energy to the other approach. Good evaluators need to encourage themselves to generate more ideas; good idea generators need to encourage themselves to test their ideas thoroughly. Since end users do it all, they must ensure that the balance between divergent and convergent thinking is appropriate throughout the problem-solving process.

An understanding of these concepts is just as important to members of a problem-solving team. In this situation, members can afford to specialize in their preferred thought process: idea generators can take a lead role in that phase, while strong evaluators can take a lead role when that becomes the primary activity of the group. But people need to understand their own strengths and the strengths of others on the team, and they need to appreciate that the other types make an important contribution. Finally, teams work best when they are aware of which type of thinking they are stressing at each point in the process. It is disruptive and inefficient to have one member of a team evaluating ideas during a brainstorming session; it is just as disruptive to have someone offering great new ideas during the preparation of the final presentation to the client.

2.2.2 The Six-Stage Problem-Solving Process

We now describe a six-stage problem-solving process (Figure 2.1) that begins with a mess and ends with implementation of a solution. This process can be used to solve (or explore) almost any problem, from the most well-structured to the most ill-structured. Since not all problem solving involves the use of formal models, we first describe the process in its most general form. Subsequently, we discuss how formal modeling fits within this overall framework. Throughout this section, we illustrate the stages of the process with the following example.

EXAMPLE
Invivo Diagnostics

Invivo Diagnostics is a $300M pharmaceutical company built on the strength of a single product that accounts for over 75 percent of revenues. In 18 months, the patent for this product will expire, and the CEO wants to explore ways to plug the expected $100–$200M revenue gap as revenues from this product decline. ∎

The six stages in the problem-solving process are:

- Exploring the mess
- Searching for information
- Identifying a problem
- Searching for solutions
- Evaluating solutions
- Implementing a solution

Divergent thinking tends to dominate early in this process, while convergent thinking comes to dominate later on, but there is a role for each type of thinking in every stage of the process.

Stage 1: Exploring the Mess　As we have said, problems do not appear to us in the form of well-posed problem statements. Rather, we find ourselves in various messes, out of which problems occasionally emerge. It often takes a special effort to rise above the press

FIGURE 2.1 The Creative
Problem-Solving Process
Source: After Couger,
*Creative Problem Solving
and Opportunity Finding*

Exploring the mess
    Divergent phase
        Search mess for problems and opportunities.
    Convergent phase
        Accept a challenge and undertake systematic efforts to respond to it.

Searching for information
    Divergent phase
        Gather data, impressions, feelings, observations; examine the situation from many
        different viewpoints.
    Convergent phase
        Identify the most important information.

Identifying a problem
    Divergent phase
        Generate many different potential problem statements.
    Convergent phase
        Choose a working problem statement.

Searching for solutions
    Divergent phase
        Develop many different alternatives and possibilities for solutions.
    Convergent phase
        Select one or a few ideas that seem most promising.

Evaluating solutions
    Divergent phase
        Formulate criteria for reviewing and evaluating ideas.
    Convergent phase
        Select the most important criteria. Use the criteria to evaluate, strengthen, and
        refine ideas.

Implementing a solution
    Divergent phase
        Consider possible sources of assistance and resistance to proposed solution.
        Identify implementation steps and required resources.
    Convergent phase
        Prepare the most promising solution for implementation.

of day-to-day activities and begin a problem-solving process. In this sense, the most important aspect of this phase may be more psychological than intellectual. The divergent thinking in this phase involves being open to the flow of problems and opportunities in the environment; the convergent phase distills a specific problem out of the mess. During this phase, we ask questions such as the following:

- What problems (or opportunities) do we face?
- Where is there a gap between the current situation and the desired one?
- What are our stated and unstated goals?

This stage will be complete when we have produced a satisfactory description of the situation and when we have identified (although not necessarily gathered) the key facts and data.

    In the Invivo example, management in the pharmaceutical company is well aware that one drug has provided the bulk of their profits over the past decade. Nevertheless, most of their day-to-day attention is devoted to tactical issues, such as resolving conflicts with suppliers or allocating R&D funds to the development of new drugs. As the date approaches on which their major drug loses its patent protection and alternative drugs can begin to compete, the managers gradually shift attention to the situation facing them. While the threat is obvious, the problem is not well defined. Each member of management probably explores this mess individually, in an informal way. They might make rough estimates of the magnitude of the threat (how much will profits fall when the patent expires?), and they might consider alternatives to improve outcomes (should we institute a cost-cutting program in manufacturing?). Eventually, management as a whole realizes the importance of the issue and creates a task force to address it. All of this activity comes under the heading of *exploring the mess*.

Stage 2: Searching for Information   Here we mean information in the broadest sense: opinions, raw data, impressions, published literature, and so on. In this phase, we cast about widely for any and all information that might shed light on what the problem really is. Examining the situation from many different points of view is an important aspect of this phase. We might survey similar companies to determine how they approach related problems. We might search the literature for related academic research. The search itself at this stage is divergent. Eventually, we begin to get a sense that some of the information is more relevant, or contains suggestions for solutions, or might otherwise be particularly useful. This is the convergent part of this phase. In this stage, we should expect to be using diagnostic skills, prioritizing, and constructing diagrams or charts. During this phase, we ask questions such as the following:

- What are the symptoms and causes?
- What measures of effectiveness seem appropriate?
- What actions are available?

This stage will be complete when we have found and organized relevant information for the situation at hand and when we have made some initial hypotheses about the source of the problem and potential solutions.

    The task force at Invivo holds several meetings to get to know each other and to get organized. They also hire a consultant to gather information and to bring an outside perspective to the discussion. The CEO charges the group to "find a strategy to deal with the patent situation"; the task force recognizes, however, that this is not a problem statement, but only a vague indication of senior management's discomfort with the future of the company. The consultant, meanwhile, begins interviewing key managers inside the firm and gathering information externally. She collects information on general trends in the pharmaceutical industry as well as case studies on the transition off patent for other drugs. A rough picture emerges of the rate at which generics have invaded a market once patent protection has been lost. She also collects specific information on strategies that other market-dominating firms have used to limit their losses during similar transitions. The consultant interviews economists specializing in industry structure. Inside the firm, she interviews the scientists who develop new drugs, and she begins to formulate a picture of how the firm's portfolio of new drugs will contribute to future revenues. If the problem-solving process is to work well here, a broad search for information must precede any effort to close in on a specific problem that can be resolved. However, even while this search goes on, the members of the task force begin to form opinions as to the real problem they face and the solutions they prefer.

Stage 3: Identifying a Problem   In the divergent portion of this phase, we might pose four or five candidate problem statements and try them on for size. We will eventually choose one of these statements, perhaps somewhat refined, as our working problem statement. As mentioned before, there is a significant benefit for any problem-solving group to have an unambiguous statement of the problem they are solving. This is not to say that we can't modify or even replace one problem statement with another if the evidence suggests this is necessary. All problem statements should be viewed as tentative, although as time passes, the cost and risk of changing the problem statement increase. In this stage, we should be asking whether the situation fits a standard problem type, or whether we should be breaking the problem into subproblems. During this phase, we ask questions such as the following:

- Which is the most important problem in this situation?
- Is this problem like others we have dealt with?
- What are the consequences of a broad versus narrow problem statement?

    This stage will be complete when we have produced a working problem statement.

    The consultant to Invivo holds a series of meetings with the task force to present and discuss her preliminary research. The group now has a shared understanding of the financial state of their own firm, as well as a general idea of the state of the industry. They discuss how other firms fared when major drugs came off patent and what strategies were used to smooth the transition. At this point, the consultant leads an effort to define a problem statement that can serve as an organizing theme for the future efforts of the task force. In the discussion that ensues, two major points of view emerge. One group focuses on preserving the revenue-generating power of the patent drug as long as possible. They ask whether it would be possible to extend the patent, slow the introduction of generic competitors, or perhaps make an alliance with competitors that would share the profits from this category of drugs without significantly reducing its revenues. The other group focuses on a different issue: how to generate more revenue from other drugs now in the development pipeline. They ask whether the firm should increase its R&D spending, narrow its efforts to just the most promising drugs, or look for quicker ways to get regulatory approval. The consultant recognizes that no one is looking at reducing costs or shrinking the firm as possible strategies.

The task force has reached a critical stage in the problem-solving process. How they define the problem here will determine in large measure the solutions they eventually recommend. The consultant, recognizing this, makes an effort to have the group debate a wide range of problem statements. Here are some candidate problem statements they may consider:

- In what ways might we slow the decline in revenues from our patented drug?
- In what ways might we increase the chances of success of R&D on new products?
- In what ways might we increase market share for our existing products?
- In what ways might we resize the firm to match declining profits?
- In what ways might we develop more products with the same investment?
- In what ways might we partner with other firms?

Eventually, the task force comes to the conclusion that protecting the revenues from the existing drug is both difficult and risky. The most effective strategy probably involves developing a portfolio of new drugs as quickly and effectively as possible. Accordingly, they adopt the problem statement: "In what ways might we reduce the time to market for the six drugs currently under development?"

Stage 4: Searching for Solutions   Again, there is a divergent aspect to this phase, in which a deliberately open-ended process searches for good, even radical, solutions. Brainstorming or other creativity-enhancing techniques might be particularly useful, since the team has a well-considered problem statement to serve as a focal point for the creation of solutions. Prior to this point, it is premature to consider solutions. It can even be dangerous to do so, since superficially appealing solutions often gain support on their own, even if they solve the wrong problem. The convergent part of this phase involves a tentative selection of the most promising candidate solutions. The selection process must be tentative at this point, because criteria have not yet been established for a careful comparison of solutions. Nonetheless, there are costs to considering too many solutions, so some pruning is often necessary. During this phase, we ask questions such as the following:

- What decisions are open to us?
- What solutions have been tried in similar situations?
- How are the various candidate solutions linked to outcomes of interest?

This stage will be complete when we have produced a list of potential solutions and perhaps a list of advantages and disadvantages for each one.

Having decided to focus their efforts on improving the R&D process, the task force at Invivo first forms a subcommittee composed mainly of scientists from the R&D division, along with a few business experts. The consultant conducts extensive interviews within the R&D group to uncover inefficiencies and possible ways to improve the process of bringing drugs to market. The subcommittee eventually develops a list of potential solutions, along with an evaluation of their advantages and disadvantages. Three areas for potential improvement stand out:

- Hire outside firms to conduct clinical trials and develop applications for Food and Drug Administration (FDA) approvals. This will speed up the approval process, although it will also increase costs.
- Invest a higher percentage of the R&D budget in drugs with the most promise of winning FDA approval. This should reduce the time required for the most promising drugs to reach the market, but it may also reduce the number of drugs that do so.

- Focus the drug portfolio on drugs in the same medical category. This should help develop an expertise in just one or two medical specialties, rather than spreading efforts over many technical areas and markets.

Stage 5: Evaluating Solutions This stage can be considered the culmination of the process, as it is here that a preferred solution emerges. Any evaluation of the candidate solutions developed in the previous phase requires a set of criteria with which to compare solutions. Usually, many criteria could be relevant to the outcome; some divergent thinking is useful in this phase to ensure that all relevant criteria, even those that are not obvious, are considered. Once the most important criteria are identified, the various solutions can be evaluated and compared on each criterion. This can lead directly to a preferred alternative. More often, this process leads to changes—and improvements—in the solutions themselves. Often, an aspect of one solution can be grafted onto another solution, or a particularly negative aspect of a generally attractive solution can be removed once the weakness has been recognized. So this phase, while generally stressing convergent thinking, still involves considerable creativity. During this phase, we ask questions such as the following:

- How does this solution impact each of the criteria?
- What factors within our control could improve the outcomes?
- What factors outside our control could alter the outcomes?

This stage will be complete when we have produced a recommended course of action, along with a justification that supports it.

During this phase, the Invivo task force develops a set of criteria with which to evaluate each of the previously proposed solutions. The overall goal is to ensure that the firm remains profitable into the future, even as the main drug goes off patent and its revenues are lost. However, it is difficult to anticipate how any one solution will impact profits directly. For example, how much additional profit will the firm realize if it saves two months in the development process for a particular drug? For this reason, each solution is measured against many criteria, and the results are synthesized by the task force. Here are some of the criteria they develop:

- R&D cost reduction
- Increase in market share
- Months of development time saved
- Increase in probability of FDA approval

After extensive discussion, the task force finally decides that the one most critical area for improvement is how R&D funds are allocated over time. In the past, the firm has generally been very slow to cancel development of any particular drug. Each drug has the passionate support of the scientists working on it, and the commitment of this group to its own drug has superseded the business judgment needed to recognize that other drug-development teams can make better use of scarce R&D resources. With a more business-oriented allocation process, fewer drugs will be developed, but each will get increased R&D funding. Hopefully, more drugs will then come to market quickly.

Stage 6: Implementing a Solution This stage is included to remind us that a solution is useless if it cannot be implemented. Political resistance, departures from established tradition, and high personal cost or risk are some of the many reasons apparently rational solutions do not get implemented in real organizations. In the divergent portion of this phase, the problem-solving team identifies potential sources of resistance and support. As this phase proceeds and specific implementation plans for the proposed solution are developed, the thinking style turns from divergent toward convergent. In this stage, we should expect to perform change management and focus on communication. During this phase, we ask questions such as the following:

- What are the barriers to successful implementation?
- Where will there be support and motivation, or resistance and conflict?
- Are the resources available for successful implementation?

This stage will be complete when we have produced an implementation plan and executed enough of it to begin evaluating how well it is succeeding.

To implement its plan, the task force at Invivo must first convince senior management to support its recommended solution. The consultant has a major role to play here in developing an effective presentation and in convincing both scientists and executives that this solution will work. The task force's role ends when it has won approval and has appointed a new committee to manage the implementation of the new R&D budget allocation process. Of course, the problem-solving process does not really end here, as the new committee must carry the plan forward, monitor its impacts, modify it as needed, and solve a new set of problems as they arise. To this extent, no problem-solving process ever really ends; it just flows into a subsequent process.

Every successful problem-solving effort starts with a mess and concludes with an implemented solution. Sometimes the cycle will be repeated more than once, so that the implementation itself creates a new situation and paves the way for follow-on problems to be identified. Nevertheless, the process passes through the stages we have outlined here. Knowledge of these stages is helpful in planning the overall tasks and resources, allocating effort, and setting expectations about progress. Within each stage, an awareness of the contributions from divergent and convergent thinking is helpful in balancing the need for creativity with the need for closure.

It is worth repeating that only rarely are these six stages followed in a strict sequence. Most problem-solving processes move back and forth from one stage to another, perhaps rethinking the problem statement while evaluating solutions, or returning to an information-gathering mode while searching for solutions. As in any creative endeavor, it is important for a problem-solving team (or individual) to remain flexible. That means remaining open to discoveries and to evidence that past work needs to be rethought.

2.2.3 Mental Models and Formal Models

The problem-solving process described earlier is generic in that it does not specifically address how formal modeling is used within the overall framework. Informal modeling, often called *mental modeling*, goes on constantly during problem solving. That is, problem solvers construct quick, informal mental models at many different points in the process. For example, when a potential solution is proposed, everyone on the team runs that idea through a mental model to get a quick first impression of its attractiveness.

As an example, consider the following question:

> Would a tax on carbon emissions in developed countries significantly reduce global warming?

What mental models do you use to evaluate this question? How do you think a tax would affect actual emissions of carbon? What effect would it have on economic growth and quality of life? How would developing countries react to such a policy, and what would be the long-term impact on global temperature? Usually, when we consider questions like this, we use mental models to link causes (the tax) with their effects (changes in global temperature).

Mental models help us to relate cause and effect, but often in a highly simplified and incomplete way. Mental models also help us to determine what might be feasible in a given situation, but our idea of what is possible is often circumscribed by our personal experiences. Finally, mental models are always influenced by our preferences for certain outcomes over others, although those preferences may not be acknowledged or even understood. One source of confusion and debate on topics such as global warming is that we all use different mental models, based on different assumptions and preferences for outcomes, and we have limited means of sharing those models because they are informal and hidden from view. So, while mental models may be useful, even necessary, they can also be extremely limiting. A common pitfall is to reject an unusual idea because it appears at first to be unworkable. Effective divergent thinking can help overcome this pitfall and allow unusual ideas to persist long enough to get a thorough hearing. But in some circumstances, mental models are simply not robust enough to provide sufficient insight, and formal models are called for.

Formal models provide the same kind of information as mental models. In essence, they link causes to effects and help us evaluate potential solutions. Once a set of potential solutions and a set of criteria have been identified, a formal model can be used to measure how well each solution performs according to the criteria. Formal models are undoubtedly costlier and more time-consuming to build than mental models, but they have the great advantage of making our assumptions, logic, and preferences explicit and open to debate.

Mental models were used extensively during the problem-solving process in our pharmaceutical company example. Every member of the task force was experienced in the industry, so each of them had developed mental models to think through the implications of the various proposals. For example, they each had some idea of the development and testing protocols for new drugs, the current process used to allocate R&D funds, and the profit streams new drugs typically generate. Using this experience, they were able to make rough, qualitative assessments of the impact the new R&D-allocation process would have on new-drug success, as well as the profit impact of introducing fewer drugs sooner. However, given the complexity of the drug-development process and the interaction of the various competing companies in the market, mental models would simply not support quantitative estimates of the overall profit impact of the proposed solution.

How could Invivo use formal modeling in its problem-solving process? With a formal model, it could track the progress of each of the six drugs through the various stages of development. One of the key assumptions it needs to agree on is how the new R&D process affects the completion time and probability of success at each stage. They would probably want to add to this basic model a module that projects the introduction of competing products in each medical category. This requires discussion and agreement on a set of assumptions about the plans of their competitors. Finally, they can complete the model by adding a financial component to determine their profits under any scenario. Taken as a whole, this model projects a stream of new-drug introductions by the firm and its competitors, then determines the price and market share for each drug, and ultimately calculates the resulting profits. Unlike mental models, a formal model built along these lines can help analyze whether the firm will be able to generate enough revenues from new drugs to offset the loss in revenues from its blockbuster drug.

2.3   INFLUENCE CHARTS

As we have pointed out, model building and analysis are used within the broader context of problem solving. To be successful, this process must begin with recognition of a problem and end with implementation of a solution. At a minimum, modeling should help in evaluating alternative solutions, but it also can provide the analyst with an enhanced intuitive understanding of the problem and the forces at work within it.

A key challenge modelers face in the problem-solving process is how to translate an initial, vague understanding of a problem into a concrete model. A mathematical model, of course, requires specific numerical inputs and outputs along with the precise relationships that connect them. Many modelers make the mistake of plunging into the details of a model before they think through the role the model will play in the overall process. We recommend a different approach, using the power of visualization to develop a broad understanding of the critical inputs, outputs, and relationships in a chart before building an initial model. An **influence chart** is a simple diagram that shows what outcome variables the model will generate and how these outputs are calculated from the necessary inputs. Influence charts are not designed to provide numerical results or insights into which particular solutions are desirable. Rather, they can help to bring clarity to the initial stages of the model formulation process.

Influence charts are particularly powerful in the early, conceptual stages of a modeling effort. They encourage the modeler or modeling team to focus on major choices, such as what to include and what to exclude from the model, rather than on details that may ultimately turn out to be unimportant. Influence charts provide a high-level view of the entire model that can be comprehended at one glance. This high-level perspective, in turn, supports modeling in teams by facilitating communication among team members. As a result, areas of agreement and disagreement among team members surface early. Influence charts can also be highly effective in communicating the essence of the modeling approach to clients.

Influence charts are flexible, so they support the frequent revision that effective modeling requires. We often encourage our student teams to devote the first hour in the life of a model to working out an influence chart. In addition, we ask them not to turn on the computer until all members of the team agree that their chart represents a suitable initial description of their model.

2.3.1 A First Example

To illustrate how influence charts are built, we begin with a highly simplified example.

EXAMPLE
A Pricing Decision

Determine the price we should set for our product so as to generate the highest possible profit this coming year. ∎

Since our plan will ultimately be measured by its profitability, we define Profit as the outcome measure and enclose it in a hexagon to distinguish it from other variables in the chart (Figure 2.2a). Next we ask what we need to know to determine Profit. The major components of Profit, Total Revenue and Total Cost, are drawn as variables enclosed in circles to the left of Profit and connected to it by arrows (Figure 2.2b). These arrows identify which variables are required to calculate the outcome. Next, Total Cost is determined by Fixed Cost and Variable Cost, which are drawn to the left of Total Cost (Figure 2.2c). Variable Cost in turn is the product of Quantity Sold and Unit Cost (Figure 2.2d). Now we turn to Total Revenue, which is the product of Quantity Sold and Price. We add Price and enclose it in a box to show it is our decision variable (Figure 2.2e) . Finally, Price Elasticity, along with the price we set, determines Quantity Sold, so in Figure 2.2f, we add the Price Elasticity variable and an arrow from Price to Quantity Sold.

Traditionally, influence charts are built from right to left, using diagrammatic conventions that distinguish the roles of different types of variables (Figure 2.3). For example, we use hexagons to represent outputs and boxes to represent decisions, as indicated in our example. We also use circles to represent other variables. As we complete the layout, we can identify certain of the variables as inputs. These are shown in the diagram as triangles. Later, we will also use double circles to represent variables that are random.

While this is a highly simplified example, its development does involve a number of modeling choices. For example, we can see in the influence chart that Fixed Cost is assumed to be a known quantity, because there are no variables that are needed to determine Fixed Cost. In another situation, we might face a set of choices as to which production technology to choose for the coming year. In that case, Fixed Cost would not be known but would be influenced by our technology choices, and the chart would have to reflect those complexities. Another modeling choice is evident in how Quantity Sold is determined. In our chart, both Price and Price Elasticity influence Quantity Sold. This reflects our modeling judgment that we face a price-dependent market. In many situations, we might assume instead that Sales are independent of Price, at least within a reasonable range of prices. One final modeling decision is evident in our chart: because Quantity Sold determines Revenue, we are assuming that production and sales are simultaneous. If, on the other hand, it were our practice to produce to stock, and to sell from inventory, we would need to modify the chart to reflect this practice. This example illustrates that influence charts

FIGURE 2.2a Start the Influence Chart with the Objective (Profit)

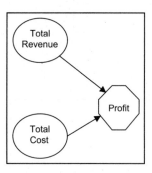

FIGURE 2.2b Decompose Profit into Total Revenue and Total Cost

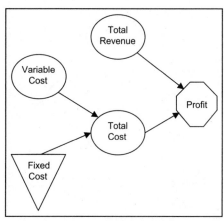

FIGURE 2.2c Decompose Total Cost into Variable Cost and Fixed Cost

FIGURE 2.2d Decompose Variable Cost into Quantity Sold and Unit Cost

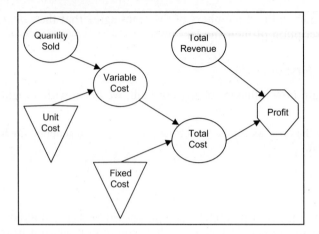

FIGURE 2.2e Decompose Total Revenue into Quantity Sold and Price

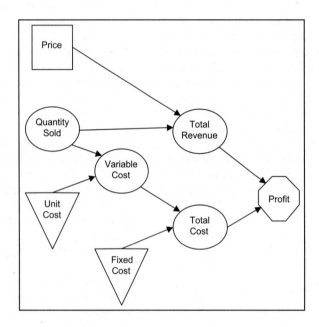

FIGURE 2.2f Decompose Quantity Sold into Price and Price Elasticity

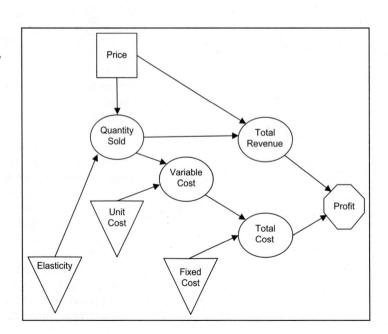

FIGURE 2.3 Symbols Used in Influence Charts

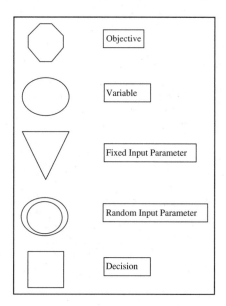

help the modeler make explicit decisions about what is included in thc model and how the variables interact to determine the output.

2.3.2 An Income Statement as an Influence Chart

An income statement is a standard accounting framework that is widely used for reporting on the past performance of a company. The bottom line in an income statement is Retained Earnings, which is roughly the difference between revenue and costs, adjusted for taxes and dividends. A simple income statement is shown in the form of an influence chart in Figure 2.4.

If our purpose were simply to record the historical performance of a company, then the relationships depicted in Figure 2.4 would be sufficient. Moreover, the related spreadsheet would consist entirely of numbers; no formulas would be needed because all variables are already determined. However, Figure 2.4 would be inadequate if our purpose were to make projections into the future because it reveals nothing about how critical variables such as Sales Revenue and Cost of Goods Sold will be determined. (A projected income statement is known as a *pro forma* income statement; the Latin phrase *pro forma* literally means "as a formality," but the meaning in accounting is "provided in advance.") In other words, Figure 2.4 represents only a static accounting framework and not a *model* of the future. To convert a static income statement into a model, we need to determine how underlying variables such as Quantity Sold evolve over time. In a simple model, we could assume that Unit Cost and Price are constant and that Quantity Sold is determined by Initial Sales and Sales Growth Rate. Figure 2.5 shows an influence chart for this model.

Even in this case, where accounting rules determine much of the model structure, an influence chart is useful for depicting the underlying forces that drive the results.

2.3.3 Principles for Building Influence Charts

An influence chart is not a technical flowchart that must conform perfectly to a rigid set of rules. Rather, it is a somewhat free-form visual aid for thinking conceptually about a model. We offer the following guidelines for constructing such charts:

- Start with the outcome measure. To decide which variable this is, ask what single variable the decision maker will use to measure the success of a plan of action.

- Decompose the outcome measure into a small set of variables that determine it *directly*. Each of these influencing variables should be independent of the others, and together they should be sufficient to determine the result.

FIGURE 2.4 Influence Chart for a Static Income Statement

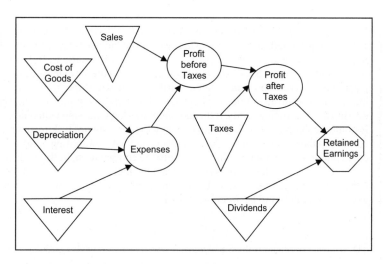

FIGURE 2.5 Influence
Chart for an Income
Statement Model

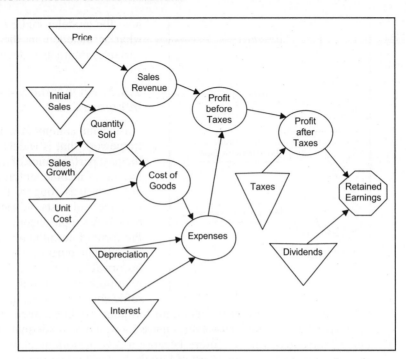

- Take each variable in turn and repeat this process of decomposition. For each variable, ask, "What do I need to know to calculate . . . ?"
- Identify input data and decisions as they arise.
- Make sure that each variable appears only once in the diagram.
- Highlight special types of elements with consistent symbols. For example, we use squares for decision variables and double circles for random variables, but any consistent code will work.

The most common error in drawing influence charts is to draw an arrow from the output back to the decisions. The thinking here seems to be that the outcome will be used to determine the best decisions. Remember, however, that an influence chart is simply a *description* of how we will calculate outcomes for *any* set of decisions and other parameters. It is not intended to be used to find the best decisions. That is a separate process, requiring an actual model, not simply a diagram.

2.3.4 Two Additional Examples

In this section, we present two detailed exercises in building influence charts for unstructured problems. Read each case and draw an influence chart before proceeding. We will then describe the process of building an influence chart and discuss some of our modeling choices. Keep in mind, however, that there is no one correct diagram, just as there is no one correct model.

EXAMPLE
*The S.S.
Kuniang*

In the early 1980s, New England Electric System (NEES) was deciding how much to bid for the salvage rights to a grounded ship, the S.S. *Kuniang*.[1] If the bid was successful, the ship could be repaired and outfitted to haul coal for the company's power-generation stations. But the value of doing so depended on the outcome of a U.S. Coast Guard judgment about the salvage value of the ship. The Coast Guard's judgment involved an obscure law regarding domestic shipping in coastal waters. If the judgment indicated a low salvage value, and if NEES submitted the winning bid, then NEES would be able to use the ship for its shipping needs. If the judgment was high, the ship would be considered too costly for use in domestic shipping. The Coast Guard's judgment would not be known until after the winning bid was chosen, so there was considerable risk associated with submitting a bid. If the bid were to fail, NEES could purchase either a new ship or a tug/barge combination, both of which were relatively expensive alternatives. One of the major issues was that the higher the bid, the more likely that NEES would win. NEES judged that a bid of $2 million would definitely not win, whereas a bid of $12 million definitely would win. Any bid in between was possible. ∎

[1] D. E. Bell, "Bidding for the S.S. *Kuniang*," *Interfaces* 14 (1984): 17–23.

FIGURE 2.6 S.S.
Kuniang Influence Chart

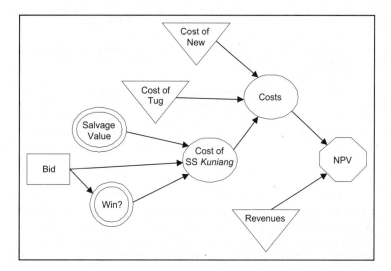

The goal here is to select an amount to bid for the S.S. *Kuniang* that will allow NEES to supply coal to its plants in the most economical way. We assume that the amount of coal to be shipped is fixed and that NEES will either use the *Kuniang* or buy a new ship or a tug/barge combination. That is, we explicitly rule out the possibility that NEES can avoid meeting the demand for shipped coal. We further assume that the outcome measure is the Net Present Value (NPV) of profits from this shipping operation over an appropriate time period (in the case of a ship, perhaps 20 years).

Our influence chart starts with an outcome measure for NPV and two influences: Costs and Revenues (Figure 2.6). Since the revenues are independent of the ship chosen, that part of the diagram does not need to be developed further. The costs incurred in coal shipping depend on which option is chosen. Apparently, NEES can always buy a new ship or a tug/barge combination, and it may have the option to buy the *Kuniang* if its bid wins. The costs of the *Kuniang* are the essential part of the model. These costs are dependent on the salvage value set by the Coast Guard, which is unpredictable and is therefore shown as a random variable (a double circle). The cost is also influenced by the size of the bid and by whether it wins the auction. In Figure 2.6, we have shown the outcome of the auction as the random variable "Win?" We have in mind a simple model in which the probability of winning increases as our bid increases. But this is an area of the diagram where further elaboration could be productive. We could, for example, add modules for the bids of our competitors. We could also add a module for the auction process itself. Whether to add further detail is always the modeler's judgment. But this simple influence chart is sufficiently detailed to support the building of a prototype model.

One additional point to notice here is that the numerical information in the problem statement, which places some limits on reasonable bids, plays no role at all in constructing the influence chart. In fact, we routinely ignore all available numerical data when we build influence charts because the goal is to develop a problem *structure*, not to solve the problem. Problem structure is not influenced by the values of parameters. This principle conflicts with another that many of us learned in early math classes, which was to use all the given data to solve the problem. This may be an appropriate problem-solving heuristic for simple math problems in school, but it is not necessarily helpful in structuring real business decisions.

EXAMPLE
Automobile
Leasing

During the 1990s, leasing grew to 40 percent of new-car sales. Nowadays, the most popular leases are for expensive or midrange vehicles and terms of 24 or 36 months. The most common form of leasing is the closed-end lease, where the monthly payment is based on three factors:

- *Capitalized Cost*: the purchase price for the car, net of trade-ins, fees, discounts, and dealer-installed options.

- *Residual Value*: the value of the vehicle at the end of the lease, specified by the leasing company (the "lessor") in the contract. The customer has the right to purchase the vehicle at this price at the end of the lease.

- *Money Factor*, or *Rate*: the interest rate charged by the leasing company.

A lower residual value results in higher monthly payments. Therefore, a leasing company with the highest residual value usually has the lowest, and most competitive, monthly payment. However, if the actual end-of-lease market value is lower than the contract residual value, the customer is likely to return the car to the lessor. The lessor then typically sells the vehicle, usually at auction, and realizes a "residual loss."

On the other hand, if the actual end-of-lease market value is greater than the contract residual, the customer is more likely to purchase the vehicle. By then selling the vehicle for the prevailing market value, the customer in essence receives a rebate for the higher monthly payments. (Of course, the customer may also decide to keep the car.) When customers exercise their purchase option, the lessor loses the opportunity to realize "residual gains." ■

The primary challenge for companies offering a closed-end lease is to select the residual value of the vehicle. Intelligent selection means offering competitive monthly payments on the front end without ignoring the risk of residual losses on the back end. In approaching this problem from a modeling perspective, the first task is to find ways to cut it down to size. After all, any leasing company offers leases on dozens of vehicles at any one time. Furthermore, unless it is just starting to do business, the company has an existing portfolio of hundreds of leases on its books, and the risk characteristics of this portfolio may influence the terms offered on new leases. We can become overwhelmed by complexity if we start by trying to model the entire problem. It is vital in modeling an ill-structured problem of this type to start simple and add complexity sparingly.

One reasonable approach is to develop an influence chart for a specific lease on a single type of vehicle. Once a prototype model based on this diagram is tested and proved, we can expand on it by bringing in excluded aspects of the problem.

An example will make the problem more concrete. Consider new Honda Accord models, which sell for $25,000. Also consider only three-year leases, and assume the money rate is fixed at 5 percent. Given these assumptions, our goal is to determine the best contract residual value (CRV) for a single lease on this single class of vehicles.

The CRV is clearly our decision variable. How will we determine whether we have made a good choice? Once we have chosen the CRV (and the other terms of the lease), we will offer it to the leasing market. Some number of customers will purchase our lease and pay us the monthly lease payments for three years. (A few will default during this period, but we ignore that factor in our initial prototype.) Our monthly lease revenues will be the product of the monthly payment and the number of leases sold. The monthly payment, in turn, will depend on the term, the money factor, and the CRV.

At the end of three years, all our leases will expire. Some customers will buy their vehicles at the CRV; others will return their vehicles and take a new lease with us; still others will return their vehicles and not purchase another lease with us. (We ignore the value of follow-on leases in our initial prototype.) When all is said and done, we will have made some level of profit. Profit, then, is our outcome measure, and it is influenced by three factors: lease revenues, our cost of borrowing (to pay for new vehicles), and the residual value of vehicles at the end of the lease (Figure 2.7).

FIGURE 2.7 Automobile Leasing Influence Chart

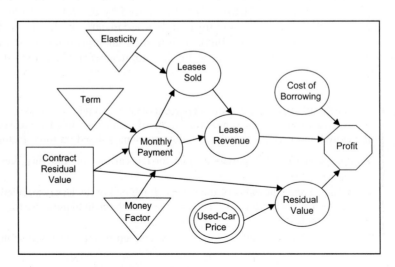

So far, this is a rather straightforward influence chart. But two parts of it deserve additional attention. First, what determines how many leases are sold? Presumably, customers are sensitive to the monthly payment, and that influence is shown in the diagram, but what else influences volume? One simple approach is to assume a value for demand elasticity: volume increases (or decreases) by *x* percent when our monthly payments decrease (or increase) by 1 percent. This relationship is sufficient to generate some realistic aspects of the lease market—namely, a decline in volume with increasing payments—and it may be sufficient for a prototype model. But it does not explicitly include any information about our competitor's monthly payments. In particular, the elasticity is probably different when our payments are above the competition than when they are below. This may be a fertile area for refinement in later prototypes.

We should also consider what factors determine the residual value of the vehicle to the leasing company. When a lease expires, the contract allows the customer to purchase the vehicle for the CRV or to return it to the leasing company. The customer's decision at this point is crucial to determining the profitability of the lease. If used-car prices are high relative to the CRV, it is in the customer's interest to buy the car at the CRV and then sell it for the higher market price. But if used-car prices are low, customers will tend to return their leased vehicles and buy a cheaper equivalent used car. In this case, the leasing company will have to sell the vehicle at the low market price. And, of course, some customers will lease a new vehicle regardless of used-car prices, and some may not behave in an economically rational manner at all. Should we include all of these factors in our influence chart?

One approach would be to assume that all vehicles will be purchased if used-car prices exceed the CRV, and none will be purchased if the reverse holds. But how do we know how much used cars will be worth three years from now? In our chart, we model used-car prices as a random variable—for example, a normal distribution with a mean of $15,000 and a standard deviation of $2,000. Alternatively, we might assume that this class of vehicles loses a random amount of its value each year, where the annual loss is uniformly distributed between 8 and 12 percent. This slightly more detailed model will also generate a distribution of values three years from now. In further refinements of the chart, we might expand on these ideas and model the fundamental determinants of used-car values: new-vehicle quality, the macro economy, and so on. In any case, a random value for used-car prices captures one of the essential features of this problem—namely, the uncertainty surrounding residual losses and residual gains. This influence chart is probably sufficiently detailed to support construction of a prototype model. Working with this model will help us discover whether we have captured the essential trade-offs in the problem.

As we have stressed before, the influence chart documents the simplifying assumptions made during the modeling process. Here are some of the critical assumptions embodied in Figure 2.7:

- One vehicle/one lease term
- No lease defaults
- No follow-on leases
- Rational behavior of customers at lease end
- Random used-car prices

We recommend that the modeler or one member of the modeling team record each assumption as it is made during the process of developing an influence chart. This is useful for two reasons. First, it focuses attention and discussion on assumptions as they are being made. Second, each assumption should be viewed as a potential area for later refinement of the model.

2.4 CRAFT SKILLS FOR MODELING

Successful modelers can draw on both technical and craft skills in their work. **Technical skill** refers to the ability to carry out specific, narrow, well-defined tasks in the modeling process. This includes, for example, calculating present values, or linking balance sheets and income statements correctly, or identifying a tail probability in the results of a simulation model. Proper use of technical skill leads to a correct result and allows little room for creativity. In contrast, **craft skill** does not lead to a single correct result and does require creativity. Some examples of craft skill are making useful simplifications in a complex problem, designing a prototype, or brainstorming ways to increase demand for a new product. Craft skills develop slowly, over time and with experience, whereas technical skills can be learned at one pass. In playing the piano, technical skill is developed by practicing scales, while real craft is needed to interpret the music while playing it. Craft skills are harder to describe and teach than technical skills, but they are just as important to successful modeling. In fact, it is the high level of craft skill that distinguishes the expert modeler from the journeyman. In this section, we describe some of the most important craft skills and discuss the role that these skills play in modeling. The modeling cases that appear later in the book provide opportunities to practice these skills in ill-structured problem situations.

Craft skills are rarely discussed in books on spreadsheets or management science. One reason may be the common perception that modeling is an art that cannot be taught, only learned through long experience. Another reason may be that expert modelers, like experts in all fields, are largely unconscious of their own craft skills. There is also no well-accepted theory or classification for the craft skills in modeling. Nevertheless, we have found that awareness of these skills is essential to the successful development of truly skilled modelers. We commonly encounter highly skilled spreadsheet users whose craft skills are weak. As a consequence, they cannot successfully employ modeling in new and ill-structured situations. On the other hand, we rarely encounter analysts with good craft skills who cannot learn enough Excel to become good modelers. Furthermore, craft skills *can* be learned, despite the impediments we have cited. The first step in this process is to identify the skills themselves so that the modeler-in-training can begin to develop an awareness of modeling on a higher level than the merely technical.

It is helpful to classify craft skills into useful rules of thumb, or **modeling heuristics**. In general, a heuristic is an approach, a strategy, or a trick that has often proved effective in a given situation. A widely cited example from general problem solving is to write down everything we know about a problem. Heuristics are thought to be one of the most common ways humans deal with the complexities of the world around them, so it should not be surprising to find that modelers have their own. A modeling heuristic is a rule of thumb that experienced modelers use to help them overcome the inevitable difficulties that arise in modeling. We believe that novices can improve their modeling abilities by observing how these heuristics are used in a number of different situations. However, the only way to acquire these skills is to practice them on new problems.

In this section, we describe eight fundamental heuristics and illustrate how they can be used in practice. For the novice modeler, our purpose here is to raise awareness of the role these skills play so that they can be called on routinely in modeling work. With practice and refinement they can become as familiar as technical skills. Implementing these ideas will lead to a stronger personal tool kit of modeling skills. The modeling cases provide an opportunity to begin practicing these skills. In fact, we initiate that process in this chapter.

Throughout this section, we will refer to four modeling cases that describe ill-structured problems. One involves assisting a friend in planning for retirement, another deals with determining how many draft TV commercials to commission, the third requires evaluating the feasibility of towing icebergs to Kuwait for drinking water, and the fourth involves determining the profitability of a new production process. Short synopses of these cases are given here, while the complete versions can be found in the collection of modeling cases at the end of the book. Before proceeding any further, it would be helpful to read these synopses and give some thought to how to model them.

EXAMPLE
*Retirement
Planning*

The client currently is 46 years old, with an income of about $126,000 per year. His goal is to retire between age 62 and 67 and to have enough savings to live comfortably in about the same fashion he does now (with some money available for expanded travel). The client's accumulated savings for retirement total $137,000. His employer contributes around $10,000 per year into the retirement fund, while he has been contributing $7,500. How much should he be saving? ∎

EXAMPLE
*Draft TV
Commercials*

The client directs TV advertising for a large corporation. His budget for a single ad campaign is typically around $10 million. Under current procedures, a single TV advertisement is commissioned for about $500,000, and the remainder of the budget is spent on airing the ad. The client is considering a new approach, in which two or more draft commercials (at about the same cost) would be commissioned from different agencies. The best of these drafts would then be aired using the remainder of the budget. Is this new plan more effective than the old procedure? ∎

EXAMPLE
Icebergs for Kuwait

Drinking water is in short supply in Kuwait and is therefore very expensive. One suggested remedy is to tow icebergs from Antarctica to Kuwait (a distance of about 9,600 kilometers) and melt them for freshwater. The volume of an iceberg ranges from about 500,000 cubic meters to more than 10 million cubic meters. Theoretical analysis suggests that an idealized spherical iceberg would lose about 0.2 meter of radius per day during transport, although this amount increases with the speed of towing and the distance from the pole. Fuel costs for towboats depend on the size of the boat, the speed, and the volume of the iceberg being towed. Would it be cost-effective to tow icebergs to Kuwait for freshwater, and, if so, how should this be done?   ∎

EXAMPLE
The Racquetball Racket

A new and cheaper process has been invented for manufacturing racquetballs. The new ball is bouncier but less durable than the major brand. Unit variable costs of production for the new process will run about $0.52, while the current process costs $0.95. A new plant would cost between $4 million and $6 million. We have 14 years of data on the number of racquetball players in the United States, the average retail price of balls, and the number of balls sold. The number of players is expected to increase about 10 percent per year for 10 years and then level off. In a recent survey, 200 players were asked to use both balls over several months, and their preferences were assessed at several different prices for the new ball. What is the net present value of an investment in a new plant to manufacture balls using this new process? What is the best price for the new ball, and how might the competitor react to introduction of a new ball?   ∎

2.4.1 Simplify the Problem

Without a doubt, the most important heuristic in all modeling is to *simplify*. Simplification is the very essence of modeling. We should never criticize a model for being simple, only for being too simple for the purposes at hand. Remember: a model that is too simple can often be modified to better suit the desired purposes.

A model that is more complex than necessary, however, already represents a waste of some modeling effort. Worse yet, a model may be so complex that it cannot be simplified effectively. It is, in fact, much harder to detect when a model is more complex than needed than it is to detect when a model is too simple. Overly simple models make us uncomfortable and motivate us to improve them; overly complex models may simply confuse and overwhelm us.

In discussing the importance of simplicity in models, Michael Pidd offers the following aphorism: "Model simple, think complicated."[2] By this, he reminds us that models are not independent of their users. So the right question to ask about a model is not whether the model by itself is adequate, but whether the user can discover helpful insights with the model. Simple models can support rigorous, critical thinking on the part of the user. Simple models are also more transparent and therefore easier to understand and apply. Users (and their managers) are more likely to trust simple models and implement the recommendations that are developed from their analysis. A modeling team will find that a simple model facilitates communication within the team, while only the modeling experts may understand a complex model.

There is no more useful tool in the modeler's kit than "keeping it simple." Thus, we try to cut away all complexity that is not essential. Never stop asking whether any particular aspect of a model is necessary for achieving the goals at hand. Novice modelers are often amazed at the simplicity of experts' models, particularly the simplicity of an expert's *first* model. Two other heuristics we will discuss later, decomposition and prototyping, are themselves powerful tools for keeping models simple.

How does one go about simplifying situations for modeling? One approach is to focus on the connections between the key decisions and the outcomes that result from those decisions. Then, ask what central trade-offs make these decisions difficult and build a model to explore those trade-offs. In the Retirement Planning case, for example, increasing one's savings rate reduces current disposable income but increases one's assets at retirement. If that trade-off makes the problem difficult, focus the modeling effort on that issue and leave out anything that seems peripheral.

In the Draft TV Commercials case, money spent on creative work will increase the quality of the advertisement, while money spent on buying airtime will increase the

---

[2] M. Pidd, *Tools for Thinking: Modelling in Management Science* (Chichester: John Wiley and Sons, 1996), p. 95.

number of consumers who see the advertisement. If the budget is limited, there is an inevitable trade-off between spending money on creative work and spending money on airtime. Focus the modeling effort on illuminating this trade-off.

In the Icebergs for Kuwait case, we know that large icebergs will provide more water, but they may take longer and cost more to transport. Small icebergs provide less water but may be more efficient to move. Here is an essential trade-off to capture in the model.

The goal in the Racquetball Racket case is not to make a highly accurate forecast of profits from the venture, but rather to understand the risks introduced by various factors such as the competitor's response to our entry. This argues for a simple but highly flexible model. Obviously, the pricing decision will be a key factor. A high price may provide attractive margins but also limit our market share. On the other hand, a low price may provide a large market share but leave us with very tight margins. The relationship between price and profitability is one important aspect of the problem, but it helps to keep this relationship simple because we are interested in understanding how it is affected by the competitive response.

Simplification by its nature involves making assumptions. Boldness and self-confidence in making assumptions is a mark of an experienced modeler. Many modelers, however, make assumptions but do not recognize that they are doing so. For example, in the Racquetball Racket case, many student modelers assume that sales will immediately reach a steady state. But if they don't realize this is an assumption, they miss the opportunity to test the sensitivity of their results to it. Thus, it is important both to make assumptions and to recognize them as they are being made. Every assumption should be revisited at some point in the analysis, to see if an alternative assumption would substantially change the results or provide new insights.

This discussion is summarized well by Morgan and Henrion:

> There are some models, especially some science and engineering models, that are large or complex because they need to be. But many more are large or complex because their authors gave too little thought to why and how they were being built and how they would be used.[3]

2.4.2 Break the Problem into Modules

One of the fundamental ways to approach any type of problem solving is to decompose the problem into simpler components. The decomposition approach is basic to Western science and, some would say, to Western thought itself. The challenge, of course, is to know where to draw the lines; that is, which are the most productive components to create? One approach is to divide the problem into components that are as *independent* of each other as possible.

In the Retirement Planning case, it is natural to decompose the problem into a working-life module and a retirement module. Within the working-life module, we will want to keep track of salary and other income as well as accumulating retirement assets. In the retirement module, we will follow the accumulated assets as they are drawn down for consumption. We may also track certain aspects of consumption, such as travel expenses. These modules are nearly independent: the only necessary connection is that the final assets from the working-life module become the initial assets in the retirement module.

In the Draft TV Commercials case, one module can be devoted to determining the quality of the advertisement that is ultimately aired, while another can be devoted to determining the impact of a budget for airing an advertisement of a given quality. These modules are largely independent: the quality of the advertisement chosen depends on the distribution of quality in the population from which advertisements are drawn, as well as on the number of drafts purchased. Meanwhile, the impact of a given budget in creating audience impressions depends on the size of the budget and the quality of the ad being aired. This latter module requires some assumption about the influence of incremental advertising dollars on impact. The simplest assumption would be that impact is proportional to advertising spending, although we might expect diminishing returns to set in eventually.

---

[3] M. G. Morgan and M. Henrion, *Uncertainty: A Guide to Dealing with Uncertainty in Quantitative Risk and Policy Analysis* (Cambridge, UK: Cambridge University Press, 1992), p. 289.

In the Icebergs for Kuwait case, a productive approach would be to create three modules. The first determines the supply of icebergs at the edge of the ice cap in Antarctica (by size, shape, etc.). The second module determines how large the iceberg is when it arrives in Kuwait, given its size and shape at the start of the trip, the speed at which it is towed, melting rates, and other factors. Finally, the third module converts the iceberg into a certain quantity of drinking water and a corresponding economic value.

In the Racquetball Racket case, a typical decomposition is to determine annual dollar sales of our ball by multiplying the number of users by the average number of balls purchased per year. The number purchasing our ball is the total number of users multiplied by our share of the market. Our share, in turn, is a function of our price and quality relative to the competitor's price and quality. There are, of course, other ways to decompose sales: by geographic region, by age of buyer, by product type, and so on. Choosing among these methods in a given situation depends on two things: how effective it is to build a model of one component and how easy it is to extend the model for one component to cover all the other components.

Why does the decomposition heuristic work? The great advantage of decomposing a problem is that the components are simpler to deal with than the whole. In addition, the process provides a natural structure for the analysis, thereby allowing the analyst to focus effort on one area at a time. Finally, this heuristic naturally leads us to think in terms of modules, and from there, it is a short step to discover the *interchangeability* of modules. For example, we can change our approach to modeling market share in the Racquetball Racket case without changing any other module. This leads us naturally to another powerful heuristic: *prototyping*.

2.4.3 Build a Prototype and Refine It

A **prototype** is just a working model. A prototype of a new car, for example, is a working model of the car, built to test design concepts prior to high-volume manufacturing. A prototype of a computer program is a working model that can be used to test whether the program works as intended. It can also be used to test the reactions of the users, who may not be able to specify their needs in the abstract but may discover their needs through experimenting with the prototype. A prototype of a model (in our sense) is nothing more than a working version of a model. As a working model, it should take data and inputs from the user and produce key outputs in response. However, the prototype is very likely to need further refinements because there will probably be gaps between its current performance and the desired results. These gaps describe the tasks that remain, either in terms of interaction with the user or in terms of analysis yet to be done, if the prototype is to be elevated to a finished model. Prototyping is an essential part of an effective modeling approach, especially when modeling is performed under tight limits on the available time and budget.

What would a prototype for the Retirement Planning case look like? In this case, the essential concern is to explore the relationship between working life savings and retirement assets. We might take as our objective the number of years that we can live off our retirement assets before they are exhausted. In order to estimate this result, it will be useful to simplify at the start some of the many complexities of the problem. For a first prototype, we could make the following assumptions:

- Income grows at a constant rate during the working years.
- The savings rate is a constant percentage of annual income in the working years.
- Retirement assets provide a fixed rate of return.
- The retirement date is fixed.
- Post-retirement consumption is a fixed percentage of income in the final year of work.

Using these assumptions, we can rather easily build a model that accomplishes the following tasks:

- Project our income (at some assumed growth rate) from the present to retirement.
- Calculate our retirement contributions (given a constant savings rate).
- Accumulate our retirement assets (at some assumed rate of return).
- Project our assets as they are drawn down during retirement (at the assumed consumption rate).
- Determine the year in which they are exhausted.

FIGURE 2.8 Sketch of Results for the Retirement Planning Case

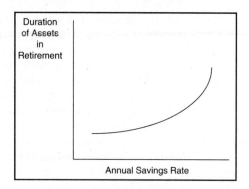

This simple model allows us to create a plot that shows how long our assets last as a function of our savings rate (Figure 2.8). If that relationship is the essential summary of our analysis, we have completed our first prototype. We can now test the model, varying decisions and parameters in an attempt to gain insight into the problem. Eventually, we may want to build a refined model, if the first prototype proves inadequate in some way.

In an initial approach to the Draft TV Commercials problem, we might avoid the complexities of sampling from a population of potential drafts and simply assume that advertisement quality increases with the number of draft ads, but with diminishing returns. We might implement this relationship using a power function:

$$Quality = a(Number\ of\ drafts)^b$$

We might also assume that the total budget is fixed and that each draft advertisement costs a fixed percentage of the budget. It follows that each additional draft advertisement reduces the budget available for airing by the same amount. If we assume that the total impact created by an advertisement is the product of the quality of the advertisement (in impressions per dollar spent on airing) and the airing budget, we have the basis for a prototype. From this simple model, we can plot a graph that relates the total number of impressions created to the number of draft advertisements (Figure 2.9).

Are we content with this first prototype? Probably not. Assuming that we have or can acquire some data on the variability of ad quality, we might later refine the portion of the model in which the quality of the best draft is determined. Sampling from a distribution of ad quality will give us the average quality of the best advertisement as a function of the number of drafts. We expect this function to have the same concave shape as the power function in our first prototype. But it will be better in at least two ways: first, it more closely resembles the actual process by which the best advertisement is created; second, it allows us to test the sensitivity of the results (total impressions created) to the variability in the distribution of quality.

A prototype for the Icebergs for Kuwait problem could be a model for the radial shrinking of a spherical iceberg of fixed initial size being towed at constant speed from the ice pack to Kuwait. If we calculate the final volume of the iceberg and multiply by the price of water, then we can compute an initial estimate of the value of the project.

This is the information the client wants, so our simple model is a legitimate prototype. Is this approach highly simplified? Of course it is. But the model's simplicity is its strength, not its weakness. If we have built our prototype quickly, we have time left over to refine it. Rather than having a number of separate pieces to integrate, we can work with one unified model.

Before refining this model, we would want to use it to explore the problem. For example, we would want to test the sensitivity of the final cost to the initial size of the iceberg, the towing speed, and the size of the boat. These tests will give us ideas not only about the ultimate results the model will generate, but also about where improvements might be warranted. We might, for example, want to test towing strategies that involve changes in speed over the trip. On the other hand, perhaps the weakest part of the model is the assumption that the iceberg is spherical and melts with a constant radius. Does the submerged portion of an iceberg melt faster or slower than the visible part? Does the ratio of these parts change with size? Every assumption is an opportunity to improve the analysis. The trick to effective prototyping is to find those improvements that lead to significant improvements in the results, not merely to a more elegant, more complex, or more "realistic" model.

FIGURE 2.9 Sketch of Results for the Draft TV Commercials Case

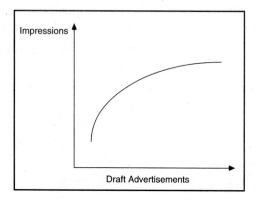

In the Racquetball Racket case, the objective is to help the client make a go/no-go decision. A highly accurate forecast of the NPV is not necessarily required, especially if the estimated NPV is clearly positive or negative. Thus, a prototype should give us a first, rough estimate of project NPV. It will move us closer to that goal if we assume that

- our competitor will price at its current level,
- our price and our competitor's price both remain constant over the life of the product,
- no third competitor will enter, and
- total demand for balls will grow at a constant percentage rate, independent of prices.

The only remaining component involves our market share, which we could model as an S-shaped function of our price. The following function is useful in this context:

$$Share = b + (a - b)(Price^c/(d + Price^c))$$

We can use the market research data to help us determine plausible values for the parameters $a, b, c,$ and d. With this module in place, we have a full prototype, because the model can generate an NPV for any price we choose. With the model, we can develop a chart showing how project NPV varies with our price and whether there is a price we can charge at which the project looks attractive (Figure 2.10). Once again, we are not done with the analysis. These results are only the first in what will most likely be a long sequence of estimates for project NPV, but this prototype supports the next stage in the analysis, which involves testing the sensitivity of our results to our assumptions.

In general, how do we know when we have a completed prototype? If we have

- decomposed the problem into modules,
- built at least a simple model for every module, and
- coordinated the modules so that they work together to generate results in the form we think the client wants,

then we have a prototype. If we cannot provide at least a tentative answer to the client's major questions, we don't have a prototype. If one or more modules are missing, we don't have a prototype. But once our ideas come together in a working model, the event marks a key milestone, for then the emphasis will shift from creation to refinement, in collaboration with the client.

The cyclic nature of prototyping is worth some elaboration. Many people think that prototyping involves building one model after another until we are satisfied that we have the final model, and *then* carrying out the analysis. This is a fundamental misconception. It is essential to use each successive prototype to answer the managerial questions in the problem before refining the model further. This discipline helps keep the modeler's attention on the *problem*, and not exclusively on the model or the modeling process. One reason modelers sometimes hesitate to use prototypes in this way is that they are embarrassed by the shortcomings of their early models and don't want to see them being used "for real." But this is the only way that a modeler can see the value of each successive refinement.

Why is prototyping such a powerful idea? One reason is that a prototype keeps the entire problem in the mind of the modeler. It is impossible to perfect a module in isolation because it has value only as part of the entire model. In most situations, we cannot know how well a module works until it is integrated with the others, so it is vital to build prototypes in which every major component is represented. Prototyping also helps avoid the seduction of modeling for its own sake. Remember that the task is to provide management with *insight*. Modeling is merely a means to that end. One way to maintain focus on the managerial question at hand is to use a series of prototypes to generate tentative answers to the client's questions. By using each model to provide an answer and by performing sensitivity analysis on each model, the focus will remain, appropriately, on the problem rather than on the model.

FIGURE 2.10 Sketch of Results for the Racquetball Racket Case

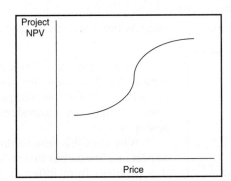

Prototyping is a particularly critical tool for novice modelers, who often struggle psychologically with the vagaries of the creative process. Many of our students have never struggled as hard as they do in modeling ill-structured problems. Some of them suffer from all the symptoms of depression when they have worked for a week and feel they have nothing to show for it. For these students, as for most modelers, having a working prototype, *no matter how primitive*, is a great psychological boost. Once we have a prototype, we have not only a tentative answer for the client, but also a road map for future work.

Finally, prototyping is an essential tool for the practicing analyst who operates under severe time constraints. Once a prototype is up and running, the analyst should ask this question: Where would my model benefit most from additional work? Or, to put it more precisely: Where should I focus my efforts to most improve the quality of my advice to the client? This is an impossible question to answer in the abstract. But with a prototype and some skill in sensitivity analysis, we can get a fair idea of which modules or which components within a given module have the biggest impact on the results. Thus, the prototype is itself a necessary tool in the analyst's efforts to use time effectively.

2.4.4 Sketch Graphs of Key Relationships

One of the reasons modeling is so difficult for many people is that it appears to be highly abstract or mathematical, and they cannot find a way to express their thoughts in these terms. Most people have good intuitions about the modeling challenges they face, but they lack the skills to represent those intuitions in a useful way. The ability to change representation systems is one of the powerful heuristics that experts suggest for general problem solving. Good problem solvers can look at a problem from many angles—inventing analogies, drawing pictures, hypothesizing relationships, or perhaps carrying out suggestive physical experiments.

Novice modelers rarely use drawings or sketches to represent their understanding of a problem. They haven't discovered that visual depictions of models are often much easier to work with than verbal or mathematical ones. When it comes to creating a relationship between variables, sketching a graph is a very useful first step.

The inability to visualize the relation between variables is a common stumbling block in modeling. Ask a manager whether the relation between advertising and sales is linear or concave, and you may get a puzzled look. Yet if we draw coordinate axes and label the horizontal axis "Advertising," and the vertical "Sales," most anyone will say the graph slopes up and probably "bends over" at some point. So the *intuition* for a concave relation in this case is widely shared; what many people lack is a representation system within which they can express their intuition. Such people lack the mathematical sophistication to select a plausible family of functions to represent a given graphical relation.

Here is another example of the power of visualization. When one of our students is completely stuck about how to start a modeling problem, we might draw a simple diagram (Figure 2.11) consisting of a box with one arrow coming in from the top and another going out to the right. Along with the drawing, we'll say that the way we see the problem, we have some decisions to make (arrow going into box), then the future will evolve in some way (inside the box), and in the end, we'll have some outcomes (arrow going out of box). The model we need to build is going to transform alternative decisions into outcomes we can evaluate. This simple picture does wonders—it focuses the novice on three key issues:

- What *decisions* do we have?
- How will we evaluate *outcomes*?
- What system of *relationships* connects the decisions to the outcomes?

FIGURE 2.11 Visualization of the Modeling Process

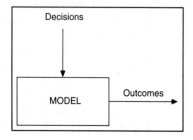

To an experienced modeler, this picture would seem trivial. To a struggling novice, however, it can be a revelation. Somehow, the picture itself is far more powerful than an equivalent verbal or algebraic description.

Why does this visualization heuristic work? We suspect one reason has to do with the power of looking at a problem from different viewpoints. Somehow,

FIGURE 2.12 Useful Functions for Modeling

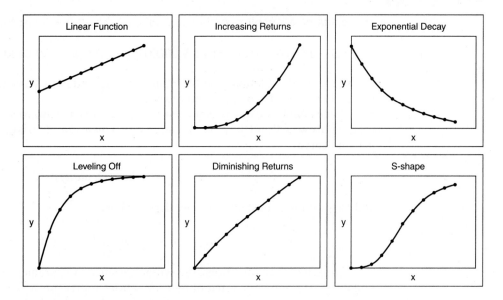

changing how we look at a problem often helps us overcome a sense of being stuck, of having no useful knowledge about a particular issue. (Novice modelers usually are able to sketch a graph for a relation, even when they say they know nothing about the mathematical function involved.)

Visualization probably works by *externalizing* the analysis—that is, by moving the focal point of analysis from inside the mind to an external artifact (such as a graph or equation). This is clearly essential for modeling in groups, where thoughts in the mind cannot be debated unless they are represented outside the mind. But it is also crucial for the solo modeler because it is far easier to test and refine an external artifact than an inchoate idea in the mind.

Sketching graphs is also a powerful heuristic because there is only a small set of possible relations between two variables that are useful in a typical modeling problem, and common sense can rule out most of them. The most often used is the simple straight line (with either positive or negative slope). In the spirit of prototyping, we often suggest that the *first* relation we would propose between *any* variables is a linear one. Build a working prototype first and gain some experience with it. Come back later and refine the linear relation if theory or intuition suggests a more complex relation and if model testing suggests that the results will be sensitive to this relation.

In order to make full use of this heuristic, the modeler also needs to know a few useful families of functions (also depicted in Figure 2.12). Here is a basic list:

- Linear function, showing constant returns (positive or negative), $y = a + bx$
- Power function with increasing returns, $y = ax^b$ with $b > 1$
- Exponential function, representing decline and decay, $y = ae^{-bx}$
- Exponential function, representing leveling off at an asymptote, $y = a(1 - e^{-bx})$
- Power function, with diminishing returns, $y = ax^b$ with $b < 1$
- The S-shaped curve, for rapid, then slowing growth, $y = b + (a - b)(x^c/(d + x^c))$

This use of graphs to select a family of curves to represent a relation is closely related to the parameterization heuristic discussed next.

2.4.5 Identify Parameters and Perform Sensitivity Analysis

We have seen that sketching a graph is a powerful way to express one's intuitions about the relationship between two variables. (The idea could be extended to three variables, although it gets more complicated.) But there is no direct way as yet to enter a sketch into a spreadsheet. Some explicit formula must be created to stand for the sketch in the model itself. This could take the form of a traditional mathematical function, for example:

$$D5 = \$A\$1 + \$A\$2 * D4$$

or it could be a complex combination of spreadsheet functions, for example:

$$D5 = IF((D2 - D1) > \$E\$4, VLOOKUP(E7, Data, 3), VLOOKUP(E7, Data, 2))$$

In either case, the relations involve input numbers, and these parameters play an essential role in spreadsheet modeling and analysis.

For example, we might hypothesize that there is a downward-sloping relation between the quantity we sell and the price we can charge. This assumption is consistent with the linear demand curve

$$Price = a - b \times (Quantity)$$

and also with the constant-elasticity demand curve

$$Price = a \times (Quantity)^b \quad (b < 0)$$

In each of these functions, the symbols a and b are parameters that stand for as-yet-undetermined numbers. Each of these functions represents a *family* of relations having the common property of sloping downward; the linear family declines at a constant rate, while the constant-elasticity family declines at a decreasing rate. When we implement one of these families in a spreadsheet model, we choose particular values of the parameters; that is, we select one from among the family of curves. Rarely will we know the values of these parameters exactly. This is where sensitivity analysis comes in. With sensitivity analysis, we can determine plausible ranges for the parameters and test the impact of changing parameter values on model outputs. In fact, we will recommend in Chapter 4 that testing the sensitivity of the critical outputs to model parameters is an essential step in any modeling activity. One reason we can be creative in the functional relationships we put in our models is that we have confidence that we can eventually test our results with respect both to the functions we have used and to the parameters that drive those functions.

Parameterization plays a key role in one of our favorite short modeling problems, called *Hot and Thirsty*.[4] The goal is to model the temperature of a warm beer as it cools over time in a refrigerator. Common sense leads to a difference equation of the form

$$T_{t+1} = T_t - Heat\ loss\ over\ the\ interval(t, t+1)$$

where T_t represents the temperature of the beer at time t. What factors influence the heat loss? Clearly, the type of beer may be relevant, as are the material used in its container, the shape of the container, the humidity of the refrigerator, how frequently it is opened, and so on. So many factors influence heat loss that one might think the only feasible approach is to gather data on all of them, a daunting task. However, there is an easier way.

A little understanding of thermodynamics (or some experience with refrigerators) will suggest that heat loss is proportional to the temperature difference between the beer and the air in the refrigerator, with the constant of proportionality depending on all the factors cited above; that is:

$$T_{t+1} = T_t - k \times \left(T_t - T_{fridge}\right)$$

If, for the moment, we assume some arbitrary value for the constant of proportionality k, it is straightforward to build a spreadsheet model for this relation. Then, as we choose different values of the parameter k, we can graph different decline curves for the temperature (see Figure 2.13). It is surprising but true that we can use common sense and a little experience with beer to determine plausible values for k within a rather narrow range, just based on the time it takes to cool to refrigerator temperature. We could also determine k rather accurately by cooling a beer for, say, 15 minutes and then determining its temperature. We can then use the family of curves in Figure 2.13 to read off the value

---

[4] A. Starfield, K. Smith, and A. Bleloch, *How to Model It* (New York: McGraw-Hill, 1990), 54–69.

FIGURE 2.13 Tempera-
ture of Beer over Time

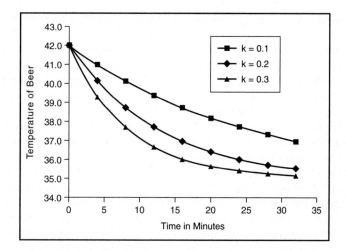

FIGURE 2.13 Temperature of Beer over Time

of k that gives us this temperature. This looks like sleight of hand, as if we were manufacturing knowledge out of ignorance. After all, we know that k depends on a long list of factors, none of which is known in this problem. Yet here we lump all these influences into a single number. What really has happened is that we have used intuition and common sense to build a structure (or model) that is more general than needed for the immediate purpose, and then we have specialized it to the case at hand by varying the single number k. We have also saved a lot of effort by building a model structure before we tried to collect data, because, using this approach, we never have to know the type of beer, its container, or anything about the refrigerator.

Why is parameterization such a powerful heuristic? We believe its power comes, as the previous example suggests, from our ability to select one from a family of curves by using sensitivity analysis. Parameterization also reduces the vagueness in a relation to a single dimension, which itself is a great simplification. Then, if we can find ways (such as the graphical approach described earlier) to display the implications of a particular choice for the parameter, we can bring to bear our usually considerable intuition about the problem. So the power of parameterization, in part, lies in building links between our rational knowledge and our intuition.

2.4.6 Separate the Creation of Ideas from Their Evaluation

Jim Evans, who has written extensively on the role of creativity in management science, points out in his book *Creative Thinking*[5] that one of the important emotional blocks to creativity is the tendency to judge ideas before they receive an adequate hearing. Many modelers we have worked with show a marked *preference* for judging ideas over generating them, especially if generating ideas means coming up with wild notions that probably will not work. But some wild notions actually do work, and others spark the mind to generate additional creative solutions. It is, therefore, essential to have methods available that help *quiet the critical voice* during the most creative phases of the problem-solving process.

The "quiet the critic" heuristic is based on the distinction, discussed earlier, between divergent and convergent thinking. Divergent thinking involves generating alternative problem statements, approaches, and possible solutions, with a minimum of evaluation. Convergent thinking, on the other hand, involves the rational analysis of these alternatives, with the goal of choosing the best (and rejecting the rest). Each stage of the problem-solving process involves both divergent and convergent thinking. However, it is generally most effective to stress divergent types of thinking early in the modeling process and to gradually shift to more convergent thinking as the model and analysis take shape.

The quintessential divergent-thinking process is **brainstorming**, in which a group generates as many ideas on an issue as possible, without any critical evaluation. The most effective brainstorming sessions involve a facilitator, who can set the ground rules and

---

[5] J. R. Evans, *Creative Thinking* (Cincinnati: South-Western, 1991).

remind participants not to criticize the ideas of others. The purpose of not criticizing ideas is to prevent premature selection of obvious or mundane approaches to a problem. Some participants always seem to have difficulty refraining from evaluating their own ideas or those of others during such a session. It is often equally difficult for them to show overt enthusiasm for ideas, from whatever source. Fostering a climate in which ideas are celebrated, regardless of their source or their apparent usefulness, should be a goal of modeling teams and individuals.

It's difficult to appreciate the power of brainstorming without seeing it in action. We recall a class session in which we were analyzing the problem of how to configure a highway tunnel to accommodate the maximum traffic volume. We had determined the optimal speed and heading for cars to follow, but were stuck on how to ensure that drivers would actually follow our solution. We then had a short brainstorming session focused on how to accomplish this. Among many other creative ideas, one student suggested installing rows of lights in the tunnel that would blink on and off at a speed set by the traffic engineers to guide drivers to the correct speed. This student was from another country, and the other students' first reaction was that this solution must be something she had seen in use in her home country. Once they began to realize it was not a known solution but something she had invented on the spot, they were more willing to think of alternatives beyond their own experience.

Why does this heuristic work? Apparently, our educational systems encourage students to criticize their own ideas and those of others, but not to create ideas or to appreciate their own and others' creative ideas. This imbalance can be so extreme that an open-ended project such as modeling becomes overwhelming because the pitfalls of every approach seem so clear to the modeler. When the critical faculty is so strong, the modeler needs reassurance that mistakes and blind alleys are a necessary part of the creative process. By finding ways to "quiet the critic," the novice modeler gains time to find a solution that eventually will stand up to their own scrutiny and to the scrutiny of others.

2.4.7 Work Backward from the Desired Answer

Most modeling projects proceed from the ground up: make assumptions, gather data, build a prototype, and so on. This is a reasonable approach in many ways, and to some extent, there is no alternative. But the bottom-up approach can lead to difficulties, especially in the hands of creative individuals. Creative exploration of a problem with a succession of models sometimes leaves the modeling team in a quandary about which approach among many to take and which results to show the client.

One way to break through this dilemma is to *work backward from the desired answer*. That is, imagine the *form* the answer will take, and then work backward from that point to select the model and analysis necessary to generate the chosen form of answer. An example will clarify this point.

It is clear in the Retirement Planning case that the client wants to know how his savings during his working life will influence his retirement years. But there are many ways to measure the quality of retirement living; which ones are best suited to this client? Would he like to know his asset level at retirement, or the number of years his assets will hold out, or the maximum amount he can afford to spend if he lives to 75, or the probability of running out of money before he is 90? Before we can focus our modeling, we must have an answer (even a tentative one) to this question. We also need to know how the client thinks about his savings decision—in terms of a constant percentage of his income or a constant dollar amount, or perhaps a percentage rising at a certain rate. Until we settle this question, we are also not ready to think about how we are going to present our results. If, after sufficient thought, we decide we want to show the client how his final assets depend on his (constant percentage) savings rate and how this relationship itself depends on the returns he can earn on his assets, we can sketch the chart shown in Figure 2.14 . Notice that we do not need a model, nor do we need any data, to sketch this chart because it is only an illustration. But the chart has considerable value because it focuses our modeling effort on a clear end product.

We sometimes facetiously call this the "PowerPoint heuristic." Here's the idea: most decision makers are very busy, so they cannot sit through a long-winded presentation. In fact, we like to imagine that our client is so busy that we have to condense our entire presentation to *one* PowerPoint slide. If that's all we have, that one slide must contain the

FIGURE 2.14 Sketch of Results for Retirement Analysis

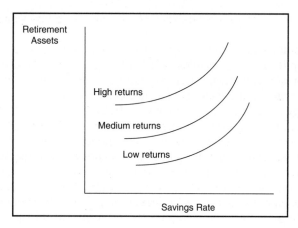

essential message we have to deliver. What is that message? Is it a number, a table, a chart, a procedure, a recommendation? Sketching out what that one slide might look like involves making decisions about the critical outputs, thus focusing the modeling effort on the essential message.

The power of this heuristic lies not just in being able to organize one's thoughts at the end of a modeling effort, but also in organizing the work itself by asking periodically: What will our final results look like?

2.4.8 Focus on Model Structure, not on Data Collection

As we mentioned in Chapter 1, novice modelers often spend a high proportion of their time searching for and analyzing *data*. Expert modelers, however, spend most of their time working on the *structure* of their models. This contrast has significant implications for the appropriate conduct of a modeling project.

Why do novices emphasize data analysis over model structure? This attitude appears to be based on three beliefs. First, novices assume that the available data are an accurate indicator of the information needed in the modeling process. Second, they believe that obtaining data moves the process forward in a productive direction. Third, they believe that the available data will ultimately improve the quality of the recommendations developed as a result of modeling. From these beliefs, it seems to follow logically that data collection and analysis should be an important and early activity in any modeling project. But these beliefs are not supported by experience. As Mosteller, Fienberg, and Rourke state it, "Although we often hear that data speak for themselves, their voices can be soft and sly."[6]

Novice modelers tend to accept, without critical screening, any data provided to them. By contrast, expert modelers know that most data contain hidden biases and errors. Perhaps the biggest single problem with empirical information is that it reports on the *past*, whereas modeling looks to the *future*. Even if we have accurate data on the growth in sales over the past 10 years, can we be sure next year's growth will follow the same pattern? Other common sources of biases and errors in empirical data include:

- Sampling error (e.g., a phone survey does not contact the homeless)
- Differences in purpose (e.g., accounting profits do not correspond to economic profits)
- Masking (e.g., actual sales may not reflect underlying customer demand)
- Inappropriateness (e.g., growth rates for one product may not predict those for another)
- Definitional differences (e.g., demand histories do not reveal price elasticity)

Experts look at all data skeptically, asking where the information came from and who gathered it (and with what motivations). They try to determine all the ways in which it may be flawed for the purpose they have in mind. Even when high-quality data are available, the modeler must use judgment before incorporating the data into a model. Sometimes, good judgment involves discarding parts of the data as irrelevant or misleading; sometimes it involves choosing how to summarize the data (whether to use the average or the worst case, for example). Experts, then, are much more skeptical than novices about the accuracy and appropriateness of data, and therefore more skeptical about the usefulness of data in a modeling effort.

While novices believe that collecting data will move the modeling process forward beneficially, they seldom recognize that data collection can also be distracting and limiting.

[6] F. Mosteller, S. E. Fienberg, and R. E. K. Rourke, as quoted in Jonathan G. Koomey, *Turning Numbers into Knowledge* (Oakland, CA: Analytics Press, 2001), p. 86.

For example, if the corporate database records sales by industry and by company size, most likely a model for sales will relate it to these two driving variables, rather than to less readily available, but perhaps more important, factors. A better model results in most cases if it is built up from first principles, without being overly influenced by the available data.

The Racquetball Racket case provides another example of how the availability of data can limit modeling creativity. The market research firm has given us information on the percentage of people who would buy our ball at various prices. They present the data in the form of a ratio of our competitor's price to our price. Does this imply that we should use the price *ratio* as the driving variable in our model of market share? The implication of such an approach would be that consumers do not react to the actual level of prices but only to relative prices. In other words, our share would be the same if we charged $5 and the competition $10, or if we charged $1 to their $2. Is this a plausible model, or might consumers react instead to the *difference* in prices? If we focus first on the data as presented, we may not even recognize the relevance of this question.

Thus, experts first build an appropriate model structure and use data to refine that model. The principle, in essence, is to let the model tell us what data we need rather than letting the data dictate our model.

Novice modelers often think they cannot build a useful model without acquiring good data first. Worse, they often feel that collecting good data, or at least better data than they currently have, is necessary before they even begin to *think* about a model. In either case, their premise is that data hold the key to a successful analysis. Some companies foster this attitude by emphasizing "data-driven decision making." A popular textbook even offers the advice that "one of the *first jobs* of an analyst is to gather exactly the *right data* and summarize the data appropriately." [Emphases added.] But how can a modeler identify the right data before building an initial model within which these questions can be answered? Most important, how can the modeler know what data will have the biggest impact on the ultimate recommendations that flow out of the modeling process? As Clifford Stoll says, "Minds think with ideas, not information. No amount of data, bandwidth, or processing power can substitute for inspired thought."[7]

Inexperienced modelers appear to believe that the quality of a model's recommendations depends critically on the quality of the model's data. But the managerial recommendations that evolve from modeling and analysis are often driven far more by the structure of the model than by the specific parameters in it. Therefore, it is imperative to get the model structure right, but it may be quite acceptable to work with rough parameter estimates. Once the modeling process has begun and a prototype provides us a basis for determining which data would be desirable, we can address the question of whether rough parameter estimates are sufficient. The precision needed for the numerical inputs can be determined only through testing the model itself. This is an additional benefit from sensitivity analysis, beyond the plausibility tests that we mentioned earlier. Sensitivity tools can help identify which parameters require precise values—that is, the ones for which data analysis would be most beneficial. Experts, then, focus on getting model structure right and on acquiring only data that they anticipate will materially affect their conclusions.

Based on our observations of expert modelers, we believe that data collection should rarely be the main concern in modeling. It is quite possible to build models, analyze models, and draw insights from models without relying on data analysis or statistical methods at all. In fact, we endorse that approach as a first cut. Data collection should ideally be undertaken only after a model-based determination has been made as to precisely which data are needed and with what level of precision. We have come to this point of view after observing problem-solving teams waste large amounts of precious time and effort on poorly conceived data collection expeditions, and observing novice modelers in a research setting become distracted from model structuring by the lack of data or by an excess of data. This is not to say that data collection is irrelevant; there are circumstances in which empirical data have a major impact on the quality of model-based recommendations. However, most business analysis takes place under a fairly severe time constraint. In such circumstances, modelers seldom have the luxury to search for the best possible data. Sometimes, we can find only data that were collected for other purposes and may not be tailored to our needs. At other times, very little data are available at all. At the extreme,

---

[7] As quoted in J. G. Koomey, *Turning Numbers into Knowledge: Mastering the Art of Problem Solving*. (Oakland, CA: Analytics Press, 2001), p. 101.

little or no data at all may be available. Nevertheless, we can usually structure a model without data and explore it for insight before concluding that data is critical. We must remember that *modeling* is central, not data.

2.5 SUMMARY

Effective modeling takes place within a larger problem-solving process. Modeling can be useful both in finding a good solution and in facilitating communication as the solution is developed, refined, and implemented. Therefore, it is important to recognize the larger context in which modeling occurs. We organize the problem-solving process into six stages:

1. Exploring the mess
2. Searching for information
3. Defining the problem
4. Searching for solutions
5. Evaluating solutions
6. Implementing a solution

Although it's convenient to describe these stages as if they were separate and occurred in a strict sequence, that is seldom the case. In fact, we can't always identify the specific activities at each stage until after the fact. Nevertheless, every implemented solution comes about through some version of this problem-solving process. Generally speaking, the bigger the problem at hand or the larger the team working on it, the more important it is to use a structured problem-solving process.

Mental modeling is an essential tool in problem solving. A mental model allows us to trace the consequences of a course of action without actually implementing it. In that way, mental models save us the time and cost, not to mention the occasionally disastrous consequences, of actually trying out alternative solutions to a problem.

Formal models provide the same kind of benefits as mental models. A formal model is a laboratory within which we can search for the best solution, without incurring the time and cost of trial-and-error approaches. Formal models are costlier and more time-consuming to build than mental models, but they have the great advantage that they make our assumptions, logic, and preferences explicit. They also allow us to search among many more solutions than would otherwise be possible. Finally, an effective formal model can help communicate the reasoning behind a solution and in that way help to motivate an individual or organization to act.

Influence charts offer the modeler a bridge between an ill-structured problem and a formal model. A formal model is usually precise and quantitative, but an influence chart is conceptual, abstract, and nonnumerical. It helps the modeler decide what is to be included in the model and what is to be excluded. It also helps focus attention on outputs, inputs, and the logic that connects them. Finally, it helps a modeler or modeling team to surface and recognize the assumptions behind the model and its limitations.

Modeling heuristics are rules of thumb that help in the design and use of models. They enhance pure technical skill by enabling us to invent models for new and unfamiliar situations. They also play a major role in the craft of modeling. Our list of modeling heuristics includes:

1. Simplify the problem.
2. Break the problem into modules.
3. Build a prototype and refine it.
4. Sketch graphs of key relationships.
5. Identify parameters and perform sensitivity analysis.
6. Separate the creation of ideas from their evaluation.
7. Work backward from the desired answer.
8. Focus on model structure, not on data collection.

Some of the items on the list are useful to help a modeling effort get off to a good start. If we think in terms of the chronological steps in a typical modeling project, the last heuristic may be the first one to apply: focus first on structuring a model rather than on obtaining data. The first model ought to be simple. It should be guided mainly by the desire to capture an essential trade-off in the problem. Simplification, by its nature, involves making assumptions about the problem, and these should be explicit. In any stage of model development, there should be a companion phase in which those assumptions are subjected to sensitivity analysis so that we can determine which ones need refinement. Devising a model structure made up of modules enables us to focus on the components of the model as a means of overcoming complexity in the overall problem. An ideal structure contains independent modules and allows interchangeable substitutes for the original module.

In building an initial model structure, we might start with visual representations, such as diagrams or graphs, for the inputs and also for the outputs. Visualizing the outputs, in the sense of working backward, keeps us focused on the precise requirements of the problem. Then, in order to convert graphical representations to mathematical representations, we might want to draw on a small family of familiar functions, specifying parameters as needed. Parameters used in this way are numerical assumptions, and, as with structural assumptions, they deserve sensitivity analysis. Sensitivity testing will tell us which parameters or which functional relationships are most critical to the ultimate outcomes.

Some of the heuristics on our list may be applied repeatedly during a modeling project. Developing a good model is a multistep process involving successive refinement. We start with a first prototype, and we test it to determine how well it addresses the problem. This testing may suggest we do some data collection, and it might stimulate our thinking about enrichments to the model. At various stages in the process, especially when the project is team-based, we may need some creative input from brainstorming activity. However, with the repeated cycles of model enhancement and model testing, we will have compiled some analysis, perhaps overly simple, that we can bring to bear on the problem. As we improve the model, we continually add to our store of knowledge and insight about the problem, so that at every stage in the process, we have an answer for the client and a sense of whether our analysis is adequate. Prototyping thus creates an important dialogue with the client and helps ensure that the focus remains on the problem rather than the model.

SUGGESTED READINGS

For more information on problem solving and creativity, consult the following books:

Adams, J. L. 2001. *Conceptual Blockbusting*. Reading, MA: Addison-Wesley.
Couger, J. D. 1995. *Creative Problem Solving and Opportunity Finding*. Danvers, MA: Boyd & Fraser.
Evans, J. R. 1991. *Creative Thinking*. Cincinnati: South-Western.

Very little has been written on the craft aspects of modeling, whether in business or science. The original work on heuristics in problem solving is the following:

Polya, G. 1971. *How to Solve It*. Princeton, NJ: Princeton University Press.

This little classic, which is still in print 60 years after it was written, is focused on problem solving in mathematics, but it still provides worthwhile reading. Three more recent books that discuss some of the ideas in this chapter are:

Pidd, M. 2003. *Tools for Thinking: Modelling in Management Science*. 7 ed. Chichester: John Wiley & Sons.
Koomey, J. G. 2008. *Turning Numbers into Knowledge: Mastering the Art of Problem Solving*. 7 ed. Oakland, CA: Analytics Press.
Powell, S.G. and R.J. Batt 2008. *Modeling for Insight*. Hoboken: John Wiley & Sons..

The following classic articles are still relevant after many years and remain worth reading:

Geoffrion, A. M. 1976. "The Purpose of Mathematical Programming Is Insight, Not Numbers." *Interfaces* **7**, 81–92.
Little, J. D. C. 1970. "Models and Managers: The Concept of a Decision Calculus." *Management Science* **16**, B466–B485.
Morris, W. T. 1967. "On the Art of Modeling." *Management Science* **13**, B707–717.
Urban, G. L. 1974. "Building Models for Decision Makers." *Interfaces* **4**, 1–11.

EXERCISES

PROBLEM FORMULATION

The four short cases we have analyzed in this chapter (Retirement Planning, Draft TV Commercials, Icebergs for Kuwait, and Racquetball Racket) are reproduced with full details toward the end of this book. For each of these cases, prepare for building a model by reading the full case and answering the following questions.

1. Explore the mess by answering the following questions:

a. What do we know?

b. What can we assume?

c. What could the results look like?

d. What information can be brought to bear?

e. What can we ask the client?

f. Are there any similar situations or problems?

2. Formulate one or more problem statements.

3. What are the decisions, outcomes, and relationships in the problem?

4. Draw an influence chart for the problem.

5. In what ways could we simplify the problem?

6. What modules will we need to build?

7. What are the key relationships in the problem? Draw their graphs.

8. What are the parameters of the problem?

INFLUENCE CHARTS

Draw influence charts for each of the following problems.

1. The Boeing Company faces a critical strategic choice in its competition with Airbus Industries for the long-haul flight segment: Should it design and build a super-747 model that can carry 550 passengers at speeds around 350 mph, or a plane that can fly at 95 percent of the speed of sound but carry only about 350 passengers? As a member of Boeing's Planning Group, your task is to build a model to investigate the trade-offs involved in this decision.

2. The Red Cross provides about 40 percent of the replacement blood supply for the United States. The available donor base has been shrinking for years, and although increased advertising has kept Red Cross supplies adequate, the time is approaching when demand will outstrip supply. For many years, the Red Cross has refused to pay donors for blood because to do so would "put the blood supply of the country at risk"; however, Red Cross management has begun to consider changing its policy. Evaluate the impacts of a policy under which the Red Cross would offer each of its donors a set fee.

3. Your client is the planning office of a major university. Part of the job of the planning office is to forecast the annual donations of alumni through the university's long-established giving program. Until now, the forecast has been made subjectively. The client wants you to develop a more objective approach. The Planning Office can make data available for the past 10 years that shows for each alumni class in that year:

• The number of living alumni in the class
• The number of givers
• Total direct donations from the class
• Other gifts for the class (e.g., employer matching)

4. Congress is considering a new law that will grant amnesty to the roughly 13 million illegal aliens in the United States. Under this law, anyone who has entered the country illegally in the past can apply for permanent residence status and a green card, which conveys the right to work. This law, if passed, can be expected to have significant impacts on industries that currently rely on illegal workers (such as hospitality, meat packing, and construction). It may also have impacts on wages, school enrollments, healthcare costs, and the future rate of illegal immigration.

5. A major pharmaceutical manufacturer is facing a difficult decision concerning one of its hearing-enhancement products. The product has been on the market less than two years, and reports have recently begun to come in that the product may cause serious hearing loss in certain users. The number and severity of these reports are not sufficiently high to warrant a recall order from the FDA, but if the reports continue this could eventually happen. In the meantime, management is considering issuing a voluntary recall to limit the potential damages. However, any such recall will probably destroy the future market for this product, which may be entirely safe, and it will also hurt sales of all other products sold by this company and depress its stock price.

SKETCHING GRAPHS

Sketch graphs for the relationships described in each of the following problems and select one or more of the families of functions discussed in Section 2.4.4 to represent it.

1. The relationship between the effectiveness of a new drug and the amount spent on R&D.

2. The relationship between the cost of manufacturing a product and the cumulative quantity produced.

3. The relationship between the time it takes to complete a project and the number of people assigned to work on it.

4. The relationship between the probability that the FDA will approve a given drug and the number of patients enrolled in the clinical trials of the drug.

5. The relationship between the sales of a given brand of cereal in a grocery store and the amount of shelf space devoted to displaying it.

3 Spreadsheet Engineering

3.1 INTRODUCTION

Builders of ships, bridges, and skyscrapers all spend considerable time and money planning the structure before they order concrete and steel. Even the builder of a modest house starts with blueprints and a plan of activities. Without detailed planning, complex structures cannot be built efficiently, and they sometimes fail in use. The same is true of spreadsheet models. Spreadsheets can be as important to a business as bridges are to a road network. If a business relies on a spreadsheet, the business should devote sufficient resources to ensuring that the spreadsheet is suitably *engineered*.

Advance planning can speed up the process of implementing a complex design. Some years ago, the auto industry learned that investing more resources in preproduction activities saved a great deal of time and money when a new car was being prepared for manufacturing. One of the major sources of efficiency in this case was avoiding cycles of rework and redesign. Without good planning, the need for design improvements is detected only after implementation has begun, and much of the implementation effort is wasted. The same is true of spreadsheet models: extra time spent in planning can actually *reduce* the overall time required to perform a spreadsheet analysis.

Sometimes, at the outset, it seems that a spreadsheet project will be fairly straight-forward. The flexibility of the spreadsheet environment seduces us into believing that we can jump right in and start entering formulas. Then, as we move further into the process of building the spreadsheet, it turns out that the project is a bit more complicated than it seemed at first. We encounter new user requirements, or we discover obscure logical cases. We redesign the spreadsheet on the fly, preserving some parts of the original design and reworking others. The smooth logical flow of the original spreadsheet gets disrupted. Rather quickly, a simple task becomes complicated, driven by a cycle of unanticipated needs followed by rework and additional testing. Before long, we face a spreadsheet containing "spaghetti logic," and as a result, we have reason to worry that the spreadsheet contains errors.

In addition to speeding up the design process, advance planning can help the designer avoid critical errors in a design. A mistake in the design of a building or bridge can cause it to collapse; a bug in a spreadsheet can lead to poor decisions and substantial monetary losses. As we pointed out in Chapter 1, research suggests that many spreadsheets actually in use contain hidden errors. Learning how to avoid bugs is an essential aspect of spreadsheet modeling. Many analysts spend 80 percent of their time building (and fixing) models, and only 20 percent using them for analysis. With good design skills, this ratio can be reversed, so that analysts can spend the majority of their effort improving actual decisions.

In this chapter, we offer guidelines for the engineering of spreadsheets. Our motivation is to improve both the efficiency and the effectiveness with which spreadsheets are created. An *efficient* design process uses the minimum time and effort to achieve results. An *effective* process achieves results that meet the users' requirements. Although spreadsheet modeling is a creative process, and thus cannot be reduced to a simple recipe, every spreadsheet passes through a predictable series of stages. Accordingly, we organize our guidelines around these phases:

- Designing
- Building
- Testing

In this chapter, and several later chapters, we draw on the following example to illustrate our precepts and methods.

EXAMPLE
The Advertising Budget Decision

As product-marketing manager, one of our jobs is to prepare recommendations to the Executive Committee as to how advertising expenditures should be allocated. Last year's advertising budget of $40,000 was spent in equal increments over the four quarters. Initial expectations are that we will repeat this plan in the coming year. However, the committee would like to know whether some other allocation would be advantageous and whether the total budget should be changed.

Our product sells for $40 and costs us $25 to produce. Sales in the past have been seasonal, and our consultants have estimated seasonal adjustment factors for unit sales as follows:

Q1: 90%	Q3: 80%
Q2: 110%	Q4: 120%

(A seasonal adjustment factor measures the percentage of average quarterly demand experienced in a given quarter.)

In addition to production costs, we must take into account the cost of the sales force (projected to be $34,000 over the year, allocated as follows: Q1 and Q2, $8,000 each; Q3 and Q4, $9,000 each), the cost of advertising itself, and overhead (typically around 15 percent of revenues).

Quarterly unit sales seem to run around 4,000 units when advertising is around $10,000. Clearly, advertising will increase sales, but there are limits to its impact. Our consultants several years ago estimated the relationship between advertising and sales. Converting that relationship to current conditions gives the following formula:

$$Unit\ sales = 35 \times seasonal\ factor \times \sqrt{(3,000 + Advertising)}$$

■

Although this problem is not ill structured in the terms we discussed in Chapter 2, it is still good practice to begin the process of building a spreadsheet model by drawing an influence chart. The key output measure is Profit, which decomposes readily into Revenue and Cost (see Figure 3.1). Revenue depends on Price and Units Sold, while Cost depends on Overhead, Sales Expense, Cost of Goods, and Advertising. The Cost of Goods depends on the Unit Cost and Units Sold. Finally, Units Sold depends on the Seasonal Factors and Advertising.

Drawing the influence chart helps us to clearly identify outputs (Profit) and decisions (Advertising). It also helps lay bare the essential relationships that connect the two. Finally, it should help us to recognize assumptions as we make them. Two assumptions in particular may be relevant later: one is that units sold are identical to units produced, so we

FIGURE 3.1 Influence Chart for the Advertising Budget Problem

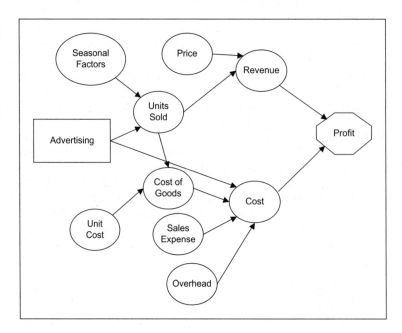

ignore the timing of production and inventory; the second is that price is considered a parameter, not a decision variable, and it does not influence unit sales.

3.2 DESIGNING A SPREADSHEET

The essential first step in developing any spreadsheet model is to *design* it. In this section, we offer some tips on good design practices for single-worksheet models. In the next section, we discuss how to design an effective workbook composed of interconnected worksheets. We begin with eight guidelines for designing a worksheet.

3.2.1 Sketch the Spreadsheet

Carpenters have the saying, "Measure twice, cut once." That is, since planning is inexpensive and miscut wood is useless, plan carefully to avoid waste and rework. A similar piece of advice applies to spreadsheets: careful planning tends to result in far less time spent correcting mistakes.

Turn the computer *off* and *think* for a while before hitting any keys. This advice may seem harsh at the start, but we have seen many modelers create a spreadsheet in a flurry of keystrokes, only to discover at some later point that their design is flawed and in need of wholesale revision. To those who are relatively new to spreadsheet modeling, we recommend beginning with a sketch of their spreadsheet before entering anything into the computer. We also believe this is a good first step for experienced modelers. A sketch should show the physical layout of major elements and should contain at least a rough indication of the flow of calculations. Instead of laboriously writing out formulas with cell addresses, we use variable names to indicate how calculations will be performed. For example, we might write: *Profit = Total Revenue − Total Cost*. In order to show the logic for calculating unsold goods, we might write: IF(*Stock > Demand, Stock − Demand,* 0). The acid test for whether a sketch is sufficiently detailed is whether someone else could build a spreadsheet from it without any significant redesign.

An influence chart often provides a useful starting point for a spreadsheet design, as we illustrated earlier. The process of constructing an influence chart helps to identify the key outputs and inputs, as well as the logic that connects them. These are all critical ingredients in the spreadsheet model, but a spreadsheet provides a somewhat different view. For one thing, a spreadsheet has to be populated with numbers, while an influence chart involves only the *names* of parameters, variables, and relationships. Also, the physical design of the spreadsheet is usually different from that of the influence chart. Whereas an influence chart begins with outputs and works back to inputs, a spreadsheet typically starts with inputs and works toward outputs.

For the Advertising Budget example, a sketch of the spreadsheet might include four major sections (Parameters, Decisions, Outputs, and Calculations), row headings for the entries in the Calculations section, and a brief indication of how each row in the model will be calculated. For example, we could note the equation, *Gross Margin = Revenue − Cost of Goods*. Figure 3.2 shows an initial sketch along these lines. In this sketch, we have not listed each of the parameters or the values of the decision variables. Nor have we shown specific cell addresses. The level of detail that is appropriate for a sketch depends on the complexity of the problem and the preferences of the designer.

The normal logical flow would require calculations to precede outputs. Why have we placed calculations at the bottom of the spreadsheet? The reason has to do with the use we envision for the model. We expect to vary some of the decision variables, and we'll want to know the consequences for the output measure. Since we want to see the effects of varying decisions on the output, it makes sense to place these items close together in the spreadsheet. In addition, we may also want to alter one or more of the input parameters and revisit the relationship between decisions and output. Therefore, it also makes sense to have inputs in close proximity to the output and decisions. The one part of the spreadsheet we won't be examining or altering, once we've tested it, is the set of calculations. Therefore, we place the calculations in a secondary location.

Part of the thinking process, then, is anticipating what use will be made of the model. We will return to this point later, but for now, the planning process should take this into consideration when the model structure is sketched.

FIGURE 3.2 Sketch of
Spreadsheet for the
Advertising Budget
Problem

FIGURE 3.2 Sketch of Spreadsheet for the Advertising Budget Problem

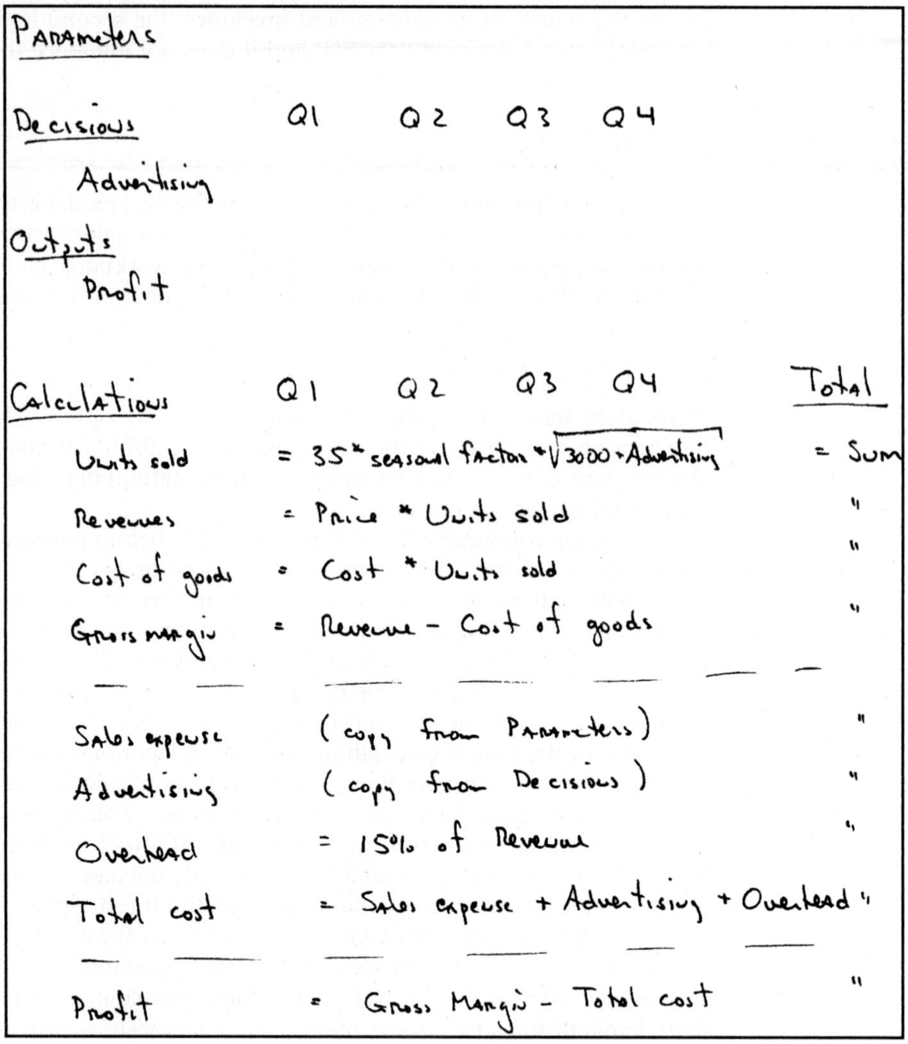

3.2.2 Organize the Spreadsheet into Modules

Modules bring together groups of similar items, and they separate unlike items. Modularization is a basic principle of good design and a useful first step in organizing information. In spreadsheets, this means separating data, decision variables, outcome measures, and detailed calculations. If an influence chart has been constructed, as discussed in Chapter 2, then a lot of this work will already have been done. An influence chart will have identified the outcome measure (or measures) of major interest as well as the data and decisions that make up the inputs. Most importantly, the influence chart will also have organized the major steps in the calculations required to produce the outputs.

Along with grouping and separating, the next step is to consider the flow of information in the model—that is, to specify which information will need to pass from one group to another. Data and decisions will serve as inputs to some of the calculations, and a small number of the calculations will eventually be highlighted as outputs. After these key linkages are identified, the additional development of one module can go on somewhat independently of modifications in other modules. Keep in mind that formulas should generally reference cells located above and to the left.

Figure 3.3* displays our spreadsheet for the Advertising Budget example. Following the layout in our initial sketch, we use four modules and surround each one with a border for clarity. The detailed calculations are simple enough to include in a single block, but even here, we use blank lines to separate gross margin, costs, and profits. We highlight values of decision variables (the quarterly advertising expenditures) and the output

---

* To download spreadsheets for this chapter, go to the Student Companion Site at www.wiley.com/college/powell.

FIGURE 3.3 The Advertising Budget Spreadsheet

	A	B	C	D	E	F	G	H	I	J
1	Advertising Budget Model									
2	SGP/KRB									
3	1/1/2013									
4										
5	PARAMETERS									
6				Q1	Q2	Q3	Q4			Notes
7		Price	$40.00							Current price
8		Cost	$25.00							Accounting
9		Seasonal		0.9	1.1	0.8	1.2			Data analysis
10		OHD rate	0.15							Accounting
11		Sales Parameters								
12			35							Consultants
13			3000							
14		Sales Expense		8000	8000	9000	9000			Consultants
15		Ad Budget	$40,000							Current budget
16										
17	DECISIONS							Total		
18		Ad Expenditures		$10,000	$10,000	$10,000	$10,000	$40,000		sum
19										
20	OUTPUTS									
21		Profit	$69,662							
22										
23	CALCULATIONS									
24		Quarter		Q1	Q2	Q3	Q4	Total		
25		Seasonal		0.9	1.1	0.8	1.2			
26										
27		Units Sold		3592	4390	3192	4789	15962		given formula
28		Revenue		143662	175587	127700	191549	638498		price*units
29		Cost of Goods		89789	109742	79812	119718	399061		cost*units
30		Gross Margin		53873	65845	47887	71831	239437		subtraction
31										
32		Sales Expense		8000	8000	9000	9000	34000		given
33		Advertising		10000	10000	10000	10000	40000		decisions
34		Overhead		21549	26338	19155	28732	95775		rate*revenue
35		Total Fixed Cost		39549	44338	38155	47732	169775		sum
36										
37		Profit		14324	21507	9732	24099	69662		GM-TFC
38		Profit Margin		9.97%	12.25%	7.62%	12.58%	10.91%		pct of revenue
39										

measure (annual profit) with color shading. Models that are more complex may, of course, contain many more modules and require layouts that are more elaborate.

As planned, the modules for parameters, decisions, and outputs are in close proximity. Therefore, we can change the value of an input and immediately see the impact on the output in the same Excel window.

3.2.3 Start Small

Do not attempt to build a complex spreadsheet all at once. Isolate one part of the problem or one module of the spreadsheet; then design, build, and test that one part. Once that part of the model is in good shape, go on to the next one. By making (and correcting) many little mistakes in each module, and thus keeping the mistakes local if they occur, it is possible to avoid making really large and complex mistakes that require much more effort to detect and correct.

If we were building a model to cover 100 customers, it would make sense to start with a model for one customer, or perhaps a few customers. If the model structure is the same or similar for each of the customers, it should be easy to replicate this initial building block. Then, when the basic building block is working, the model can be expanded to include the remaining customers. Similarly, if we were building a complex model to cover 12 months, we would start by building a model for the first month; then we would expand it to 2 months and ultimately to all 12.

In the Advertising Budget example, we start by creating the Parameters and Decisions modules, because those simply organize and display the information we have gathered. Since we do not know at the outset what values we will ultimately choose for the decision variables, we enter convenient values (last year's expenditures of $10,000 each quarter seem appropriate), simply to hold a place and to assist us in debugging the logic of the spreadsheet. When we begin work on the financial logic, we focus on the first quarter. Only when the profit in the first quarter has been calculated successfully should we move on to the rest of the year. (Recursive formulas, which use a previous value to calculate the current value, facilitate this process.)

3.2.4 Isolate Input Parameters

Place the numerical values of key parameters in a single location and separate them from calculations. This means that formulas contain only cell references, not numerical values. It also means that a parameter contained in several formulas appears only once as a numerical value in the spreadsheet, although it may appear several times as a cell reference in a formula.

Parameterization offers several advantages. First, placing parameters in a separate location makes it easy to identify them and change them. It also makes a particular scenario immediately visible. Parameterization ensures that changing a numerical value in one cell is sufficient to induce a change throughout the entire model. In addition, parameterization is required for effective sensitivity analysis, as we discuss in Chapter 4. Finally, it is relatively easy to document the assumptions behind parameters, or the sources from which they were derived, if those parameters appear in a single location.

In our audits of spreadsheets, we frequently observe a tendency to bury parameters in cell formulas and to replicate the same parameter in multiple cells. This makes identifying parameters difficult, because they are not immediately visible. It's also difficult to know whether all numerical values of a parameter have been changed each time an update is required. By contrast, the habit of using a single and separate location considerably streamlines the building and debugging of a spreadsheet.

In our sample spreadsheet, all the parameters are located in a single module (cells B6:G15). Notice, for example, that price is referenced in cells D28:G28. When price is changed in C7, it is automatically changed in these other cells as well.

3.2.5 Design for Use

While designing a spreadsheet, try to anticipate who will use it and what kinds of questions they will want to address. Make it easy to change parameters that can be expected to change often. Make it easy to find key outputs by collecting them in one place. Include graphs of the outputs to make it easier to learn from the spreadsheet.

In our example spreadsheet, we have anticipated that when we move into the analysis phase, we will primarily be changing one or more values in the Parameters module or the Decisions module and observing the effect on the key output, annual profits. That is why we have copied the value of profits from cell H37 to cell C21, where it can be read more conveniently. In a larger model, the outputs may be scattered over many locations in different worksheets. It is very helpful to gather them together and place them near the inputs so that the details of the model itself do not interfere with the process of analysis. We will have more to say about this principle when we discuss workbooks in the next section.

3.2.6 Keep It Simple

Just as good models should be simple, good spreadsheets should be as simple as possible while still getting the job done. Complex spreadsheets require more time and effort to build than simple ones, and they are *much* more difficult to debug. Some of our earlier guidelines, such as modularization and parameterization, help keep models simple.

Long formulas are a common symptom of overly complex spreadsheets. The most serious constraint on effective spreadsheet modeling is not computing power, but human brainpower. Therefore, there is little to be gained from minimizing the number of cells in a spreadsheet by writing a long formula in one cell. It is better to decompose a complex calculation into its intermediate steps and to display each step in a separate cell. This makes it easier to spot errors in the logic and to explain the spreadsheet calculations to others. Overall, it is a more efficient use of the combined human–computer team.

In the Advertising Budget example, we could calculate Gross Margin (cell D30) in a single row rather than use three rows to calculate its components (Units Sold, Revenue, and Cost of Goods). However, the detail helps in checking the logic, and it may eventually prove helpful during analysis. Later on, for example, we may decide that it would be more realistic to model sales as a function of price. Instead of modifying a complicated Gross Margin formula, we will find it easier to work with the formula for Units Sold.

3.2.7 Design for Communication

Spreadsheets are often used long after the builder ever thought they would be, and frequently by people who are not familiar with them. Logical design helps users understand what the spreadsheet is intended to accomplish and how to work with it effectively. The look and the layout of a spreadsheet often determine whether its developer or another user can understand it several months or years after it was built. Visual cues that reinforce the model's logic also pay dividends when the spreadsheet gets routine use in a decision-support role.

The use of informative labels and the incorporation of blank spaces can go a long way toward conveying the organization of a spreadsheet. The specialized formatting options in Excel (outlines, color, bold font, and so on) can also be used to highlight certain cell entries or ranges for quick visual recognition. This facilitates navigating around the spreadsheet, both when building the spreadsheet and when using it. However, formatting tools should be applied with care. If used to excess, formatting can confuse, obscure, and annoy rather than help. In our example spreadsheet, we use various formatting tools to improve readability, including bold font, borders, color shading, and capitalization. Within a team or an organization, or when creating a series of spreadsheets, it also helps to use these formatting tools consistently. For example, we use yellow shading and a border to designate cells that represent decision variables in virtually all of our spreadsheet models.

Sometimes large spreadsheets can be reorganized with the help of split windows. For example, if we were to display the Advertising Budget spreadsheet at normal size, it would not fit within one (laptop) window. As a result, the lower part of the Calculations module would drop out of view. If we wanted to preserve the top portion of the spreadsheet, but also view the quarterly profit levels and the profit-margin percentages, we could split the window vertically, as shown in Figure 3.4. (To split a screen, select a row or column and choose View▶Window▶Split.)

3.2.8 Document Important Data and Formulas

Spreadsheets have become widespread in the business world because they are easy to build and use. Originally, many analysts learned to build spreadsheets because their corporate information technology departments could not serve their needs in a timely fashion. One reason for the lack of a timely response is that information technology professionals use a careful and time-consuming design process for creating computing applications, including extensive documentation. Spreadsheet users rarely apply the same level of effort to their applications. The question, then, is: How can we preserve the benefits of using spreadsheets, while also gaining the benefits of a careful design process?

One answer to this question is to find *practical* ways to document a spreadsheet. Creating separate documentation or user manuals is often impractical. But it is neither difficult nor time consuming to record the source of each important parameter and explain

FIGURE 3.4 Split-Window Display in the Advertising Budget Spreadsheet

	A	B	C	D	E	F	G	H	I	J
1	Advertising Budget Model									
2	SGP/KRB									
3	1/1/2013									
4										
5	PARAMETERS									
6				Q1	Q2	Q3	Q4			Notes
7		Price	$40.00							Current price
8		Cost	$25.00							Accounting
9		Seasonal		0.9	1.1	0.8	1.2			Data analysis
10		OHD rate	0.15							Accounting
11		Sales Parameters								
12			35							Consultants
13			3000							
14		Sales Expense		8000	8000	9000	9000			Consultants
15		Ad Budget	$40,000							Current budget
16										
17	DECISIONS							Total		
18		Ad Expenditures		$10,000	$10,000	$10,000	$10,000	$40,000		sum
37		Profit		14324	21507	9732	24099	69662		GM -TFC
38		Profit Margin		9.97%	12.25%	7.62%	12.58%	10.91%		pct of revenue
39										

3.3 3.4

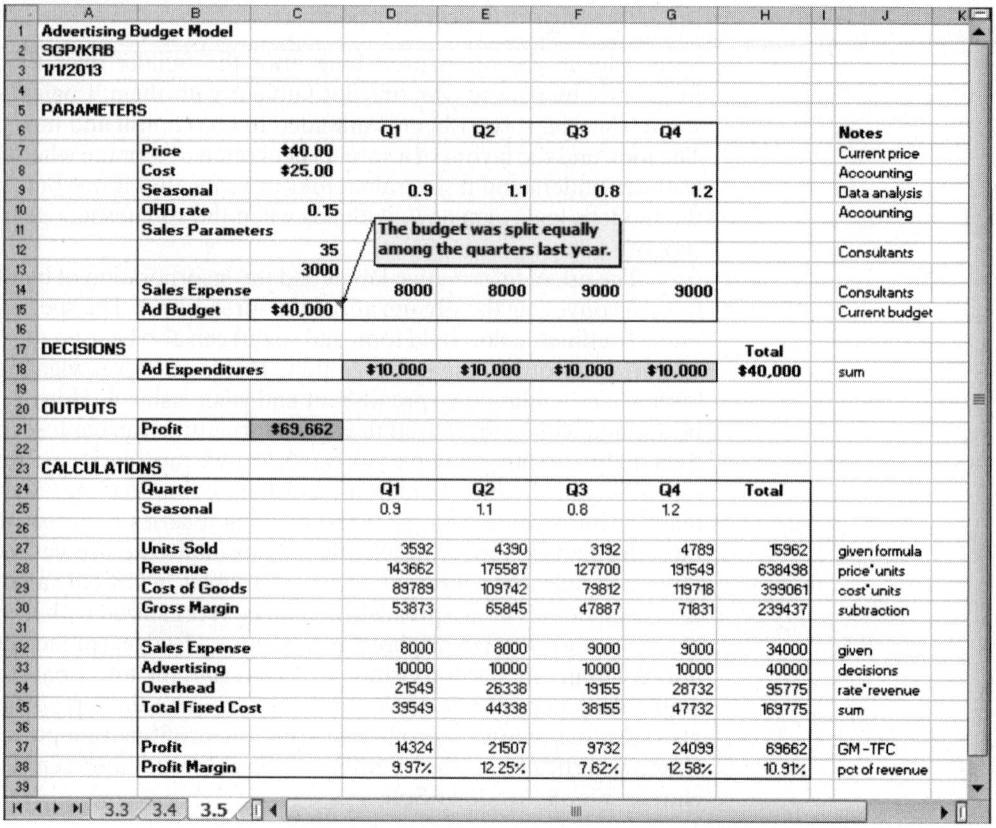

FIGURE 3.5 Comment Window for the Budget Parameter

each important calculation in the spreadsheet itself. A design sketch or influence chart of the spreadsheet provides documentation, in a fashion, for every important relationship in the model. Transferring this information to the actual spreadsheet helps preserve the underlying logic of the model and ultimately helps convey that logic to users of the spreadsheet.

In our example spreadsheet, we have documented both input parameters and the model logic in column J (refer to Figure 3.3). We have noted the source of each of the parameters: the accounting department, consultants, and so on. For each formula, we have provided a short explanation of the arithmetic, such as *Revenue = Price*Units*.

At the detailed level, we can provide documentation within individual cells by inserting cell comments. The command Review▸Comments▸New Comment brings up a small window in which we can describe the contents of the cell where the cursor is located. Figure 3.5 shows an example in which the Comment window explains that last year the budget was distributed equally among the quarters. The format of the comment is controlled by a selection from the File▸Options▸Advanced menu. In the Display Section within this menu are three buttons controlling the display of cell comments. A comment can be displayed permanently by clicking on Comments and indicators. Or we can click on No comments or indicators, in which case there will be a red triangle in the upper right-hand corner of the cell, but the comment will be displayed only when the cursor is placed within that cell. If we click on No Comments, then neither the comment nor the indicator will be visible at all.

Finally, it may be worth creating a separate module to list the assumptions in the model, particularly the structural simplifications adopted at the outset of the model-building process. In the Advertising Budget example, we assumed that production quantities would be equal to demand quantities each quarter and that there would be no inventory. That is, we assumed that we could ignore the detailed timing problems that might arise in the supply chain when we attempt to meet demand directly from production. These assumptions will not be obvious to another user of the model but may significantly influence the results. Thus, they should be noted on the spreadsheet itself.

Workbooks offer additional options for effective documentation, as they do for most of the other guidelines. We now turn to the question of how to design workbooks effectively.

3.3 DESIGNING A WORKBOOK

Although many effective spreadsheet models use only a single worksheet, it is often desirable to use multiple worksheets in a workbook. In fact, the multisheet format can be exploited to better accomplish many of the goals discussed in the previous section, such as modularization and ease of use. Most of the design principles described above apply equally well to the design of workbooks. However, some additional issues arise, as we discuss below. (The Northern Museum model is available with the book. We recommend that the reader open this model and explore it before reading on.)

EXAMPLE
Northern Museum Capital Campaign

The Northern Museum is a 115-year-old natural history museum located in northern New England. It houses extensive natural history, historical, and ethnological collections in a 20,000-square-foot building. It also houses a planetarium and weather station.

The physical plant of the Museum has grown increasingly inadequate for its programs and collections, and the Board has begun planning seriously for a major capital campaign. This campaign will attempt to raise several million dollars over a six-year period. In order to raise this money, the Board will have to authorize significant expenditures for consultants and other expenses. In a typical campaign, expenses exceed donations for at least the first two years. The Board is concerned that the campaign and ongoing revenue shortfalls from operations may have serious impacts on its endowment.

In order to understand the financial implications of the capital campaign, the Board and the executive director asked the treasurer to construct a planning model. This model would link the short-term budgeting perspective the Board had traditionally taken to finances with a long term planning perspective. It would allow the Board and the director to make explicit their assumptions about the future growth of the Museum in the context of the capital campaign and to evaluate the consequences of those assumptions on its financial health.

An early step in the process of developing this model was to construct an influence chart (Figure 3.6). This chart shows that a central purpose of the model was to track the evolution of the endowment and how it is influenced by both operating results and the capital campaign. The critical assumption that drives the model is that shortfalls between operating revenues and costs will be made up by withdrawals ("Drawdowns") from the endowment. This process had actually been going on at the Museum for several years, and the Board was concerned that expenses associated with the capital campaign not be allowed to reduce the endowment to a dangerous level before it could be built up from donations. ∎

FIGURE 3.6 Influence Chart for Northern Museum Model

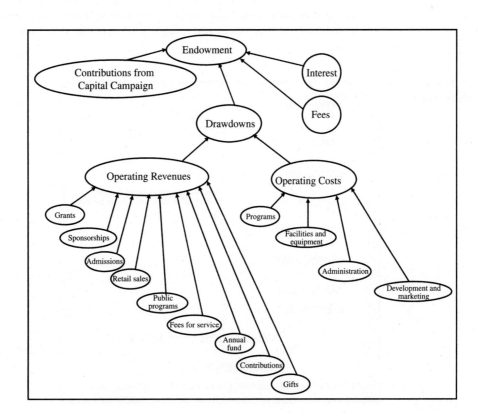

3.3.1 Use Separate Worksheets to Group Similar Kinds of Information

Workbooks should be designed to make a model easy to understand and use. Individual worksheets should each have a well-defined purpose and be given descriptive names. They should also appear in a natural order. Assumptions, calculations, and results should be placed on separate worksheets whenever possible. This allows users to view assumptions and results without being distracted by the details of the calculations.

The Northern Museum workbook consists of 10 worksheets appearing in the following order:

Overview: Describes the purpose and assumptions behind the model

Instructions: Gives step-by-step instructions for using the model

Log of changes: Records the major changes made to the model over time

Guide to sheets: Shows the logical relationships among the worksheets and provides hyperlinks to navigate directly to any worksheet

Influence chart: Depicts the fundamental logic of the model itself

Assumptions: Provides some historical data and records assumptions used in the model

Long-term Model: Projects revenues, costs, endowment, and critical ratios from 2006 to 2016

Short-term results: Summarizes projections one and three years out in the same format as the Long-term Model worksheet

Historical data: Records historical data

Ratio charts: Provides graphical depiction of the ratios calculated in the Long-term Model worksheet

Figure 3.7 shows the Guide to sheets. This simple worksheet helps the user to understand the structure of the workbook and to determine which worksheets provide inputs to other sheets. For example, it shows that the Long-term Model sheet takes its inputs only from the Assumptions sheet. If we examine cell F30 in the Long-term Model sheet, we see that it references cell F30 on the Assumptions sheet (using the formula =Assumptions!F30). In Excel, a reference to a cell on another worksheet begins with the name of that worksheet followed by an exclamation mark. When entering formulas that contain references to other worksheets, the references themselves become complicated, and most users find it convenient to create these references by pointing and clicking. The complexity of multisheet references reinforces the importance of keeping formulas

FIGURE 3.7 Northern Museum Model: Guide to Sheets

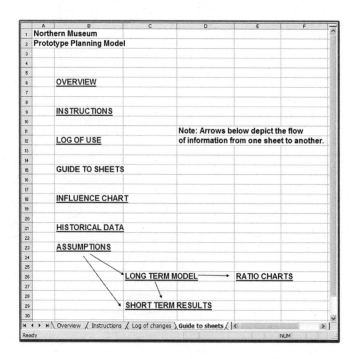

and worksheet names simple, so that someone examining the logic for the first time can follow the calculations. Another way to make formulas look simple is to use range names.

3.3.2 Design Workbooks for Ease of Navigation and Use

The purpose of a structured workbook is to facilitate understanding by users, so any form of structural help for finding their way around the workbook is beneficial. Using revealing names for individual worksheets is one helpful approach. (To change a worksheet name, double-click on the name tab at the bottom of the spreadsheet and edit the name, or right-click on the worksheet name and select `Rename`.)

The Northern Museum workbook illustrates a number of techniques for assisting the user with navigation and use. We pointed out previously that the worksheet named Guide to sheets (Figure 3.7) shows the logical relationships among the worksheets. It also provides an easy way to navigate to a particular worksheet. Each of the cells that displays a worksheet name also has a hyperlink, so that when the user clicks on the worksheet name, the display moves to the corresponding worksheet. (A hyperlink can be added to a cell by choosing Insert►Links►Hyperlink.) The Influence chart sheet also uses hyperlinks to take the user from a given variable such as Revenues to the exact location in the Long-term Model sheet where that variable is calculated (cell A26). Finally, the Long-term Model sheet illustrates another use of hyperlinks for navigation. The phrase `Return to Influence chart` appears near the upper left corner of the worksheet. This phrase is created using Word Art (Insert►Text►WordArt). A hyperlink can be associated with WordArt by highlighting the WordArt object and choosing Insert►Links►Hyperlink. Click on this phrase and Excel returns to the Influence chart sheet.

Another approach to navigation aids is to use buttons. A button is one of the Form Controls that can be selected from the Developer tab. Select Developer► Controls►Insert to display the menu of choices. For example, we can create a command button that will invoke a particular macro. (Macros are also covered in Appendix 2.) In the Ratio charts sheet, we have created a Command Button called `Go to Guide`, whose purpose is to take the user back to the Guide to sheets. It calls on the following macro that was created using the Record Macro procedure (Developer►Code►Record Macro):

```
ActiveSheet.Shapes("CommandButton1").Select
Sheets("Guide to sheets").Select
ActiveSheet.Range("A1").Select
```

In worksheets with many rows it is often difficult to recognize the large-scale structure among all the details. The Excel Group and Outline option (Data► Outline►Group) can be used in these cases to help the user understand the structure and navigate to the desired location quickly. Grouping simply provides a display option in which the rows that provide details can be hidden in the display. Figure 3.8 shows how

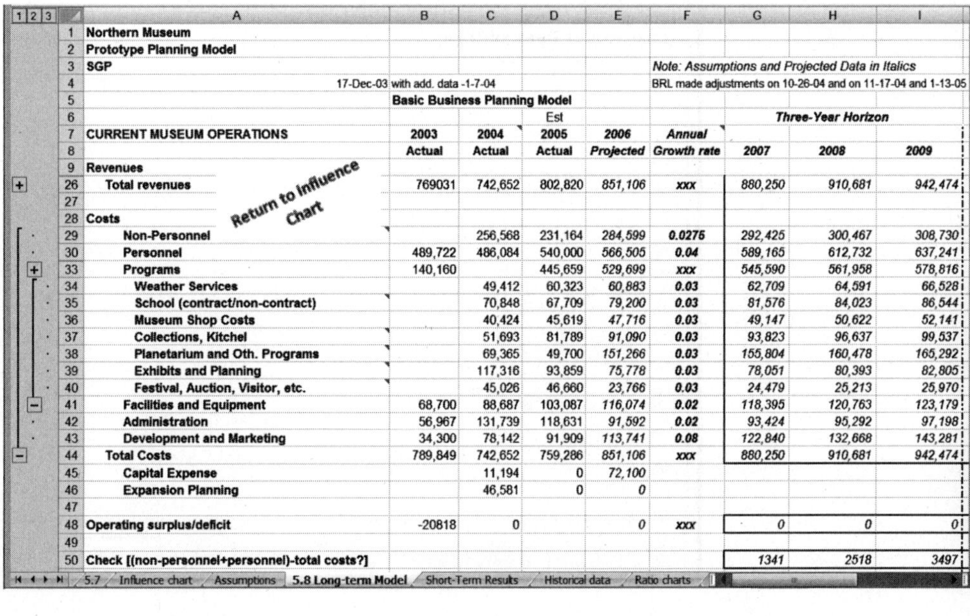

	A	B	C	D	E	F	G	H	I
1	Northern Museum								
2	Prototype Planning Model								
3	SGP					Note: Assumptions and Projected Data in Italics			
4	17-Dec-03	with add. data -1-7-04				BRL made adjustments on 10-26-04 and on 11-17-04 and 1-13-05			
5		Basic Business Planning Model							
6				Est				Three-Year Horizon	
7	CURRENT MUSEUM OPERATIONS	2003	2004	2005	2006	Annual			
8		Actual	Actual	Actual	Projected	Growth rate	2007	2008	2009
9	Revenues								
26	Total revenues	769031	742,652	802,820	851,106	xxx	880,250	910,681	942,474
27									
28	Costs								
29	Non-Personnel		256,568	231,164	284,599	0.0275	292,425	300,467	308,730
30	Personnel	489,722	486,084	540,000	566,505	0.04	589,165	612,732	637,241
33	Programs	140,160		445,659	529,699	xxx	545,590	561,958	578,816
34	Weather Services		49,412	60,323	60,883	0.03	62,709	64,591	66,528
35	School (contract/non-contract)		70,848	67,709	79,200	0.03	81,576	84,023	86,544
36	Museum Shop Costs		40,424	45,619	47,716	0.03	49,147	50,622	52,141
37	Collections, Kitchel		51,693	81,789	91,090	0.03	93,823	96,637	99,537
38	Planetarium and Oth. Programs		69,365	49,700	151,266	0.03	155,804	160,478	165,292
39	Exhibits and Planning		117,316	93,859	75,778	0.03	78,051	80,393	82,805
40	Festival, Auction, Visitor, etc.		45,026	46,660	23,766	0.03	24,479	25,213	25,970
41	Facilities and Equipment	68,700	88,687	103,087	116,074	0.02	118,395	120,763	123,179
42	Administration	56,967	131,739	118,631	91,592	0.02	93,424	95,292	97,198
43	Development and Marketing	34,300	78,142	91,909	113,741	0.08	122,840	132,668	143,281
44	Total Costs	789,849	742,652	759,286	851,106	xxx	880,250	910,681	942,474
45	Capital Expense		11,194	0	72,100				
46	Expansion Planning		46,581	0	0				
47									
48	Operating surplus/deficit	-20818	0		0	xxx	0	0	0
49									
50	Check [(non-personnel+personnel)-total costs?]						1341	2518	3497

FIGURE 3.8 Northern Museum Model: Outlining

grouping is used in the Northern Museum Long-term Model sheet. The details behind the calculation of Revenues are grouped so that rows 10 to 25 are hidden. Similarly, the details under Personnel Costs have been grouped so that rows 31 and 32 are hidden. Other groupings have been created, but they are not active in the view shown in Figure 3.8. By selecting among the + and − symbols to the left of the worksheet, the user can tailor the display.

3.3.3 Design a Workbook as a Decision-Support System

Frequently, a spreadsheet evolves from a single use by its developer to repeated use by multiple users or a team. When this evolution takes place, the spreadsheet has become a decision-support system. A **decision-support system** is an integrated information system that provides data, analytics, and reporting capabilities over an extended period of time to multiple users. The Northern Museum model is a decision-support system because the Board and the executive director regularly use it to address a variety of budget and planning issues. In fact, one of the keys to its success is that it has helped the various interested parties at the Museum focus on a common way to think about and plan for the future.

Effective decision-support systems are designed to present information in a manner that is most useful to decision makers. Often, this means using graphs instead of tables of numbers, as in most Excel models. In the National Museum model, nine ratios are calculated in the Long-term Model sheet. These ratios indicate how the Museum is performing over time on important aspects of its operation, such as the ratio of general admission revenues to total expenditures (row 62). Museum professionals track this ratio carefully and compare it to the results of similar museums to understand the financial health of the operation. In order to make this information most useful, the tables in the Long-term Model sheet are displayed in the form of graphs in the Ratio charts sheet. While the treasurer, who is most familiar with the model, concentrates on the Assumptions and Long-term Model sheets, other users naturally concentrate on the graphical summaries in the Ratio graphs sheet.

If a workbook will be used by multiple users, it is important to protect the contents of the workbook from unwanted changes. In the Advertising Budget example, if we wanted to protect all the cells other than the decision variables, we would first lock all cells, then unlock the cells for the advertising allocation, and finally protect the entire worksheet. The details are as follows. First, we select the entire worksheet. Then, we select Home▶Font$\searrow$, choose the Protection tab, and check the box for Locked (Figure 3.9). Next, we repeat the

FIGURE 3.9 The Protection Tab in the Format Cells Window

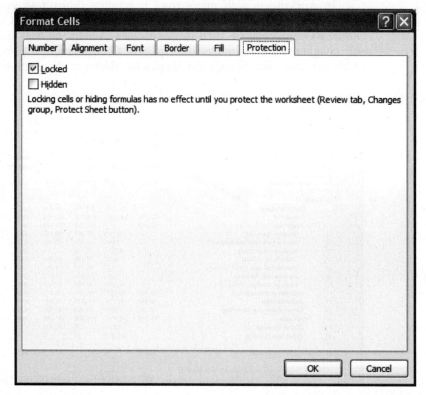

FIGURE 3.10 The Protect
Sheet Window

process for the decision variables, first selecting the range C18:F18. Again, we select Home▶Font↘ and choose the Protection tab, but this time we uncheck the box for Locked. Finally, we protect the entire worksheet, using Review▶Changes▶Protect Sheet. At the top of the Protect Sheet window (Figure 3.10), we check the box for Protect worksheet. In the lower window, there is a list of actions that can be allowed users. If we check only the box for Select unlocked cells, then a user will be able to select and modify only the decision variable cells. It will not be possible to select other cells. On the other hand, if we check the boxes for Select locked cells and Select unlocked cells, then the user will be able to select any of the locked cells (e.g., to verify a formula) but will not be permitted to alter the contents of those cells.

It can also be useful to ensure that only legitimate values are used as inputs. This process is called **data validation**, a technique that is highly recommended for workbooks available to multiple users over an extended period. To invoke data validation, highlight the cells involved and click on Data▶Data Tools▶Data Validation. The Data Validation window contains three tabs, as shown in Figure 3.11. On the first tab, we can restrict the allowable inputs to a cell—for example, to require a number (as opposed to text) and one that lies between certain minimum and maximum values. In the Advertising Budget example, we require a user to enter a price that lies between unit cost (cell C8) and $100. On the second tab, we have an option of creating an input message that will appear whenever the cursor is placed on this cell. This message functions like a cell comment. On the third tab, we can design an error alert for the case of an invalid entry. An example for the Advertising Budget spreadsheet is shown in Figure 3.12, which shows the error alert when we attempt to enter a price greater than $100 or less than the unit cost.

FIGURE 3.11 The Data
Validation Window

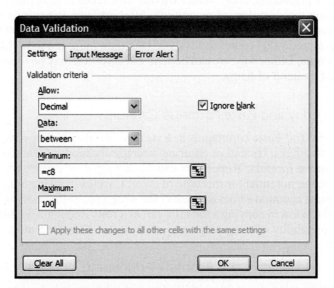

FIGURE 3.12 Error Alert
Produced by Data
Validation

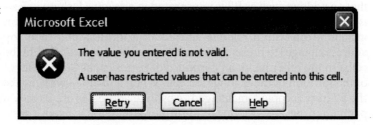

3.4 BUILDING A WORKBOOK

The second stage in creating a useful spreadsheet model is actually building it. Since most spreadsheet users do not consciously design their spreadsheets, they merge the designing and building processes. The usual result is that a great deal of time and energy are wasted fixing mistakes and redesigning a model that should have been designed once at the start.

A well-*designed* spreadsheet should be easy and quick to *build*. However, speed is not the only criterion here. Most bugs in spreadsheets are introduced during the building process. Therefore, learning to build spreadsheets without introducing errors is also vital. All of the guidelines in this section are designed to make the building process routine, repeatable, and error-free.

3.4.1 Follow a Plan

Having gone to the trouble of sketching the spreadsheet, we should follow the sketch when building. With a sufficiently detailed sketch, the building process itself becomes largely mechanical and therefore less prone to mistakes.

3.4.2 Build One Worksheet or Module at a Time

Rather than trying to build an entire workbook in one pass, it is usually more efficient to build a single worksheet or module and test it out before proceeding. For one thing, as we build the first module, we may discover that the design itself can be improved, so it is best to have made a limited investment in the original design before revising it. Another rationale for this advice is to localize the potential effects of an error. If we make an error, its effects are likely to be limited mainly to the module we're building. By staying focused on that module, we can fix errors early, before they infect other modules that we build later.

3.4.3 Predict the Outcome of Each Formula

For each formula entered, predict the numerical value expected from it before pressing the Enter key. Ask what order of magnitude to expect in the result, and give some thought to any outcomes that don't correspond to predictions. This discipline helps to uncover bugs: without a prediction, every numerical outcome tends to look plausible. At the same time, a prediction that is orders of magnitude different from the calculated number provides an opportunity to catch an error. For example, if we predict $100,000 for annual revenue, and the calculated value comes to $100,000,000, then there is a flaw either in our intuition or in our formula. Either way, we can benefit: our intuition may be sharpened, or we may detect an error in need of fixing.

3.4.4 Copy and Paste Formulas Carefully

The Copy-and-Paste commands in Excel are not simply time-savers; they are also helpful in avoiding bugs. Instead of entering structurally similar formulas several times, we copy and paste a formula. Repetition can be a source of errors, and copying formulas can diminish the potential for this type of error. Careless copying is also a source of bugs. One of the most common errors is to select the wrong range for copying—for example, selecting one cell too few in copying a formula across a row. Recognizing this problem keeps us alert to the possibility of a copying error, and we are therefore more likely to avoid it.

3.4.5 Use Relative and Absolute Addressing to Simplify Copying

Efficient copying depends on skillful use of relative and absolute addressing. Remember that an address such as B7 is interpreted in a *relative* fashion in Excel: if the highlighted cell is A6, then B7 is read as the cell one row down and one column to the right. When we include a cell with a relative address in a formula and then copy the formula, the cell address changes to preserve the relative position between the highlighted cell and the input cell. On the other hand, an *absolute* address, such as $B$6, refers to the cell B6 regardless of the location of the highlighted cell. When a formula with an absolute address is copied, the address is copied unchanged. Absolute addresses are usually used when referring to a parameter, because the location of the parameter is fixed.

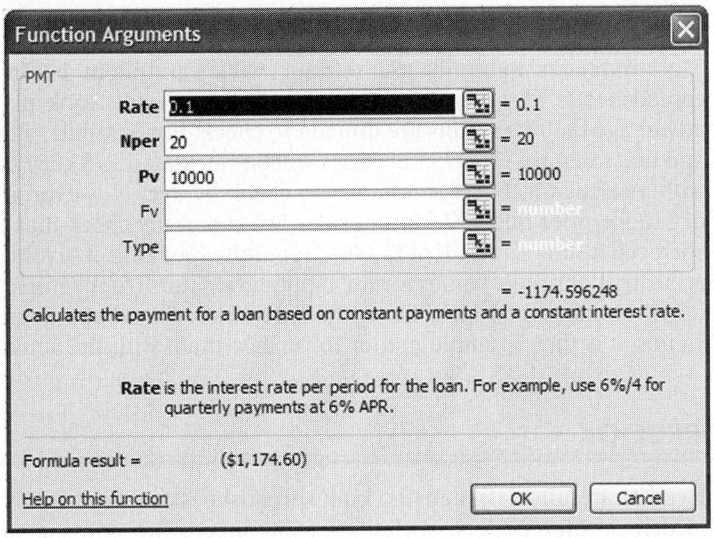

FIGURE 3.13 Function
Arguments Window

3.4.6 Use the Function Wizard to Ensure Correct Syntax

The button f_x to the left of the formula bar or on the Formulas ribbon brings up the Insert Function window, which contains a complete listing of all the functions built into Excel. It is not necessary to memorize the exact syntax of an occasionally-used function, or to guess at the correct syntax, because help is available. For example, we might want to calculate the payment on a car loan once in a while, but it is difficult to memorize the exact form of the PMT function. Whenever this function is needed, click on the Insert Function button and select PMT. A window then appears that shows what inputs the function needs and in what order (see Figure 3.13). This window even calculates the value of the function when its inputs are specified, thus providing quick feedback on whether the results are as expected.

3.4.7 Use Range Names to Make Formulas Easy to Read

Any cell or range of cells in a spreadsheet can be given a name. This name can then be used in formulas to refer to the contents of the cell. If cell B6 is named VblCost, we can use either B6 or VblCost interchangeably in any formula. Obviously, it is easier to understand a formula that uses range names than one that uses cell addresses. Formulas containing descriptive names are easier for the developer to debug and easier for new users to understand.

Range names require extra work to enter and maintain, so they may not be worth the effort in simple spreadsheets destined for one-time use. But in a spreadsheet that will become a permanent tool or be used by other analysts after the designer has moved on, it is a good idea to use range names to help subsequent users understand the details. Some firms require that all major spreadsheets use range names throughout.

We can assign a name to a cell or a range of cells by selecting Formulas▶Defined Names▶Define Name and specifying the relevant cell range (see Figure 3.14). For example, in the spreadsheet of Figure 3.3, we have assigned the name TotProfit to cell H37. This allows us to use the formula =TotProfit in C21, our main output cell. (To view all the range names in use, look in the pull-down window at the top of the spreadsheet, to the left of the formula window.) As a more ambitious example, we can assign the name Price to cell C7 and the name Sales to the range D27:G27 (by highlighting the four-cell range before defining the name). Then, the revenue formulas in cells D28:G28 can be entered as =Price*Sales. This makes the formulas easier to interpret and reduces the possibility for errors.

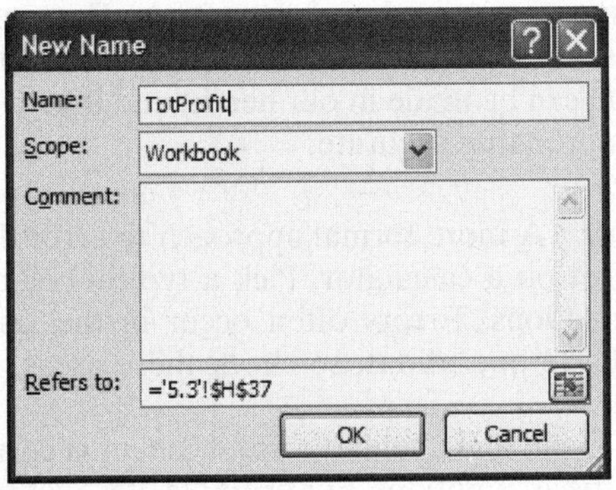

FIGURE 3.14 New Name
Window

3.4.8 Choose Input Data to Make Errors Stand Out

Most modelers naturally use realistic values for input parameters as they build their spreadsheets. This has the advantage that the results look plausible, but it has the disadvantage that the results are difficult to check. For example, if the expected price is $25.99 and unit sales are 126,475, revenues will be calculated as $3,287,085.25. We could check this with a calculator, but it is not easy to check by eye. However, if we input arbitrary values of $10 for price and 100 for unit sales, we can easily check that our formula for revenue is correct if it shows a result of $1,000. Generally speaking, it saves time in the long run to input arbitrary but simple values for the input parameters (for example, 1, 10, and 100) during the initial building sequence. Once the spreadsheet has been debugged with these arbitrary values, it is then a simple matter to replace them with the actual input values.

3.5   TESTING A WORKBOOK

Even a carefully designed and built spreadsheet may contain errors. Errors can arise from incorrect references in formulas, from inaccurate copying and pasting, from lack of parameterization, and from a host of other sources. There is no recipe to follow for finding all bugs. When a bug is found late in the analysis phase, the user must backtrack to fix the bug *and* to repeat most or all of the previous analysis. This can be avoided by carefully testing the spreadsheet before using it for analysis.

The tips we offer here can help an end user test whether a model is correct. However, common sense and the experience of thousands of professional programmers suggest that one of the most effective ways to find errors in a model is to give it to an outsider to test. Another pair of eyes can often find errors that have eluded the builder, who is so immersed in the details that errors are no longer detectable. Finding another pair of eyes may be impractical for many end users who work on their own, but it should be feasible in almost any company, especially when the spreadsheet is large, complex, and important. Formal code inspection, as practiced by professionals, is rarely carried out for spreadsheet models. However, some sophisticated companies practice *peer review*, in which important spreadsheet models are examined in detail by individuals or teams other than the builders. We suspect this practice will become more common as the risks of spreadsheet errors become more widely appreciated.

3.5.1   Check That Numerical Results Look Plausible

The most important tool for keeping a spreadsheet error-free is a skeptical attitude. As we build the spreadsheet, we transform input parameters into a set of intermediate results that eventually lead to final outcomes. As these numbers gradually appear, it is important to check that they look reasonable. We offer three distinct ways to accomplish this:

- Make rough estimates
- Check with a calculator
- Test extreme cases

Make Rough Estimates   In an earlier section, we recommended predicting the rough magnitude of the result of each formula before pressing Enter. This helps catch errors as they are made. Similarly, it is a good idea to scan the completed spreadsheet and to check that critical results are the correct order of magnitude. For example, in the Advertising Budget example, if we sell about 3,000 units in Q3 at $40 each, we should make about $120,000. This calculation can be made in our heads, and it helps to confirm that the value in cell F28 ($127,700) is probably accurate.

Check with a Calculator   A more formal approach to error detection is to check some portion of the spreadsheet on a calculator. Pick a typical column or row and check the entire sequence of calculations. Errors often occur in the last row or column due to problems in Copy-and-Paste operations, so check these areas, too.

Test Extreme Cases   If the logic behind a spreadsheet is correct, it should give logical results even with unrealistic assumptions. For example, if we set Price to $0, we should have zero revenues. Extreme cases such as this are useful for debugging because the correct results are easy to predict. Note, however, that just because a spreadsheet gives zero revenues when we set Price to $0 does not guarantee that the logic will be correct for all cases.

In the Advertising Budget example, if we price at cost, we should get a Gross Margin of zero. We can make this test by entering $25 for Price in C7 and then observing that Gross Margin in D30:G30 becomes zero. Testing extreme cases is one of the tools professional programmers use that end users can easily adopt as their own.

3.5.2   Check That Formulas Are Correct

Most spreadsheet errors occur in formulas. We can reduce the possibility of errors by making formulas short and using multiple cells to calculate a complex result. We can also reduce errors by using recursive formulas wherever possible, so that successive formulas in a row or column have the same form. Yet another good idea is to design the spreadsheet so that formulas use as inputs only cells that are above and to the left and are as close as possible. But having taken all these precautions, we still need to test that formulas are correct before beginning the analysis. We offer seven ways to perform this testing:

- Check visually
- Display individual cell references
- Display all formulas
- Use the Excel Auditing Tools
- Use Excel Error Checking
- Use error traps
- Use auditing software

Check Visually   Most end users check formulas one at a time, by highlighting each cell in a row or column in sequence and visually auditing the formula. This procedure can work fairly well, especially if the formulas are recursive so that many cell references change in a predictable way or do not change at all from cell to cell. A visual check also works best if range names are used. This method is extremely tedious, however, and tedious methods encourage carelessness. Several better methods are described in the following sections.

Display Individual Cell References   Another way to check formulas is to use the cell-edit capability, invoked either by pressing the F2 key or by double-clicking on the cell of interest. This reveals the formula in the cell, displayed with color-coded cell references. Each cell that appears in the formula is highlighted by a selection border, which is color-coded to the cell reference in the formula. Often, the locations of the cell references in a formula give visual clues to whether a formula is correctly structured. When an error is found, it is often possible to drag a highlighted border to a different cell as a means of correcting the address in the formula. This method is preferred to scanning formulas because it provides stronger visual clues for locating logical errors.

Display All Formulas   Another excellent device is to display all the formulas in the spreadsheet by holding down the Control key and pressing the tilde key ($\sim$) on the upper-left corner of the main keyboard (Control + $\sim$). This displays all the spreadsheet formulas, as shown in Figure 3.15, making them easier to scan. Usually, successive formulas in a row or column have some consistent pattern. For example, one cell reference is absolute and does not change, while another is relative and changes from D28 to E28 to F28, and so on. If there is an error, it can often be detected as a break in a pattern. (Return the spreadsheet to its normal form by pressing Control + $\sim$ again.)

In the spreadsheet for the Advertising Budget example, note the similar structure in the four formulas for Gross Margin in the range D30:G30. A copying error would show up as a break in the pattern here.

Use the Excel Auditing Tools   Another useful and underutilized set of debugging tools in Excel is available on the ribbon under Formulas▶Formula Auditing. These options can be used to identify the cells used to calculate a given cell (its **predecessors**) or the cells it is used to calculate (its **dependents**). The Trace Precedents option draws colored arrows to the predecessors of a given cell. Invoking the Trace Precedents option again from this point will

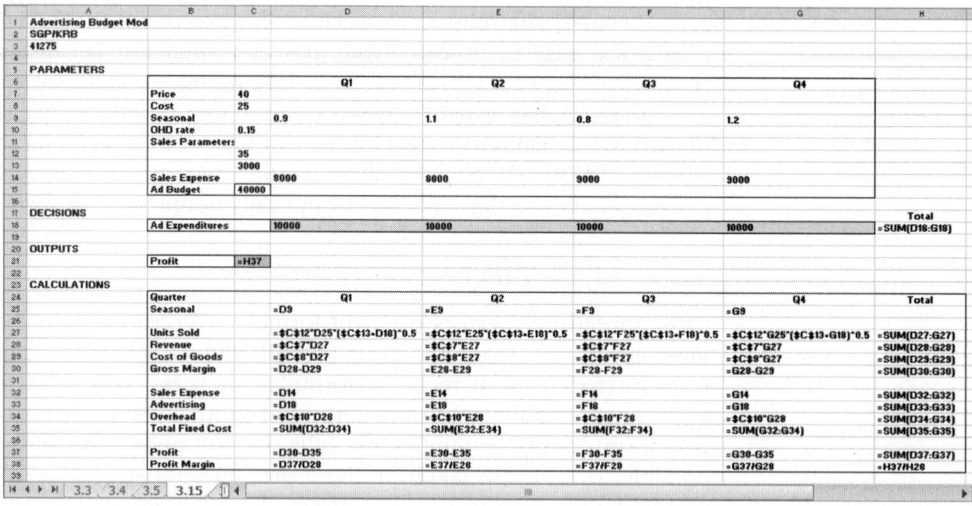

FIGURE 3.15   Displaying Formulas in the Advertising Budget Spreadsheet

identify the predecessors of the predecessors, and so on, reaching backward into the logic of the calculations. The Trace Dependents option works similarly, but in the forward direction. The arrows convey a pattern of information flow, which should conform to the underlying logic of the model. For debugging purposes, the auditing tools can be used to display the information flows related to a group of cells. If these cells have a parallel or recursive structure, there should be a distinctive pattern in the arrows produced by the auditing tools. As with displaying formulas, bugs often show up as unexpected breaks in the pattern of these arrows.

In the spreadsheet for the Advertising Budget example, suppose we select cell H38. Next, we choose the option for Trace Precedents several times in succession. The cells that are used to calculate profit are highlighted, then their predecessors are highlighted, and so on, as shown in Figure 3.16. Again, an error in the formulas would show up as a break in these visual patterns. (Use the Remove Arrows option to erase the auditing arrows.)

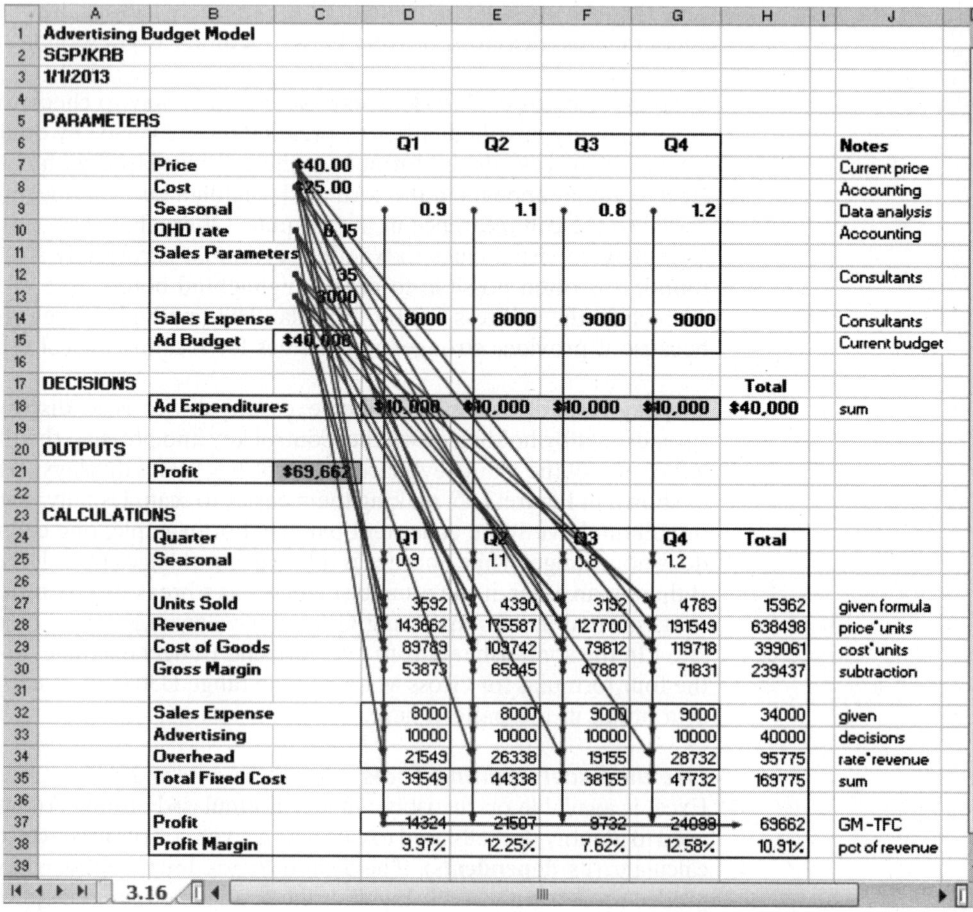

FIGURE 3.16   Using the Auditing Toolbar in the Advertising Budget Spreadsheet

FIGURE 3.17 The Error
Checking Window

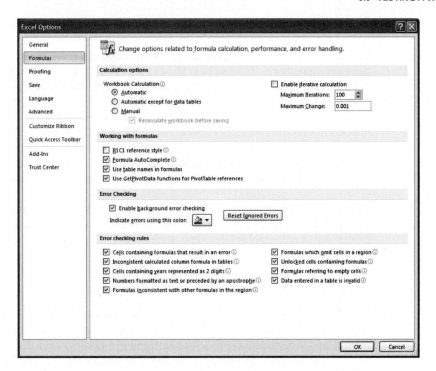

Use Excel Error Checking This is the spreadsheet equivalent of grammar checking in word processing. Error checking is managed from the Formulas tab of the Excel Options menu. The single check box under Error Checking (see Figure 3.17) chooses whether the tool is enabled or disabled. If it is enabled, then all cells that are identified as possibly containing an error are flagged with a colored triangle. (The color can be chosen under Error Checking.) The Error checking rules comprise a list of nine types of checks. Although the user can choose which of these rules to activate, we generally recommend keeping all nine boxes checked.

Three of these categories of possible errors seem to be most prevalent: formulas inconsistent with other formulas in the region, formulas which omit cells in a region, and formulas referring to empty cells. Inconsistent formulas are those that violate a pattern. For example, a recursive formula that is copied across a row but that changes its pattern of references to absolute addresses would be flagged under this category. Often, these potential errors are consciously designed into the spreadsheet, and although they are not errors, they are nonetheless indicative of poor programming practice. Formulas that omit cells in a region also violate an expected pattern. Finally, formulas that refer to empty cells are either wrong outright or at least indicate dangerous programming practice. While this Error Checking capability can highlight only certain well-defined categories of potential errors (and the user can determine which categories by using the check boxes), it is a useful tool—one that should be employed during the design and testing phases of spreadsheet construction.

Use Error Traps Error traps are formulas added to a spreadsheet that warn the user of potential errors. They can check for errors in input data or for errors in formulas.

A simple application is to check that row sums and column sums are consistent. For example, in cell H30 in the Advertising Budget spreadsheet we calculate total Gross Margin by adding up the four quarterly values for gross margin. But total Gross Margin can also be calculated by subtracting total Cost of Goods from total Revenue. If these two calculations do not give the same result, we have an error. An error trap can be set by entering an IF statement that checks the cells in question and returns a warning if an error occurs. For example, the statement

```
IF(SUM(D30:G30)<>(H28 – H29), "Warning:row and
column totals do not match"," ")
```

returns the warning text when there is an error and returns a blank value otherwise.

The Long-term Model sheet of the Northern Museum workbook uses a different kind of error checking. In this situation there are two ways to calculate total costs, and both are of interest to important model users. One approach is to divide total costs into personnel and non-personnel costs. This is done in rows 29 and 30. The alternative is to break total costs down by programs, which is done in rows 34–40. The workbook designer decided that both approaches should be shown on the worksheet and even that inconsistent projections could be allowed. But to highlight these inconsistencies when they occur, the difference in total costs between the two methods is calculated in row 50.

Any number of error traps can be added to a workbook to improve its safety. It is important that the results of these error checks be clearly visible to the user. One way to do this is to create an overall error trap that checks whether *any one* of the individual traps is true, and returns a warning. This trap can be placed in a prominent place near the outputs, so a user will be unlikely to trust outputs that result from a model with errors.

Use Auditing Software A number of Excel add-ins are available for auditing spreadsheets. These add-ins typically provide a set of tools for detecting errors and displaying model structure graphically. One such tool is Spreadsheet Professional (www.spreadsheetinnovations.com).

3.5.3 Test That Model Performance Is Plausible

For many end users, the analysis phase begins while testing is still in progress. This is natural and perhaps unavoidable, although we have stressed the importance of taking a careful and structured approach to designing, building, and testing a spreadsheet *before* using it for analysis. However, if analysis begins before testing is complete, it is at least desirable to retain a skeptical attitude toward the early results from using the model. Many minor bugs come to light during analysis. More importantly, actually using the model can reveal major logical flaws. These types of errors, which usually cannot be uncovered by the most meticulous checking of formulas, can destroy the credibility of the entire modeling process.

If a spreadsheet model is logically sound and built without errors, it should react in a plausible manner to a range of input values. Thus, sensitivity testing, which we discuss in Chapter 4, can be a powerful way to uncover logical and mechanical errors. In our Advertising Budget example, if profit were to go *down* as we increased the price, we could be fairly sure we had a bug in the model. But even if we have confirmed that profits rise with price, would we expect that relationship to be linear or nonlinear? We can test our intuition and the model by calculating profit for a range of prices and graphing the results. In this model as it is currently built, that relationship is in fact linear. We might conclude that this is as we expected and intended. On the other hand, we might decide that demand should instead depend on price (which, in our model, it does not) and that the model needs further refinement.

3.6 SUMMARY

Spreadsheets are important throughout business, and important tools deserve careful engineering. Although spreadsheet modeling is not a science, we can enumerate a set of guidelines for designing, building, and testing our spreadsheets. Our guidelines have evolved from our observations working with both experienced and inexperienced model builders. These guidelines are designed to make the process of spreadsheet development both more efficient and more effective.

The available evidence suggests strongly that most spreadsheets in use contain errors and that their developers are overconfident about the reliability of their models. The implication is that we should be humble about our ability to develop spreadsheets that correctly implement the models we have conceived. Care and effort are required to build models successfully. Some useful lessons can be learned from professional programmers—most importantly, *be skeptical* and *test thoroughly*.

Here is a summary list of the guidelines given in this chapter:

Designing a Spreadsheet

1. Sketch the spreadsheet.
2. Organize the spreadsheet into modules.
3. Start small.
4. Isolate input parameters.
5. Design for use.
6. Keep it simple.
7. Design for communication.
8. Document important data and formulas.

Designing a Workbook

1. Use separate spreadsheets to group like information.
2. Design workbooks for ease of navigation and use.
3. Design a workbook as a decision-support system.

Building a Workbook

1. Follow a plan.
2. Build one module at a time.
3. Predict the outcome of each formula.
4. Copy and Paste formulas carefully.
5. Use relative and absolute addressing to simplify copying.
6. Use the Function Wizard to ensure correct syntax.
7. Use range names to make formulas easy to read.
8. Choose input data to make errors stand out.

Testing a Workbook

1. Check that numerical results look plausible.
2. Check that formulas are correct.
3. Test that model performance is plausible.

SUGGESTED READINGS

The most thoughtful writing on spreadsheet design has appeared not in books but in journal articles. We list some useful articles here. More information can be found in references compiled in the Edwards and Panko articles.

Caine, D. J., and A. J. Robinson. 1993. "Spreadsheet Modeling: Guidelines for Model Development." *Management Decision* **31**, 38–44.

Conway, D. G., and C. T. Ragsdale. 1997. "Modeling Optimization Problems in the Unstructured World of Spreadsheets." *Omega* **25**, 313–322.

Edwards, J. S., P. N. Finlay, and J. M. Wilson. 2000. "The Role of OR Specialists in 'Do It Yourself' Spreadsheet Development." *European Journal of Operational Research* **127**, 14–27.

Panko, R. R. 1999. "Applying Code Inspection to Spreadsheet Testing." *Journal of Management Information Systems* **16**, 159–176.

The following short monographs and websites contain more detailed recommendations for best practices in spreadsheet design, building, and testing:

BPM Analytical. 2004. "Best Practice Spreadsheet Modelling Standards." http://www.bpmglobal.com/bpm_standards.html.

Mailbarrow . Undated. "52 Easy Ways to Prevent Spreadsheet Problems." http://www.AccessAnalytic.com.au/whitepapers.php.

Raffensperger, J. F., 2002. "The Art of the Spreadsheet." http://john.raffensperger.org/ArtofTheSpreadsheet/index.html.

Read, N., and J. Batson. 1999. "Spreadsheet Modeling Best Practice." http://www.eusprig.org/smbp.pdf.

EXERCISES

The following exercises refer to the cases in the back of this book. Read the case description carefully, sketch an appropriate spreadsheet on paper, and then build and test a prototype model. The purpose of the model is specified in the question.

1. Refer to the XYZ Company case. Design a spreadsheet that will allow an analyst to predict the month in which the cash balance falls below zero, signaling a need to borrow money.

2. Refer to the Medical Supplies for Banjul case. Design a spreadsheet that will enable you to request the required funds from your team's finance officer, order supplies from the home office, and ensure dissemination of appropriate quantities to each village. Your final order to the home office should specify the number of packages required of each item.

3. Refer to the Reid's Raisins case. Design a spreadsheet that will allow the firm to project profit for base-case conditions; the open market grape price is $0.30.

4. Refer to the Big Rig Rental Company case. Design a spreadsheet that will allow the firm to determine the Net Present Value of cash flows over the five-year period.

5. Refer to the Flexible Insurance Coverage case. Design a spreadsheet that will allow an individual employee with estimated annual medical expenses of $400 to compare the total expenses under each plan.

6. Refer to the Snoey Software Company case. Design a spreadsheet that will determine the annual profit when the prices for the Educational, Large-Scale, and Professional versions are $100, $300, and $500, respectively.

7. Refer to the Cox Cable and Wire Company case. In the role of Meredith, design a spreadsheet with which to find a machine schedule and a corresponding inventory and shipment schedule that meets demand. What is the profit contribution of this schedule?

8. Refer to the BMW Company case. Design a spreadsheet that will allow the firm's managers to estimate what percentage of the firm's net income 10 years into the future will be devoted to disposal of vehicles, assuming there are no changes in trends and policies.

9. Refer to the ERP Decision case. Design a spreadsheet that will assist the Board in evaluating the net benefits of implementing the ERP system.

10. Refer to the Retirement Planning case. Review the problem statement and influence chart that were generated for this case in conjunction with the corresponding exercise in Chapter 2. (If this has not yet been done, develop the problem statement and influence chart as preliminary steps.) Design a spreadsheet to estimate the impact on Davidson's retirement of increasing his annual retirement savings by 10 percent.

11. Refer to the Draft TV Commercials case. Review the problem statement and influence chart that were generated for this case in conjunction with the corresponding exercises in Chapter 2. (If this has not yet been done, develop the problem statement and influence chart as preliminary steps.) Design a spreadsheet to determine the impact on ad quality of paying for three draft commercials.

12. Refer to the Icebergs for Kuwait case. Review the problem statement and influence chart that were generated for this case in conjunction with the corresponding exercises in Chapter 2. (If this has not yet been done, develop the problem statement and influence chart as preliminary steps.) Design a spreadsheet to estimate the economic value of the freshwater produced by towing the largest possible iceberg using the largest available boat.

13. Refer to the Racquetball Racket case. Review the problem statement and influence chart that were generated for this case in conjunction with the corresponding exercises in Chapter 2. (If this has not yet been done, develop the problem statement and influence chart as preliminary steps.) Design a spreadsheet to evaluate the Net Present Value of selling the new ball at $0.65, assuming the competitor does not change price.

4 Analysis Using Spreadsheets

4.1 INTRODUCTION

In the previous chapter, we pointed out that spreadsheet models often play a critical role in business planning and analysis. Because of their importance, spreadsheets should not be created haphazardly. Instead, they should be carefully engineered. We recommended a process for designing, building, and testing a spreadsheet that is both efficient and effective. Not only does this process minimize the likelihood that the spreadsheet contains errors, but it also prepares the user to investigate the business questions at hand in the analytic phase of the modeling process. In this chapter we provide a structure for this investigation and present the essential Excel tools that support analysis. Advanced methods, and the Excel tools that go with them, are elaborated in later chapters.

We have found that, over time, most analysts develop their own informal approaches to the analytic phase of modeling. Many of us have favorite tools that we tend to rely on, even when they are not really adequate to the task. But it is difficult to develop a *complete* set of analytic tools simply through experience. An analyst who does not know a particular tool generally does not think to ask the business question that the tool helps answer. By the same token, an analyst with a complete analytic toolkit would be more likely to ask the right questions.

Although Excel itself has thousands of features, most of the analysis done with spreadsheets falls into one of the following five categories:

- Base-case analysis
- What-if analysis
- Breakeven analysis
- Optimization analysis
- Risk analysis

Within each of these categories, there are specific Excel tools—such as the Goal Seek tool—and add-ins—such as Analytic Solver Platform—which can be used either to automate tedious calculations or to find powerful business insights that cannot be found any other way. Some of these tools are quite complex and will be given more complete treatment in later chapters. Here, we provide only a brief introduction to these tools so as to give the reader an overview of the process of spreadsheet analysis. By contrast, some of the other tools we describe in this chapter are extremely simple, yet they seem to be underutilized by the majority of analysts.

Once again, we draw on the Advertising Budget example, which was introduced in Chapter 3, to illustrate the different kinds of analysis. Here is a sample of the kinds of questions we answer in this chapter:

- If we follow last year's plan to spend the same amount on advertising in each quarter, how much profit can we expect to make?
- How much will profit change if our product costs turn out to be 10 percent higher or lower than we have assumed?
- If our product costs rise, at what point will profit reach zero?
- What is the maximum profit we can make with an advertising budget of $40,000?
- How likely is it that we will lose money if price and cost are uncertain?

4.2 BASE-CASE ANALYSIS

Almost every spreadsheet analysis involves measuring outcomes relative to some common point of comparison, or **base case**. Therefore, it's worth giving some thought to how the base case is chosen. A base case is often drawn from current policy or common practice, but many other alternatives are available. Where there is considerable uncertainty in the decision problem, it may be appropriate for the base case to depict the most likely scenario; in other circumstances, the worst case or the best case might be a good choice.

Sometimes, several base cases are used during the course of analysis. For example, we might start the analysis with a version of the model that takes last year's results as the base case. Later in the analysis, we might develop another base case using a proposed plan for the coming year. At either stage, the base case is the starting point from which an analyst can explore the model using the tools described in this chapter, and thereby gain insights into the corresponding business situation. The base case also sets the tone for presenting results to decision makers.

In the Advertising Budget example, most of the input parameters such as price and cost are forecasts for the coming year. These inputs would typically be based on previous experience, modified by our hunches as to what will be different in the coming year. But what values should we assume for the decision variables in the base case? Our ultimate goal is to find the best values for these decisions, but that is premature at this point. A natural alternative is to take last year's advertising expenditures ($10,000 in each quarter) as the base-case decisions, both because this is a simple plan and because initial indications point to a repeat for this year's decisions.

4.3 WHAT-IF ANALYSIS

Once a base case has been specified, the next step in analysis often involves nothing more sophisticated than varying one of the inputs to determine how the key outputs change. Assessing the change in outputs associated with a given change in inputs is called **what-if analysis**. The inputs may be *parameters*, in which case we are asking how sensitive our base-case results are to forecasting errors or other changes in input values. Alternatively, the inputs may be *decision variables*, in which case we are exploring whether changes in our decisions might improve our results, for a given set of parameters. Finally, there is another type of what-if analysis, in which we test the effect on the results of changing some aspect of our model's *structure*. For example, we might replace a linear relationship with a nonlinear one. In these three forms of analysis, the general idea is to alter an assumption and then trace the effect on the model's outputs.

We use the term **sensitivity analysis** interchangeably with the term *what-if analysis*. However, we are aware that sensitivity analysis sometimes conveys a distinct meaning. In the optimization models of Chapters 8–12, we use the term sensitivity analysis more narrowly to mean the effect of changing a parameter on the *optimal* outcome. (In optimization models, the term *what-if analysis* is seldom used.)

When we vary a *parameter*, we are implicitly asking what would happen if there were an unexpected change in that parameter or if our forecast of that parameter were wrong. That is, what if we had made a different numerical assumption at the outset, but everything else remained unchanged? This kind of questioning is important because the parameters in our model represent assumptions or forecasts about the environment for decision making. If the environment turns out to be different from what we had assumed, then it stands to reason that the results will also be different. What-if analysis measures that difference and helps us appreciate the potential importance of each numerical assumption.

In the Advertising Budget model, for example, if unit cost rises to $26 from $25, then annual profit drops to $53,700. In other words, an increase of 4 percent in the unit cost will reduce profit by nearly 23 percent. Thus, it would appear that profits are quite sensitive to unit cost, and in light of this insight, we may decide to monitor the market conditions that influence the material and labor components of cost.

When we vary a *decision variable*, we are changing inputs that we control. First, we'd like to know whether changing the value of a decision variable would lead to an improvement in the results. If we locate an improvement, we can then try to determine what value of the decision variable would result in the largest improvement. This kind of questioning is different from asking about a parameter, because we can act directly on what we learn. What-if analysis can thus lead us to better decisions.

In the Advertising Budget model, if we spend an additional $1,000 on advertising in the first quarter, then annual profit rises to $69,882. In other words, an increase of 10 percent in the advertising expenditure during Q1 will translate into an increase of roughly 0.3 percent in annual profit. Thus, profits seem quite insensitive to small changes in advertising expenditures in Q1, all else being equal. Nevertheless, we have identified a way to increase profits. We might guess that the small percentage change in profit reflects the fact that expenditures in the neighborhood of $10,000 are close to optimal, but we will have to gather more information before we are ready to draw conclusions about optimality.

In addition to testing the sensitivity of results to parameters and decision variables, there are situations in which we want to test the impact of some element of model structure. For example, we may have assumed that there is a linear relationship between price and sales. As part of what-if analysis, we might then ask whether a nonlinear demand relationship would materially alter our conclusions. As another example, we may have assumed that our competitors will not change their prices in the coming year. If we then determine that our own prices should increase substantially over that time, we might ask how our results would change if our competitors were to react by matching our price increases. These what-if questions are more complex than simple changes to a parameter or a decision variable because they involve alterations in the underlying structure of the model. Nonetheless, an important aspect of successful modeling is testing the sensitivity of results to key assumptions in the model's structure.

In the Advertising Budget model, the nonlinear relationship between advertising and sales plays a fundamental role. In the spirit of structural sensitivity analysis, we can ask how different our results would be if we were to replace this relationship with a linear one. For example, the linear relationship

$$Sales = 3,000 + 0.1(Advertising \times Seasonal\ Factor)$$

lies close to the nonlinear curve for advertising levels around $10,000. When we substitute this relationship into the base-case model, holding advertising constant at $10,000 each quarter, we find that profit changes only slightly, to $70,000. But in this model, if we then increase Q1 advertising by $1,000, we find that profit *decreases*, while in the base-case model it increases. Evidently, this structural assumption does have a significant impact on the desired levels of advertising.

We have illustrated what we might call a "one-at-a-time" form of what-if analysis, where we vary one input at a time, keeping other inputs unchanged. We could, of course, vary two or more inputs simultaneously, but these more complex experiments become increasingly difficult to interpret. In many cases, we can gain the necessary insights by varying the inputs one at a time.

It is important not to underestimate the power of this first step in analysis. Simple what-if exploration is one of the most effective ways to develop a deeper understanding of the model and the system it represents. It is also part of the debugging process, as we pointed out in the previous chapter. When what-if analysis reveals something unexpected, we may have found a useful insight or perhaps discovered a bug.

Predicting the outcome of a what-if test is an important part of the learning process. For example, in the Advertising Budget model, what would be the result of doubling the selling price? Would profits double as well? In the base case, with a price of $40, profits total $69,662. If we double the price, we find that profits increase to $612,386. Profits increase by much more than a factor of two when prices double. After a little thought, we should see the reasons. For one, costs do not increase in proportion to volume; for another, demand does not decline as price increases. Thus, the sensitivity test helps us to understand the nature of the cost structure—that it's not proportional—as well as one possible limitation of the model—that no link exists between demand and price.

4.3.1 Benchmarking

During what-if analysis, we repeatedly change inputs and observe the resulting change in outputs. This can get confusing unless we keep a record of the results in some organized fashion. One simple solution to this problem is to **benchmark** sensitivity results against the base case by keeping a record of the base-case outcome on the spreadsheet.

FIGURE 4.1 The Advertising Budget Spreadsheet

	A	B	C	D	E	F	G	H	I	J
1	Advertising Budget Model									
2	SGP/KRB									
3	1/1/2013									
4										
5	PARAMETERS									
6				Q1	Q2	Q3	Q4			Notes
7		Price	$40.00							Current price
8		Cost	$25.00							Accounting
9		Seasonal		0.9	1.1	0.8	1.2			Data analysis
10		OHD rate	0.15							Accounting
11		Sales Parameters								
12			35							Consultants
13			3000							
14		Sales Expense		8000	8000	9000	9000			Consultants
15		Ad Budget	$40,000							Current budget
16										
17	DECISIONS							Total		
18		Ad Expenditures		$10,000	$10,000	$10,000	$10,000	$40,000		sum
19										
20	OUTPUTS									
21		Profit	$69,662		Base case	$69,662				
22										
23	CALCULATIONS									
24		Quarter		Q1	Q2	Q3	Q4	Total		
25		Seasonal		0.9	1.1	0.8	1.2			
26										
27		Units Sold		3592	4390	3192	4789	15962		given formula
28		Revenue		143662	175587	127700	191549	638498		price*units
29		Cost of Goods		89789	109742	79812	119718	399061		cost*units
30		Gross Margin		53873	65845	47887	71831	239437		subtraction
31										
32		Sales Expense		8000	8000	9000	9000	34000		given
33		Advertising		10000	10000	10000	10000	40000		decisions
34		Overhead		21549	26338	19155	28732	95775		rate*revenue
35		Total Fixed Cost		39549	44338	38155	47732	169775		sum
36										
37		Profit		14324	21507	9732	24099	69662		GM-TFC
38		Profit Margin		9.97%	12.25%	7.62%	12.58%	10.91%		pct of revenue
39										

Base case value of profit recorded as a fixed number.

4.1

FIGURE 4.2 The Paste Special Window

In the Advertising Budget spreadsheet, we benchmark the base-case profit of $69,662 on the spreadsheet in cell F21, as shown in Figure 4.1*. Note that this cell contains the *number* $69,662, not a cell reference to profit in C21. We construct this entry by selecting C21 and choosing Home▶Clipboard▶Copy, then selecting F21 and choosing Home▶Clipboard▶Paste▶Paste Special with the option Values, as shown in Figure 4.2. With this design, the result of any new sensitivity test appears in C21, while the base-case value is maintained in F21. If we wish, we can add a cell to measure the difference in profit between the base case and the sensitivity test, or the percentage difference, if that is more useful.

4.3.2 Scenarios

Up to this point, we have viewed each parameter in our model as independent of all the others. But it is often the case that certain *sets* of parameters go together in some natural way. For example, in the airline industry during a recession, we might expect passenger miles to be low and interest rates also to be low. Thus, in using a model to forecast future airline profitability, we might want to analyze a recession, and to do so, we would choose low values for these two inputs. Furthermore, when we perform what-if analysis, we would vary both parameters up and down *together*, not independently.

In general, we can think of a **scenario** as a story about the future decision-making environment translated into its effects on several of the model's parameters. More

* To download spreadsheets for this chapter, go to the Student Companion Site at www.wiley.com/college/powell.

FIGURE 4.3 The Scenario Manager Window

specifically, a scenario is a set of parameters that describes an internally consistent view of the future. In our airline example, the story involves a recession and the impact the recession has on specific parameters affecting demand and investment. In the oil industry, a scenario might depict the breakup of the OPEC cartel and its impacts on production and exploration worldwide. In the semiconductor business, a scenario might involve a breakthrough in optical technology that leads to the first chip powered by light. To translate these stories into useful terms, we would have to determine how such events influence specific parameters in a coordinated fashion.

In the Advertising Budget example, we can construct an optimistic scenario in which prices are high ($50) and costs are low ($20), yielding a profit of $285,155. Similarly, we can construct a pessimistic scenario, in which prices are low ($35) and costs are high ($30), leading to a loss of $77,991. Each scenario tells a coherent story that has meaning to the decision makers and is implemented in the model through a set of two or more parameters. Excel's Scenario Manager provides a way to record the inputs and outputs of multiple scenarios. We select Data▶Data Tools▶What-If Analysis▶Scenario Manager and enter the first scenario by clicking on the Add button and entering the information required in the Add Scenario window and (after clicking OK) the Scenario Values window. Thereafter, we can use the Edit button to change the details, or the Add button to enter another scenario. Figure 4.3 shows the window for the Scenario Manager after the optimistic and pessimistic scenarios have been added. If we click on the Show button, the values corresponding to the selected scenario are placed in the spreadsheet. If we click on the Summary button, we obtain the summary table shown in Figure 4.4.

When scenarios involve a large number of parameters, it is convenient to switch from one set of parameters to another all at once. This can be accomplished using the Excel CHOOSE function. CHOOSE selects a value from a range based on an index number. The index number is the number of the scenario, and the range contains the inputs for a given parameter. This is illustrated in Figure 4.5. In cell C6 we enter the number of the scenario, 1, 2, or 3 in this case. In L7:N7 we enter the values for the price parameter for three scenarios: Optimistic (1), Base Case (2), and Pessimistic (3). The CHOOSE function is entered in cell C7, as =CHOOSE (C6, L7, M7, N7) and the appropriate price is entered depending on the scenario chosen in C6. The appropriate value for cost is entered in cell C9 using the same approach. This method can be used to enter any number of parameters for a given scenario simply by changing the index number in cell C6.

FIGURE 4.4 The Summary Produced by the Scenario Manager

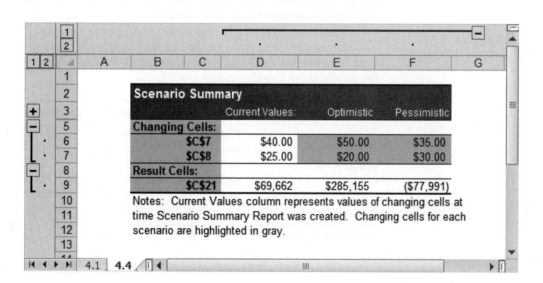

FIGURE 4.5 Use of the CHOOSE Function to Implement Scenarios

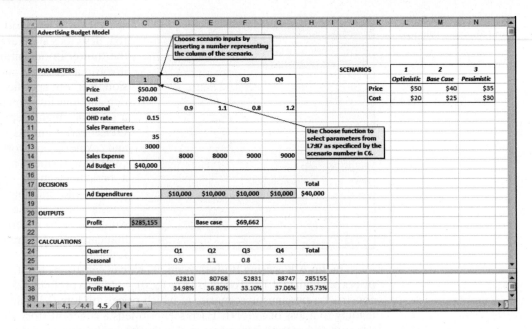

As an application of scenario analysis, consider the Heineken Brewery case.[1] The modeling task in this case was to develop a forecast for Heineken profits over the five years 1999–2003. Because of uncertainty over the strategies that major players in the beer industry would pursue over this time period, no single base case was considered appropriate. Three scenarios were developed, as described in the following.

Business As Usual The industry avoids major price wars, and financial returns improve slightly. Heineken's performance is the same as in the late 1990s, and in the near future, the company makes two major acquisitions and some small ones. Heineken continues to globalize and augments its market share by 8 percent over the five years.

Price War The industry price wars started by Miller and Busch continue worldwide, dropping returns toward the cost of capital. Heineken's performance is stable but with weaker margins and no new acquisitions.

Market Discipline The industry consolidates and avoids price wars. Heineken improves gross margins through an aggressive mergers-and-acquisitions program. It becomes a leader in the drive for industry consolidation.

These alternative futures were then translated into appropriate sets of input parameters. For the Price War scenario, two adjustments were made to the Business As Usual assumptions: revenue growth would be 0 percent (rather than 2 percent), and 1 percent (rather than 3 percent) of revenue growth would come from acquisitions. In the Market Discipline scenario, growth by acquisitions was increased so that Heineken augments its market share by 15 percent.

The results of the Heineken scenario analysis are summarized in the following table. To focus on just one result, we can see that equity per share is 19.3 guilders lower in the Price War scenario and 40.5 guilders higher in the Market Discipline scenario, relative to the Business As Usual scenario.

Result	Units	Price War	Business As Usual	Market Discipline
Average annual growth	Percentage	2.4	5.6	7.0
Average ROIC	Percentage	13.0	13.1	14.2
Company value	NLG Billion*	29.8	35.8	48.8
Equity value	NLG Billion	27.5	33.5	46.2
Equity value per share	NLG	87.6	106.9	147.4
Probability	Percentage	15.0	60.0	25.0

* Netherlands guilders

[1] T Copeland, T. Koller, and J. Murrin, *Valuation* (New York: John Wiley and Sons, 2005), 253.

Several aspects of this case are noteworthy. First, scenarios should describe the major events that could impact the company or individual in the future. The story told in each scenario should be believable and coherent, although credible scenarios are not necessarily highly likely. (In fact, one of the strengths of scenario analysis is to focus attention on important but unlikely futures.) Second, the description of each scenario must be sufficiently complete to suggest plausible values for all the input parameters. Often, the parameters of a business-as-usual scenario are set first, and the parameters of the other scenarios are selected as changes from the base values.

4.3.3 Parametric Sensitivity

Simple what-if analysis requires changing one input and observing the resulting value of the output. But we often wish to understand how the output varies over a *range* of inputs. We could type in a series of input values and record the outputs manually, but an automatic procedure would be more efficient.

Analytic Solver Platform can be used to automate this form of what-if analysis, which we refer to as **parametric sensitivity**. It recalculates the spreadsheet for a series of values of an input cell and generates either a table or a graph of the resulting values of an output cell. This allows the analyst to perform several related what-if tests in one pass rather than entering each input value and recording each corresponding output.

We illustrate the use of parametric sensitivity analysis in the Advertising Budget model by showing how variations in unit cost (cell C8) affect profit (cell C21). To avoid confusion, it is helpful to designate a separate portion of the worksheet for sensitivity values. In the Advertising Budget model, we can use the top portion of column H for this purpose. Place the cursor on cell H8 (in the same row as the cost) and then choose Analytic Solver Platform▶Parameters▶Sensitivity. The Function Arguments window opens for the PsiSenParam sensitivity function (Figure 4.6). Enter a Lower value of 20 and an Upper value of 30, and click OK. Then change the contents of cell C8 so that it references H8. At this point, both cells display the value 25, because the PsiSenParam function displays the midrange value by default.

To create a table for profit as a function of unit cost in the range from $20 to $30, select cell C21 in the spreadsheet in Figure 4.1 and then select Analytic Solver Platform ▶Analysis▶Reports▶Sensitivity▶Parameter Analysis. This opens the Sensitivity Report window (Figure 4.7). Select cell C21 in the Result cells window and click on the ">" button. This step places the reference to C21 in the window to the right. Similarly, select cell H8 from the Parameters window and use the corresponding arrow button to place it in the window to its right. Choose 11 Major Axis Points and click OK. Analytic Solver Platform will then create a new sheet named Sensitivity Analysis Report that contains the table shown in Figure 4.8. (The column headings have been edited.)

The first column of Figure 4.8 lists the 11 values for unit cost that have been entered in the model. We specified the range of values ($20–$30) when we entered the PsiSenParam function in cell H8. We specified the number of values to calculate in the table when we specified 11 Major Axis Points in the Sensitivity Report window. The second column in the table shows the profit (cell C21) that corresponds to each of the values for unit cost in the first column. The table shows that profit ranges from about $150,000 to –$10,000 for costs from $20 to $30.

FIGURE 4.6 PsiSen-Param Function Arguments

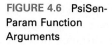

FIGURE 4.7 Sensitivity Report Window

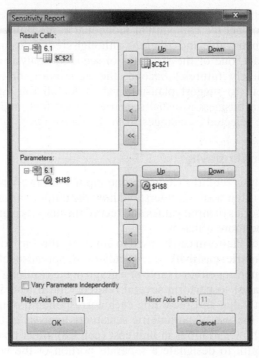

Parametric sensitivity will work correctly only if the input has been placed in a single location. By contrast, if an input parameter had been embedded in several cells, the tool would have given incorrect answers when we tried to vary the input. Thus, the use of single and separate locations for parameters (or for decisions), which we advocated in Chapter 3, makes it possible to take advantage of this capability.

We can also create a graph for the relationship between unit cost and profit. If we had not already done so, we would enter the function =PsiSenParam (20, 30) in cell H8. Then select cell C21 and select Analytic Solver Platform▶Analysis▶Charts▶Sensitivity Analysis▶Parameter Analysis. This opens the Sensitivity Report window (Figure 4.7). Again, select cell C21 in the Result cells window and click on the corresponding arrow button, placing the reference to C21 in the window to the right. (This step may not be necessary if the Sensitivity Report Table has just been created.) Select cell H8 from the Parameters window and place it in the window to its right. Choose 11 Major Axis Points, and click OK. The resulting chart (Figure 4.9) shows graphically the same results that were shown in tabular form in Figure 4.8. Alternatively, a graph can be constructed from the Sensitivity Report worksheet using the normal charting features in Excel.

We can also use these tools to analyze the sensitivity of an output to two inputs. This option gives rise to a two-way table or a three-dimensional chart, in contrast to the one-way sensitivity table illustrated in Figure 4.8 and the two-dimensional chart in Figure 4.9. To demonstrate this feature, we build a table showing how profits are affected by both Q1 advertising and Q2 advertising. To vary Q1 advertising from $5,000 to $15,000 we enter the function =PsiSenParam (5000, 15000) in cell D19 (and edit cell D18 to reference cell D19). To also vary Q2 advertising over the same range we can copy this function to E19 (and edit cell E18 to reference cell E19). To create the two-way sensitivity chart, highlight cell C21 and select Analytic Solver Platform▶Analysis▶Reports▶Sensitivity▶Parameter Analysis. Use the buttons to select cell C21 as the Result cell and cells D19:E19 as the Parameter cells. Check the box Vary Parameters Independently, choose 11 Major Axis Points and 11 Minor Axis Points, and click OK. Analytic Solver Platform will then create a new sheet named Sensitivity Analysis Report that contains the table shown in Figure 4.10. A quick check that helps us confirm our work is to look up the profit value in the table corresponding to advertising expenditures of $10,000 in both Q1 and Q2. In the center of the table, we see that this value is $69,662, as expected.

FIGURE 4.8 Parametric Sensitivity Report: Profit as a Function of Cost

	A	B
1	Cost (C8)	Profit (C21)
2	$20.00	$149,474
3	$21.00	$133,512
4	$22.00	$117,549
5	$23.00	$101,587
6	$24.00	$85,625
7	$25.00	$69,662
8	$26.00	$53,700
9	$27.00	$37,737
10	$28.00	$21,775
11	$29.00	$5,812
12	$30.00	($10,150)
13		

By studying Figure 4.10, we can make a quick comparison between the effect of additional spending in Q1 and the effect of the same spending in Q2. As we can observe in the table, moving across a row generates more profit than moving the same distance down a column. This pattern tells us that we can gain more from spending additional dollars in Q2 than from the same additional dollars in Q1. This observation suggests that, starting with the base case, we could improve profits by shifting dollars from Q1 to Q2. We can also note from the table that the relationship between profits and advertising expenditures is not linear. Instead, profits show diminishing returns.

We can also create a chart to show the sensitivity of profit to Q1 and Q2 advertising. As before, select cell

FIGURE 4.9 Parametric Sensitivity Chart: Profit as a Function of Cost

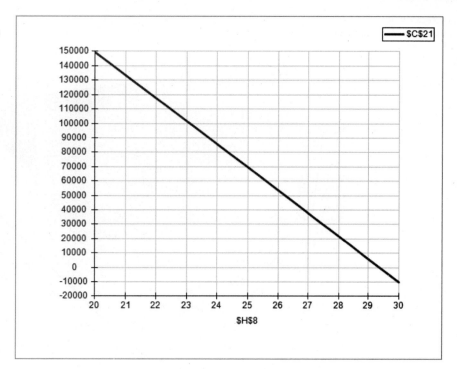

FIGURE 4.10 Parametric Sensitivity Table: Profit as a Function of Q1 and Q2 Advertising

Profit ($C$21)											
					Q2 Advertising ($E$19)						
Q1 Advertising ($D$19)											
	5000	6000	7000	8000	9000	10000	11000	12000	13000	14000	15000
5000	$64,180	$65,060	$65,838	$66,529	$67,145	$67,695	$68,186	$68,625	$69,017	$69,366	$69,676
6000	$64,718	$65,598	$66,376	$67,067	$67,683	$68,233	$68,725	$69,164	$69,555	$69,904	$70,214
7000	$65,173	$66,053	$66,831	$67,522	$68,138	$68,688	$69,179	$69,618	$70,010	$70,359	$70,669
8000	$65,557	$66,437	$67,215	$67,906	$68,522	$69,072	$69,563	$70,002	$70,394	$70,743	$71,053
9000	$65,879	$66,759	$67,537	$68,228	$68,844	$69,394	$69,885	$70,324	$70,716	$71,065	$71,375
10000	$66,147	$67,027	$67,805	$68,496	$69,112	$69,662	$70,153	$70,592	$70,984	$71,333	$71,643
11000	$66,367	$67,247	$68,025	$68,716	$69,332	$69,882	$70,374	$70,813	$71,204	$71,553	$71,863
12000	$66,544	$67,424	$68,203	$68,894	$69,510	$70,060	$70,551	$70,990	$71,382	$71,731	$72,040
13000	$66,683	$67,563	$68,341	$69,033	$69,648	$70,198	$70,690	$71,129	$71,520	$71,869	$72,179
14000	$66,787	$67,667	$68,445	$69,136	$69,752	$70,302	$70,793	$71,232	$71,624	$71,973	$72,283
15000	$66,858	$67,738	$68,517	$69,208	$69,824	$70,374	$70,865	$71,304	$71,696	$72,045	$72,354

C21 and then select Analytic Solver Platform▶Analysis▶Charts▶ Sensitivity Analysis▶Parameter Analysis. Use the arrow buttons to select cell C21 as the Result cell and cells D19:E19 as the Parameter cells. Check the box Vary Parameters Independently, choose 11 Major Axis Points and 11 Minor Axis Points, and click OK. The resulting chart (Figure 4.11) shows graphically the same results that were tabulated in Figure 4.10. In the chart, both the nonlinearity in the relationship between advertising and profit, and the stronger impact of Q2 advertising, are more easily recognized than in the table.

4.3.4 Tornado Charts

Another useful tool for sensitivity analysis is the **tornado chart**. In contrast to the information produced by parametric sensitivity, which shows how sensitive an output is to one or perhaps two inputs, a tornado chart shows how sensitive the output is to several different inputs. Consequently, it shows us which parameters have a major impact on the results and which have little impact.

Tornado charts are created by changing input values one at a time and recording the variations in the output. The simplest approach is to vary each input by a fixed percentage of its base-case value, such as ±10 percent. For each parameter in turn, we increase the base-case value by 10 percent and record the output, then we decrease the base-case value

FIGURE 4.11 Parametric
Sensitivity Chart: Profit as
a Function of Q1 and Q2
Advertising

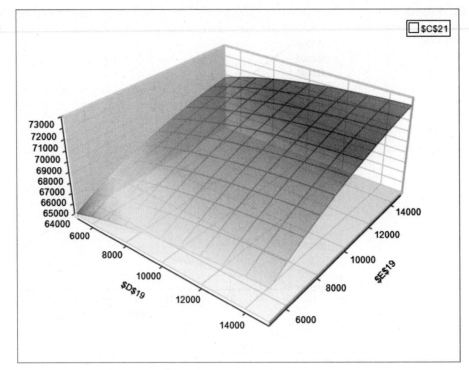

by 10 percent and record the output. Next, we calculate the absolute difference between these two outcomes and display the results in the order of these differences.

Analytic Solver Platform can be used to generate a tornado chart for any cell in a spreadsheet. For the Advertising Budget example in Figure 4.1, highlight cell C21 and select Analytic Solver Platform▶Parameters▶Parameters▶Identify. The results are shown in Figure 4.12.

FIGURE 4.12 Tornado
Chart for Profit

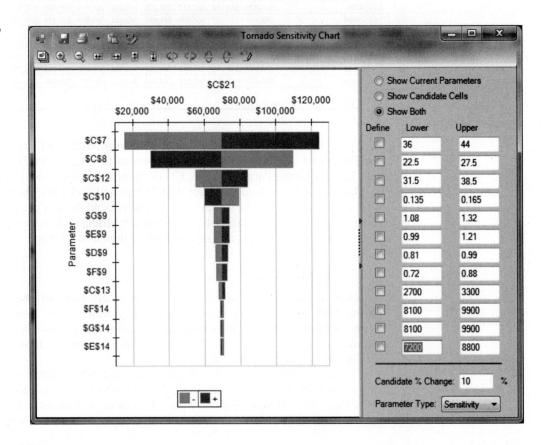

The horizontal axis at the top of the chart shows profits (cell C21), and the bars in the chart show the changes in profit resulting from ± 10 percent changes in each input. After calculating the values, the bars are sorted from largest to smallest for display in the diagram. Thus, the most sensitive inputs appear at the top, with the largest horizontal spans. The least sensitive inputs appear toward the bottom, with the smallest horizontal spans. Drawing the chart using horizontal bars, with the largest span at the top and the smallest at the bottom, suggests the shape of a tornado, hence the name. In our example, we can see that price (cell C7) has the biggest impact (a range of more than $108,000), with unit cost (cell C8) next (a range of nearly $80,000), and the other inputs far behind in impact on profit.

The Tornado Chart tool in Analytic Solver Platform actually calculates the change in the output caused by a change in every input that influences the output. However, it displays only the twelve parameters with the largest impacts. That is why, for instance, the parameter in cell D18 (Q1 advertising) does not appear in the chart: a ± 10 percent change in that cell has a smaller impact on profit than the parameters that are displayed.

On the right of Figure 4.12, the parameters are listed again, this time with the ranges over which they vary. For example, cell C7 (price) ranges from 36 to 44 (± 10 percent around the base case value of 40). Unit cost (cell C8) ranges from 22.5 to 27.5 (± 10 percent around the base-case value of 25). If we wish to change the ranges, we can change the Candidate % Change value in the lower right corner (enter the new number and press the Tab key). When input cells are given by PsiSenParam functions, the upper and lower limits for tornado charts are the upper and lower limits given in the function. We can also use this window to enter PsiSenParam functions for any number of inputs, simply by checking the Define boxes to the left of the Lower limit. Tornado charts are an extremely useful tool for determining quickly which parameters are most important in a model. Nevertheless, they have several limitations. First, it is not always realistic to vary each parameter by the same percentage. A 10 percent range may be realistic for one parameter, while 20 percent is realistic for another and 5 percent for a third. The critical factor is the size of the forecast error or uncertainty for each parameter. If these ranges are significantly different, we can assign different ranges to each parameter using the PsiSenParam functions. An additional pitfall arises in models with significant nonlinearities. If the output is related to an input in a nonlinear fashion, the degree of sensitivity implied by a tornado chart may be misleading. In general, we must be cautious about drawing conclusions about the sensitivity of a model outside the range of the parameters tested in a tornado chart. We must also remember that a tornado chart gives the sensitivity of an output when each input is varied *by itself*, leaving all other inputs fixed. In Chapter 14, we will show how to use Monte Carlo simulation to determine the sensitivity of an output when all inputs can vary together over ranges specified by probability distributions.

4.4 BREAKEVEN ANALYSIS

Many managers and analysts throw up their hands in the face of uncertainty about critical parameters. If we ask a manager to directly estimate market share for a new product, the reply may be: "I have *no idea* what market share we'll capture." A powerful strategy in this situation is to reverse the sense of the question: instead of asking "What will our market share be?" ask, "How high does our market share have to get before we turn a profit? " The trick here is to look for a **breakeven value**, or cutoff level for a parameter—that is, a target value of the output at which some particularly interesting event occurs, such as reaching zero profits or making a 15 percent return on invested assets. Managers who cannot predict market share can often determine whether a particular breakeven share is likely to occur. This is why breakeven analysis is so powerful.

Even if we have no idea of the market share for the new product, we should be able to build a model that calculates profit given some *assumption* about market share. Once market share takes the role of a parameter in our model, we can use parametric sensitivity analysis to construct a table or graph of profit as a function of market share. Then, from the table or graph, we can find the breakeven market share quite accurately.

New capital investments are usually evaluated in terms of their net present value, but the appropriate discount rate to use is not always obvious. Rather than attempting to determine the appropriate discount rate precisely, we can take the breakeven approach and ask how high the discount rate would have to be in order for the project to have an

FIGURE 4.13 The Goal Seek Window

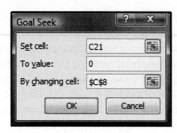

NPV of zero. (This discount rate is generally known as the **internal rate of return**.) If the answer is 28 percent, we can be confident that the project is a good investment. On the other hand, if breakeven occurs at 9 percent, we may want to do further research to establish whether the appropriate discount rate is clearly below this level.

Breakeven values for parameters can be determined manually, by repeatedly changing input values until the output reaches the desired target. This can often be done fairly quickly by an intelligent trial-and-error search in Excel. In the Advertising Budget model, suppose we want to find the breakeven cost to the nearest penny. Recall from Figure 4.8 that profit goes to zero somewhere between $29 and $30. By repeating the search between these two costs in steps of $0.10, we can find the breakeven cost to the nearest dime. If we repeat the search once more, in steps of $0.01, we will obtain the value at the precision we seek.

Excel also provides a specialized tool called **Goal Seek** for performing this type of search. Three pieces of information are required: the output-cell address, the target level sought, and the input-cell address. To determine the breakeven cost in the Advertising Budget example, we select Data▶Data Tools▶ What-if Analysis▶Goal Seek. The Set Cell is Profit in C21; the To Value is the profit target of zero; and the Changing Cell is unit cost, in C8. With these three specifications, the Goal Seek window takes the form shown in Figure 4.13. The tool locates the desired unit cost as $29.36, and the corresponding results are displayed on the spreadsheet (see Figure 4.14). Choosing the OK button in the Goal Seek Status window preserves these values in the spreadsheet; choosing the Cancel button returns the spreadsheet to its base case.

The Goal Seek tool searches for a prescribed level in the relation between a single output and a single input. Thus, it requires the parameter or decision being varied to

FIGURE 4.14 Using the Goal Seek Tool in the Advertising Budget Example

	A	B	C	D	E	F	G	H	I	J
5	PARAMETERS									
6				Q1	Q2	Q3	Q4			Notes
7		Price	$40.00							Current price
8		Cost	$29.36							Accounting
9		Seasonal		0.9	1.1	0.8	1.2			Data analysis
10		OHD rate	0.15							Accounting
11		Sales Parameters			If the cost is set to $29.36 . . .					
12			35							Consultants
13			3000							
14		Sales Expense		8000	8000	9000	9000			Consultants
15		Ad Budget	$40,000							Current budget
16										
17	DECISIONS							Total		
18		Ad Expenditures		$10,000	$10,000	$10,000	$10,000	$40,000		sum
19										
20	OUTPUTS				. . . then the profit equals the target figure of $0.					
21		Profit	$0							
22										
23	CALCULATIONS									
24		Quarter		Q1	Q2	Q3	Q4	Total		
25		Seasonal		0.9	1.1	0.8	1.2			
26										
27		Units Sold		3592	4390	3192	4789	15962		given formula
28		Revenue		143662	175587	127700	191549	638498		price*units
29		Cost of Goods		105463	128899	93745	140617	468724		cost*units
30		Gross Margin		38199	46688	33955	50932	169775		subtraction
31										
32		Sales Expense		8000	8000	9000	9000	34000		given
33		Advertising		10000	10000	10000	10000	40000		decisions
34		Overhead		21549	26338	19155	28732	95775		rate*revenue
35		Total Fixed Cost		39549	44338	38155	47732	169775		sum
36										
37		Profit		-1350	2350	-4200	3200	0		GM -TFC
38		Profit Margin		-0.94%	1.34%	-3.29%	1.67%	0.00%		pct of revenue
39										

4.1 / 4.4 / 4.5 / 4.8 / 4.9 / 4.10 / 4.11 / 4.12 / **4.14**

reside in a single location, reinforcing one of the design principles we introduced in Chapter 3.

One warning should be added. If we invoke Goal Seek when there is more than one breakeven point, the value returned by the Goal Seek tool may depend on where we start. A simple example illustrates this feature. Suppose our model contains the formula $y = x^2 - 5x + 6$, and we want to find the value of x for which $y = 0$. If we set up this search on a spreadsheet and initially assign $x = 7$, then Goal Seek produces the result $x = 3$ as the desired value. However, if we initially assign $x = 1$, then Goal Seek returns the value $x = 2$. Thus, we may need to be alert to the possibility of more than one breakeven point, because Goal Seek can return only one value. If we suspect that there may be a second breakeven level, we can perform a preliminary parametric sensitivity analysis to see whether multiple breakeven points are a possibility.

4.5 OPTIMIZATION ANALYSIS

Another fundamental type of managerial question asks what decision variables achieve the best possible value of an output. In fact, we might claim that the fundamental management task is to make choices that result in optimal outputs. Analytic Solver Platform provides a variety of powerful tools for this purpose, allowing us to optimize models with many decision variables and with constraints on the choice of decision variables. Optimization is a complex subject, and we devote Chapters 8–12 to it and to the use of Analytic Solver Platform for this purpose. However, we can provide a glimpse of its power by demonstrating a simple application in the Advertising Budget example.

Suppose we wish to maximize total profits with an advertising budget of $40,000. We already know that, with equal expenditures in every quarter, annual profits come to $69,662. The question now is whether we can achieve a higher level of annual profits. By using Analytic Solver Platform we can find that a higher level is, in fact, attainable. An optimal reallocation of the budget produces annual profits of $71,447. The chart in Figure 4.15 compares the allocation of the budget in the base case with the optimal allocation. As we can see, the optimal allocation calls for greater expenditures in quarters Q2 and Q4 and for smaller expenditures in Q1 and Q3.

This is just one illustration of the power of optimization. Among the many questions we could answer with Analytic Solver Platform in the Advertising Budget example are these:

- What would be the impact of a requirement to spend at least $8,000 each quarter?
- What would be the marginal impact of increasing the budget?
- What is the optimal budget size?

Chapters 8–12 develop the techniques to answer these and a host of related questions for a variety of spreadsheet models.

FIGURE 4.15 Comparison of Base Case and Optimal Allocations

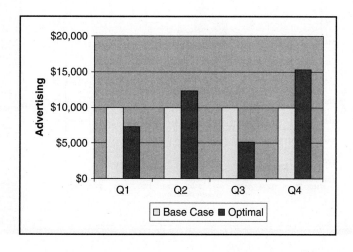

4.6 SIMULATION AND RISK ANALYSIS

Uncertainty often plays an important role in analyzing a decision because with uncertainty comes risk. Until now, we have been exploring the relationship between the inputs and outputs of a spreadsheet model as if uncertainty were not at issue. However, risk is an inherent feature of all managerial decisions, so it is frequently an important aspect in modeling. In particular, we might want to recognize that some of the inputs are subject to uncertainty. In other words, we might want to associate probability models with some of the parameters. When we take that step, it makes sense to look at outputs the same way—with probability models. The use of probability models in this context is known as **risk analysis**.

Analytic Solver Platform has the capability of performing Monte Carlo simulation for risk analysis. This tool allows us to generate a probability distribution for any output cell in a spreadsheet, given probability assumptions about some of the input cells. Simulation and risk analysis are the subjects of Chapters 14 and 15. Here, we simply illustrate how Analytic Solver Platform can help us answer an important question about risk.

We return to the base case in the Advertising Budget example, in which we assumed equal expenditures of $10,000 for advertising each quarter. Our analysis, which assumed that all parameters are known exactly, showed an annual profit of $69,662. However, we might wonder about the distribution of profits if there's uncertainty about the unit price and the unit cost. Future prices depend on the number of competitors in our market, and future costs depend on the availability of raw materials. Since both the level of competition and raw material supply are uncertain, so, too, are the parameters for our price and cost. Suppose we assume that price is normally distributed with a mean of $40 and a standard deviation of $10, and that unit cost is equally likely to fall anywhere between $20 and $30. Given these assumptions, what is the probability distribution of annual profits; specifically, what is the *average* profit? And how likely is it that profits will be *negative*?

Figure 4.16 shows the probability distribution for profits in the form of a histogram, derived from the assumptions we made about price and cost. The graph shows us the extreme range of possible outcomes, from a loss of about $350,000 to a profit of around $450,000. The mean profit is $69,657, while the probability of a loss is about 32 percent. This exposure may cause us to reevaluate the desirability of the base-case plan.

Chapters 14 and 15 develop the techniques to address uncertain elements in the analysis, for a variety of spreadsheet models. There, we show how to:

- Determine which inputs require probability models.
- Select appropriate probability models for those inputs.
- Configure Analytic Solver Platform to generate a histogram for any output cell.

FIGURE 4.16 Distribution of Profit in the Advertising Budget Example

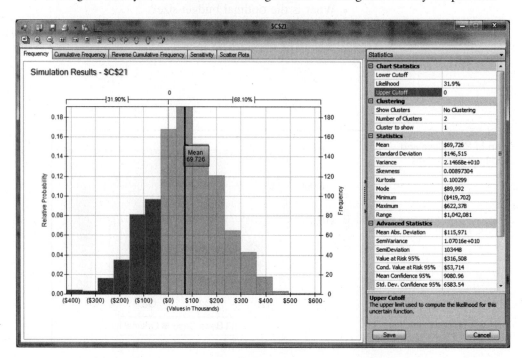

4.7 SUMMARY

The process of analyzing a spreadsheet model has several identifiable steps. The first step is to construct a base case, which becomes a key point of comparison for all of the subsequent analyses. The next step is what-if analysis: changing inputs and tracing the effects on one or more of the outputs. Early in the development of a spreadsheet, this step is an aid in debugging the model, as we mentioned in Chapter 3. Once the spreadsheet has been debugged and tested, what-if analysis helps us discover how sensitive an output is to one or more of the inputs. Parametric sensitivity analysis using Analytic Solver Platform helps us automate this type of sensitivity analysis.

A tornado chart provides another form of what-if analysis, treating several of the inputs at once. Scenario analysis can be used to analyze the outputs for a set of inputs that together tell a story. Whatever tool we use, probing for sensitivities helps provide useful insight to support management decisions. In the Advertising Budget example, our early probing revealed that profits respond in straight-line fashion to changes in the unit cost and that profits show diminishing returns to additional advertising expenditures.

A related step involves inverting the analysis, where we start with a target for a particular output and "back into" the input value that achieves that target level of performance. The most prominent form is breakeven analysis, which aims at a target of zero, but the concept can be applied to any target level. Excel provides the Goal Seek tool to automate the search for a single input value that achieves a desired output value. Breakeven analysis provides us with an early indication of risk: we can determine how much of a cushion there is in any one of our parameter forecasts. Should the actual value turn out to be worse than our base-case assumption, breakeven analysis tells

us how much of a difference we can tolerate before our output measure reaches a critical level. In the Advertising Budget example, we found that the $25 unit cost could increase to more than $29 before we would face negative profits.

The most ambitious forms of analysis are optimization and simulation. Optimization methods look for the best value of an output by searching through various combinations of the decisions. Simulation methods allow some of the inputs to be treated as probabilistic, tracing the implications for outputs. These two methods represent advanced techniques of modeling, and we devote several later chapters to them. In our analysis framework, they play the role of powerful tools capable of delivering further insights. In the Advertising Budget example, the insight obtained from optimization was that the allocation of advertising expenditures across the four quarters should not be equal but rather should reflect the size of the seasonal factors. In fact, further optimization analysis reveals that the $40,000 budget itself is probably too small. With a larger budget, we could substantially increase profits.

The progression from a base-case to a what-if and a breakeven analysis, and then to optimization and simulation analyses, represents a logical and increasingly sophisticated set of methods for *experimenting* with a spreadsheet model. This kind of experimentation provides the opportunity for the same kind of learning that a scientist derives from laboratory experiments. Indeed, the spreadsheet is an analyst's electronic laboratory, and in supporting management decisions with laboratory work, the analyst is serving as a *management scientist*. In the following chapters, we begin to develop the management scientist's advanced modeling tools.

EXERCISES

1. Refer to the XYZ Company case. From the corresponding exercise in Chapter 3, review the design of a spreadsheet that will allow an analyst to predict monthly cash needs and profitability for the first five months of the year.

a. In what month does the cash balance fall below zero, signaling a need to borrow money?

b. What is the profit, as a percentage of sales, in April?

c. Suppose the monthly increment in sales is 600—instead of 500, as in the base case. How does this change affect the answers in (a) and (b)? Construct a table to examine the month in which the cash balance disappears as a function of the monthly increment in sales.

d. Suppose the monthly increment in sales is 300—instead of 500, as in the base case. How does this change affect the answers in (a) and (b)? Construct a graph showing the profitability percentage in (b) as a function of the monthly increment in sales.

e. Starting with the base case, suppose that unit cost runs higher than originally thought. What level of unit cost will lead the firm to run out of cash by the end of March?

2. Refer to the Medical Supplies for Banjul case. From the corresponding exercise in Chapter 3, review the design of a spreadsheet that will enable you to request the required funds

from your team's finance officer, order supplies from the home office, and ensure dissemination of appropriate quantities to each village. Your final order to the home office should specify the number of packages required of each item.

a. The population figures will show that there are 3,000 children, 2,500 teenagers, 500 seniors, and 9,000 other adults in the population. If there were no stock on hand, what amount would be required for ordering supplies?

b. Using the parameters in (a), construct a graph showing how the amount required for the order would vary if the unit cost of a package of bandages rose by $0.25, $0.50, and so on, up to $3.00 per package.

c. Following up on (a), a check on stock shows an inventory of 124 packages of A-bandages, 16 packages of B-bandages, 82 packages of C-bandages, 72 rolls of tape, and 4 hearing aids. What amounts will be required for ordering supplies?

3. Refer to the Reid's Raisins case. From the corresponding exercise in Chapter 3, review the design of a spreadsheet that will allow the firm to determine how many grapes to buy under contract and how much to charge for the raisins they sell.

a. What is the profit projected for the base-case conditions, assuming a market price of $0.30 for the open-market grape price?

b. What is the breakeven value of the open-market grape price?

c. Construct a table showing how profit varies as a function of the price set for raisins. Cover a range from $1.80 to $2.80 in steps of $0.10.

d. Construct a tornado chart for the analysis in (a). List the relevant parameters in descending order of their impact on annual profit.

4. Refer to the Big Rig Rental Company case. Design a spreadsheet that will provide the owner with the five-year economic analysis requested.

a. What is the Net Present Value of the firm's cash flows over the five-year period?

b. Construct a tornado chart for the analysis in (a). List the relevant parameters in descending order of their impact on the Net Present Value.

c. What is the internal rate of return for the cash flows in (a)?

d. Construct a table to show how profit varies with the base rental rate, currently $1,000 per month.

5. Refer to the Flexible Insurance Coverage case. From the corresponding exercise in Chapter 3, review the design of a spreadsheet that will allow an individual employee to compare the annual expenses for each plan and thereby choose the cheapest alternative.

a. Consider the case of a single employee with estimated annual expenses of $400. Which plan is the cheapest? What is the total annual cost associated with this plan?

b. For the analysis in (a), construct a table to show the best plan and the associated cost for annual expenses ranging from $100 to $1,200 in steps of $100.

c. Consider the case of a married employee with estimated annual expenses of $1,000 and an equal amount for the spouse. Which plan is the cheapest? What is the total annual cost associated with this plan?

d. For the analysis in (c), construct a table to show the best plan and the associated cost for annual expenses ranging from $100 to $1,500 in steps of $100 for the employee, assuming that the employee's expenses and the spouse's expenses are the same.

e. For the analysis in (d), find the level of expenses at which the cost is the same under Plan 1 and Plan 2.

6. Refer to the Snoey Software Company case. From the corresponding exercise in Chapter 3, review the design of a spreadsheet for the desired five-year economic analysis mentioned in the case.

a. Consider a recommendation that the prices for the Educational, Large-Scale, and High-Speed versions should be $75, $275, and $475, respectively. What annual profit would these prices achieve?

b. Construct three separate sensitivity analyses, starting from the base case in (a). For each analysis, vary the price above and below the base case, and find the best price for the version being analyzed. When these prices are used in combination, what annual profit is achieved?

c. For the pricing in (a), consider the set of prices that the five segments would be willing to pay for the three products. If each of these prices could vary by 15 percent, which one would have the greatest dollar impact on the annual profit?

7. Refer to the Cox Cable and Wire Company case. In the role of Meredith, design a spreadsheet that will evaluate the profitability of any particular production and delivery schedule.

a. Find a machine schedule and a corresponding inventory and shipment schedule that meets demand. What is the profitability of this schedule?

b. Suppose that material costs for both products were to rise by a specific percentage. At what percentage increase would profitability drop to zero?

c. Construct a table showing how profitability varies with changes in the selling price of Plastic reels. Repeat for Teflon reels. Which price has a greater effect on profitability?

8. Refer to the BMW Company case. From the corresponding exercise in Chapter 3, review the design of a spreadsheet that will allow BMW management to estimate the cost of disposal a decade into the future (i.e., in 1999) as a percentage of net income.

a. What percentage is predicted for 1999, assuming there are no changes in trends and policies?

b. How does the percentage change as a function of BMW's market share in 1999? (Consider a range from 5 percent to 8 percent.)

c. Construct a tornado chart for the analysis in (a). List the relevant parameters in descending order of their impact on the disposal cost.

d. Consider three scenarios, called Slow, Medium, and Fast, characterized by different landfill costs in 1999 (600, 1200, and 1800DM, respectively) and by different landfill percentages (60 percent, 50 percent, and 40 percent, respectively). For these scenarios, and assuming that incineration costs will run double landfill costs, construct a scenario table for BMW's disposal cost in 1999 and the percentage of its net income that this figure represents.

9. Refer to the ERP Decision case. From the corresponding exercise in Chapter 3, review the design of a spreadsheet that will assist the Board in understanding the likely costs and benefits of implementing ERP.

a. Develop a base case. You may create any data you need for this purpose. Why is this base case appropriate for this situation?

b. How sensitive are the benefits of ERP in the base case to the efficiency gains?

c. Break the total benefits down into the contribution from efficiency gains, inventory turns, and CRM.

10. Refer to the Retirement Planning case. From the corresponding exercise in Chapter 3, review the design of a spreadsheet for this problem.

a. Develop a base case. You may create any data you need for this purpose. Why is this base case appropriate for this situation?

b. Perform an appropriate sensitivity analysis. Which parameters have the most significant impact on the results? Can you find applications for the Parametric Sensitivity, Tornado Chart, and Scenario Manager tools?

c. Identify applications of the Goal Seek tool in this situation. (For example, find the savings rate needed to ensure that assets do not run out before age ninety.)

d. Identify potential applications of *optimization* in this case.

e. Identify potential applications of *simulation* in this case.

11. Refer to the Draft TV Commercials case. From the corresponding exercise in Chapter 3, review the design of a spreadsheet for this problem.

a. Develop a base case. You may create any data you need for this purpose. Why is this base case appropriate for this situation?

b. Perform an appropriate sensitivity analysis. Which parameters have the most significant impact on the results? Can you find applications for the Parametric Sensitivity, Tornado Chart, and Scenario Manager tools?

c. Identify applications of Goal Seek in this situation. (For example, what percentage of the overall budget should be devoted to draft commercials in order to achieve a preset target number of impressions?)

d. Identify potential applications of *optimization* in this case.

e. Identify potential applications of *simulation* in this case.

12. Refer to the Icebergs for Kuwait case. From the corresponding exercise in Chapter 3, review the design of a spreadsheet for this problem.

a. Develop a base case. You may create any data you need for this purpose. Why is this base case appropriate for this situation?

b. Perform an appropriate sensitivity analysis. Which parameters have the most significant impact on the results? Can you find applications for the Parametric Sensitivity, Tornado Chart, and Scenario Manager tools?

c. Identify applications of Goal Seek in this situation. (For example, how large an iceberg should they tow in order to break even at the current price for pure water?)

d. Identify potential applications of *optimization* in this case.

e. Identify potential applications of *simulation* in this case.

13. Refer to the Racquetball Racket case. From the corresponding exercise in Chapter 3, review the design of a spreadsheet for this problem.

a. Develop a base case. You may create any data you need for this purpose. Why is this base case appropriate for this situation?

b. Perform an appropriate sensitivity analysis. Which parameters have the most significant impact on the results? Can you find applications for the Parametric Sensitivity, Tornado Chart, and Scenario Manager tools?

c. Identify applications of Goal Seek in this situation. (For example, what percentage of the market must they achieve to break even on their investment?)

d. Identify potential applications of *optimization* in this case.

e. Identify potential applications of *simulation* in this case.

5 Data Exploration and Preparation

5.1 INTRODUCTION

Well-prepared business analysts need to know how to use data to derive business insights and to improve business decisions in a variety of contexts. In one context, the analyst is called upon to *describe* the current situation. For example, the task might be to discover which products contributed most to profit over the past year. In another context, the analyst may be asked to *predict* the future situation. In this case, it may be useful to project sales by product line over the next year. In yet another context, the analyst might be called upon to *prescribe* specific actions the organization should take to achieve its goals. In this case the task might be to recommend a pricing strategy for each product line in order to increase profits. The first of these tasks, describing the past, is simply a matter of extracting and summarizing the appropriate data; it involves no modeling at all. At the other extreme, the pricing task may involve sophisticated management science modeling supported, of course, by relevant data. Whether the task at hand is primarily descriptive, predictive, or prescriptive, an analyst needs to command a range of data-related skills.

In this chapter, we focus on the basic skills needed to understand a data set, to explore individual variables and groups of variables for insights, and to prepare data for more complex analysis. Most of these skills relate to the descriptive tasks mentioned above. However, these same skills are necessary for any predictive or prescriptive task that involves data. Whether simple or complex, any management science model rests on a foundation of numerical assumptions. These numbers are often derived from raw data, which must be understood and explored before reliable estimates can be entered into the model. Furthermore, effective sensitivity analysis relies on the plausible range for a given variable, and this range can often be estimated from data.

In Chapter 6, we present a set of predictive models that rely heavily on data for their effectiveness. Some of these models are used for classification methods, which predict the category for an individual case. For example, we might want to predict which of a set of corporations will default on their bonds, which of our customers will respond to a promotion campaign, or which qualified voters will actually vote on Election Day. Other methods focus on numerical prediction. For example, we might want to predict the size of the next purchase from an existing customer, the value of the stock for a company going public, or the annual donations from members of a nonprofit organization. Both classification and prediction methods are based on past associations between outcomes and the variable to be predicted, and usually require large amounts of data to be effective. In Chapter 7, we present a special class of prediction methods called time-series methods. These rely on past values of the variables themselves to predict future values. Again, well-understood and well-prepared datasets are the keys to success in using these methods.

This chapter covers four main topics: database structure, types of variables, data exploration, and data preparation. We should also say a word about our coverage of software skills. Throughout this and the next two chapters, we use a variety of tools from Excel as well as the Excel add-in XLMiner. In a number of cases, a given data operation can be performed in several alternative ways in Excel and XLMiner. In most cases, we present the one method we think is most straightforward, flexible, and effective. When two alternative methods have competing advantages, we present both, but our intent is not to provide exhaustive coverage.

Finally, we offer an admonition to always maintain a skeptical attitude toward data. Datasets used for teaching purposes are usually carefully selected to be relevant to the problem at hand, free of bias, and without missing values or errors. Datasets encountered in the real world are another story: they may not be relevant to the problem, they may have been collected or processed in biased ways, and they often contain missing values and errors. Thus, when working with real data, it is crucial to explore the dataset carefully and prepare it for analysis, and to never lose sight of the fundamental assumption behind all data analysis: that the future will be enough like the past to make past data relevant.

5.2 DATABASE STRUCTURE

When the only data available to us are a few numbers or a few names, we can store them on slips of paper. But when the data grow to hundreds, thousands, or millions of data points, it is essential to store data in a structured format designed for easy access and manipulation. Most complex organizational data today are stored in relational databases and accessed using sophisticated database management systems, but data analysis is often carried out in spreadsheets. For our purposes, a database is a two-dimensional file (often called a flat file) consisting of rows and columns. Each row, or **record**, contains information on a single entity, which could be an individual customer, product, or company, depending on the database. Each column, or **field**, contains a specific type of information on each record, such as the name of a customer, the cost of a product, or the ticker symbol for a company. Depending on the context, records are also referred to as cases or instances, while fields may be referred to as variables, descriptors, or predictors. Most databases also contain a **data dictionary**, which documents each field in detail.

As examples, we'll work with three databases:

- Analgesics.xlsx, with data on retail sales of painkillers.
- Applicants.xlsx, with data on one year's pool of MBA applicants.
- Executives.xlsx, with data on executive compensation for a sample of companies.

Figure 5.1 shows a portion of the Analgesics database. This database contains 7,517 records, each of which describes sales at one of six different stores for a particular painkiller during a one-week period. The database has eight fields, starting with ID number and ending with SALES. The data dictionary describes the fields as follows:

Field Name	*Description*
ID	Record number
ITEM	Item number
UPC	Uniform Product Code
DESCRIPTION	Description
SIZE	Items per container
STORE	Store number
WEEK	Week number
SALES	Sales volume in cases

We might use this database to answer such questions as the following:

- What were the market shares of the various brands?
- What were the weekly sales volumes at the different stores?

We use the past tense here to emphasize that although we are interested in projecting into the future, the data actually tell us something about the past.

Figure 5.2 shows a portion of the Applicants database. This database contains 2,917 records, each of which describes an applicant to an MBA program. The database

FIGURE 5.1 First Portion of the Analgesics Database*

	A	B	C	D	E	F	G	H
1	ID	ITEM	UPC	DESCRIPTION	SIZE	STORE	WEEK	SALES
2	1	6122741	2586610502	ALEVE CAPLETS	24 CT	101	383	0
3	2	6122741	2586610502	ALEVE CAPLETS	24 CT	101	384	0
4	3	6122741	2586610502	ALEVE CAPLETS	24 CT	101	385	0
5	4	6122741	2586610502	ALEVE CAPLETS	24 CT	101	386	0
6	5	6122741	2586610502	ALEVE CAPLETS	24 CT	101	387	0
7	6	6122741	2586610502	ALEVE CAPLETS	24 CT	101	388	0
8	7	6122741	2586610502	ALEVE CAPLETS	24 CT	101	389	0
9	8	6122741	2586610502	ALEVE CAPLETS	24 CT	101	390	0
10	9	6122741	2586610502	ALEVE CAPLETS	24 CT	101	391	0
11	10	6122741	2586610502	ALEVE CAPLETS	24 CT	101	392	0
12	11	6122741	2586610502	ALEVE CAPLETS	24 CT	103	383	0
13	12	6122741	2586610502	ALEVE CAPLETS	24 CT	103	384	0
14	13	6122741	2586610502	ALEVE CAPLETS	24 CT	103	385	0
15	14	6122741	2586610502	ALEVE CAPLETS	24 CT	103	386	0
16	15	6122741	2586610502	ALEVE CAPLETS	24 CT	103	387	0
17	16	6122741	2586610502	ALEVE CAPLETS	24 CT	103	388	0
18	17	6122741	2586610502	ALEVE CAPLETS	24 CT	103	389	0
19	18	6122741	2586610502	ALEVE CAPLETS	24 CT	103	390	0
20	19	6122741	2586610502	ALEVE CAPLETS	24 CT	103	391	0
21	20	6122741	2586610502	ALEVE CAPLETS	24 CT	103	392	0
22	21	6122751	2586610504	ALEVE CAPLETS	50 CT	102	383	0
23	22	6122751	2586610504	ALEVE CAPLETS	50 CT	102	384	0
24	23	6122751	2586610504	ALEVE CAPLETS	50 CT	102	385	0
25	24	6122751	2586610504	ALEVE CAPLETS	50 CT	102	386	0
26	25	6122751	2586610504	ALEVE CAPLETS	50 CT	102	387	0
27	26	6122751	2586610504	ALEVE CAPLETS	50 CT	102	388	0
28	27	6122751	2586610504	ALEVE CAPLETS	50 CT	102	389	0
29	28	6122751	2586610504	ALEVE CAPLETS	50 CT	102	390	0
30	29	6122751	2586610504	ALEVE CAPLETS	50 CT	102	391	0

5.1

FIGURE 5.2 First Portion of the Applicants Database

	A	B	C	D	E	F	G	H	I
1	ID	ROUND	AGE	SEX	CITZ CODE	1ST CONTACT	JOB MONTHS	INDUSTRY	INDUSTRY DESC.
2	1	1	30	M	U	Email	84	260	Finan Serv-Diversified
3	2	1	29	M	U	Phone call	86	370	Government
4	3	1	27	M	U	Phone call	40	260	Finan Serv-Diversified
5	4	1	30	M	U	Email	48		
6	5	1	32	M	U	Home Page	85	290	Finan Serv-Invest Mgt/Research
7	6	1	26	M	U	Home Page	32	280	Finan Serv-Invest Bk/Brokerage
8	7	1	29	M	U	Phone call	60	10	Accounting
9	8	1	27	F	U		44	220	Entertainment/Leisure/Media
10	9	1	29	M	U	Phone call	66	40	Agribusiness
11	10	1	31	M	U	Letter	78	420	Nonprofit
12	11	1	27	M	U	Phone call	24	460	Retail
13	12	1	27	M	U	Phone call	51	370	Government
14	13	1	28	M	U		26	230	Environmental Services
15	14	1	30	M	U	Phone call	72	20	Advertising/Marketing Services
16	15	1	27	F	U	Phone call	48	420	Nonprofit
17	16	1	25	M	U	Home Page	31	260	Finan Serv-Diversified
18	17	1	24	F	U	Phone call	24	210	Energy/Utilities
19	18	1	28	M	U	Phone call	31	400	Law
20	19	1	27	M	N	Home Page	54	80	Construction
21	20	1	26	M	U	Letter	32	230	Environmental Services
22	21	1	24	M	U	World Wide Web	24	580	Other Services
23	22	1	27	M	U	Phone call	46	260	Finan Serv-Diversified
24	23	1	28	M	U	Home Page	50	160	Consumer Gds-Food/Beverage
25	24	1	28	M	U	Home Page	60	10	Accounting
26	25	1	29	M	U	Phone call	30	370	Government
27	26	1	27	M	U		48	120	Consulting-Strategy/Management
28	27	1	26	M	U	Phone call	36	260	Finan Serv-Diversified
29	28	1	28	F	U	Home Page	44	260	Finan Serv-Diversified
30	29	1	35	M	U	Phone call	146	220	Entertainment/Leisure/Media

5.1 5.2

* To download spreadsheets for this chapter, go to the Student Companion Site at www.wiley.com/college/powell.

contains 20 fields, each of which is described in more detail in the following data dictionary:

Field Name	Description
ID	Record number
ROUND	Round number (1–5) in which application was received
AGE	Age
SEX	Gender
CITZ CODE	U (U.S.) or N (non-U.S.)
1ST CONTACT	How first made contact with admissions
JOB MONTHS	Tenure in current (or most recent) job
INDUSTRY	Industry code number
INDUSTRY DESC.	Industry description
DECISION	Admission Committee decision
GMAT	Test score
PCT	Percentile
OLD	Old GMAT score, if previously taken
DEGREE	Previous degree
MJR	Major (abbreviated)
MAJOR	Major
DEG2	2nd previous degree
MJR2	2nd previous major
DEG3	3rd previous degree
MJR3	3rd previous major

We might use this database to answer such questions as the following:

- What proportion of the applicants had nonprofit work experience?
- What was the average GMAT score for accepted applicants?

Figure 5.3 shows a portion of the Executives database. This database contains 100 records, each of which describes the financial background of an executive. The database

FIGURE 5.3 First Portion of the Executives Database

	A	B	C	D	E	F	G	H	I
1	ID	EXECID	GENDER	SALARY	BONUS	OTHER	SHARES	CONAME	TICKER
2	108	01512	MALE	1000.000	2400.000	284.179	617.072	AMERICAN EXPRESS	AXP
3	151	01542	MALE	631.733	1124.421	0.000	48.300	AMGEN INC	AMGN
4	166	01060	MALE	475.400	0.000	25.600	194.583	ANDREW CORP	ANDW
5	217	01538	MALE	980.000	1557.710	14.377	161.445	ATLANTIC RICHFIELD CO	ARC
6	314	00111	MALE	750.000	825.000	294.770	183.031	BAXTER INTERNATIONAL INC	BAX
7	381	02633	MALE	1093.079	1900.800	0.000	21.136	BOEING CO	BA
8	447	01258	MALE	636.500	975.000	3.500	402.261	CIGNA CORP	CI
9	498	02821	MALE	700.000	1000.000	0.000	50.510	CHAMPION INTERNATIONAL CORP	CHA
10	516	00197	MALE	1350.000	1965.000	0.000	.	CHEVRON CORP	CHV
11	586	00778	MALE	1000.000	8732.474	448.577	17500.746	CITIGROUP INC	C
12	609	02079	MALE	750.000	861.000	0.000	1667.160	COMPUTER ASSOCIATES INTL INC	CA
13	767	02328	MALE	334.511	177.582	0.552	16.445	DOMINION RESOURCES INC	D
14	776	01504	MALE	850.000	1100.000	0.000	308.486	DOVER CORP	DOV
15	791	02272	MALE	425.000	226.250	0.000	2569.562	DOW JONES & CO INC	DJ
16	809	02238	MALE	723.000	376.834	0.000	172.819	DUN & BRADSTREET CORP	DNB
17	822	00315	MALE	771.018	463.200	0.000	224.861	EASTERN ENTERPRISES	EFU
18	921	01337	MALE	800.000	0.000	55.556		FIRST UNION CORP (N C)	FTU
19	988	02741	MALE	1050.000	1560.000	97.036	616.694	GENERAL ELECTRIC CO	GE
20	1016	00418	MALE	620.000	952.468	0.000	334.430	GENUINE PARTS CO	GPC
21	1063	02277	MALE	410.040	92.258	0.000	57.860	GRAINGER (W W) INC	GWW
22	1106	02424	MALE	312.500	177.470	24.000	91.066	HARRIS CORP	HRS
23	1121	02437	MALE	527.300	290.015	12.815		HASBRO INC	HAS
24	1153	01208	MALE	980.769	3000.000	104.984	34796.756	HOME DEPOT INC	HD
25	1211	02567	MALE	260.000	1120.000	0.000	3012.109	INTEL CORP	INTC
26	1214	02569	MALE	323.471	85.266	54.165	50.849	INTERGRAPH CORP	INGR
27	1220	01549	MALE	2000.000	7200.000	66.376	965.986	INTL BUSINESS MACHINES CORP	IBM
28	1307	01305	MALE	877.308	804.169	0.000	167.635	KNIGHT-RIDDER INC	KRI
29	1329	00555	MALE	1185.577	3331.968	0.000	46497.711	LIMITED INC	LTD
30	1351	02793	MALE	180.000	407.457	2.823	75.648	LONGS DRUG STORES INC	LDG

H ◀ ▶ H / 5.1 / 5.2 / **5.3** / | ◀ | IIII | ▶ |

contains 19 fields, each of which is described in more detail in the following data dictionary:

Field Name	Description
ID	Record number
EXECID	Executive ID number
GENDER	Male or Female
SALARY	Annual salary
BONUS	End of year bonus
OTHER	Other compensation
SHARES	Shares owned
CONAME	Company name
TICKER	Ticker abbreviation
INDDESC	Industry description
STATE	State where company HQ located
ZIP	Zip code
AREA	Telephone area code
SALES	Annual sales
PRETAX	Pretax profits
ASSETS	Total assets
ROA	Return on assets
MKTVAL	Market value of stock
DIVYIELD	Dividend yield for the year

We might use this database to answer such questions as the following:

- What was the average salary among these executives?
- What proportion of compensation was due to annual bonuses?

5.3 TYPES OF DATA

Despite the almost infinite variety of data in databases, there are only a few common types of data. The most basic type is **nominal data**, which simply names the category of a record. The GENDER field in the Executives database is nominal data: it takes only the two values M (for Male) and F (for Female). Likewise, the CITZ CODE field in the Applicants database is nominal: it takes on the values U (for US) and N (for non-US). The DESCRIPTION field in the Analgesics database is also nominal: it takes over 90 distinct values, from ADVIL to TYLENOL X/STRGH LIQ. Note that nominal data are simply names; they have no natural order and cannot be treated as numbers. In some cases, nominal variables actually appear as numbers: for example, the categories Male and Female might be represented by 0 and 1 respectively. But these numbers should be understood as simply codes for the related words, not as numbers subject to addition or multiplication. An example is the STORE field in the Analgesics database, where the six stores are given the numbers 100 to 105; in this case the *average* store number makes no practical sense.

A second type of data, known as **ordinal data**, also identifies the category of a record, but in this case there is a natural order to the values. A simple example would be a sales variable in which the values were High, Medium, and Low. These values are clearly not numbers, but there is a definite order: we can say that High is greater than Medium, and Medium is greater than Low. Again, we could code these values using numbers, such as 3, 2, and 1. This coding preserves the order of the values, but we should avoid calculating differences or averages because these are meaningless. When we ask survey respondents to rank alternatives from Least Preferred (1) to Most Preferred (7), we are using an ordinal scale: Most Preferred is preferred to Least Preferred, but the difference of 6 is not meaningful.

Nominal variables and ordinal variables are both referred to as **categorical variables**. The other main type of data is **numerical data**. This category itself can be further divided into interval data and ratio data. **Interval data** conveys a sense of the differences between values. The Fahrenheit and Celsius temperature scales provide common examples. We can say that 80 degrees Fahrenheit is 40 degrees warmer than 40 degrees Fahrenheit, so differences in degrees make sense. However, we cannot say that 80 degrees Fahrenheit is *twice* as warm as 40 degrees Fahrenheit. (These measurements correspond to 25 degrees Celsius and 5 degrees Celsius, so in Celsius the same temperature would appear to be five times as hot.) Interval data is based on a scale with an arbitrary zero point, which is why ratios are not meaningful. **Ratio data**, on the other hand, is based on a scale with a meaningful zero point, so differences, ratios, and any other algebraic calculation make sense. If a bank account increases from $1,000 to $2,000 not only has it increased by $1,000, but it also contains twice as much money. In our sample databases, the field SALARY in the Executives database and the field AGE in the Applicants database are both ratio variables.

5.4 DATA EXPLORATION

A database is a highly structured means for storing raw data, but it does not automatically reveal the patterns and insights that we seek. These must be ferreted out by a process of exploration. Although exploration is a creative process, and somewhat different from one situation to the next, some common approaches can be used in most situations. In this section, we describe a logical approach to the task of exploring a database, along with the software tools needed at each stage. This five-step process proceeds as follows:

- Understand the data.
- Organize and subset the database.
- Examine individual variables and their distributions.
- Calculate summary measures for individual variables.
- Examine relationships among variables.

5.4.1 Understand the Data

Remembering our earlier admonition to be skeptical of the data, the first step in data exploration is to understand the data we have: how are the fields defined, what types of data are represented, and what units are the data in?

For example, in scanning the Analgesics database we observe that the DESCRIPTION field is a nominal variable that defines both the brand (e.g., Aleve) and the type of analgesic (caplet, tablet, etc.). The SIZE field is somewhat ambiguous, so we consult the data dictionary to find that SIZE refers to "Items per container." Does this mean the number of bottles per case or the number of pills in a bottle? We may have to give this question additional thought. Similarly, the SALES field is ambiguous: this is defined as "Sales volume," but is that in units of bottles or cases? It's hard to know for sure; more investigation is needed before we draw final conclusions from this dataset.

Examining the Applicants database, we note that the AGE field is in integers; perhaps the actual age is rounded to the nearest year. The CITZ CODE field takes on the values U for US and N for non-US, but we might want to know more about how this value is assigned. Does it represent the country of birth, the country of citizenship, the country where the applicant currently lives, or perhaps the country where the most recent degree was received? The conclusions we draw might depend on how this variable is coded.

The Executives database gives financial information on 100 executives and their firms. The SALARY field seems clear enough, but what units apply? Most of the values are between 500 and 2,000, so we might infer that these are actual salaries between $500,000 and $2,000,000, and thus the data are in thousands of dollars. We can also infer that the BONUS and OTHER variables are in similar units, but we cannot know for sure.

It is vital not to skip over this first step in data exploration. Most databases contain ambiguities or hidden pitfalls, and it is important not to assume that our data are either defined in the manner we would like or measured in the units we would expect. Furthermore, our application of more sophisticated exploration techniques often depends on the data type and the coding method, so it is worthwhile to understand those issues at the start.

FIGURE 5.4 The Sort
Window

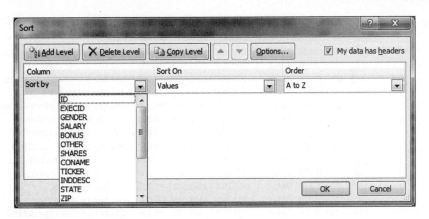

5.4.2 Organize and Subset the Database

The next step after understanding the data is to organize the database and to create subsets of it. Two Excel tools are particularly helpful here: **Sort** and **Filter**. These can be found on the Home ribbon in the Editing group and on the Data ribbon in the Sort & Filter group. Sorting and Filtering a database can be particularly helpful when we have a question that applies to a subset of a database, such as those records with the highest values on a variable or those records that satisfy a complex set of restrictions. We give an example of sorting using the Executives database and another using the Applicants database.

Question: In the Executives database, do any duplicate records appear?

Suppose we wish to determine whether any executive (identified by the number in column B) is represented more than once in the sample. We begin by selecting the database. (Exploiting the range name, we do this by clicking the drop-down menu of range names, located directly above column A, and selecting the name Data.) Then, we choose Home▶Editing▶Sort & Filter▶Custom Sort, which opens the Sort window (Figure 5.4). This window has three drop-down windows: Column, Sort On, and Order. Here we sort by the EXECID column, sort on Values, and sort in the order A to Z. (This field was entered as text, so it must be sorted in alphabetical order.) When we click on OK, the sorting procedure is carried out, producing the results shown in Figure 5.5. Then, when we scan the ID numbers in the sorted list, we can see that no two adjacent entries match. Therefore, no executive appears twice in the list.

EXCEL TIP
The Sort Command

When we sort a list with column headings, we check the box My data has headers in the Sort window. If we need to sort by rows instead of columns, we click on the Options button and choose Sort left to right. Although the Sort operation can be reversed by the Undo command, it is often a good idea to save the data to a new worksheet before sorting, so that the sorted data can be saved and analyzed separately. ∎

Question: In the Applicants database, how does work experience vary among the applicants in successive rounds?

In the previous example, we chose one basis for sorting—the executive identification number. Sometimes we want to sort on a second or third criterion. When two sort criteria are specified, ties on the first criterion are broken by the second; when three criteria are specified, ties on the second criterion are broken by the third. To sort on additional criteria, click on Add Level in the Sort window. In the Applicants database, for example, we can sort first by Round, then by Industry Description, and finally by Job Months (see Figure 5.6 for the entries in the Sort window) to get a sense of how applications arrive over time from people in different industries and with different lengths of service in their current job. The first portion of the result appears in Figure 5.7. Looking deeper into this worksheet, we might observe, for example, that the applicants with relatively fewer months in advertising tend to apply in the first two rounds.

The Filtering capabilities in Excel allow us to probe a large database and extract a portion of it that deals with the specific records in which we are interested. We may simply

FIGURE 5.5 The Executives Database sorted by the EXECID field

	A	B	C	D	E	F	G	H	I
1	ID	EXECID	GENDER	SALARY	BONUS	OTHER	SHARES	CONAME	TICKER
2	2611	00006	MALE	683.462	412.768	0.000	207.828	ADC TELECOMMUNICATIONS INC	ADCT
3	4666	00029	MALE	750.000	1012.500	0.000	641.691	ALLTEL CORP	AT
4	2702	00074	MALE	875.000	1000.000	22.100	2234.402	ARROW ELECTRONICS INC	ARW
5	5562	00085	MALE	324.389	80.563	0.000	16632.050	ATMEL CORP	ATML
6	314	00111	MALE	750.000	825.000	294.770	183.031	BAXTER INTERNATIONAL INC	BAX
7	2766	00140	MALE	509.734	77.257	0.000	354.541	BOB EVANS FARMS	BOBE
8	2777	00152	MALE	700.000	317.665	0.000	39.928	KEYSPAN CORP	KSE
9	5588	00167	MALE	820.677	500.000	45.687	1208.415	CALLAWAY GOLF CO	ELY
10	516	00197	MALE	1350.000	1965.000	0.000		CHEVRON CORP	CHV
11	2962	00223	MALE	1000.000	0.000	0.000	255.198	CMS ENERGY CORP	CMS
12	2654	00246	MALE	1357.026	2162.508	91.721	1517.168	AFLAC INC	AFL
13	5865	00313	MALE	933.333	5554.350	300.034	6033.567	TRIARC COS INC -CL A	TRY
14	822	00315	MALE	771.018	463.200	0.000	224.861	EASTERN ENTERPRISES	EFU
15	9283	00393	MALE	1000.000	2750.000	143.698	643.966	FREEPRT MCMOR COP&GLD -CL B	FCX
16	5067	00398	MALE	205.000	0.000	56.891	9040.113	HUMANA INC	HUM
17	16384	00415	MALE	550.000	275.000	60.703	48.542	BARNES GROUP INC	B
18	1016	00418	MALE	620.000	952.468	0.000	334.430	GENUINE PARTS CO	GPC
19	10891	00474	MALE	410.004	400.000	0.000	1469.256	HORACE MANN EDUCATORS CORP	HMN
20	3296	00482	MALE	450.000	0.000	0.000	151.477	HUNT (JB) TRANSPRT SVCS INC	JBHT
21	3367	00522	MALE	750.000	0.000	46.067	740.528	KANSAS CITY SOUTHERN INDS	KSU
22	1329	00555	MALE	1185.577	3331.968	0.000	46497.711	LIMITED INC	LTD
23	4837	00563	MALE	1051.946	0.000	712.393	17308.998	LOEWS CORP	LTR
24	1459	00608	MALE	369.231	0.000	77.757	141.572	MCKESSON HBOC INC	MCK
25	1679	00705	MALE	730.769	0.000	159.776		OGDEN CORP	OG
26	5415	00731	MALE	800.000	10662.500	0.000	1185.531	PAINE WEBBER GROUP	PWJ
27	4903	00741	MALE	689.178	448.630	0.000	216.999	PPL CORP	PPL
28	9594	00749	MALE	990.000	698.465	128.496	1075.749	FORT JAMES CORP	FJ
29	586	00778	MALE	1000.000	8732.474	448.577	17500.746	CITIGROUP INC	C
30	10955	00791	MALE	773.085	975.000	0.000	4931.348	QUALCOMM INC	QCOM

|◄ ◄ ► ►| 5.1 / 5.2 / 5.3 / 5.4 / **5.5** /

want to view the extracted portion temporarily, or we may want to store it separately for further analysis. As an illustration, we use the Applicants database.

Question: In the Applicants database, what are the characteristics of the applicants from nonprofit organizations?

Suppose we want to view only the applicants who worked in nonprofit organizations. We first select the database and then choose Home►Editing►Sort & Filter►Filter. This selection adds a list arrow to the title of each column. If we click on the Industry Description list arrow, we see a list of all the possible entries in this column, each one next to a checked box. The first step is to uncheck the box for Select All; this step removes all the checks. Then we can check Nonprofit, and we see the subset of the database that contains Nonprofit entries (Figure 5.8). Filtering does not actually *extract* any records: it merely *hides* rows that do not match the filter criteria. Thus, in Figure 5.8, we see that applicants from the Nonprofit sector appear in rows 11, 16, 87, 103, and so on. If we wish to extract the filtered records, we can copy and paste this subset to a different sheet.

FIGURE 5.6 Sorting by Three Fields

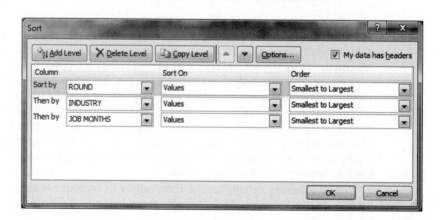

FIGURE 5.7 The Applicants Database Sorted by Round, Industry, and Job Months

	A	B	C	D	E	F	G	H	I
1	ID	ROUND	AGE	SEX	CITZ CODE	1ST CONTACT	JOB MONTHS	INDUSTRY	INDUSTRY DESC.
2	1637	1	25	M	U	Letter	22	10	Accounting
3	470	1	26	M	U	Letter	35	10	Accounting
4	91	1	26	F	U	Letter	36	10	Accounting
5	1694	1	27	M	U	Home Page	36	10	Accounting
6	1585	1	28	M	U	Phone call	37	10	Accounting
7	1638	1	27	M	U	Home Page	40	10	Accounting
8	392	1	24	F	U	Home Page	43	10	Accounting
9	1846	1	28	M	N	Phone call	44	10	Accounting
10	46	1	27	M	U	Phone call	45	10	Accounting
11	118	1	25	M	U	Phone call	48	10	Accounting
12	184	1	27	M	U	Test Score Tape (DNU)	48	10	Accounting
13	371	1	27	F	U	Phone call	48	10	Accounting
14	1793	1	27	F	U	Home Page	48	10	Accounting
15	1710	1	28	M	U	Phone call	49	10	Accounting
16	115	1	28	F	U	Phone call	56	10	Accounting
17	249	1	27	M	N	Home Page	56	10	Accounting
18	7	1	29	M	U	Phone call	60	10	Accounting
19	24	1	28	M	U	Home Page	60	10	Accounting
20	1906	1	29	M	U	Reapplicant	60	10	Accounting
21	1584	1	29	M	U	Phone call	66	10	Accounting
22	1626	1	29	M	U	Phone call	67	10	Accounting
23	504	1	29	M	U	Reapplicant	72	10	Accounting
24	1689	1	29	M	U	Home Page	75	10	Accounting
25	1518	1	29	M	N	Phone call	78	10	Accounting
26	1726	1	32	M	U	Email	82	10	Accounting
27	130	1	30	F	N	Phone call	100	10	Accounting
28	338	1	32	M	N	Email	102	10	Accounting
29	515	1	35	M	U	Reapplicant	120	10	Accounting
30	370	1	35	M	U	Home Page	144	10	Accounting

5.1 / 5.2 / 5.3 / 5.4 / 5.5 / 5.6 / 5.7

Alternatively, to restore the view of the entire database, we can either choose Select All using the list arrow again or choose Home▶Editing▶Sort & Filter▶Clear. While we are viewing a filtered subset of the database, the triangle corresponding to the list arrow we used displays the Filter symbol. This is a reminder that the information on the screen is filtered.

Question: In the Applicants database, what are the ages of the oldest applicants?

One of the options on the arrow list is Number Filters. This option allows us to use numerical criteria for filtering. (In a text field, the Text Filters option appears in the same place.) For example, to find the ten oldest applicants, we filter on Age, and from its arrow list, we select Number Filters▶Top 10 (see Figure 5.9). This window provides three

FIGURE 5.8 Filtering the Applicants Database to Highlight Nonprofit Backgrounds

	A	B	C	D	E	F	G	H	I
1	ID	ROUN	AGE	SEX	CITZ CO	1ST CONTACT	JOB MONT	INDUSTI	INDUSTRY DESC.
11	10	1	31	M	U	Letter	78	420	Nonprofit
16	15	1	27	F	U	Phone call	48	420	Nonprofit
87	86	1	29	M	U	Test Score Tape (DNU)	4	420	Nonprofit
103	102	1	27	M	U	World Wide Web	30	420	Nonprofit
174	173	1	26	M	U	Home Page	37	420	Nonprofit
176	175	1	28	M	U	Phone call	60	420	Nonprofit
209	208	1	32	F	U	Home Page	108	420	Nonprofit
328	327	1	30	M	U	Phone call	62	420	Nonprofit
336	335	1	35	M	U	Phone call		420	Nonprofit
344	343	1	27	M	U	Phone call	44	420	Nonprofit
375	374	1	32	M	U	Home Page	88	420	Nonprofit
412	411	1	27	F	U	Phone call	48	420	Nonprofit
428	427	1	29	F	U	Phone call	62	420	Nonprofit
454	453	1	29	F	N	Test Score Tape (DNU)	56	420	Nonprofit
470	469	1	32	M	N	World Wide Web	61	420	Nonprofit
521	520	1	29	U	U	Home Page	72	420	Nonprofit
578	577	2	26	M	U	Test Score Tape (DNU)	26	420	Nonprofit
614	613	2	30	M	U	Home Page	6	420	Nonprofit
686	685	2	37	M	U	Letter	144	420	Nonprofit
748	747	2	28	F	U	Phone call	60	420	Nonprofit
825	824	2	29	M	N	Letter	58	420	Nonprofit
990	989	2	29	F	U	Phone call	67	420	Nonprofit
998	997	2	32	M	U	Reapplicant	98	420	Nonprofit
1120	1119	3	28	F	U	Phone call	35	420	Nonprofit
1172	1171	3	26	M	U	Home Page	36	420	Nonprofit
1184	1183	3	25	F	U	Phone call	38	420	Nonprofit
1202	1201	3	32	F	U	Email	84	420	Nonprofit
1229	1228	3	31	M	N	Home Page	15	420	Nonprofit
1263	1262	3	27	F	U	Phone call	68	420	Nonprofit

5.1 / 5.2 / 5.3 / 5.4 / 5.5 / 5.6 / 5.7 / 5.8

FIGURE 5.9 The Top 10
Autofilter Window

FIGURE 5.9 The Top 10
Autofilter Window

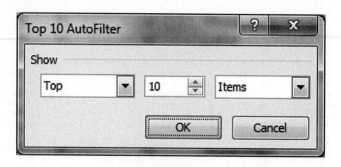

FIGURE 5.10 The Custom Autofilter Window

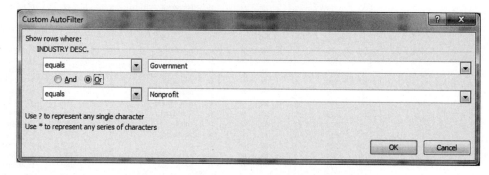

sets of options. The left-hand window allows us to choose from the `Top` or `Bottom` of the records; the right-hand window allows us to choose a fixed number of `Items` (records) or a `Percent` of all records, and the middle window allows us to select the actual number of records (e.g., 10 items or 10 percent).

> *Question*: Isolate the applicants who worked in either the Nonprofit or Government sectors.

Another option under `Number Filters` or `Text Filters` is the Custom filter, which allows us to filter data using compound criteria. For example, to isolate the applicants who worked in *either* the Nonprofit *or* Government sectors, we select the Custom Filter option and click the Or button in the Custom AutoFilter window to set up the appropriate logical structure (see Figure 5.10).

> *Question*: Isolate the applicants who worked in either the Nonprofit or Government sectors and had GMAT scores above 700.

For more complicated compound criteria, such as the one posed in this question, we use the Custom Filter on more than one field. We first filter the Industry Description field for Nonprofit and Government, and then we filter the GMAT field for scores above 700. The result of these filtering steps is shown in Figure 5.11.

FIGURE 5.11 The Applicants Database after Filtering

	A	B	C	D	E	F	G	H	I	J	K
1	ID	ROUN	AGE	SEX	CITZ CO	1ST CONTACT	JOB MONT	INDUSTI	INDUSTRY DESC.	DECISION	GMA
13	12	1	27	M	U	Phone call	51	370	Government	Cancel Enrollment	760
26	25	1	29	M	U	Phone call	30	370	Government	Deny	750
103	102	1	27	M	U	World Wide Web	30	420	Nonprofit	Deny	750
122	121	1	28	M	U	Letter		370	Government	Wait List Deny	720
209	208	1	32	F	U	Home Page	108	420	Nonprofit	Deny	740
263	262	1	32	M	U	Home Page	97	370	Government	Deny	770
323	322	1	32	M	U	Letter	76	370	Government	Wait List Deny	710
412	411	1	27	F	U	Phone call	48	420	Nonprofit	Wait List Deny	710
578	577	2	26	M	U	Test Score Tape (DNU)	26	420	Nonprofit	Deny	730
769	768	2	29	M	U	Email	62	370	Government	Deny	730
863	862	2	30	M	U	World Wide Web	84	370	Government	Deny	750
1128	1127	3	31	M	U	Phone call	78	370	Government	Deny	730
1184	1183	3	25	F	U	Phone call	38	420	Nonprofit	Deny	710
1229	1228	3	31	M	N	Home Page	15	420	Nonprofit	Deny	740
1251	1250	3	28	M	U	Home Page	61	370	Government	Deny	780
1259	1258	3	30	F	N	Letter	86	370	Government	Deny	720
1322	1321	4	28	M	N	World Wide Web	61	370	Government	Deny	730
1497	1496	1	30	F	U	Phone call	82	370	Government	Withdraw before Decision	770
1532	1531	1	26	F	U	Letter	50	370	Government	Withdraw after Decision	710
1561	1560	1	27	F	U	Phone call	48	420	Nonprofit	Deny	720
1574	1573	1	25	M	U	Email	38	420	Nonprofit	Deny	720
1609	1608	1	33	M	U	Phone call	115	420	Nonprofit	Withdraw after Decision	740
1654	1653	1	32	M	U	Home Page	98	370	Government	Enrolling	750
1809	1808	1	29	M	U	Phone call	24	370	Government	Deny	720
1834	1833	1	29	M	U	Home Page	63	370	Government	Wait List Deny	730
1844	1843	1	27	M	U	Home Page	46	420	Nonprofit	Withdraw after Decision	710
1846	1845	1	26	M	U	Home Page	38	420	Nonprofit	Deny	760
2101	2100	2	31	M	U	Phone call	48	420	Nonprofit	Wait List Deny	720
2113	2112	2	32	F	N	Test Score Tape (DNU)	89	370	Government	Deny	710

5.4.3 Examine Individual Variables and their Distribution

We now focus on the details of individual variables. For numerical variables, we typically want to know the range of the records from lowest to highest and the areas where most of the outcomes lie. For categorical variables with a small number of distinct values (such as Male/Female or High/Medium/Low), we typically want to know how many records fall into each category. Precise calculations require the use of Excel functions, which we cover in the next section. First, we use charts to generate visual summaries of the data.

> *Question*: In the Applicants database, what are typical values for JOB MONTHS and what is the range from lowest to highest?

A common way to summarize the entire set of values for a numerical variable is to use a **histogram**. A histogram is created by sorting the values from low to high, grouping them into **bins** (for example, all values between 10 and 20), and displaying the number of values in each bin as a bar chart. To create a histogram in XLMiner we choose Explore▶Chart Wizard and the screen shown in Figure 5.12 appears.

This wizard offers us eight distinct types of charts. We choose Histogram, and in subsequent windows choose the Frequency option for the Y-axis and JOB MONTHS as the X-axis variable. When we select Finish, the chart in Figure 5.13 appears.

This chart shows that JOB MONTHS ranges from a low of 0 to a high around 280. The modal (most common) value appears to be about 40 months, and most records lie in a range from about 20 to 120 months. (Experiment with the Bins slider below the X-axis label to change the number of bins and the look of the chart.)

> *Question*: Which are the most common decisions in the Applicants database?

DECISION is a categorical variable with values such as Admit, Deny, Cancel Enrollment, and Withdraw after Decision. To display the frequencies of these values, we use a Variable chart in the XLMiner Chart Wizard and select the DECISION variable. The result is shown in Figure 5.14.

This chart shows that the vast majority of these applicants received the Deny decision. Roughly 200 are Enrolling, while another 200 or so were given the decision Wait List Deny.

Histograms provide a useful visual overview of all the values of a variable. In many ways these charts represent a variable better than any single summary measure, such as the mean, median, minimum, or maximum. However, individual measures such as those are vital when we want to know specific facts about a variable.

FIGURE 5.12 XLMiner Chart Wizard

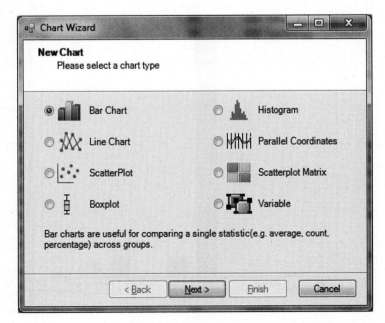

FIGURE 5.13 Histogram of JOB MONTHS

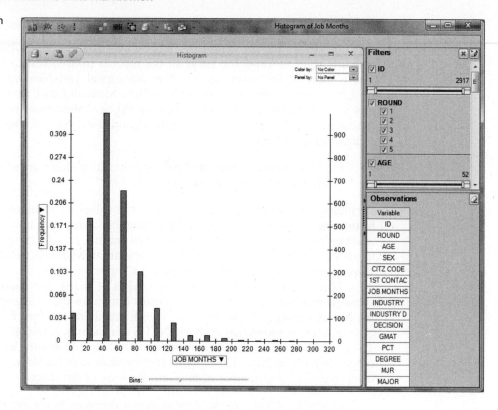

5.4.4 Calculate summary measures for individual variables

Excel provides a number of functions that are useful for investigating individual variables. Some functions can be used to summarize the values of a numerical variable; others can be used to identify or count specific values for both numerical and categorical variables.

Question: What is the average age in the Applicants database?

FIGURE 5.14 Histogram of DECISION

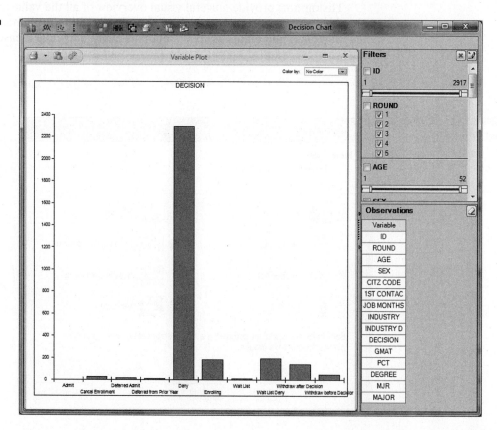

The most common summary measure of a numerical variable is its average or mean, which can be calculated with the AVERAGE function in Excel. In the Applicants database, we find that

$$\text{AVERAGE}\,(\text{C2}:\text{C2918}) = 28.97.$$

Other useful summary measures are the median, minimum, and maximum. Those measures for the AGE variable are calculated with Excel functions as follows:

$$\text{MEDIAN}\,(\text{C2}:\text{C2918}) = 28$$

$$\text{MIN}\,(\text{C2}:\text{C2918}) = 1$$

$$\text{MAX}\,(\text{C2}:\text{C2918}) = 52$$

The minimum age in this dataset is 1 year. Presumably this is an error. In fact, any ages below 20 for MBA applicants are highly suspect.

Question: How many applicants have ages less than 20 in the Applicants database?

Excel provides the COUNTIF function for such questions. The COUNTIF function calculates the number of cells in a range that satisfy a given criterion. Here we can use:

$$\text{COUNTIF}\,(\text{C2}:\text{C2918}, "< 20") = 5$$

The quotation marks are necessary as part of the criterion.

Question: What percentage of the applicants were given the DENY decision?

DECISION is a categorical variable, so we cannot calculate values as if it were a numerical variable. But we can count the number of times DENY appears and divide that result by the number of non-blank cells, as follows:

$$\text{COUNTIF}\,(\$\text{J}\$2:\$\text{J}\$2918, "\text{Deny}")/\text{COUNT}\,(\$\text{J}\$2:\$\text{J}\$2918) = 0.79$$

The COUNT function does not count blank cells or cells containing text, so this approach will work correctly if the range is known to hold only numbers.

Excel provides a number of related functions. For example, COUNTA records the number of nonempty cells in a range, and COUNTBLANK counts empty cells. (Cells containing zero are ignored.)

Question: What is the average age of the applicants from the nonprofit sector?

This question asks for an average in a subset of the database. Intuitively, we might think of first filtering the data and then using the AVERAGE function. However, Excel's AVERAGE function does not adjust for the fact that we have filtered the data: it makes the calculation for the hidden cells as well as the visible cells. To make this calculation for just the visible cells, we can use the function $\text{SUBTOTAL}\,(1, \text{C2}:\text{C2918})$ because it ignores the hidden cells in the specified range.

The SUBTOTAL function performs the calculations for one of Excel's more familiar functions according to the first argument inside the parentheses, while ignoring hidden cells. In our example, the argument 1 specifies the average value. The list below gives the functions that can be calculated with the SUBTOTAL function:

1. AVERAGE
2. COUNT
3. COUNTA
4. MAX
5. MIN
6. PRODUCT
7. STDEV
8. STDEVP

9. SUM

10. VAR

11. VARP

5.4.5 *Examine Relationships among Variables*

Up to this point we have examined variables one at a time, but in many cases the relationships among variables are more important to the analysis than the properties of one variable. For example, variables that are highly correlated with each other generally should not be used in data mining, so identifying those variables is a key step in data exploration. Graphical methods can track relationships among as many as four or five variables simultaneously.

Question: How long have older applicants held their current job?

To answer this question we use XLMiner to create a scatterplot between AGE and JOB MONTHS in the Applicants database. Select Explore▶Chart Wizard▶Scatterplot Matrix; select the variables AGE and JOB MONTHS; then click on Finish. The results appear in Figure 5.15.

On the main diagonal we find the histograms of the two variables AGE and JOB MONTHS. The scatterplots are shown in the off-diagonals. (These charts may be referred to as *X-Y charts* in Excel.) In the scatterplot on the lower left, each record is plotted with its AGE value on the X-axis and its JOB MONTHS value on the Y-axis. (The axes are reversed in the plot on the upper right.) As we might have guessed, older applicants tend to have spent more time in their current job, although the relationship is less well-defined at lower ages. (To generate the scatterplot between two variables without the histograms, use the Scatterplot chart option in XLMiner.)

Question: To what extent do executives with higher salaries work in firms with higher return on assets (ROA)?

In this case we follow the same steps to create a scatterplot for SALARY and ROA in the Executives database. The results are shown in Figure 5.16.

Again, we find the histograms in the diagonal cells and the scatterplots in the off-diagonal cells. If there were a strong (positive) relationship between salary and ROA, we would see the data points lying near a straight line with positive slope. But here we see something like a random cloud of points with very little apparent association.

FIGURE 5.15 Scatterplot Matrix for AGE and JOB MONTHS

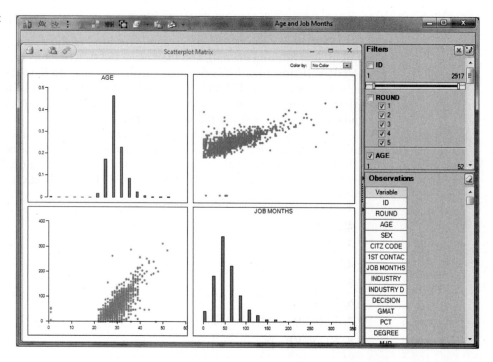

FIGURE 5.16 Scatterplot Matrix for SALARY and ROA

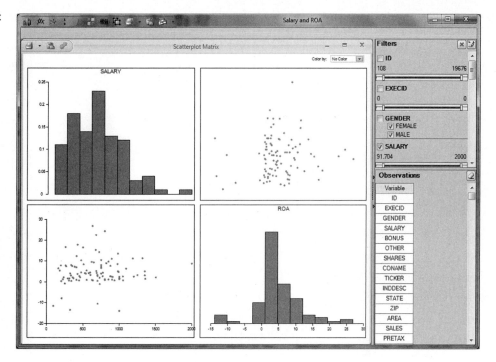

Scatterplots provide a strong visual indication of the degree to which two variables are correlated. However, they do not provide a precise numerical estimate of that correlation. For numerical precision we can use the CORREL function in Excel. For example, in the Applicants database, we find that

$$\texttt{CORREL(C2:C2918,G2:G2918)} = 0.72$$

which confirms the high degree of correlation we observe in Figure 5.15. On the other hand, in the Executives database, we find that

$$\texttt{CORREL(D2:D101,Q2:Q101)} = 0.07$$

which confirms the low degree of correlation we observe in Figure 5.16.

Question: How does the distribution of GMAT scores of applicants compare across the five application rounds?

This question asks us to compare five distributions, which is a difficult task because each distribution contains so much information. One solution is to summarize the distributions by various statistics, such as mean, median, and so on. We use the Boxplot option in XLMiner to generate this chart. (A boxplot is also known as a *box-and-whiskers plot*.) Select Explore▶Chart Wizard▶Boxplot; select the variables GMAT and ROUND; then click on Finish. The results appear in Figure 5.17.

Each of the five distributions for ROUNDS 1-5 is summarized in the vertical dimension by its mean, median, maximum, 75th percentile, 25th percentile, and minimum. The green rectangle highlights the range from the 75th to the 25th percentile. The mean is shown by a solid horizontal line and the median by a dashed horizontal line. The maximum and minimum values are shown by the horizontal lines connected to the green rectangle. (Place the cursor over one of the green rectangles to display the exact values of these statistics.) This chart shows that the mean (and most of the other statistics) of these distributions decline from Round 1 to Round 5. Also, the variability (as measured by the range from 75th to 25th percentile) appears to increase.

Question: How does the distribution of SALARY for executives compare among Males and Females?

We answer this question using a boxplot of SALARY and GENDER in the Executives database. The results are shown in Figure 5.18.

FIGURE 5.17 Boxplot of GMAT and ROUND

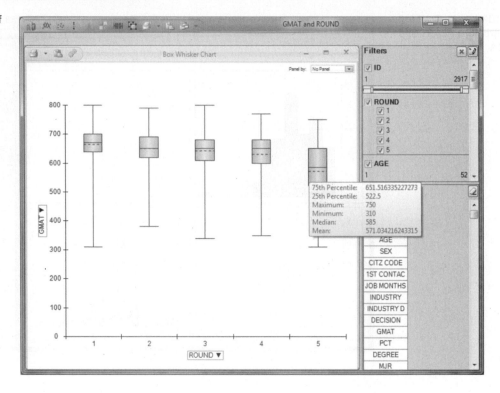

Among this sample of 100 executives, male salaries are generally higher than female salaries (with means, for example, of 685.62 versus 500.84), but the lowest salary for males is well below that for females. However, only two females appear in this database, so the results for this group may not be representative.

Question: How does the variability of GMAT scores compare across rounds?

We observed in Figure 5.17 that the variability of GMAT scores appeared to increase from Round 1 to Round 5. This conclusion was based on the range from the 25th to the 75th percentile. A more common measure of variability is the standard deviation. We use a

FIGURE 5.18 Boxplot of SALARY and GENDER

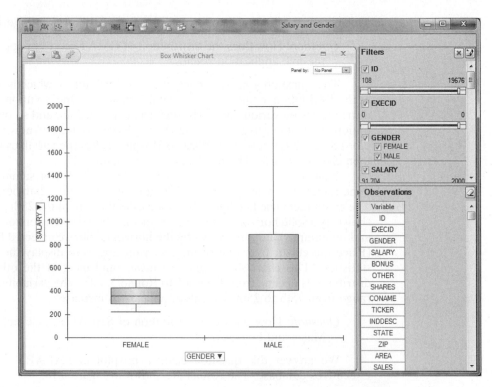

FIGURE 5.19 Bar Chart of the Standard Deviation of GMAT by ROUND

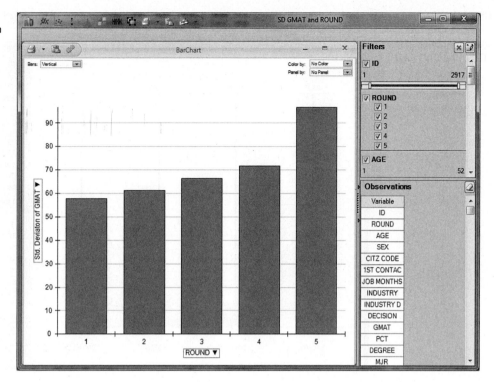

Bar Chart in XLMiner to show how the standard deviation varies across rounds. Select Explore▶Chart Wizard▶Bar Chart; select the variables GMAT and ROUND; then click on Finish. (The chart will first appear with COUNT of GMAT on the vertical axis. Double click on this box and a menu of statistics will appear. Then select Std. Deviation.) The results shown in Figure 5.19 demonstrate clearly that the standard deviation increases steadily across rounds.

> *Question*: Is the salary of an individual executive related in a systematic way to the firm's sales, assets, or dividend yield?

We would often like to know whether a group of variables is tightly or loosely interconnected. This is a more complex question than simply asking whether pairs of variables are correlated. It requires us to somehow track the values of records on multiple variables and compare them as a group. One way to do this is with a Parallel Coordinates chart. Select Explore▶Chart Wizard▶Parallel Coordinates; select the variables SALARY, SALES, ASSETS, and DIVYIELD; then click on Finish. The results are shown in Figure 5.20

The four variables are shown on the horizontal axis, while the vertical axis depicts the range of values for each variable. For example, the SALARY variable ranges from 91.704 to 2000 in this sample. The values for each record are plotted on these four vertical axes, and a line is drawn (representing a given record) connecting each of the four points. (Highlight an individual record by drawing a rectangle with the cursor around any one line.) If, hypothetically, high salaries were associated with low sales, high assets, and low dividend yields, the chart would show bands of lines in a W-pattern. The results in this case are more complex. Salaries seem to be loosely correlated to sales, and sales to assets, but dividend yields vary widely among firms with similar assets.

Up to this point we have illustrated some of the most useful types of charts in XLMiner without going into detail about how charts can be specialized. Four options are available for most charts that allow us to address complex questions:

- Filtering
- Coloring
- Paneling
- Details-on-demand

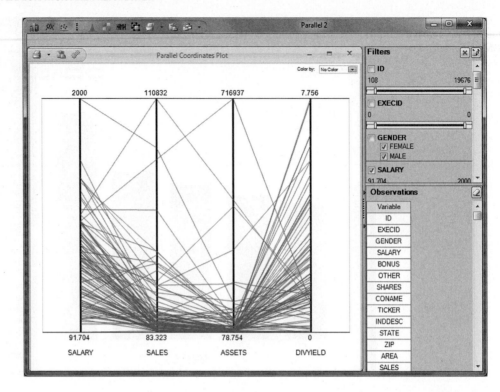

Each chart is accompanied by a control panel on the right-hand side. (This panel can be displayed or hidden by clicking on the vertical space to the right of the chart itself.) The upper half of the control panel is devoted to **filters**. Each variable is given a filter, in the form of a slider for numerical variables or a checkbox for categorical variables. By using these sliders and checkboxes we can include or exclude any combination of values from the chart. For example, by checking Male but not Female, we can specialize the chart so it displays the data for Males only.

Coloring and Paneling are controlled by drop-down lists at the upper right of the chart. **Coloring** allows us to apply distinct colors to the different values of a categorical variable. **Paneling** creates a separate chart for each distinct value of a categorical variable. Figure 5.21 shows the mean for GMAT scores over the five rounds colored by sex and paneled by citizen code.

Although charts are generally an excellent way to capture an entire variable (or multiple variables) at one time, they are not as useful for identifying specific records. Yet there are times when we would like to understand more about a few specific points on a chart, such as outlying values. XLMiner provides an option called **details-on-demand** to make this form of exploration possible. In Figure 5.22 we have created a scatterplot of AGE and JOB MONTHS. Two records are of particular interest: the ones in the upper right of the chart with high values for both AGE and JOB MONTHS. To learn more about these records we draw a rectangle around them using the cursor. XLMiner then colors them differently from the other points and displays their values on all variables in the Observations pane of the control panel located on the lower right. Here we can see that these records both represent Females from the US.

Most of the methods we have discussed to this point involve charts. When more precision is needed, we turn to **cross-tabulation tables**, or cross-tabs. A cross-tabulation is a table that shows how one variable is distributed across another. For example, we might create a table showing how the average GMAT of applicants varies by application round. Another cross-tab would show analgesic sales by store and by brand.

Cross-tabs are created in Excel using the Pivot Table wizard, which is located on the Insert ribbon. To appreciate how pivot tables work, we return to the Analgesics database and specifically to an edited version where we have combined all of the item descriptions into single-word brand names. (The modified data are saved as a separate worksheet with a new database name, such as BrandData.) In what follows we describe the construction of three pivot tables, each elaborating on the one before.

Question: What are total sales of painkillers, and how do they break down by brand name and by store?

FIGURE 5.21 Bar Chart for Mean of GMAT Illustrating Paneling by CITZ CODE and Coloring by SEX

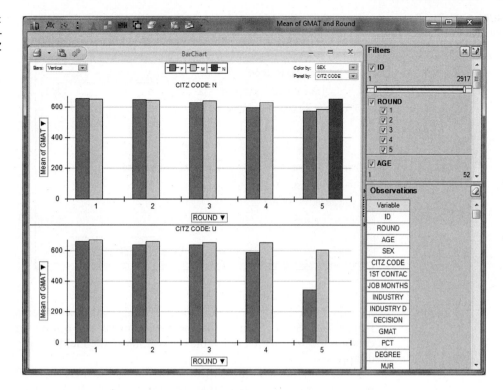

First select the database and then choose Insert▶Tables▶Pivot Table▶Pivot Table, which opens the Create Pivot Table window (Figure 5.23).

Place the Pivot Table report in a new worksheet and click OK. The new worksheet will have a template for the pivot table and a panel (Pivot Table Field List) on the right containing the field names (Figure 5.24).

The Pivot Table Field List contains a drop-down menu that offers different layouts; we have shown the "stacked" layout in Figure 5.24. Next, drag the list item SALES to the Values box. A simple pivot table appears with the title Sum of Sales in cell A3 and the value 9,432 in cell A4. (If a different title appears, such as Count of SALES, double-click

FIGURE 5.22 Scatterplot of AGE and JOB MONTHS Showing Detail on Demand

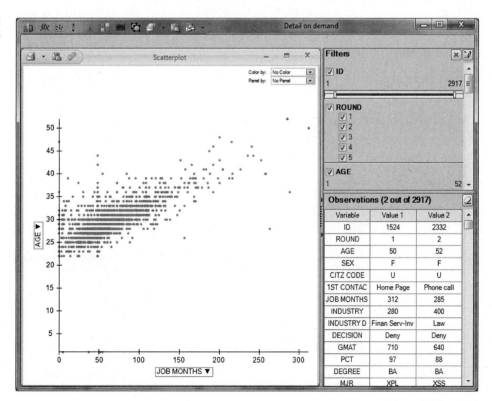

FIGURE 5.23 The Create
Pivot Table Window

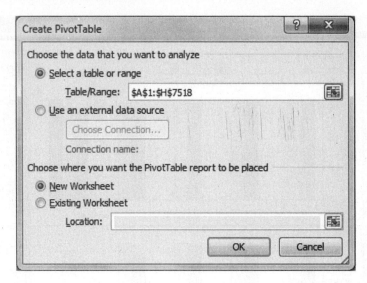

on that name, and the Value Field Settings window appears, similar to the one in Figure 5.25. Select Sum in the main window of this option and click OK.) When the cursor is located on the pivot table (cells A3:A4), the Field List remains visible; otherwise it disappears.

Extend the pivot table by dragging the list item DESCRIPTION to the Row Labels box. A more detailed pivot table appears in cells A3:B12, showing the breakdown of sales by brand name. Extend the pivot table again by dragging the list item STORE to the Column Labels box. The pivot table now shows a sales breakdown by both brand name and store, as shown in Figure 5.26.

Pivot tables can be modified easily after they are built. For example, we can use the filtering arrows in the row or column headings to limit our table to particular row and column entries. We can also edit the table using the Pivot Table Field List. (If the Pivot Table template and Field List are not visible, click anywhere in the pivot table to display them.) We can, for example, substitute WEEK for STORE in the Column Labels box to obtain a breakdown of sales by brand and by week.

Question: In the Applicants database, how does the average GMAT score vary according to the round in which the application is filed?

FIGURE 5.24 The Pivot
Table Template

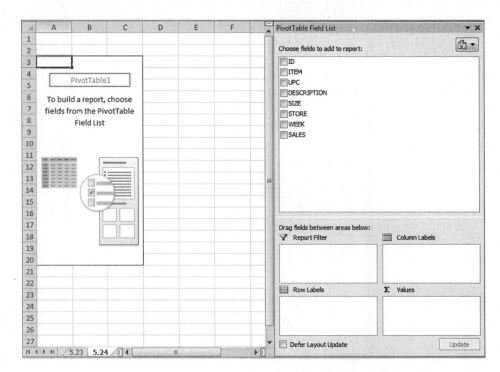

FIGURE 5.25 The Value
Field Settings Window

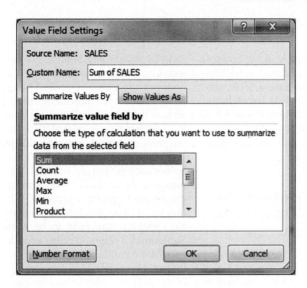

In developing a strategy for round-by-round selections, it is helpful to know whether systematic differences exist among the rounds. To probe this topic, we return to the Applicants database and set up a pivot table. The Pivot Table shows average GMAT scores broken down by ROUND. Figure 5.27 displays the result. Evidently, there is a trend toward lower GMAT scores during the course of the overall admission process.

FIGURE 5.26 Pivot Table
Showing Sales by Brand
Name and by Store
Number

	A	B	C	D	E	F	G	H	I	J
1										
2										
3	**Sum of SALES**	**Column Labels** ▾								
4	**Row Labels** ▾		100	101	102	103	104	105	**Grand Total**	
5	ADVIL		434	469	499	207	301	226	2136	
6	ALEVE		229	169	274	106	125	93	996	
7	ANACIN		105	64	93	29	11	63	365	
8	BAYER		213	223	312	65	111	95	1019	
9	BUFFERIN		32	32	46	8	26	12	156	
10	EXCEDRIN		211	235	444	132	188	115	1325	
11	MOTRIN		120	128	183	76	98	60	665	
12	TYLENOL		737	543	705	270	222	293	2770	
13	**Grand Total**		2081	1863	2556	893	1082	957	9432	
14										
15										
16										

⁞◀ ◀ ▶ ▶⁞ ╱ 5.23 ╱ 5.24 ╱ 5.25 ╱ **5.26** ╱

FIGURE 5.27 Pivot Table
Showing Average GMAT
Scores by Round

	A	B	C	D	E	F	G	H
1								
2								
3	**Row Labels** ▾	**Average of GMAT**						
4	1	665.1						
5	2	650.8						
6	3	642.8						
7	4	629.5						
8	5	537.5						
9	(blank)	675.0						
10	**Grand Total**	**651.5**						
11								
12								
13								
14								
15								
16								

⁞◀ ◀ ▶ ▶⁞ ╱ 5.23 ╱ 5.24 ╱ 5.25 ╱ 5.26 ╱ **5.27**

5.5 SUMMARY

The ability to use data intelligently is a vital skill for business analysts. Although complex data is typically stored in sophisticated databases with specialized data management tools, analysts tend to perform most of their data analysis in Excel. In this chapter, we presented the tools needed to understand Excel databases, to explore data, and to prepare it for further analysis.

We organized the data exploration task into five steps:

- Understand the data.
- Organize and subset the database.
- Examine individual variables and their distributions.
- Calculate summary measures for individual variables.
- Examine relationships among variables.

The first step is the most important: before undertaking any analysis it is crucial to understand the database and how it was defined, collected, and scaled; whether it is numerical or categorical; whether it contains missing or erroneous values; and so on. Then we can organize and subset the data in various ways by sorting and filtering the data. The focus then shifts to individual variables and how are they are distributed. Distributions provide a useful graphical overview of individual variables; but when we want more detail, we calculate summary measures such as the mean, minimum, maximum, etc. Finally, we explore how variables are related to each other using scatterplots, boxplots, and other graphical aids provided by XLMiner.

Careful preparation of the raw data is often required before data mining can succeed. Missing values may have to be removed or replaced with average values for data mining algorithms to perform properly. Likewise, numerical variables may need to be converted to categorical variables, or categorical variables may need to be converted to numerical form. Sometimes a single variable must be transformed or multiple variables combined into a new variable in order to capture the information needed for data mining to succeed. Normalization of the data may also be required or recommended. We discuss the important details of data preparation in the chapter appendix.

SUGGESTED READINGS

A great deal has been written about the best ways to use charts in presentations, but much less has been written about how to explore data itself. The books listed below are some of our favorites.

Few, S. C. 2004. *Show Me the Numbers: Designing Tables and Graphs to Enlighten*. Oakland, CA: Analytics Press.

Few, S. C. 2009. *Now You See It: Simple Visualization Techniques for Quantitative Analysis*. Oakland, CA: Analytics Press.

Koomey, J. G. 2008. *Turning Numbers into Knowledge: Mastering the Art of Problem Solving*. Oakland, CA: Analytics Press.

EXERCISES

1. The database *Dish.xlsx* contains a transaction history describing more than 4,000 purchases of detergent at a number of stores in a grocery chain over a period of several weeks.

a. How many records are in this database?

b. How many fields are in this database?

c. Is the field SALE nominal or numerical?

d. Is the variable PRICE measured on an interval or ratio scale?

e. Which field contains blank cells, and how many does it contain?

f. What is the highest price in the database?

g. How many records pertain to the description SUNLIGHT GEL 2.49?

h. Create a histogram of the PRICE variable and interpret it.

i. What is the average price?

j. Are higher priced products generally more profitable?

k. Does profit vary systematically across stores?

l. In week 387, which stores had average profit over 18?

2. The database *Tissue.xlsx* contains a transaction history describing more than 3,700 purchases of facial tissues at a number of stores in a grocery chain over a period of several weeks.

a. How many records are in this database?

b. How many fields are in this database?

c. Is the field STORE nominal or numerical?

d. How many records have a price exceeding 5?

e. Which field contains blank cells, and how many does it contain?

f. For what percentage of records does profit equal zero?

g. What is the second-highest value for profit?

h. Compare the average price across stores.

i. Compare the distribution of profit across the weeks.

j. Describe the relationship between price and profit for items on sale (SALE = S).

k. How much average profit did STORE 102 make in WEEK 390?

3. The database *Population.xlsx* contains data on the populations of the 50 states from 1990 to 1999.

a. How many records are in this database?

b. How many fields are in this database?

c. Are there any missing data?

d. Which state was ranked 25th in population in 1993?

e. Which state had the largest percentage increase in population from 1990 to 1999?

f. Which states had populations of more than 1 million and less than 2 million in 1995?

g. Create a histogram of the populations by state for 1999 and interpret it.

4. The database *Executives.xlsx* contains salary and company data on a number of executives.

a. How many records are in this database?

b. How many fields are in this database?

c. Are there any missing data?

d. Is the STATE field nominal or ordinal?

e. Among the top five executives in terms of Salary, how many work in the oil industry?

f. How many executives work for companies in California or New York and have sales less than 4,000?

g. Compare the salaries of male and female executives.

h. Does having a high return on assets predict a high bonus?

i. Which two states have the highest average salaries?

5. The database *Applicants.xlsx* contains a description of an MBA applicant pool.

a. How many records are in this database?

b. How many fields are in this database?

c. Are there any missing data?

d. Is the ROUND field nominal or ordinal?

e. What decision was made on the top four candidates by GMAT?

f. Among enrolling students, what is the average GMAT score? What is the average in the applicant pool as a whole?

g. How many in the applicant pool represented Financial Services in terms of job background? What was their average age?

h. Create a histogram for Job Months and interpret it.

6. The database *Boston Housing.xlsx** contains demographic, environmental, and housing data on a number of towns in the Boston area.

a. How many records are in this database?

b. How many fields are in this database?

c. Is the field RAD ordinal or numerical?

d. Is the field RM interval or ratio?

e. How many fields have missing data?

f. What is the lowest level of NOX among these towns?

g. How many towns have NOX below 4.0?

h. Does a histogram of MEDV reveal any unusual features of the data?

i. Is the median value of homes related to their proximity to the Charles River?

j. Does the distance of a town to Boston have an influence on the median values of homes?

7. The database *German Credit.xlsx*** contains data on prior applicants for credit, including whether they proved to have good or bad credit.

a. How many records are in this database?

b. How many fields are in this database?

c. Is the field HISTORY nominal or ordinal?

d. Is the field PRESENT_RESIDENT nominal or ordinal?

e. How many records are male, divorced, and unskilled resident?

f. Which record number has the highest credit amount?

g. What percentage of records has less than 100DM in a savings account?

h. How does the credit amount compare for those who own their residence versus those who do not?

i. How are the amount of credit and the duration of the loan related?

8. The database *Universal Bank.xlsx**** contains information on a large number of current bank customers.

a. How many records are in this database?

b. How many fields are in this database?

c. How many fields have missing data?

d. Are there any cells coded as text in the Education field?

e. What is the lowest value of Age?

f. How many records have Experience of 2 or less and a personal loan?

g. How is Income distributed?

h. Does the distribution of Income change with Education?

i. Is there a relationship between Income and Mortgage?

9. The database Book *Club.xlsx*[†] contains data on a number of current customers of a direct-mail book club.

a. How many records are in this database?

b. How many fields are in this database?

c. How many fields have missing data?

d. What is the highest value for the amount spent on all products?

e. How many records are females who first purchased 2 months ago?

f. What is the overall distribution of the amount spent on all products?

g. Does the distribution of the amount spent on all products change substantially with the number of Italian books purchased?

h. How are the amounts spent on all purchases and the number of purchases related?

10. The database *Income.xlsx*[‡] contains average personal income data for a number of states over the years 1929–1999.

a. How many records are in this database?

b. How many fields are in this database?

c. What was the absolute increase in the personal income of Maine over this period?

d. What was the percentage increase in the personal income of California over this period?

e. In what years was the personal income of Illinois at, or under, 399 and that of Massachusetts at, or over, 613?

f. Plot the personal income for Connecticut over this time period.

g. Create a histogram of average personal income by state for 1999 and interpret it.

---

* Source: UCI Machine Learning Repository (http://archive.ics.edu.edu/ml).

** Source: UCI Machine Learning Repository (http://archive.ics.edu.edu/ml).

*** Source: Cytel, Inc. 2005

† Source: Shmueli, G., N. R. Patel, and P. C. Bruce. 2010. *Data Mining for Business Intelligence.* New Jersey: John Wiley & Sons, p. 367.

‡ Source: U.S. Department of Commerce, Bureau of Economic Analysis (http://www.bea.gov/bea/regional/spi/).

APPENDIX 5.1 DATA PREPARATION

Most raw data collected by analysts contains missing values, inconsistent data (for example, values in one field recorded as both numbers and text), or other types of problematic data. Some of these data problems will rule out the use of certain data mining tools; others will bias any analysis done on the data. For these reasons, careful cleaning of raw data is an important step in data analysis. Raw data, even when cleaned, is also not necessarily in the appropriate form for the intended analysis. For example, some data mining tools require that categorical variables be transformed into numerical variables. In this appendix we discuss a variety of approaches to cleaning and transforming data.

A.5.1 HANDLING MISSING DATA

Individual values can be missing from a database for many reasons. Missing values may be more common among variables that are difficult to collect or that subjects do not wish to divulge. For example, all the names and addresses may be present in a database, but a significant percentage of family incomes may be missing because respondents chose not to reveal that information. If there is no systematic pattern to the missing data, and only a small percentage of records are affected, the simple solution of removing all such records will suffice. But this procedure will introduce a bias if the missing data are not randomly distributed. If, for example, wealthier families are less likely to divulge their incomes, then removing records with missing income data may mean that wealthy families are under-represented in the database.

The first step in dealing with missing data is to locate it. The COUNTBLANK function can be used to count the number of blank cells in a column. If the count of blank cells is not zero, we can locate individual blank cells by inserting a new column of formulas parallel to the column of data that will highlight the blank cells. A formula such as

$$IF(ISBLANK(A2) = TRUE,"BLANK",0)$$

will show the highly-visible word BLANK if A2 is a blank cell and 0 if it is not. Having located the blank cells, we can detect whether patterns occur in the blank cells by sorting or filtering the database on an important variable and then checking whether the pattern of blank cells in any other variable appears to be concentrated.

Another common data quality problem involves a variable with both numerical and text entries. These cells can be counted and located using the ISNUMBER, and ISTEXT functions. For example, we can use the formula

$$IF(ISNUMBER(A2) = TRUE,1,0)$$

to locate individual cells with numerical entries, and then we can SUM the column of such formulas to count the number of numerical cells. In most cases, either the text or the numerical entries are the result of formatting errors and can easily be fixed by correcting them individually.

XLMiner provides a utility for dealing with missing data called Missing Data Handling (Data Analysis▶Transform▶Missing Data Handling). Figure 5A1 shows the Missing Data Handling window.

This utility provides a number of options for dealing with missing data in categorical and numerical data. For categorical variables, the choices are to ignore the missing data (No treatment), delete the record, replace the missing data with the modal value, or replace the missing data with a user-specified value. For numerical data the same choices are available. However, instead of replacing missing data with the modal value, the options include using the mean or median. Any one of these choices can bias the ultimate results, so the careful analyst will repeat the analysis using different approaches to missing data.

A.5.2 BINNING CONTINUOUS DATA

Some data mining methods require all-categorical data. To meet this requirement, we transform continuous (numerical) data into categorical form, a process known as **binning**.

FIGURE 5A1 The
Missing Data
Handling Window

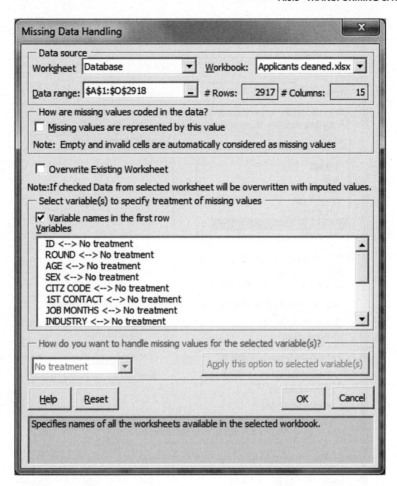

The basic idea is simple: define a number of intervals ("bins") that cover the range of the variable, and then assign a value to each interval.

XLMiner provides the Bin Continuous Data utility to automate this process (Data Analysis▶Transform▶Bin Continuous Data). Figure 5A2 shows the Bin Continuous Data window.

The main options provided here are to define the bins in terms of equal numbers of values (`Equal count`) or by equal length (`Equal interval`), and to assign values to bins using the rank, mean, or median of the bin.

A.5.3 TRANSFORMING CATEGORICAL DATA

Just as numerical data sometimes need to be transformed into categorical data, the opposite transformation is often required. Multiple linear regression, for example, accepts only numerical variables. A categorical variable such as MONTHS, which takes on the 12 values January through December, can be transformed into 12 so-called **dummy variables**, each of which takes on only the values 0 and 1. The first dummy variable is 1 when the month is January and 0 otherwise; the second is 1 when the month is February and 0 otherwise; and so on. For any given value of the original categorical variable, only one of the dummy variables takes on the value 1. XLMiner provides the Create Dummies utility to automate this process (Data Analysis▶Transform▶Transform Categorical Data ▶Create Dummies).

A related transformation involves assigning sequential numbers to the values of an ordinal variable. Thus a variable that takes on the values Low, Medium, and High could be transformed into a numerical variable taking on the values 1, 2, and 3. XLMiner provides the Create Category Scores utility to automate this process (Data Analysis▶Transform▶Transform Categorical Data▶Create Category Scores).

Finally, some categorical variables have too large a number of distinct values to be useful in data mining. (XLMiner limits categorical variables to 30 distinct values.) The

FIGURE 5A2 The Bin Continuous Data Window

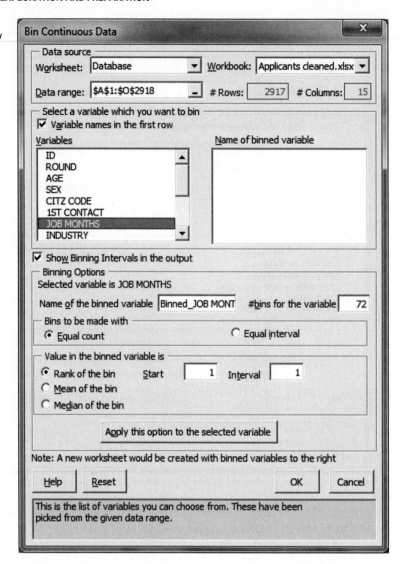

solution is to reduce the number of categories by combining some values into the same category. XLMiner provides the Reduce Categories utility to automate this process (Data Analysis▶Transform▶Transform Categorical Data▶Reduce Categories). Using this utility we can either define up to 29 categories for the most frequent values and then include all the remaining values in the 30th category, or manually assign values to categories (up to the limit of 30).

A.5.4 FUNCTIONAL TRANSFORMATIONS

We have emphasized that the raw data collected by analysts are generally not in a form suitable for analysis and require careful cleaning. But there is another important sense in which raw data are not suitable for analysis. The analyst's job is not only to acquire data but also to ensure that the *information* contained in the data is available for the analytic methods used to derive insights. One way to improve the information content of the data is to transform it. We can transform data in an unlimited number of ways, depending on the context. Some involve a single variable, such as taking the logarithm or square root of the original data; others involve combining more than one variable into a new variable. Unfortunately, analysts largely overlook these options. We give one example here as an illustration.

If we are trying to identify individuals who are likely to default on home loans, we may suspect that neither their income nor the size of their mortgage by itself is critical.

Rather, it is when income is relatively low *and* the size of the mortgage relatively high that individuals are most likely to default. To test this idea, we can create a new variable from the two original ones (INCOME and SIZE OF MORTGAGE), using a formula with logic such as this:

If(INCOME < 100, 000 and SIZE OF MORTGAGE >1, 000) then HIGH RISK;

else LOW RISK

This creates a categorical variable with values High Risk and Low Risk from two existing numerical variables.

A.5.5 NORMALIZATIONS

Rescaling a variable, or **normalization**, is required for a number of data mining methods such as neural networks. It can also be used in other contexts to make variables more nearly comparable to each other.

The **linear normalization** is the most common. This approach rescales a variable so that its values all lie between 0 and 1. The original values of the variable are transformed using the following formula, where X_{new} is the new value, X_{old} is the old value, and Min and Max are the minimum and maximum values of this variable in the dataset:

$$X_{new} = (X_{old} - Min)/(Max - Min)$$

The **Z-score normalization** is used to adjust variables for differences in their variability as well as their scale. Without adjustment, a variable with a high variance relative to others is likely to have a larger impact. Imagine that we have two variables (Variable 1 and Variable 2) that both have a mean of 100, but standard deviations of 50 and 100, respectively. These could represent student test scores, for example. A value of 200 on Variable 1 lies two standard deviations above the mean, while an outcome of 200 on Variable 2 lies only one standard deviation above its mean. In a sense, the outcome of 200 on Variable 1 is more unusual than the same numerical outcome on Variable 2. To reflect this, we transform the original values using the following formula, where X_{new} is the new value, X_{old} is the old value, and the Mean and Standard Deviation are calculated from the values of this variable in the dataset:

$$X_{new} = (X_{old} - Mean)/Standard\ Deviation$$

6 Classification and Prediction Methods

6.1 INTRODUCTION

In the previous chapter, we discussed three types of tasks that analysts engage in: descriptive, predictive, and prescriptive. This chapter is devoted to predictive methods, including both classification and numerical prediction. We use the term **classification** when the task is to predict which class an individual record will occupy; we use the term **prediction** when the task is to predict a numerical outcome for an individual record. For example, classification applies when we wish to predict whether a particular customer will buy; prediction applies when we wish to forecast how much they will spend.

Previously, we offered the admonition to maintain a skeptical attitude toward data. With a skeptical attitude, we are motivated to spend the time needed to carefully explore our data. Here, we offer another admonition: *do not expect magic* from the methods presented in this chapter. The success of any of these methods depends on carefully selected, cleaned, and prepared data. Even then there are pitfalls that only the skeptical analyst can avoid.

The methods we present here originated in a variety of fields. Some come from classical statistics, others from the more recently developed fields of machine learning, artificial intelligence, or decision analysis. As a broad generalization, we could say that in the world of classical statistics, computing was difficult and data were scarce. Moreover, the focus was more on building explanatory models, which suggest the factors that influence the outcome variable, than on predictive models, which aim for accurate predictions on new data. The methods of classical statistics were developed under those constraints. But the more recently developed approaches, which are often referred to collectively as **data mining**, have arisen in a world where large amounts of data are readily available and computing power is essentially unlimited. Moreover, the data mining approach focuses more on predictive modeling than on explanatory modeling. Within the data mining approach, a model is fit using one part of the database and tested using a different part of the database. Since a well-trained analyst needs some facility with a variety of methods, in this chapter we have included the most practical and reliable methods from both schools of thought.

We begin the chapter with a discussion of issues that are common to all classification and prediction approaches: over-fitting, partitioning, and performance measurement. Then we present six widely-used approaches to classification and prediction:

- *k*-Nearest Neighbor
- Naïve Bayes
- Classification and Prediction Trees
- Multiple Linear Regression
- Logistic Regression
- Neural Networks

6.2 PRELIMINARIES

6.2.1 The Problem of Over-fitting

Behind all data analysis is the notion that the data we observe result from two influences: **patterns** and **noise**. The patterns are the stable, underlying relationships that persist and that we can expect to observe both in the existing data and in new data generated by the same process. Noise reflects the transient, random effects of factors that will not be observed in new data. The goal of data analysis is to fit models to the patterns and not to the noise. A model is **over-fit** when it matches the available data so well that it reflects not only the patterns but the noise as well. Over-fit models do not predict the future well because they reflect temporary effects too closely.

We can illustrate the problem of over-fitting using a simple example. The task is to predict sales given the data below:

Year	Sales
1	10
2	19
3	27
4	29
5	45
6	23
7	35
8	42
9	39
10	56

If we fit a model to this entire dataset, we have no additional data for testing it. Instead, we fit models to the first five data points and test how well they predict the remaining five data points. (This process, called *partitioning*, is described in more detail in the next section.)

Figure 6.1 shows one model for this data. Here we have fit a fourth-order polynomial function $(y = 1.208x^4 - 13.08x^3 + 47.79x^2 - 60.91x + 35)$ to the five data points. This function goes precisely through each point, so the fit is perfect.

Figure 6.2 shows an alternative model: a linear fit $(y = 7.9x + 2.1)$. In this case the model does not fit the data nearly as well.

FIGURE 6.1 Polynomial Function Fit to Sales Data

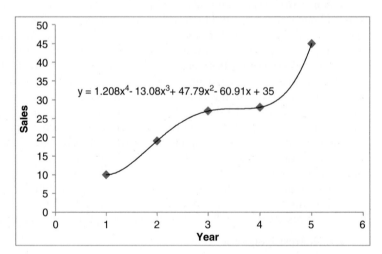

FIGURE 6.2 Linear Function Fit to Sales Data

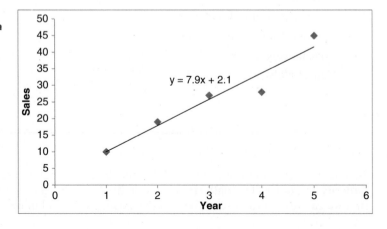

FIGURE 6.3 Sales Data and Linear Function

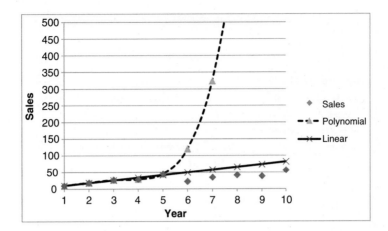

Which model does a better job of predicting the remaining data for years 6 through 10? As Figure 6.3 shows, the linear function does a reasonable job of predicting the values over this time period, even though sales appear to have dropped below the trend of the first five years. The polynomial function, on the other hand, predicts sales of 2,785 in Year 10, almost *fifty times* the actual value. As it happens, the underlying pattern in this data is closer to a linear trend than it is to the highly nonlinear shape of the polynomial. The polynomial fits both the pattern and the noise, so it diverges dramatically from the actual data in the later years. The linear function, despite its relatively poor fit to the early data, does not incorporate the noise to such an extent.

6.2.2 Partitioning the Database

The fundamental strategy used in all classification and prediction methods to avoid the problem of over-fitting is to develop a model on one portion of data and test it on another. Without testing our models on a separate set of data, we will generally be overly optimistic as to how well they will predict. This process of creating subsets of the data for different purposes is called **partitioning**. The first partition, called the **training partition**, is used to develop the model. If different methods are to be tested and compared (such as logistic regression and neural networks), they are both developed on the training partition. The second partition is the **validation partition**, which is used to assess how well the model performs on new data. In some cases we also use the validation partition to fine-tune the model; in these cases we use a third partition called the **test partition** for a final, independent test of the performance of the model.

XLMiner provides several utilities for partitioning a database. The Standard Data Partition window is shown in Figure 6.4 (Data Mining▶Partition▶Standard Partition). All the variables in the database are listed so that some or all of them can be partitioned. Records can be selected for the various partitions in one of two ways: randomly or by using a partition variable. The random option is most commonly used as it ensures that the partitions are unbiased samples from the given data. Records will then be assigned randomly to each partition using either default percentages specified in the window or percentages specified by the user. A partition variable is created by the user and would typically be a categorical variable with codes for the training and validation partitions.

The Data Partition utility creates a new worksheet with information on how the partitioning was carried out and the records for the various partitions collected together. Figure 6.5 shows a typical Data Partition Sheet. The actual data records begin in row 19 with the training partition. Of the first ten records in the original database, records numbered 1, 4, 5, 6, 9, and 10 fall in the training partition; records 2, 3, 7 and 8 appear below in the validation partition.

XLMiner also provides two specialized utilities for partitioning: Time Series Partition and Partition with Oversampling. The Time Series Partition utility is used to divide data with a time element into early and late samples. Partition with Oversampling is used for classification tasks where the class of interest, say those who purchase an expensive car, is rare in the database. This utility allows the analyst to develop a training sample in which the rare attribute is much more common, thus leading to better models.

FIGURE 6.4 Standard
Data Partition Window

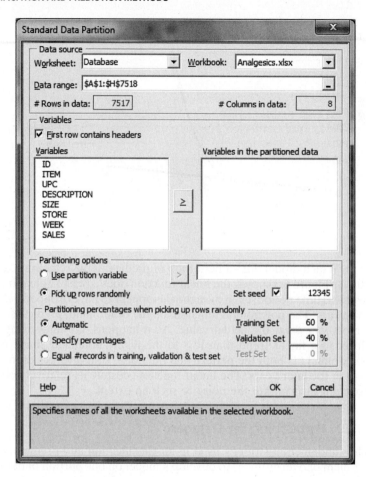

6.2.3 Performance Measures

The ultimate goal of data analysis is to predict the future. When the task at hand is to classify new instances—for example, to predict whether a registered voter will actually vote on Election Day—we naturally measure predictive accuracy by the percentage of instances correctly classified. When the task is numerical prediction—say, predicting the

FIGURE 6.5 Data
Partition Sheet

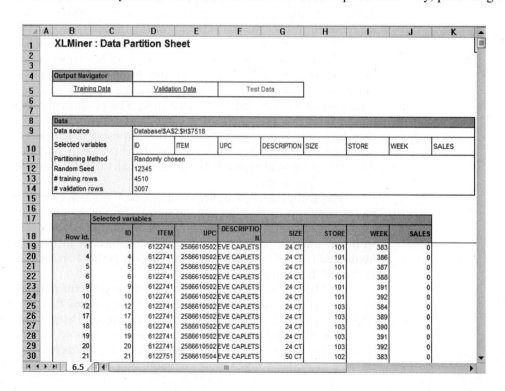

FIGURE 6.6 Classification Matrix

Classification Confusion Matrix		
	Predicted Class	
Actual Class	1	0
1	326	94
0	40	140

Error Report			
Class	**# Cases**	**# Errors**	**% Error**
1	420	94	22.38
0	180	40	22.22
Overall	600	134	22.33

number of votes received by the winner in each state—predictive accuracy will reflect the numerical differences between the actual outcomes and the predictions.

For classification, the predictive accuracy of a model on any given set of data is usually summarized in a **classification matrix** (sometimes called a confusion matrix). Figure 6.6 shows a typical classification matrix from XLMiner.

This chart shows that 600 records were in the dataset. The actual outcome variable (e.g., Vote/No Vote) for each record was either 0 or 1. Likewise, the model predicted the outcome as either 0 or 1. The four combinations of these outcomes are summarized in the upper panel of the chart. We see that 326 records were actually 1s and predicted 1s; 140 were actually 0s and predicted 0s. The errors are in the off-diagonal cells: 40 records were actually 0s but were predicted 1s; 94 were actually 1s but were predicted 0s. These outcomes are summarized in the lower panel, where the overall error rate is reported as 22.33 percent $((40+94)/600)$.

Another commonly-used summary of the predictive performance of a classification model is the **lift chart**. These charts are most helpful if we are interested in the accuracy of our classification on a particular *subset* of the records. Many classification methods generate a probability for each record that it is classified as a 1. Then a rule is used to assign a prediction (0 or 1) to this probability. The rule usually is: if the probability estimate exceeds 0.5, the prediction is 1; if not, the prediction is 0. The lift chart provides a comparison of the predictive performance of a model on those records with the highest probability of being a 1. The performance of the algorithm is compared to that of a naïve model, in which the classification is based solely on the average number of 1s in the data.

Figure 6.7 shows a typical lift chart. The lower line, which is always a straight line, shows the performance of the naïve model. The slope of this line is given by the percentage of 1s in the data. For example, if 1s represent 25 percent of the records, this line has a slope of 0.25, and the naïve model classifies records by assigning every fourth one as a 1. The upper curve represents the performance of the algorithm. It is based on the probabilities computed for each record, sorted from highest to lowest. This curve goes up one unit for every record in this sorted list that correctly predicts a 1, and it goes to the right one unit for every record incorrectly classified as a 0. The more accurate the model is in predicting 1s, the higher the predicted response curve is above the naive response curve.

A closely-related summary of predictive performance is the **decile-wise lift chart**. This type of chart is also created by ranking all the records in terms of the probability of being classified as a 1, from highest to lowest probability. The records are then divided into deciles (groups of 10 percent), and the *factor* by which each decile outperforms a classification based on the naïve model is calculated. For example, if in the top 10 percent we have 100 1s, and the underlying percentages would predict 25, this factor is 4. Figure 6.8 shows a typical decile-wise lift chart. It

FIGURE 6.7 Lift Chart

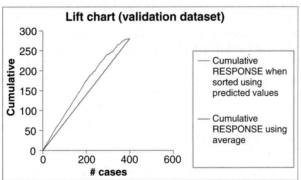

FIGURE 6.8 Decile-Wise Lift Chart

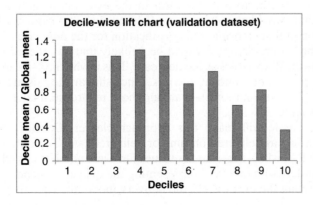

FIGURE 6.9 Perform-
ance Measures for
Numerical Prediction

Total sum of squared errors	RMS Error	Average Error
94.73245727	0.729523691	0.181623702

shows that the top ten percent of records outperform the average assignment by a factor of about 1.3.

Classification matrices and lift charts focus on different aspects of the performance of an algorithm. The classification matrix treats each record and type of error equally, and gives a summary measure of the overall accuracy of the algorithm. Both types of lift charts, by contrast, focus on that subset of records for which the probability of being a 1 is highest. This is relevant when, for example, we have a limited budget for marketing to customers and want to identify that subset with the highest probability of purchasing.

When the task is prediction, model performance can be evaluated by a number of alternative measures. All of them make use of the difference (or error, e_i) between the actual value on each record and the predicted value. XLMiner routinely reports three summary measures: Total sum of squared errors, Root-mean-squared error (RMS Error), and Average error (Figure 6.9).

These are calculated as follows:

$$\text{Total sum of square errors} = \sum e_i^2$$

$$\text{RMS Error} = \text{SQRT} \sum [(1/n)e_i^2]$$

$$\text{Average Error} = \sum e_i$$

Each of these measures can be used to compare the predictive performance of alternative models since lower error is always better. Average error can be misleading, however, because positive and negative errors can cancel each other out, resulting in an unrealistically low overall error. Probably the most useful of these three error measures is the RMS error because it is an average error *in the same units* as the underlying variable, and by squaring the errors we penalize large errors relatively more than small ones.

6.3 THE *K*-NEAREST NEIGHBOR METHOD

The motivating idea behind the *k*-Nearest Neighbor method is to base the classification of a new case (or the numerical prediction for a new case) on those records in the database that are *most similar* to the new case. In the extreme, if there were one record in the database that was identical in every field to the new case, we could use the known classification of that record as our classification for the new case. But in a database with a large number of predictors, it would be unlikely that any record would have exactly the same values on all variables as the new case. This is why the *k*-Nearest Neighbor method is based on similar, not identical, records. Once similar records are identified, the method computes the most common class among those records and takes that as its classification for the new case.

An example will make this approach clearer. Consider the task of classifying customer orders as delivered on time or delivered late. The outcome variable of interest is DELIVERY, which takes on the values On Time and Late. We have a database of past customer orders with one field representing the delivery outcome and a number of other fields describing the order itself, the delivery mode, the customer, and so on. To predict whether a new order will be delivered on time or late, we compare its values on all fields except DELIVERY (which is unknown) to similar records in the database. (Later, we elaborate on the meaning of "similar.") If we find five records that are similar, and four are On Time while one is Late, we predict that the new order will be On Time.

The *k*-Nearest Neighbor approach can be used both for classification and for numerical prediction. In most cases, the classification task is based on *majority voting* among similar records; the prediction task is based on *averaging* the known values of the outcome variable for similar records.

As simple as this idea is, it is embedded in some very familiar products. One example is Pandora, a music radio service on the Internet. Pandora allows its users to build customized lists of songs. Pandora's Music Genome Project uses an algorithm very similar to the *k*-Nearest Neighbor method to identify new songs that should appeal to the user and highlight them to be either included or excluded from the existing song list.

6.3.1 Overview of the *k*-Nearest Neighbor Algorithm

There are three major questions that must be addressed to implement the *k*-Nearest Neighbor algorithm. These are:

- How to define similarity between records?
- How many neighboring records to use?
- What classification or prediction rule to use?

We illustrate the implications of these choices using the situation of a college that wants to predict whether incoming students will successfully graduate. It has a database of past students that includes their high school grade-point average (GPA) and their standardized test scores (TEST SCORE), as well as whether they graduated (Y) or failed to graduate (N). Figure 6.10 shows a graph of the data, with GPA on the horizontal axis, TEST SCORE on the vertical axis, and the graduation result as Y or N. The solid dot represents a new student whose graduation outcome we are trying to predict.

FIGURE 6.10 Data on Graduation Success

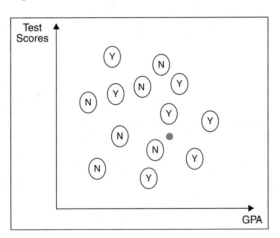

In this example we define similarity between records by the straight-line distance between the corresponding points in the graph. Figure 6.11 shows the four nearest neighbors to the new record, using this definition of similarity.

If we rely only on the closest record, which lies to the lower left of the new record and is N, our classification would be N. If we take into account the *two* closest records, including the second closest which is directly above the new record, we would have to break a tie between one Y and one N. If we use the three closest records, we would have two Ys and one N; our prediction by majority vote would be Y. And if we include the four closest records, we would have three Ys, one N, and a classification of Y. This example shows that the prediction we make generally depends on the number of nearest neighbors we take into account. The prediction also depends on the definition of distance and the classification rule.

In most applications of the *k*-Nearest Neighbor approach, the predictor variables are measured on different numerical scales. In our example,

FIGURE 6.11 Four Nearest Neighbors to New Record

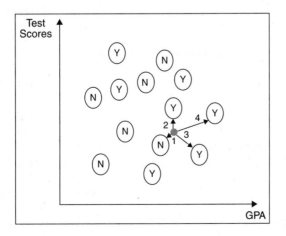

the values for GPA are around 4.0 and those for Test Scores are around 700. A GPA of 3.0 is very different from one of 4.0, while a test score of 699 is almost identical to one of 700. To ensure that one variable does not dominate the others merely because of its scale, k-Nearest Neighbor algorithms typically call for normalizing the predictors. The usual normalization is by z-scores (see Chapter 5, Section A.5.5 for more details).

The distance between records can also be defined in different ways. The most common is the **Euclidean distance**, where the distance between two records X and Y (with values x_i and y_i on the ith variable, respectively) is given by

$$Distance = [(x_1 - y_1)^2 + (x_2 - y_2)^2 + \ldots + (x_n - y_n)^2]^{1/2} \qquad (6.1)$$

As with all data mining methods, over-fitting is a major issue with the k-Nearest Neighbor approach. If we use just one neighbor ($k = 1$), our results are sure to be very sensitive to the particular data we are using; we are certainly over-fitting to the noise. At the other extreme, we could use all n records in the database ($k = n$). In this case, if the majority of the records were 1s on the outcome variable, we would predict a 1 for *every* new case. Here, we would be over-smoothing the data because all new cases would receive the same classification. Somewhere in between $k = 1$ and $k = n$ lies the best choice for k. It is common to choose the k that maximizes the classification accuracy on the validation sample.

6.3.2 An Application of the k-Nearest Neighbor Algorithm

We illustrate the application of the k-Nearest Neighbor approach using a database with 30 variables and 1,000 records on the credit rating assigned to previous applicants for credit (*German Credit.xlsx*).[*] The task is to use this dataset to create a method for rating the credit of new applicants. The outcome variable is Response (column AF), which takes on the value 0 when the credit rating was poor and 1 when it was good. The variables in the database are described in the following table:

Variable Name	Description	Type	Coding
OBS#	Observation number	Categorical	
CHK_ACCT	Checking account status	Categorical	0: <= 0 DM
			1: 0< . . . <200 DM
			2: => 200 DM
			3: no account
DURATION	Duration of credit in months	Numerical	
HISTORY	Credit history	Categorical	0: no credits taken
			1: all credits at this bank paid back duly
			2: existing credits paid back duly till now
			3: delay in paying off in the past
			4: critical account
NEW_CAR	Purpose of credit	Binary	0: No
			1: Yes
USED_CAR	Purpose of credit	Binary	0: No
			1: Yes
FURNITURE	Purpose of credit	Binary	0: No
			1: Yes
RADIO/TV	Purpose of credit	Binary	0: No
			1: Yes
EDUCATION	Purpose of credit	Binary	0: No
			1: Yes
RETRAINING	Purpose of credit	Binary	0: No
			1: Yes
AMOUNT	Credit amount	Numerical	
SAV_ACCT		Categorical	0: < 100 DM

[*] Source: UCI Machine Learning Repository (http://archive.ics.uci.edu/ml).

	Average balance in savings account		
			1: 100< . . . <500 DM
			2: 500< . . . <1000 DM
			3: => 1000 DM
			4: unknown/no savings account
EMPLOYMENT	Present employment Since	Categorical	0: unemployed
			1: < 1 year
			2: 1 <= . . . < 4 years
			3: 4 < . . . < 7 years
			4: >= 7 years
INSTALL_RATE	Installment rate as % disposable income	Numerical	
MALE_DIV	Applicant is male and divorced	Binary	0: No 1: Yes
MALE_SINGLE	Applicant is male and single	Binary	0: No 1: Yes
MALE_MAR_WID	Applicant is male and widowed	Binary	0: No 1: Yes
CO_APPLICANT	Application has a co-applicant	Binary	0: No 1: Yes
GUARANTOR	Application has a guarantor	Binary	0: No 1: Yes
PRESENT_RESIDENCE			
	Present residence since . . . years	Categorical	0: < 1 year
			1: 1< . . . <= 2 years
			2: 2< . . . <= 3 years
			3: > 4 years
REAL_ESTATE	Applicant owns real estate	Binary	0: No 1: Yes
PROP_UNKNOWN	Applicant owns no property (or unknown)	Binary	0: No 1: Yes
AGE	Age in years	Numerical	
OTHER_INSTALL	Applicant has other installment plan credit	Binary	0: No 1: Yes
RENT	Applicant rents	Binary	0: No 1: Yes
OWN_RES	Applicant owns residence	Binary	0: No 1: Yes
NUM_CREDITS	Number of existing credits at this bank	Numerical	
JOB	Nature of job	Categorical	0: unemployed/unskilled – non-resident
			1: unskilled – resident
			2: skilled employee/official
			3: management/self-employed/highly qualified
NUM_DEPENDENTS			
	Number of people for whom liable to provide maintenance	Numerical	
TELEPHONE	Applicant has phone in his or her name	Binary	0: No 1: Yes
FOREIGN	Foreign worker	Binary	0: No 1: Yes
RESPONSE	Credit rating is good	Binary	0: No 1: Yes

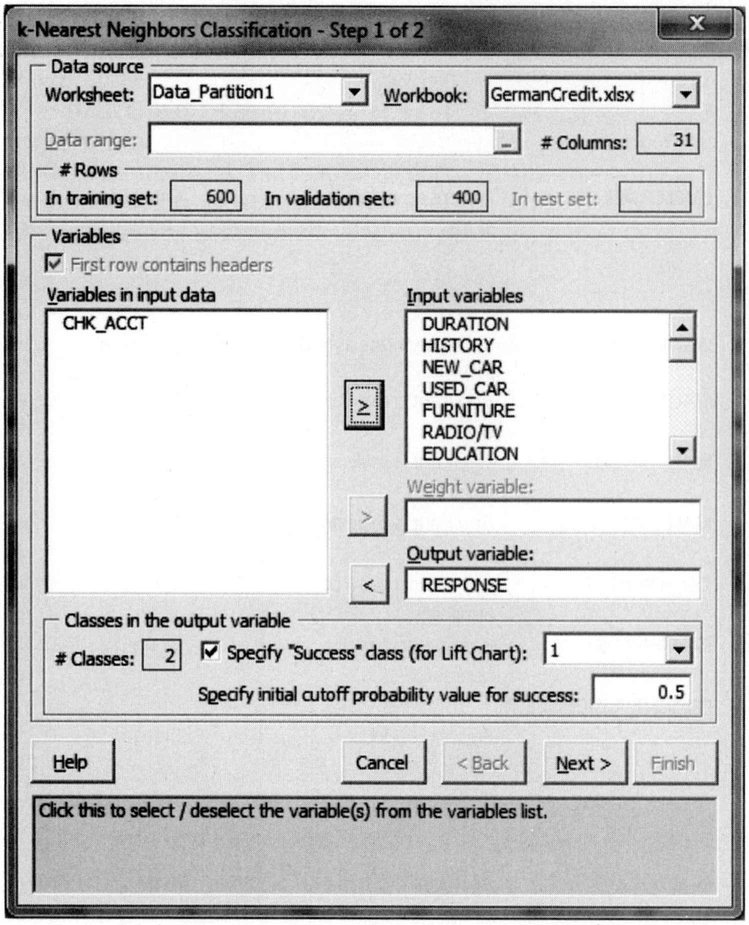

FIGURE 6.12 First
k-Nearest Neighbor
Classification Window

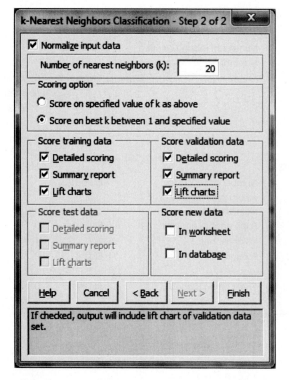

The first step is to partition the database into 600 training records and 400 validation records (using the Standard Partition utility in XLMiner). Then, select the *k*-Nearest Neighbor algorithm for classification: Data Mining▶Classify▶*k*-Nearest Neighbors. (If the task were numerical prediction rather than classification, we would select Data Mining▶Predict▶ *k*-Nearest Neighbors.) This brings up a window similar to that shown in Figure 6.12.

FIGURE 6.13 Second
k-Nearest Neighbor
Classification Window

In this window, we select RESPONSE as the Output variable and move all the other relevant variables into the Input variables category. We also confirm that there are two classes for the output variable: "Success" is a 1 (representing good credit), and the probability cutoff for the classification rule is 0.5.

When we click on OK, a second window appears, shown in Figure 6.13. Here, we chose to normalize the variables (using *z*-scores), we request up to 20 nearest neighbors (all cases from 1 to 20 will be computed), and we ask for the best alternative for *k* between 1 and 20 to be scored on both the training and validation partitions.

The Validation Error Log is shown in Figure 6.14. The first column shows the values of *k* that were tested from 1 to 20. The second and third columns show the error rates on the training and validation records, respectively. The error is zero on the training

FIGURE 6.14 Validation Error Log for *k*-Nearest Neighbor Algorithm

Validation error log for different k

Value of k	% Error Training	% Error Validation	
1	0.00	42.00	
2	20.17	31.75	
3	19.83	35.50	
4	24.83	33.00	
5	23.83	35.25	
6	25.17	33.25	
7	25.67	33.75	
8	25.83	33.00	
9	25.50	34.25	
10	27.33	33.50	
11	26.00	33.75	
12	27.83	32.00	
13	27.83	32.25	
14	27.33	32.00	
15	26.67	33.00	
16	27.17	30.75	<--- Best k
17	27.00	31.50	
18	27.00	30.75	
19	27.83	32.00	
20	28.17	31.00	

data for $k = 1$ because in this case the training data is matched against itself, so no errors can occur. The error on the training data starts out around 20 percent for low values of k and gradually increases as k increases. The error on the validation data shows a quite different pattern. In this case, the validation data is matched with the training data. The error rate for $k = 1$ is quite high, suggesting a high degree of noise in the data. The error rate then falls with k, reaching a minimum for $k = 16$ ($k = 18$ gives the same error rate). However, the error rate is between 30 and 35 percent for most values of k.

Figure 6.15 shows the classification matrix for both the training and the validation records. Since we specified that these matrices be displayed for the "best" value of k, they are computed for $k = 16$, which has the lowest error on the validation data. As we would expect, the error rate is somewhat higher on the validation data than on the training data. In

FIGURE 6.15 Classification Matrices for Training and Validation Partitions

Training Data scoring - Summary Report (for k=16)

Cut off Prob.Val. for Success (Updatable)	0.5

Classification Confusion Matrix		
Predicted Class		
Actual Class	1	0
1	411	9
0	154	26

Error Report			
Class	# Cases	# Errors	% Error
1	420	9	2.14
0	180	154	85.56
Overall	600	163	27.17

Validation Data scoring - Summary Report (for k=16)

Cut off Prob.Val. for Success (Updatable)	0.5

Classification Confusion Matrix		
Predicted Class		
Actual Class	1	0
1	270	10
0	113	7

Error Report			
Class	# Cases	# Errors	% Error
1	280	10	3.57
0	120	113	94.17
Overall	400	123	30.75

addition, the great majority of the errors (92 percent, 113/123) are cases in which the actual class was 0, but our model predicted 1.

It seems likely in this situation that the consequences of misclassifying someone who is a poor credit risk as a good credit risk (Actual = 0, Predicted = 1) far outweigh those of the opposite error. Yet this is the error our method makes most often. We can change these error rates by changing the cutoff probability in the classification rule, which was set at 0.5 initially. If we set the cutoff to 0.75, the error rate goes up somewhat, but the costly errors are far less common. In particular, the total number of errors on the 400 records in the validation sample increases from 123 to 146, but the percentage in the high-risk category drops from 92 to 23 percent.

6.3.3 Strengths and Weaknesses of the *k*-Nearest Neighbor Algorithm

The major advantage of the *k*-Nearest Neighbor algorithm is its simplicity. It requires essentially no assumptions as to the form of the model and few assumptions about the parameters. Only one parameter is estimated (*k*), and we can test all reasonable values for that parameter. This method has been found to perform well in situations where there is a large training database, and where there are many combinations of predictor variables that distinguish the class outcomes.

One drawback is that the method provides no information on which predictors are most effective in making a good classification. The only practical approach is to edit the database in advance, removing predictors that would intuitively appear to have little value. The method also can suffer from long computational times because the number of records required for a sufficiently large training database increases faster than linearly with the number of variables.

6.4 THE NAÏVE BAYES METHOD

The Naïve Bayes method is similar to the *k*-Nearest Neighbor approach in that it bases the classification of a new case on similar records in the database. However, it is restricted to situations in which all the predictor variables are categorical. (Numerical variables can be converted to categorical variables by binning; for details see Chapter 5, Section A.5.2.) With categorical variables, several records in the database are usually *identical* to the new case, and the more prevalent class among these records is taken as the classification for the new case.

Consider the task of predicting a school's admissions decision based on a single test score. The test scores range from 450 to 800 and are binned into three categories: Low (450–600), Medium (601–700), and High (701–800). The following data are available on 300 past decisions:

		Test Score		
		Low (450–600)	**Medium (601–700)**	**High (701–800)**
	Y	10	30	60
Admission				
	N	90	70	40

How would we categorize a new applicant with a test score of 650 using the logic of the Naïve Bayes method? This score falls in the Medium range, and the proportion of records that were admitted in that range is 30 percent, while 70 percent were not admitted. Since the proportion not admitted is higher, that is the category we choose for this applicant. The same logic applies when we have many more predictor variables: find the records that have the same values on all predictors and assign the category that is most prevalent among those records.

Spam filtering is an everyday application in which the Naïve Bayes algorithm is often used. The task is to classify individual emails as Spam or Not Spam. A very large database of actual emails is assembled in which a record is a single email, and the fields reflect whether each distinct word appears in that email. All the predictors are categorical variables with two values: Word Appeared, and Word did not Appear. Experts also classify each record as Spam or Not Spam. New emails are then classified by breaking them down into individual words and identifying those records with identical words. The algorithm makes its classification based on whether Spam is more frequent than Not Spam in that subset of records.

6.4.1 Overview of the Naïve Bayes Algorithm

To understand how the Naïve Bayes approach works (and why it is "naïve") requires a bit of algebra. We assume we are attempting to classify an outcome variable Y that takes on the values 1 and 0. Our data consists of two (categorical) predictors X_1 and X_2. (For example, we might want to classify companies as to whether they will default on their debts, given data on prior defaults and company size.) In practice, we would have many more predictors, but the main points can be made with just two.

We use the notation $P(Y = 1|X_1, X_2)$ to represent the probability that the outcome is 1 given specific values for the two predictors X_1 and X_2 (e.g., the probability a given company defaults given that it had No Prior Defaults and was Small). Although we use the language of probability, we measure these probabilities using proportions of records in the database.

Bayes Rule, which is a standard probability formula, allows us to rewrite this probability in a more useful form:

$$P(Y = 1|X_1, X_2) = P(X_1, X_2|Y = 1) * P(Y = 1)/$$

$$[P(X_1, X_2|Y = 1) * P(Y = 1) + P(X_1, X_2|Y = 0) * P(Y = 0)] \quad (6.2)$$

In words, this says that we can rewrite the probability $P(Y = 1|X_1, X_2)$ as a ratio. In the numerator, we have the probability of getting the data given the outcome, $P(X_1, X_2|Y = 1)$, multiplied by the probability of getting the outcome, $P(Y = 1)$. If we think in terms of proportions of records in the database, the probability $P(X_1, X_2|Y = 1)$ is the proportion of records with the specific values for X_1 and X_2 among all those for which $Y = 1$. And the probability $P(Y = 1)$ is just the proportion of records in the database with $Y = 1$. The denominator consists of two terms, the numerator and its complement for $Y = 0$.

Using another probability formula, the chain rule, we can rewrite $P(X_1, X_2|Y = 1)$ in this form:

$$P(X_1, X_2|Y = 1) = P(X_1|Y = 1) * P(X_2|Y = 1, X_1) \quad (6.3)$$

In words, this says that the probability of getting the specific outcomes for X_1 and X_2, given $Y = 1$, is the product of the probability of getting X_1 given the outcome $Y = 1$, $P(X_1|Y = 1)$, and the probability of getting X_2 given *both* $Y = 1$ *and* X_1, $P(X_2|Y = 1, X_1)$.

Now, we can begin to see the problem that arises in estimating these probabilities using proportions of the database: the number of records satisfying the conditions gets smaller, and therefore the probability estimated from the proportion of records is more subject to noise. In fact, probabilities of the form $P(X_2|Y = 1, X_1)$ will get closer and closer to zero as the number of predictors increases. For example, if we had 30 predictors in our database, we would need to estimate $P(X_{30}|Y = 1, X_1, X_2, X_3, \ldots X_{29})$, and there might well be no records at all satisfying these conditions.

An example will make this clearer. Suppose we are attempting to predict the vote of a specific individual. We have information on the previous votes of other individuals, including data on race, gender, ethnic background, political affiliation, state of residence, whether they voted in the last two elections, marital status, and number of children. The individual in question is white, male, Hispanic, Democrat, from Ohio, voted in the last election, did not vote in the election before that, is divorced, and has one son. To predict his vote, we look in the database for similar voters, but we find no one with exactly his values on all predictors: what can we do? Surely the probability that he will vote is not zero, even though the formulas above would give that result.

One solution to this problem is to assume that knowing the specific value for X_1 does not change the probability for X_2. In other words,

$$P(X_2|Y = 1, X_1) = P(X_2|Y = 1) \qquad (6.4)$$

This assumption is known as **class-conditional independence**. It makes it much less likely that the constituent probabilities will be zero because it is based on larger fractions of the database. Remarkably, this assumption provides the basis for a powerful classification algorithm even though it is almost never precisely true and is often grossly inaccurate. This is why the method is known as *Naïve* Bayes. The justification for making this assumption is simply that it works. But it works only if our goal is classification, not if we are trying to accurately estimate probabilities of class membership.

Here's an example with which we can compare the accurate approach using the full Bayes Rule, and the approximate approach using the Naïve Bayes approach assuming class-conditional independence. The task is to classify firms as to whether they will default on their debts (Default = Yes) or not (Default = No). The data we have is the prior default history and company size:

Prior Default	Company Size	Default
DYes	Small	Yes
DNo	Small	Yes
DNo	Large	Yes
DNo	Large	Yes
DNo	Small	Yes
DNo	Small	Yes
DYes	Small	No
DYes	Large	No
DNo	Large	No
DYes	Large	No

We take a new firm that has defaulted in the past (Prior Default = DYes) and is small (Company Size = Small) and estimate the probability it will not default in the future (Default = No). Using the full Bayes Rule we have:

$$
\begin{aligned}
P(\text{No}|\text{DYes}, \text{Small}) &= P(\text{No}) * P(\text{DYes}|\text{No}) * P(\text{Small}|\text{DYes}, \text{No})/ \\
&\quad [P(\text{No}) * P(\text{DYes}|\text{No}) * P(\text{Small}|\text{DYes}, \text{No}) + \\
&\quad P(\text{Yes}) * P(\text{DYes}|\text{Yes}) * P(\text{Small}|\text{DYes}, \text{Yes})] \\
&= (4/10 * 3/4 * 1/3)/ \\
&\quad [4/10 * 3/4 * 1/3 + 6/10 * 1/6 * 1/1] \\
&= 0.50
\end{aligned}
$$

Using the Naïve Bayes approach we have:

$$
\begin{aligned}
P(\text{No}|\text{DYes}, \text{Small}) &= P(\text{No}) * P(\text{DYes}|\text{No}) * P(\text{Small}|\text{No})/[P(\text{No}) * P(\text{DYes}|\text{No}) \\
&\quad * P(\text{Small}|\text{No}) + P(\text{Yes}) * P(\text{DYes}|\text{Yes}) * P(\text{Small}|\text{Yes})] \\
&= (4/10 * 3/4 * 1/4)/ \\
&\quad [4/10 * 3/4 * 1/4 + 6/10 * 1/6 * 4/6] \\
&= 0.53
\end{aligned}
$$

It happens that the probabilities calculated in these two ways are close in this case, but that is not generally true. For a full picture, we show in the table below the estimated probabilities under both the tull Bayes Rule and Naïve Bayes for all four combinations of predictors:

	Full Bayes	Naïve Bayes	Classification (*cutoff = 0.5*)
P(No|DYes, Small)	0.50	0.53	No
P(No|DYes, Large)	1.00	0.87	No
P(Yes|DYes, Small)	0.00	0.07	Yes
P(Yes|DYes, Small)	0.33	0.31	Yes

As the last column in the table shows, the classification we would make for each case is the same whether we use the the full Bayes Rule or the Naïve Bayes method. For example, if we use a cutoff probability of 0.5, then whenever the estimated probability is 0.5 or higher, we classify the case as No, otherwise as Yes. Both sets of probabilities therefore give the same classification outcomes because both are either above or below 0.5. With a larger number of predictors, we can expect that the estimated probabilities would differ more and more, but the classifications would continue to be similar.

6.4.2 An Application of the Naïve Bayes Algorithm

We illustrate the application of the Naïve Bayes approach using a database (*Universal-Bank.xlsx*)[*] containing 14 variables and 5,000 records on bank customers who were made a personal loan offer. The outcome variable is Personal Loan, which takes on the value 0 when the offer was rejected and 1 when it was accepted. The task is to use this dataset to create a method for predicting whether new cases will respond positively to a loan offer. The variables in the database are described in the table below.

Variable	Description
ID	customer ID
Age	age in completed years
Experience	years of professional experience
Income	annual income ($000)
ZIPCODE	home zip code
Family	size of family
CCAvg	average monthly spending on credit cards ($000)
Education	1: undergraduate; 2: graduate; 3: advanced degree
Mortgage	value of house mortgage ($000)
Personal Loan	did customer accept personal loan offer? (1: Yes; 0: No)
Securities Account	did customer have securities account? (1: Yes; 0: No)
CD Account	did customer have CD account? (1: Yes; 0: No)
Online	did customer use online banking? (1: Yes; 0: No)
CreditCard	did customer use Universal credit card? (1: Yes; 0: No)

The first step is to examine the database for numerical variables because this method requires categorical variables. We find five: Age, Experience, Income, CCAvg, and Mortgage, which we convert to categorical variables (using 3 bins in each case) with the XLMiner utility Bin Continuous Variables. Next, we partition the data using the Standard Partition.

We then select the Naïve Bayes algorithm (Data Mining▶Classify▶Naïve Bayes). The first input window appears as in Figure 6.16. We specify Personal Loan as the outcome variable and all the other variables (except ID and zip code, which we exclude as irrelevant) as inputs (being careful to include only the binned versions of Age, Experience, Income, CCAvg, and Mortgage). There are two classes for the outcome variable and the cutoff for classification is 0.5.

The second input window (Figure 6.17) gives us a choice for calculating class probabilities: Choose According to relative occurrences in training data. The final input window allows us to choose the level of detail in the output. We specify complete results on both the training and the validation data (Figure 6.18).

The results of running the Naïve Bayes algorithm are summarized in the classification matrices shown in Figure 6.19. The overall classification error rate is 6.37 percent on the training data and 5.95 percent on the validation data. In both cases, there are more than twice as many Actual 1s classified as 0s than the reverse.

Figure 6.20 shows the actual and predicted classes for each record (in this case, for the training data). This report allows us to examine errors such as record number 19, for which the estimated probability of success was 0.434, so the prediction was 0, but the actual value was 1. Since the values of all the predictor variables are also shown here, this provides a convenient means for trying to understand the reasons behind classification errors.

[*] Source: Cytel, Inc. 2005.

FIGURE 6.16 First Naïve
Bayes Window

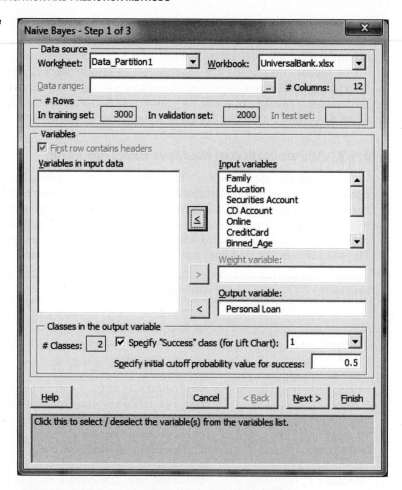

FIGURE 6.17 Second
Naïve Bayes Window

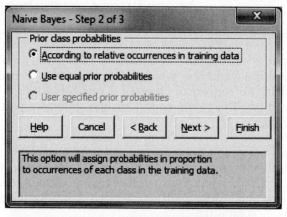

Finally, the lift chart and decile-wise list chart provide visual summaries of the accuracy of this approach (Figure 6.21). In particular, the decile-wise chart shows that if we were to target the top 10 percent of the validation sample, we would achieve about a 700 percent improvement in classification accuracy over random classification.

6.4.3 Strengths and Weaknesses of the Naïve Bayes Algorithm

The Naïve Bayes algorithm is remarkably simple and often gives classification accuracy as good as or better than more sophisticated algorithms. It requires no assumptions other than class-conditional independence, and we have seen that the algorithm can perform well even when that assumption is violated.

Several downsides to this approach should be kept in mind. One is that a very large number of records may be needed to obtain

FIGURE 6.18 Third
Naïve Bayes Window

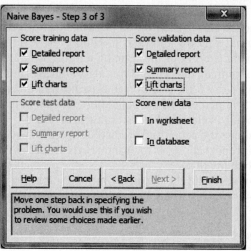

FIGURE 6.19 Classification Matrices for Training and Validation Data

Training Data scoring - Summary Report

Cut off Prob.Val. for Success (Updatable)	0.5

Classification Confusion Matrix

	Predicted Class	
Actual Class	1	0
1	156	130
0	61	2653

Error Report

Class	# Cases	# Errors	% Error
1	286	130	45.45
0	2714	61	2.25
Overall	3000	191	6.37

Validation Data scoring - Summary Report

Cut off Prob.Val. for Success (Updatable)	0.5

Classification Confusion Matrix

	Predicted Class	
Actual Class	1	0
1	108	86
0	33	1773

Error Report

Class	# Cases	# Errors	% Error
1	194	86	44.33
0	1806	33	1.83
Overall	2000	119	5.95

good results. Another potential pitfall is that the method estimates a probability of zero for any new case with a predictor value missing from the training database. To use our earlier example, if the new voter whose vote we wish to predict has 15 children, and no record in the training data has 15 children, the result will be a probability of zero (regardless of the values of the other predictors). (This problem can be somewhat mitigated by careful binning.) Finally, this method is only suitable for classification, not for estimating class probabilities.

Row Id.	Predicted Class	Actual Class	Prob. for 1 (success)	Family	Education	Securities Account	CD Account	Online	CreditCard	Binned_Age	Binned_Experience	Binned_Income	Binned_CC Avg	Binned_Mortgage
1	0	0	0.001214055	4	1	1	0	0	0	1	1	2	2	1
4	0	0	0.454926457	1	2	0	0	0	0	1	1	3	3	1
5	0	0	0.003462409	4	2	0	0	0	1	1	1	2	2	1
6	0	0	0	4	2	0	0	1	0	1	1	1	1	3
9	0	0	0.004869015	3	2	0	0	1	0	1	1	2	1	3
10	0	1	0.46225673	1	3	0	0	0	0	1	1	3	3	1
12	0	0	0.003771046	3	2	0	0	1	0	1	1	2	1	1
17	1	1	0.60414012	4	3	0	0	0	0	1	1	3	3	3
18	0	0	0.006030049	4	1	0	0	0	0	2	2	2	3	1
19	0	1	0.434003163	2	3	0	0	0	0	2	2	3	3	1
20	0	0	0	1	2	1	0	0	1	3	3	1	1	1
21	0	0	0	4	2	0	0	1	0	3	3	1	1	3
23	0	0	0.000927473	1	1	0	0	1	0	1	1	2	2	3
26	0	0	0	3	1	0	0	1	0	2	2	1	1	3
27	0	0	0.002242151	4	3	0	0	0	0	2	2	2	1	1
29	0	0	0.02048296	1	3	0	0	1	1	3	3	2	3	1
30	1	1	0.910003999	1	2	0	1	1	1	1	1	3	3	1
31	0	0	0	1	3	0	0	1	0	3	3	1	2	3
32	0	0	0	1	2	0	0	1	0	2	2	1	2	1
35	0	0	0.003767977	4	3	0	0	1	0	1	1	2	2	1

FIGURE 6.20 Predicted and Actual Classes for Each Record

FIGURE 6.21 Lift Charts for Naïve Bayes Algorithm

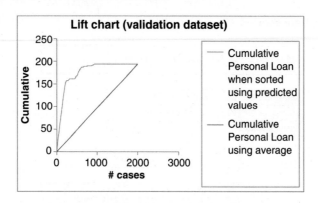

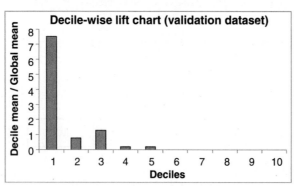

6.5 CLASSIFICATION AND PREDICTION TREES

The tree approach to classification is based on the observation that there are subsets of the records in a database that contain mostly 1s or 0s. If we can identify these subsets, then we can classify a new record by determining the majority outcome in the subset it most resembles. The same approach can be used for numerical prediction although the prediction is made by *averaging* the values of the outcome variable in the subset, not by majority voting as in classification. (This class of algorithms is often referred to by the acronym CART, for Classification and Regression Tree. We prefer the term *prediction* to *regression* because the word *regression* often is taken to imply linear regression, an entirely different algorithm.)

When compared to other methods, classification and prediction trees are particularly simple to understand and explain to others. The process used to create them can be described in several equivalent ways: as recursive partitioning, as creating trees, or as defining a set of logical rules.

Imagine the task is to predict the purchase behavior ($Y = 1$ or $Y = 0$) of individuals about whom we know three facts: their age, income, and education. A typical classification tree could take the form of Figure 6.22. In this tree, circular nodes represent the partitioning of records, while rectangular nodes represent collections of records with similar values for the outcome variable. Starting at the top, the tree indicates that we first want to distinguish records for which INCOME exceeds 107.6 from those for which INCOME is less than this value. The records in the second group (INCOME $\leq$ 107.6) are immediately classified $Y = 0$. The ones in the first group (INCOME > 107.6) are then further split by those for

FIGURE 6.22 Classification Tree

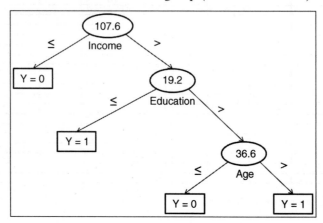

whom EDUCATION exceeds 19.2 from those for whom EDUCATION does not exceed 19.2. The second group is classified $Y = 1$, while the first group is once again divided, this time by AGE, using an age of 36.6 as the split point. These two remaining groups can now be classified as either $Y = 0$ or $Y = 1$. Given this tree, we classify a new record by starting at the top and taking the branch at each circular node that corresponds to the new record's values until we reach a rectangular node, where the classification is made.

This example suggests qualitatively how a classification tree algorithm works. First, it must decide on which variable to make the initial split (INCOME in our example). Then, it must decide at what value to make the split (107.6 in our example). This initial split defines two subsets of records. These subsets are then assigned a classification or split further (usually with different variables and split points). This process is carried out recursively until the subsets of records are sufficiently homogeneous, by which we mean they contain either mostly 1s or mostly 0s.

6.5.1 Overview of Classification and Prediction Trees

The general outline of the classification and prediction tree algorithm is simple to describe. We first describe the approach used for classification with numerical predictor variables. Then, we describe how to use categorical predictor variables for classification, and finally how this algorithm is applied to numerical prediction.

The following steps describe the algorithm:

1. Pick a predictor variable.

2. Sort its values from low to high.

3. Define a set of **split points** as the midpoints between each pair of values.

4. For each split point, divide the records into two sets: those having values above and those below the split point.

5. Evaluate the **homogeneity** of the records in each of these subsets. (Homogeneity measures the extent to which the records are mostly 1s or 0s.)

6. Repeat this process for all split points for this variable.

7. Choose the split point for this variable that gives the most homogeneous subsets.

8. Repeat this process for all variables.

9. Split on the variable with the highest homogeneity.

10. Repeat the entire process for each subset of records created by this split.

This basic outline is used for all tree algorithms. However, categorical variables are treated somewhat differently. Instead of sorting them as we do with numerical variables, all possible subsets are created and evaluated for homogeneity. For a categorical variable with two outcomes, Y and N, there is only one possible split point: between Y and N. For a categorical variable with three outcomes, say H, M, and L, there are three possible splits: {H} and {M, L}; {M} and {H, L}; and {L} and {H, M}.

When the task at hand is numerical prediction, not classification, essentially the same algorithm can be used. The major difference is that the "homogeneity" of a subset of records is usually measured by the variance (sum of squared deviations from the mean) of the outcome variable for those records.

FIGURE 6.23 Illustration of Homogeneity

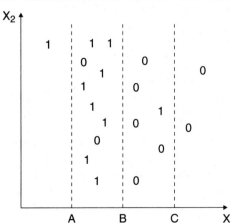

Measuring the degree of homogeneity of groups of records is an essential element of this approach. Homogeneity, again, reflects the extent to which a subset is predominantly either 1s or 0s. The goal of the algorithm is to create subsets of records with a high degree of homogeneity.

An example will make this concept clearer. Consider the case where we have two predictor variables, X_1 and X_2, and the outcomes are Y and N. Figure 6.23 shows a plot of 19 records. We consider three alternative split points for X_1: A, B, or C. (The algorithm considers all possible split points; here we illustrate just these three.)

Each time we split, we form two subsets of records: the group to the right and the group to the left of the split point. If we split at A, the group to the left has one record with a Y; the group to the right has 18 records with 9 Ys and 9 Ns. Splitting at B we have 9 Ys and 2 Ns to the left; 1 Y and 7 Ns to the right. Finally, splitting at C we have 10 Ys and 7 Ns to the left; 0 Ys and 2 Ns to the right. These results are displayed in the following table:

Split Point	Left Group		Right Group	
	Ys	Ns	Ys	Ns
A	1	0	9	9
B	9	2	1	7
C	10	7	0	2

If we had to choose among these three split points, which would create the most homogeneous subsets? The group on the right for split point A is problematic because it is evenly divided between Ys and Ns, and is therefore not homogeneous. Likewise, split point C creates a highly nonhomogeneous group on the left. Only point B creates two relatively homogeneous subsets, and it is the one we would choose among these three.

In XLMiner, homogeneity is computed using a variant of the **Gini index**. If we define p_0 as the proportion of records in the subset with $Y = 0$ and p_1 as the proportion of records with $Y = 1$, then the Gini Index is

$$\text{Gini Index} = 1 - p_0^2 - p_1^2 \qquad (6.5)$$

This formula reaches its minimum value of zero when either p_0 or p_1 is 1. These are the extremes of perfect homogeneity. Its maximum occurs when $p_0 = p_1 = 0.5$, which is the least homogeneous possibility. Because the most homogeneous cases are ones with the lowest values of the Gini index, the algorithm seeks to *minimize* the Gini score.

The Gini Index for each of these subsets is shown in the table below. The overall index is the weighted average of the indices for the left and right groups, where the weights are the number of records in each group. These numerical results confirm our previous observation that B is the split point for which *both* subsets are relatively homogenous.

Split Point	Left Group	Right Group	Weighted Average
A	0.00	0.50	0.47
B	0.33	0.22	0.26
C	0.48	0.00	0.43

Over-fitting is a particular problem with classification and prediction trees since we can achieve a *perfect* fit on any dataset simply by continuing to divide records until the final subsets contain only one record each. Such a tree will perfectly classify training data, but it is likely to perform poorly on validation data. This is because smaller subsets contain fewer records, which are less representative of the underlying patterns and more influenced by noise. The solution to this problem is to **prune** the tree—to remove nodes at the bottom that divide small subsets into even smaller subsets, until the resulting tree no longer over-fits the data. This requires partitioning the database into three partitions: a training partition, a validation partition, and a test partition. The procedure is this: fit a full tree to the training data (for a perfect fit), prune this tree using validation data to minimize classification error, test the resulting tree on the test data.

6.5.2 An Application of Classification and Prediction Trees

We illustrate the application of the classification and prediction tree approach using a database with 25 variables and 3,120 records on the donation histories of members of a nonprofit organization (*Fundraising.xlsx*)[*]. The outcome variable is TARGET-B (column W), which takes on the value 1 when the individual has donated and 0 otherwise. The task is to use this data to create a method for predicting the donations from new members. The variables in the database are described in the following table:

---

[*] Source: Shmueli, G., N. R. Patel, and P. C. Bruce. 2010. *Data Mining for Business Intelligence*. New Jersey: John Wiley & Sons, page 387.

Variable	Description
ZIP	Zip code group
HOMEOWNER	0: not homeowner, 1 homeowner
NUMCHLD	number of children
INCOME	household income
GENDER	0: Male, 1: Female
WEALTH	wealth rating from 0-9 lowest to highest
HV	average home value in neighborhood
ICmed	median family income in neighborhood
ICavg	average family income in neighborhood
IC15	percent of population earning less than $15,000 in neighborhood
NUMPROM	number of promotions received to date
RAMNTALL	lifetime gifts to date
MAXRAMNT	largest gift to date
LASTGIFT	most recent gift
TOTALMONTHS	months from last donation
TIMELAG	months between first and second donation
AVGGIFT	average size of donation
TARGET_B	0: nondonor, 1: donor

The first step is to examine the predictor variables in the database. We note that ZIPCODE has been converted from a 5-digit code to four dummy variables by region. The WEALTH variable is an index variable, ranging from 1 to 9, depending on median family wealth and area population. This is technically an ordinal categorical variable, but we will interpret it as numerical for the purposes of developing a tree model. The remaining variables are either numerical or binary, and therefore in an appropriate format for the classification tree algorithm.

We select the Classification Tree algorithm (Data Mining▸Classify▸Classification Tree). The first input window appears as in Figure 6.24. We specify TARGET-B as the

FIGURE 6.24 First Classification Tree Window

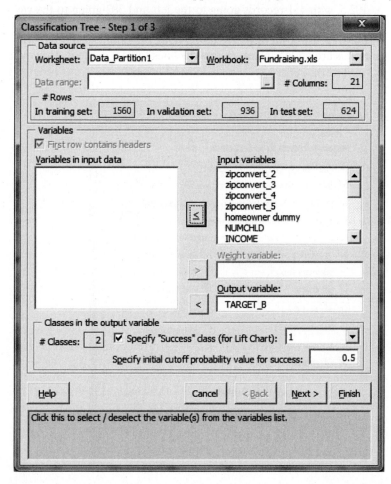

FIGURE 6.25 Second Classification Tree Window

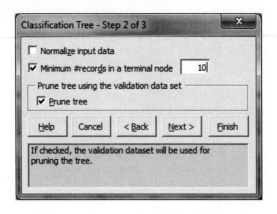

outcome variable and all the other variables as inputs. There are two classes for the outcome variable and the cutoff for classification is 0.5.

On the second input window (Figure 6.25) we specify 10 for Minimum #records in a terminal node. This choice controls the depth of the tree that is fit to the training data. With 1,560 records in the training partition we might expect that it will take a very complex tree to separate the records into perfectly homogeneous subsets, and doing so will lead to extreme over-fitting. Thus we allow the algorithm to stop when the subsets contain 10 records. We also check the box Prune tree so the trees constructed on the training data will be pruned on the validation data.

Finally, on the third input window (Figure 6.26) we choose options in the top panel (Trees) for how the trees will be displayed in the output. In most cases we choose a small number (in this case 5) for Maximum # levels to be displayed so that the displayed trees are not too complex. We also choose to report all the available detail for all three partitions: training, validation, and test.

The full classification tree developed on the training partition is shown in Figure 6.27. The first split is on the variable MAXRAMNT, which measures the maximum donation given to date. The split value is 14.5; 727 records are less than or equal to this value and go down the left branch, while 833 records are greater than this value and go down the right branch $(727 + 833 = 1, 560,$ which is the total number of records in the partition). The left branch then splits on INCOME, at a value of 4.5. with 521 records going to the left and 206 going to the right $(521 + 206 = 727,$ which is the number of records splitting left above this node). The right branch splits on RAMNTALL, which is the total of gifts lifetime. The split value is 102.5, with 451 records going to the left and 382 going to the right.

The training log (Figure 6.28) shows how the error rate declines as we add nodes to the tree using the training data. With zero nodes the error rate is 50 percent; after 119 nodes are added the error rate declines to 24.8 percent. However, we are more interested

FIGURE 6.26 Third Classification Tree Window

Classification Tree - Step 3 of 3

Trees
Maximum # levels to be displayed: 5

☑ Full tree (grown using training data)
☑ Best pruned tree (pruned using validation data)
☑ Minimum error tree (pruned using validation data)
☑ Tree with specified number of decision nodes: 20

Score training data
☑ Detailed report
☑ Summary report
☑ Lift charts

Score validation data
☑ Detailed report
☑ Summary report
☑ Lift charts

Score test data
☑ Detailed report
☑ Summary report
☑ Lift charts

Score new data
☐ In worksheet
☐ In database

Help   Cancel   < Back   Next   Finish

If checked, output will include detail scoring of test data set.

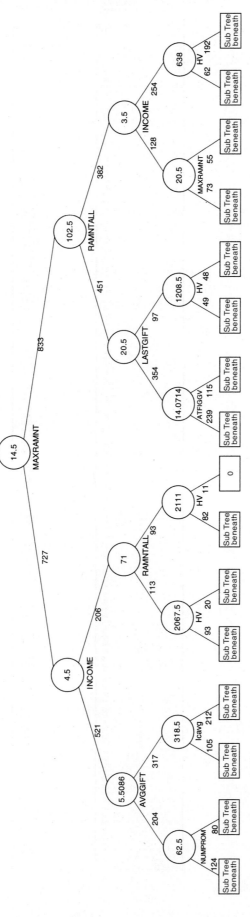

FIGURE 6.27 Full Classification Tree Fit to Training Data

Training Log (Growing the full tree using training data)

# Decision Nodes	% Error
0	49.62
1	43.78
2	43.78
3	43.53
4	43.08
5	43.08
6	43.08
7	42.05
8	42.05
9	40.9
10	40.9
11	40.71
12	40.13
13	40.13
14	39.81
15	39.17
16	39.04
17	39.04
18	38.72
19	38.08
20	37.69
21	37.69
22	37.69
23	37.37
24	36.86
25	36.86
26	36.79
27	36.28
28	36.28
29	36.03
30	35.96
31	35.96
32	35.45
33	35.45
34	35.13
35	34.87
36	34.87
37	34.36
38	34.29
39	34.29
40	33.97
41	33.85
42	33.85
43	33.27
44	33.27
45	32.88
46	32.88
47	32.88
48	32.56
49	32.31
50	31.99
51	31.79
52	31.54
53	31.47
54	31.47
55	30.9
56	30.9
57	30.64
58	30.64
59	30.64
60	30.64
61	30.45
62	30.45
63	30.45
64	30.06
65	29.94
66	29.94
67	29.68
68	29.62
69	29.62
70	29.62
71	29.62
72	29.36
73	29.36
74	28.97
75	28.91
76	28.91
77	28.65
78	28.59
79	28.59
80	28.59
81	28.59
82	28.59
83	28.59
84	28.4
85	28.08
86	28.08
87	27.82
88	27.69
89	27.63
90	27.63
91	27.37
92	27.37
93	26.99
94	26.73
95	26.73
96	26.73
97	26.73
98	26.73
99	26.73
100	26.6
101	26.6
102	26.15
103	26.15
104	26.15
105	26.03
106	25.9
107	25.9
108	25.83
109	25.58
110	25.58
111	25.32
112	25.32
113	25.32
114	25.32
115	25.06
116	25.06
117	25.06
118	25.06
119	24.81

FIGURE 6.28   Training Log

FIGURE 6.29 Prune Log
Using Validation Data

# Decision Nodes	% Error
119	51.282051
118	51.282051
117	51.282051
116	51.282051
115	51.282051
114	51.282051
113	51.282051
112	51.282051
111	51.282051
110	51.282051
109	51.282051
108	51.282051
107	51.282051
106	51.282051
105	51.282051
104	51.282051
103	51.282051
102	51.282051
101	51.282051
100	51.282051
20	43.376068
19	43.376068
18	43.376068
17	44.230769
16	44.551282
15	43.376068
14	43.376068
13	43.376068
12	43.376068
11	43.376068
10	42.948718
9	42.948718
8	42.948718
7	42.094017
6	42.094017
5	42.094017
4	42.094017 <-- Min. Err. Tree Std. Err. 0.016137415
3	43.696581
2	43.696581
1	43.696581 <-- Best Pruned Tree
0	49.679487

in the error rates on the validation partition, which are displayed in Figure 6.29. As we prune away branches from the 119 used in the full tree, the error rate on the validation data declines. It reaches its minimum with four nodes; this is the Minimum Error Tree. The Best Pruned Tree, however, has only one node. (The Best Pruned Tree generally has fewer nodes than the Minimum Error Tree. It accounts for the variability in the estimates of the error rate.)

These results suggest that the full tree is extremely over-fit to the training data, and that the best trees for classifying new records have a small number of branches (but do not perform terribly well). This conclusion is supported by the classification matrices (Figure 6.30), which show that the misclassification is lowest on the training data but increases for both the validation and test data.

Finally, we examine the lift charts for the test data (Figure 6.31). As expected, the lift chart shows that the classification tree performs only slightly better than the average, and the decile-wise lift chart shows that this approach is about 10 percent better than a naïve model on the first decile of the records.

FIGURE 6.30 Classification Matrices for all Three Partitions

Training Data scoring - Summary Report (Using Full Tree)

Cut off Prob.Val. for Success (Updatable)	0.5

Classification Confusion Matrix		
	Predicted Class	
Actual Class	1	0
1	604	182
0	205	569

Error Report			
Class	# Cases	# Errors	% Error
1	786	182	23.16
0	774	205	26.49
Overall	1560	387	24.81

Validation Data scoring - Summary Report (Using Best Pruned Tree)

Cut off Prob.Val. for Success (Updatable)	0.5

Classification Confusion Matrix		
	Predicted Class	
Actual Class	1	0
1	255	216
0	193	272

Error Report			
Class	# Cases	# Errors	% Error
1	471	216	45.86
0	465	193	41.51
Overall	936	409	43.70

Test Data scoring - Summary Report (Using Best Pruned Tree)

Cut off Prob.Val. for Success (Updatable)	0.5

Classification Confusion Matrix		
	Predicted Class	
Actual Class	1	0
1	171	132
0	146	175

Error Report			
Class	# Cases	# Errors	% Error
1	303	132	43.56
0	321	146	45.48
Overall	624	278	44.55

6.5.3 Strengths and Weaknesses of Classification and Prediction Trees

The classification and prediction tree approach has the great advantage of being easy to understand and explain to others. Its results are transparent and can be interpreted as explicit If-Then rules. These rules can be directly programmed for automatic classification or prediction of new cases.

In addition to these advantages, this approach is based on few assumptions and works well even with missing data and outliers. Finally, it identifies the most important predictor variables because the early splits are based on those variables that increase the homogeneity of the subsets of the records the most.

FIGURE 6.31 Lift Charts for Test Data

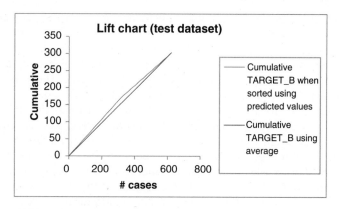

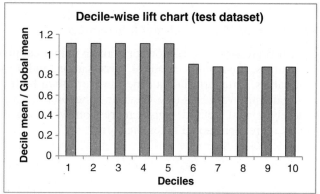

Among the few disadvantages of trees is this: accurate results can require very large databases. In addition, this approach allows partitioning of only individual variables, not pairs or groups of variables. This approach will miss relationships between variables; the solution is to define new variables by combining existing ones.

A limitation specific to XLMiner is that only binary categorical variables are allowed. Thus categorical variables with more than two values must be replaced with dummy variables.

6.6 MULTIPLE LINEAR REGRESSION

Linear regression is one of the most widely-used tools from classical statistics, and when used appropriately, it is an important tool in the business analyst's toolkit. This method is ubiquitous in the natural and social sciences, where it is more often used for *explanatory modeling* than for *predictive modeling*. The goal of explanatory modeling is to determine whether specific variables influence the outcome variable. (It is also called inferential modeling because the goal is to *infer* from the data the existence and strength of relationships between variables.) Here are some typical questions of this type that linear regression has been used to answer:

- Do the data support the claim that women are paid less than men in comparable jobs?
- Is there evidence in the data that price discounts and rebates lead to higher long-term sales?
- Do data support the idea that firms that outsource their manufacturing overseas have higher profits?
- Do the available epidemiological data support the notion that smoking is associated with lung cancer?

Linear regression was originally developed to answer questions of scientific interest. For example, agricultural experimenters wanted to know which treatments lead to higher crop yields, medical experts wanted to know whether certain drugs lead to improvements in health, and economists wanted to identify the key determinants of firms' profitability. In most of these cases, the models were not used for prediction. The focus instead was on determining which specific factors could reliably be said to influence the outcome variable.

When linear regression was developed, data were scarce, so all the available data were typically used to fit the model. This left no unused data with which to test the predictive accuracy of the model. Indirect methods, therefore, had to be developed that would suggest which predictor variables had the strongest relationship to the outcome variable. These methods, known as inferential statistics, have been used for decades to help select the variables to include in the best fitting model.

Our focus in this chapter, by contrast, is on *predicting* the outcome variable, not primarily on *explaining* it. This difference in emphasis causes us to use linear regression in a somewhat different way than it is used for explanatory modeling. As with other methods, we are less interested in how well the model fits the data than in how well it predicts with new data. This is why we create a model using a training dataset and test its predictive power on a validation dataset. A model that fits the training data very well but has poor predictive accuracy on the validation data would hardly be considered adequate.

6.6.1 Overview of Multiple Linear Regression

Multiple linear regression is a method for making numerical predictions using numerical predictor variables. It cannot be used for classification, and it cannot employ categorical predictor variables. Categorical data can, however, often be transformed into numerical data by using dummy variables (see Chapter 5, Section A.5.3.) (In the next section, we discuss a closely related method, logistic regression, which can be used for classification.)

A linear regression model takes the form

$$Y = b_0 + b_1 X_1 + b_2 X_2 + \ldots + b_q X_q + e \tag{6.6}$$

where the outcome variable is Y, the explanatory variables are $X_1, X_2, \ldots, X_q$; the parameters to be estimated from the data are $b_0, b_1, b_2, \ldots, b_q$, and e represents a random error term that accounts for all the unobserved factors that influence the outcome Y.

This model is based on two strong assumptions. One is that the effect of each predictor variable X_i is *additive* to those of other predictors. The other assumption is that the effect of each predictor is *proportional* to its value, with the proportionality factor given by the coefficient b_i.

These assumptions may seem excessively restrictive, especially when compared to algorithms such as Classification and Prediction Trees or Naïve Bayes that assume very little about the form of the model or its parameters. However, by suitably transforming the original data we can adapt the linear regression model to a wide variety of situations. A simple example illustrates this point.

The relationship between the speed of a vehicle and the distance it takes to bring that vehicle to a stop is crucial to traffic safety. Figure 6.32 shows a set of experimental data on this relationship. It is clear from these data that stopping distance increases with speed at an increasing rate: the relationship is not linear. A straight line fit to these data, as shown in the figure, consistently under- or over-predicts stopping distance.

FIGURE 6.32 Stopping Distance as a Function of Speed

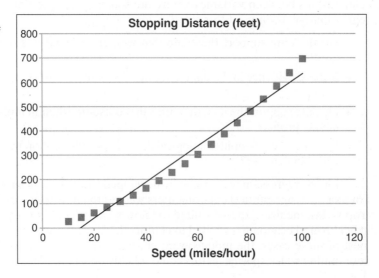

FIGURE 6.33 Stopping Distance as a Function of Speed Squared

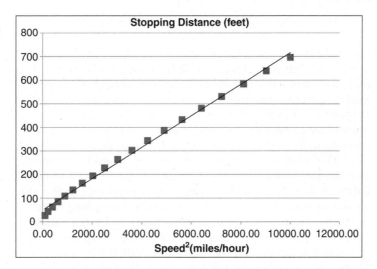

However, the figure does suggest that the relationship between stopping distance and speed might be quadratic, so that if we plotted stopping distance against the *square* of speed it would appear linear. Figure 6.33 confirms this hunch and shows that a straight line fits this transformed data very well.

The lesson to draw from this example is that we should avoid using the raw data at our disposal in a linear regression model until we have confirmed that a linear relationship is plausible. Creating a scatterplot of each predictor against the outcome variable is an important step in this process. If the relationship does not appear to be linear, either from the data or from background knowledge, we should transform the predictor (as we did in the example above by squaring it) to more closely satisfy the linearity assumption.

In multiple linear regression, we assume the data are given and the task is to determine the "best" values for the regression coefficients b_i. This becomes a form of optimization. The objective function to be minimized is the sum (over all the records) of the squared errors between the data and the regression function. The decision variables are the coefficients b_i. In effect, the algorithm adjusts the values for the b_i until it finds the smallest possible total error. Fortunately, under the assumption of linearity, this process is straightforward: unless the predictor variables are almost perfectly correlated, all that is required is solving a set of simple algebraic equations. Unlike more complex search algorithms, multiple linear regression always finds an answer quickly and reliably.

The practical challenge in using multiple linear regression is not in solving for the parameters but in determining which predictor variables to use, particularly when a large database with scores of potential predictor variables is available. One approach would be to use *all* the available predictors; after all, why throw away perfectly good data? But this approach is likely to lead to over-fitting and eventually to poor predictions. To see why this is so, consider that every predictor X_i is correlated to the outcome Y to some degree: either weakly, strongly, or somewhere in between. If we add dozens of predictors to our model, some of which are weakly correlated, we are fitting the model to the noise represented by the weakly correlated variables. As always with over-fitting, the result will be poor predictions.

There are three complementary approaches to selecting predictors for a regression model:

- pre-processing the data
- use of inferential statistics
- search to select the best subset of predictors

In pre-processing the data, we ask a series of questions to help us eliminate potentially problematic predictor variables. If, for example, a predictor X on its face does not have any influence on the outcome Y, then we eliminate it from our data at the outset. For example, sunspots surely do not influence store sales. In the same manner, we would eliminate from further consideration variables in our dataset that contain numerous missing values, or that are expensive to collect, or that are likely to be recorded inaccurately, or that will not be available at the time predictions must be made. Finally, we eliminate variables that are highly correlated with other predictor variables because including them will add little to the overall predictive accuracy of the model.

The second approach is to use inferential statistics to determine predictor variables whose apparent influence on the outcome variable may be due to chance. This approach requires running the multiple regression algorithm and examining the p-value of each regression coefficient. These p-values can be used to answer this question: Could this value for b_i have arisen due to random sampling if the actual parameter value was zero? (If $b_i = 0$ then the predictor variable has no influence on the outcome variable.) The p-value measures the probability in repeated sampling from the data that an observed value at least as large as b_i could have arisen even though the true value is zero. A p-value above 0.05 is customarily taken to indicate that the variable in question should be eliminated from the model.

This approach to variable selection cannot be followed mechanically; p-values provide only a rule of thumb. Certainly it is a mistake to believe that a very low p-value indicates that the variable in question is important in the model or that the regression coefficient is accurate. The five percent cutoff is nothing more than a convention, and there are many instances where we would choose to keep a variable in a model even though it failed this test. On the other hand, a high p-value can be taken as a warning that this coefficient deserves careful scrutiny and might not belong in the model. The final arbiter, of course, is predictive accuracy on the validation data, so we can always compare the accuracy of models with and without a particular variable.

The third approach to selecting predictors is to systematically search over different subsets of variables from all of those in the dataset and attempt to determine the best collection. If we had to do this by hand, it would be impractical because the number of subsets of variables is huge even for a modest number of predictors. But most software for multiple linear regression offers one or more automated approaches to this problem. We will describe the approaches available in XLMiner in more detail in the following section. Here we give a brief overview.

The two most common approaches to automated subset selection are *forward selection* and *backward elimination*. In forward selection, variables are added into the regression model one a time, starting with the one that most improves the fit of the model to the data. Under backward elimination, a model is first run with *all* the variables, and then they are eliminated one by one, starting with the one that makes the smallest contribution to the fit.

As with the use of p-values, these search methods should be used only to provide suggestions for variables to include or exclude. They should never be relied on as providing the final word. Do not expect any of these search methods to serve up the best model automatically. We should examine the contribution each predictor variable makes to the model, and we should always test predictive accuracy on validation data.

6.6.2 An Application of Multiple Linear Regression

We illustrate the application of the multiple linear regression approach using a database with 9 variables and 398 records on the mileage and other characteristics of automobile models (*MPG.xlsx*)*. The outcome variable is MPG, which measures fuel efficiency in miles per gallon. The potential predictor variables include a number of measurements of the physical features of the vehicle, such as horsepower and weight, as well as the year of the model and the region of origin ($1 = $ US, $2 = $ Europe, $3 = $ Asia). The task is to use the data to predict the fuel efficiency of a new vehicle. The variables in the database are described in the following table:

Variable	Description
MPG	fuel efficiency in miles per gallon
CYLINDERS	number of cylinders
DISPLACEMENT	engine displacement in cubic inches
HORSEPOWER	engine horsepower
WEIGHT	vehicle weight in pounds
ACCELERATION	acceleration in feet per second squared
YEAR	model year
ORIGIN	country of origin ($1 = $ US, $2 = $ Europe, $3 = $ Asia)
NAME	model name

* Source: UCI Machine Learning Repository (http://archive.ics.uci.edu/ml)

We first examine the predictor variables and consider the effect we would expect each to have on mileage. CYLINDERS, DISPLACEMENT, HORSEPOWER, WEIGHT, and ACCELERATION are all numerical variables, and we intuitively expect each of them to have a negative impact on mileage. By a negative impact, we mean that the associated regression coefficient should be negative, so MPG should decrease as each of these variables increases. YEAR is also numerical, and we might expect fuel efficiency to improve with the model year (under the influence of technological change and government regulations) so its coefficient would be positive. ORIGIN is a categorical variable although the values it takes on are numerical, so we must be careful about how we use it in a regression model. To see why this is so, consider that the ORIGIN variable takes on the values 1 for US, 2 for Europe, and 3 for Asia. If we include it in the regression, then the estimated coefficient will measure the effect on MPG of a 1-unit increase in ORIGIN, that is, going from US to Europe, and from Europe to Asia. But we have no reason to believe that these effects are equal. A better approach is to create dummy variables (see Chapter 5, Section A.5.3) for all three possible outcomes. We use only two of the dummy variables in the regression (those for Europe and Asia) because the information contained in the third variable is redundant and adds no information. The coefficients of these dummy variables in the regression will measure the impact on MPG of a vehicle coming from Europe (relative to being from the US), and coming from Asia (also relative to coming from the US).

We partition the resulting dataset and select the multiple regression procedure for the prediction task in XLMiner (Data Mining▶Predict▶Multiple Linear Regression). The first input screen appears as in Figure 6.34.

We select MPG as the Output variable, and all of the remaining variables as inputs other than NAME and ORIGIN_1 (US), which is redundant with the dummies for Europe and Asia.

The second input window (Figure 6.35) gives us the option to force the constant term in the regression to be zero. The constant term reflects the value of the outcome variable when all the predictor variables are zero. Because we have no reason to believe this value is

FIGURE 6.34 First Multiple Linear Regression Window

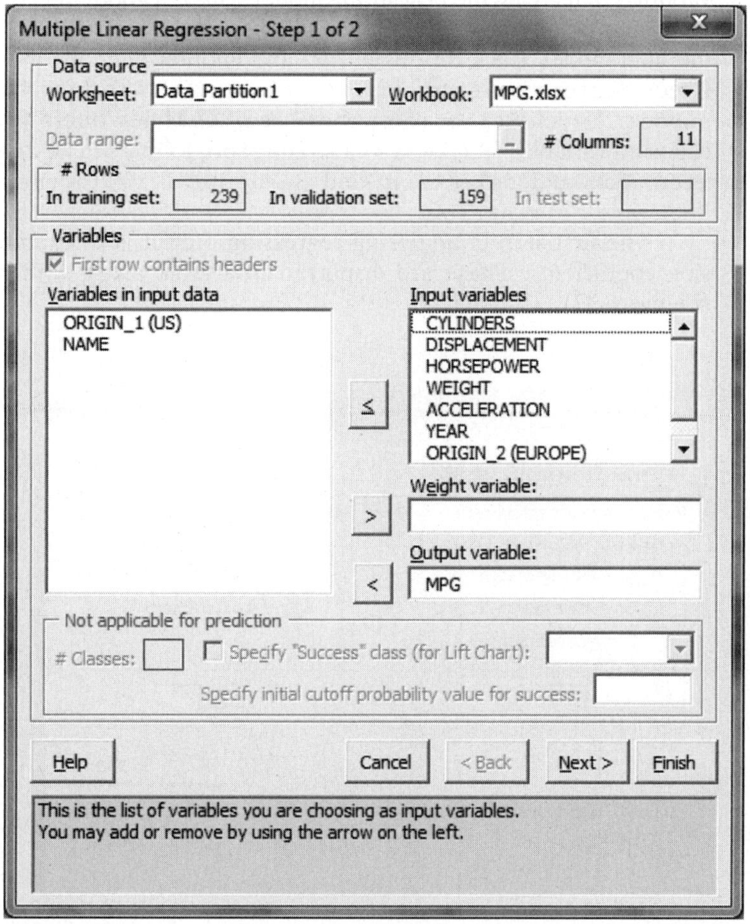

FIGURE 6.35 Second Multiple Linear Regression Window

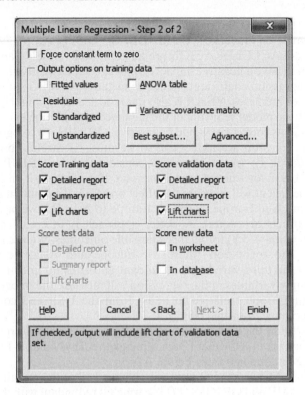

zero, we leave this box unchecked. This window also gives us options for how the results on the training data will be displayed. We choose to display all the scoring results for both the training and validation datasets.

The Best subset option in this window allows us to run the regression algorithm on subsets of the predictor variables. In each case the algorithm will attempt to choose those variables that create the best-fitting model. This is a good procedure to use when we have a large number of predictor variables and we suspect that many of them will not be useful in the final model. Click on this button and another window opens, shown in Figure 6.36. Check Perform best subset selection and choose 8 for the Maximum size of best subset. Under Selection procedure, XLMiner offers five different methods for choosing variables (Backward elimination, Exhaustive search, Stepwise selection, Forward selection, and Sequential replacement). Accept the default, Backward elimination.

The first step in analyzing regression output is to examine the estimated regression coefficients. These are displayed in a table along with their associated *p*-values (Figure 6.37).

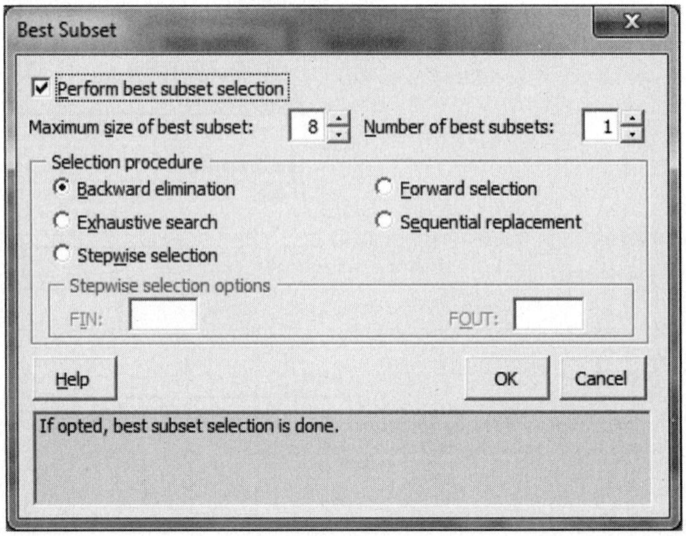

FIGURE 6.36 Best Subset Window for Linear Regression

FIGURE 6.37 Estimated Regression Coefficients and *p*-Values

The Regression Model

Input variables	Coefficient	Std. Error	p-value	SS
Constant term	-10.63756657	5.63866806	0.06048214	135269.7031
CYLINDERS	-0.87675035	0.38984695	0.02546228	9097.974609
DISPLACEMENT	0.02932786	0.01001434	0.00374738	615.5471191
HORSEPOWER	-0.03307875	0.01755075	0.06072474	239.9298706
WEIGHT	-0.00602707	0.00088837	0	479.6585083
ACCELERATION	0.02440948	0.12455896	0.84480882	2.32501674
YEAR	0.70097178	0.06264555	0	1316.237549
ORIGIN_2 (EUROPE)	2.70879459	0.69464511	0.00012651	24.82397842
ORIGIN_3 (ASIA)	3.59014463	0.6924535	0.00000047	280.2293396

The regression equation takes the following form when we substitute in the estimated parameters:

$$MPG = -10.64 - 0.88\,CYLINDERS + 0.03\,DISPLACEMENT - 0.03$$
$$HORSEPOWER - 0.01\,WEIGHT + 0.02\,ACCELERATION + 0.70\,YEAR$$
$$+ 2.71\,ORIGIN\_2(EUROPE) + 3.59\,ORIGIN\_3(ASIA)$$

Recall that a regression parameter measures the effect on the outcome variable of increasing the predictor variable by *one unit*. So the coefficient of –0.88 on CYLINDERS means that fuel efficiency decreases by 0.88 miles per gallon for every additional cylinder added to a vehicle. Likewise, the coefficient of –0.01 on WEIGHT means that fuel efficiency decreases by 0.01 miles per gallon for every increase of one pound of WEIGHT. To interpret these coefficients properly, it is important to keep in mind the units of the predictor variable. For example, we might be surprised at how small the effect of WEIGHT seems to be until we realize that 0.01 here means 0.01 miles *per pound*, so increasing the weight of a car by 100 pounds decreases fuel efficiency by 1 mile per gallon. Most of the regression coefficients are relatively small except for CYLINDERS and YEAR; increasing the model year by one year appears to increase fuel efficiency by 0.70 miles per gallon, or 7 miles per gallon each decade.

We expected the coefficients on the first five variables to be negative, but this is not the case for DISPLACEMENT and ACCELERATION. It is possible that our intuition is wrong about the effects of these factors, but we should also seriously question keeping predictor variables in the model when the regression coefficients have the opposite sign from what we expected. In this context it is useful to examine the *p*-values in the fourth column of Figure 6.37. Recall that *p*-values roughly measure the probability that the true regression coefficient is zero. The *p*-values in this regression are quite low (below 5 or 10 percent) except for ACCELERATION, whose *p*-value is 0.84. This is another indication, in addition to the unexpected sign of the coefficient, that we might want to consider eliminating this variable from the model.

The regression algorithm provides an estimate of how well the model fits the data in the form of the R^2 statistic. This measure reflects the percentage of the variability in the output variable that is accounted for by the regression equation (R^2 lies between 0 and 1). The higher the R^2 the better the model fits the data. The R^2 in this case is 0.83, indicating that the model accounts for 83 percent of the variability in MPG. There is no magic level for R^2 that indicates a good enough fit. After all, it is really the prediction accuracy on the validation data that measures how well the model performs. But R^2 can be used as a rough indication of which of two regression models is likely to perform better.

The predictive accuracy of the regression model is summarized in terms of the RMS error in the table shown in Figure 6.38 (for details on performance measures for prediction models, see Section 6.1.3). As we would expect, the error is somewhat higher on the validation data (3.50) than on the training data (3.17), but the difference is not dramatic. It is helpful to observe in this context that the average value of MPG in this database is 23.8, so this level of error is about 15 percent of the average value. For another perspective, we can use the information given in the Scoring worksheet, where the difference between the actual and predicted values is listed for every record, to calculate that the average

FIGURE 6.38 Regression Accuracy on Training and Validation Data

Training Data scoring - Summary Report

Total sum of squared errors	RMS Error	Average Error
2397.721649	3.167381909	-3.83544E-06

Validation Data scoring - Summary Report

Total sum of squared errors	RMS Error	Average Error
1946.325514	3.498719905	-0.597126923

absolute error is 2.40. The RMS error is higher than the average absolute error because it penalizes large errors relatively more than small ones.

The results of the best subset selection process are shown in Figure 6.39. Recall that we specified in setting up the algorithm that XLMiner should search for the best subsets of predictor variables, up to a limit of 8. The rows of this table report the results of those searches for 1 through 8 predictors (a constant is also included in each case). The ninth row of this table summarizes the results when the best 8 variables are included. When we compare this row to the one above, we see that the first variable to be excluded is ACCELERATION, which is not surprising given our previous conclusion that the sign of the coefficient for this variable is the opposite of what we would expect. The next variable to be eliminated as we scan the rows of this table is CYLINDERS, followed by DISPLACEMENT. At each stage we track the performance of the model by examining the R^2 value (in the fourth column of the table), which decreases as each variable is eliminated.

As we look at the R^2 values, we can see that the value associated with the best subset drops off very little from eight predictors ($R^2 = 0.83$) to two predictors ($R^2 = 0.81$), but drops off much more when only one predictor remains. Thus, the two-predictor subset, with YEAR and WEIGHT in the model, may capture most of the predictive capability we can provide based on this dataset.

6.6.3 Strengths and Weaknesses of Multiple Linear Regression

Multiple linear regression is a very well-known and accepted model for prediction. It is easy to implement and the resulting regression equation is easy to interpret. Under the assumptions of this approach, each of the regression coefficients measures the (constant) per unit impact of the corresponding predictor variable. Some analysts consider it a strength of the regression approach that inferential statistics (p-values and R^2) are available. However, within the context of a data mining approach, these measures provide only rough guidance. Certainly a regression model with a high R^2 but low predictive accuracy on validation data is not worthy of serious consideration.

A number of alternative approaches to prediction should be considered in addition to multiple linear regression. These include k-Nearest Neighbor, Prediction Trees, and

Best subset selection

	#Coefs	RSS	Cp	R-Squared	Adj-R Squared	Probability	Model(Constant present in all models) 1	2	3	4	5	6	7	8	9
Choose Subset	2	4294.993164	176.9946137	0.702860102	0.701606347	0	Constant	WEIGHT	*	*	*	*	*	*	*
Choose Subset	3	2740.752686	29.90504074	0.810368699	0.808780008	0.00002467	Constant	WEIGHT	YEAR	*	*	*	*	*	*
Choose Subset	4	2622.385986	20.55078697	0.818575845	0.816259792	0.0009032	Constant	WEIGHT	YEAR	ORIGN_3 (ASIA)	*	*	*	*	*
Choose Subset	5	2517.041504	12.44568062	0.825863878	0.822887192	0.02417886	Constant	WEIGHT	YEAR	ORIGN_2 (EUROPE)	IGN_3 (ASIA)	*	*	*	*
Choose Subset	6	2491.280029	11.97452736	0.82764613	0.823947549	0.03171313	Constant	HORSEPOWER	WEIGHT	YEAR	I_2 (EUROPE)	IGN_3 (ASIA)	*	*	*
Choose Subset	7	2451.044189	10.11492825	0.83042976	0.826044323	0.07968456	Constant	DISPLACEMENT	HORSEPOWER	WEIGHT	YEAR	I_2 (EUROPE)	IGN_3 (ASIA)	*	*
Choose Subset	8	2398.12207	7.03840637	0.834091064	0.82906352	0.84480196	Constant	CYLINDERS	DISPLACEMENT	HORSEPOWER	WEIGHT	YEAR	I_2 (EUROPE)	IGN_3 (ASIA)	*
Choose Subset	9	2397.72168	8.99999905	0.834118764	0.828349882	1	Constant	CYLINDERS	DISPLACEMENT	HORSEPOWER	WEIGHT	ACCELERATION	YEAR	I_2 (EUROPE)	IGN_3 (ASIA)

FIGURE 6.39 Best Subset Selection for Multiple Linear Regression

Neural Networks. Many data mining analysts build competing models using two or more distinct approaches and implement the one that is most effective.

6.7 LOGISTIC REGRESSION

Logistic regression, which is a statistical approach to the classification of categorical outcome variables, is very widely used in data mining. As the name implies, it is similar in many ways to multiple linear regression: it assumes a certain functional form for the relationship between the outcome and the predictor variables, and it uses the data to estimate the parameters of this relationship. Usually the outcome variable is binary, but logistic regression can also be used when the outcome has more than two values.

When the outcome variable is binary, it takes on two values that we can denote as Success/Failure, Yes/No, or 1/0, depending on the context. For example, we might wish to classify flights into those that will be delayed and those that will not, or classify companies into those that will default on their bonds and those that will not, or classify employees into those who will be promoted and those who will not.

The logistic regression model uses the data to produce a *probability* that a given case falls into one of these two classes. If we denote this probability by q, then the formula estimates

$$q = \text{Prob}(Y = 1) \tag{6.7}$$

where Y is the outcome variable. We then classify records as 1s when $q \geq 0.5$, and 0s when $q < 0.5$.

Probabilities like q, of course, are required to be between 0 and 1. This is why multiple linear regression cannot be used for the classification task: it can produce values that fall outside the acceptable range for probabilities. Logistic regression solves this problem, while preserving many of the benefits of multiple linear regression, by transforming the probability q into a form that can be estimated using a linear model.

6.7.1 Overview of Logistic Regression

To explain how logistic regression works, we begin with an example using one predictor variable. Assume we are attempting to predict which customers will default on their credit cards based on the size of their balances. The outcome variable is Y, which takes on the values 1 for default and 0 for no default. The predictor variable is X, which measures the size of their balance.

Our approach will be to transform the predictor value X for a specific customer into a probability q that the customer will default. Then, given q, we will classify that customer as $Y = 1$ or $Y = 0$ by comparing q to a cut-off probability that we choose. (The cut-off probability is usually 0.5; we will explain later why we sometimes use a higher or lower value.) The classification rule then is

$$\text{If } q \geq 0.5, Y = 1;$$

$$\text{if } q < 0.5, Y = 0.$$

As is usual in data mining, we fit our model to a training dataset and then test its classification accuracy on a validation dataset.

We pointed out above that we cannot use linear regression directly to calculate q, because there is no way to guarantee that a linear function of X such as $b_0 + b_1 X$ will produce a result between 0 and 1. But we can ensure this condition if we relate X to q in a nonlinear fashion. Logistic regression gets its name from the logistic curve, which is an S-shaped curve often used to model the growth of populations or the growth of market share for a new product. The logistic curve takes the form

$$q = 1/[1 + e^{(-b_0 - b_1 X)}] \tag{6.8}$$

FIGURE 6.40 Logistic
Function of One Variable

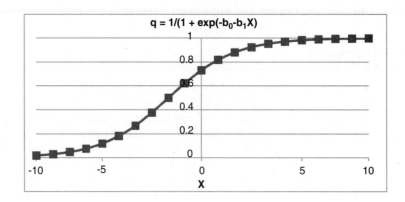

where the coefficients b_0 and b_1 are estimated from the data. Figure 6.40 shows a plot of this relationship for the parameters $b_0 = 1.0$ and $b_1 = 0.5$. Note that q falls between 0 and 1 regardless of the value of X.

Although the logistic function does accomplish our goal of generating an acceptable probability, the logistic regression algorithm actually uses an equivalent form based on *odds*, not probability. The odds of an event that occurs with probability q are simply $q/(1 - q)$. (This quantity is called the *odds in favor*, as opposed to the *odds against*, which are often quoted in gambling.) So, for example, if $q = 0.5$, the corresponding odds are

$$q/(1 - q) = 0.5/(1 - 0.5) = 0.5/0.5 = 1.0$$

Odds of 1.0 are usually stated as 1:1. Likewise, when $q = 0.1$, the odds of the event are $0.1/(1 - 0.1) = 0.1/0.9 = 1/9 = 1 : 9$. And when $q = 0.9$, the odds of the event are $0.9/(1 - 0.9) = 0.9/0.1 = 9/1 = 9 : 1$. Figure 6.41 shows how odds and probability are related.

An algebraically equivalent form of the logistic function is

$$\ln[q/(1 - q)] = -b_0 - b_1 X \qquad (6.9)$$

In this form, the natural logarithm of the odds is a linear function of the predictor X. This form of the relationship is the one used in the logistic regression algorithm. When we have multiple predictors $X_1, X_2, \ldots X_q$, the model takes the form

$$\ln[q/(1 - q)] = -b_0 - b_1 X_1 - b_2 X_2 - \ldots - b_q X_q \qquad (6.10)$$

As in multiple linear regression, we estimate the values of the regression coefficients $b_1, b_2, \ldots, b_q$ using training data, and we assess the classification accuracy of the model on validation data.

FIGURE 6.41 Odds and
Probability

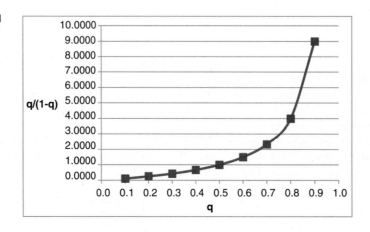

6.7.2 An Application of Logistic Regression

We illustrate the application of the logistic regression approach using a database with 27 variables and 132 records on the financial condition of banks, some of which have declared bankruptcy (*Bankruptcy.xlsx*)*. The outcome variable is DECLARED, which takes on the value 1 when the bank has declared bankruptcy and 0 otherwise. The task is to use this database to create a method for predicting bankruptcy among banks. The variables in the database are described in the following table:

Variable	Description
NO	ID number
DECLARED	1: declared bankruptcy; 0 otherwise
YR	year of bankruptcy
R1	CASH/CURDEBT
R2	CASH/SALES
R3	CASH/ASSETS
R4	CASH/DEBTS
R5	CFFO/SALES
R6	CFFO/ASSETS
R7	CFFO/DEBTS
R8	COGS/INV
R9	CURASS/CURBEDT
R10	CURASS/SALES
R11	CURASS/ASSETS
R12	CURDEBT/DEBTS
R13	INC/SALES
R14	INC/ASSETS
R15	INC/DEBTS
R16	UBCDEP/SALES
R17	INCDEP/ASSETS
R18	INCDEP/DEBTS
R19	SALES/REC
R20	SALES/ASSETS
R21	ASSETS/DEBTS
R22	WCFO/SALES
R23	WCFO/ASSETS
R24	WCFO/DEBTS

The first step is to partition the database into 79 training records and 53 validation records (using the Standard Partition utility in XLMiner). We then select the logistic regression algorithm for classification: Data Mining▶Classify▶Logistic Regression. This brings up the window shown in Figure 6.42.

We identify the Output variable as Declared, and move all the other relevant variables into the Input variables category (excluding the irrelevant variables ID and YR). We also confirm that there are two classes for the output variable, "Success" is a 1 (representing good credit), and the probability cutoff for the classification rule is 0.5.

When we click on OK, a second window appears, shown in Figure 6.43.

We ignore the options in this window except for Best subset. We click on this button and another window opens, shown in Figure 6.44. We check Perform best subset selection and choose 10 for the Maximum size of best subset. Under this option the logistic regression algorithm runs on subsets of the predictor variables. This is a good procedure to use when we have a large number of predictor variables and we suspect that many of them will not be useful in the final model. Under Selection procedure XLMiner offers five different methods for choosing variables; we accept the default Backward elimination. Under this method, a logistic regression model will be created with a constant and the best 10 predictors. Then predictors are eliminated from

* Source: University of Virginia Darden School Foundation, 1988. Cited in Shmueli, G., N. R. Patel, and P. C. Bruce. 2010. *Data Mining for Business Intelligence*. New Jersey: John Wiley & Sons, page 390.

FIGURE 6.42 First Logistic Regression Window

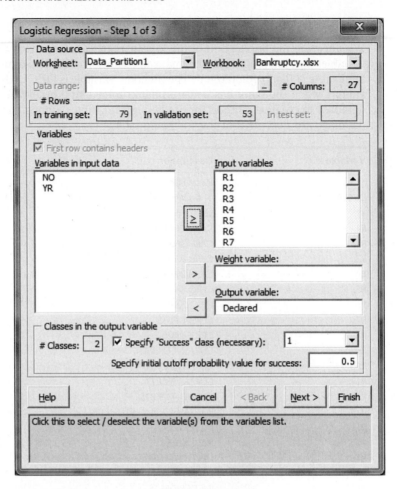

FIGURE 6.43 Second Logistic Regression Window

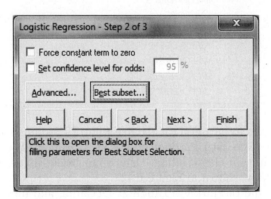

FIGURE 6.44 Best Subset Window for Logistic Regression

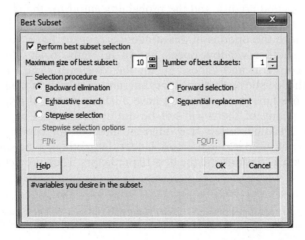

FIGURE 6.45 Third
Logistic Regression
Window

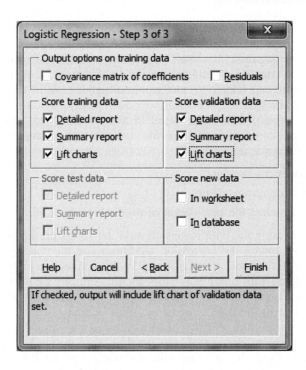

the model one by one. The eliminated predictors are those that contribute the least to the fit (R^2) of the model to the data.

We click OK and the final window opens, allowing us to select the level of detail in the output for both the training and validation partitions (Figure 6.45).

To assess the results of this procedure, we first examine the estimated regression coefficients b_i. These are displayed in a table along with their standard errors, p-values, and odds (Figure 6.46).

We begin by evaluating the sign and magnitude of each of these coefficients and testing them against our intuition and knowledge of the application area. For *continuous* predictor variables, a positive coefficient means that a higher value for the variable

FIGURE 6.46 Logistic
Regression Output

Input variables	Coefficient	Std. Error	p-value	Odds
Constant term	0.94022244	11.45125103	0.93456203	*
R1	-72.5627213	43.50226974	0.09531145	0
R2	239.3921661	147.3618164	0.10426495	*
R3	-248.003448	140.2663422	0.07704595	0
R4	152.2921753	84.22820282	0.07059248	*
R5	62.8237648	38.32469559	0.10116117	1.92316E+27
R6	-239.699112	132.5966187	0.07064826	0
R7	97.11029053	72.98288727	0.18332401	*
R8	0.20126833	0.11925387	0.0914631	1.22295284
R9	3.16049457	12.9766655	0.80757773	23.58225441
R10	-52.4358826	39.23118591	0.18135756	0
R11	31.32620811	38.54645538	0.41639748	4.02531E+13
R12	-42.6215744	35.76930618	0.2334305	0
R13	184.1763458	194.9337006	0.34475318	*
R14	-1117.86804	617.1432495	0.07008529	0
R15	596.4025269	339.3278198	0.07881561	*
R16	-219.07251	158.6295929	0.1672692	0
R17	60.28596497	204.8086243	0.76848841	1.52007E+26
R18	211.1898956	200.7417908	0.29277778	*
R19	-0.05616639	0.04893949	0.2511048	0.94538182
R20	0.23155816	2.3573463	0.92175102	1.26056266
R21	6.15925217	13.79048634	0.65514183	473.0740967
R22	88.58720398	113.0458527	0.43325165	*
R23	565.6481934	309.3605652	0.06748305	*
R24	-425.693054	287.3888245	0.13854149	0

indicates a higher probability that $Y = 1$, and vice versa; a negative coefficient means that a higher value for the variable indicates a lower probability that $Y = 1$, and vice versa. For *binary categorical* predictor variables, a positive coefficient means a higher probability when $X = 1$ versus $X = 0$, and vice versa. In this case, we might question the positive coefficient on R8: COGS/INV: why would a higher Cost of Good Sold have a *positive* impact on good credit?

As we explained in more detail in Section 6.5, there are three complementary approaches to selecting predictors for a regression model, whether multiple linear regression or logistic regression:

- pre-processing the data
- use of inferential statistics
- search to select the best subset of predictors

Pre-processing the data means considering which predictor variables to use in the model *before* running the regression algorithm and eliminating any that do not prove acceptable. Variables that do not have a plausible connection to the output or ones that are highly correlated with other predictors should certainly be excluded. We also consider eliminating variables that are measured inaccurately, contain many missing values, or will not be available at the time a prediction must be made.

Use of inferential statistics means eliminating variables whose *p*-values exceed a cutoff, usually 5 or 10 percent. The *p*-values are listed in the fourth column of Figure 6.46. Note, for example, that the estimated coefficient for R9: CURASS/CURDEBT is 3.16, with a *p*-value of 0.81. This value indicates that the probability in repeated sampling is 81 percent that the true coefficient for this variable is zero. At the very least we can conclude that the true coefficient could be either positive or negative, and the case for including it in a final model is weak.

The third approach to selecting predictors, searching for the best subset, takes us to another portion of the XLMiner output, shown in Figure 6.47.

When we set up the algorithm, we specified that XLMiner should search for the best subsets of predictor variables, up to a limit of 10. The nine rows of this table report the results of those searches for 1 through 10 predictors (a constant is included in each case). To interpret this table we can start in the last row: this row shows the 10 variables that together fit the data best. As we move up a row, we see which variable among these 10 was eliminated as contributing the least to a good fit (R14). Four variables consistently appear among these alternative models: R5, R6, R11, and R12. These four probably belong in any model with a small number of predictors.

In multiple linear regression, the regression coefficients b_i have a convenient interpretation as the (constant) incremental impact of the corresponding predictor variable on the outcome variable. The same is *not* true in logistic regression, because the model is not linear. In logistic regression, the *odds* of the outcome $Y = 1$ change by the constant *factor* e^{bi} when the predictor X_i changes by 1. (For categorical variables, when X_i changes from 0 to 1 the odds of $Y = 1$ go up by the factor e^{bi}.) This factor is reported in the last column of Figure 6.46 (under the confusing heading "Odds"). So, in our example, the value of e^{bi} for the R8 variable is 1.22, which indicates that the odds increase by 22 percent for every increase of one unit in the ratio COGS/INV. The value of e^{bi} for R19 is 0.95, indicating that the odds decrease by 5 percent as the ratio SALES/REC increases by one unit.

Best subset selection

	#Coeffs	RSS	Cp	Probability	1	2	3	4	5	6	7	8	9	10	11
					Model (Constant present in all models)										
Choose Subset	2	61.88358307	-11.948802	0.99305761	Constant	R2	*	*	*	*	*	*	*	*	*
Choose Subset	3	61.65716171	-10.1794958	0.99092835	Constant	R2	R5	*	*	*	*	*	*	*	*
Choose Subset	4	61.31307983	-8.53006935	0.98914176	Constant	R5	R6	R11	*	*	*	*	*	*	*
Choose Subset	5	60.57032776	-7.28683567	0.99044251	Constant	R5	R6	R11	R12	*	*	*	*	*	*
Choose Subset	6	60.46712112	-5.39198971	0.98611212	Constant	R5	R6	R11	R12	R23	*	*	*	*	*
Choose Subset	7	60.0524025	-3.81453323	0.98415732	Constant	R5	R6	R11	R12	R16	R23	*	*	*	*
Choose Subset	8	59.25661087	-2.62533975	0.98676395	Constant	R5	R6	R11	R12	R14	R16	R23	*	*	*
Choose Subset	9	59.07365799	-0.81174457	0.98163474	Constant	R2	R5	R6	R11	R12	R14	R16	R23	*	*
Choose Subset	10	58.80073547	0.91018343	0.97635508	Constant	R1	R2	R5	R6	R11	R12	R14	R16	R23	*
Choose Subset	11	58.54005051	2.64457989	0.96920836	Constant	R1	R2	R5	R6	R8	R11	R12	R14	R16	R23

FIGURE 6.47 Best Subset Selection for Logistic Regression

FIGURE 6.48 Classification Matrices for Logistic Regression

Training Data scoring - Summary Report

Cut off Prob.Val. for Success (Updatable)	0.5

Classification Confusion Matrix		
	Predicted Class	
Actual Class	1	0
1	36	1
0	1	41

Error Report			
Class	# Cases	# Errors	% Error
1	37	1	2.70
0	42	1	2.38
Overall	79	2	2.53

Validation Data scoring - Summary Report

Cut off Prob.Val. for Success (Updatable)	0.5

Classification Confusion Matrix		
	Predicted Class	
Actual Class	1	0
1	20	9
0	9	15

Error Report			
Class	# Cases	# Errors	% Error
1	29	9	31.03
0	24	9	37.50
Overall	53	18	33.96

The classification matrices for the logistic regression model are shown in Figure 6.48 for both the training and validation partitions. Among the 79 records in the training data set this model makes 2 classification errors for an overall error rate of 2.5 percent. Among the 53 records in the validation dataset it misclassifies 18 records, for an error rate of 34.0 percent. As usual, the model performs less well on the validation data than on the training data, but in this case the difference is dramatic. This is a model that is extremely over-fit to the training data and performs relatively poorly on the validation data.

The lift charts for the validation partition are shown in Figure 6.49. The decile-wise lift chart shows that the logistic regression model improves predictive accuracy by a factor of about 1.7 over the average accuracy on the top 10 percent of records.

An additional sign of an over-fit model is the large number of coefficients with high p-values (none of the coefficients have p-values below the traditional cut-off of 0.05). We should not be surprised by this because many of the variables in the database involve identical accounting measures (such as Sales, Assets, and Debts). This suggests that some of the variables may be highly correlated; for example, the correlation between CURASS/DEBT and ASSETS/DEBTS is 76 percent. An alternative model with only nine predictor variables (chosen to be relatively uncorrelated with each other) has a much higher error rate on the training data (17.7 percent) but a much lower error rate on the validation data (17.0 percent). This is likely to be a much better model for making predictions.

6.7.3 Strengths and Weaknesses of Logistic Regression

Logistic regression is a well-known and widely used technique, especially in marketing. It is easy to implement and fairly straightforward to interpret, although a facility with the concept of odds is necessary. When the data include a large number of predictor variables,

FIGURE 6.49 Lift Charts for Logistic Regression

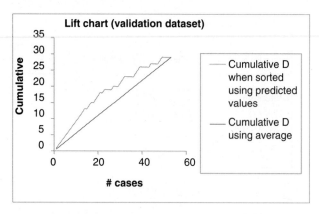

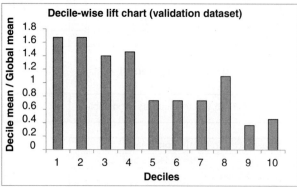

it is necessary to reduce them to the most important ones using a combination of pre-processing, inferential statistics, and best subset selection.

Several approaches to classification should be considered in addition to logistic regression. These include *k*-Nearest Neighbor, Naïve Bayes, Classification Trees, and Neural Networks. Many data mining analysts build competing models using two or more distinct approaches and implement the most effective one.

6.8 NEURAL NETWORKS

Neural networks are an outgrowth of research within artificial intelligence into how the brain works. The brain is composed of complex networks of interconnected neurons. Each neuron is connected to a number of other neurons that send electrical impulses (or signals) into it, and it in turn sends electrical impulses out to a number of other neurons. Just how a neuron transforms the input signals into an output signal is not fully understood, but a type of learning called *reinforcement learning* seems to be involved. Reinforcement learning occurs over time when the learner takes in information and alters its internal state based on the difference between its actual output and its desired output. One can imagine learning to ride a bicycle as a process of reinforcement learning. After all, we don't learn to ride by listening to lectures or reading a book. We learn to ride by getting on a bicycle, straying too far to the left and trying various corrective actions until we regain the proper heading, then straying too far to the right and repeating the process. Over time, through this reinforcement process, our minds and bodies learn to ride. This is more or less how a neural network learns to perform its task.

Neural networks can be used for classification and for prediction. They accept as inputs both continuous and ordinal variables. Both multiple linear regression models and logistic regression models have the structure of simple neural networks, although the optimization algorithms used to estimate the parameters in those models are quite different from the learning algorithms used in neural networks.

Neural networks have been applied in an extremely wide variety of areas, ranging from financial applications to controlling robots. Within finance, they have been used to predict the bankruptcy of firms; to trade on currency, stock or bond markets; and to predict credit card fraud. Neural network models have a reputation for being complex and difficult to understand intuitively, but also for providing high predictive accuracy.

6.8.1 Overview of Neural Networks

A neural network has three components: a network structure, a set of input-output parameters, and a learning algorithm. The network structure is equivalent to the model in other data mining approaches. The network consists of **nodes**, which are analogous to neurons. At each node, a set of parameters governs how the node translates input data into an output to the next nodes in the network. Finally, a variety of learning algorithms can be used in neural networks. These algorithms use the data on the outcome variable and the predictor variables to determine the input-output parameters through a process similar to reinforcement learning. The only choice the modeler has to make is the network structure; once that is determined, the algorithm does the rest.

An example will make this clearer. Consider a college that is trying to determine which of its prospective incoming students will ultimately graduate. It has data on the high school GPA and Test Scores of a number of students, and on whether they graduated. Figure 6.50 shows a typical neural network structure for this situation. Nodes 1 and 2 are *input nodes*: they take in the data on the two predictor variables GPA and Test Scores for a particular student. Node 6 is the *output node*: it produces the output probability from which we will make the classification of the student as Graduating or Not Graduating. Nodes 3, 4, and 5 are *hidden layer nodes* that stand between the input and output nodes and transform the input values into the output value.

All neural networks have input, hidden, and output nodes. There must be one input node for each predictor variable and one output node for classification of a variable with two values. In between we can have any number of hidden layers, each of which can contain any number of nodes. However, simple networks with one hidden layer work quite well in many applications. (XLMiner includes an option to test models with varying numbers of layers and nodes.)

As we have said, each node in a neural network takes in input numbers from all upstream nodes that are connected to it, transforms that data into an output value, and sends the output to every downstream node it is connected to. For example, node 4 in Figure 6.50 takes in data from nodes 1 and 2 and sends its output to node 6. Each node has two sets of associated parameters: a *bias (θ) and weights ($w_1, w_2, \ldots$)*. The bias is a single number, whereas there is one weight for each input node (see Figure 6.51). The output is computed using the logistic function

$$y = 1/[1 + e^{(-\theta - w_1 X_1 - w_2 X_2 - \ldots - w_q X_q)}] \quad (6.11)$$

FIGURE 6.50 Simple Neural Network

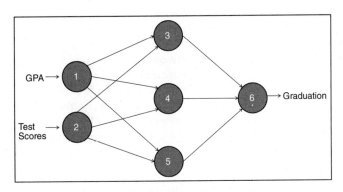

FIGURE 6.51 Computation of Output at a Node

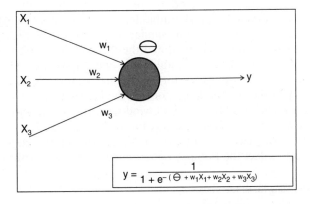

$$y = \frac{1}{1 + e^{-(\theta + w_1 X_1 + w_2 X_2 + w_3 X_3)}}$$

In this formula, the X_i are the inputs from upstream nodes, the parameters w_i and θ are determined from the data, and the output y is the value sent to downstream nodes. In most neural networks, the raw predictor variables are normalized to the range from 0 to 1. The logistic function then ensures that the output y of each node in the network remains between 0 and 1.

Many different types of learning algorithms can be used in neural networks to determine the parameters θ and w_i at each node. We describe here the method of *back propagation* used in XLMiner. The first step in determining the parameters is to pick initial values. These are randomly selected between -0.5 and $+0.5$. Next, each record is run through the network to determine the output value for these initial parameter values. When the output is in error, that is, when the network predicts $Y = 1$ for a record for which $Y = 0$ (or vice versa), the values of the parameters are adjusted to better match the correct output. This process is repeated for all of the records in the training dataset, which is referred to as one *epoch*. The training process then continues over a number of epochs chosen by the user. Training stops when the weights are no longer changing significantly, or when the misclassification rate is acceptable, or when the maximum number of epochs has been reached. Once the training has been completed, the final network is used on the validation data to assess its classification accuracy.

6.8.2 An Application of Neural Networks

We illustrate the application of neural networks using a database with 16 variables and 4,985 records on the effectiveness of a direct mail campaign to sell wireless phone service (*EastWest.xlsx*)[*]. The outcome variable is PHONESALE, which takes on the value 1 when a customer agrees to buy a phone contract, and 0 otherwise. The task is to use this database to develop a method for classifying new customers by whether they will purchase or not. The variables in the database are described in the following table:

Variable	Description
ID#	unique identifier
Topflight	indicates whether flyer is Topflight (1) or not (0)
Balance	miles eligible for award travel
Qual_miles	miles qualifying for Topflight
cc1_miles	has member used frequent flyer card (1 = Yes, 0 = No)
cc2_miles	has member used Rewards card (1 = Yes, 0 = No)
cc3_miles	has member used Business card (1 = Yes, 0 = No)
Bonus_miles	miles earned from bonus
Bonus_trans	number of bonus transactions
Flight_miles_12mo	number of flight miles last 12 months
Flight_trans_12	number of flight transactions last 12 months
Online_12	online purchases last 12 months
Email	email address on file (1 = Yes, 0 = No)
Club_member	airline club member (1 = Yes, 0 = No)
Any_cc_miles_12mo	added miles on any credit card (1 = Yes, 0 = No)
PHONESALE	purchased in response to direct mail campaign

The first step is to partition the database into 60 percent (2,991) training records and 40 percent (1,994) validation records (using the Standard Partition utility in XLMiner). We then select the neural network algorithm for classification: Data Mining▶Classify▶Neural Network. This brings up a window similar to that shown in Figure 6.52.

In this window we have identified the Output variable as PHONE SALE, and moved all the other relevant variables into the Input variables category. We also confirm that there are two classes for the output variable, "Success" is a 1 (representing a phone sale), and the probability cutoff for the classification rule is 0.5.

When we click on OK a second window appears, shown in Figure 6.53.

In this window we check the box for Normalize input data, so all the predictor variables are normalized to fall between 0 and 1 (for more details see Chapter 5, Section A.5.5). We also select the Manual option under Network architecture, and choose a

[*] Source: Resampling Stats, Inc. 2005.

FIGURE 6.52   First
Neural Network Window

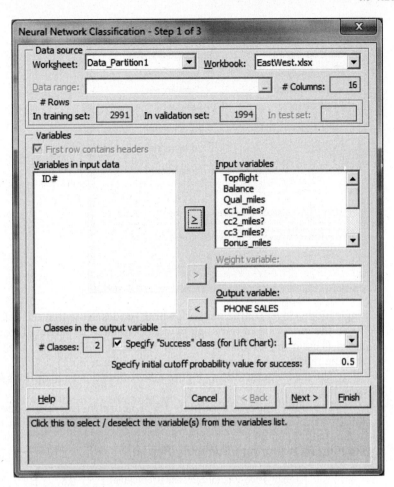

FIGURE 6.53   Second
Neural Network Window

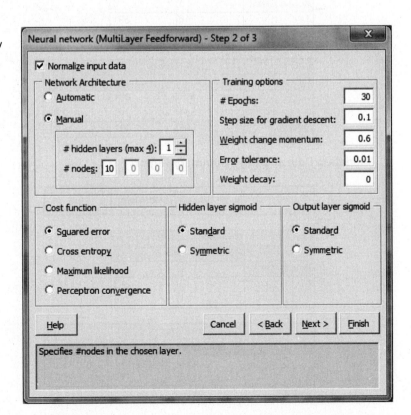

FIGURE 6.54 Third Neural Network Window

single hidden layer for the network with 10 nodes. Note that the default number of epochs is 30, so the input-output parameters will be updated by passing through the training data 30 times. (Under the `Automatic` option, XLMiner searches over the number of hidden layers and the number of nodes for models that perform well.)

The final input window (Figure 6.54) offers the usual options for displaying details for both training and validation data.

The most important outputs for a neural network are the classification matrices for the training and validation partitions. Figure 6.55 shows that the overall error rate is

FIGURE 6.55 Classification Matrices for Neural Network

Training Data scoring - Summary Report

Cut off Prob.Val. for Success (Updatable)	0.5

Classification Confusion Matrix		
	Predicted Class	
Actual Class	1	0
1	16	391
0	10	2574

Error Report			
Class	**# Cases**	**# Errors**	**% Error**
1	407	391	96.07
0	2584	10	0.39
Overall	2991	401	13.41

Validation Data scoring - Summary Report

Cut off Prob.Val. for Success (Updatable)	0.5

Classification Confusion Matrix		
	Predicted Class	
Actual Class	1	0
1	5	243
0	11	1735

Error Report			
Class	**# Cases**	**# Errors**	**% Error**
1	248	243	97.98
0	1746	11	0.63
Overall	1994	254	12.74

FIGURE 6.56 Lift Charts for Neural Network

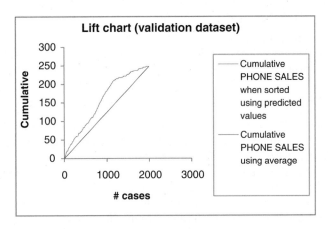

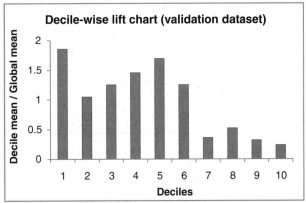

13.4 percent on the training data and 12.7 percent on the validation data. The great majority of errors in both cases are actual 1s classified as 0s. This may indicate that the neural network is setting too high a cutoff for classifying cases, and that lowering the cutoff might improve the performance of the model.

The lift charts for the validation dataset are shown in Figure 6.56. The decile-wise lift chart shows that the neural network performs about 70 percent better than the average classification on the top 10 percent of the cases.

We commented earlier that neural networks can appear to be complex and hard to understand intuitively. One contributing factor is that it is difficult to relate the network structure to any specific features of the problem itself, and the input-output parameters are not easy to interpret. These parameters are reported in the model output, as shown in Figure 6.57. Here the top table shows the weights at the hidden layer nodes. So the value of −1.27 in the first cell represents the weight on the first input variable (Topflight) at Node 1 (in the hidden layer). The values in the bottom table represent the weights on the output

Inter-layer connections weights

Hidden Layer # 1	Input Layer														
	Topflight	Balance	Qual_miles	cc1_miles?	cc2_miles?	cc3_miles?	Bonus_miles	Bonus_trans	Flight_miles_12mo	Flight_trans_12	Online_12	Email	Club_member	Any_cc_miles_12mo	Bias Node
Node # 1	-1.26888	-0.521952	-0.500775	0.0504865	-0.960643	0.19123	0.471247	0.230036	-0.605145	-0.00310082	-0.381642	0.898314	-1.02632	-0.557609	-0.71998
Node # 2	-0.415826	0.281331	-0.132404	0.224407	-0.274082	0.175251	0.257998	-0.245295	-0.207111	-0.0428865	-0.570688	0.115005	-0.798496	-0.182563	-0.599523
Node # 3	-0.606482	-0.346143	-0.428211	0.239136	-0.341649	0.0391274	0.433343	-0.248349	-0.0533675	-0.0131345	-0.0706507	-0.291621	-0.761374	-0.19301	-0.752636
Node # 4	2.83627	2.18589	0.386613	-0.57445	0.660958	-0.184517	-1.90795	-1.59632	-0.16358	-0.162792	-1.24851	0.048337	0.0220563	-1.01026	-0.373526
Node # 5	-0.216231	0.221634	-0.0598451	0.046953	-0.0505927	-0.216557	-0.0534339	-0.271672	-0.283615	0.130407	0.261381	-0.281946	-0.252978	-0.227955	-0.643868
Node # 6	-0.474873	0.322736	0.259249	0.38886	-0.00959488	0.14296	-0.807199	-0.0847936	0.35581	0.0452288	-0.206198	-0.673137	0.555938	-0.268357	-0.935843
Node # 7	-0.338404	0.597929	0.341455	0.139753	0.00729393	0.148224	-1.04514	-0.0212707	-0.13685	0.170048	-0.33268	-0.503064	0.796175	-0.22694	-0.965298
Node # 8	0.0229727	0.594877	0.066968	0.266679	0.0582912	-0.322123	-0.282886	-0.453696	0.0578073	-0.107503	0.293959	-0.23851	-0.207362	-0.00656528	-0.64518
Node # 9	-0.531628	-0.18146	-0.215265	0.222575	-0.223252	0.166299	0.235117	-0.0971159	-0.0282929	-0.105447	-0.380705	-0.0727286	-0.451626	-0.328063	-0.864976
Node # 10	-0.131846	0.215764	-0.0758814	0.115726	-0.030707	-0.0278689	-0.0853493	-0.165909	-0.174273	0.00647592	-0.0447191	-0.347186	-0.180851	-0.200236	-0.630423

Output Layer	Hidden Layer # 1										
	Node # 1	Node # 2	Node # 3	Node # 4	Node # 5	Node # 6	Node # 7	Node # 8	Node # 9	Node # 10	Bias Node
1	-0.911189	-0.117039	-0.280877	-1.54116	-0.168917	-0.321988	-0.442434	-0.145818	-0.124954	-0.0566348	0.345543
0	0.902308	0.136452	0.266758	1.54274	0.170604	0.325626	0.450494	0.162422	0.16118	0.0052299	-0.348467

FIGURE 6.57 Input-output Parameters for Neural Network

node for each hidden layer node. Thus the first entry of –0.91 represents the weight of Node 1 in the output.

Because neural networks are difficult to interpret, their value lies entirely in their predictive power.

6.8.3 Strengths and Weaknesses of Neural Networks

Neural networks have been highly successful in a number of applications and have been unsuccessful in many more. Their advantage is that they are very flexible because the fundamental structure of the model (the number of hidden layers and nodes) is chosen by the user. Thus they can capture complex relationships between the inputs and the outputs (much more so than linear regression, for example). However, this approach has several disadvantages. The models are difficult to interpret, and therefore hard to justify to skeptics. They also provide limited insight into the underlying relationships. Further, there is no mechanism within this algorithm for choosing the best predictor variables, so the modeler must carefully pre-process predictor variables and in many cases experiment with different sets of predictors to see which offers the most effective model.

For the classification task, alternative algorithms to neural networks include *k*-Nearest Neighbor, Naïve Bayes, Classification Trees, and Logistic Regression. For prediction, we can consider Prediction Trees or Multiple Linear Regression.

6.9 SUMMARY

In this chapter we presented a variety of methods for building models from large databases for classifying cases or making numerical predictions. Classification methods apply when the task is to predict which class an individual record will occupy, for example, *whether* a customer will buy a certain product. Prediction methods apply when the task is to predict a numerical outcome for an individual record, for example, *how much* a customer will buy.

We presented the following six methods in this chapter:

- *k*-Nearest Neighbor
- Naïve Bayes
- Classification and Prediction Trees
- Multiple Linear Regression
- Logistic Regression
- Neural Networks

For each of these methods we provided an intuitive overview of the approach, followed by an example of how the method is applied using XLMiner. Many of these methods can be applied to the same situation, and it is quite common for analysts to construct models using competing methods and then select the most effective one.

SUGGESTED READINGS

Many of the topics introduced in this chapter are covered in more detail and at a higher level of mathematical sophistication in the following book:

Shmueli, G., N. R. Patel, and P. C. Bruce. 2010. *Data Mining for Business Intelligence*. New Jersey: John Wiley & Sons.

The following book is one of the bibles in this area, with extensive coverage of a wide variety of methods and descriptions of numerous applications:

Nisbet, R., J. Elder, and G. Miner. 2009. *Handbook of Statistical Analysis and Data Mining Applications*. London: Elsevier.

WEKA is an open-source software platform on the Web for data mining. As such, it does not require that the analyst have access to any particular software product. The following book is a useful guide to data mining in general and WEKA in particular:

Witten, I. H., E. Frank, and M. A. Hall. *Data Mining: Practical Machine Learning Tools and Techniques*. Massachusetts: Elsevier.

EXERCISES

In each of the following exercises, the goal is to develop a classification or prediction model for the given situation and data. Follow these steps:

1. Examine the data descriptions and explore the data.

2. Clean the data as needed.

3. Transform the data as needed (e.g., create dummy variables for categorical variables).

4. Partition the data.

5. Run the specified algorithm.

6. Interpret the results and choose the best model (e.g., choose the best *k* in the *k*-Nearest Neighbor method).

1. *K*-NEAREST NEIGHBORS—CLASSIFICATION

The database *Low Birth Weight.xlsx*[*] consists of data on 189 women, 59 of whom had low-birth-weight babies. The data provided include basic demographic information (e.g., age of mother) as well as detailed information on the mother's behavior prior to the birth (e.g., smoking status). The goal is to create a *k*-Nearest Neighbor model to classify births as low risk.

[*]Source: University of Massachusetts Statistical Software Information (http://www.umass.edu/statdata/statdata/index.html).

2. *K*-NEAREST NEIGHBORS—PREDICTION

The database *Forest Fires.xlsx*[*] contains information on the weather and ground conditions before the start of a number of forest fires. The goal is to create a *k*-Nearest Neighbor model to predict the size of a forest fire.

3. NAÏVE BAYES—CLASSIFICATION

The database *Bank Marketing.xlsx*[**] contains information on the results of a direct marketing campaign by a Portuguese bank. The purpose of the campaign was to enroll customers in a bank term deposit account. The data include demographic information (e.g., marital status) as well as financial information (e.g., size of balance). The goal is to create a Naïve Bayes model to determine which customers will enroll.

4. NAÏVE BAYES—CLASSIFICATION

The database *Spambase.xlsx*[**] contains detailed information on the words used in a large number of emails. The emails are classified as Spam or Not Spam. The goal is to create a Naïve Bayes model to determine whether individual emails are spam or not.

5. CLASSIFICATION AND PREDICTION TREES—CLASSIFICATION

The database *Boston Housing.xlsx*[**] contains information on 506 census tracts around the city of Boston. The data include housing-related information (e.g., average rooms per dwelling) as well as demographic information (e.g., per capita crime rate). The goal is to create a Classification Tree model to predict which census tracts have a median home price above $30,000.

6. CLASSIFICATION AND PREDICTION TREES—PREDICTION

The database *Automobile Losses.xlsx*[**] contains information on the average loss payment per insured year for a number of makes and models of cars. It also contains data on the physical characteristics of the vehicles (e.g., weight) and the price. The goal is to create a Prediction Tree model to predict the loss payment on a vehicle.

7. MULTIPLE LINEAR REGRESSION—PREDICTION

The database *Wine Quality.xlsx*[**] contains data on the chemical properties of nearly 5,000 wines. It also has a quality score for each wine that is based on the opinions of experts. The goal is to create a Multiple Linear Regression model which predicts the quality score.

8. MULTIPLE LINEAR REGRESSION—PREDICTION

The database *Airfares.xlsx*[***] contains information on the airfare on 638 routes in the United States. In addition, it contains data on the length of the route, the average income in the starting and ending cities, whether Southwest Airlines flies on the route, and other variables. The goal is to create a Multiple Linear Regression model which predicts the airfare along a given route.

9. LOGISTIC REGRESSION—CLASSIFICATION

The database *ICU Data.xlsx*[†] contains information on 200 subjects from a much larger study of the survival of patients admitted to an intensive care unit (ICU) of a hospital. The data provided include basic demographic information (e.g., age and sex) as well as detailed medical data (e.g., blood gas measurements). The goal is to create a Logistic Regression model to determine which patients admitted to the ICU will live.

10. LOGISTIC REGRESSION—CLASSIFICATION

The database *German Credit.xlsx*[**] contains information on the credit risk of 1,000 customers. The data include demographic information (e.g., gender) and financial information (e.g., savings account balance). The goal is to create a Logistic Regression model to classify customers by credit risk.

11. NEURAL NETWORKS—CLASSIFICATION

The database *Credit Approval.xlsx*[**] contains information on a large number of individuals who have applied for credit cards, including whether they were approved. The data include demographic data (e.g., age) and financial data (e.g., income). The goal is to create a Neural Network model to classify applicants by credit worthiness.

12. NEURAL NETWORKS—CLASSIFICATION

The database *Voting Records.xlsx*[**] contains data on the voting records for 435 members of the U.S. House of Representatives on 16 important pieces of legislation. The goal is to create a Neural Network model to classify members by party (Republican or Democrat).

[*]Source: UCI Machine Learning Repository (http://archive.ics.uci.edu/ml).
Citation: P. Cortez and A. Morais. "A Data Mining Approach to Predict Forest Fires using Meteorological Data." In J. Neves, M. F. Santos and J. Machado Eds., New Trends in Artificial Intelligence, Proceedings of the 13th EPIA 2007—Portuguese Conference on Artificial Intelligence, December, Guimaraes, Portugal, pp. 512-523, 2007. APPIA, ISBN-13 978-989-95618-0-9. Available at: http://www.dsi.uminho.pt/~pcortez/fires.pdf.
[**]Source: UCI Machine Learning Repository (http://archive.ics.uci.edu/ml).
[***]Source: Shmueli, G., N. R. Patel, and P. C. Bruce. 2010. Data Mining for Business Intelligence. New Jersey: John Wiley & Sons, page 134.
[†]Source: University of Massachusetts Statistical Software Information (http://www.umass.edu/statdata/statdata/index.html).

7 Short-Term Forecasting

7.1 INTRODUCTION

The physicist Nils Bohr once quipped, "Prediction is very difficult, especially about the future." While prediction, or forecasting, is always difficult, some kinds are more difficult than others. Long-term forecasting is the most difficult because information is limited, competing trends exist, and many variables can influence future outcomes. An example would be forecasting the development of new technologies. A decade ago, could we have developed good forecasts for the sales of cholesterol-reducing drugs? Or the demand for downloadable music? Or the uses for geographic information systems? Forecasting those phenomena at that early stage would certainly have been challenging.

Short-term forecasting is another matter. Predicting the volume of activity in an established market is relatively manageable when we have access to good records based on recent observations. For example, what if we want to predict how much gas we'll use in our car next month? Or the interest rate on 6-month CDs next week at our local bank? Or the number of callers requesting maintenance service on their kitchen appliances tomorrow? When quantities such as these play the role of input parameters in our models, the task becomes one of making intelligent extrapolations from the history of observations. Practical techniques are available for this kind of short-term forecasting.

Regression analysis can sometimes be useful in short-term forecasting because it represents a general modeling approach to predicting the value of one variable based on knowledge of other variables. In particular, if we know the future values of the explanatory variables, we may be in a good position to predict the future value of the response variable. However, when we want to forecast the routine behavior of parameters in the short run, regression may be of limited usefulness. Although it does afford us an opportunity to "explain" one variable's behavior in terms of several other variables, it still leaves us with the task of finding or predicting *those* values. In short, regression replaces the problem of forecasting the response variable with the problem of forecasting the explanatory variables. The alternative we will explore in this chapter is to base the forecast of a variable on its own history, thereby avoiding the need to specify a causal relationship and to predict the values of explanatory variables.

Our focus in this chapter is on time-series methods for forecasting. For our purposes, a **time series** is a set of observations taken at regular intervals over time. The use of time-series methods presumes that the future will be enough like the past that we can obtain reasonably accurate forecasts by using only past values to predict future values.

Finally, a note on terminology. Some people use the term **forecasting** to imply the use of a routine computational method, preferring to reserve the term **prediction** to suggest the use of subjective judgment in addition to calculations. In that sense, we are dealing here with forecasting techniques.

7.2 FORECASTING WITH TIME-SERIES MODELS

The basic problem in short-term forecasting is to estimate the value of an important parameter, such as next week's demand for a product. Two features of short-term forecasting are important. First, we make use of historical data for the phenomenon we wish to forecast. In other words, we have some recent data on hand, and we assume that the near-term future will resemble the past. That assumption makes it sensible to project

FIGURE 7.1 Three Components of Time-Series Behavior

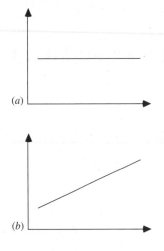

historical observations into the future. Second, we seek a routine calculation that may be applied to a large number of cases and that may be automated, without relying on any qualitative information about the underlying phenomena. Short-term forecasts are often used in situations that involve forecasting many different variables at frequent intervals. Some inventory systems, for example, track thousands of items. To forecast demand for each item every day requires efficient methods that do not require manual intervention.

At the outset, we hypothesize a model for systematic behavior in the time series of interest. The major components of such a model are usually the following:

- A base level
- A trend
- Cyclic fluctuations

Figure 7.1 shows these three basic categories in graphical form: a base level in Figure 7.1a, a trend in Figure 7.1b, and cyclical fluctuations in Figure 7.1c. Thus, we start by adopting one of these models, or a combination of them, as a representation of the process we're forecasting. Later, we will see how we might choose one of the models based on how well the forecasts match our observations.

By adopting one of the models in Figure 7.1, we assume that future observations will be samples drawn from a probability distribution whose mean value follows the model. The simplest case is the model for a constant mean (Figure 7.1a), without trend or cyclic effects. In that case, our model becomes:

$$x_t = a + e_t \tag{7.1}$$

where x_t represents the observed value for time period t and a represents the mean value. Later on, when we introduce other factors, we'll refer to a as the **base value**. The term e represents randomness. In other words, the actual observations can be thought of as a systematic but unknown mean value (a), modified by a random or "noise" term (e). The random term captures all of the uncertainty, and our purpose is to forecast the nonrandom term—the mean value—as precisely as possible. In order to produce that forecast, we can draw on the existing observations, x_t, x_{t-1}, x_{t-2}, and so on.

7.2.1 The Moving-Average Model

If we were perfectly confident of our assumption that the model in (7.1) would remain unchanged forever, then we could use our entire history of observations to construct a forecast. The more of our past data we used, the more precise our forecast would tend to be. However, we may suspect that there has been, or will be, some systematic change in the mean of the process (that is, a change in a). If such a change occurred without our realizing it, then some of the data used in the construction of the forecast could be outdated when we drew on the entire history. To guard against this possibility, we can limit ourselves to only the most recent observations in order to construct a forecast. In particular, the n-period **moving average** builds a forecast by averaging the observations in the most recent n periods:

$$A_t = (x_t + x_{t-1} + \ldots + x_{t-n+1})/n$$

where x_t represents the observation made in period t and A_t denotes the moving average calculated after making the observation in period t. If we let F_{t+1} represent the forecast for period $(t + 1)$, then our forecasting procedure sets $F_{t+1} = A_t$. Of course, for the model in (7.1) there is no difference between the mean demand in period t and the mean demand in period $(t + 1)$, so we could also think of A_t as a forecast for the mean value of demand at period t as well as at period $(t + 1)$. However, when there is a trend or a seasonality factor, it is important to be clear about the target period for the forecast. We adopt the following convention for the steps in forecasting:

1. Make the observation in period t.
2. Carry out the necessary calculations.
3. Use the calculations to forecast period $(t + 1)$.

The formula in (7.2) simply takes the average of the n most recent observations. One period from now, there will be a new observation to include in the average, while the oldest observation will be dropped. Thus, in the event that a systematic change occurs in the underlying process, the oldest data point, which reflects how the process looked prior to the change, will be purged from the forecast calculation.

EXAMPLE
*Curtis
Distributors (1)*

Curtis Distributors is a distributor of office products. Among the many items it handles is a particular folding table that is in constant demand. The actual demands in each of the previous 10 weeks have been tracked by Curtis's information system, as reproduced in the following table:

Week	1	2	3	4	5	6	7	8	9	10
Sales	73	106	76	89	106	113	96	66	104	73

Now the distributor's task is to develop a forecast for week 11 (and beyond) from this history. ■

For the purposes of illustration, we use a 4-week moving average. In the worksheet of Figure 7.2*, we find the observations in column B and the moving average in column C. The forecast calculations appear in column D, using the moving average at period t as the forecast for period $(t + 1)$. The first forecast we can calculate occurs after the fourth observation, so we see entries in the Forecast column starting in week 5. Cell C8 contains the formula AVERAGE(B5:B8), and this formula has been copied to the cells below it. The last calculation in column C contains the moving average after the observation in week 10, a value of 85.50, which becomes our forecast for week 11. (Given our model of constant mean demand, this value is also our forecast, at this stage, for week 12 and beyond.)

In our example, the largest forecast (101) occurs after an observation (96) that is lower than the previous two observations. However, we can understand why that might be the case here: the 4-week moving average has just dropped the observation of 76 from week 3 and added the observation of 96 from week 7. As a result, the moving average is larger than before. With two observations above 100 from weeks 5 and 6 also included in

FIGURE 7.2 Worksheet for Calculating Moving Averages

	A	B	C	D	E	F	G
1	**Moving Average Example**						
2							
3	Period		**4-week Moving Average**				
4	t	Observed	A(t)	Forecast	Error	Deviation	Percent
5	1	73					
6	2	106					
7	3	76					
8	4	89	86.00				
9	5	106	94.25	86.00	20.00	20.00	19%
10	6	113	96.00	94.25	18.75	18.75	17%
11	7	96	101.00	96.00	0.00	0.00	0%
12	8	66	95.25	101.00	-35.00	35.00	53%
13	9	104	94.75	95.25	8.75	8.75	8%
14	10	76	85.50	94.75	-18.75	18.75	25%
15	11			85.50			
16							

7.2

*To download spreadsheets for this chapter, go to the Student Companion Site at www.wiley.com/college/powell.

FIGURE 7.3 Moving-Average Calculations in a Stylized Example

t	Observed	A(t)	Forecast	Error	Deviation	Percent	A(t)	Forecast	Difference	Deviation	Percent
			4-week Moving Average					6-week Moving Average			
1	100										
2	100										
3	100										
4	100	100.00									
5	100	100.00	100.00	0.00	0.00	0%					
6	100	100.00	100.00	0.00	0.00	0%	100.00				
7	100	100.00	100.00	0.00	0.00	0%	100.00	100.00	0.00	0.00	0%
8	100	100.00	100.00	0.00	0.00	0%	100.00	100.00	0.00	0.00	0%
9	100	100.00	100.00	0.00	0.00	0%	100.00	100.00	0.00	0.00	0%
10	180	120.00	100.00	80.00	80.00	44%	113.33	100.00	80.00	80.00	44%
11	180	140.00	120.00	60.00	60.00	33%	126.67	113.33	66.67	66.67	37%
12	180	160.00	140.00	40.00	40.00	22%	140.00	126.67	53.33	53.33	30%
13	180	160.00	160.00	20.00	20.00	11%	153.33	140.00	40.00	40.00	22%
14	180	180.00	180.00	0.00	0.00	0%	166.67	153.33	26.67	26.67	15%
15	180	180.00	180.00	0.00	0.00	0%	180.00	166.67	13.33	13.33	7%
16	180	180.00	180.00	0.00	0.00	0%	180.00	180.00	0.00	0.00	0%
17	180	180.00	180.00	0.00	0.00	0%	180.00	180.00	0.00	0.00	0%
18	180	180.00	180.00	0.00	0.00	0%	180.00	180.00	0.00	0.00	0%
19	180	180.00	180.00	0.00	0.00	0%	180.00	180.00	0.00	0.00	0%
20	180	180.00	180.00	0.00	0.00	0%	180.00	180.00	0.00	0.00	0%
				MSE	MAD	MAPE			MSE	MAD	MAPE
For periods 10-15				2000.00	33.33	18.5%			2696.30	46.67	25.9%

the moving average, we can see why the forecast might peak at this stage. The low observation of 66 in week 8 causes the moving average to drop, for similar reasons.

How many periods' worth of observations should we include in the moving average? There is no definitive answer to this question, but there is a trade-off to consider. Suppose the mean of the underlying process remains stable. If we include very few data points, then the moving average exhibits more variability than if we include a larger number of data points. In that sense, we get more *stability* from including more points. Suppose, however, there is an unanticipated change in the mean of the underlying process. If we include very few data points, our moving average will tend to track the changed process more closely than if we include a larger number of data points. In that case, we get more *responsiveness* from including fewer points.

A stylized example, containing no randomness, helps to demonstrate the responsiveness feature. Suppose the mean of a process is stable at 100 and then jumps to 180 in period 10, where it remains. In Figure 7.3, we see that the 4-week moving average detects the change and raises the forecast in column D to 120 for period 11. After week 13, the 4-week moving average has fully recovered, and the forecast stays at 180 thereafter.

For comparison, a 6-week moving average is calculated for the same observations and shown in column I, with forecasts in column J. Here, we see that the change is detected in period 10, but the response is more gradual. Full recovery occurs only after week 15. As the example suggests, the longer moving average responds more slowly to a step change in the mean. If there were randomness in the observations, in addition to the systematic change in the mean, the results might be harder to discern, but the essence of the comparison would be similar. To the extent that we value responsiveness in our forecasts, we prefer a shorter moving average to a longer one.

The other side of the trade-off, as mentioned above, involves stability. We return to the data from the Curtis Distributors example in Figure 7.2 and compute a 6-week moving average for comparison with the original 4-week moving average. In Figure 7.4, we can see that the 4-week moving average fluctuates more than the 6-week moving average. In the five weeks in which both methods generate forecasts, the 4-week moving average forecasts range from a low of 85.50 to a high of 101.00. The range for the 6-week moving average is 91.00 to 97.67, a much tighter interval. To the extent that we value a small range in our forecast, we prefer a longer moving average to a shorter one.

To resolve the trade-off, we have to consider what is likely to happen in the process that generates the observations. If we are confident in the model of a stable mean—that is, a constant value of *a*—then we should value stability in the forecast and prefer a longer

FIGURE 7.4 Comparison of 4-week and 6-week Moving Averages

Period	Observed	4-week Moving Average						6-week Moving Average				
t		A(t)	Forecast	Error	Deviation	Percent		A(t)	Forecast	Difference	Deviation	Percent
1	73											
2	106											
3	76											
4	89	86.00										
5	106	94.25	86.00	20.00	20.00	19%						
6	113	96.00	94.25	18.75	18.75	17%		93.83				
7	96	101.00	96.00	0.00	0.00	0%		97.67	93.83	2.17	2.17	2%
8	66	95.25	101.00	-35.00	35.00	53%		91.00	97.67	-31.67	31.67	48%
9	104	94.75	95.25	8.75	8.75	8%		95.67	91.00	13.00	13.00	13%
10	76	85.50	94.75	-18.75	18.75	25%		93.50	95.67	-19.67	19.67	26%
			85.50						93.50			

moving average. To the extent that we believe that the value of *a* is subject to change, we should value responsiveness and prefer a shorter moving average.

7.2.2 Measures of Forecast Accuracy

How good are the forecasts produced by a moving-average calculation? There is no universal measure of performance for forecast accuracy, but several measures are used frequently. We suggest three measures:

- MSE: the Mean Squared Error between forecast and actual
- MAD: the Mean Absolute Deviation between forecast and actual
- MAPE: the Mean Absolute Percent Error between forecast and actual

The MSE is a traditional squared-error calculation that echoes results in statistics; the MAD looks only at absolute error sizes, without squaring them; and the MAPE looks at relative error sizes. The relevant formulas are as follows (where F_t represents the forecast and x_t the actual observation), assuming that forecasts have been calculated for periods u through v. The number of periods is therefore $(u - v + 1)$.

$$MSE = \frac{1}{(u - v + 1)} \sum_{t=u}^{v} (F_t - x_t)^2$$

$$MAD = \frac{1}{(u - v + 1)} \sum_{t=u}^{v} |F_t - x_t| \tag{7.2}$$

$$MAPE = \frac{1}{(u - v + 1)} \sum_{t=u}^{v} \left| \frac{F_t - x_t}{x_t} \right|$$

The MAD and MAPE calculations are similar: one is absolute, and the other is relative. We usually reserve the MAPE for comparisons in which the magnitudes of two cases are different. For example, we might be evaluating forecasts for two of a distributor's products, a standard product that sells about 100 per period and a custom product that sells about 10 per period. The forecast deviations for the standard product are likely to be much larger than the deviations for the custom product, so a comparison seeking a small value of the MAD would intrinsically favor the custom product. A fairer comparison might be the MAPE because it adjusts for the differences in scale.

In Figure 7.3, we have included the calculations of these three measures, covering periods 10–15, where there are forecast errors. Here, we can see that all three measures are lower for the 4-week moving average than for the 6-week alternative. Thus, the more responsive 4-week moving average is preferred here.

In Figure 7.5, we have extended the Curtis Distributors example through 20 periods in order to allow for a longer comparison interval. Here, the three error measures, calculated for periods 11–20, happen to be smaller for the 6-week moving average. Such a result is typical when the mean is stable and we observe the process for a relatively long interval.

FIGURE 7.5 Extended
Comparison of 4-week
and 6-week Moving
Averages

	A	B	C	D	E	F	G	H	I	J	K	L	M
1	**Moving Average Example**												
2													
3	Period		**4-week Moving Average**						**6-week Moving Average**				
4	t	Observed	A(t)	Forecast	Error	Deviation	Percent		A(t)	Forecast	Difference	Deviation	Percent
5	1	73											
6	2	106											
7	3	76											
8	4	89	86.00										
9	5	106	94.25	86.00	-20.00	20.00	19%						
10	6	113	96.00	94.25	-18.75	18.75	17%		93.83				
11	7	96	101.00	96.00	0.00	0.00	0%		97.67	93.83	-2.17	2.17	2%
12	8	66	95.25	101.00	35.00	35.00	53%		91.00	97.67	31.67	31.67	48%
13	9	104	94.75	95.25	-8.75	8.75	8%		95.67	91.00	-13.00	13.00	13%
14	10	73	84.75	94.75	21.75	21.75	30%		93.00	95.67	22.67	22.67	31%
15	11	97	85.00	84.75	-12.25	12.25	13%		91.50	93.00	-4.00	4.00	4%
16	12	112	96.50	85.00	-27.00	27.00	24%		91.33	91.50	-20.50	20.50	18%
17	13	117	99.75	96.50	-20.50	20.50	18%		94.83	91.33	-25.67	25.67	22%
18	14	84	102.50	99.75	15.75	15.75	19%		97.83	94.83	10.83	10.83	13%
19	15	79	98.00	102.50	23.50	23.50	30%		93.67	97.83	18.83	18.83	24%
20	16	62	85.50	98.00	36.00	36.00	58%		91.83	93.67	31.67	31.67	51%
21	17	60	71.25	85.50	25.50	25.50	43%		85.67	91.83	31.83	31.83	53%
22	18	92	73.25	71.25	-20.75	20.75	23%		82.33	85.67	-6.33	6.33	7%
23	19	68	70.50	73.25	5.25	5.25	8%		74.17	82.33	14.33	14.33	21%
24	20	87	76.75	70.50	-16.50	16.50	19%		74.67	74.17	-12.83	12.83	15%
25													
26					MSE	MAD	MAPE				MSE	MAD	MAPE
27		For periods 11-20			477.63	20.30	25.3%				399.35	17.68	22.8%

Sheet tabs: 7.2 / 7.3 / 7.4 / 7.5

EXCEL TIP
*Moving-
Average
Calculations*

Moving averages are simple enough to calculate on a spreadsheet, and we don't necessarily need specialized software or commands to do the work. However, Excel's Data Analysis tool does contain an option for calculating moving averages (Data▶Analysis▶Data Analysis▶Moving Average). Excel assumes that the data appear in a single column, and the tool provides an option of recognizing a title for this column, if it is included in the data range. Other options include a graphical display of the actual and forecast data and a calculation of the standard error after each forecast. (This is equivalent to the square root of the MSE; however, Excel pairs the forecast F_{t+1} and the observation x_t. In the calculations of Figure 7.2, we adopted a more intuitive convention in which the forecast F_{t+1} is compared with the next observation, x_{t+1}.) ∎

7.3   THE EXPONENTIAL SMOOTHING MODEL

All time-series forecasts involve weighted averages of historical observations. In the case of a four-period moving average, the weights are 0.25 on each of the last four observations and zero on all of the previous observations. But if the philosophy is to weight recent observations more than older ones, then why not allow the weights to decline gradually as we go back in time? This is the approach taken in **exponential smoothing**.

For the stable-demand model (7.1), exponential smoothing involves taking a weighted average of the latest observation x_t and our previous forecast S_{t-1}:

$$S_t = \alpha x_t + (1 - \alpha)S_{t-1} \tag{7.3}$$

The parameter α is a number between zero and one, called the **smoothing constant**. We refer to S_t as the **smoothed value** of the observations, and we can think of it as our "best guess" as to the value of the mean. Our forecasting procedure sets the forecast $F_{t+1} = S_t$.

Similarly, one period previously, we would have made the calculation

$$S_{t-1} = \alpha x_{t-1} + (1 - \alpha)S_{t-2}$$

Substituting this equation into (7.3) yields

$$S_t = \alpha x_t + \alpha(1 - \alpha)x_{t-1} + (1 - \alpha)^2 S_{t-2}$$

Continuing to substitute in this way, we can eventually express (7.3) as follows:

$$S_t = \alpha x_t + \alpha(1 - \alpha)x_{t-1} + \alpha(1 - \alpha)^2 x_{t-2} + \alpha(1 - \alpha)^3 x_{t-3} + \cdots \tag{7.4}$$

Because $\alpha < 1$, the term $\alpha(1 - \alpha)^t$ declines as t increases. Thus, we can see that the forecast is a weighting of all the observations, applying the largest weight to the most recent observation, the second largest weight to the second most recent observation, and so on. The exponential smoothing formula is not as drastic as the moving-average formula because it doesn't discard old data after n periods. Instead, the exponential smoothing calculation simply gives less weight to observations as they become older. Indeed, the exponential decay exhibited by the weights in (7.4) is the basis for the name of the forecasting technique.

As written in (7.3), the new forecast is a weighted average of the most recent observation and the last smoothed value. Another way to express the same relationship is the following:

$$S_t = S_{t-1} + \alpha(x_t - S_{t-1}) \tag{7.5}$$

In other words, our new smoothed value (S_t) is equal to our old one (S_{t-1}), modified by an amount proportional to the difference, or error, between our latest observation and our previous best guess. Thus, we are willing to adjust our best guess in the direction of that difference, and in some sense, the value of α describes the strength of that adjustment. A larger value of α gives more weight to the adjustment. However, there is likely to be some randomness in the difference between the last observation x_t and our last forecast (which is equivalent to S_{t-1}), so we do not want to make the value of α too large.

The forecasting process described by (7.4) strikes something of a balance between stability (by including all observations) and responsiveness (by weighting recent observations most heavily). However, this balance can be influenced by the choice of the smoothing constant. When α is large (close to 1), the forecasts are responsive but tend to be volatile; when α is small (close to 0), the forecasts tend to be stable but relatively unresponsive. Most analysts opt for a conservative choice—that is, a relatively small value of α. This means using a stable forecast and accepting the risk that the true mean may change. When evidence mounts that a systematic change has occurred in the mean, it would then make sense to manually override the calculated value of S_{t-1}, essentially reinitializing the calculations.

We can get an additional perspective by examining the coefficients in the expression (7.4). Figure 7.6 shows the weight applied to observation x_{t-k} (the observation that is k periods old) for two values of the smoothing constant, $\alpha = 0.2$ and $\alpha = 0.6$. The use of the larger value, $\alpha = 0.6$, leads to 99 percent of the weight being placed on the most recent five observations, whereas the use of the smaller value, $\alpha = 0.2$, leads to only 67 percent of the weight being placed on the same observations. The graph also shows that the weights for $\alpha = 0.2$ are almost identical from period to period, while for $\alpha = 0.6$, the weights decline rapidly for earlier periods.

FIGURE 7.6 Comparison of Weights Placed on k-Year-Old Data

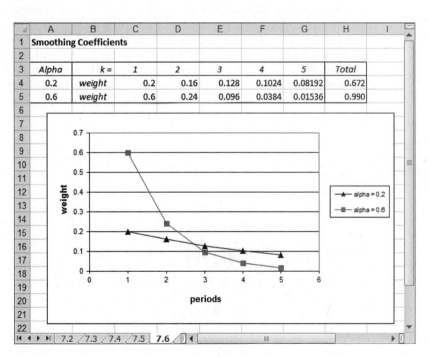

FIGURE 7.7   Worksheet for Exponential Smoothing Calculations

Exponential Smoothing Example

Alpha 0.2   Initial value S(1) = X(1)

								4-week Moving Average				
Period												
t	Observed	S(t)	Forecast	Error	Deviation	Percent		A(t)	Forecast	Difference	Deviation	Percent
1	73	73.00										
2	106	79.60	73.00									
3	76	78.88	79.60									
4	89	80.90	78.88					86.00				
5	106	85.92	80.90	-25.10	25.10	24%		94.25	86.00	-20.00	20.00	19%
6	113	91.34	85.92	-27.08	27.08	24%		96.00	94.25	-18.75	18.75	17%
7	96	92.27	91.34	-4.				101.00	96			
8	66	87.02	92.27	26.27	26.27	40%		95.25	101.00	35.00	35.00	53%
9	104	90.41	87.02	-16.98	16.98	16%		94.75	95.25	-8.75	8.75	8%
10	73	86.93	90.41	17.41	17.41	24%		84.75	94.75	21.75	21.75	30%
11	77	84.94	86.93	9.93	9.93	13%		80.00	84.75	7.75	7.75	10%
12	119	91.76	84.94	-34.06	34.06	29%		93.25	80.00	-39.00	39.00	33%
13	84	90.20	91.76	7.76	7.76	9%		88.25	93.25	9.25	9.25	11%
14	71	86.36	90.20	19.20	19.20	27%		87.75	88.25	17.25	17.25	24%
15	88	86.69	86.36	-1.64	1.64	2%		90.50	87.75	-0.25	0.25	0%
16	97	88.75	86.69	-10.31	10.31	11%		85.00	90.50	-6.50	6.50	7%
17	69	84.80	88.75	19.75	19.75	29%		81.25	85.00	16.00	16.00	23%
18	117	91.24	84.80	-32.20	32.20	28%		92.75	81.25	-35.75	35.75	31%
19	80	88.99	91.24	11.24	11.24	14%		90.75	92.75	12.75	12.75	16%
20	73	85.79	88.99	15.99	15.99	22%		84.75	90.75	17.75	17.75	24%
				MSE	MAD	MAPE				MSE	MAD	MAPE
	For periods 5-20			391.99	17.47	19.7%				409.02	16.66	19.1%

$$S(t) = \alpha x(t) + (1-\alpha)S(t-1)$$

$$A(t) = [X(t)+X(t-1)+X(t-2)+X(t-3)]/4$$

7.7

To illustrate the calculations for exponential smoothing, we return to the Curtis Distributors example. In Figure 7.7, we show the calculation of the smoothed value in column C. The parameter $\alpha = 0.2$ appears in cell C3. The initial smoothed value S_1 is taken to be equal to the first observation in cell C6. The Excel implementation of the exponential smoothing formula in (7.3) appears in cell C7 as: $C\$3 * B7+(1-\$C\$3) * C6$. Then this formula is copied to the cells below. The smoothed value becomes the forecast for the following period in column D.

In cells E28:G28, we calculate the three error measures covering periods 5–20 for the exponential smoothing approach. Comparable measures for the 4-week moving-average method are calculated in cells K28:M28. We see that the accuracies of the two procedures are roughly comparable. The MSE favors exponential smoothing, whereas the two absolute deviation methods favor the moving average. Although there is no theoretical reason to prefer exponential smoothing, some research suggests that, across a wide spectrum of applications, exponential smoothing tends to produce more accurate forecasts than moving averages. One of the questions we have not explored in this comparison is whether the error measures could be improved for a different choice of the smoothing constant. (We may already suspect, based on a different calculation in Figure 7.5, that an alternative moving average may achieve better error measures.)

Figure 7.8 displays the smoothed and averaged data against the actual observations. The graph provides a good reminder that the two forecasting methods serve to estimate the

FIGURE 7.8   Comparison of Smoothed and Averaged Forecasts

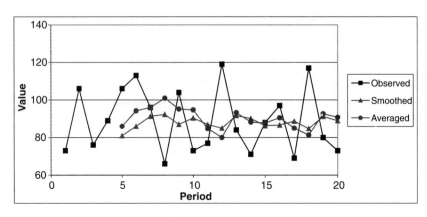

FIGURE 7.9 Exponential Smoothing Calculations in a Stylized Example

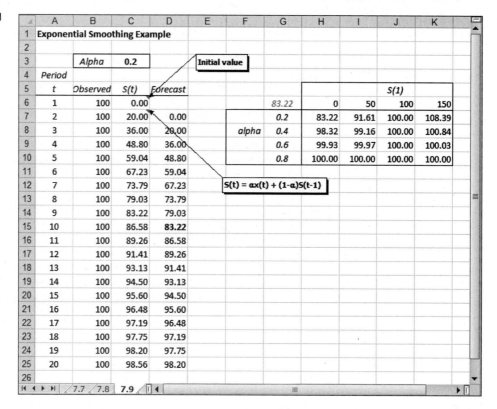

mean of the underlying process. In this example, the process also has quite a bit of randomness, reflected by the fact that the time series for the observations fluctuates more drastically than either of the forecasts.

It's helpful to look at a stylized example (with no randomness) to appreciate how exponential smoothing works. For example, imagine that we were tracking a process for which the observations were stable at 100, with no variability. In other words, the observation in each period is exactly 100. How does exponential smoothing perform?

In Figure 7.9, we show the calculations for the case of $\alpha = 0.2$ and an initial value of $S_1 = 0$. The observations appear in column B, the calculation of S_t in column C, and the forecast in column D. As the table shows, the forecast underestimates the observation from the outset, but the gap gradually narrows. After approximately 20 periods, the forecasts are virtually on target. Thus, the responsiveness feature of exponential smoothing can eventually overcome an inaccurate initialization of the smoothed value.

In addition, we would expect that the forecast would be better if the initial value of S_1 were larger. The sensitivity table in Figure 7.9 shows how the value of the forecast after period 10 varies with α and with S_1. When $S_1 = 100$, the forecasts are on target for any choice of α (and this turns out to be the case in every period). In a sense, this is exactly how we would hope a forecasting procedure would operate: if we start with a good guess for the mean, then the procedure stays on target; if we start with a poor guess, then the procedure at least converges to the figure we desire, and it converges faster for larger values of the smoothing constant.

One remaining concern we might have about the exponential smoothing formula is how it performs when we are wrong about the underlying model—that is, when the mean is not constant. In the next two sections, we examine how to adapt the exponential smoothing model to the trend and cyclical effects pictured in Figure 7.1.

EXCEL TIP
Implementing Exponential Smoothing

Excel's Data Analysis tool contains an option for calculating forecasts using exponential smoothing. The Exponential Smoothing module resembles the Moving-Average module, but instead of asking for the number of periods, it asks for the damping factor, which is the complement of the smoothing factor, or $(1 - \alpha)$. Again, there is an option for chart output and an option for a calculation of the standard error. ∎

7.4   EXPONENTIAL SMOOTHING WITH A TREND

In the previous discussion, we assumed in equation (7.1) that the underlying model is stable. But what if that isn't the case: how will the procedure perform? To shed some light on this problem, consider another stylized case, without any variability. Suppose that we have been operating with a stable mean of 100 for some time but that an upward trend occurs and then persists. Figure 7.10 illustrates this case. The observations (column B) remain at 100 until period 4 and then increase by 10 each period. The value of $S_1 = 100$, as would be the case if there were a past history of stable behavior not shown in the figure.

Once the trend begins, the value of S_t increases, but the forecast always lags behind the corresponding observation. Given the form of (7.5), this pattern is not surprising, because we are always updating our best guess by a fraction of the forecast error. In fact, as the example shows, the forecast error $(F_t - x_t)$ eventually stabilizes at a gap of approximately 50. (In general, for other values of the smoothing constant, the size of the gap would be a factor of $1/\alpha$ multiplied by the trend, if we waited long enough). When randomness is present and we assume the model for a stable mean when in reality a trend exists, our forecasts will tend to underestimate the actual mean. Therefore, it will be necessary to modify the basic model if we want to generate accurate forecasts in the presence of a trend.

Our introduction to moving average and exponential smoothing methods for forecasting was based on a model with a stable mean, $x_t = a + e_t$. The exponential smoothing model for this case is sometimes referred to as *simple* exponential smoothing. Now, however, we consider a model with a linear trend:

$$x_t = a + bt + e_t \tag{7.6}$$

where a is called the **base value**, b is the **trend**, and t is the time period. The observation is assumed to be drawn from a probability distribution with a mean value of $a + bt$. In other words, the mean value follows a straight line with a slope of b, and variability exists as well. We can think of the parameter a as the initial value.

When a trend is present, we have two tasks—to forecast the mean and to forecast the trend. Loosely speaking, we ask: where is the process now and how fast is it changing? To answer these questions, we use **Holt's method**, shown in the following formulas:

$$S_t = ax_t + (1 - a)(S_{t-1} + T_{t-1}) \tag{7.7}$$

$$T_t = \beta(S_t - S_{t-1}) + (1 - \beta)T_{t-1} \tag{7.8}$$

FIGURE 7.10 Exponential Smoothing Calculations with a Trend in the Data

	A	B	C	D	E	F	G	H	I
1	Basic Model with Trend in Data				Trend	10			
2									
3		Alpha	0.2		Initial value				
4	Period								
5	t	Observed	S(t)	Forecast	Error				
6	1	100	100.00				Sensitivity of Error to a at t=25		
7	2	100	100.00				a	Error	
8	3	100	100.00	100.00	0.00			-49.63	
9	4	110	102.00	100.00	-10.00		0.1	-90.15	
10	5	120	105.60	10... S(t) = ax(t) + (1-a)S(t-1)			0.2	-49.63	
11	6	130	110.48	105.00	-24.40		0.3	-33.32	
12	7	140	116.38	110.48	-29.52		0.4	-25.00	
13	8	150	123.11	116.38	-33.62		0.5	-20.00	
14	9	160	130.49	123.11	-36.89		0.6	-16.67	
15	10	170	138.39	130.49	-39.51		0.7	-14.29	
16	11	180	146.71	138.39	-41.61		0.8	-12.50	
17	12	190	155.37	146.71	-43.29		0.9	-11.11	
18	13	200	164.29	155.37	-44.63				
19	14	210	173.44	164.29	-45.71				
29	24	310	270.37	260.46	-49.54				
30	25	320	280.30	270.37	-49.63				

7.7 / 7.8 / 7.9 / 7.10

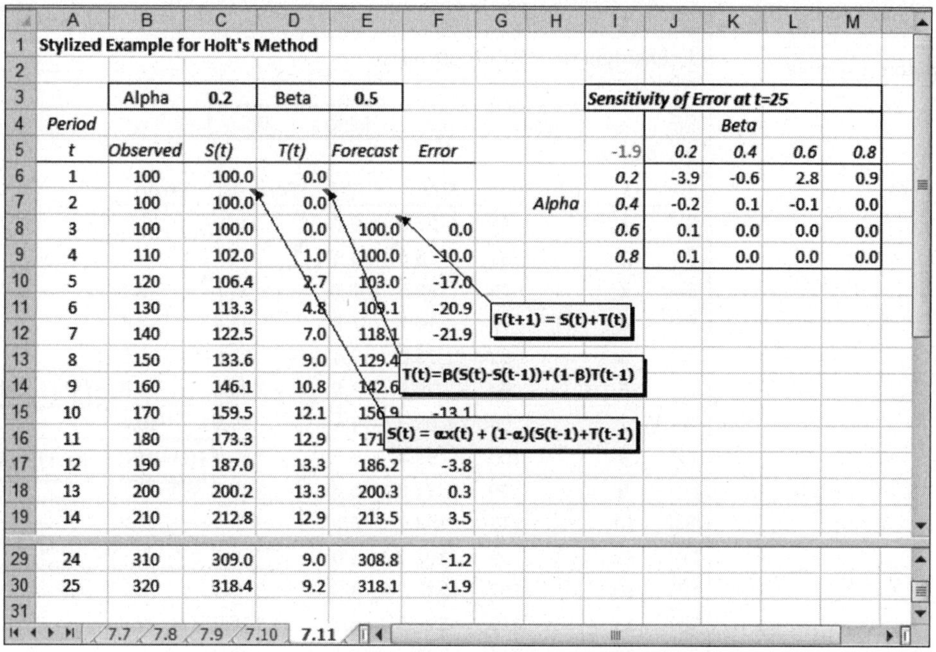

FIGURE 7.11 Holt's Method with a Trend in the Data

t	Observed	S(t)	T(t)	Forecast	Error
1	100	100.0	0.0		
2	100	100.0	0.0		
3	100	100.0	0.0	100.0	0.0
4	110	102.0	1.0	100.0	10.0
5	120	106.4	2.7	103.0	-17.0
6	130	113.3	4.8	109.1	-20.9
7	140	122.5	7.0	118.1	-21.9
8	150	133.6	9.0	129.4	
9	160	146.1	10.8	142.6	
10	170	159.5	12.1	156.9	-13.1
11	180	173.3	12.9	171	
12	190	187.0	13.3	186.2	-3.8
13	200	200.2	13.3	200.3	0.3
14	210	212.8	12.9	213.5	3.5
24	310	309.0	9.0	308.8	-1.2
25	320	318.4	9.2	318.1	-1.9

As before, S_t is the **smoothed value** after the observation has been made in period t, calculated as a weighted average of the observation in period t and the forecast for period t. Then T_t is the **estimated trend**. Equation (7.8) is similar to the calculation in simple exponential smoothing, but because we cannot observe the trend directly, we use the difference in the two most recent smoothed values as a proxy. Then we weight that value along with our previous best guess for the trend to calculate a new estimate of the trend. These calculations allow us to construct the forecast for period $(t + 1)$ from the following formula:

$$F_{t+1} = S_t + T_t \tag{7.9}$$

We can easily imagine using a different smoothing constant for the smoothed value and for the estimated trend because we may want to trade off responsiveness and stability differently for the two factors. In Holt's method, especially if we initialize the trend forecast at zero, it makes sense to use a relatively large smoothing factor β in the trend equation (7.8), whereas a smaller factor α is still reasonable for the main equation (7.7).

Figure 7.11 shows how Holt's method works in the stylized trend example from Figure 7.10. In the calculations shown, we set $\alpha = 0.2$ as before, but we take $\beta = 0.5$ for greater responsiveness in the trend estimate. In the calculations, we observe a warm-up period, but eventually the forecast becomes quite accurate.

EXAMPLE
Curtis Distributors (2)

The following table displays historical data on the orders placed for a relatively new product stocked by Curtis Distributors. Obviously, there are fluctuations in week-to-week figures, but there is clearly an upward trend in the observations. The task is to develop a forecast for week 21 (and beyond).

Week	1	2	3	4	5	6	7	8	9	10
Sales	66	69	75	72	92	83	94	105	90	112

Week	11	12	13	14	15	16	17	18	19	20
Sales	99	107	120	114	138	124	146	143	131	151

FIGURE 7.12 Holt's Method for the Curtis Distributors Example

A	B	C	D	E	F	G	H
1	Example for Holt's Method						
2							
3		Alpha	0.2	Beta	0.5		
4	Period						
5	t	Observed	S(t)	T(t)	Forecast	Error	
6	1	66	66.0	0.0			
7	2	69	66.6	0.3			
8	3	75	68.5	1.1	66.9	-8.1	
9	4	72	70.1	1.3	69.6	-2.4	
10	5	92	75.6	3.4	71.5	-20.5	
11	6	83	79.8	3.8	79.0	-4.0	F(t+1) = S(t)+T(t)
12	7	94	85.7	4.8	83.6	-10.4	
13	8	105	93.4	6.3	90.5	T(t)=β(S(t)-S(t-1))+(1-β)T(t-1)	
14	9	90	97.8	5.3	99.7	9.7	
15	10	112	104.9	6.2	103.1	8.9	
16	11	99	108.7	5.0	S(t) = αx(t) + (1-α)(S(t-1)+T(t-1))		
17	12	107	112.3	4.3	113.7	6.7	
18	13	120	117.3	4.7	116.7	-3.3	
19	14	114	120.4	3.9	122.0	8.0	
20	15	138	127.0	5.2	124.3	-13.7	
21	16	124	130.6	4.4	132.3	8.3	
22	17	146	137.2	5.5	135.0	-11.0	
23	18	143	142.8	5.5	142.7	-0.3	
24	19	131	144.9	3.8	148.3	17.3	
25	20	151	149.1	4.0	148.7	-2.3	
26							

⊢ ◀ ▶ ▶⊢ / 7.7 / 7.8 / 7.9 / 7.10 / 7.11 / **7.12** /

Figure 7.12 shows the calculations for Holt's method, using $\alpha = 0.2$ and $\beta = 0.5$. The forecast for period 21 is obtained from (7.9):

$$F_{21} = S_{20} + T_{20} = 149.1 + 4.0 = 153.1$$

By using the most recent estimated trend, we can calculate forecasts for later periods:

$$F_{22} = S_{20} + 2T_{20} = 157.1$$
$$F_{23} = S_{20} + 3T_{20} = 161.1$$

In this way, we can extrapolate to any number of future periods, under the assumption that the base value and the trend in the model of (7.6) remain unchanged.

7.5 EXPONENTIAL SMOOTHING WITH TREND AND CYCLICAL FACTORS

We can take the exponential smoothing model further and include a *cyclical* factor, as anticipated by Figure 7.1. This type of factor is usually called a "seasonal" factor, but a literal interpretation of that term may seem restrictive. A seasonal factor suggests a cycle containing four periods, one for each season in the year. However, we can also conceive of a cycle containing 12 periods, one for each month in the year. We can even conceive of a cycle containing 52 periods, one for each week in the year. Therefore, we rely on the term *cyclical* as a reminder that the number of periods in a cycle need not be four.

For a cyclical effect, there are two types of models: an additive model and a multiplicative model. The form of the additive model is as follows:

$$x_t = a + d_t + e_t \tag{7.10}$$

When a trend is included, the more general form of the additive model becomes

$$x_t = a + bt + d_t + e_t \tag{7.11}$$

Adapting the terminology introduced earlier, we call a the **base value**, b the **trend**, d_t the **cyclical factor**, and t the time period. The observation is assumed to be drawn from a probability distribution with a mean value of $a + bt + d_t$, with $b = 0$ if there is no trend. In these two models, the cyclical factor adds to (or subtracts from) the mean value an amount that depends on the position of time t in the cycle. Thus, if the cycle is quarterly, with four periods in the cycle, the effect would be represented by one of the four values d_1, d_2, d_3, d_4, depending on where in the cycle period t falls. Usually, we require that the four values of d_t sum to zero.

For the model in (7.10), we need two smoothing formulas. The first produces the smoothed value using observations from which the seasonal effect has been removed. The second produces the estimated cyclical factor. For flexibility, we use different smoothing constants in the two formulas:

$$S_t = \alpha(x_t - C_{t-p}) + (1 - \alpha)S_{t-1} \tag{7.12}$$

$$C_t = \gamma(x_t - S_t) + (1 - \gamma)C_{t-p} \tag{7.13}$$

where p represents the number of periods in a cycle. Incorporating the trend, with the more general model in (7.11), we need three smoothing formulas. The first produces the smoothed value, the second produces the trend estimate, and the third produces the estimated cyclical factor. Three smoothing constants are employed (α for the smoothed value, β for the trend, and γ for the cyclical factor):

$$S_t = \alpha(x_t - C_{t-p}) + (1 - \alpha)(S_{t-1} + T_{t-1}) \tag{7.14}$$

$$T_t = \beta(S_t - S_{t-1}) + (1 - \beta)T_{t-1} \tag{7.15}$$

$$C_t = \gamma(x_t - S_t) + (1 - \gamma)C_{t-p} \tag{7.16}$$

For the additive model, the forecast takes the following form:

$$F_{t+1} = (S_t + T_t) + C_{t+1-p} \tag{7.17}$$

where S_t is the smoothed value, T_t is the estimated trend, and C_{t+1-p} is the estimated cyclical factor for period $(t + 1)$, which would have been estimated most recently at period $(t + 1 - p)$.

For a multiplicative factor, the form of the model is as follows:

$$x_t = ad_t + e_t \tag{7.18}$$

When a trend is included, the more general form of the multiplicative model becomes the following:

$$x_t = (a + bt)d_t + e_t \tag{7.19}$$

Following the structure of the additive models, we can anticipate that we again need three smoothing formulas for the model in (7.19), as follows:

$$S_t = \alpha(x_t/C_{t-p}) + (1 - \alpha)(S_{t-1} + T_{t-1}) \tag{7.20}$$

$$T_t = \beta(S_t - S_{t-1}) + (1 - \beta)T_{t-1} \tag{7.21}$$

$$C_t = \gamma(x_t/S_t) + (1 - \gamma)C_{t-p} \tag{7.22}$$

For the multiplicative model, the forecast takes the following form:

$$F_{t+1} = (S_t + T_t)C_{t+1-p} \tag{7.23}$$

where, again, S_t is the smoothed value, T_t is the estimated trend, and C_{t+1-p} is the estimated cyclical factor for period $(t + 1)$, which would have most recently been estimated at period $(t + 1 - p)$. We have presented four variations of the cyclical model, depending on which type of cyclical factor is assumed and whether a trend is assumed. In our examples, we emphasize the multiplicative model with a trend because that seems to be the most widely used in practice. This version is often referred to as the **Holt-Winters method**.

First, we demonstrate the cyclical model with another stylized example. The observations in Figure 7.13 exhibit both cyclic fluctuation (over four periods) and a trend, but no randomness. We start with a history of four quarterly observations of demand. Based on the first cycle of observations, the components of the forecast are initialized as follows:

$$S_t = (x_1 + x_2 + x_3 + x_4)/4, \text{ for } t = 1 \text{ to } 4$$
$$T_t = \qquad\qquad 0, \text{ for } t = 1 \text{ to } 4$$
$$C_t = 4x_t/(x_1 + x_2 + x_3 + x_4), \text{ for } t = 1 \text{ to } 4$$

Thus, the smoothed values S_t are initialized in the first four periods as the average observation in the first four periods. The trend T_t is initialized at zero. Finally, for each of the first four periods, the cyclical factor is initialized as the ratio of the observation in period t to the average of the first four observations. Then, starting with the second cycle (period 5), formulas (7.20)–(7.22) are used to compute new values of S_t, T_t, and C_t each time a new observation is made.

FIGURE 7.13 Stylized Model with Trend and Cyclic Fluctuations

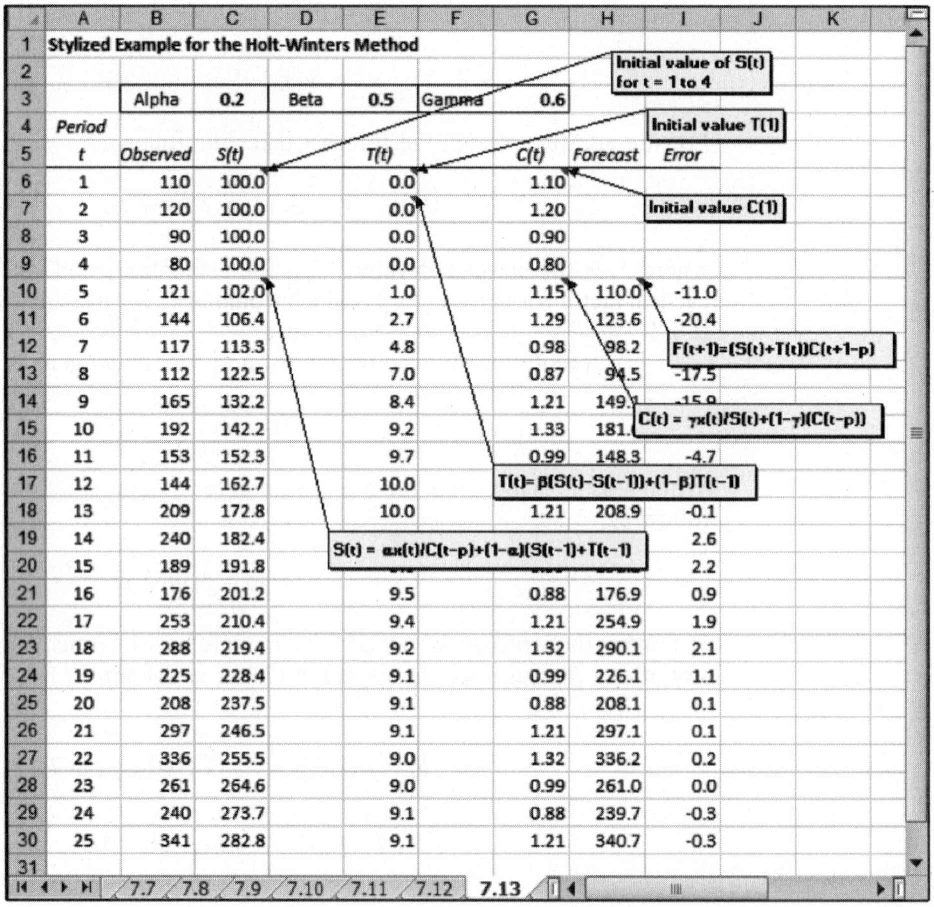

In Figure 7.13, we take the three smoothing constants to be $\alpha = 0.2$, $\beta = 0.5$, and $\gamma = 0.6$. We use a relatively large value of β because the initial trend estimate is zero, and we can expect that the forecasting procedure will have to respond to the data to produce a good trend estimate. We use a relatively large value of γ because we have an opportunity to update our estimates of the individual cyclical factors only once for every four observations. Nevertheless, as the error values in column I demonstrate, the forecasts become fairly accurate after period 12.

EXAMPLE
Town of Lincoln

The town of Lincoln tracks its water use on a quarterly basis so that it can anticipate capacity needs in its town water system and in its water treatment plant. The following table shows a three-year history of water use (in thousands of gallons), and the town wants to forecast water use in each of the upcoming four quarters.

						Quarter						
	1	**2**	**3**	**4**	**5**	**6**	**7**	**8**	**9**	**10**	**11**	**12**
Sales	8,216	9,196	3,768	4,032	7,481	7,889	3,996	3,764	6,664	7,011	4,356	3,565

∎

Figure 7.14 contains the calculations for exponential smoothing using the Holt-Winters model for this time series. To initialize the calculations, we use the same convention as in Figure 7.13. Then, for the observations starting in period 5, we invoke (7.20)–(7.22). We can clearly detect a higher-than-average seasonal factor in each of the first two periods of the cycle, with lower values in the last two periods. We also detect a slight negative trend. Our forecasts for the next four quarters are as follows:

$$F_{13} = (S_{12} + T_{12})C_9 = (5,649.8 - 29.5)(1.19) = 6,682.3$$
$$F_{14} = (S_{12} + T_{12})C_{10} = (5,649.8 - 29.5)(1.31) = 7,337.6$$
$$F_{15} = (S_{12} + T_{12})C_{11} = (5,649.8 - 29.5)(0.71) = 4,016.8$$
$$F_{16} = (S_{12} + T_{12})C_{12} = (5,649.8 - 29.5)(0.63) = 3,555.1$$

In the spreadsheet, this set of formulas provides a general and powerful way to create forecasts with exponential smoothing. In particular, if there is no trend, then we can set all T-values equal to zero. If there is no cyclical behavior, then we can set all C-values equal to one in the multiplicative model. Alternatively, we can allow the formulas to calculate these values, and, if there is not too much volatility in the observations, we expect to see calculations of T_t near zero and calculations of C_t near one.

FIGURE 7.14 The Holt-Winters Method for the Town of Lincoln Example

	A	B	C	D	E	F	G	H	I	J	K	L
1	Example for the Holt-Winters Method											
2												
3		Alpha	0.2	Beta	0.5	Gamma		0.6				
4	Period											
5	t	Observed	S(t)		T(t)		C(t)	Forecast	Error			
6	1	8216	6303.0		0.0		1.30					
7	2	9196	6303.0		0.0		1.46					
8	3	3768	6303.0		0.0		0.60					
9	4	4032	6303.0		0.0		0.64					
10	5	7481	6190.2		-56.4		1.25	8216.0	735.0			
11	6	7889	5988.5		-129.1		1.37	8949.2	1060.2			
12	7	3996	6024.4		-46.6		0.64	3502.8	F(t+1)=(S(t)+T(t))C(t+1-p)			
13	8	3764	5959.1		-55.9		0.63	3824.0	60.0			
14	9	6664	5791.8		-111.6		1.19	7358.4	694.4			
15	10	7011	5564.6		-169.4		1.31	7804.5	793.5			
16	11	4356	5683.6		-25.2		0.71	3437.3	-918.7			
17	12	3565	5649.8		-29.5		0.63	3592.3	27.3			
18												

7.7 7.8 7.9 7.10 7.11 7.12 7.13 **7.14**

7.6 USING XLMiner FOR SHORT-TERM FORECASTING

In this chapter, we have provided an Excel-based approach to fitting moving average or exponential smoothing models to time series data and making forecasts. We mentioned that Excel provides built-in tools for this purpose in its Data Analysis tool, but we prefer to build our own models.

XLMiner also provides the capability for computing forecasts using moving averages and exponential smoothing. As we've mentioned, implementing time-series forecasting methods on a spreadsheet is relatively straightforward. Compared to using specialized software like XLMiner, building custom spreadsheets allows us a great deal of flexibility. We can design the spreadsheets to suit our purposes, and the calculations are transparent. We also don't need to master new software; our knowledge of Excel will suffice. However, we always face the need to debug our own spreadsheets and the risk that some logical errors might occur. XLMiner has been debugged and has an interface that is only a slight variation from the interface used for other data mining applications. XLMiner automatically reports measures of forecast accuracy and is designed to take inputs from Excel. Thus, for certain kinds of applications, it may make sense to rely on XLMiner rather than on our own custom spreadsheet models.

XLMiner offers several forecasting procedures, organized into the following categories:

- Nonseasonal data with no trend
  - Moving Average
  - Simple Exponential Smoothing
- Nonseasonal data with a trend
  - Double Exponential Smoothing
- Seasonal data with no trend
  - Seasonal Additive
  - Seasonal Multiplicative
- Seasonal data with a trend
  - Holt-Winters' Additive
  - Holt-Winters' Multiplicative

The moving average method corresponds to the method presented in section 7.2.1, and simple exponential smoothing corresponds to the method presented in section 7.3. The "double smoothing" method corresponds to Holt's method of section 7.4, and the four seasonal methods correspond to the methods of section 7.5. Details on how to use the various methods in XLMiner are described in the built-in Help facility.

XLMiner uses the same summary measures—MSE, MAD, and MAPE—to evaluate the accuracy of time series forecasts. XLMiner uses the term Root Mean Squared Error (RMSE) in place of MSE, but the calculation is identical.

One difference in XLMiner is that the trend and seasonal models are initialized by a regression method. The software then computes errors as early as the first period, whereas in cases such as Figure 7.12, our Excel model waits until the second seasonal cycle to begin recording error values. For this reason, the specific results in XLMiner's calculations may not precisely match those in our Excel models.

Although an important feature of XLMiner is its ability to partition the data, this is not necessarily relevant for time series applications. When applying time series methods, we prefer to base our forecasts on more data rather than less, and on as much recent data as possible. For these reasons, the partitioning step is usually skipped when using XLMiner to produce time series forecasts.

7.7 SUMMARY

Moving averages and exponential smoothing are widely used for routine short-term forecasting. They rely on historical observations of a particular process, and they project the pattern of observations into the future. By making projections from past data, these methods assume that the future will resemble the past.

However, the exponential smoothing procedure is sophisticated enough to permit representations of a linear trend and a cyclical factor in its calculations. Thus, if we are sure that historical data exhibits a trend or follows a systematic cycle, we can build those structures into the exponential smoothing calculations.

Exponential smoothing procedures are adaptive. If the underlying process changes, and the size of a trend or the size of a seasonal factor changes, then the calculations will respond to this change and eventually produce accurate forecasts. Even if we fail to notice that a trend exists and rely on the basic exponential smoothing model, it will respond somewhat to the actual pattern in the observations, although its forecasts will exhibit a systematic lag.

Implementing an exponential smoothing procedure requires that initial values be specified and a smoothing factor be chosen. In most cases, when forecasts will be calculated for an extended period, the results eventually become insensitive to the initial values. Therefore, it is often reasonable to use coarse estimates or default values (zero) for initial values. At the same time, the smoothing factor should be chosen to trade off stability and responsiveness in an appropriate manner.

Although specialized software for moving-average and exponential smoothing procedures is available, routine forecasting is easy to adapt to the spreadsheet, as a means of tracking and predicting future values of key parameters. Although Excel contains a Data Analysis tool for calculating moving-average forecasts and exponentially smoothed forecasts, the tool does not accommodate the most powerful version of exponential smoothing, which includes trend and cyclical components. Fortunately, the formulas for these calculations are straightforward, and they lend themselves easily to spreadsheet use. Even without an add-in to perform the work, analysts can adapt exponential smoothing techniques to spreadsheets without extensive preparation.

SUGGESTED READINGS

A comprehensive source on forecasting methods is the textbook by Makridakis, Wheelwright, and Hyndman:

Makridakis, S., S. C. Wheelwright, and R. J. Hyndman. 1998. *Forecasting: Methods and Applications*. New York: John Wiley & Sons.

The following article reviews progress in research over the first quarter century of time-series forecasting developments:

Armstrong, J. S. 1984. "Forecasting by Extrapolation: Conclusions from Twenty-Five Years of Research." *Interfaces* **14**, 52–66.

EXERCISES

1. For the moving-average example in Figure 7.2, compute the three error measures based on the forecasts for periods 5–10.

a. What is the value of MSE?

b. What is the value of MAD?

c. What is the value of MAPE?

2. Consider the stylized example of Figure 7.3, in which there is a jump in the mean value. Using the same worksheet as a template, enter the exponential smoothing calculations for these periods. Assume that $S_1 = 100$.

a. Take $\alpha = 0.2$. Calculate the forecasts generated by exponential smoothing, and compute the values of MSE, MAD, and MAPE for periods 10–15.

b. Repeat the calculations in part (a) but with $\alpha = 0.6$.

c. If we suspect that there might be a jump in the underlying process, which of the two values of α examined in parts (a) and (b) would be preferred?

3. Brad's Burritos provides a simple set of lunch offerings in a college town. The shop has recently decided to implement a forecasting system and is testing the use of exponential smoothing methods. The owner is willing to assume that by now, the number of customers who come to the shop at lunchtime (noon to 2 P.M.) does not exhibit trends or cyclic effects on weekdays. Data collection has gone on for two weeks (10 weekdays), counting the number of lunchtime customers. The observations are shown in the table.

Day	M	T	W	T	F	M	T	W	T	F
Customers	108	130	96	144	136	113	120	119	120	106

a. Compute a forecast for the number of lunchtime customers on the next weekday by using a 3-day moving average. What is the forecast? What is the MAD for the last five observations?

b. Compute a forecast for the number of lunchtime customers on the next weekday by using exponential smoothing with $\alpha = 0.3$. What is the forecast? What is the MAD for the last five observations?

4. Garish Motors sells new and used automobiles. Sales of new cars over the past 50 weeks are given in the following table (week 50 is the most recent).

Week	Sales	Week	Sales
1	36	26	48
2	42	27	40
3	50	28	55
4	59	29	49
5	72	30	58
6	54	31	52
7	49	32	57
8	37	33	51
9	59	34	54
10	41	35	53
11	53	36	47
12	42	37	44
13	52	38	47
14	55	39	37
15	45	40	51
16	69	41	58
17	64	42	58
18	44	43	39
19	64	44	42
20	59	45	33
21	55	46	50
22	30	47	68
23	60	48	53
24	53	49	44
25	47	50	43

a. Compute a forecast for sales next week by using a 4-week moving average. What is the forecast? What is the MSE for the last five observations?

b. Can you reduce the MSE for the last five observations by changing the moving-average window? (Try 5- to 10-week windows.)

c. Compute a forecast for sales next week by using exponential smoothing with $\alpha = 0.25$. What is the forecast? What is the MSE for the last five observations?

d. Can you improve the MSE for the last five observations by changing the smoothing constant α?

5. Data covering the most recent 30 days are given in the following table for the price per gallon of regular gasoline at a local station.

Day	Price	Day	Price
1	2.53	16	2.46
2	2.35	17	2.60
3	1.91	18	2.10
4	2.20	19	2.01
5	1.77	20	2.14
6	3.26	21	2.03
7	1.63	22	2.68
8	2.73	23	2.59
9	2.41	24	2.99
10	2.72	25	2.94
11	2.87	26	1.77
12	1.49	27	2.62
13	2.92	28	3.19
14	3.53	29	3.01
15	2.74	30	2.10

a. Compute a forecast for the next day's price by using a 3-day moving average. What is the forecast? What is the MSE for the last five observations?

b. Can you reduce the MSE for the last five observations by changing the moving-average window? (Try 4- to 10-day windows.)

c. Compute a forecast for the next day's price by using exponential smoothing with $\alpha = 0.25$. What is the forecast? What is the MSE for the last five observations?

d. Can you improve the MSE for the last five observations by changing the smoothing constant α?

6. Contributions to the disaster relief fund for a national charity average around $1 million a month and do not exhibit trend or seasonal effects. Data on the most recent 12 months is given in the following table.

Month	Contributions
1	1,074,844
2	780,433
3	1,082,218
4	1,009,653
5	1,066,739
6	1,297,010
7	978,685
8	1,108,218
9	1,019,778
10	999,380
11	1,041,070
12	821,189

a. Compute a forecast for next month's contributions by using a 4-month moving average. What is the forecast? What is the MSE for the last five observations?

b. Can you reduce the MSE for the last five observations by changing the moving-average window? (Try 5- to 7-week windows.)

c. Compute a forecast for next month's contributions by using exponential smoothing with $\alpha = 0.25$. What is the forecast? What is the MSE for the last five observations?

d. Can you reduce the MSE for the last five observations by changing the smoothing constant α?

7. Consider the example of Figure 7.7, in which the smoothing constant was taken to be $\alpha = 0.2$. Repeat the calculations for smoothing constants between 0.1 and 0.9, in steps of 0.1.

a. Identify the α–value that achieves the smallest value of MSE.

b. Identify the α–value that achieves the smallest value of MAD.

8. Consider the example of the new product at Curtis Distributors, which was analyzed using Holt's method in Figure 7.12. Repeat the forecasts using one smaller value of α than the value of 0.2 used in the figure, and also one larger value. Then do the same, using one smaller value of β than the value of 0.5 used in the figure, and also one larger value. (This means nine pairs of values in all, one of which is illustrated in the figure.)

a. Which pair (α, β) achieves the smallest value of MSE?

b. Which pair (α, β) achieves the smallest value of MAD?

9. Consider the stylized example in Figure 7.13. Repeat the forecasts using the additive model with trend, using the same smoothing constants.

a. What is the value of MSE corresponding to the multiplicative model in Figure 7.13?

b. What is the value of MSE corresponding to the additive model with the same smoothing constants?

10. Consider the example of the town of Lincoln, which was analyzed using a multiplicative model in Figure 7.14. Repeat the forecasts using the additive model, with the same smoothing constants.

a. What is the value of MSE corresponding to the multiplicative model in Figure 7.12?

b. What is the value of MSE corresponding to the additive model with the same smoothing constants?

11. The operations manager at a manufacturing facility is about to begin an energy-efficiency initiative. As this program begins, it will be helpful to have benchmark data on energy use, in order to determine whether the initiative is having an effect. The facilities department has provided data on the monthly energy use (in kilowatt hours) over the past three years, as shown in the following table:

Year 1	Usage	Year 2	Usage	Year 3	Usage
Jan	31,040	Jan	24,540	Jan	32,410
Feb	28,720	Feb	26,560	Feb	21,380
Mar	20,540	Mar	22,060	Mar	20,370
Apr	22,260	Apr	16,220	Apr	18,300
May	11,550	May	12,920	May	10,020
Jun	13,100	Jun	9,740	Jun	11,420
Jul	14,790	Jul	10,160	Jul	10,020
Aug	12,360	Aug	12,740	Aug	11,800
Sep	12,890	Sep	9,240	Sep	13,120
Oct	9,790	Oct	11,220	Oct	10,410
Nov	14,840	Nov	13,780	Nov	13,510
Dec	14,610	Dec	19,040	Dec	17,340

a. Use the Holt-Winters method to estimate the monthly usage for the coming 12 months. Use smoothing parameters of $\alpha = 0.3$, $\beta = 0.4$, and $\gamma = 0.5$.

b. For the forecasting problem in (a), which value of α achieves the minimum value of MSE, holding the other smoothing parameters constant?

12. The town of Hillside has a surface reservoir that supplies water to the homes in the town's central residential district. A committee of residents is concerned about the system's capacity and wants to project future use. The town's water department has promised to develop its best forecast of water use in the next two years. The department has collected quarterly data on water use (in millions of gallons) over the past decade, as shown in the following table:

Year	Q1	Q2	Q3	Q4
1	55	34	39	65
2	59	54	46	46
3	41	38	33	65
4	37	36	35	51
5	34	21	23	60
6	39	27	23	47
7	42	25	21	55
8	23	22	25	40
9	28	26	21	53
10	30	25	21	54

a. Use the Holt-Winters method to estimate the quarterly water use for the coming eight quarters. Use smoothing parameters of $\alpha = 0.3$, $\beta = 0.4$, and $\gamma = 0.5$

b. For the forecasting problem in (a), which value of α achieves the minimum value of MSE, holding the other smoothing parameters constant?

13. Big Box, the local discount retailer, is negotiating a major expansion with the Planning Board. It has been asked as part of this process to develop a sales forecast for the next several years. Quarterly sales data for the past 10 years are given in the following table:

Year	Q1	Q2	Q3	Q4
1	94.28	83.80	115.23	125.71
2	97.89	87.02	119.65	130.52
3	104.45	92.84	127.66	139.26
4	111.11	98.77	135.81	148.15
5	115.56	102.72	141.24	154.08
6	121.47	107.97	148.47	161.96
7	127.90	113.69	156.33	170.54
8	134.20	119.29	164.02	178.93
9	141.00	125.33	172.33	188.00
10	148.94	132.39	182.04	198.59

a. Develop an appropriate forecast using a moving-average approach.

b. Develop an appropriate forecast using a simple exponential smoothing approach.

c. Develop an appropriate forecast using exponential smoothing with a trend (Holt's method).

d. Develop an appropriate forecast using exponential smoothing with trend and cyclicality (the Holt-Winters method).

e. Which of the four forecasts developed above would you recommend using?

14. Coastal Fuel Oil is a distributor of fuel-oil products in the Northeast. It contracts with shippers for deliveries of home heating oil and distributes product in its own trucks. Since its storage capacity is limited, and purchasing storage for fuel oil it cannot store itself is expensive, accurate demand forecasts are valuable. Monthly data covering the past 10 years are given in the table below.

a. Develop an appropriate forecast using a moving-average approach.

b. Develop an appropriate forecast using a simple exponential smoothing approach.

c. Develop an appropriate forecast using exponential smoothing with trend (Holt's method).

d. Develop an appropriate forecast using exponential smoothing with trend and cyclicality (Holt-Winters method).

e. Which of the four forecasts developed above would you recommend using?

Year	Jan	Feb	Mar	Apr	May	Jun	Jul	Aug	Sep	Oct	Nov	Dec
1	194.92	222.77	250.62	278.46	306.31	334.15	222.77	250.62	278.46	306.31	334.15	362.00
2	203.71	232.81	261.92	291.02	320.12	349.22	232.81	261.92	291.02	320.12	349.22	378.32
3	209.84	239.81	269.79	299.77	329.74	359.72	239.81	269.79	299.77	329.74	359.72	389.70
4	213.67	244.19	274.71	305.24	335.76	366.28	244.19	274.71	305.24	335.76	366.28	396.81
5	219.20	250.52	281.83	313.15	344.46	375.77	250.52	281.83	313.15	344.46	375.77	407.09
6	230.43	263.34	296.26	329.18	362.10	395.02	263.34	296.26	329.18	362.10	395.02	427.93
7	237.36	271.27	305.17	339.08	372.99	406.90	271.27	305.17	339.08	372.99	406.90	440.81
8	241.77	276.31	310.85	345.39	379.93	414.47	276.31	310.85	345.39	379.93	414.47	449.01
9	252.63	288.72	324.81	360.90	396.99	433.08	288.72	324.81	360.90	396.99	433.08	469.17
10	260.01	297.16	334.30	371.45	408.59	445.73	297.16	334.30	371.45	408.59	445.73	482.88

8 Nonlinear Optimization

8.1 INTRODUCTION

Optimization is the process of finding the best set of decisions for a particular measure of performance. For example, in the Advertising Budget example of Chapter 3, we measure performance in terms of annual profit, and optimization allows us to set advertising expenditures in the four quarters so that we achieve the *maximum* annual profit.

In Chapter 4, we introduced a framework for spreadsheet analysis in which optimization represents one of the higher-order levels of analysis, generally coming after a base case has been established, some what-if questions have been explored, and perhaps some back-solving calculations have been made. In this chapter, we'll assume that the steps in that framework have already been carried out. However, the entire framework does not necessarily apply to every spreadsheet model. There are spreadsheets that do not lend themselves to optimization. In some models, for example, the purpose is to explore past relationships or to forecast future outcomes. But managers and analysts generally use models to *improve* future operations. We refer to the levers they use to bring about improved performance as **decision variables**. If there are decision variables in a model, it is natural to ask what the *best* values of those variables are. The measure of performance that defines our notion of "best" is called the **objective function**, or simply the **objective**. Once we have specified the objective in a model, it is also natural to ask what the best value of that objective is. This chapter explores in some detail how to answer these questions by building and analyzing optimization models.

Optimization refers both to the goal of finding the best values of the decision variables and to a set of procedures that accomplish that goal. These procedures are known as **algorithms** and are usually implemented by software. In the case of Excel, the optimization software is known as **Solver**. A version of Solver (referred to as the Standard Solver) is built into every copy of Excel. In this book, we use **Analytic Solver Platform**, which contains a more advanced optimization capability than the Standard Solver in Excel. Analytic Solver Platform is available to users of this book and should be installed before proceeding with this chapter. It is this software that we refer to as Solver.

These days, the word "solver" is often a generic reference to optimization software, whether or not it is implemented in a spreadsheet. However, optimization tools have been available on computers for several decades, predating the widespread use of spreadsheets and even personal computers. Before spreadsheets, optimization was available through stand-alone software but was often accessible only by technical experts. Managers and business analysts had to rely on those experts to build and interpret optimization models. Building such models typically meant constructing algebraic statements to define the problem mathematically. Now, however, the spreadsheet permits end users to develop their own models without having to rely on algebra. Moreover, the same end users can then use Solver themselves to find optimal solutions for the models they build.

Finding the optimal values of decision variables in a spreadsheet model can sometimes present a challenge. Although Solver is a very powerful and highly sophisticated piece of software, it is still possible to formulate otherwise acceptable spreadsheet models for which Solver cannot find the optimal solution. To use Solver effectively, end users should understand how to formulate spreadsheet models that exploit the power of Solver while avoiding its pitfalls. This chapter and the four that follow are designed to provide that understanding.

One way to avoid some of the pitfalls is to follow the principles of spreadsheet design covered in Chapter 3. For instance, it remains desirable to modularize the spreadsheet, to isolate parameters, and to separate decision variables from calculations and intermediate calculations from final results. In the chapters on optimization, we also advocate some additional guidelines for optimization models. These guidelines help us to debug our own models, and when we're finished debugging and testing, the guidelines help us communicate our results to others. Solver actually permits users considerable flexibility in designing models, but if we were to use all of that flexibility, we might confuse the people we want to communicate with, as well as ourselves. For that reason, it is good practice to impose some discipline on the building of optimization models.

Optimization problems are categorized according to the algorithm used to solve them. In the optimization chapters, we discuss the main categories: nonlinear, linear, integer, and nonsmooth optimization problems. In each case, we provide several examples, give advice on how to formulate models appropriately, show how to find solutions, and illustrate how to interpret the results.

In this chapter, we concentrate on the nonlinear solver, which is the default option when we invoke Solver. We begin by demonstrating the optimization approach in the Advertising Budget example. We next provide general principles for building models for Solver. Then, we elaborate on the use of the nonlinear solver and provide additional examples.

8.2 AN OPTIMIZATION EXAMPLE

Recall that in the Advertising Budget example of Chapters 3 and 4, the goal is to plan the spending of advertising dollars over the coming year. Planning is done on a quarterly basis, so we must choose advertising expenditures for each of the four quarters. Whatever plan we devise, we will evaluate it in terms of annual profits. Also, we have an annual advertising budget of $40,000 that we should not exceed. Figure 8.1* reproduces the spreadsheet model that we initially developed in Chapter 3. On the right-hand side of the screen, we find the **task pane**, which holds a summary of the model we'll be building. If this window is not visible, click on the Model icon in the Analytic Solver Platform ribbon. (A second click will hide the task pane.)

8.2.1 Optimizing Q1

We first consider a limited optimization question: What is the best choice of advertising expenditures in the first quarter (Q1)? For the moment, we ignore the existence of the budget, and we assume that the expenditures in the three other quarters remain at $10,000. In Figure 8.2, we show a table of Q1 expenditures and the corresponding annual profits, along with a graph of the relationship. (The table and graph are produced using the Parametric Sensitivity tool described in Chapter 4.) The results show that expenditures beyond the base-case level of $10,000 can increase annual profits; but eventually such expenditures become counterproductive, and annual profits drop. The results also show that the maximum profit level is achieved for expenditures of about $17,000. With two or three systematic refinements

FIGURE 8.1 Base-Case Model for the Advertising Budget Example

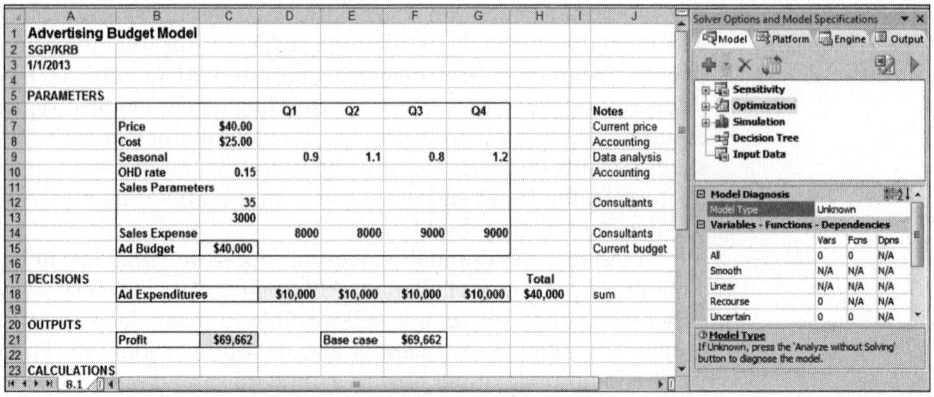

*To download spreadsheets for this chapter, go to the Student Companion Site at www.wiley.com/college/powell.

FIGURE 8.2 Parametric Sensitivity Results for Varying Q1 Expenditures

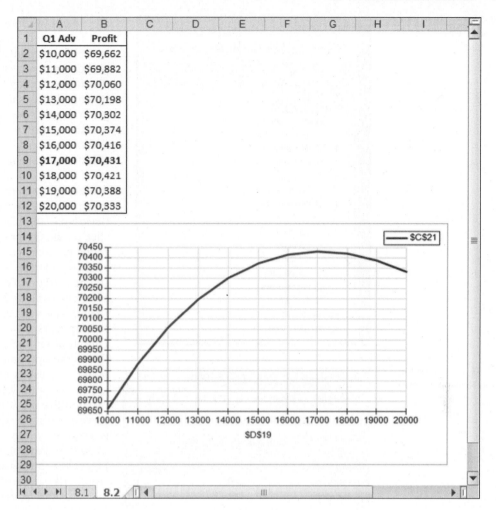

	A	B
1	**Q1 Adv**	**Profit**
2	$10,000	$69,662
3	$11,000	$69,882
4	$12,000	$70,060
5	$13,000	$70,198
6	$14,000	$70,302
7	$15,000	$70,374
8	$16,000	$70,416
9	**$17,000**	**$70,431**
10	$18,000	$70,421
11	$19,000	$70,388
12	$20,000	$70,333

of the table, we could easily determine the optimal expenditures to a higher level of precision. However, we would not be able to extend the sensitivity table to more than two variables, which is our goal given that we have four decision variables.

To illustrate the optimization approach to this problem, we access Solver on the Analytic Solver Platform tab, and we start with the Optimization Model group on the ribbon. The group contains three pull-down menus that describe the model, which we usually specify in the following order:

FIGURE 8.3 Task Pane with Decision Variable Specified

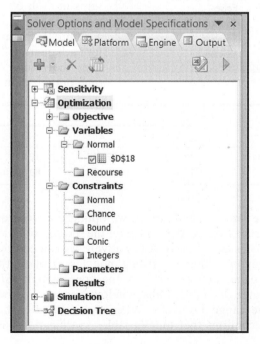

- Decisions
- Objective
- Constraints

For each specification, we have to select the relevant cells in the worksheet before clicking on a menu. For example, our decision is represented by cell D18, so we select that cell and click on the Decisions menu and select Normal. In the task pane, we can immediately see a confirmation of the choice, listed under Variables, as shown in Figure 8.3.

We can specify the objective function by selecting our objective (cell C21) and returning to the ribbon, clicking on the Objective menu, selecting Max and then Normal from the submenu. The updated task pane appears in Figure 8.4.

FIGURE 8.4 Task Pane Updated with Objective Specified

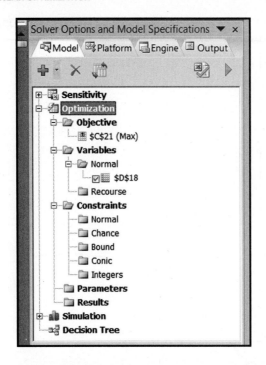

FIGURE 8.5 Selection of the Nonlinear Solver

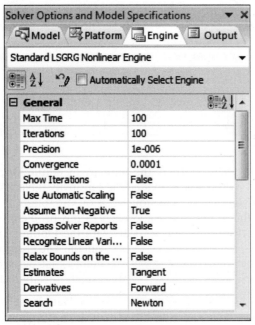

Next, we move to the Engine tab of the task pane and select the Standard LSGRG Nonlinear Engine from the pull-down menu near the top, or confirm that it has already been selected (perhaps by default), as shown in Figure 8.5. As a general rule, we uncheck the box for `Automatically Select Engine` so that we can make an explicit choice suitable for the problem we are solving.

Finally, to implement the solution procedure, we move to the Optimize menu on the ribbon and select `Solve Complete Problem` (or we can simply click on the Optimize icon). If no technical problems are encountered, Solver displays a message at the bottom of the task pane stating, `Solver found a solution. All constraints and optimality conditions are satisfied`. (This same message appears in the results window on the Output tab in the task pane.) We refer to this as the optimality message, and at this point, the results of the optimization run appear on our worksheet. The optimal expenditure in Q1 is $17,093, and the corresponding revenue is $70,431. This is essentially the same result we found using the Parametric Sensitivity tool in Figure 8.2, but with somewhat more precision. It suggests that we'd like to increase the advertising expenditure in Q1, but of course, that would push total expenditures beyond the budget.

8.2.2 Optimization Over All Four Quarters

If we optimized the advertising expenditures in each of the other quarters individually, as we did with Q1, we would find a different optimal level of expenditures for each quarter. The table below summarizes the results of those four one-at-a-time optimization runs.

	Quarter			
	1	**2**	**3**	**4**
Expenditures	17,093	27,016	12,876	32,721
Profits	70,431	73,171	69,806	75,284

We obtain the same expenditures if we optimize all four quarters simultaneously. To do so, we could start from scratch and enter the specifications as we did earlier, but this time selecting four cells as decisions. Alternatively, we can edit the model we've just run. To illustrate one way of editing an existing model, we work with the task pane.

In the task pane, double-click on the specification ($D$18) of the decision variable. The Change Variable Cells window appears, allowing us to change the specification to the range D18:G18. When we click OK, that window disappears, and the task pane confirms that the Variables specification has been edited, and the model contains four decision variables. Again, we can run the optimization by clicking on the Optimize icon. The optimality message then appears at the bottom of the task pane, and the optimal solution to the edited model appears in the worksheet, showing a profit of $79,706.

Unfortunately, this result is infeasible, because it calls for total expenditures of more than $40,000. Although this solution is infeasible, it is useful to explore our model in this way. For one thing, this solution immediately suggests that we may want to lobby for a larger budget. It also reveals an interesting structure in the solution, in that the expenditure profile reflects the seasonal factors, with the highest and lowest values coming in the last two quarters.

Having provided a glimpse of Solver's capability by optimizing our decisions without any restrictions on them, we turn next to Solver's real power, the optimization of decision variables *simultaneously*, in the presence of *constraints*. We return to the Advertising Budget example but this time intending to satisfy the original $40,000 budget. How should we allocate this budget across the four quarters?

8.2.3 Incorporating the Budget Constraint

To investigate this question, we return to the task pane, and verify that the variables are specified as D18:G18 and the objective cell is specified as C21. Next, we move to the Constraints menu in the ribbon. From the submenu, we select Normal Constraint and then the icon for "<=" to obtain the Add Constraint window. Here, we enter the constraint H18 ≤ C15, as shown in Figure 8.6, and click OK. In filling out the Add Constraint window, we follow one of our design guidelines for Solver models by referencing a *formula* in the left-hand window and referencing a *number* in the right-hand window when specifying constraints. In this case, cell H18 contains a formula, and cell C15 contains a number. By relying on cell references rather than entering numbers directly, we ensure that the key parameters are visible on the worksheet itself, rather than in the less accessible windows of the Solver interface.

At this point, the model has been specified well enough to solve (see Figure 8.7), but it is always a good habit to examine the main options in Solver before proceeding. The main options are displayed as True/False selections in the General section of the Engine tab on the task pane, shown in Figure 8.5. In this example, the decision variables must be nonnegative, so the Assume Non-Negative option must be True. The other True/False options can be left at their default values and similarly with the remaining options.

Although the optimization of a model such as the Advertising Budget model can be done quickly and smoothly, we don't advocate running Solver without forethought. We recommend pausing before running Solver, in order to think about what the outcomes might be. In the case at hand,

- Should we expect the budget to be allocated equally across the quarters?
- If so, why should this occur?
- If not, should we expect one of the allocations to be zero?

These kinds of questions are informal hypotheses that can be very valuable to an analyst. They provide an opportunity for us to test our intuition with respect to the model. Only two things can happen, and they are both good. Either our intuition will be confirmed, in which case our confidence in the model will increase; or else our intuition will be contradicted, in which case we can learn something unexpected about the situation that might improve our understanding.

In this example, we have already explored the differences among the quarters, so we should expect the allocations to be unequal across quarters, reflecting differences in the

FIGURE 8.6 Entering Constraint Information in the Add Constraint Window

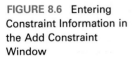

FIGURE 8.7 The Complete Optimization Model

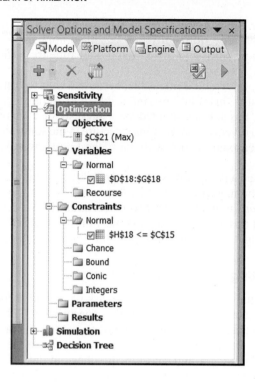

seasonal factors. Our limited examination of the relationship between Q1 expenditures and profit (Figure 8.1) revealed decreasing marginal returns, suggesting that nonzero expenditures could be productive in any quarter.

By entering the addresses of the decision variables and the objective and by specifying a constraint, we have prepared the model for optimization. When we click the Optimization icon on the ribbon, or equivalently, the green triangle icon in the task pane, Solver searches for the optimal expenditures and displays the results in the worksheet. We could restore the decision variables (by clicking the "Re-do" icon on the Output tab), but normally we keep the optimal solution. In this case, we observe that the optimal profit is $71,447, as shown in Figure 8.8. As we can see in the figure, the optimal allocation contains different expenditures in each quarter, and in every quarter the expenditure exceeds $5,000. The highest expenditures occur in Q4 and Q2, as we might have predicted, given their high seasonal factors. Finally, we note that the entire $40,000 advertising budget is used.

FIGURE 8.8 The Optimal Allocation in the Advertising Budget Model

	A	B	C	D	E	F	G	H	I	J
1	**Advertising Budget Model**									
2	SGP/KRB									
3	1/1/2013									
4										
5	PARAMETERS									
6				Q1	Q2	Q3	Q4			**Notes**
7		Price	$40.00							Current price
8		Cost	$25.00							Accounting
9		Seasonal		0.9	1.1	0.8	1.2			Data analysis
10		OHD rate	0.15							Accounting
11		Sales Parameters								
12			35							Consultants
13			3000							
14		Sales Expense		8000	8000	9000	9000			Consultants
15		Ad Budget	$40,000							Current budget
16										
17	DECISIONS							Total		
18		Ad Expenditures		$7,273	$12,347	$5,117	$15,263	$40,000		sum
19										
20	OUTPUTS									
21		Profit	$71,447		Base case	$69,662				
22										
23	CALCULATIONS									
24		Quarter		Q1	Q2	Q3	Q4	Total		
25		Seasonal		0.9	1.1	0.8	1.2			
26										
27		Units Sold		3193	4769	2523	5676	16161		given formula
28		Revenue		127709	190777	100905	227038	646430		price*units
29		Cost of Goods		79818	119236	63066	141899	404019		cost*units
30		Gross Margin		47891	71542	37840	85139	242411		subtraction
31										
32		Sales Expense		8000	8000	9000	9000	34000		given
33		Advertising		7273	12347	5117	15263	40000		decisions
34		Overhead		19156	28617	15136	34056	96965		rate*revenue
35		Total Fixed Cost		34430	48963	29253	58319	170965		sum
36										
37		Profit		13461	22578	8587	26820	71447		GM -TFC
38		Profit Margin		10.54%	11.83%	8.51%	11.81%	11.05%		pct of revenue
39										

As we mentioned earlier, most of our general guidelines about effective spreadsheet design apply to the specific case of building models for use with Solver. In addition, Solver requires specific information about our optimization problem, so we must be able to identify decision variables, an objective, and the constraints (if any). The process of identifying these elements is called **formulating** an optimization problem.

8.3.1 Formulation

Every optimization model is made up of decision variables, an objective function, and (possibly) a set of constraints. Before setting up a worksheet for optimization, it is a good idea to identify these elements, at least in words if not in symbols. To get started, we can ask three key questions:

- What must be decided?
- What measure should we use to compare alternative sets of decisions?
- What restrictions limit our choice?

To guide us toward decision variables, we ask ourselves, "What must be decided?" Decision variables must be under the control of the decision maker. (Quantitative inputs that are *not* under the decision maker's control are treated as parameters.) From the start, we should be explicit about the units in which we measure each decision variable. Common examples of decision variables would include quantities to buy, quantities to deploy, quantities to produce, and quantities to deliver (or combinations of the above list). Whatever the decision variables are, once we know their numerical values, we should have a resolution of the problem. In Solver models, the Variables cells contain the values of decision variables.

In the Advertising Budget model of Figure 8.8, the decision variables are the advertising expenditures in each of the four quarters. Once we know their values, we have a resolution of the budget allocation problem. The specific values appear in the range D18:G18.

To guide us toward an objective function, we ask ourselves, "What measure should we use to compare alternative sets of decisions?" Imagine that two consultants have come to us with their recommendations on what action to take (i.e., what decision variables to use), and we must choose which action we prefer. For this purpose, we need a yardstick—a single performance measure that tells us which action is better. That quantity is affected by the choice of decision variables, and it will normally be obvious whether we wish to maximize or minimize. Maximization criteria usually focus on such measures as profit, revenue, return, or efficiency. Minimization criteria usually focus on cost, time, distance, size, or investment. In Solver models, the Objective contains a reference to the objective function cell and a direction (max or min). In the model of Figure 8.8, the objective function cell is C21, which we want to maximize.

In many optimization models, the formula for the objective function cell directly references decision-variable cells. In complicated cases, there may be intermediate calculations, and the logical relation between objective function and decision variables may be indirect. In such cases, we might want to use the Trace Dependents command (Formulas▶Formula Auditing▶Trace Dependents) to confirm that each decision variable is linked to the objective function. Similarly, we can use the Trace Precedents option to confirm that the objective function is ultimately linked to each decision variable.

To guide us toward constraints, we ask ourselves, "What restrictions limit our choice of decision variables?" Seldom are we free to choose any set of decisions we like; instead, we may have to respect certain limitations that are intrinsic to the decision problem. For example, we may look for capacities that provide upper limits on certain activities or commitments that place lower limits on other activities. Sometimes, we may specify equations to ensure consistency among a set of variables.

A constraint consists of a comparison between one measured quantity and a parameter of the problem. The measured quantity depends on the decision variables, and the role of the constraint is to make sure that the decision variables, alone or in combination, meet the requirements of the problem. By convention, each constraint involves a relationship between a measured quantity on the left-hand side (or LHS) and a parameter of the problem on the right-hand side (or RHS.) We refer to the parameter as the **constraint constant**, the **RHS constant,** or simply the RHS. Constraints appear in three varieties in optimization models:

$$LHS \leq RHS \quad \text{(less-than constraint)}$$
$$LHS \geq RHS \quad \text{(greater-than constraint)}$$
$$LHS = RHS \quad \text{(equality constraint)}$$

We use less-than constraints to represent capacities or ceilings or in places where we find it necessary to say "at most" or "no more than" a certain quantity. For example, we might require that labor hours scheduled must be no more than the labor hours available. In that case, the number of hours scheduled would make up the LHS, and the number of hours available would be the RHS of a less-than constraint.

We use greater-than constraints to represent commitments or thresholds or in places where we find it necessary to say "at least" or "no less than" a certain quantity. For example, we might require that components purchased must be at least as large as the obligation in the purchasing contract. In that case, components purchased would make up the LHS, and the contractual commitment would be the RHS of a greater-than constraint.

Finally, we use equality constraints to represent material balance or simply to define related variables consistently. For example, we might include a material-balance constraint that end-of-month inventory must equal start-of-month inventory plus production minus demand. In symbols, this relationship translates into the following algebraic expression:

Ending Inventory = Starting Inventory + Production − Demand

In such a case, the demand level usually plays the role of a given parameter, and the other quantities are usually related to decision variables. To be consistent with the convention of placing parameters on the right-hand side, we can rewrite the expression as:

Starting Inventory + Production − Ending Inventory = Demand

Like the objective function, the LHS is a formula that references the decision variables directly, or else we can use the Formula Auditing group of tools to trace the linkage back to the decision variables through one or more intermediate quantities. We reference the LHS formula on the left-hand side of the Add Constraint window, while we reference the RHS constant on the right-hand side of the window.

In the Advertising Budget model, there is only one constraint: The total advertising expenditure over the year must be at most $40,000. The left-hand side of this less-than constraint amounts to the sum of the quarterly expenditures and appears in cell H18. (With the Trace Precedents option, we can quickly see how this quantity is linked directly to the decision variables.) The right-hand side of the constraint corresponds to the parameter in cell C15.

8.3.2 Layout

We prefer a disciplined approach to building optimization models, and we advocate conformance to a relatively standardized model template. Standardization helps us in several ways. First, it enhances our ability to communicate with others. A standardized structure provides a common language for describing optimization problems and reinforces our understanding about how these models are shaped. This is especially true when spreadsheet models are being shown to someone knowledgeable about optimization. Second, it improves our ability to diagnose errors while we are building the model. A standardized structure has certain recognizable features that make it easier to spot modeling errors or simple typographical errors than in an unstructured approach. Third, it permits us to "scale up" the model more easily. That is, we may later want to expand a model by adding variables or constraints, allowing us to move from a prototype to a practical size, or from a "toy" version to an "industrial strength" version.

Here are the main elements of our structured approach:

- Organize the worksheet into modules. We suggest using separate portions of the worksheet for decision variables, objective function, and constraints; but sometimes other forms of organization are more appropriate. For data-intensive models, it is also a good idea to devote a separate module to the input data.

- Place all decision variables in a single row (or column) of the worksheet if possible. (It is sometimes advantageous to use a rectangular range for decision variables.)
- Use color highlighting or borders for the decision variable cells.
- Place the objective function in a single cell, also highlighted.
- Arrange constraints to facilitate visual comparison of left-hand and right-hand sides. For the most part, "left" and "right" can be respected in the layout, although other formats occasionally make more sense. Sometimes, it is also helpful to calculate the difference between the left- and right-hand sides for each constraint, or at least to indicate whether the constraint has been met exactly.

On occasion, there are reasonable exceptions to these guidelines. However, the standard features provide a useful starting point for the several reasons we have enumerated.

SOLVER TIP
Ranges for Decision Variables

When we add or edit information about the decision variables of our model, we could reference those cells one at a time. We prefer, however, to arrange the worksheet so that all the decision variables are in adjacent cells, since this allows us to make a single reference to their range. Using a single range makes data entry efficient and reduces clutter in the Solver interface. Because most optimization problems have several decision variables, it saves time if we place them in adjacent cells. This design also makes the task pane description easier to interpret if someone else is trying to follow our work, or if we are reviewing it after not having seen it for a long time. ∎

8.3.3 Interpreting Results

Just as there are three modules in our worksheet, there are three kinds of information to examine in the optimization results. First, there are the optimal values of the decision variables. They tell us the best course of action. Second, there is the optimal value of the objective function, which tells us the best level of performance we can achieve. Third, there are the constraint outcomes. In particular, a constraint in which the left-hand side equals the right-hand side is called a **tight**, or **binding**, constraint. Prior to solving the model, *every* constraint is a potential limitation on the set of decisions, but optimization generally leads to an outcome where only *some* of the constraints are actually binding. These are the true economic limitations in the model: they are the constraints that actually prevent us from achieving even better levels of performance.

We can think of the solution to an optimization problem as providing what we might call **tactical** information and **strategic** information. By tactical information, we mean that the optimal solution prescribes the best possible set of decisions under the conditions given. Thus, if the model represents an actual situation, its optimal decisions represent a plan to be implemented. By strategic information, we mean that the optimal solution tells us what factors could lead us to even better levels of performance. If we are not faced with the need to implement a course of action immediately, we can think about altering one of the problem's parameters in a way that could improve the situation. Thus, if the model represents a situation with given parametric conditions, we can examine the possibility of changing the "givens" in order to raise the level of performance. In the Advertising Budget example, the tactical information consists of the specific allocation of $40,000 to four quarters. The strategic information, based on our discussion earlier, is that an increase in the budget would be economically desirable. If we can expand the budget, we can raise the level of profit achieved.

8.4 MODEL CLASSIFICATION AND THE NONLINEAR SOLVER

Optimization models come in only a few basic types or categories. It is important to recognize the category into which a model falls, because the algorithm used to optimize the model should match its type. The fundamental distinction among models arises from linearity.

Every algebraic relationship in a model is either **linear** or **nonlinear**. In a linear relationship, each variable is multiplied by a constant, such as the straight line

$$y = ax + b$$

where x and y represent variables, or the plane

$$z = ax + by$$

where x, y, and z represent variables.

Any relationship that is *not* of this form is nonlinear; for example, the power function

$$y = ax^b$$

when $b \neq 1$, or the product function

$$z = axy$$

where x, y, and z represent variables.

Optimization problems are classified as linear if the objective function and all the constraints are linear functions of the decision variables. If any one of these components is not linear, the problem is classified as a nonlinear optimization problem. We also refer to linear optimization as **linear programming** and to nonlinear optimization as **nonlinear programming**. As the default choice, the Engine tab of the task pane always shows the selection of the nonlinear solver (Standard LSGRG Nonlinear) when we first enter information describing our model. The nonlinear solver can be used for both linear problems or for nonlinear problems, although it is not always the best algorithm to use for linear problems. The main alternative is the linear solver (Standard LP/Quadratic), which is specialized for linear constraints and either linear or quadratic objectives. We examine linear models in the next chapter.

The algorithm used by Solver for nonlinear optimization is called the **LSGRG algorithm** (short for Large-Scale Generalized Reduced Gradient), which is often likened to hill climbing in the fog. Because of the fog, we can't tell where the peak is located relative to our starting point, so we can use only the conditions close around us to choose a search direction. One practical approach, or heuristic, would be to follow the steepest path we can see. After we proceed a short distance in that direction, we look again for the steepest path available from our new location and proceed in that direction. Again, after a short distance, we reach the limit of what we were able to see in the fog, and we reassess which direction is the steepest, modifying our path as we go. Eventually, we come to a point from which no path leads up. As far as we can tell, this must be the peak, so we stop.

The LSGRG algorithm uses a very similar procedure to locate a maximum for an objective function. It starts at the point represented by the values in the decision variable cells, tests different directions in which it could modify those variables, and selects the direction that goes up most steeply—that is, in which the objective function increases the fastest. After moving in that direction, the procedure tests different directions from its new location and again selects the steepest path. Eventually, the procedure comes to a point where no step in any direction goes up. At that point, the procedure stops. (In a minimization problem, we could think of the procedure as descending into a crater, looking for the lowest point.)

The LSGRG algorithm has some additional intelligence built into its procedure. For example, it is capable of adjusting the size of its steps—taking large steps while steep paths are available, but then taking smaller steps as the path levels out. The algorithm can also cope with constraints. However, hill climbing in the fog has one serious limitation. When we stop the search, fog obscures our long range view, so we can't see whether another location some distance away is higher than where we stopped. In other words, the fog may prevent us from seeing a higher peak than the one we found. In an analogous fashion, the LSGRG algorithm may stop at a solution that we call a **local optimum**. This point is better than any other point close by, but there could well be an even better solution some distance away, unseen by the search procedure. Although we wish to find the highest peak, or **global optimum**, the LSGRG algorithm will not guarantee that we always find it with one run, except in special circumstances.

FIGURE 8.9 Graph
of a Hypothetical
Performance Measure

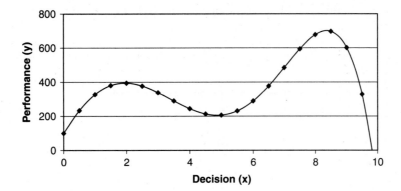

A graphical interpretation should underscore this point. Figure 8.9 shows a graph of a hypothetical performance measure, where the single decision variable is plotted along the horizontal axis. The actual formula for performance is the following:

$$f(x) = 100 + 300x - 60x^2 - 17.5x^3 + 5.32x^4 - 0.33x^5$$

The maximum value of the function is about 700, attained when $x = 8.36$. However, if we begin our hill-climbing procedure at points below $x = 4.85$, Solver will stop at the point $x = 1.95$, where the function reaches a local optimum of about 395. On the other hand, if we start above $x = 4.85$, our hill-climbing procedure will take us to the global optimum, as desired.

As our graph shows, the final solution produced by the LSGRG algorithm may depend on where it started. This would be true in problems where there are several local optima distinct from the global optimum. In such cases, there can never be a guarantee that a single run of Solver has found the optimal solution, so it makes sense to rerun Solver several times, starting with a different initial solution each time. The **initial solution** is the set of values of the decision variables in the worksheet when Solver begins its search. If Solver finds the same solution from many different initial solutions, that should increase our confidence that we have found the global optimum. On the other hand, there is no recipe for how many initial solutions to try or where they should be located.

In many practical cases, the objective function has only one local optimum, which is also a global optimum. A figure corresponding to Figure 8.9 for this type of function would exhibit only one peak. Such functions are sometimes referred to as shaped like an "inverted bowl." (In minimization problems, the analogy would be a "bowl-shaped" function.) For these kinds of functions, the LSGRG algorithm in Solver is perfectly reliable when the model contains either no constraints or a set of linear constraints. We use the term *reliable* to mean that the algorithm finds the global optimum.

8.5 NONLINEAR PROGRAMMING EXAMPLES

Because nonlinear functions include a wide variety of possible relationships, many different kinds of problems lend themselves to solution with the nonlinear solver. The Advertising Budget example was such a problem, in which the nonlinearity arose in the function relating sales and advertising. Thus, we found ourselves confronting a nonlinear objective function and (in the case of the advertising budget) a linear constraint. In this section, we illustrate the formulation and solution of nonlinear programs related to some other common problem structures. Each involves the maximization or minimization of a nonlinear objective function.

8.5.1 Facility Location

A common logistics problem is to locate a facility that serves many customer sites. The customer sites already exist, so their locations are known. The service facility is to be centrally located according to some measure of "central." Most often, the location problem arises in two dimensions, as in the case of the Kilroy Paper Company.

EXAMPLE
Kilroy Paper Company

Kilroy Paper Company distributes specialty papers to big-box stores in ten major U.S. metropolitan areas and plans to consolidate its warehouses into one national distribution center (DC). To identify a suitable location, Kilroy's distribution manager first maps the ten stores on a two-dimensional grid, so that coordinates (x_k, y_k) can be associated with each site. These values are shown in the following table:

Site (k)	x_k	y_k
1	5	41
2	20	10
3	44	48
4	60	58
5	100	4
6	138	80
7	150	40
8	170	18
9	182	2
10	190	56

For any distribution center location (x, y), it is possible to calculate the distance from the DC to each of the stores and to sum the distances. This total can be thought of as a proxy for the total annual cost incurred by Kilroy's trucks, since they will make regular trips to the individual stores. Minimizing the sum of distances therefore represents an objective that is consistent with minimizing annual distribution cost. Kilroy wishes to determine the location that achieves the minimum sum of distances. ∎

To begin the analysis, we ask, "What must be decided?" The answer is clearly the site for the distribution center, which is given by a pair of coordinates (x, y). In the worksheet of Figure 8.10, we place initial guesses for the coordinates (x, y) in cells C4 and D4.

To develop an objective function, we ask, "What measure of performance can we use?" As the problem statement indicates, the measure of interest is the sum of the distances between the distribution center and the various stores. This measure takes some effort to construct. The straight-line distance in two dimensions (also known as the **Euclidean distance**) between the distribution center and the kth store is given by

$$Distance = \sqrt{\left[(x\text{-}distance)^2 + (y\text{-}distance)^2\right]}$$

FIGURE 8.10 Model for the Kilroy Paper Company Example

	A	B	C	D	E	F	G
1	**Locating a Distribution Center**						
2							
3	**Decisions**		*x*	*y*			
4		Location	10.0	10.0			
5							
6	**Result**		Sum	1059.1			
7							
8	**Data**				**Calculations**		
9		Site (k)	x(k)	y(k)	x-dist	y-dist	Distance
10		1	5	41	-5.000	31.000	31.401
11		2	20	10	10.000	0.000	10.000
12		3	44	48	34.000	38.000	50.990
13		4	60	58	50.000	48.000	69.311
14		5	100	4	90.000	-6.000	90.200
15		6	138	80	128.000	70.000	145.890
16		7	150	40	140.000	30.000	143.178
17		8	170	18	160.000	8.000	160.200
18		9	182	2	172.000	-8.000	172.186
19		10	190	56	180.000	46.000	185.785
20							

8.10

FIGURE 8.11 Optimal Solution for the Kilroy Paper Company Example

	A	B	C	D	E	F	G
1	Locating a Distribution Center						
2							
3	Decisions		x	y			
4		Location	114.1	35.2			
5							
6	Result		Sum	670.6			
7							
8	Data				Calculations		
9		Site (k)	x(k)	y(k)	x-dist	y-dist	Distance
10		1	5	41	-109.071	5.828	109.226
11		2	20	10	-94.071	-25.172	97.380
12		3	44	48	-70.071	12.828	71.235
13		4	60	58	-54.071	22.828	58.692
14		5	100	4	-14.071	-31.172	34.201
15		6	138	80	23.929	44.828	50.815
16		7	150	40	35.929	4.828	36.252
17		8	170	18	55.929	-17.172	58.506
18		9	182	2	67.929	-33.172	75.596
19		10	190	56	75.929	20.828	78.734
20							

8.10   8.11

or

$$D_k(x, y) = \sqrt{\left[(x - x_k)^2 + (y - y_k)^2 \right]}$$

For each store k, this distance is calculated in column G of Figure 8.10 (using the Excel function SQRT). The sum of these distances is the measure of performance:

$$f(x, y) = \sum_{k=1}^{10} D_k(x, y)$$

This sum is calculated in cell D6 of the worksheet.

The optimization problem is to find the decision variables (x, y) that minimize the objective function $f(x, y)$. The problem has no explicit constraints. In Figure 8.10, the decision variables appear in cells C4 and D4, and the objective function appears in cell D6. For Solver, we enter the following specifications:

> Variables: C4:D4
> Objective: D6 (minimize)
> Constraints: None

The optimal solution, as displayed in Figure 8.11, is the location (114.1, 35.2), for which the objective function reaches a minimum of approximately 670.6. This location is the central site for Kilroy's distribution center.

SOLVER TIP
Objective Cell
Options

By default, Solver provides us with the opportunity to *maximize* an objective cell. We can instead choose to *minimize*, by double-clicking the cell reference of the objective in the task pane. This opens the Change Objective window, where we can select the button for the Min option. (We can also select the objective cell and use the pull-down Objective menu on the ribbon, if we prefer.) A third option in the Change Objective window allows us to specify a target value and for our variables find a set of values that achieves that target. This capability is similar to that of the Goal Seek tool, except that Solver can handle many variables at once. However, it is the maximization and minimization modes for which Solver is primarily used.   ∎

8.5.2   Revenue Maximization

A common business problem involves maximizing revenue in the presence of a demand curve. A **demand curve** is simply a function that relates demand volume to price. But because revenue is the product of price and volume, and volume depends on price, revenue is generally a nonlinear function of price. In some cases, volume depends as well on another product's price. We illustrate with the following example:

Coastal Telephone Company (CTC) is a regional supplier of long-distance telephone services. CTC is trying to determine the optimal pricing structure for its daytime and evening long distance calling rates. The daytime price applies from 8:00 A.M. to 6:00 P.M., and the evening price applies the rest of the time. With the help of a consultant, the company has estimated the average demand for phone lines (per minute) as follows:

$$Daytime\ Lines\ Demanded = 600 - 5000 \times Day\ Price + 300 \times Evening\ Price$$
$$Evening\ Lines\ Demanded = 400 + 600 \times Day\ Price - 2500 \times Evening\ Price$$

CTC wants to find prices that maximize its revenue. ∎

To determine the decision variables in this problem, we ask, "What must be decided?" Here, the answer is obviously the pair of prices, which we write as *DP* for the daytime price and *EP* for the evening price.

To determine the objective function, we ask, "What measure should we use?" As stated, CTC is interested in maximizing its total revenue. Total revenue consists of a daytime component and an evening component. The daytime component per minute is $DD \times DP$, where *DD* represents daytime demand. Similarly, the evening component per minute is $ED \times EP$, where *ED* represents evening demand. Noting that there are 600 minutes in the daytime period and 840 minutes in the evening period, we can write our objective function as follows:

$$Revenue = 600DD \times DP + 840ED \times EP$$

Since *DD* is a function of both *DP* and *EP*, the objective function is nonlinear because it involves products of decision variables (i.e., $DP \times DP$ and $DP \times EP$). Moreover, *DD* is not, strictly speaking, a decision variable. Rather, we can view it as a *derived* variable, or an intermediate variable, in the sense that its value is determined once we know the values of the decision variables.

A formal statement of the optimization problem is shown below, including the demand curve constraints:

$$\text{Maximize } Revenue = 600DD \times DP + 840ED \times EP$$

Subject to
$$DD = 600 - 5000DP + 300EP$$
$$ED = 400 + 600DP - 2500EP$$

In the worksheet shown in Figure 8.12, we devote column B to daytime variables and column C to evening variables. Model construction takes the following steps.

- We place the daytime and evening prices in row 4. Since we do not know the optimal prices when we are building the worksheet, we can place initial guesses (such as $0.10) in these cells.

- The demand parameters appear in the next module, with demands calculated in row 10. The revenues are calculated in row 14 from the demands in row 10.

- These last two figures are summed to obtain total revenue in cell B15.

FIGURE 8.12 Model for the Coastal Telephone Company Example

	A	B	C	D	E
1	**Coastal Telephone Company**				
2					
3	**Decisions**	Day Price	Eve Price		
4		0.100	0.100		
5					
6	**Demand**				
7	parameters	600	400		
8		-5000	-2500		
9		300	600		
10	demand	130.000	210.000		
11					
12	**Objective**				
13	parameters	600	840	minutes/day	
14	revenue	7,800	17,640		
15	total	25,440			
16					

To find a solution to the problem, we invoke Solver and specify:

Variables: B4:C4
Objective: B15 (maximize)
Constraints: None

The optimal prices turn out to be roughly $DP = 0.070$ and $EP = 0.091$, with maximum revenue of $28,044 per day. (When the objective is a quadratic function, as it is here, and no constraints apply, the LSGRG algorithm reliably finds the global optimum. This could be confirmed by running Solver from a variety of initial values for the decision variables.)

SOLVER TIP
Settings for the Solver Options

Before we run Solver, we should verify the main options, which can be found on the Engine tab of the task pane. Five options take on values of True or False:

Show Iterations. This option stops the nonlinear solver at each step of its search, displaying the latest solution found. Since there is no reason to intervene in the search procedure, except possibly when a model needs debugging, this option usually should be set to False.

Use Automatic Scaling. This option may be invoked (set to True) if numerical difficulties are encountered in finding an optimal solution. One possible cause is a formulation containing numbers of rather different magnitudes. However, it is something of a last resort for troubleshooting.

Assume Non-Negative. This option should be True whenever variables are nonnegative (which is in the vast majority of applications). It is possible to enter explicit constraints that force decision variables to be positive or zero, but the check box is an easier mechanism and avoids clutter in the model specification.

Bypass Solver Reports. This option provides an advantage only when Solver is called by a macro, but this is an advanced use. Set it to False.

Recognize Linear Variables. In complicated nonlinear models, this option allows the solution algorithm to take advantage of linear structure and speed up what might otherwise be a lengthy search; most of the time, such an advantage is not needed. Set it to False.

In summary, we usually assume that variables are nonnegative, but otherwise these options can usually be set to False (their default values) without compromising the search for an optimum. ∎

8.5.3 Curve Fitting

As another example of optimization without constraints, we describe a general approach to regression, or, more accurately, the process of fitting a function to observed data points. We consider the example of Van Winkle's Pharmacy.

EXAMPLE
Van Winkle's Pharmacy

Van Winkle's Pharmacy, a chain of drugstores, owns pharmacies in different types of locations, such as shopping malls, grocery stores, and independent storefronts. Stores in different types of locations are open for different hours, and the company can therefore study a natural experiment to see how revenue varies with store hours. For a sample of 10 stores, the following data show the number of hours the store is open each week and the average revenue:

Store	Hours	Revenue
1	40	5,958
2	44	6,662
3	48	6,004
4	48	6,011
5	60	7,250
6	70	8,632
7	72	6,964
8	90	11,097
9	100	9,107
10	168	11,498

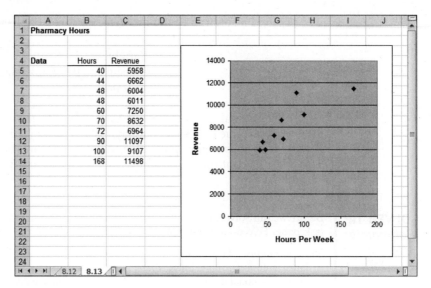

FIGURE 8.13 Data for the Van Winkle's Pharmacy Example

The given data appear in cells B5:C14 in the worksheet of Figure 8.13. The scatter plot in Figure 8.13 suggests a nonlinear relationship, so we will work with a simple nonlinear function. Recalling our list of functions in Figure 2.12, we first hypothesize that the relationship takes the form of the power curve with diminishing returns

$$Revenue = a \times Hours^b$$

∎

What must be decided? Here, the decision variables are the parameters a and b. What measure should we use? The traditional objective function is the sum of squared differences between the model and the data. What constraints apply? None: the choices for a and b are not restricted at all.

In the worksheet of Figure 8.14, we reserve cells D1 and D2 for the parameters a and b, respectively, and we enter the formula for *Revenue* into cells D5:D14. As tentative values, we set $a = 1,000$ and $b = 0.5$, knowing those arbitrary choices can likely be improved. We now have the observed values and the model values for *Revenue* next to each other in columns C and D. In column E, we calculate the difference between model and observation and in column F, the square of each difference. The sum of these squared differences appears in cell F2 and represents the objective function. We invoke Solver and specify:

Variables:	D1:D2
Objective:	F2 (minimize)
Constraints:	None

FIGURE 8.14 Model for Curve Fitting in the Van Winkle's Pharmacy Example

	A	B	C	D	E	F	G
1	Pharmacy Hours		a	1000		Sum of Squared Differences	
2			b	0.5		9,993,184	
3							
4	Data	Hours	Revenue	Model	Difference	Sq. Diff.	
5		40	5958	6325	-367	134363	
6		44	6662	6633	29	827	
7		48	6004	6928	-924	854152	
8		48	6011	6928	-917	841262	
9		60	7250	7746	-496	245983	
10		70	8632	8367	265	70437	
11		72	6964	8485	-1521	2314297	
12		90	11097	9487	1610	2592638	
13		100	9107	10000	-893	797449	
14		168	11498	12961	-1463	2141778	
15							

FIGURE 8.15 Optimal Solution for the Van Winkle's Pharmacy Example

	A	B	C	D	E	F	G
1	**Pharmacy Hours**		a	1022.0345		*Sum of Squared Differences*	
2			b	0.4817852		7,554,649	
3							
4	**Data**	Hours	Revenue	Model	Difference	Sq. Diff.	
5		40	5958	6044	-86	7372	
6		44	6662	6328	334	111650	
7		48	6004	6599	-595	353747	
8		48	6011	6599	-588	345470	
9		60	7250	7348	-98	9549	
10		70	8632	7914	718	515249	
11		72	6964	8022	-1058	1120079	
12		90	11097	8933	2164	4683482	
13		100	9107	9398	-291	84689	
14		168	11498	12067	-569	323363	
15							

8.12 / 8.13 / 8.14 / **8.15**

No constraints need be specified, not even nonnegativity of the decision variables (although we expect the optimal value of b to be greater than zero because revenue should increase with hours). The optimal model parameters turn out to be $a = 1,022$ and $b = 0.482$, with a minimum sum of squares approximately equal to 7.55 million, as shown in Figure 8.15. (When the objective is in the form of a sum of squared differences, the LSGRG algorithm reliably finds the global optimum. This could be confirmed by running Solver from a variety of initial values for the decision variables.) By way of comparison, standard regression software does not achieve a sum of squares as small as this value.

The model that we have built is quite flexible because of its modular structure. For example, we could easily modify the worksheet to fit an alternative model of diminishing returns in the form

$$Revenue = a + b \times log(Hours)$$

This modification requires that we enter the model function into cell D5 and then copy it throughout the column below. Thus, column D serves as a module corresponding to the *form* of the model we wish to fit.

A second module corresponds to the measure of fit. Although minimizing the sum of squared differences would be the typical objective function for regression analysis, other measures of fit are sometimes appropriate. For example, we could minimize the sum of *absolute* differences. Under this criterion, large deviations between the function and the data have less influence on the results than they would under the least-squares criterion. For this criterion, we calculate the absolute difference between model and observation in column F, as shown in Figure 8.16. The function in cell F2 does not have to change. When we run Solver, we do not have to modify the model specification, because the necessary modifications have all been made on the worksheet. The objective-function cell and decision-variable cells remain the same. Thus, column F is a module corresponding to the *criterion* for the model we wish to fit. Together, the modules for form and criterion give us a handy tool for fitting a model to data, a tool that provides flexibility unavailable in the standard approaches to regression.

FIGURE 8.16 Second Revenue Model for the Van Winkle's Pharmacy Example

	A	B	C	D	E	F	G
1	**Pharmacy Hours**		a	1022.0345		*Sum of Absolute Differences*	
2			b	0.4817852		6500	
3							
4	**Data**	Hours	Revenue	Model	Difference	Abs. Diff.	
5		40	5958	6044	-86	86	
6		44	6662	6328	334	334	
7		48	6004	6599	-595	595	
8		48	6011	6599	-588	588	
9		60	7250	7348	-98	98	
10		70	8632	7914	718	718	
11		72	6964	8022	-1058	1058	
12		90	11097	8933	2164	2164	
13		100	9107	9398	-291	291	
14		168	11498	12067	-569	569	
15							

8.12 / 8.13 / 8.14 / 8.15 / **8.16**

FIGURE 8.17 Optimal
Solution for the Second
Revenue Model

	A	B	C	D	E	F	G	H
1	**Pharmacy Hours**		a	1106.404		*Sum of Absolute Differences*		
2			b	0.4577308		5718		
3								
4	**Data**	Hours	Revenue	Model	Difference	Abs. Diff.		
5		40	5958	5987	-29	29		
6		44	6662	6254	408	408		
7		48	6004	6508	-504	504		
8		48	6011	6508	-497	497		
9		60	7250	7208	42	42		
10		70	8632	7735	897	897		
11		72	6964	7836	-872	872		
12		90	11097	8678	2419	2419		
13		100	9107	9107	0	0		
14		168	11498	11548	-50	50		
15								

8.12 / 8.13 / 8.14 / 8.15 / 8.16 / **8.17**

Starting with the *a* and *b* values of Figure 8.16, Solver produces a solution with an objective function of 5,718, as shown in Figure 8.17. However, at the bottom of the task pane, we read the message: Solver has converged to the current solution. All constraints are satisfied. This message indicates that Solver may not have reached even a local optimum. In fact, Solver's stopping criterion is related to the Convergence parameter on the Options menu, for which the default is usually 0.00001. This means that Solver will stop when the last few solutions in its hill-climbing procedure have been unable to improve the objective function by more than 0.001 percent. In response to this stopping message, we should simply rerun Solver, starting from the latest solution, hoping to obtain the optimality message. In this instance, a second run produces no improvement, and further runs do not change the outcome.

Unlike the minimization of the sum of squares, this nonlinear program has several local optima. If we had started the search at a different pair of values for *a* and *b*, Solver could have produced a different solution. The following table summarizes some alternative results:

Starting Values		Final Values		
a	b	a	b	Objective
1,022	0.482	1,148	0.450	5,711
1,500	0.5	1,147	0.450	5,711
1,500	0	1,116	0.456	5,716
1,000	1	1,130	0.453	5,714
1,000	0	1,150	0.449	5,711
2,000	2	1,138	0.452	5,712

This example illustrates one of the potential problems with the nonlinear solver: its final solution may depend on the initial solution. As a result, we normally want to try out a variety of initial solutions, to give us the best chance to find the global optimum.

SOLVER TIP
*Solutions
from the
LSGRG
Algorithm*

The LSGRG algorithm may stop with the message, Solver has converged to the current solution. All constraints are satisfied. We refer to this result as the *convergence message*. The convergence message indicates that the algorithm should be rerun from the stopping point. This message may then reappear, in which case Solver should be rerun once more. Eventually, the algorithm should conclude with the message, Solver found a solution. All constraints and optimality conditions are satisfied, but this will not always be the case. We refer to this result as the *optimality message*. This message signifies that Solver has found a local optimum. (If the convergence message persists, it may be helpful either to invoke the Automatic Scaling option or to increase the Convergence parameter by a factor of 10.) To help determine whether the local optimum is also a global optimum, Solver should be restarted at a different set of decision variables and rerun. If several widely differing initial solutions lead to the same local optimum, that is some evidence that the local optimum is likely to be a global optimum, but in general there is no way to know for sure.

Although there are conditions under which we can guarantee that the LSGRG algorithm is reliable—that is, it finds a global optimum—the theoretical details are beyond the scope of our treatment. It is always a good idea to try starting with different sets of decision variables, to see whether Solver will always converge to the same local optimum. If we encounter two different local optima in this process, we know that we had better test a variety of initial solutions if we hope to find the global optimum. ∎

8.5.4 Economic Order Quantity

A basic inventory problem requires balancing ordering costs and carrying costs to minimize total costs. We are given a product's annual demand, D, and we need to determine the quantity to order, Q.

Suppose that a fixed ordering cost of K is incurred with each order, independent of the order size. If the quantity ordered is Q then the *number* of orders placed per year is D/Q. It then follows that the ordering cost per year is

$$Ordering\ cost = (Cost\ per\ order) \times (Orders\ per\ year) = KD/Q$$

By placing orders so that replenishment occurs just as stock is depleted, we ensure that the inventory level fluctuates between a low of zero and a high of Q. The average inventory is therefore $Q/2$. Suppose also that items held in inventory incur an annual carrying cost of h. (This cost is often expressed as a percentage of the product's unit cost, in the form $h = ic$, where i denotes the carrying cost percentage, and c denotes an item's cost.) Then, the annual inventory carrying costs are

$$Inventory\ cost = (Carrying\ charge) \times (Average\ Inventory) = hQ/2$$

Then, the average total cost (ATC) is the sum of these two components:

$$ATC = Ordering\ cost + Inventory\ cost = KD/Q + hQ/2 \qquad (8.1)$$

The formula for ATC represents the annual total of ordering and holding costs, provided that demand D and holding cost h are annual figures. If those are weekly figures, then ATC represents the *weekly* total of ordering and holding costs. The formula thus adapts to the time scale of the input parameters.

The economic order-quantity model is a single-item model. If we have two items in an inventory system, we can analyze them separately, as two independent problems, to find optimal order quantities and optimal costs for the system. However, in most multiproduct inventory systems, interactions among the items occur. For example, the items may compete for a limited resource, as we see in the case of the Woodstock Appliance Company.

EXAMPLE
Woodstock
Appliance
Company

The Woodstock Appliance Company carries four products. The annual demands for these products range from 300/year for a high-end vacuum cleaner to 30,000/year for a table fan. The order cost, holding cost, and purchase cost are known for each of the four products as well as how much space each product occupies. The numerical information is summarized in the following table:

Product	1	2	3	4
Demand/yr.	5,000	10,000	30,000	300
Order cost	400	700	100	250
Holding cost	10%	10%	10%	10%
Purchase cost	500	250	80	1,000
Space/unit	12	25	5	20

Woodstock stores inventory in its warehouse, which contains 12,000 square feet that can be dedicated to any combination of the four products. The problem is to find the order quantities that minimize cost while respecting the limit on storage space. ∎

What must be decided? We want to determine the four order quantities, and these serve as decision variables in our model. How do we measure performance? We evaluate a set of order quantities by calculating the total annual cost across all four products. For product j, the total annual cost is given by a function ATC_j, which follows equation (8.1). The sum of the four functions ATC_j serves as the objective function. What constraints apply? The only important constraint is the ceiling on storage space. In words, we require that the storage space consumed must be less than or equal to the space available. (Note that the space requirements are given in row 10 of the worksheet.) In addition, we might want to add the constraints $Q_j \geq 1$, just to be explicit that order quantities of less than 1 are not feasible. An algebraic formulation of our problem becomes:

$$Minimize\ ATC = ATC_1 + ATC_2 + ATC_3 + ATC_4$$

subject to

$$12Q_1 + 25Q_2 + 5Q_3 + 20Q_4 \leq 12,000$$
$$Q_1 \geq 1$$
$$Q_2 \geq 1$$
$$Q_3 \geq 1$$
$$Q_4 \geq 1$$

In Figure 8.18, the individual product costs are calculated in cells B17:E17. Cell B18 then sums the four individual product costs in order to determine the cost for the product line. The space required for each product is calculated in cells B21:E21, and the total space used is calculated in cell F21.

We invoke Solver and specify:

Variables:	B10:E10
Objective:	B18 (minimize)
Constraints:	F21 ≤ H21
	B10:D10 ≥ 1

The solution achieves an annual cost of $43,916. Once again, we test this solution by choosing different values of the initial decision variables. The results indicate that the solution is likely to be a global optimum.

FIGURE 8.18 Optimal Solution for the Wood-stock Appliance Company Example

	A	B	C	D	E	F	G	H
1	Economic Order Quantity							
2								
3	Parameters	Product 1	Product 2	Product 3	Product 4			
4	Demand	5000	10000	30000	300			
5	Fixed cost	400	700	100	250			
6	Holding cost	10%	10%	10%	10%			
7	Purchase cost	500	250	80	1000			
8	Space	12	25	5	20			
9	Decisions							
10	Order quantity	272	643	784	37			
11								
12	Objective							
13	Orders/yr.	18.4	15.6	38.3	8.0			
14	Ordering cost/yr.	7,366	10,886	3,829	2,004			
15	Avg. Inventory	135.8	321.5	391.8	18.7			
16	Carrying cost/yr.	6,788	8,038	3,134	1,871			
17	Total product cost	14,154	18,924	6,963	3,875			
18	Total cost	43,916						
19								
20	Constraint							
21	Avg. Space required	1,629	8,038	1,959	374	12,000	<=	12,000
22								

8.18

Solver Tip
Avoid Discontinuous Functions

A number of functions familiar to experienced Excel programmers should be avoided when using the nonlinear solver. These include logical functions (such as IF or AND), mathematical functions (such as ROUND or CEILING), lookup and reference functions (such as CHOOSE or VLOOKUP), and statistical functions (such as RANK or COUNT). In general, any function that *changes discontinuously* is to be avoided. For example, the IF function

$$\text{IF}(X<0,0,1)$$

jumps abruptly from 0 to 1 when the variable X reaches 0.

The problem these functions create for the hill-climbing algorithm in Solver is that they can turn a smooth hill into one with abrupt cliffs. Since the hill-climbing procedure cannot "see" beyond its immediate surroundings, when it comes to a cliff, it simply stops. Thus, the Solver may stop prematurely when used on models that include these functions.

For an example, consider the Advertising Budget model. Suppose we ensure that the figures for Units Sold (row 27 of the worksheet in Figure 8.8) are integers by using the ROUND function in making those calculations. When we implement Solver starting from the base case, it stops almost immediately at an objective of $69,668. By using the round-off function, for what is essentially a cosmetic purpose, we have introduced a discontinuous function that undermines the nonlinear solver.

Analytic Solver Platform contains an Evolutionary Engine, which is better suited to nonlinear optimization problems that have discontinuities, as would be the case if the model were to use the IF, CHOOSE, or ROUND functions. We defer coverage of the Evolutionary Engine until Chapter 12. ■

8.6 SENSITIVITY ANALYSIS FOR NONLINEAR PROGRAMS

Sensitivity analysis involves testing our initial assumptions to see what impact they have on our conclusions. In previous chapters we have recommended performing sensitivity analysis on all of the numerical inputs to a model, whether they are parameters or decision variables. Sensitivity analysis of one or two decision variables (perhaps using the Parametric Sensitivity tool) can lead us to the optimal values of those variables, but this approach cannot be used for more than two variables. An optimization procedure such as Solver performs this kind of search in a sophisticated manner and can handle large numbers of decision variables and constraints. Thus, we can think of optimization as an ambitious form of what-if analysis with respect to decision variables.

In optimization models, two types of sensitivity analysis are often confused. Consider, for example, the Advertising Budget model from Section 8.2.3, which led to a maximum profit of $71,447. We first ask how the results change when the price drops by 10 percent, to $36. A simple what-if analysis gives us the answer: the new profit is $16,500. This, of course, assumes that the advertising allocation does not change. In other words, if we fix the budget allocation and then vary the price, the result is a profit of $16,500. But what would happen if we could optimize the budget allocation *after* the price dropped to $36? Would the optimal profit still be $16,500? A run of Solver at the lower price answers this question. In fact, the optimal profit at a price of $36 is $17,376, not $16,500. So in general, there is a difference between the sensitivity of a model to a parameter *without* re-optimization (which we call parametric sensitivity) and the sensitivity *with* re-optimization (which we call optimization sensitivity).

Because these two types of sensitivity are different, it is important to recognize which one is appropriate for a given situation. In the Advertising Budget example, we might find ourselves in the situation where we do not know next year's price at the present time, but we will know it before we have to implement our advertising plan. In this case, we would like to vary the price and determine both the optimal advertising plan and optimal profit for each possible price. In other words, we need to run Solver for each value of the price that we wish to study. For this purpose, the capabilities for sensitivity analysis can be extended to include re-optimization.

We illustrate Optimization Sensitivity by revisiting the Advertising Budget example of Figure 8.8. In our first sensitivity analysis, we vary the unit price, which is $40.00 in the base case. To avoid confusion, it is helpful to designate a separate portion of the worksheet for sensitivity values. In the Advertising Budget model, we can use the top portion of column H for this purpose. Place the cursor on cell H7 (in the same row as the price) and then choose Analytic Solver Platform▶Parameters▶Optimization. The Function Arguments window opens for the PsiOptParam sensitivity function. Enter a Lower value of 30 and an Upper value of 40, and click OK, as we did in the case of parametric sensitivity analysis (see Section 4.3.3). Then change the contents of cell C7 so that it references H7. At this point, both cells display the value 30, because the PsiOptParam function displays its Lower value by default.

To create a table for optimal profit as a function of price in the range from $30 to $40, select Analytic Solver Platform▶Analysis▶Reports▶Optimization▶Parameter Analysis. The Multiple Optimizations Report window opens (Figure 8.19). Recall from Chapter 4 that when we performed parametric sensitivity, we had to designate the result we intended to track by selecting it. But in the case of optimization sensitivity, the decision variables and objective-function cells automatically appear on the left-hand side in the Result Cells window. Next, use the arrow buttons to copy the cell addresses to the window on the right. (The double arrow copies all of the cell references, but we could expand the original list and copy the cell references one at a time if we preferred.) Our custom is to place the objective cell at the top of the list, using the Up button. Next, in the Parameters section of the window, we move the cell address $H$7 to the right-hand window, so that the display resembles Figure 8.20. Below these windows, we leave the drop-down menu at its default, to read Vary All Selected Parameters Simultaneously. Finally, we choose 21 Major Axis Points and click OK.

We obtain a new worksheet named Analysis Report that contains the table shown in Figure 8.21. (The column headings have been edited and some formatting has been changed.) We can also display these results graphically by following the command path Analytic Solver Platform▶Analysis▶Charts▶Multiple Optimizations ▶Parameter Analysis. Alternatively, we can build our own customized Excel chart based on the report table.

FIGURE 8.19 Report
Setup Dialog Window

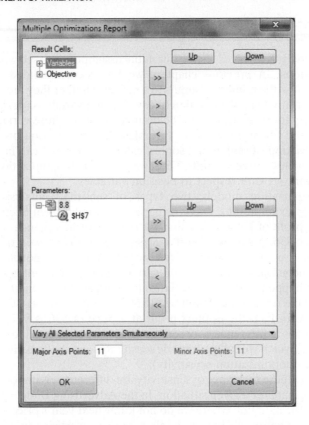

The table shows in one place how the optimal solution (that is, the objective function value and the optimal values of the decision variables) varies with the unit price. At relatively low prices (at or below $32.00), the margins are so small that it is best not to spend anything on advertising. As the unit price increases, it first becomes desirable to spend advertising money in Q4; in Q2 as well; then, in Q1 as well; and, at a price of $34.50, it becomes desirable to spend advertising money in all four quarters. When the price rises to $37.00, the advertising budget is completely spent, and the allocation of the $40,000 budget

FIGURE 8.20 Report
Setup Dialog Window
Completed

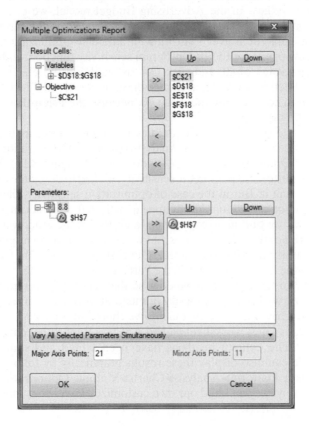

FIGURE 8.21 Optimization Sensitivity Report for Price

	A	B	C	D	E	F	G
1	**Price**	**Objective**	**Change**	**$D$18**	**$E$18**	**$F$18**	**$G$18**
2	$30.00	-$30,166		$0	$0	$0	$0
3	$30.50	-$26,907	$6,517.89	$0	$0	$0	$0
4	$31.00	-$23,648	$6,517.89	$0	$0	$0	$0
5	$31.50	-$20,389	$6,517.89	$0	$0	$0	$0
6	$32.00	-$17,130	$6,517.89	$0	$0	$0	$0
7	$32.50	-$13,871	$6,518.16	$0	$0	$0	$39
8	$33.00	-$10,511	$6,720.85	$0	$447	$0	$1,101
9	$33.50	-$6,875	$7,271.23	$0	$1,475	$0	$2,325
10	$34.00	-$2,902	$7,946.11	$773	$2,636	$0	$3,708
11	$34.50	$1,487	$8,778.44	$1,640	$3,932	$666	$5,249
12	$35.00	$6,330	$9,685.58	$2,597	$5,361	$1,422	$6,950
13	$35.50	$11,626	$10,592.76	$3,643	$6,924	$2,249	$8,810
14	$36.00	$17,376	$11,499.96	$4,779	$8,621	$3,147	$10,830
15	$36.50	$23,580	$12,407.14	$6,005	$10,452	$4,115	$13,009
16	$37.00	$30,237	$13,313.80	$7,273	$12,346	$5,117	$15,263
17	$37.50	$37,105	$13,736.64	$7,273	$12,346	$5,117	$15,263
18	$38.00	$43,974	$13,736.64	$7,273	$12,346	$5,117	$15,263
19	$38.50	$50,842	$13,736.64	$7,273	$12,346	$5,117	$15,263
20	$39.00	$57,710	$13,736.65	$7,273	$12,346	$5,117	$15,263
21	$39.50	$64,578	$13,736.65	$7,273	$12,346	$5,117	$15,263
22	$40.00	$71,447	$13,736.65	$7,273	$12,346	$5,117	$15,263
23							

8.21

remains the same as price rises even further. Thus, we can see that the base-case result (that the budget should be completely spent) is dependent, in part, on the fact that the unit price is sufficiently high. That is not an insight we could reach without doing this kind of sensitivity analysis.

Optimization sensitivity can also show the effects on the optimal solution of altering the budget. This is a common type of sensitivity analysis, in which we explore the consequences of altering a constraint that is binding in the base case. Figure 8.22 shows how optimal profit changes when we increase the budget from $30,000 to $100,000 in steps of $5,000. These inputs are shown in column A, with the corresponding optimal profit given in column B. In column C, we have inserted a calculation of the rate at which profit changes, per unit change in the budget. (In cell C3, we enter the formula =(B3-B2)/(A3-A2) and then copy the formula to the rest of the column below.) For example, the first nonblank entry indicates that, from $30,000 to $35,000, the additional $5,000 expenditure increases profit by an average of $0.51 per dollar.

A graphical perspective on these results is shown in Figure 8.23. The top chart plots the optimal profit as a function of the budget. In this graph, we can see that optimal profit expands as the budget increases. However, the graph reveals **diminishing marginal returns**, reflecting the fact that the profit function gets flatter as the budget increases. Eventually, profit actually levels out, because the advertising budget is more than we can effectively

FIGURE 8.22 Sensitivity of Optimal Results to Budget Levels

	A	B	C	D	E	F	G	H	I	J	K
1	**Budget**	**Objective**	**Change**	**$D$18**	**$E$18**	**$F$18**	**$G$18**	**Q1**	**Q2**	**Q3**	**Q4**
2	$30,000	$66,715.5		$5,298	$9,395	$3,556	$11,751	17.7%	31.3%	11.9%	39.2%
3	$35,000	$69,277.5	0.512	$6,285	$10,871	$4,337	$13,507	18.0%	31.1%	12.4%	38.6%
4	$40,000	$71,446.8	0.434	$7,273	$12,346	$5,117	$15,263	18.2%	30.9%	12.8%	38.2%
5	$45,000	$73,279.0	0.366	$8,261	$13,822	$5,898	$17,020	18.4%	30.7%	13.1%	37.8%
6	$50,000	$74,817.5	0.308	$9,249	$15,298	$6,678	$18,776	18.5%	30.6%	13.4%	37.6%
7	$55,000	$76,097.3	0.256	$10,237	$16,773	$7,459	$20,532	18.6%	30.5%	13.6%	37.3%
8	$60,000	$77,146.8	0.210	$11,224	$18,249	$8,239	$22,288	18.7%	30.4%	13.7%	37.1%
9	$65,000	$77,989.6	0.169	$12,212	$19,724	$9,020	$24,044	18.8%	30.3%	13.9%	37.0%
10	$70,000	$78,645.7	0.131	$13,200	$21,200	$9,800	$25,800	18.9%	30.3%	14.0%	36.9%
11	$75,000	$79,131.8	0.097	$14,188	$22,676	$10,580	$27,556	18.9%	30.2%	14.1%	36.7%
12	$80,000	$79,462.3	0.066	$15,176	$24,151	$11,361	$29,312	19.0%	30.2%	14.2%	36.6%
13	$85,000	$79,649.9	0.038	$16,163	$25,627	$12,141	$31,068	19.0%	30.1%	14.3%	36.6%
14	$90,000	$79,705.6	0.011	$17,093	$27,016	$12,876	$32,721	19.0%	30.0%	14.3%	36.4%
15	$95,000	$79,705.6	0.000	$17,093	$27,016	$12,876	$32,721	18.0%	28.4%	13.6%	34.4%
16	$100,000	$79,705.6	0.000	$17,093	$27,016	$12,876	$32,721	17.1%	27.0%	12.9%	32.7%
17											

8.21 8.22

FIGURE 8.23 Graphical Display of the Sensitivity Results

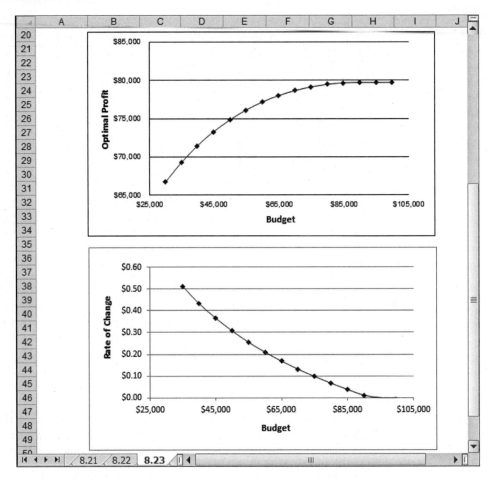

use. The bottom chart plots the rate of change in profit as a function of the budget. Here, we observe diminishing returns in the form of a declining rate of change. The rate of change in profit reaches zero when the budget exceeds a useful level, around $90,000.

We have added four columns in Figure 8.22 (columns H:K) with formulas that translate the quarterly expenditures into percentages of the overall budget. As we can see, the percentage split changes very slightly over this range. For a budget of $30,000, the optimal expenditure in Q4 is about 39 percent of the year's budget, and for a budget of $90,000, this figure drops to about 36 percent.

Perhaps the most important feature of these results is a qualitative one. *When we relax a binding constraint, the objective function cannot get worse.* In fact, it usually gets better, as illustrated in Figure 8.22. This is an intuitive but important result, and we will encounter it in both linear and nonlinear optimization models.

SOLVER TIP
Which Kind of Sensitivity Analysis?

It is easy to confuse parametric sensitivity and optimization sensitivity. Both types of analysis explore the results of varying an input parameter (or two input parameters), but they answer different questions.

Optimization sensitivity answers questions about how the *optimal solution* changes with a change in a parameter. In this case, the sensitivity tool varies an input parameter *and* reruns Solver to determine the optimal values of the decision variables for modified values of that parameter. The output can trace the implications for a result cell (or several result cells). However, it is not appropriate to use this form of the tool unless the decision maker actually has the opportunity to optimize decisions in response to a parameter change.

Parametric sensitivity answers questions about how specific outputs change with a change in a parameter. In this case, the sensitivity tool varies an input parameter and traces the implications through the model to a result cell (or several result cells). If there are decision variables in the model, they remain fixed when the input parameter changes, and they are not "reoptimized".

Parametric sensitivity can also be used to answer questions about how specific outputs change with a change in one or two *decision variables*. This usage amounts to a simple search for optimal decision variables. It is a form of what-if analysis that explores the change in outputs when an input is varied, where the input just happens to be a decision variable. For this purpose, Solver itself would be a more powerful tool. However, parametric sensitivity may be appropriate if we are interested in the nonoptimal values of the decision variables as well as the optimal values. ∎

8.7* THE PORTFOLIO OPTIMIZATION MODEL

A **portfolio** is a collection of assets. In a stock portfolio, the investor chooses the stocks, and the dollar value of each, to hold in the portfolio at the start of an investment period. Over this period, the values of the stocks may change. At the end of the period, performance can be measured by the total value of the portfolio. For a given size (or dollar value) of the portfolio, the key decision is how to allocate the portfolio among its constituent stocks.

The performance of individual stocks can be measured in two ways: return and risk. **Return** is the percentage growth in the value of the stock. **Risk** is the variability associated with the returns on the stock. The information on which stock performance is evaluated is a series of historical returns, typically compiled on a monthly basis. This history provides an empirical distribution of a stock's return performance. For stock k in the portfolio, this return distribution can be summarized by a mean (r_k) and a standard deviation (s_k).

The performance of a portfolio of stocks is also measured in terms of return and risk. When we create a portfolio of stocks, our goals are usually to maximize the mean return and to minimize the risk. Both goals cannot be met simultaneously, but we can use optimization to explore the trade-offs involved.

EXAMPLE *Advising Ms. Womack*

Suppose we are providing investment advice to Ms. Womack, who has some savings to invest and very clear ideas about her preferred stocks. In fact, she has identified stocks in five different industries that she believes would constitute a good portfolio. The performance of the five stocks in two recent years is summarized by the means and standard deviations of monthly stock prices, as shown in the following table:

Stock	Mean	St. Dev.
National Computer	0.0209	0.0981
National Chemical	0.0121	0.0603
National Power	0.0069	0.0364
National Auto	0.0226	0.0830
National Electronics	0.0134	0.0499

Ms. Womack is stumped only by the question of how to allocate her investment among these five stocks. National Computer Company and National Auto Company stocks have achieved the best average returns in the two-year period, but they also have relatively high volatility, as measured by their standard deviations. National Power Company is the least volatile, but it also has the lowest average return. Ms. Womack wishes to navigate between these different extremes. Our task is to organize the quantitative information so that we can help her make the allocation decision. ■

Figure 8.24 shows a worksheet containing the monthly returns for Ms. Womack's five stocks over the last two years. The data can be found in columns I through N. The mean

	A	B	C	D	E	F	G
1	**Portfolio Model**						
2							
3	**Data Summary**	*Computer*	*Chemical*	*Power*	*Auto*	*Electronic*	
4	*Avg. Return*	0.0209	0.0121	0.0069	0.0226	0.0134	
5	*St. Deviation*	0.0981	0.0603	0.0364	0.0830	0.0499	
6							
7	**Covariances**						*Proportions*
8	*Computer*	0.0092	-0.0006	0.0003	0.0026	0.0012	0.132
9	*Chemical*	-0.0006	0.0035	0.0000	-0.0006	0.0003	0.304
10	*Power*	0.0003	0.0000	0.0013	0.0006	-0.0001	0.158
11	*Auto*	0.0026	-0.0006	0.0006	0.0066	0.0017	0.225
12	*Electronic*	0.0012	0.0003	-0.0001	0.0017	0.0024	0.181
13							
14	**Proportions**						
15		0.132	0.304	0.158	0.225	0.181	1.000
16							
17	**Calculations**						
18		0.000161	-0.000025	0.000006	0.000077	0.000028	
19		-0.000025	0.000322	-0.000002	-0.000038	0.000016	
20		0.000006	-0.000002	0.000032	0.000020	-0.000004	
21		0.000077	-0.000038	0.000020	0.000333	0.000070	
22		0.000028	0.000016	-0.000004	0.000070	0.000078	
23							
24	*Portfolio Variance*	**Risk**	0.00122		Risk ceiling	0.0015	
25							
26	*Weighted Average*	**Return**	0.0150		Return floor	0.015	
27							
28							
29							

Data (columns I–N)

Month	*Computer*	*Chemical*	*Power*	*Auto*	*Electronic*
1	0.22816	-0.07205	0.01730	0.22266	0.08202
2	0.09134	0.02588	0.05646	0.01278	-0.03499
3	-0.01288	-0.04771	0.02280	0.00379	0.01662
4	-0.17196	0.06342	0.00000	0.04101	-0.07496
5	0.16557	0.03670	0.00510	0.07576	-0.00810
6	-0.00789	0.01372	0.02244	0.06817	0.05446
7	-0.04909	0.05960	0.06583	-0.07143	-0.08607
8	0.22967	-0.02083	0.00812	-0.02564	0.01712
9	0.10117	0.00681	0.02360	0.12632	-0.00510
10	-0.10530	-0.05128	0.00865	0.16406	0.08376
11	-0.02767	0.04730	-0.02926	-0.05593	0.04890
12	0.00813	-0.01247	0.00893	0.01327	0.08498
13	0.05323	0.11894	-0.00885	0.15493	0.09790
14	0.05364	0.00197	-0.06917	-0.07317	-0.00382
15	-0.01818	-0.04479	-0.06473	-0.08640	-0.01546
16	-0.09556	0.04366	0.01384	-0.07952	0.03534
17	0.02459	0.08765	0.00259	0.03665	0.02402
18	-0.06400	-0.03260	-0.01379	-0.03535	-0.02736
19	0.01393	0.05736	0.06993	0.01316	0.04604
20	0.10971	0.08680	0.02588	-0.00260	0.05501
21	-0.06464	0.05025	0.00645	-0.05990	-0.00350
22	0.01114	-0.06070	0.01603	0.08357	-0.03981
23	0.01610	-0.12925	0.04076	-0.00257	-0.03415
24	0.01188	0.06094	-0.06442	0.01856	0.00763

8.24

FIGURE 8.24 The Portfolio-Optimization Model

returns are calculated using the AVERAGE function in cells B4:F4, and the standard deviations are calculated using the STDEV function in cells B5:F5.

The next task is to combine the individual stock behaviors into a summary for the portfolio as a whole—that is, the portfolio mean and variance. For the portfolio mean, we use a weighted average of individual stock returns. Thus, if we allocate a proportion p_k of our portfolio to stock k, then the return on the five-stock portfolio is the following weighted average:

$$R = p_1 r_1 + p_2 r_2 + p_3 r_3 + p_4 r_4 + p_5 r_5$$

This calculation lends itself to the SUMPRODUCT formula and appears in the worksheet in cell C26. The proportions themselves, highlighted as decision variables, appear in cells B15:F15, with their sum in cell G15.

For the portfolio variance, we use a standard statistical formula for the variance of a sum. For this purpose, we must know the covariance σ_{kj} between every pair of stocks (k, j). The covariance values are calculated from the historical data with Excel's COVAR function. These figures appear in the worksheet in cells B8:F12.

EXCEL MINI-LESSON
The COVAR Function

The COVAR function in Excel calculates the covariance between two equal-sized sets of numbers representing observations of two variables. The covariance measures the extent to which one variable tends to rise or fall with increases and decreases in the other variable. If the two variables rise and fall in unison, their covariance is large and positive. If the two variables move in opposite directions, then their covariance is negative. If the two variables move independently, then their covariance is close to zero. The basic form of the function is the following:

COVAR(Array1,Array2)

- *Array1* references the observations of the first variable.
- *Array2* references the observations of the second variable.

■

In cell C11 of Figure 8.24, the function =COVAR($M5:$M28,$K5:$K28) finds the covariance between the returns of National Auto Company and those of National Chemical Company. In this case, the function generates the value −0.0006. The fact that it is a small number in absolute value indicates that the two sets of returns are nearly independent; the fact that it is negative indicates that there is a slight tendency for National Auto's returns to go up when National Chemical's returns go down, and vice versa.

A convenient way to calculate the portfolio variance V, is to weight all the covariances $\sigma_{k,j}$ by the corresponding proportions p_k and p_j. The value of the product $p_k \sigma_{kj} p_j$ is computed as the (k, j)th element of the array in cells B18:F22. (For this purpose, it is convenient to replicate the proportions from row 15 in cells G8:G12.) Then the elements of this array are summed in cell C24 to form V. Thus, the risk measure V appears in cell C24, and the return measure R appears in C26.

The portfolio optimization problem is to choose the investment proportions so that we minimize risk subject to a floor (lower bound) on the return. That is, we want to minimize V subject to a minimum value of R, with the p-values as the decision variables. A value for the lower bound appears in cell F26. We invoke Solver and specify the model as follows.

Variables: B15:F15
Objective: C24 (minimize)
Constraints: C26 ≥ F26
G15 = 1

For a return floor of 1.5 percent, Solver returns the solution shown in Figure 8.24. All five stocks appear in the optimal portfolio, with allocations ranging from 30 percent of the portfolio in National Chemical to 13 percent of the portfolio in National Computer.

For this model, the worksheet layout is a little different from the others we have examined, mainly due to the close relationship between the historical data and the elements of the analysis. The worksheet, as constructed, could easily be adapted to the optimization of any five-stock portfolio. For this purpose, we need only the set of returns

FIGURE 8.25 Graphs of the Efficient Frontier in the Portfolio Example

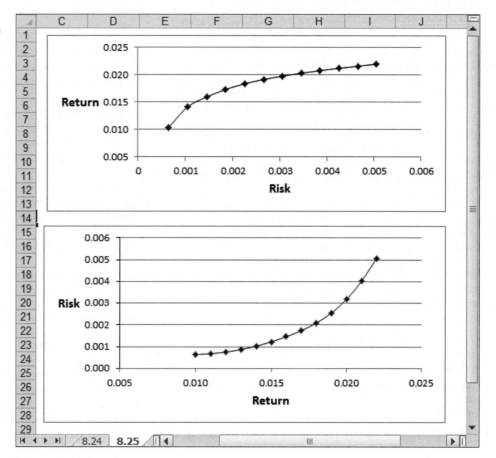

data, which we can copy into the data section of the worksheet. For a data collection period of longer than 24 periods, the formulas for average, standard deviation, and covariance would have to be adjusted. The Calculations section separates the decision variables from the objective function, but the logic of the computations flows from Proportions to Calculations to Risk and Return.

Beyond a single optimization of the portfolio model, investors are usually interested in the trade-off between risk and return. If we minimize risk subject to a floor on the return, we can repeat the optimization for several values of the floor. This process traces out points along the so-called **efficient frontier**, which plots the best risk achievable for any desired level of return. A complementary approach is available if we maximize return subject to a ceiling on risk. Results from the Optimization Sensitivity tool for these two approaches, along with summary plots, are shown in Figure 8.25. Both plots describe the same risk-return trade-off; they just happen to take slightly different forms. By exploring Ms. Womack's preferences as they play out in these graphs, we can make a more persuasive recommendation on how her investment funds should be allocated.

SOLVER TIP
The Solver Parameters Window

In this chapter, we have entered information about the optimization model from either the ribbon or the task pane. These two parts of the interface offer very similar options, but they are not identical. For example, the ribbon does not offer the Change Constraint option, and the task pane does not offer the Optimization Sensitivity tool. For that reason, it is helpful to be familiar with both parts of the interface.

A third part of the interface exists. It is called the Solver Parameters window, and it can be accessed from the Add-Ins tab, where an icon can be found for Premium Solver. Prior to version 9 of the software, this window was the primary interface, and it has been retained to help users who became familiar with older versions. The Solver Parameters window contains buttons for adding, changing, and deleting parts of the model. Clicking on one of these buttons opens a window similar to one that can be opened from the ribbon or the task pane. Similarly, the Model and Options buttons provide access to a number of options that can also be found on the task pane. For our purposes in this book, however, the Solver Parameters window is redundant, and we rely on the ribbon and the task pane when we want to enter, run, or edit our optimization models. ∎

8.8 SUMMARY

We introduced optimization in Chapter 4 as one phase in a general analytic procedure for spreadsheet models. Optimization answers the question, "What's the best we can do?" or to put it more formally, "What values of the decision variables lead to the best possible value of the objective?" In a sense, optimization is simply a sophisticated tool for performing what-if analysis.

In Excel, optimization is carried out using Solver. Solver is actually a collection of optimization procedures, and in this chapter, we illustrated the use of the nonlinear solver, which is Solver's default choice.

To develop facility with Solver, it helps to practice formulating, solving, and interpreting optimization problems. Formulation and layout for optimization require some additional considerations that tend not to arise in simpler kinds of modeling, and we mentioned a number of principles that bear repeating. These are guidelines for the model builder and, in our experience, the craft skills exhibited by experts:

- Follow a standard form whenever possible.
- Enter cell references in the Solver windows; keep numerical values in cells.
- Try out some feasible (and infeasible) possibilities as a way of debugging the model and exploring the problem.
- Test intuition and suggest hypotheses before running Solver.

Along with our examples, these guidelines provide help in learning how to implement optimization analyses in spreadsheet models.

Sometimes, difficulties arise in using the nonlinear solver to find optimal solutions. The most frequent difficulties and the appropriate responses are listed below:

- The search doesn't move away from the initial solution. This symptom usually indicates that the model contains some discontinuity, most likely caused by the use of one of Excel's special functions (IF, MAX, ROUND, LOOKUP, etc.). To avoid the problem, avoid the use of discontinuous Excel functions.
- The search stops at an inferior solution. This symptom occurs when the problem contains local optima. To help circumvent this difficulty, rerun the search from a number of different initial solutions. Doing so will either provide evidence of local optima or build confidence that a global optimum has been found.
- An infeasible solution occurs. This symptom arises when the initial set of decision variables is infeasible, and the nonlinear solver cannot locate a feasible solution, let alone an optimal one. To avoid this problem, make sure the initial values of the decision variables are feasible in the constraints. (Very rarely, the nonlinear solver starts with a feasible solution and then goes infeasible. Should this happen, rerun with a very different starting solution.)
- Solver claims that no feasible solution exists, even when the initial values of the decision variables are feasible. This symptom suggests a scaling problem. Try rerunning after invoking Automatic Scaling. Occasionally, the difficulty can be resolved by resetting the Convergence parameter on the Engine tab to a value ten times larger than the default value.

Thus, a little troubleshooting effort can overcome unexpected behavior by the nonlinear solver.

SUGGESTED READINGS

Some advanced perspectives on optimization techniques, along with some guidance in constructing optimization models, can be found in several books. A partial list is given below.

A book that fleshes out the coverage in our optimization chapters, retaining an emphasis on spreadsheet modeling, is the following:

Baker, K.R. 2011. *Optimization Modeling with Spreadsheets (Second Edition)* Hoboken, NJ: John Wiley & Sons.

A thorough discussion of applications can be found in the following book:

Williams, H. P. 1999. *Model Building in Mathematical Programming*, 4th ed. Chichester: John Wiley & Sons.

If we want to explore alternatives to Excel as the software platform, we are drawn to algebraic modeling languages. Two popular and accessible approaches are represented by AMPL and LINDO, described in the following books:

Fourer, R., D. F. Gay, and B. W. Kernighan. 2003. *AMPL: A Modeling Language for Mathematical Programming*. Belmont, CA: Duxbury Press.

Schrage, L. 1997. *Optimization Modeling with LINDO*, 5th ed. Belmont, CA: Duxbury Press.

For a more theoretical treatment of optimization, the following books provide up-to-date treatments:

Rardin, R. L. 1998. *Optimization in Operations Research*. Upper Saddle River, NJ: Prentice-Hall.

Winston, W. L. and M. Venkataramanan. 2003. *Introduction to Mathematical Programming*. 4th ed. Belmont, CA: Duxbury Press.

EXERCISES

1. *Location Problem (revisited).* Return to the Kilroy Paper Company example introduced in this chapter. Upon further consideration, the logistics manager points out that the trucks do not make an equal number of trips to the various stores. Thus, a better proxy for total distribution costs would be obtained by weighting the distance from distribution center to store k by the annual number of trips to store k (represented as n_k). The expanded set of input data is as follows:

	Coordinates		Trips
Site (k)	x_k	y_k	n_k
1	5	41	12
2	20	10	20
3	44	48	15
4	60	58	27
5	100	4	8
6	138	80	16
7	150	40	10
8	170	18	18
9	182	2	25
10	190	56	14

a. Find the optimal location for Kilroy's distribution center in this expanded version of the problem.

b. What is the optimal value of the objective function?

2. *Location Problem with Two Sites.* Oliveira Office Supply has a large retail system consisting of twelve stores spread around the country, often in direct competition with Kilroy. However, managers at Oliveira have decided to use two national distribution centers. When Oliveira's stores are mapped on the same grid as Kilroy's, the store locations occur at the coordinates listed in the following table. As in the previous exercise, there are also data to indicate how many trips are made annually to each store:

	Coordinates		Trips
Site (k)	x_k	y_k	n_k
1	2	96	21
2	5	41	12
3	20	10	20
4	44	48	15
5	60	58	27
6	100	4	8
7	122	94	21
8	138	80	16
9	150	40	10
10	170	18	18
11	182	2	25
12	190	56	14

a. Find the optimal location for Oliveira's two distribution centers in this expanded version of the problem.

b. What is the optimal value of the objective function?

3. *Cost Modeling.* General Widget Corporation has collected data on the daily output and daily production cost of widgets produced at its factory. (Data

for the study are shown in the table below.) The company believes that daily output (DO) and daily production cost (PC) ought to be linearly related. Thus, for some numbers a and b:

$$PC = a + b \times DO$$

	Output	Production Cost
Day 1	5,045	2,542
Day 2	6,127	2,812
Day 3	6,360	2,776
Day 4	6,645	3,164
Day 5	7,220	4,102
Day 6	9,537	4,734
Day 7	9,895	4,238
Day 8	10,175	4,524
Day 9	10,334	4,869
Day 10	10,855	4,421

a. Build a least-squares model to estimate the parameters a and b in the linear relationship. In other words, minimize the sum of squared differences between the model's predicted values and the observations. What are the best values of the parameters a and b for this criterion? What is the minimum value of the objective function? (Verify your results by using Excel's Regression tool.)

b. Suppose, instead, that a better criterion is thought to be minimizing the sum of absolute deviations between the model's predicted values and the observations. What are the best values of the parameters a and b for this criterion? What is the minimum value of the objective function?

c. Suppose, instead, that a better model than the linear model is thought to be the power function

$$PC = a(DO)^b$$

Using the sum of absolute deviations (as in the previous part), what values of a and b provide the best fit? What is the minimum value of the objective function?

4. *Curve Fitting with Constraints.* A bank's economist has been interested in developing a production function for the bank. The model recognizes three explanatory variables, which are measures of resources available to the bank. These are Labor Hours, Operating Expenses, and Capital Expenses. The response variable, which measures output activity, is a weighted average of the transactions processed by all departments in the course of a month. The economist's model takes the form:

$$Q = a_0 x_1^{a_1} x_2^{a_2} x_3^{a_3}$$

Because the fitted curve is a production function, it represents the ideal output level that could be achieved for any choice of inputs. Thus, the notion is to fit the model to actual data as well as possible, subject to the requirement that the predicted value be at least as large as the observed value for each combination of inputs in the data set.

Branch	Labor Hours	Operating Expenses	Capital Expenses	Output
1	34,515	6,543	591	289,130
2	49,960	11,830	550	506,808
3	20,652	3,464	427	143,653
4	49,024	7,603	478	385,421
5	36,923	8,723	830	253,525
6	28,967	4,606	474	219,992
7	28,452	7,425	182	193,284
8	45,911	8,013	790	257,253
9	26,890	14,662	447	173,266
10	47,376	7,576	764	326,752
11	57,913	12,035	875	478,533
12	43,477	7,255	1,109	337,643
13	49,786	10,909	405	244,127
14	30,045	4,264	479	139,447
15	56,579	8,895	840	380,206
16	43,824	12,690	801	178,769
17	33,823	4,143	381	216,168

a. What are the best-fitting values of a_0, a_1, a_2, and a_3?

b. Using the model determined in part (a), what ideal output is predicted for Branch 2? for Branch 4?

5. *Profit Maximization with Demand Curves.* Campbell Motors is an auto dealership that specializes in the sale of station wagons and light trucks. Because of its reputation for quality and service, Campbell has a strong position in the regional market, but demand remains somewhat sensitive to price. While evaluating the new models, Campbell's marketing consultant has come up with the following demand curves:

$$Truck\ Demand = 500 - 18(Truck\ Price\ in\ thousands)$$
$$Wagon\ Demand = 400 - 11\ (Wagon\ Price\ in\ thousands)$$

The dealership's unit costs are $20,000 for trucks and $25,000 for wagons. Each truck requires three hours of prep labor, and each wagon requires two hours of prep labor. The current staff can supply 250 hours of labor.

a. Determine prices at which Campbell Motors can maximize the profit it generates from combined sales of trucks and wagons.

b. What is the marginal value of the current staff's labor hours?

6. *Allocation.* A regional beer distributor has $100,000 to spend on advertising in four markets, where each market responds differently to advertising. Based on observations of each market's response to several advertising initiatives, the distributor has estimated the sales response by fitting a power curve $R = ax^b$, where R represents sales revenue, and x represents advertising dollars, both measured in thousands. The estimated curves are described in the following table:

Market	Sales Revenue
Domestic	$100x^{0.4}$
Premium	$80x^{0.5}$
Light	$120x^{0.3}$
Microbrew	$60x^{0.6}$

a. Determine how the advertising dollars should be allocated to the four markets so that the sales revenue for the distributor is maximized.

b. If the distributor had $1,000 of additional funds in the advertising budget, by how much could total revenue be increased?

c. If the distributor had $2,000 of additional funds in the advertising budget beyond the base case in part (a), by how much could total revenue be increased?

d. Construct a graph showing the optimal total revenue as a function of the advertising budget, for budget sizes in the range $50,000 to $150,000.

7. *Selecting an Advertising Budget.* A well-known charity is interested in conducting a television campaign to solicit contributions. The campaign will be conducted in two metropolitan areas. Past experience indicates that, in each city, the total contributions are a function of the amount of money expended for TV advertisements. Specifically, the charity has estimated response functions that indicate the percentage of the population making a donation as a function of the dollars spent on TV advertising. The form of this function is $y = 1 - \exp(-\alpha x)$, where x represents the advertising expenditure (in thousands of dollars), y represents the percentage donating, and α is a parameter that differs from city to city. The charity has earmarked a fund of $400,000 for advertising between the two cities and wants to determine the best allocation of these funds.

	City 1	City 2
Response parameter (α)	0.006	0.004
Population	750,000	600,000
Average donation per donor	$2.00	$1.50

a. Suppose the charity decides to maximize total donations, given its budget limit on advertising. How should advertising funds be spent, and what amount will be raised in donations as a result?

b. Is the budget binding in the solution of (a)? If so, how much additional budget would the charity like to obtain? If not, how much of the budget should actually be spent?

c. Suppose the charity maximizes total donations net of the cost of advertising. (This would make sense if surplus advertising funds can be put toward the charity's other services.) From the perspective of this objective, how should advertising funds be spent, and what amount will be raised in donations as a result?

8. *Joint ordering.* A firm uses the policy of ordering two particular items at a time because they come from the same supplier. The characteristics of these items are shown in the following table:

Item	Demand	Fixed Cost	Unit Cost	Holding Cost
1	800/year	$3	$10	30%
2	40/year	$3	$12	30%

a. Find the optimal cycle length for the joint orders. What are the optimal order quantities for the two items? What is the average annual cost for the two items combined?

b. Suppose the two items are managed independently, and each uses its own optimal order quantity. What is the average annual cost for the two items combined?

c. Suppose that there is a savings in the fixed cost due to joint ordering. Instead of $6, the ordering cost is only $3 because some activities cover both items. Which strategy (joint or independent) is preferable?

9. *Ordering Fuels.* Three liquid fuels are stored in tanks for use in a blending process. Each fuel is characterized by a demand rate, a fixed replenishment cost, and a unit cost. Inventory carrying costs are assessed at the rate of 12 percent per year.

In order to save money on insurance rates, the operating policy is to limit the average value of stock on hand to no more than $7,500.

Fuel	Demand	Fixed Cost	Unit Cost
1	1,000/year	$100	$150
2	250/year	$175	$100
3	500/year	$150	$120

a. What are the optimal order quantities for the three items when they are ordered jointly, assuming that the fixed ordering costs are incurred for each item? What is the average annual cost for the three items combined?

b. Suppose the items are managed separately, but the overall limit on stock value still holds. What are the order quantities for the individual items? What is the average annual cost for the three items combined?

c. Suppose the stock limit in the base case is relaxed. If the limit is raised by $500, what is the impact on the optimal average annual cost?

10. *Learning-Based Production Planning.* Many labor-intensive production operations experience a learning curve effect. The learning curve specifies that the cost to produce a unit is a function of the unit number; that is, as production volume increases, the cost to produce each unit drops. One form of the learning curve is as follows: $C_i = a(i)^b$ where C_i is the cost of unit i, a is called the first unit cost, and b is the learning "slope" parameter. The total cost of producing a batch of size x can then be approximated by $(ax^{1+b})/(1+b)$. Now consider a production setting where there is learning. We have the following single-product production-planning data: demands for the next five periods are 100, 150, 300, 200, 400. Holding cost per unit per period is $0.30 and production cost follows a learning curve with $a = 15$ and $b = -0.2$.

a. Assume that there is no transfer of learning between time periods and that, at most, one batch is produced per time period. Solve the production-planning problem of minimizing the sum of production and inventory costs, while satisfying demand. What are the optimal batch sizes?

b. Solve the same production-planning problem, ignoring the learning curve, that is, assume that every unit costs $15 dollars.

c. Assume we must have an ending inventory in period 5 of at least 50. Re-solve the problem in part (a). What are the optimal batch sizes? How much of a required ending inventory in period 5 induces a change in the optimal batch sizes?

11. *Predicting Sales.* Managers at Office Products, Inc. are planning their sales campaigns for the coming year. As one part of this effort, they are attempting to determine the

relationship between the number of sales reps that are assigned to a product and the sales of that product. The subjective estimates of a group of experienced managers are summarized in the following table, which relates sales effort to sales:

Sales Reps	Sales (000)
50	433
75	478
100	545
125	745
150	987
175	1,156
200	1,235
225	1,288
250	1,345

a. Build a least squares model to fit an S-shaped curve to this data set. An appropriate function has the form

$$Sales = b + (a - b)(Reps^c/(d + Reps^c))$$

What values of the four parameters a, b, c, and d minimize the sum of squared differences between the model's predicted values and the observations? (Good initial solutions for the four parameters are helpful in achieving a good fit.) In general, the parameter b represents the lowest level of the function and a its highest level.

b. Determine whether there are local optima in the optimization problem in part (a) by providing Solver different initial values for the four parameters.

12. *Financial Planning.* Managers at Industrial Supply, Inc. are planning a sales campaign for the coming year in which they must determine how many sales representatives they will assign to seven product lines. S-shaped sales response functions of the form

$$\%Sales = b + (a - b)(\%Reps^c/(d + \%Reps^c))$$

have been fitted to subjective data provided by a group of experienced managers. (Both variables *Sales* and *Reps* have been measured relative to base levels. Thus %*Reps* represents the ratio between proposed reps and base reps, while %*Sales* represents the ratio between proposed sales and base sales.) The fitted values for the four parameters for each product are given in the following table:

	Response Parameters			
	a	b	c	d
Product A	1.6574	0.4722	2.0322	1.1954
Product B	1.3792	0.1493	2.5622	0.4562
Product C	1.2798	0.3101	2.3345	0.4033
Product D	1.0971	0.4497	3.0420	0.1910
Product E	1.2527	0.5603	1.7734	0.5576
Product F	1.1152	0.5899	2.8685	0.2851
Product G	2.0276	0.1575	1.7337	1.0381

The following table gives the current number of reps assigned to each product and current sales, along with the contribution margin on each product. The cost of each rep is $63,000 per year.

	Current Reps	Current Sales	Contribution Margin
Product A	96.8	214,400	0.70
Product B	142.4	36,500	0.55
Product C	52.7	21,200	0.72
Product D	24.1	37,200	0.72
Product E	27.3	38,000	0.62
Product F	29.7	14,600	0.53
Product G	56.8	11,200	0.52

a. Build a financial model to calculate the total net profit over all seven product lines for any proposed allocation of reps. What is the optimal allocation of reps and resulting optimal profit if we use no more reps than we currently have?

b. What is the optimal allocation of reps and the resulting optimal profit if we can hire an unlimited number of reps?

9 Linear Optimization

9.1 INTRODUCTION

In Chapter 8, we introduced optimization with Solver, and we focused on nonlinear programming. The nonlinear solver is the default algorithm in Solver, and it can be applied to a variety of optimization problems. *Linear* programming is a special case for which certain mathematical conditions must hold, but it is much more widely used in practice than nonlinear programming. Because of the mathematical structure of a linear program, it is possible to harness a more powerful algorithm (called the *simplex method*) for linear problems than for nonlinear problems, and we can accommodate larger numbers of variables and constraints. In this chapter, we cover the use of the linear solver, and we examine several examples that illustrate the wide applicability of linear programming models. In the fifty years or so that computers have been available for this kind of decision support, linear programming has proven to be a valuable tool for understanding business decisions.

As in the previous chapter, our optimization models contain a set of decision variables, an objective function, and a set of constraints. (In fact, we strongly recommend reading our general introduction to Solver in Sections 8.1 through 8.4 before proceeding.) In the case of linear models, we can impose additional design guidelines on our worksheets that lead to a more standardized approach than we were able to adopt with nonlinear models. These additional guidelines help us develop models efficiently, debug our models quickly, and communicate our results effectively.

9.1.1 Linearity

The term "linear" in linear programs refers to a feature of the objective function and the constraints. A linear function exhibits three properties:

- additivity
- proportionality
- divisibility

By **additive**, we mean that the contribution from one decision gets added to (or sometimes subtracted from) the contributions of other decisions. In an additive function, we can separate the contributions that come from each decision. By **proportional**, we mean that the contribution from any given decision grows in proportion to the value of the corresponding decision variable. When a decision variable doubles, its contribution to the objective also doubles. By **divisible**, we mean that a fractional decision variable is meaningful.

As an example, suppose that we compute profit from the function

$$Profit = (Unit\ Revenue) \times (Quantity\ Sold) - (Unit\ Cost) \times (Quantity\ Purchased)$$

where *Unit Revenue* and *Unit Cost* are parameters known to be 100 and 60, whereas *Quantity Sold* and *Quantity Purchased* are decisions, which we'll denote by x and y, respectively. In symbols, we can simply write:

$$Profit = 100x - 60y$$

219

where x and y are decision variables. Note that *Profit* separates into two additive terms, which we can call total revenue and total cost. The total revenue term ($100x$) is proportional to the decision variable *Quantity Sold*. Likewise, the total cost term ($60y$) is proportional to the decision variable *Quantity Purchased*. Fractional values for the decisions could well make sense. Suppose, for example, that the product is fuel and that the unit of measurement is gallons. Then certainly a fractional value such as $x = 72.4$ is plausible. Even if we think of discrete items, such as televisions, the unit of measurement could be dozens, in which case a fractional value such as $x = 15.5$ would also be meaningful. In summary, our *Profit* function exhibits all three of the linearity properties.

We turn now to an algebraic perspective. When we have several decision variables, we may give them letter names, such as x, y, and z, or we may number them and denote them by x_1, x_2, x_3, and so on. When there are n decision variables, we can write a linear objective function as follows:

$$z = c_1 x_1 + c_2 x_2 + \cdots + c_n x_n$$

where z represents the value of the objective function, and the c's are a set of given parameters called **objective function coefficients**. Note that the x's appear in separate terms (i.e., they are additive), they appear with exponents of 1 (i.e., their contributions to the objective function are proportional), and they are not restricted to integers (i.e., they are divisible). In a worksheet, we recognize the structure of z as a calculation that could be made by the SUMPRODUCT function. Thus, for spreadsheet purposes, we can recognize a linear function if it consists of a sum of pairwise products—where one of the pairs in each product is a parameter and the other is a decision variable.

For a constraint to be linear, its left-hand side must be a linear function. In other words, the left-hand side can be represented by a SUMPRODUCT function made upof a sum of pairwise products, where one element of each product is a parameter and the other is a decision variable. In most cases, we will actually use the SUMPRODUCT formula, although, as we will see in the next chapter, we sometimes prefer the SUM formula.

EXCEL MINI-LESSON *The SUMPRODUCT Function*	The SUMPRODUCT function in Excel takes the pairwise products of two sets of numbers and sums the products. This operation is sometimes called the "scalar product." For our purposes, the form of the function is the following: SUMPRODUCT(*Array1,Array2*) • *Array1* references the first set of numbers. • *Array2* references the second set of numbers.

The two arrays must have identical layouts. Specifically, if *Array1* comprises a set of numbers in a single row, then *Array2* must also be a set of numbers in a single row. Both arrays must be of the same size.

Suppose, for example, that we had three items with unit prices of 2, 3, and 4 and with sales volumes of u, v, and w, respectively. Then total revenue would come to $2u + 3v + 4w$, which could be computed from the formula SUMPRODUCT({2,3,4},{u,v,w}). When the volumes are $u = 30$, $v = 33$, and $w = 36$, the total revenue function takes on the value 303. ∎

9.1.2 Simplex Algorithm

The solution procedure for linear models is referred to as the **simplex algorithm**, or the linear solver. The simplex algorithm employs a strategy that shares some of the features of hill climbing, but it is able to exploit the special properties of linearity to find an optimal solution efficiently. For instance, if we can imagine a diamond that represents the set of feasible decision variables, then the simplex algorithm can be viewed as a procedure for moving along the edges of the diamond's surface until an optimal point is encountered. The simplex algorithm does not require a starting point in the worksheet; to put it another way, it determines its own starting solution. This means that Solver ignores the initial information in the decision variable cells when solving a linear model. Once the solution procedure finds a **feasible solution**, one that satisfies all the constraints, it proceeds from there to an optimal solution. An **optimal solution** must satisfy all constraints and its objective function must equal the best value that can be achieved. Moreover, the simplex method *guarantees* that it will find a global optimum (if there is one), and in that sense, the simplex method is completely reliable. We cannot say the same for nonlinear optimization algorithms (such as LSGRG), except in special circumstances.

In mathematical terms, linear models are a special case of nonlinear models, and, in principle, the LSGRG algorithm could be used as a solution procedure for the examples we present here. However, the simplex algorithm is especially suited to linear models, and it avoids numerical problems that sometimes affect the performance of the LSGRG algorithm. The linear solver is the preferred choice for any linear programming problem.

Linear programming models come in many sizes and shapes, but there are only a few standard types. It is helpful, therefore, to think in terms of a few basic structures when learning how to build and interpret linear programming models. In this chapter and the next, we present four different types. Most linear programming models are, in fact, combinations of these four types, but understanding the building blocks helps to clarify the key modeling concepts. In our framework, the four types are:

- *allocation* models
- *covering* models
- *blending* models
- *network* models

We cover the first three types in this chapter and network models separately in Chapter 10.

9.2   ALLOCATION MODELS

The allocation model calls for maximizing an objective (usually profit) subject to less-than constraints on capacity. Consider the Veerman Furniture Company as an example.

EXAMPLE
Veerman Furniture Company

Veerman Furniture Company makes three kinds of office furniture: chairs, desks, and tables. Each product requires some labor in the parts fabrication department, the assembly department, and the shipping department. The furniture is sold through a regional distributor, who has estimated the maximum potential sales for each product in the coming quarter. Finally, the accounting department has provided some data showing the profit contributions on each product. The decision problem is to determine the product mix—that is, to maximize Veerman's profit for the quarter by choosing production quantities for the chairs, desks, and tables. The following data summarizes the parameters of the problem:

Department	Hours per Unit			Hours Available
	Chairs	Desks	Tables	
Fabrication	4	6	2	1,850
Assembly	3	5	7	2,400
Shipping	3	2	4	1,500
Demand Potential	360	300	100	
Profit	$15	$24	$18	

■

9.2.1   Formulation

As recommended in the previous chapter, we approach the formulation of the optimization model by asking three basic questions. To determine the decision variables, we ask, "What must be decided?" The answer is the product mix, so we define decision variables as the number of chairs, desks, and tables produced. For the purposes of notation, we use C, D, and T to represent the number of chairs, the number of desks, and the number of tables respectively, in the product mix.

Next we ask, "What measure can we use to compare alternative sets of decision variables?" To choose between two different product mixes, we would calculate the total profit contribution for each one and choose the higher profit. To calculate profit, we add the profit from chairs, the profit from desks, and the profit from tables. Thus, an algebraic expression for total profit is:

$$Profit = 15C + 24D + 18T$$

To identify the model's constraints, we ask, "What restrictions limit our choice of decision variables?" In this scenario, there are two kinds of limitations: one due to production capacity and the other due to demand potential. In words, a production capacity constraint states that the number of hours *consumed* in the fabrication department must be less than or equal to the number of hours *available*. In symbols, we write:

$$Fabrication\ hours\ consumed = 4C + 6D + 2T \leq 1,850\ (\text{Fabrication hours available})$$

Similar constraints hold for the assembly and shipping departments:

$$Assembly\ hours\ consumed = 3C + 5D + 7T \leq 2,400\ (\text{Assembly hours available})$$
$$Shipping\ hours\ consumed = 3C + 2D + 4T \leq 1,500\ (\text{Shipping hours available})$$

Another type of constraint relates to demands. We require that the number of chairs *produced* must be less than or equal to the estimated demand *potential* for chairs. In symbols, we write:

$$Chairs\ produced = C \leq 360\ (\text{Chair demand potential})$$

Similar constraints hold for desks and tables:

$$Desks\ produced = D \leq 300\ (\text{Desk demand potential})$$
$$Tables\ produced = T \leq 100\ (\text{Table demand potential})$$

We now have six constraints that describe the restrictions limiting our choice of decision variables C, D, and T. The entire model, stated in algebraic terms, reads as follows:

$$\text{Maximize } z = 15C + 24D + 18T$$

subject to

$$
\begin{aligned}
4C + 6D + 2T &\leq 1,850 \\
3C + 5D + 7T &\leq 2,400 \\
3C + 2D + 4T &\leq 1,500 \\
C\ \ \ \ \ \ \ \ \ \ \ &\leq 360 \\
D\ \ \ \ \ \ &\leq 300 \\
T &\leq 100
\end{aligned}
$$

9.2.2 Spreadsheet Model

This algebraic statement reflects a widely used format for linear programs. Variables appear in columns, constraints appear as rows, and the objective function appears as a special row at the top of the model. We will adopt this layout as a standard for spreadsheet display.

A worksheet for this allocation problem appears in Figure 9.1.* Notice the three modules in the worksheet:

- a highlighted row for the decision variables (B5:D5)
- a highlighted single cell for the objective function value (E8)
- a set of constraint relationships (rows 11–16)

---

*To download spreadsheets for this chapter, go to the Student Companion Site at www.wiley.com/college/powell.

FIGURE 9.1 Spreadsheet Model for the Veerman Furniture Company Example

	A	B	C	D	E	F	G	H
1	**Allocation: Furniture Production**							
2								
3	**Decision Variables**							
4		C	D	T				
5	Product mix	100	200	50				
6								
7	**Objective Function**				*Total*			
8	Profit	15	24	18	$7,200			
9								
10	**Constraints**				*LHS*		*RHS*	
11	Fabrication	4	6	2	1700	<=	1850	Not Binding
12	Assembly	3	5	7	1650	<=	2400	Not Binding
13	Shipping	3	2	4	900	<=	1500	Not Binding
14	Chair market	1	0	0	100	<=	360	Not Binding
15	Desk market	0	1	0	200	<=	300	Not Binding
16	Table market	0	0	1	50	<=	100	Not Binding
17								

9.1

In the Constraints module, cells containing the symbol <= have no function in the operation of the worksheet; they are intended as a visual aid, helping to convey a sense of the information in the constraints. We place them between the left-hand side value of the constraint (a formula) and the right-hand side value (a parameter). To the right of each constraint parameter, we construct a cell that displays the status of the constraint. In cell H11, for example, the formula is `IF(E11=G11,"Binding","Not Binding")`. The constraint is **binding** if it is satisfied as an equality; otherwise, it is nonbinding. (Although this status indicator is a desirable feature of linear programming models for most beginners, we will often omit it, so that we can focus on the information in the constraints themselves.)

Figure 9.2 shows the formulas in this model. Note here that, aside from labels, the model contains only two kinds of cells: those containing a number (either a parameter or a decision variable) and those containing a SUMPRODUCT formula.

The set of values for the decision variables in Figure 9.1 was an arbitrary one. We could try different sets of three values in order to see whether we could come up with a good product mix by trial and error. Such an attempt might also be a useful debugging step, to provide some assurance that the model is correct. For example, suppose we start by fixing the number of desks and tables at zero and varying the number of chairs. For fabrication capacity, chairs consume 4 hours each, and there are 1,850 hours available, so we could put $1,850/4 = 462.5$ chairs into the mix (that is, into cell B5), and the result would be feasible for the first constraint. However, we can see immediately—by comparing LHS and RHS values—that this solution violates the ceiling on chair demand. So we can reduce the number of chairs to 360, which will give us a feasible product mix and a profit of $5,400. (Recall that a feasible solution must satisfy *all* constraints.) Keeping the number of chairs fixed, we can now add desks to the product mix (by entering a number into cell C5). Using trial and error (or Excel's Goal Seek tool), we can determine that it is possible to raise the number of desks to 68, achieving a profit of $7,032. However, this choice consumes all of the remaining fabrication capacity, leaving no room for tables in the product mix. Similar kinds of explorations, with other values of the decision variables, can help us confirm that the model is working properly and give us a feel for the profit that might be achievable.

FIGURE 9.2 Formulas in the Veerman Furniture Company Worksheet

	A	B	C	D	E	F	G	H
1	**Allocation: Furniture**							
2								
3	**Decision Variables**							
4		C	D	T				
5	Product mix	100	200	50				
6								
7	**Objective Function**				*Total*			
8	Profit	15	24	18	=SUMPRODUCT($B$5:$D$5,B8:D8)			
9								
10	**Constraints**				*LHS*		*RHS*	
11	Fabrication	4	6	2	=SUMPRODUCT($B$5:$D$5,B11:D11)	<=	1850	=IF(E11=G11,"Binding","Not Binding")
12	Assembly	3	5	7	=SUMPRODUCT($B$5:$D$5,B12:D12)	<=	2400	=IF(E12=G12,"Binding","Not Binding")
13	Shipping	3	2	4	=SUMPRODUCT($B$5:$D$5,B13:D13)	<=	1500	=IF(E13=G13,"Binding","Not Binding")
14	Chair market	1	0	0	=SUMPRODUCT($B$5:$D$5,B14:D14)	<=	360	=IF(E14=G14,"Binding","Not Binding")
15	Desk market	0	1	0	=SUMPRODUCT($B$5:$D$5,B15:D15)	<=	300	=IF(E15=G15,"Binding","Not Binding")
16	Table market	0	0	1	=SUMPRODUCT($B$5:$D$5,B16:D16)	<=	100	=IF(E16=G16,"Binding","Not Binding")
17								

9.1 9.2

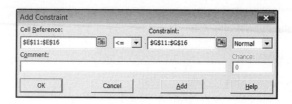

Although we will not discuss this step as we build other models in this chapter, we wouldn't
skip it unless we were dealing with a familiar type of problem.

9.2.3 Optimization

Once we are satisfied that the model is valid, we proceed to the optimization procedure and
specify:

Variables:	B5:D5
Objective:	E8 (maximize)
Constraints:	E11:E16 $\leq$ G11:G16

To enter this specification from the ribbon, we first highlight the decision variables
(B5:D5) and, from the ribbon, select Analytic Solver Platform▶Decisions▶Normal. Next,
we highlight the objective function cell (E8) and select Objective▶Max▶Normal. Then, we
highlight the left-hand side of the constraints (E11:E16) and select Constraints▶Normal
Constraint▶<=. The Add Constraint window opens, and we fill out the required information as shown in Figure 9.3 and click OK to close the window. In this last step, it is good
practice to enter cell references rather than numbers. We usually do *not* enter the right-hand
side constants as numbers in the Add Constraint window, even though Solver permits us to
do so. At this stage, the full model is specified in the task pane on the Model tab, as shown in
Figure 9.4.

Moving to the Engine tab of the task pane, we select the Standard LP/Quadratic
algorithm from the pull-down menu near the top, as shown in Figure 9.5. The default
parameters are sufficient for our needs, except for the Assume Non-Negative option,
which should be set to True because our decision variables will be meaningful in this model
only if they are nonnegative.

FIGURE 9.5 Algorithm Selection and Options Settings

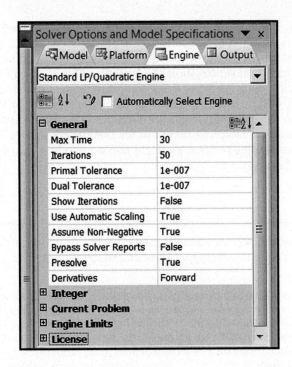

As we mentioned in Chapter 8, this is an excellent opportunity to test our intuition by posing some simple hypotheses. For example,

- Do we expect the optimal solution to call for producing all three products?
- Will the optimal solution consume all of the available hours?
- Should desks, which have the highest profit margin, be produced at the maximum amount the market allows?

With questions such as these, along with our tentative answers, we can proceed to implement the solution procedure by clicking on the Optimize icon.

As shown in Figure 9.6, the optimal solution calls for no chairs, 275 desks, and 100 tables. Evidently, the profit margin on chairs is not high enough for us to devote scarce resources to their production. The maximum profit contribution is $8,400, and the two binding constraints are fabrication hours and the demand ceiling for tables. (We also have unused time in assembly and shipping and unmet demand in chairs and desks.) These results—decision variables, objective function, and binding constraints—are the three key pieces of information provided in the solution.

Recall the distinction made in Chapter 8 between tactical and strategic information in the solution to an optimization problem. If we are faced with implementing a production

FIGURE 9.6 Optimal Solution for the Veerman Furniture Company Model

	A	B	C	D	E	F	G	H
1	Allocation: Furniture Production							
2								
3	Decision Variables							
4			C	D	T			
5	Product mix	0	275	100				
6								
7	Objective Function				Total			
8	Profit	15	24	18	$8,400			
9								
10	Constraints				LHS		RHS	
11	Fabrication	4	6	2	1850	<=	1850	Binding
12	Assembly	3	5	7	2075	<=	2400	Not Binding
13	Shipping	3	2	4	950	<=	1500	Not Binding
14	Chair market	1	0	0	0	<=	360	Not Binding
15	Desk market	0	1	0	275	<=	300	Not Binding
16	Table market	0	0	1	100	<=	100	Binding
17								

9.1 / 9.2 / 9.6

plan for the next quarter at Veerman Furniture, we would pursue the tactical solution, producing no chairs, 275 desks, and 100 tables. (We might first want to make sure that our marketing department approves the idea of bringing a limited range of products to the market in order to maximize short-term profits. This is one of the places where the simplifications in a model could be assessed against the realities of the actual situation.) On the other hand, if there is time to adjust the resources available at Veerman Furniture, we should explore the possibility of acquiring more fabrication capacity or expanding the demand potential for tables, as these are the binding constraints. In addition, if there is time to adjust marketing policies, we might also want to look into the possibility of raising the price on chairs.

9.3 COVERING MODELS

The covering model calls for minimizing an objective (usually cost) subject to greater-than constraints on required coverage. Consider Dahlby Outfitters as an example.

EXAMPLE
Dahlby
Outfitters

Dahlby Outfitters wishes to introduce packaged trail mix as a new product. The ingredients for the trail mix are seeds, raisins, flakes, and two kinds of nuts. Each ingredient contains certain amounts of vitamins, minerals, protein, and calories. The marketing department has specified that the product be designed so that a certain minimum nutritional profile is met. The decision problem is to determine the optimal product composition—that is, to minimize the product cost by choosing the amount for each of the ingredients in the mix. The following data summarizes the parameters of the problem:

	Grams per Pound					Nutritional
Component	Seeds	Raisins	Flakes	Pecans	Walnuts	Requirement
Vitamins	10	20	10	30	20	20
Minerals	5	7	4	9	2	10
Protein	1	4	10	2	1	15
Calories	500	450	160	300	500	600
Cost/pound	$4	$5	$3	$7	$6	

■

9.3.1 Formulation

What must be decided? Here, the answer is the amount of each ingredient to put into a package of trail mix. For the purposes of notation, we use $S, R, F, P,$ and W to represent the number of pounds of each ingredient in a package.

What measure will we use to compare sets of decision variables? This should be the total cost of a package, and our goal is the lowest possible total cost. To calculate the total cost of a particular composition, we add the cost of each ingredient in the package:

$$Cost = 4S + 5R + 3F + 7P + 6W$$

What restrictions limit our choice of decision variables? In this scenario, the main limitation is the requirement to meet the specified nutritional profile. Each dimension of this profile gives rise to a separate constraint. An example of such a constraint would state, in words, that the number of grams of vitamins *provided* in the package must be greater than or equal to the number of grams *required* by the specified profile. In symbols, we write:

$$Vitamin\ content = 10S + 20R + 10F + 30P + 20W \geq 20\ (\text{Vitamin floor})$$

Similar constraints must hold for the remainder of the profile:

$$Mineral\ content = 5S + 7R + 4F + 9P + 2W \geq 10\ (\text{Mineral floor})$$
$$Protein\ content = 1S + 4R + 10F + 2P + 1W \geq 15\ (\text{Protein floor})$$
$$Calorie\ content = 500S + 450R + 160F + 300P + 500W \geq 600\ (\text{Calorie floor})$$

In this basic scenario, no other constraints occur although we could imagine that there might also be limited quantities of the ingredients available, expressed as less-than constraints, or a weight requirement for the package, expressed as an equality constraint. Putting the algebraic statements together in one place, we obtain the following model:

$$\text{Minimize } z = 4S + 5R + 3F + 7P + 6W$$

subject to

$$
\begin{aligned}
10S + 20R + 10F + 30P + 20W &\geq 20 \\
5S + 7R + 4F + 9P + 2W &\geq 10 \\
1S + 4R + 10F + 2P + 1W &\geq 15 \\
500S + 450R + 160F + 300P + 500W &\geq 600
\end{aligned}
$$

9.3.2 Spreadsheet Model

A worksheet for this model appears in Figure 9.7. Again, we see three modules:

- a highlighted row for the decision variables (B5:F5)
- a highlighted single cell for the objective function value (G8)
- a set of constraint relationships (rows 11–14)

If we were to display the formulas in this worksheet, we would again see that the model is made up of only numbers and cells containing the SUMPRODUCT formula.

9.3.3 Optimization

Once we are satisfied that the model is valid, we proceed to optimize the model. We invoke Solver and specify:

Variables:	B5:F5
Objective:	G8 (minimize)
Constraints:	G11:G14 $\geq$ I11:I14

As in Figure 9.5, we select the linear solver and specify nonnegative variables. After contemplating some hypotheses about the problem (for example, will the solution require all five ingredients?), we run Solver and obtain a solution. The optimal solution, shown in Figure 9.8, calls for 1.32 pounds of flakes, 0.33 pound of raisins, and 0.48 pound of seeds, with no nuts at all. Evidently, nuts are prohibitively expensive, given the nature of the required nutritional profile and the other ingredients available. The optimal mix achieves all of the nutritional requirements at a minimum cost of $7.54. The three binding constraints in this solution are the requirements for minerals, protein, and calories.

FIGURE 9.7 Worksheet for the Dahlby Outfitters Model

	A	B	C	D	E	F	G	H	I	J
1	Covering: Trail Mix Composition									
2										
3	Decision Variables									
4		S	R	F	P	W				
5	Amounts	0.50	0.40	0.30	0.70	0.20				
6										
7	Objective Function						Total			
8	Cost	4	5	3	7	6	$11.00			
9										
10	Constraints						LHS		RHS	
11	Vitamins	10	20	10	30	20	41	>=	16	Not Binding
12	Minerals	5	7	4	9	2	13.2	>=	10	Not Binding
13	Protein	1	4	10	2	1	6.7	>=	15	Not Binding
14	Calories	500	450	160	300	500	788	>=	600	Not Binding
15										

FIGURE 9.8 Optimal Solution for the Dahlby Outfitters Model

	A	B	C	D	E	F	G	H	I	J
1	**Covering: Trail Mix Composition**									
2										
3	**Decision Variables**									
4		S	R	F	P	W				
5	Amounts	0.48	0.33	1.32	0.00	0.00				
6	Floor levels	0.15	0.15	0.15	0.15	0.15				
7	**Objective Function**						*Total*			
8	Cost	4	5	3	7	6	$7.54			
9										
10	**Constraints**						*LHS*		*RHS*	
11	Vitamins	10	20	10	30	20	24.642	>=	16	Not Binding
12	Minerals	5	7	4	9	2	10	>=	10	Binding
13	Protein	1	4	10	2	1	15	>=	15	Binding
14	Calories	500	450	160	300	500	600	>=	600	Binding
15										

9.7 **9.8**

FIGURE 9.9 Optimal Solution for the Amended Dahlby Outfitters Model

	A	B	C	D	E	F	G	H	I	J
1	**Covering: Trail Mix Composition**									
2										
3	**Decision Variables**									
4		S	R	F	P	W				
5	Amounts	0.39	0.15	1.36	0.15	0.15				
6	Floor levels	0.15	0.15	0.15	0.15	0.15				
7	**Objective Function**						*Total*			
8	Cost	4	5	3	7	6	$8.33			
9										
10	**Constraints**						*LHS*		*RHS*	
11	Vitamins	10	20	10	30	20	27.97	>=	16	Not Binding
12	Minerals	5	7	4	9	2	10.0791	>=	10	Not Binding
13	Protein	1	4	10	2	1	15	>=	15	Binding
14	Calories	500	450	160	300	500	600	>=	600	Binding
15										

9.7 9.8 **9.9**

Of course, we might decide that a trail mix without nuts is not an appealing product. If we wish, we can amend the model in order to force nuts into the optimal mix. One way is to specify a minimum amount of nuts. In Figure 9.9, we show an amended model that requires at least 0.15 pound of *each* ingredient. The value of 0.15 is placed in row 6, just below the corresponding decision variable. Using the ribbon, we add the constraint that the range B5:F5 must be greater than or equal to the range B6:F6. A requirement that a particular decision variable must be greater than or equal to a given number, such as we have here, is called a **lower bound** constraint. Similarly, a requirement that a particular decision variable must be less than or equal to a given number is called an **upper bound** constraint. It is usually convenient to locate the upper or lower bound on the worksheet in close proximity to the corresponding decision variable, as we have done in row 6. In the task pane, lower bound constraints and upper bound constraints appear in the Bounds subsection of the model's constraints.

After including the lower bound constraints, a new run of Solver produces the optimal solution shown in Figure 9.9. The lower bounds create an optimal solution that contains all five of the ingredients, as expected. We might have anticipated that nuts would appear at their lower limit, because before we added the lower bound constraints the optimization process kept nuts completely out of the mix. The minimum cost is also $0.79 higher in the amended model than in the original, at $8.33. This fact reflects an intuitive principle that complements the one we stated earlier: *When we add constraints to a model, the objective function cannot improve.* In most cases, as in this example, the objective function will get worse when we add a constraint.

9.4 BLENDING MODELS

Blending relationships are very common in linear programming applications, yet they remain difficult for beginners to identify in problem descriptions and to implement in spreadsheet models. Because of this difficulty, we begin with a special case—the representation of proportions. As an example, let's return to the product mix example of Veerman Furniture which was introduced earlier in this chapter. Recall from Figure 9.6 that the optimal product mix consisted of no chairs, 275 desks, and 100 tables. Suppose that this outcome is unacceptable because of the imbalance in volumes. For more balance, the Marketing Department might require that each of the products must make up at least 25 percent of the total units sold.

9.4.1 Blending Constraints

When we describe outcomes in terms of proportions, and when we place a floor (or ceiling) on one or more of those proportions, we are using blending constraints of a special type. Because the total number of units sold is $C + D + T$, a direct statement of the requirement for chairs is the following:

$$\frac{C}{C + D + T} \geq 0.25 \tag{9.1}$$

This greater-than constraint has a parameter on the right-hand side and all the decision variables on the left-hand side, as is usually the case. Although this is a valid constraint, it is not in *linear* form, because the quantities C, D, and T appear in both the numerator and denominator of the fraction. (In effect, the ratio divides decision variables by decision variables.) However, we can convert the nonlinear inequality to a linear one with a bit of algebra. First, multiply both sides of the inequality by $(C + D + T)$, yielding:

$$C \geq 0.25(C + D + T)$$

Next, collect terms involving the decision variables on the left-hand side, so that we get:

$$0.75C - 0.25D - 0.25T \geq 0 \tag{9.2}$$

This form conveys the same requirement as the original fractional constraint, and we recognize it immediately as a linear form. The coefficients on the left-hand side of (9.2) turn out to be either the complement of the floor $(1 - 0.25)$ or the floor itself (but with a minus sign). In a similar fashion, the requirement that the other products must respect the floor leads to the following two constraints:

$$-0.25C + 0.75D - 0.25T \geq 0$$
$$-0.25C - 0.25D + 0.75T \geq 0$$

Appending these three constraints to the product mix model (in rows 17–19) gives rise to the linear program described in Figure 9.10. Note that the first of the three new

FIGURE 9.10 Product Mix Model with Added Constraints

	A	B	C	D	E	F	G
1	**Allocation: Furniture Production**						
2							
3	**Decision Variables**						
4			C	D	T		
5	Product mix		0	275	100		
6							
7	**Objective Function**				Total		
8	Profit	15	24	18	$8,400		
9							
10	**Constraints**				LHS		RHS
11	Fabrication	4	6	2	1850	<=	1850
12	Assembly	3	5	7	2075	<=	2400
13	Distribution	3	2	4	950	<=	1500
14	Chair market	1	0	0	0	<=	360
15	Desk market	0	1	0	275	<=	300
16	Table market	0	0	1	100	<=	100
17	Chair fraction	0.75	-0.25	-0.25	-93.75	>=	0
18	Desk fraction	-0.25	0.75	-0.25	181.25	>=	0
19	Table fraction	-0.25	-0.25	0.75	6.25	>=	0
20							

9.10

	A	B	C	D	E	F	G
1	**Allocation: Furniture Production**						
2							
3	**Decision Variables**						
4			C	D	T		
5	Product mix	100	200	100			
6							
7	**Objective Function**				*Total*		
8	Profit	15	24	18	$8,100		
9							
10	**Constraints**				*LHS*		*RHS*
11	Fabrication	4	6	2	1800	<=	1850
12	Assembly	3	5	7	2000	<=	2400
13	Distribution	3	2	4	1100	<=	1500
14	Chair market	1	0	0	100	<=	360
15	Desk market	0	1	0	200	<=	300
16	Table market	0	0	1	100	<=	100
17	Chair fraction	0.75	-0.25	-0.25	0	>=	0
18	Desk fraction	-0.25	0.75	-0.25	100	>=	0
19	Table fraction	-0.25	-0.25	0.75	0	>=	0
20							

`9.10` **9.11**

constraints is not satisfied by the existing solution. A Solver run produces the solution in Figure 9.11, where we can see that the new optimal mix becomes 100 chairs, 200 desks and 100 tables. Thus, swapping chairs and tables for desks in the product mix, we can achieve the best possible level of profit, at $8,100. Also, as we might have expected, chairs comprise exactly 25 percent of the optimal output in this solution.

Whenever we encounter a constraint in the form of a lower limit or an upper limit on a proportion, we can take the following steps:

1. Write the fraction that expresses the constrained proportion.
2. Write the inequality implied by the lower bound or upper bound.
3. Multiply both sides of the inequality by the denominator and collect terms.
4. The result is a linear inequality, ready to incorporate in the model.

In Step 3, it is not actually necessary to collect terms because Solver allows us to leave a SUMPRODUCT formula on both sides of the inequality. However, we recommend collecting terms so that the variables appear on the left-hand side of the inequality and a constant appears on the right. This format is consistent with allocation and blending constraints and may make it easier to debug a model.

In general, the blending model involves mixing materials with different individual properties and describing the properties of the blend with weighted averages. We might be familiar with the phenomenon of mixing if we have spent time in a chemistry lab mixing fluids with different concentrations, but the concept extends beyond lab work. Consider the Diaz Coffee Company as an example.

EXAMPLE
The Diaz Coffee Company

The Diaz Coffee Company blends three types of coffee beans (Brazilian, Colombian, and Peruvian) into ground coffee to be sold at retail. Suppose that each kind of bean has a distinctive aroma and strength, and the company has a chief taster who can rate these features on a scale of 1 to 100. The features of the beans are tabulated as follows:

Bean	Aroma Rating	Strength Rating	Cost/lb.	Pounds Available
Brazilian	75	15	$0.50	1,500,000
Colombian	60	20	$0.60	1,200,000
Peruvian	85	18	$0.70	2,000,000

The company would like to create a blend that has an aroma rating of at least 78 and a strength rating of at least 16. Its supplies of the various beans are limited, however. The available quantities are specified above. All beans are delivered under a previously arranged purchase agreement. Diaz wants to make four million pounds of the blend at the lowest possible cost. ∎

9.4.2 Formulation

Suppose, for example, that we blend Brazilian and Peruvian beans in equal quantities of 25 pounds each. Then we should expect the blend to have an aroma rating of 80, just half way between the two pure ratings of 75 and 85. Mathematically, we take the weighted average of the two ratings:

$$\text{Aroma rating} = \frac{25(75) + 25(85)}{25 + 25} = 80$$

Now suppose that we blend the beans in amounts B, C, and P. The blend will have an aroma rating calculated by a weighted average of the three ratings, as follows:

$$\text{Aroma rating} = \frac{B(75) + C(60) + P(85)}{B + C + P}$$

To impose a constraint that requires an aroma rating of at least 78, we write:

$$\frac{B(75) + C(60) + P(85)}{B + C + P} \geq 78 \tag{9.3}$$

This greater-than constraint has a parameter on the right-hand side of (9.3) and all the decision variables on the left-hand side, as is usually the case. Although this is a valid constraint, it is not in *linear* form, because the quantities B, C, and P appear in both the numerator and denominator of the fraction. If we were to include this form of the constraint in Solver, we would be forced to use the nonlinear solver to get a solution. However, we can convert the nonlinear inequality to a linear one by following the steps listed earlier and thus satisfy the linear solver. First, multiply both sides of the inequality by $(B + C + P)$, yielding:

$$75B + 60C + 85P \geq 78(B + C + P)$$

Next, collect terms on the left-hand side, so that we get:

$$-3B - 18C + 7P \geq 0 \tag{9.4}$$

This form conveys the same requirement as the original fractional constraint in (9.3), and we recognize it immediately as a linear constraint. The coefficients on the left-hand side turn out to be just the *differences* between the individual aroma ratings (75, 60, 85) and the requirement of 78, with the signs indicating whether the individual rating is above or below the target. In a similar fashion, a requirement that the strength of the blend must be at least 16 leads to the constraint

$$-1B + 4C + 2P \geq 0$$

Thus, blending requirements are stated initially as fractions in (9.1) and (9.3), and in that form, they lead to nonlinear constraints. We are interested in converting these to linear constraints, as in (9.2) and (9.4), because with a linear model, we can harness the power of the linear solver. As discussed earlier, this means that we can find a global optimum reliably.

Now, knowing how to incorporate the blending requirements, we return to our scenario.

- What must be decided? The decision variables are the quantities to purchase, which we can continue to represent as B, C, and P. However, due to the scale of the model, it is convenient to take the dimensions of these three quantities to be thousands of pounds.

- What measure will we use? Evidently, it is the total purchase cost of meeting our four-million-pound requirement.

- What restrictions must we meet? In addition to the blending constraints, we need a constraint that generates a four-million-pound blend, along with three constraints that limit the supplies of the different beans.

FIGURE 9.12 Worksheet for the Diaz Coffee Company Model

	A	B	C	D	E	F	G	H
1	Blending: Coffee beans							
2								
3	Decision Variables							
4		B	C	P				
5	Inputs	100	100	100			in '000	
6								
7	Objective Function				Total			
8	Cost	0.50	0.60	0.70	$180		in '000	
9								
10	Constraints				LHS		RHS	
11	Blend aroma	-3	-18	7	-1400	>=	0	Not Binding
12	Blend strength	-1	4	2	500	>=	0	Not Binding
13	Output	1	1	1	300	>=	4000	Not Binding
14	B-supply	1	0	0	100	<=	1500	Not Binding
15	C-supply	0	1	0	100	<=	1200	Not Binding
16	P-supply	0	0	1	100	<=	2000	Not Binding
17	Actual aroma	75	60	85	73.3		78	
18	Actual strength	15	20	18	17.7		16	
19								

9.4.3 Spreadsheet Model

Figure 9.12 shows the spreadsheet for our model, which contains a greater-than constraint and three less-than constraints, in addition to the blending constraints. In addition, the model has been scaled by taking the supply and output constraints, as well as the decision variables, to be in thousands of pounds. The three decision variables have been set arbitrarily to 100,000 in the figure. In a sense, the model has two key blending constraints, and it also has what we might think of as covering and allocation constraints. Each of the constraints takes the same form: a SUMPRODUCT formula on the left-hand side and a parameter on the right-hand side. This model contains both less-than and greater-than constraints, and it is helpful, when specifying the model, to keep like constraints together.

The Output constraint requires that we produce *at least* four million pounds, not *exactly* four million pounds. Thus, as formulated here, there is some flexibility in the Output constraint. Although Diaz wishes to produce four million pounds, our model allows the production of a larger quantity if this will reduce costs. (Our intuition probably tells us that we should be able to minimize costs with a four-million-pound blend, but we would accept a solution that lowered cost while producing more than this amount because we could simply throw away the excess and remain better off.) In many situations, it is a good idea to use the weaker form of a constraint, giving the model some additional flexibility and avoiding equality constraints. In other words, *we build the model with some latitude in satisfying the constraints of the decision problem, whenever possible*. The solution will either confirm our intuition (as this one does) or else teach us a lesson about the limitations of our intuition.

9.4.4 Optimization

We now invoke Solver and specify:

Variables:	B5:D5
Objective:	E8 (maximize)
Constraints:	E11:E13 ≥ G11:G13
	E14:E16 ≤ G14:G16

As in Figure 9.5, we select the linear solver and specify nonnegative variables. When we run Solver, we obtain the optimal blend of 1.500 million pounds of Brazilian, 520,000 pounds of Colombian, and 1.980 million pounds of Peruvian beans, for a total cost of $2.448 million (see Figure 9.13). Of the two blending constraints, only the first (aroma) constraint is binding; the optimal blend actually has better-than-required strength. The output constraint is also binding (consistent with our intuitive expectation), as is the limit on Brazilian supply.

In Figure 9.13, which displays the optimal solution, rows 17 and 18 on the worksheet are, strictly speaking, not part of our Solver model. (In other words, the model's constraints

FIGURE 9.13 Optimal Solution for the Diaz Coffee Company Model

▲	A	B	C	D	E	F	G	H
1	**Blending: Coffee beans**							
2								
3	**Decision Variables**							
4		B	C	P				
5	Inputs	1500	520	1980			in '000	
6								
7	**Objective Function**				*Total*			
8	Cost	0.50	0.60	0.70	$2,448		in '000	
9								
10	**Constraints**				*LHS*		RHS	
11	Blend aroma	-3	-18	7	0	>=	0	Binding
12	Blend strength	-1	4	2	4540	>=	0	Not Binding
13	Output	1	1	1	4000	>=	4000	Binding
14	B-supply	1	0	0	1500	<=	1500	Binding
15	C-supply	0	1	0	520	<=	1200	Not Binding
16	P-supply	0	0	1	1980	<=	2000	Not Binding
17	*Actual aroma*	75	60	85	78.0		78	
18	*Actual strength*	15	20	18	17.1		16	
19								

9.12   **9.13**

and objective function are not influenced by the calculations in these two rows.) Instead, they provide a more conventional calculation of the blended properties, and we include them simply for convenience when interpreting the results. Thus, the first constraint of the model (row 11) is binding, and the aroma calculation in row 17 shows that the weighted average exactly equals the requirement of 78. The second constraint (row 12) shows that the strength requirement is not binding, but a face-value comparison of left-hand side (4,540) with right-hand side (zero) may not be very useful. However, the last row of the worksheet shows that the optimal blend's strength is 17.1 (see cell E18), giving us a clearer sense of the cushion between the strength achieved and the requirement of 16.

SOLVER TIP
Rescaling the Model

Rescaling the decisions and parameters of a model—for example, using thousands or millions as a unit of measure—has the virtue that it saves us the work of entering lots of zeros. As a consequence, we may avoid some data-entry errors, and the spreadsheet looks a little less crowded than it would with many large numbers on it. However, there is another important practical reason for rescaling. The way that Solver carries out its arithmetic sometimes makes rescaling desirable. As a guideline, the parameters in the objective function and the constraints should not differ from each other, or from the values of the decision variables, by more than a factor of 100,000. In the Diaz Coffee example, the ratio of the largest right hand-side constant to the smallest constraint coefficient would be four million if there were no rescaling. Although a model as simple as this one would likely run correctly, it is safer (as well as more convenient) to do the rescaling.

One symptom of a need for rescaling would be a response from Solver stating that there is no feasible solution to a problem in which we're sure that feasible solutions can be found. In these circumstances, we should try to multiply a constraint by some constant or redefine the decision variables using a different unit of measure. Sometimes, however, scaling problems are difficult to completely avoid when we're trying to keep the model easy for another user to understand. In these cases, we can ask Solver to perform some internal rescaling of the model if we specify the option for Automatic Scaling, which appears on the Engine tab shown in Figure 9.5. The Automatic Scaling option may be helpful; however, it is always preferable for the model builder to do the rescaling. (Unfortunately, there are also instances in which the Automatic Scaling option causes the linear solver to go awry when it would otherwise have functioned perfectly.)

Finally, if we need to display our model results in units that are more natural for our audience, we can create a separate presentation worksheet. On that sheet, the numbers can be "unscaled" and displayed in any desired format without affecting the optimization process. ∎

9.5   SENSITIVITY ANALYSIS FOR LINEAR PROGRAMS

As we stressed in Chapter 4, sensitivity analysis is a vital part of all spreadsheet modeling. In optimization modeling, some of the most valuable insights come not from the optimal solution itself, but from a sensitivity analysis around the optimal solution. As we will see, the special structure of linear programs gives rise to certain characteristic results. We again use the Optimization Sensitivity tool.

We implement the Optimization Sensitivity tool with the Veerman Furniture model to illustrate some of the features of sensitivity analysis in linear programs. Recall that the model allows us to find the profit-maximizing product mix among chairs, desks, and tables. The optimal product mix (see Figure 9.6) is made up of desks and tables, with no chairs. Two constraints are binding: fabrication hours and the tables market. The optimal total profit contribution in the base case is $8,400.

9.5.1 Sensitivity to Objective Function Coefficients

Suppose that we are using the Veerman Furniture model as a planning tool and that we wish to explore a change in the price of chairs. We might not yet know what the exact price will be, pending more information about the competition, but we want to explore the impact of a price change, which translates into a change in the profit contribution of chairs. For the time being, let's assume that if we vary the price, there will be no effect on the demand potential for chairs.

As mentioned in Chapter 8, it is helpful to designate a separate portion of the worksheet for sensitivity values. In the Veerman Furniture model, we can use column I for this purpose. Place the cursor on cell I8 (in the same row as the profit contributions), and then click on Analytic Solver Platform▶Parameters▶Optimization to open the Function Arguments window. Enter 12 and 24 as the Lower and Upper values, respectively, and click OK to close the window. Now, cell I8 contains the function `PsiOptParam(12,24)`. Next, change the contents of cell B8 so that it references I8. At this point, both cells display the value 12, because the PsiOptParam function displays its Lower value by default.

Returning to the ribbon, we click on Reports▶Optimization▶Parameter Analysis to display the report window for Multiple Optimizations. Cell I8 is specified as a parameter, and the variables and objective of the model are automatically specified as results. Using the arrow buttons, these cells are copied to the right-hand window, as shown in Figure 9.14. For the Results window, our preference is to place the objective cell at the top of the list, followed by the variables. (The Up and Down buttons can be used to sequence the list according to our preferences.) Finally, we enter 13 as the `Major Axis Points` (for steps of 1 from 12 to 24), and click OK.

The Optimization Sensitivity report appears on a new worksheet (reproduced, with some reformatting, as Figure 9.15). These results show how the optimal product mix and

FIGURE 9.14 The Multiple Optimizations Report Window

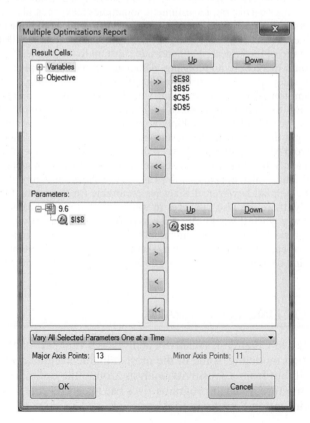

FIGURE 9.15 Sensitivity Report for a Change in Price

	A	B	C	D	E
1	Unit Profit	Total Profit	Chairs	Desks	Tables
2	12	$8,400	0	275	100
3	13	$8,400	0	275	100
4	14	$8,400	0	275	100
5	15	$8,400	0	275	100
6	16	$8,400	330	55	100
7	17	$8,730	330	55	100
8	18	$9,060	330	55	100
9	19	$9,390	330	55	100
10	20	$9,720	330	55	100
11	21	$10,050	360	40	85
12	22	$10,410	360	40	85
13	23	$10,770	360	40	85
14	24	$11,130	360	40	85
15					

9.15

the optimal profit both change as the profit contribution on chairs increases. For the range of profit contributions we chose ($12 to $24), we see two distinct profiles. For values up to $16, the base-case solution prevails, but starting at $16, the optimal mix changes, as follows:

- Chairs stay at zero until the unit profit contribution on chairs reaches $16; then, chairs enter the optimal mix at a quantity of 330.

- When the unit contribution reaches $21, the number of chairs in the optimal mix increases to 360.

- Desks and tables are not affected until the unit contribution on chairs reaches $16; then, the optimal number of desks drops from 275 to 55. When the unit profit on chairs reaches $21, the optimal number of desks drops again, to 40.

- Tables stay level at 100 until the unit contribution on chairs reaches $21; then, the optimal number of tables drops to 85.

- The optimal total profit remains unchanged until the unit contribution on chairs reaches $16; thereafter, it increases.

From this information, we can conclude that the optimal solution is insensitive to changes in the unit profit contribution of chairs, up to $16. Beyond that point, however, the profit contribution on chairs is high enough to have all three products in the mix. In effect, chairs substitute for desks (though not at a ratio of 1:1) when the profit contribution reaches $16. Subsequently, when the profit contribution reaches $21, chairs substitute for both desks and tables and are limited only by their demand potential. Thus, if we decide to alter the price for chairs, we can anticipate the impact on our product mix from the information in the sensitivity table.

In all linear programs, changes in the optimal solution lead to a distinct pattern when we vary a coefficient of a decision variable in the objective function. In some interval around the base-case value, there is no change at all in the optimal decisions, but the objective function value changes if the decision variable is positive. Outside of this interval, a different set of values for the decision variables becomes optimal. As we saw in this example, the change from one set of values to the other will not be gradual. Instead, it will often be dramatic, as illustrated by the optimal number of chairs changing from 0 to 330 when the profit contribution reaches $16.

9.5.2 Sensitivity to Constraint Constants

Turning to another question, the optimal solution to the base case revealed that two constraints are binding: fabrication hours and the demand for tables. If fabrication time limits our ability to increase profits, perhaps we should acquire more of it. How much should we pay for additional time? This is a sensitivity question that involves one of the right-hand-side constants rather than an objective function coefficient. To obtain an answer, we can invoke optimization sensitivity again. (To avoid confusion, we first reset cell B8 to the original value of 15.) Our sensitivity analysis is aimed at keeping the original model intact, except for the number of fabrication hours.

Starting with the original model, we select cell I11, return to the ribbon, and click on Parameters▶Optimization. In the Function Arguments window, we specify Lower and

FIGURE 9.16 The Multiple Optimizations Report Window

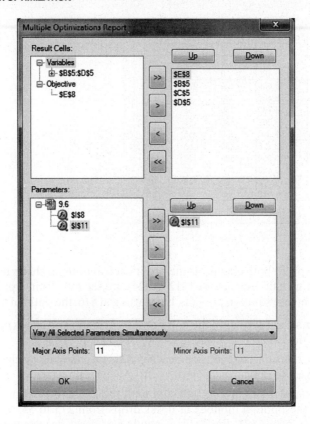

Upper values of 1,500 and 2,500. Equivalently, we can just enter the function = PsiOpt-Param(1500, 2500). Our entries in the report window are shown in Figure 9.16.

The Optimization Sensitivity report appears on a new worksheet (reproduced, with some reformatting, as Figure 9.17). The table shows how the optimal product mix and the optimal profit both change as the number of fabrication hours increases. Thus, we see the following changes in the optimal product mix:

- Chairs stay at zero until the number of fabrication hours reaches 2,000; then, chairs enter the optimal mix and continue to increase thereafter.

- Desks increase until the number of fabrication hours reaches 2,000; then, desks stay level at 300.

- Tables stay level at 100 until the number of fabrication hours reaches 2,200; then, tables drop.

- The optimal total profit increases as the number of fabrication hours increases.

From this information, we can conclude that as we increase fabrication capacity, we should alter the product mix—first by increasing the number of desks, then by adding chairs to the mix, and then by swapping chairs for tables.

FIGURE 9.17 Sensitivity Report for a Change in Fabrication Hours

	A	B	C	D	E	F
1	**Fab Hours**	**Total Profit**	**Change**	**Chairs**	**Desks**	**Tables**
2	**1500**	$7,000		0	216.67	100.00
3	**1600**	$7,400	$4.00	0	233.33	100.00
4	**1700**	$7,800	$4.00	0	250.00	100.00
5	**1800**	$8,200	$4.00	0	266.67	100.00
6	**1900**	$8,600	$4.00	0	283.33	100.00
7	**2000**	$9,000	$4.00	0	300.00	100.00
8	**2100**	$9,375	$3.75	25.00	300.00	100.00
9	**2200**	$9,750	$3.75	50.00	300.00	100.00
10	**2300**	$10,077	$3.27	77.27	300.00	95.45
11	**2400**	$10,309	$2.32	109.09	300.00	81.82
12	**2500**	$10,541	$2.32	140.91	300.00	68.18
13						

9.17

To determine how much we should be willing to pay for additional time, we examine the marginal value of additional fabrication hours. The **marginal value** is defined as the improvement in the objective function from a unit increase in the number available (i.e., an increase of 1 in the right-hand side of the fabrication constraint). We could calculate this marginal value by changing the number of fabrication hours to 1,851, re-solving the problem, and noting the improvement in the objective function. (It increases to $8,404, an improvement of $4.)

We have inserted a calculation in column C of the report to compute the change in the optimal total profit per unit change in fabrication hours. (In cell C3, we enter the formula =(B3−B2)/(A3−A2), and then copy the formula to the rest of the column below.) For example, the first nonblank entry indicates that, between 1,500 and 1,600 hours, each additional hour of fabrication capacity adds $4.00 to total profit. This calculation gives us some insight into the marginal value of fabrication hours, which is also $4.00 in the region of the base case. As the number of fabrication hours increases, the marginal value stays level for a while, then drops to $3.75, stays level at that value for a while, and then eventually drops to about $2.32. This pattern is an instance of *diminishing marginal returns*: if someone were to offer us more and more of a scarce resource, its value would eventually decline. In this case, the scarce resource (or binding constraint) is fabrication capacity. Limited fabrication hours prevent us from achieving higher total profits; that is what makes fabrication hours economically scarce.

Starting with the base case, we should be willing to pay up to $4.00 for each additional fabrication hour because profit increases by this amount. This marginal value is also called the **shadow price**. In economic terms, the shadow price is the break-even price at which it would be profitable to acquire more of a scarce resource. In other words, imagine that someone were to offer us additional fabrication hours (for example, if we could lease fabrication equipment). We can improve total profit by acquiring those additional hours, as long as their price is less than $4.00 each.

In this example, we observe that the marginal value of the scarce resource remains constant in a neighborhood around the base-case value. In particular, the $4.00 shadow price holds for additional fabrication hours until we reach 2,000 hours; then it drops to $3.75. In the interval from 1,850 hours to 2,000 hours, the incremental hours allow more desks to be manufactured. In fact, we can see from Figure 9.17 that each additional 100 hours leads to an increment of 16.67 desks in the product mix. This increment, in turn, accounts for an increase of $400.00 in total profit, since desks contribute $24.00 each.

Above 2,000 fabrication hours, the pattern is a little different. With additional hours available, there are more chairs in the optimal product mix, and the optimal profit grows by $375.00 for each additional 100 hours. Thus, the shadow price is $3.75, and this value persists until around 2,200 hours. Actually, the shadow price changes at 2,266.67 hours, but the report table is too coarse for us to see the precise change point. (We could see it more readily if we were to repeat the analysis with a step size of 1 hour.) Above 2,266.67 fabrication hours, the total profit increases at an even smaller rate ($2.32). In this interval, chairs are added to the product mix, and tables are removed from it. Chairs consume more fabrication time than do tables. Therefore, with a relatively small amount of fabrication capacity (1,850 hours), we are better off not making chairs. As fabrication capacity increases (to, say, 2,300 hours), we are willing to swap chairs for tables, in light of other capacities available, in pursuit of optimal profits.

Linear programs typically give rise to a distinct pattern in sensitivity tables when we vary the availability of a scarce resource. The marginal value of capacity remains constant over some interval of increase or decrease. (This contrasts with the marginal value in nonlinear models, such as Figure 8.23, where marginal values changed continuously as we altered the availability of a scarce resource.) Within this interval, some of the decision variables change linearly with the change in capacity, while other decision variables stay the same. If someone were to continually give us more of a scarce resource, its value would drop and eventually fall to zero. In the case of our product mix problem, we could confirm that the value of additional hours drops to zero at a capacity level of 3,000.

The Optimization Sensitivity tool has the limitation that we must specify in advance the increment with which we change the input parameter. If we choose too big an increment (too coarse a grid), we may not identify the precise point at which the solution changes. In that case, we can always refine the search and run the analysis again. An alternative is to use the Sensitivity Report, which provides information on the local sensitivity to both objective function coefficients and right-hand sides. (The chapter appendix provides some details on the information in the Sensitivity Report.)

We have illustrated the sensitivity of linear programs to two fundamental types of parameters: an objective function coefficient and a constraint constant. These cases are particularly interesting because each produces a characteristic pattern in the optimal solution. However, we should not lose sight of the fact that with the Optimization Sensitivity tool, we can analyze the sensitivity of the optimal solution to *any* parameter in the model.

SOLVER TIP
Optimization Sensitivity and Shadow Prices

Optimization sensitivity is a general purpose tool for sensitivity analysis of optimization models. It determines the sensitivity of the optimal solution to any input parameter. It allows us to calculate the change in the objective function per unit change in the input parameter, which we call the *marginal change* in the objective.

Optimization sensitivity can be used to assess the impact on the optimal solution of changes in the constraint constants, which typically represent resources. In that case, the marginal change in the objective can be interpreted as the marginal value of the resource. The marginal value of a resource is the change in the objective per unit change in the resource, which can usually be interpreted as the maximum amount we would be willing to pay to acquire additional quantities of the resource.

The marginal value of a resource is given the special name **shadow price**. In linear programs, shadow prices are constant for some range of changes in the RHS. This feature is central to our interpretation of the economic meaning in the solutions to linear optimization models. In nonlinear models, by contrast, the marginal values of resources are typically not constant. ∎

9.6   PATTERNS IN LINEAR PROGRAMMING SOLUTIONS

In linear programming models, one form of insight comes from seeing a qualitative pattern in the solution. Stated another way, the optimal solution tells a "story" about a pattern of economic priorities, and it's the recognition of those priorities that provides useful insight. When we know the pattern, we can explain the solution more convincingly than when we simply read Solver results. When we know the pattern, we can also anticipate some of the answers to "what if" questions without having to modify the worksheet. In short, the pattern provides a level of understanding that enhances decision making. Therefore, after we optimize a linear programming model, we should always try to discern the qualitative pattern in the optimal solution.

9.6.1   Identifying Patterns

Spotting a pattern involves observations about both variables and constraints. In the optimal solution, we pay special attention to which constraints are binding and which are not, as well as to which decision variables are positive and which are zero. Grasping the pattern of binding constraints and positive decision variables often allows us to reconstruct the solution in a step-by-step fashion. To the untrained observer, we seem to be solving the problem methodically, from scratch; in fact, we are only providing a retrospective interpretation of the solution, and we need to know that solution before we can devise the interpretation. Nevertheless, we are not merely reflecting information in the computer output. Rather, we are describing a set of economic imperatives at the heart of the model. When we can see those imperatives, and communicate them, then we have gained some insight. In the examples that follow, we show how to uncover these patterns.

While it can be extremely helpful to identify the pattern in the solution to a linear program, we should not assume that the pattern holds for anything other than small changes in the parameters. We can always check whether the pattern changes by rerunning Solver with new input parameters.

To illustrate the process of identifying a pattern, recall the solution of the product mix problem in Figure 9.6. The display in Figure 9.18 highlights the positive variables and the binding constraints. When we concentrate on these variables and constraints, we see that the problem becomes one of optimizing the choice of the variables D and T, subject to two constraints:

$$6D + 2T = 1,850$$
$$T = 100$$

The second equation dictates the value of T because it is a binding constraint containing only one variable. Once we know that $T = 100$, we can substitute into the first

FIGURE 9.18 Optimal
Product Mix Model,
Highlighting Elements of
the Pattern

	A	B	C	D	E	F	G
1	**Allocation: Furniture Production**						
2							
3	**Decision Variables**						
4			C	D	T		
5	Product mix		0	275	100		
6							
7	**Objective Function**				*Total*		
8	Profit		0	24	18	$8,400	
9							
10	**Constraints**				*LHS*		*RHS*
11	Fabrication	4	6	2	1850	<=	1850
12	Assembly	3	5	7	2075	<=	2400
13	Shipping	3	2	4	950	<=	1500
14	Chair market	1	0	0	0	<=	360
15	Desk market	0	1	0	275	<=	300
16	Table market	0	0	1	100	<=	100
17							

9.18

constraint and deduce that $D = 275$. The solution is constructed as if we determine T first and then D. The construction of the solution goes like this:

- First, remove C from further consideration.
- Next, let the market ceiling for tables dictate the value of T.
- Finally (with T fixed), let the fabrication capacity dictate the value of D.

This procedure describes the solution fully but does not use any numbers. In that sense, the pattern is a qualitative interpretation of the solution. However, once we supply the parameters of the constraints (in this case, that means 100 and 1,850), the pattern gives us a scheme for computing the optimal quantitative solution. It is almost as if Solver first spots the optimal pattern and then says, "Give me the numerical information in your problem." For any specification of the numbers (within certain limits), Solver could then compute the optimal solution by simply following the sequential steps in the pattern. In reality, of course, Solver cannot know the pattern until the solution is determined, because the solution is a critical ingredient in the pattern.

Let's return to the point that the patterns hold for any set of numbers within certain limits. What limits are we referring to? Suppose we make a change in the size of the market ceiling for tables and increment the ceiling by one, to 101. Then, the steps in the pattern lead us to a new optimal solution: $T = 101$ and $D = 274.667$. The impact on the objective function is an increment of $24 (-0.333) + 18 (+1) = 10$. In other words, a unit increase in the market ceiling for tables allows the optimal mix to increase profits by $10.

In effect, we have derived the shadow price for the market ceiling constraint. (We could confirm this result by rerunning Solver with a market ceiling of 101 for tables.) Thus, if we increment the ceiling by two units, the new optimal solution becomes $T = 102$ and $D = 274.333$, with an increase of $20 in the objective. How long can we continue incrementing the market ceiling for tables? To answer this question, we have to consider the impact on the constraints we have been ignoring, as well as on the decision variables. In the latter case, the optimal value of D drops 0.333 for every unit increase in the ceiling. At this rate, the ceiling could become as large as 825. But let's look at the nonbinding constraints:

- The Assembly constraint had a surplus of 325 hours in the original problem. Increasing T by one and reducing D by 0.333 consumes an additional 5.333 Assembly hours. At this rate, there is room to increase the ceiling by at most $325/5.333 = 60.9375$.
- The Shipping constraint had a surplus 550 hours in the original problem. Increasing T by one and reducing D by 0.333 consumes an additional 3.333 Shipping hours. At this rate, there is room to increase the ceiling by at most $550/3.333 = 165$.
- The chair ceiling is unaffected by the change.
- The desk ceiling had a surplus of 25 desks in the original solution, but because the change involves a reduction in the number of desks, the desk ceiling does not come into play.

Taking the tightest of the relevant limits, we conclude that the market ceiling for tables could be increased as much as 60.9375 units without changing the pattern.

In the opposite direction, suppose we *reduce* the size of the market ceiling for tables.

- Reducing the ceiling for tables directly affects the variable T. There is room to decrease the ceiling by at most 100 tables.

- The desk ceiling had a surplus of 25 desks in the original solution. Decreasing T by one and increasing D by 0.333 consumes an additional 0.333 of the surplus in the constraint. At this rate, there is room to increase the ceiling by at most $25/0.333 = 75$ tables.

Taking the tighter of these two limits, we conclude that the market ceiling for tables could be reduced by as much as 75 units without changing the pattern. Thus, the analysis of both directions leads to the conclusion that the shadow price holds for market ceilings from 25 to 160.9375. Beyond this range, the pattern changes: in particular, there is a change in the set of binding constraints or the set of nonzero variables (or both).

9.6.2 Further Examples

The following examples illustrate patterns in the optimal solution of other linear programs:

EXAMPLE
A Product Portfolio Decision

The product portfolio problem asks which products a firm should be making. If there are contracts that obligate the firm to enter certain markets, then the question is which products to make in quantities beyond the required minimum. Consider Grocery Distributors (GD), a company that distributes fifteen different vegetables to grocery stores. GD's vegetables come in standard cardboard cartons that each take up 1.25 cubic feet in the warehouse. The company replenishes its supply of frozen foods at the start of each week and rarely has any inventory remaining at week's end. An entire week's supply of frozen vegetables arrives each Monday morning at the warehouse, which can hold up to 18,000 cubic feet of product. In addition, GD's supplier extends a line of credit amounting to $30,000. That is, GD is permitted to purchase up to $30,000 worth of product each Monday. GD can predict sales for each of the fifteen products for the coming week. This forecast is expressed in terms of a minimum and a maximum level of sales. The minimum quantity is based on a contractual agreement that GD has made with a few retail grocery chains; the maximum quantity represents an estimate of the sales potential in the upcoming week. The unit cost and unit selling price for each product are known. The given data are compiled in the following table:

Product	Cost	Price	Minimum	Maximum
Whipped Potatoes (WP)	2.15	2.27	300	1,500
Creamed Corn (CC)	2.20	2.48	400	2,000
Blackeyed Peas (BP)	2.40	2.70	250	900
Artichokes (AR)	4.80	5.20	0	150
Carrots (CR)	2.60	2.92	300	1,200
Succotash (SU)	2.30	2.48	200	800
Okra (OK)	2.35	2.20	150	600
Cauliflower (CL)	2.85	3.13	100	300
Green Peas (GP)	2.25	2.48	750	3,500
Spinach (SP)	2.10	2.27	400	2,000
Lima Beans (LB)	2.80	3.13	500	3,300
Brussel Sprouts (BS)	3.00	3.18	100	500
Green Beans (GB)	2.60	2.92	500	3,200
Squash (SQ)	2.50	2.70	100	500
Broccoli (BR)	2.90	3.13	400	2,500

■

GD solves the linear programming model shown in Figure 9.19. In this model, the objective is maximizing profit for the coming week. Sales for each product are constrained by a minimum quantity and a maximum quantity. In addition, constraints come from aggregate limits on warehouse space and purchase expenditures.

We invoke Solver and specify:

Variables: C9:Q9
Objective: R11 (maximize)
Constraints: C9:Q9 $\geq$ C6:Q6
C9:Q9 $\leq$ C7:Q7
R14:R15 $\leq$ T14:T15

FIGURE 9.19 Optimal Solution for the GD Model

		WP	CC	BP	AR	CR	SU	OK	CL	GP	SP	LB	BS	GB	SQ	BR			
General Distributors																			
Data	Vegetable	WP	CC	BP	AR	CR	SU	OK	CL	GP	SP	LB	BS	GB	SQ	BR			
	Cost	2.15	2.20	2.40	4.80	2.60	2.30	2.35	2.85	2.25	2.10	2.80	3.00	2.60	2.50	2.90			
	Price	2.27	2.48	2.70	5.20	2.92	2.48	2.20	3.13	2.48	2.27	3.13	3.18	2.92	2.70	3.13			
	Min	300	400	250	0	300	200	150	100	750	400	500	100	500	100	400			
	Max	1500	2000	900	150	1200	800	600	300	3500	2000	3300	500	3200	500	2500			
Decisions	Cartons	300	2000	900	0	1200	200	150	100	750	400	2150	100	3200	100	400			
Objective	Profit $	0.12	0.28	0.30	0.40	0.32	0.18	-0.15	0.28	0.23	0.17	0.33	0.18	0.32	0.20	0.23	$3,395.50		
																	LHS		RHS
Constraints	Credit	2.15	2.20	2.40	4.80	2.60	2.30	2.35	2.85	2.25	2.10	2.80	3.00	2.60	2.50	2.90	30,000.00	<=	30,000
	Space	1.25	1.25	1.25	1.25	1.25	1.25	1.25	1.25	1.25	1.25	1.25	1.25	1.25	1.25	1.25	14,937.50	<=	18,000
Ratios		1.056	1.127	1.125	1.083	1.123	1.078	0.936	1.098	1.102	1.081	1.118	1.060	1.123	1.080	1.079			

The solution shows that all of the decision variables are positive except for artichokes, and the maximum profit is $3,395.50.

Examining the variables in the solution in more detail, we notice that all but one of the purchase quantities match either the maximum or the minimum, with lima beans as the only exception. Any product that has a nonzero minimum must appear in the solution at a positive amount, but some products are purchased at even higher levels. These can be considered high-priority products. Products purchased at their minimum levels can be considered low-priority products. In either case, however, the values corresponding to high-priority products and low-priority products are dictated by one binding constraint containing one variable.

Examining the other constraints in the solution, we see that the credit limit is binding, but the space constraint is not. In effect, the credit limit serves as a bottleneck on purchases, but we can ignore the space constraint, because other constraints dictate how much space is used. A description of the pattern could take the following form:

- Set the volume of each high-priority product equal to its maximum level.
- Set the volume of each low-priority product equal to its minimum level.
- Use the entire credit limit.

In other words, we are actually solving a simpler problem than originally given: produce the highest possible value from the fifteen products under a tight credit limit. To solve this problem, we can use a common sense rule: pursue the products in the order of highest to lowest *profit-to-cost ratio*. Meanwhile, we must meet the given minimum quantities. Therefore, we can convert the pattern into a calculation scheme for the decision variables, as follows:

- Purchase each product at its minimum sales level.
- Rank the products from highest to lowest ratio of profit to cost.
- For the highest-ranking product, raise the purchase quantity toward its maximum sales level. As we increase the purchase quantity, only two things can happen: either we reach the maximum for that product (in which case we go to the next highest priority product), or we use up the credit limit (in which case we are done).

The ranking mechanism prioritizes the products. Using these priorities, we essentially separate the products into three groups: a set of high-priority products, produced at their maximum levels; a set of low-priority products, produced at their minimum levels; and a *single* medium-priority product, produced at a level somewhere between its minimum and maximum. (This product is the one we are adding to the purchase plan when we use up the credit limit.) This procedure is complete and unambiguous, and this pattern describes the optimal solution without explicitly using any numbers. At first, the solution was just a collection of positive decision variables and binding constraints. But we were able to convert the solution into a prioritized list of allocations that establishes the values of the decision variables one at a time.

Actually, Solver's solution merely distinguishes the three priority classes; it does not reveal the profit-to-cost ratio rule explicitly. That insight might come from reviewing the makeup of the priority classes, or from some intuition about how single-constraint problems are optimized. (The profit-to-cost ratios are shown for confirmation in row 17 of Figure 9.19.) But this brings up an important point. Solver does not usually reveal the economic reason why a variable should have high priority, and it is not always necessary (or even possible) for us to know why an allocation receives high priority. We simply notice a binding constraint containing just one positive variable, and that leads us toward a better understanding of the solution.

Again, we can alter the base-case model slightly and follow the consequences for the optimal purchase plan. For example, if we raise the credit limit, the only change in the solution will be the purchase of additional cartons of the medium-priority product. Thus, the marginal value of raising the credit limit by a dollar is equivalent to the incremental profit per dollar of purchase cost for the medium-priority product, or $0.1179. We could confirm this result by rerunning Solver with one additional dollar of credit.

Suppose instead that we were to increase the amount of a low-priority product in the purchase plan. Then, following the optimal pattern, we would have to purchase less of the medium-priority product due to the tight credit limit. Consider the purchase of more squash than the 100-carton minimum. Each additional carton of squash will cost $2.50, substituting for about 0.892 cartons of lima beans in the credit constraint. The net effect on profit is as follows:

- Add a carton of squash (increase profit by $0.20).
- Remove 0.892 carton of lima beans (decrease profit by $0.2946).
- Therefore, net cost = $0.0946.

Thus, each carton of squash we force into the purchase plan, above the minimum sales level of 100, will reduce profits by 9.46 cents. If we were to rerun the model requiring 101 cartons of squash, we would confirm that profit declines by exactly this amount.

Comparing the analysis of GD's decision with the product-mix example considered earlier, we see that the optimal pattern, when translated into a computational scheme, is complete and unambiguous in both cases. We can use the pattern to determine the shadow price on a binding constraint or to derive marginal costs of introducing nonoptimal decisions. A specific feature of GD's model is the focus on one particular bottleneck constraint. This feature helps us understand the role of a binding constraint when we interpret a pattern; however, in many problems, there is more than one binding constraint.

EXAMPLE
*Production
Planning*

The production planning problem has several formulations. In one version, a company has contracted to meet a certain demand schedule and faces constraints on production capacity. The problem is to find a least-cost production plan. In our example, a company produces two products (A and B) using two types of machines (X and Y) over a planning period of three months. The products can be produced on either machine, and the following table describes the machine hours required to make a single unit of each product:

	Product A	Product B
Hours on Machine X	2.0	1.5
Hours on Machine Y	2.5	2.0

Machine capacities on X and Y are given for each of the three months. In addition, the quantities to be delivered each month, according to the contract, are also given:

Month	X-Capacity	Y-Capacity	A-Demand	B-Demand
1	140	250	50	30
2	60	80	100	60
3	150	100	50	50

The relevant costs are labor on each machine ($30.00/hour) and inventory held ($10.00/unit/month, for either product). ∎

Figure 9.20 shows a linear programming model for this problem, and its optimal solution. The variables in this model are of two kinds. One kind is the number of units of each product scheduled for production, broken down by machine and by month—for example, $AX1$. The other kind is the inventory of each product held from one month to the

FIGURE 9.20 Optimal Solution for the Production-Planning Model

Production Planning

Parameters

	Hrs/unit	A	B		$/hr	A	B		$/unit	A	B
	X	2.0	1.5	X		30	30	X		60	45
	Y	2.5	2.0	Y		30	30	Y		75	60

Decisions

			Month 1					Month 2					Month 3			
	AX1	AY1	BX1	BY1	AI1	BI1	AX2	AY2	BX2	BY2	AI2	BI2	AX3	AY3	BX3	BY3
Units	32.5	85.5	50.0	0.0	68.0	20.0	0.0	32.0	40.0	0.0	0.0	0.0	37.5	12.5	50.0	0.0

Objective

	AX1	AY1	BX1	BY1	AI1	BI1	AX2	AY2	BX2	BY2	AI2	BI2	AX3	AY3	BX3	BY3	Total Cost
$	60	75	45	60	10	10	60	75	45	60	10	10	60	75	45	60	$21,130

Constraints

	AX1	AY1	BX1	BY1	AI1	BI1	AX2	AY2	BX2	BY2	AI2	BI2	AX3	AY3	BX3	BY3	LHS		RHS		
X1	2.0	0	1.5	0	0	0	0	0	0	0	0	0	0	0	0	0	140	<=	140	X1	
Y1	0	2.5	0	2.0	0	0	0	0	0	0	0	0	0	0	0	0	214	<=	250	Y1	
X2	0	0	0	0	0	0	2.0	0	1.5	0	0	0	0	0	0	0	60	<=	60	X2	Machine
Y2	0	0	0	0	0	0	0	2.5	0	2.0	0	0	0	0	0	0	80	<=	80	Y2	Capacities
X3	0	0	0	0	0	0	0	0	0	0	0	0	2.0	0	1.5	0	150	<=	150	X3	
Y3	0	0	0	0	0	0	0	0	0	0	0	0	0	2.5	0	2.0	31	<=	100	Y3	
A1	1	1	0	0	-1	0	0	0	0	0	0	0	0	0	0	0	50	=	50	A1	
B1	0	0	1	1	0	-1	0	0	0	0	0	0	0	0	0	0	30	=	30	B1	
A2	0	0	0	0	1	0	1	1	0	0	-1	0	0	0	0	0	100	=	100	A2	Product
B2	0	0	0	0	0	1	0	0	1	1	0	-1	0	0	0	0	60	=	60	B2	Shipments
A3	0	0	0	0	0	0	0	0	0	0	1	0	1	1	0	0	50	=	50	A3	
B3	0	0	0	0	0	0	0	0	0	0	0	1	0	0	1	1	50	=	50	B3	

next—for example, $AI1$. The inventory variables allow us to express demand constraints using the basic accounting definition of inventory: final inventory must be equal to starting inventory plus production minus shipments. One such equation applies to each product in each month (rows 21–26).

Our specification of the model is as follows:

Variables:	B10:Q10
Objective:	R13 (minimize)
Constraints:	R15:R20 $\leq$ T15:T20
	R21:R26 = T21:T26

The optimal solution in Figure 9.20 leads us to the following description of the pattern:

- All product-shipment constraints are binding (because they were cast as equations in the model).

- Capacity constraints on machine X capacity are binding in each period, but machine Y capacity is binding only in month 2.

- In the optimal production plan, the following variables are positive:

$AX1, AX3$
$AY1, AY3$
$BX1, BX2, BX3$

- The positive inventory variables are $AI1$ and $BI1$.

To convert this pattern into a scheme for calculating the values of the decision variables, we again start by noticing which variables are positive and which are zero. If we focus on product-month combinations, we may not see a distinct pattern, although it becomes clear that the optimal schedule calls for overproduction in the first month, creating inventory that gets consumed in the second month ($AI2$ and $BI2$ are both zero). In the third month, production matches demand exactly. When we focus on product-machine combinations, on the other hand, a detailed pattern begins to take shape. We see that product B is never produced on machine Y ($BY1$, $BY2$, and $BY3$ are all zero), whereas product A is produced on both X and Y. Since machine-X capacity is binding in each month, it is evidently important to produce B on X and to avoid producing B on Y. In fact, we see that it is also preferable to produce B on X in an earlier period, and to hold it in inventory, as compared to producing B on Y in the period when demand occurs. This observation suggests that the solution can be constructed by the following procedure:

- First, assign X-capacity in each month to make the number of units of B-demand in the same period.

- If X-capacity is inadequate to meet current B-demand, then assign X-capacity in the previous month and hold the items in inventory.

- If X-capacity is more than adequate for B-demand, then assign X-capacity to make the number of units of A-demand in the current period.
- If X-capacity is fully consumed, then assign Y-capacity to make the remaining number of units of A-demand in the current period.
- If Y-capacity is inadequate to meet current A-demand, then assign Y-capacity in the previous month and hold the items in inventory.

Clearly, machine X has a cost advantage over machine Y in making both products: Its hourly cost is the same, and it takes less time to produce either product. It is this relative cost advantage that leads to the pattern in the optimal solution. Here again, we have interpreted the optimal solution without explicitly using a number, yet we have provided a complete and unambiguous description of the solution. This description can be viewed as a system of priorities that determines the variables one at a time, in sequence.

Again, we can test our characterization of the optimal pattern by deriving the shadow prices. For example, suppose that the capacity of X were increased by one hour in month 1. Given the optimal pattern, we should want to transfer some production of A at the margin from machine Y to machine X. The extra hour of X would accommodate 1/2 unit of A. This would reduce production of A by 5/4 of an hour on Y. In cost terms, the extra hour of X incurs a cost of $30.00, while 5/4 of an hour on Y will be saved, at a benefit of $37.50. The net benefit is $7.50, which is the shadow price on the capacity constraint for machine X in month 1. We could, of course, confirm this result by rerunning Solver with one more hour of capacity on X.

As another example of altering the problem slightly, suppose that we increase by one unit the quantity of product A to be delivered in month 1. The marginal cost of meeting this shipment is just the cost of producing one more unit of product A on Y. This amount is $75.00, which turns out to be the shadow price for the corresponding constraint. Suppose, instead, that we increase by one unit the quantity of product A to be delivered in month 2. In this case, the marginal cost is $85.00, since the marginal unit must be produced in month 1 (at a cost of $75.00) and held in inventory one month (at a cost of $10.00), because no capacity remains in month 2 under the optimal plan. Suppose now that we increase by one unit the quantity of product B to be delivered in month 2. According to the pattern, we prefer to make this unit on machine X, but X is fully committed to product B during month 2. Following the pattern, we want to make product B on X during month 1 and hold it in inventory; but to do so, we will have to transfer some production of A from machine X to machine Y. To find the marginal cost of this entire adjustment, we have to follow the economic implications of each element of the marginal change:

- Make one unit of B on X (time = 1.5 hrs.; cost = $45.00).
- Hold one unit of B one month (cost = $10.00).
- Remove 1.5 hrs. of A production from X (cost saved = $45.00; $\frac{3}{4}$ unit).
- Add 3/4 unit of A production to Y (time = $\{\frac{15}{8}\}$ hrs.; cost = $56.25).
- Therefore, net cost = $45.00 + $10.00 − $45.00 + $56.25 = $66.25.

Once again, knowing the qualitative pattern in the optimal solution allows us to anticipate how that solution will change when the problem is modified. Moreover, we can calculate shadow prices by quantifying the implications of the pattern for changes in the constraint constants.

9.6.3 Review

The foregoing examples illustrate the process of extracting insight from the solution to a linear programming problem. By focusing just on positive variables and binding constraints, we try to rebuild the optimal solution from the given parameters, with the determination of one variable at a time, if possible. At the first step, we look for a binding constraint containing a single variable. That combination allows us to deduce the value of the variable immediately. Then, with that value known, we look for another binding constraint containing just one other variable, and continue in this fashion. This construction can often be interpreted as a list of priorities, and those priorities reveal the economic forces at work.

Answers to two diagnostic questions help determine whether we have been successful at extracting a pattern:

- Is the pattern complete and unambiguous?
- Where do the shadow prices come from?

The answer to the first question takes us to a full solution of the problem, specifying all of the decision variables in the optimal solution uniquely. The second question invites us to alter one constraint constant in the original problem and trace the incremental changes in the variables, allowing us to derive the shadow price for the corresponding constraint. This derivation is not necessary except to achieve a deeper interpretation of the results, because we can determine the value of the shadow price automatically with the Optimization Sensitivity tool.

Patterns have certain limits, as suggested above. If we test our specification of a pattern by deriving shadow prices, we have to recognize that a shadow price has a limited range over which it holds. (Recall from Figure 9.16 that the shadow price on fabrication time was $4.00 up to 2,000 hours and then dropped to $3.75.) Beyond this range, a different pattern prevails. As we change a right-hand-side constant, there will eventually be a change in the shadow price. The same is true of the pattern: beyond the range in which the shadow price holds, the pattern may change. In the production-planning example, however, we were able to describe the pattern in a fairly general way, so that it holds even when the shadow price changes.

Unfortunately, it is not always the case that the pattern can be reduced to a list of assignments, in priority order. Occasionally it happens that, once we identify the positive variables and the binding constraints in the optimal solution, we might be able to say no more than that the pattern comes from solving a system of equations determined by the binding constraints and the positive variables. Nevertheless, in most cases, as the foregoing examples indicate, we can learn a great deal about the underlying economics by looking for patterns in the optimal solution.

9.7* DATA ENVELOPMENT ANALYSIS

Data Envelopment Analysis (DEA) is a linear programming application aimed at evaluating the efficiencies of similar organizational departments or *decision-making units* (DMUs, as they are called). The DMUs are characterized in terms of their inputs and outputs, but not in terms of their operating details. A DMU is considered **efficient** if it gets the most output from its inputs. In the diagram of Figure 9.21, for example, a DMU has three outputs (y_1, y_2, and y_3) and two inputs (x_1 and x_2). Its efficiency is defined as the value of its outputs divided by the value of its inputs. An efficient DMU could potentially produce greater output value from the same inputs, or it could produce the same outputs from smaller input value. The purpose of DEA is to identify efficient DMUs when there are multiple outputs and multiple inputs.

When inputs and outputs are treated as multidimensional, there is a need to use weighting factors to produce an overall efficiency measure. We compute the total value of two *inputs* x_1 and x_2 as $v_1 x_1 + v_2 x_2$. The input quantities are obtained from historical data and the weights v_1 and v_2 are determined in the analysis. Similarly, we compute the total value of three *outputs* as $u_1 y_1 + u_2 y_2 + u_3 y_3$, where the output quantities (y_1, y_2, y_3) are historical data, and the weights (u_1, u_2, u_3) are determined in the analysis. The efficiency measure is then the ratio of weighted outputs to weighted inputs:

$$E = \frac{u_1 y_1 + u_2 y_2 + u_3 y_3}{v_1 x_1 + v_2 x_2}$$

FIGURE 9.21 Conceptual Description of a Decision-Making Unit

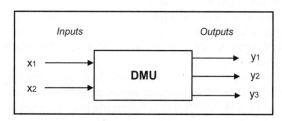

EXAMPLE

Burritoville Restaurants

Juan Pimiento has been a successful entrepreneur, developing a chain of Mexican restaurants in the southwest. A few years ago, he opened his first Burritoville store. When it became profitable and popular in its first two years, Juan built some new stores, bought similar competing stores, and eventually found himself the owner of a restaurant chain. Because some of the stores in the chain had been existing restaurants, and because he was inclined to experiment with store designs and menus, there were differences in the way the various stores operated. From his new vantage point, Juan thought that it might be a good idea to evaluate where in the chain things were going well and where they were not.

After reading up on DEA, Juan has come up with some historical data to summarize performance of his stores. The key outputs in his analysis are monthly profit and peak daily volume. The key inputs are labor hours and monthly facility cost. He has gathered the following data for the restaurants in the chain:

Store ID	Monthly Profit	Peak Volume	Labor Hours	Facility Cost
1	761	109	56	1,476
2	925	103	72	1,613
3	788	119	64	1,612
4	858	114	63	1,381
5	928	107	70	1,748
6	758	120	72	1,645
7	963	104	66	1,290
8	918	119	60	1,779
9	876	94	61	1,325
10	997	102	72	1,453

The data for monthly profit and facility cost have come directly from accounting records in the company. The average daily labor hours have been pulled together by store managers, working from daily personnel schedules. Peak volumes have been determined by having someone stand at the front door to count (and greet) customers coming into the store. With the data collection effort finished, Juan hopes that DEA can provide some insight into levels of efficiency at the various locations. ■

Let's address the efficiency analysis for Store 1. Given the historical data, we know that the efficiency measure for Store 1 takes the following form:

$$E_1 = \frac{u_1 y_1 + u_2 y_2}{v_1 x_1 + v_2 x_2} = \frac{761 u_1 + 109 u_2}{56 v_1 + 1476 v_2}$$

with the weights yet to be determined. The DEA method imposes two conditions on the analysis. First, to re-scale the efficiency measure, the denominator is set equal to 1. Thus:

$$56 v_1 + 1476 v_2 = 1$$

Second, by convention, DEA requires that output value cannot exceed input value, for any of the DMUs, or:

$$761 u_1 + 109 u_2 - 56 v_1 - 1476 v_2 \leq 0 \quad \textit{for Store 1}$$
$$925 u_1 + 103 u_2 - 72 v_1 - 1613 v_2 \leq 0 \quad \textit{for Store 2}$$

and similarly for the eight remaining DMUs.

At this stage, the analysis turns to linear programming to find the weights that produce the largest efficiency value for Store 1. Because the denominator (input value) of E_1 is scaled to 1, the optimization problem for Store 1 simplifies to maximizing the output value, $761 u_1 + 109 u_2$.

Figure 9.22 shows the worksheet for the analysis, using the standard format for an allocation model. The objective function in this model corresponds to the output value of Store 1, computed by a SUMPRODUCT formula in cell G18. The equality constraint that

FIGURE 9.22 Analysis of Store 1 in the Burritoville DEA Model

	A	B	C	D	E	F	G	H	I
1	Restaurants								
2			*Outputs*		*Inputs*				
3	Data	*DMU*	*Profit*	*Volume*	*Hours*	*Cost*			
4		Store 1	761	109	56	1476			
5		Store 2	925	103	72	1613			
6		Store 3	788	119	64	1612			
7		Store 4	858	114	63	1381			
8		Store 5	928	107	70	1748			
9		Store 6	758	120	72	1645			
10		Store 7	963	104	66	1290			
11		Store 8	918	119	60	1779			
12		Store 9	876	94	61	1325			
13		Store 10	997	102	72	1453			
14									
15								DMU	1
16	Decisions	*Weights*	0.00000	0.00917	0.01040	0.00028			
17									
18	Objective	*Efficiency*	761	109	0	0	1.000		
19									
20	Constraints	Input	0	0	56	1476	1.000	=	1
21		Store 1	761	109	-56	-1476	0.000	<=	0
22		Store 2	925	103	-72	-1613	-0.260	<=	0
23		Store 3	788	119	-64	-1612	-0.030	<=	0
24		Store 4	858	114	-63	-1381	0.000	<=	0
25		Store 5	928	107	-70	-1748	-0.241	<=	0
26		Store 6	758	120	-72	-1645	-0.113	<=	0
27		Store 7	963	104	-66	-1290	-0.097	<=	0
28		Store 8	918	119	-60	-1779	-0.036	<=	0
29		Store 9	876	94	-61	-1325	-0.147	<=	0
30		Store 10	997	102	-72	-1453	-0.224	<=	0
31									

9.22

fixes the value of inputs can be found in row 20, while the normalizing convention (requiring that output values never exceed input values) can be found in rows 21–30. We invoke Solver and specify the model as follows:

Variables:	C16:F16
Objective:	G18 (maximize)
Constraints:	G20 = I20
	G21:G30 ≤ I21:I30

When we run Solver on this model, we obtain an objective function of 1.00, as shown in the figure, along with the following weights:

Output	Profit weight (u_1)	0.0
Output	Volume weight (u_2)	0.00917
Input	Labor weight (v_1)	0.01040
Input	Facilities weight (v_2)	0.00028

With these weights, the input value is 1.0 and the output value is 1.0 for Store 1, resulting in an efficiency of 100 percent. In effect, we have imagined that the manager of Store 1 has been acting to optimize some measure of efficiency. Our model tells us that if that measure were based on weights of 0.0, 0.00917, 0.01040, and 0.00028, then indeed, Store 1 would have the highest efficiency among the stores in the chain. In other words, there is at least one set of weights for which Store 1 performs as well as any other store in the set. In that sense, we can conclude that Store 1 is operating efficiently.

Figure 9.22 shows the analysis for Store 2. The format is the same as the format for Store 1, and only two changes occur. First, the objective function now contains data for Store 2 in row 18. Second, the coefficients for the constraint on input value contain data for Store 2 in row 20. Otherwise, the parameters of the linear program remain unchanged from the analysis of Store 1. When we run Solver on this model, we obtain an objective function of 0.869, as shown in the figure, along with the following weights:

Output	Profit weight (u_1)	0.00094
Output	Volume weight (u_2)	0.0
Input	Labor weight (v_1)	0.01241
Input	Facilities weight (v_2)	0.00007

With these weights, the input value is 1.0, and the output value is 0.869, resulting in an efficiency of 86.9 percent. Note that cells G27 and G28 are zero. This means that the normalizing constraint is binding for Stores 7 and 8. In other words, Stores 7 and 8 have efficiencies of 100 percent, even at the most favorable weights for Store 2. In effect, we have imagined that the manager of Store 2 has been acting to optimize some measure of efficiency. Our model tells us that if that measure were based on weights of 0.00094, 0.0, 0.01241, and 0.00007, then Store 2 would achieve the highest efficiency it could reach, 0.869. But even then, two other stores in the chain would achieve higher efficiency values. In that sense, we can conclude that Store 2 is operating inefficiently. When we analyze other stores in the chain, we can discover which ones are operating efficiently.

We could construct similar worksheets for the analysis of other stores following the same format. However, much of the content on those worksheets would be identical, so we can design a more streamlined approach to the analysis. Figure 9.23 contains a version of the model that actually handles the analysis for all ten stores. The array in rows 4–14, as before, contains the problem data. Cell I15 contains the store number for the DMU being analyzed. Based on this choice, two adjustments must be made in the linear programming model. First, the outputs for the store being analyzed must be selected for use in the objective function, in cells C18:D18. Second, the inputs for the store being analyzed must be selected for use in the equality constraint, in cells E20:F20. These selections are highlighted in bold in Figure 9.23. The INDEX function uses the store number in cell I15 to copy the objective function coefficients from the data array into cells C18:D18. It also copies the input values from the data array into cells E20:F20. The four cells in bold format thus change when we enter a different selection in cell I15.

EXCEL MINI-LESSON
The INDEX Function

The INDEX function in Excel finds a value in a rectangular array according to the row number and column number of its location. The basic form of the function, as we use it for DEA models, is the following:

    `INDEX(Array, Row, Column)`

- *Array* references a rectangular array.
- *Row* specifies a row number in the array.
- *Column* specifies a column number in the array. If Array has just one column, then this argument can be omitted.

In the example of Figure 9.23, suppose *Array* = C4:C13 and *Row* = I15. When cell I15 contains the number 4, the function `INDEX(C4:C13, $I$15)` finds the element in the fourth row of the array in cells C4:C13. In this case, the function returns the Profit output value for Store 4, or 858. This calculation would be suitable for cell C18, and the formula could be copied to cell D18, producing the entry `INDEX(D4:D13, $I$15)` and the corresponding value of 114. ∎

The analysis of the stores in the chain requires that we solve the model in Figure 9.23 several times, once for each DMU. In our example, we vary the contents of cell I15 from 1 to 10. For each value, we save the essential results some other place before switching to a new DMU. In particular, we want to save the weights and the value of the objective function. Figure 9.24 shows a worksheet containing a summary of the ten optimizations for the ten-store example (one from each choice of cell I15). This summary can be generated automatically with one run of the Optimization Sensitivity tool.

As we can see in Figure 9.24, there are four efficient stores in our example: Stores 1, 4, 7, and 8. The other stores are inefficient, at levels ranging from 87 percent to 97 percent. This means that the inefficient stores could probably learn something by examining the way that the efficient stores are run. For this reason, DEA is often used to organize benchmarking visits within the divisions or branches of a large organization.

FIGURE 9.23 Analysis of Store 2 in the Burritoville DEA Model

	A	B	C	D	E	F	G	H	I
1	**Restaurants**								
2			*Outputs*		*Inputs*				
3	**Data**	*DMU*	*Profit*	*Volume*	*Hours*	*Cost*			
4		Store 1	761	109	56	1476			
5		Store 2	925	103	72	1613			
6		Store 3	788	119	64	1612			
7		Store 4	858	114	63	1381			
8		Store 5	928	107	70	1748			
9		Store 6	758	120	72	1645			
10		Store 7	963	104	66	1290			
11		Store 8	918	119	60	1779			
12		Store 9	876	94	61	1325			
13		Store 10	997	102	72	1453			
14									
15								**DMU**	**2**
16	**Decisions**	*Weights*	0.00094	0.00000	0.01241	0.00007			
17									
18	**Objective**	*Efficiency*	**925**	**103**	**0**	**0**	0.869		
19									
20	**Constraints**	Input	0	0	72	1613	1.000	=	1
21		Store 1	761	109	-56	-1476	-0.078	<=	0
22		Store 2	925	103	-72	-1613	-0.131	<=	0
23		Store 3	788	119	-64	-1612	-0.161	<=	0
24		Store 4	858	114	-63	-1381	-0.067	<=	0
25		Store 5	928	107	-70	-1748	-0.113	<=	0
26		Store 6	758	120	-72	-1645	-0.290	<=	0
27		Store 7	963	104	-66	-1290	0.000	<=	0
28		Store 8	918	119	-60	-1779	0.000	<=	0
29		Store 9	876	94	-61	-1325	-0.022	<=	0
30		Store 10	997	102	-72	-1453	-0.053	<=	0
31									

H ◄ ► H 9.22 **9.23**

FIGURE 9.24 Optimization Sensitivity Report for the Burritoville Example

	A	B	C	D	E	F
1	**DMU**	**Efficiency**	*Profit*	*Volume*	*Hours*	*Cost*
2	1	**1.000**	0.00027	0.00728	0.01199	0.00022
3	2	**0.869**	0.00094	0.00000	0.01241	0.00007
4	3	**0.973**	0.00000	0.00818	0.00927	0.00025
5	4	**1.000**	0.00012	0.00786	0.00000	0.00072
6	5	**0.885**	0.00095	0.00000	0.01261	0.00007
7	6	**0.907**	0.00000	0.00756	0.00856	0.00023
8	7	**1.000**	0.00104	0.00000	0.00000	0.00078
9	8	**1.000**	0.00109	0.00000	0.01440	0.00008
10	9	**0.974**	0.00111	0.00000	0.01470	0.00008
11	10	**0.946**	0.00095	0.00000	0.01254	0.00007
12						

H ◄ ► H 9.22 9.23 **9.24**

9.8 SUMMARY

Linear programming represents the most widely used optimization technique in practice. In this chapter, we have taken note of the special features of a linear program: a linear objective function and linear constraints. Linearity in the optimization model allows us to apply the simplex method as a solution procedure, which in turn guarantees finding a global optimum whenever an optimum of any kind exists. Therefore, when we have a choice, we are better off with a linear formulation of a problem than with a nonlinear formulation.

To develop facility with the linear solver, it helps to practice formulating, solving, and interpreting linear programming problems. The spreadsheet layout can be somewhat standardized, and a number of additional guidelines become helpful:

- Follow a standard form whenever possible, relying on the SUMPRODUCT function.

- Enter cell references in the Solver interface; keep numerical values in cells.

- Use a linear model in preference to a nonlinear model.

- If the model contains simple bounds, place them near the decision-variable cells.

- Show constraint relationships ($\leq$, $=$, $\geq$) on the worksheet.

- Group like constraints together (i.e., similar in logical direction).
- Align data with decisions when appropriate.
- Use the weak form of a constraint and give the model maximum flexibility.
- For blending models, add redundant but more intuitive calculations of blending constraints, outside of the Solver model.
- Explore some feasible (and infeasible) decisions as a way of debugging the model.
- Test intuition and suggest hypotheses before running Solver.
- Identify the patterns of economic priorities that appear in the solution.

Along with the technical information that we have covered, these guidelines help accelerate the process of building and applying linear programming models successfully.

One last caveat: While optimization is a powerful technique, we should not assume that a solution that is optimal for a model is also optimal for the real world. Because every model is a simplification, any optimal solution from a model must be interpreted before it can be applied in the real world. Often, the realities of the application will force changes in the optimal solution determined by the model. One powerful method for making this translation is to look for the pattern, or the economic priorities, in the optimal solution. These economic priorities are often more valuable to decision makers than the precise solution to a particular instance of the model.

SUGGESTED READINGS

Some advanced perspectives on optimization techniques, along with guidance in constructing optimization models, can be found in the following books:

Baker, K. R. 2011. *Optimization Modeling with Spreadsheets (Second Edition)* Hoboken, NJ: John Wiley & Sons.
Fourer, R., D. F. Gay, and B. W. Kernighan. 2003. *AMPL: A Modeling Language for Mathematical Programming.* Belmont, CA: Duxbury Press.

Rardin, R. L. 1998. *Optimization in Operations Research.* Upper Saddle River, NJ: Prentice–Hall.
Schrage, L. 1997. *Optimization Modeling with LINDO.* 5th ed. Belmont, CA: Duxbury Press.
Williams, H. P. 1999. *Model Building in Mathematical Programming.* 3d ed. Chichester: John Wiley & Sons.

EXERCISES

1. *Production Planning.* The Bogard Corporation produces three types of bookcases, which it sells to large office supply companies. The production of each bookcase requires two machine operations, trimming and shaping, followed by assembly, which includes inspection and packaging. All three types require 0.4 hours of assembly time, but the machining operations have different processing times, as shown in the following table, in hours per unit:

	Standard	Narrow	Wide
Trimmer	0.2	0.4	0.6
Shaper	0.6	0.2	0.5

Each machine is available 150 hours per month, and the current size of the assembly department provides capacity of 600 hours. Each bookcase produced yields a unit profit contribution as follows:

	Standard	Narrow	Wide
Profit	$8	$6	$10

a. What are the optimal production quantities for the company?

b. What is the pattern in the optimal allocation?

2. *Fertilizing the Lawn.* The facilities manager at Oxbridge University is planning to apply fertilizer to the grass in the quadrangle area in the spring. The grass needs nitrogen, phosphorus, and potash in at least the amounts given in the following table:

Mineral	Minimum Weight (lb)
Nitrogen	12
Phosphorus	14
Potash	18

Three kinds of commercial fertilizer are available, with mineral content and prices per 1,000 pounds as given in the following table. There is virtually unlimited supply of each kind of fertilizer.

Fertilizer	Nitrogen Content (lb)	Phosphorus Content (lb)	Potash Content (lb)	Price ($)
A	20	10	5	10
B	10	5	15	8
C	15	10	5	7

How much of each fertilizer should be purchased to satisfy the requirements at minimum cost?

3. *Coordinating Production and Marketing.* The Andrews Apple Products Company purchases apples from local growers and makes applesauce and apple juice. It costs $0.80 to produce a jar of applesauce and $0.60 to produce a bottle of apple juice. The company has a policy that at least 20 percent but not more than 60 percent of its output must be applesauce.

The company wants to meet but not exceed the demand for each product. The marketing manager estimates that the demand for applesauce is a maximum of 5,000 jars, plus an additional 3 jars for each $1 spent on advertising for applesauce. The maximum demand for apple juice is estimated to be 4,000 bottles, plus an additional 5 bottles for every $1 spent on advertising for apple juice. The company has $16,000 to spend on producing and advertising its two products. Applesauce sells for $1.75 per jar; apple juice sells for $1.75 per bottle. The company wants to know how many units of each product to produce, and how much advertising to spend on each product, in order to maximize profit.

a. What are the optimal quantities of applesauce and apple juice for Andrews to produce? (Rounding off is acceptable.)

b. What is the optimal amount to spend on advertising? What is the optimal profit?

c. Describe the qualitative pattern in the solution.

4. *Managing a Portfolio.* A local bank wants to build a bond portfolio from a set of five bonds with $1 million available for investment. The expected annual return, the worst-case annual return on each bond, and the "duration" of each bond are given in the following table. (The duration of a bond is a measure of the bond's sensitivity to changes in interest rates.)

	Expected Return	Worst Case Return	Duration
Bond 1	12.5%	8.0%	8
Bond 2	11.5%	7.5%	7
Bond 3	10.5%	6.8%	6
Bond 4	9.5%	7.0%	5
Bond 5	8.5%	7.4%	3

The bank wants to maximize the expected return from its bond investments, subject to three conditions:

- The average worst-case return for the portfolio must be at least 7.2 percent.
- The average duration of the portfolio must be at most 6.
- Because of diversification requirements, at most 40 percent of the total amount invested can be invested in a single bond.

a. What is the maximum return on the $1 million investment? How should the investment be distributed among the bonds to achieve this return? (Assume that bonds can be purchased in fractional amounts.)

b. What is the qualitative pattern in the optimal solution?

c. What is the marginal rate of return on the investment amount? That is, what would be the percentage return on an additional dollar invested? (Give the percentage to four significant figures.)

5. *Planning Automobile Production.* The Auto Company of America (ACA) produces four types of cars: subcompact, compact, intermediate, and luxury. ACA also produces trucks and vans. Vendor capacities limit total production capacity to at most 1.2 million vehicles per year. Subcompacts and compacts are built together in a facility with a total annual capacity of 620,000 cars. Intermediate and luxury cars are produced in another facility with capacity of 400,000; and the truck/van facility has a capacity of 275,000. ACA's marketing strategy requires that subcompacts and compacts must constitute at least half of the product mix for the four car types. The Corporate Average Fuel Economy (CAFE) standards in the Energy Policy and Conservation Act require an average fleet fuel economy of at least 27 mpg.

Profit margins, market potential, and fuel efficiencies are summarized as follows:

Type	Profit Margin ($/vehicle)	Market Potential (sales in '000)	Fuel Economy (mpg)
Subcompact	150	600	40
Compact	225	400	34
Intermediate	250	300	15
Luxury	500	225	12
Truck	400	325	20
Van	200	100	25

a. What is the optimal profit for ACA?

b. What is the pattern in the optimal allocation?

c. How much would optimal annual profits drop if the fuel economy requirement were raised to 28 mpg?

6. *Making Beer.* The Schutzberg Brewery has received an order for 1,500 gallons of 3-percent beer (that is, 3 percent alcoholic content). This is a custom order because Schutzberg does not produce a 3-percent product. They do brew the following products.

Product	Percent Alcohol	Cost per Gallon
Free	0.25	0.55
Light	2.50	0.65
Amber	4.50	0.80
Dark	6.00	0.75

There are 500 gallons of each of these products on hand. Rather than brewing a 3-percent beer from scratch, the brewmaster has decided to mix existing stocks, perhaps with some water (0 percent alcoholic content), to satisfy this small order in the shortest possible time, hoping that the taste will be adequate. In case the taste is bad and he has to throw the mixture out, he would like to minimize the cost of the mix.

a. What are the components of the least-cost blend that will result in a 3-percent beer?

b. What is the total cost for the 100 gallons of product?

c. Use the pattern in (b) to trace the effects of increasing the requirement by 10 percent. How will the optimal mix change? How will the optimal cost change?

7. *Make or Buy.* A sudden increase in the demand for smoke detectors has left Acme Alarms with insufficient capacity to meet demand. The company has seen monthly demand from its retailers for its electronic and battery-operated detectors rise to 20,000 and 10,000, respectively. Acme's production process involves three departments: fabrication, assembly, and shipping. The relevant quantitative data on production and prices are summarized as follows:

Department	Monthly Hours Available	Hours/Unit (Electronic)	Hours/Unit (Battery)
Fabrication	2,000	0.15	0.10
Assembly	4,200	0.20	0.20
Shipping	2,500	0.10	0.15

Variable cost/unit	$18.80	$16.00
Retail price	$29.50	$28.00

The company also has the option to obtain additional units from a subcontractor, who has offered to supply up to 20,000 units per month in any combination of electric and battery-operated models, at a charge of $21.50 per unit. For this price, the subcontractor will test and ship its models directly to the retailers without using Acme's production process.

a. What are the maximum profit and the corresponding make/buy levels? (Fractional decisions are acceptable.)

b. Describe the qualitative pattern in the solution.

c. Use the pattern in (*b*) to trace the effects of increasing the fabrication capacity by 10 percent. How will the optimal make/buy mix change? How will the optimal profit change?

d. For how much of a change in fabrication capacity will the pattern persist?

8. *Leasing Warehouse Space.* Cox Cable Company needs to lease warehouse storage space for five months at the start of the year. Cox knows how much space will be required in each month, and the company can purchase a variety of lease contracts to meet these needs. For example, Cox can purchase one-month leases in each month from January to May. The company can also purchase two-month leases in January through April, three-month leases in January through March, four-month leases in January and February, or a five-month lease in January. In total, there are fifteen possible leases the company could use. Cox must decide which leases to purchase and how many square feet to purchase on each lease. Since the space requirements differ month to month, it may be economical to lease only the amount needed each month on a month-by-month basis. On the other hand, the monthly cost for leasing space for additional months is much less than for the first month, so it may be desirable to lease the maximum amount needed for the entire five months. Another option is the intermediate approach of changing the total amount of space leased (by adding a new lease and/or having an old lease expire) at least once, but not every month. Two or more leases for different terms can begin at the same time.

The space requirements (in square feet) are shown in the following table:

	Month				
	Jan	Feb	Mar	Apr	May
Required space	15,000	10,000	20,000	5,000	25,000

Leasing costs (in dollars per thousand square feet) are given in the following table:

	Length of Lease				
	1	2	3	4	5
Cost ($/TSF)	$280	$450	$600	$730	$820

The task is to find a leasing schedule that provides the necessary amounts of space at the minimum cost.

a. Determine the optimal leasing schedule. What is the optimal total cost and the corresponding schedule?

b. Describe the qualitative pattern in the solution.

c. Use the pattern in (b) to trace the effects of increasing the space required for January. How will the leasing schedule change? How will the total cost change?

d. For how much of a change in January's requirement will the pattern persist?

9. *Oil Blending.* An oil company produces three brands of oils: Regular, Multigrade, and Supreme. Each brand of oil is composed of one or more of four crude stocks, each having a different viscosity index. The relevant data concerning the crude stocks are:

Crude Stock	Viscosity Index	Cost ($/barrel)	Supply Per Day (barrels)
1	20	7.10	1,000
2	40	8.50	1,100
3	30	7.70	1,200
4	55	9.00	1,100

Each brand of oil must meet a minimum standard for viscosity index, and each brand thus sells at a different price. The relevant data concerning the three brands of oil are:

Brand	Minimum Viscosity Index	Selling Price ($/barrel)	Daily Demand (barrels)
Regular	25	8.50	2,000
Multigrade	35	9.00	1,500
Supreme	50	10.00	750

Determine an optimal production plan for a single day, assuming that all oil produced during this day can be either sold or stored at negligible cost. This exercise is subject to alternative interpretations. Use a model to investigate the following distinct situations:

a. The daily demands represent potential sales. In other words, the model should contain demand ceilings (upper limits). What is the optimal profit under these assumptions?

b. The daily demands are to be met precisely. In other words, the model should contain demand constraints in the form of equalities. What is the optimal profit under these assumptions?

c. The daily demands represent minimum sales commitments, but all output can be sold. In other words, the model should permit production to exceed daily demand. What is the optimal profit under these assumptions?

10. *Coffee Blending and Sales.* Hill-O-Beans Coffee Company blends four component beans into three final blends of coffee: one is sold to luxury hotels, another to restaurants, and the third to supermarkets for store label brands. The company has four reliable bean supplies: Robusta, Javan Arabica, Liberica, and Brazilian Arabica. The following table summarizes the very precise recipes for the final coffee blends, the cost and availability information for the four components, and the wholesale price per pound of the final blends. The percentages indicate the fraction of each component to be used in each blend.

Component	Hotel	Restaurant	Market	Cost per Pound	Max Weekly Availability (lbs)
Robusta	20%	35%	10%	$0.60	40,000
Javan Arabica	40%	15%	35%	$0.80	25,000
Liberica	15%	20%	40%	$0.55	20,000
Brazilian Arabica	25%	30%	15%	$0.70	45,000
Wholesale Price Per Pound	$1.25	$1.50	$1.40		

The processor's plant can handle no more than 100,000 pounds per week, but there is virtually unlimited demand for the final blends. However, the marketing department requires minimum production levels of 10,000, 25,000, and 30,000 pounds, respectively, for the hotel, restaurant, and market blends.

a. In order to maximize weekly profit, how many pounds of each component should be purchased?

b. What is the economic value of an additional pound's worth of plant capacity?

c. How much (per pound) should Hill-O-Beans be willing to pay for additional pounds of Liberica in order to raise total profit?

d. Construct a graph to show how the optimal profit varies with the minimum weekly production level of the hotel blend.

e. Construct a graph to show how the optimal profit varies with the unit cost of Robusta beans.

11. *Coordinating Advertising and Production.* The Hawley Lighting Company manufactures four families of household lighting at its factory. The product families are table lamps, floor lamps, ceiling fixtures, and pendant lamps. The following table shows the average material costs for each of the products:

Product	Table	Floor	Ceiling	Pendant
Material cost	$66	$85	$50	$80

Each product is made in one of two production processes by purchasing components, assembling and testing the product, and, finally, packaging it for shipping. Table lamps and floor lamps go through the assembly and finishing process in Department 1, while ceiling fixtures and chandeliers go through the process in Department 2. Variable production costs and capacities (measured in units of product) are shown in the following table. Note that there are regular and overtime possibilities for each department.

Process	Regular Time Unit Cost	Regular Time Capacity	Overtime Unit Cost	Overtime Capacity
Department 1	$16	100,000	$18	25,000
Department 2	$12	190,000	$15	24,000

Average selling prices for the four products are known, and estimates have been made of the market demand for each product at these prices. These figures are shown in the following table:

Product	Table	Floor	Ceiling	Pendant
Selling price	$120	$150	$100	$160
Potential sales (000)	60	20	100	35
Advertising effect	12%	10%	8%	15%

Sales levels can also be affected by advertising expenditures. Starting with the demand levels in the table, an increase of up to $10,000 in advertising raises the demand by the percent shown in the last row. An expenditure of less than $10,000 in advertising will lead to a proportional effect on demand. For example, an increase in advertising of $5,000 for table lamps would raise demand by 6 percent, or 3,600 units. However, there is a budget limit of $18,000 on the total amount to be spent on advertising among all four products.

a. What is an optimal output plan for the company?

b. For each department, what is the marginal value of additional overtime capacity?

c. What is the marginal value of additional advertising dollars?

d. What is the marginal value of additional sales for each product?

12. *Scheduling Staff.* You are the Director of the Computer Center for Gaillard College and responsible for scheduling the staffing of the center, which is open from 8 a.m. until midnight. You have monitored the usage of the center at various times of the day and determined that the following number of computer consultants are required:

Time of Day	Minimum Number of Consultants Required To Be on Duty
8 a.m. – noon	4
Noon – 4 p.m.	8
4 p.m. – 8 p.m.	10
8 p.m. – midnight	6

Two types of computer consultants can be hired: full-time and part-time. The full-time consultants work for eight consecutive hours in any of the following shifts: morning (8 a.m. – 4 p.m.), afternoon (noon – 8 p.m.), and evening (4 p.m. – midnight). Full-time consultants are paid $14 per hour.

Part-time consultants can be hired to work any of the four shifts listed in the table. Part-time consultants are paid $12 per hour. An additional requirement is that during every time period, there must be at least one full-time consultant on duty for every part-time consultant on duty.

a. Determine a minimum-cost staffing plan for the center. How many full-time consultants and part-time consultants will be needed? What is the minimum cost?

b. After thinking about this problem for a while, you have decided to recognize meal breaks explicitly in the scheduling of full-time consultants. In particular, full-time consultants are entitled to a one-hour lunch break during their eight-hour shift. In addition, employment rules specify that the lunch break can start after three hours of work or after four hours of work, but those are the only alternatives. Part-time consultants do not receive a meal break. Under these conditions, what staffing schedule minimizes costs? What is the minimum cost?

13. *Project Scheduling.* A construction contractor is responsible for a project with seven key tasks. Some of the tasks can begin at any time, but others have predecessor tasks that must be completed previously. The individual tasks can be carried out at standard times or they can be expedited ("crashed"). The cost of executing the task increases by a certain cost per day if its time is shortened. The following table shows the information describing the tasks of the project, their standard and minimum times (in days), their standard costs, the crashing cost per day shortened, and the predecessor(s):

Task Number	Minimum Time	Standard Time	Standard Cost	Cost/ Day to Shorten	Predecessor Tasks
1	6	12	1,600	100	None
2	8	16	2,400	75	None
3	16	24	2,900	120	2
4	14	20	1,900	100	1, 2
5	14	16	3,800	140	3
6	12	16	2,900	165	3
7	2	12	1,300	60	4

The project has a deadline of 40 days, which the contractor is committed to meet.

a. If no crashing is done, how long will the project take and what will be its cost?

b. Which activities should be crashed to achieve the least-cost schedule that meets a 40-day deadline? What is the difference between its cost and the cost in part (a)?

14. *Cargo Loading.* You are in charge of loading cargo ships for International Cargo Company (ICC) at a major East Coast port. You have been asked to prepare a loading plan for an ICC freighter bound for Africa. An agricultural commodities dealer would like to transport the following products aboard this ship:

Commodity	Tons Available	Volume per Ton (cu.ft.)	Profit per Ton ($)
1	4,000	40	70
2	3,000	25	50
3	2,000	60	60
4	1,000	50	80

You can elect to load any or all of the available commodities. However, the ship has three cargo holds with the following capacity restrictions:

Cargo Hold	Weight Capacity (tons)	Volume Capacity (cu.ft.)
Forward	3,000	100,000
Center	5,000	150,000
Rear	2,000	120,000

More than one type of commodity can be placed in the same cargo hold. However, because of balance considerations, the weight in the forward cargo hold must be within 10 percent of the weight in the rear cargo hold, and the center cargo hold must be between 40 percent and 60 percent of the total weight on board.

a. Determine a profit-maximizing loading plan for the commodities. What is the maximum profit and the loading plan that achieves it?

b. Suppose each one of the cargo holds could be expanded. Which holds and which forms of expansion (weight or volume) would allow ICC to increase its profits on this trip, and what is the marginal value of each form of expansion?

15. *Evaluating Performance.* Fidelity Savings & Loans (FS&L) operates a number of banking facilities throughout its region of the country. The officers of FS&L would like to analyze the efficiency of the various branch offices using DEA. The following data set has been selected to represent appropriate input and output measures of each banking facility. (Labor Hours and Operating Costs are considered inputs; Customer Satisfaction, New Loans, and ROA are considered outputs.)

Branch	Labor Hrs.	Op. Costs	ROA	New Loans	Satisfaction
1	3.73	6.34	5.32	770	92
2	3.49	4.43	3.39	780	94
3	5.98	6.31	4.95	790	93
4	6.49	7.28	6.01	730	82
5	7.09	8.69	6.40	910	98
6	3.46	3.23	2.89	860	90
7	7.36	9.07	6.94	880	89
8	6.38	7.42	7.18	970	99
9	4.74	6.75	5.98	770	94
10	5.04	6.35	4.97	930	91

a. Which branches are efficient?

b. Which branches are inefficient? For each inefficient branch, which other branches would be good benchmarking targets?

APPENDIX 9.1 THE SOLVER SENSITIVITY REPORT

The Optimization Sensitivity tool duplicates for optimization models the functionality of the Parametric Sensitivity tool for basic spreadsheet models. That parallelism makes optimization sensitivity the vehicle of choice for most of the sensitivity analyses we might want to perform with optimization models. However, it is sometimes useful to draw on another of Solver's sensitivity tools. The Sensitivity Report is one of several reports offered automatically after a Solver run, once the optimal solution has been found. The other reports are superfluous if a model has been constructed effectively, but the Sensitivity Report sometimes provides additional insight or efficiency.

To provide access to the Sensitivity Report, we must ensure that the `Bypass Solver Reports` option is set to False on the Engine tab of the task pane. After the optimal

FIGURE 9A1 Sensitivity Report for the Allocation Example

Microsoft Excel 14.0 Sensitivity Report
Worksheet: [Figures 9.xlsx]9.6
Report Created: 8/15/2013 11:15:13 AM
Engine: Standard LP/Quadratic

Objective Cell (Max)

Cell	Name	Final Value
$E$8	Profit Total	8400

Decision Variable Cells

Cell	Name	Final Value	Reduced Cost	Objective Coefficient	Allowable Increase	Allowable Decrease
$B$5	Product mix C	0	-16	0	16	1E+30
$C$5	Product mix D	275	0	24	30.0000003	24.0000001
$D$5	Product mix T	100	0	18	1E+30	10.0000001

Constraints

Cell	Name	Final Value	Shadow Price	Constraint R.H. Side	Allowable Increase	Allowable Decrease
$E$11	Fabrication LHS	1850	4	1850	150	1650
$E$12	Assembly LHS	2075	0	2400	1E+30	325
$E$13	Shipping LHS	950	0	1500	1E+30	550
$E$14	Chair market LHS	0	0	360	1E+30	360
$E$15	Desk market LHS	275	0	300	1E+30	25
$E$16	Table market LHS	100	10	100	60.9375	75

9A1

solution has been produced, we click on the Reports icon on the ribbon, select Optimization, and then Sensitivity. The Sensitivity Report for linear programs has three sections and appears on a separate worksheet. The first section (Objective Cell) shows the optimal value of the objective function. The second section (Decision Variable Cells) refers to the coefficients in the objective function corresponding to each of the decision variables. The third section (Constraints) refers to the values of the constants on the right-hand sides. Figure 9A1 shows the Sensitivity Report for the Veerman Furniture (allocation) example, slightly reformatted. If some of the rows are hidden (that is, if the row numbers do not appear to be consecutive), the report is in outline form. Return to Analytic Solver Platform▶Reports▶Optimization and click on the portion of the menu that states Reports are outlined. This toggle switch allows the full table to be read.

In the second section, the report provides the values of the decision variables in the optimal solution (under Final Value) and the values of the coefficients in the objective function (under Objective Coefficient). The Allowable Increase and Allowable Decrease show how much we could change any one of the objective function coefficients without altering the optimal product mix—that is, without altering any of the decision variables. For example, the objective function coefficient for desks is $24 in the base case. This figure could rise to $54.00 or drop to $22.50 without having an impact on the optimal product mix. (Of course, the optimal profit would change, because the number of desks remains fixed.) A similar range is provided for the other two variables, with 1E+30 symbolizing infinity in the report's output. Finally, there is a column labeled Reduced Cost. Entries in this column are zero for variables that are not at their bound (in this case, the bounds are zero). For chairs, the reduced cost of −1 reflects the fact that the objective function coefficient of $15 would have to improve by more than $1 before there would be an incentive to use chairs in the optimal mix. However, this same information is available in the Allowable Increase column for chairs. In most cases, the Reduced Cost information in the report is redundant.

In the third section, the report provides the values of the constraint left-hand sides (under Final Value) and the right-hand side constraint constants (under Constraint R. H. Side), along with the shadow price for each constraint. The Allowable Increase and Allowable Decrease show how much we could change any one of the constraint constants without altering any of the shadow prices. For example, the number of Fabrication hours (1,850 in the base case) could change from 200 to 2,000 without affecting the shadow price of $4.00.

The ranging analysis for right-hand side constraint constants is omitted for constraints that involve a simple lower bound or upper bound. That is, if the form of the constraint is Variable ≤ Ceiling or else Variable ≥ Floor, then the sensitivity analysis will not appear. On the other hand, if the same information is incorporated into the model using the standard SUMPRODUCT constraint form, as in the case of the allocation example, then the Sensitivity Report will treat the constraint in its usual fashion and include it in the Constraints table. As an example, consider the modified version of the

FIGURE 9A2 Sensitivity Report for the Covering Example

	A	B	C	D	E	F	G	H
1	Microsoft Excel 14.0 Sensitivity Report							
2	Worksheet: [Figures 9.xlsx]9.8							
3	Report Created: 8/15/2013 11:17:00 AM							
4	Engine: Standard LP/Quadratic							
5								
6	Objective Cell (Min)							
7		Cell	Name	Final Value				
8		$G$8	Cost Total	8.332128099				
9								
10	Decision Variable Cells							
11				Final	Reduced	Objective	Allowable	Allowable
12		Cell	Name	Value	Cost	Coefficient	Increase	Decrease
13		$B$5	Amounts S	0.39	0.00	4	1.064766875	3.700000097
14		$C$5	Amounts R	0.15	0.85	5	1E+30	0.849173554
15		$D$5	Amounts F	1.36	0.00	3	2.651612992	1.720000097
16		$E$5	Amounts P	0.15	4.35	7	1E+30	4.351239669
17		$F$5	Amounts W	0.15	2.00	6	1E+30	2
18								
19	Constraints							
20				Final	Shadow	Constraint	Allowable	Allowable
21		Cell	Name	Value	Price	R.H. Side	Increase	Decrease
22		$G$11	Vitamins LHS	27.97004132	0	16	11.97004132	1E+30
23		$G$12	Minerals LHS	10.07913223	0	10	0.079132231	1E+30
24		$G$13	Protein LHS	15	0.17768595	15	7.29375	0.319166667
25		$G$14	Calories LHS	600	0.007644628	600	5836.5	8.326086957
26								

Dahlby Outfitters (covering) example, with a floor of 0.15 for each of the decision variables. Although there are four original constraints and five additional constraints limiting the decision variables to values no less than 0.15, the Sensitivity Report shows information for only the four original constraints (see Figure 9A2).

Compared to the Optimization Sensitivity report, the Sensitivity Report is more precise but less flexible. The Sensitivity Report is more precise than Optimization Sensitivity with respect to the question of where the decision variables change or where a shadow price changes. For our allocation example, recall that we could not tell precisely when the shadow price drops from $3.75 to $2.32. Only by searching on a smaller grid could we detect where the change takes place, and even that would require some careful interpolation in the table to obtain the exact value. By contrast, if we were to solve a base-case model in which there were 2,200 Fabrication hours, and if we asked for the Sensitivity Report, we would be able to see from the Allowable Increase on Fabrication hours that the shadow price holds up to 2,666.67 hours.

The Sensitivity Report is less flexible than optimization sensitivity with respect to the user's ability to tailor the analysis. The Sensitivity Report cannot "see" beyond the Allowable Increase or the Allowable Decrease. However, a coarse grid search using optimization sensitivity can show how values in the model change beyond these ranges. In addition, Optimization sensitivity can track the effect of varying a parameter on any cells in the spreadsheet. The Sensitivity Report, by contrast, does not tell us explicitly how the objective function changes when we vary one of the objective function coefficients, nor does it tell us how the decision variables change when we vary one of the constraint constants. Optimization sensitivity can even track the effect of varying a parameter that is not, strictly speaking, within the model itself. For example, suppose there were several constraint constants that represented capacities, and that these capacities could all be increased by a common percentage. Optimization sensitivity could be set up to track the decision variables and the objective function as functions of this percentage.

In addition, the Optimization Sensitivity tool can perform two-way analyses, in the same spirit as the two-way analysis in the Parametric Sensitivity tool. When we also consider the user's ability to tailor the analysis, something that is lacking in the Sensitivity Report, we conclude that the Optimization Sensitivity tool is the more valuable way of doing sensitivity analysis, in spite of the loss in precision.

10 Optimization of Network Models

10.1 INTRODUCTION

As mentioned in the previous chapter, there are four main types of linear programming structures, three of which we covered in that chapter. The fourth type is the **network model**, which is the subject of this chapter. Network models themselves fall into several categories, but what is common in our approach to all network models is that we use a diagram to help formulate and solve linear programming problems.

The network model describes patterns of flow in a connected system, where the flow might involve material, people, or funds. The system elements may be locations, such as cities, warehouses, or assembly lines; or they may be points in time rather than points in space. When we construct diagrams to represent such systems, the elements are represented by **nodes**, or circles, in the diagram. The paths of flow are represented by **arcs**, or arrows. Figure 10.1 shows a very simple diagram, in which the network elements are a factory (node 1) and two warehouses (nodes 2 and 3). The arc from node 1 to node 2 carries the flow (truckloads of goods, perhaps) from the factory to the first warehouse; similarly, the arc from node 1 to node 3 carries the flow from the factory to the second warehouse.

As we shall see, drawing a network diagram helps us formulate an appropriate linear programming model, and if we encounter difficulties in getting our model to work, the diagram can also be a helpful device for troubleshooting.

10.2 THE TRANSPORTATION MODEL

A very common supply chain involves the shipment of goods from suppliers at one set of locations to customers at another set of locations. The supplier may own several factories that fabricate component parts, while the customers could be represented by the assembly plants that build and test products. Alternatively, the supplier may be a wholesaler who stocks food in several warehouses, while the customers are a chain of grocery stores that reorder separately on a regular basis. A supply-chain structure of this sort lends itself to representation as a **transportation model**. The classic transportation model is characterized by a set of supply sources (each with known capacities), a set of demand locations (each with known requirements), and the unit costs of transportation between supply-demand pairs. A case in point is Bonner Electronics.

FIGURE 10.1 A Simple Network Diagram

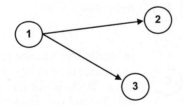

EXAMPLE
Bonner
Electronics

Bonner Electronics is planning next week's shipments from its three manufacturing plants to its four distribution warehouses and is seeking a minimum cost shipping schedule. Each plant has a potential capacity, expressed in cartons of product, and each warehouse has a week's requirement that must be met. There are twelve possible shipment routes, and for each route, the unit shipping cost is known. The following table provides the given information for this example:

| | Warehouse | | | | |
Plant	Atlanta	Boston	Chicago	Denver	Capacity
Minneapolis	$0.60	$0.56	$0.22	$0.40	9,000
Pittsburgh	0.36	0.30	0.28	0.58	12,000
Tucson	0.65	0.68	0.55	0.42	13,000
Requirement	7,500	8,500	9,500	8,000	

■

10.2.1 Flow Diagram

A flow diagram showing the possible routes is depicted in Figure 10.2. In the diagram, the node letters on the left designate manufacturing plants, which supply the product. The node letters on the right stand for warehouses, where the demands occur. In this case, all supply-demand pairs represent feasible routes for the shipment plan.

Each route of flow incurs a cost: the unit cost of flow from any plant to any warehouse is given in the table containing the parameters of the problem. The flows along each of the twelve possible routes constitute the decision variables in the model. Although the diagram does not contain labels for the arcs, it would be natural to use the notation MA for the quantity shipped on the route from Minneapolis to Atlanta, MB for the quantity shipped on the route from Minneapolis to Boston, and so on. In the network diagram, each arc represents a decision.

10.2.2 Model Formulation

The transportation model has two kinds of constraints: less-than capacity constraints and greater-than demand constraints, assuming total demand does not exceed capacity. For the Minneapolis plant, we can express the capacity constraint as follows:

$$MA + MB + MC + MD \leq 9,000$$

In words, the total amount shipped out of Minneapolis must be less than or equal to the Minneapolis capacity. For Pittsburgh and Tucson, we have similar constraints:

$$PA + PB + PC + PD \leq 12,000$$
$$TA + TB + TC + TD \leq 13,000$$

The left-hand side of these constraints simply adds the outbound shipment quantities from a given location. For that reason, we don't really need to use the SUMPRODUCT formula in a spreadsheet representation; we can use the simpler SUM formula.

For the Atlanta warehouse, the demand constraint reads:

$$MA + PA + TA \geq 7,500$$

In words, the amount received at Atlanta must be greater than or equal to the Atlanta requirement. Similarly, for the other three warehouses, the demand constraints become:

$$MB + PB + TB \geq 8,500$$
$$MC + PC + TC \geq 9,500$$
$$MD + PD + TD \geq 8,000$$

FIGURE 10.2 Diagram for Bonner Electronics

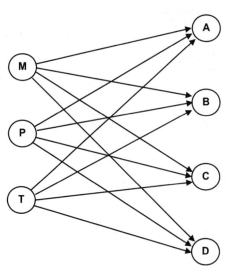

Again, the left-hand sides of these constraints can easily be expressed using the SUM formula. Putting both kinds of constraints together, and building an objective function from the same set of variables, we can create the following algebraic statement of the model:

$$\text{Minimize } z = 0.60MA + 0.56MB + 0.22MC + 0.40MD + 0.36PA + 0.30PB$$
$$+ 0.28PC + 0.58PD + 0.65TA + 0.68TB + 0.55TC + 0.42TD$$

subject to

$$MA + MB + MC + MD \leq 9,000$$
$$PA + PB + PC + PD \leq 12,000$$
$$TA + TB + TC + TD \leq 13,000$$
$$MA + PA + TA \geq 7,500$$
$$MB + PB + TB \geq 8,500$$
$$MC + PC + TC \geq 9,500$$
$$MD + PD + TD \geq 8,000$$

10.2.3 Spreadsheet Model

Figure 10.3* displays a worksheet for this problem. Notice the distinctive From/To structure in the table describing the problem's data. This structure lends itself readily to a row-and-column format, which is the essence of spreadsheet layout. Here, we adopt the convention that flow moves conceptually *from* the rows of the worksheet *to* the columns—for example, from Minneapolis to Atlanta. Because of this From/To structure, it is helpful to depart from the standard linear programming layout of the previous chapter and adopt a special format for this type of model. In particular, we can construct a model in rows and columns to mirror the table of parameters that describes the problem. In the Parameters module of the worksheet, we see all of the unit costs displayed in an array. In the Decisions module, the decision variables (shaded for highlighting) appear in an array of the same size. At the right of each decision row is the "Sent" quantity, which is simply the sum of the flows along the row. These figures align with the capacities given in the Parameters module. Below each decision column is the "Received" quantity, which is the sum down the column. These figures align with the demands given in the Parameters

FIGURE 10.3   Worksheet for the Bonner Electronics Model

	A	B	C	D	E	F	G
1	Transportation Model						
2							
3	Parameters						
4		*From/To*	Atl	Bos	Chi	Den	*Capacity*
5		Minn	0.60	0.56	0.22	0.40	9000
6		Pitt	0.36	0.30	0.28	0.58	12000
7		Tucs	0.65	0.68	0.55	0.42	13000
8		*Required*	7500	8500	9500	8000	
9							
10	Decisions						
11			Atl	Bos	Chi	Den	*Sent*
12		Minn	0	4000	5000	0	9000
13		Pitt	7500	4500	0	0	12000
14		Tucs	0	0	4500	8000	12500
15		*Received*	7500	8500	9500	8000	
16							
17	Objective						
18		Total Cost	$13,225				
19							

10.3

*To download spreadsheets for this chapter, go to the Student Companion site at www.wiley.com/college/powell.

module. The objective function, which is expressed as a SUMPRODUCT in cell C18, is the total transportation cost for the system. A useful exercise for someone encountering the transportation model for the first time is to clear the decision-variable cells C12:F14 and search by trial and error for a low-cost shipment plan.

EXCEL MINI-LESSON

The SUMPRODUCT Function

The SUMPRODUCT function in Excel takes the pairwise products of two sets of numbers and sums the products. The form of the function is the following:

SUMPRODUCT(*Array 1, Array 2*)

- *Array1* references the first set of numbers.
- *Array2* references the second set of numbers.

In the standard form for linear programs, introduced in Chapter 9, the two arrays were each laid out as one row and several columns. However, in general, the arrays can be *m* rows by *n* columns, as long as both arrays are of the same size. It is this more general structure that we employ in the transportation model and other, similar models. ∎

10.2.4 Optimization

Now, with this formulation in mind, we can invoke Solver and specify:

$$\begin{aligned}
\text{Variables:} \quad & \text{C12:F14} \\
\text{Objective:} \quad & \text{C18 (minimize)} \\
\text{Constraints:} \quad & \text{C15:F15} \geq \text{C8:F8} \quad (\textit{Received} \geq \textit{Required}) \\
& \text{G12:G14} \leq \text{G5:G7} \, (\textit{Sent} \leq \textit{Capacity})
\end{aligned}$$

On the Engine tab of the task pane, we select the Standard LP/Quadratic Engine (the linear solver) and check that the Assume Non-Negative option is set to True. We obtain the solution shown in Figure 10.4, which achieves the minimum cost of $12,025. All requirement constraints in this solution are binding, even though we permitted the model to send more than the requirement to each warehouse. This result makes intuitive sense, because shipping more than is required to any warehouse would merely incur excess cost. Once we understand why there is no incentive to exceed demand, we can anticipate that there will be some excess capacity in the solution. This follows from the fact that total capacity comes to 34,000 cartons, while total demand comes to only 33,500. In particular, capacity constraints are binding at Pittsburgh and Minneapolis, but an excess capacity of 500 cartons remains at Tucson.

FIGURE 10.4 Optimal Solution to the Bonner Electronics Model

	A	B	C	D	E	F	G
1	Transportation Model						
2							
3	Parameters						
4		From/To	Atl	Bos	Chi	Den	Capacity
5		Minn	0.60	0.56	0.22	0.40	9000
6		Pitt	0.36	0.30	0.28	0.58	12000
7		Tucs	0.65	0.68	0.55	0.42	13000
8		Required	7500	8500	9500	8000	
9							
10	Decisions						
11			Atl	Bos	Chi	Den	Sent
12		Minn	0	0	9000	0	9000
13		Pitt	3500	8500	0	0	12000
14		Tucs	4000	0	500	8000	12500
15		Received	7500	8500	9500	8000	
16							
17	Objective						
18		Total Cost	$12,025				
19							

10.3 10.4

FIGURE 10.5 Revised Flow Diagram for Bonner Electronics

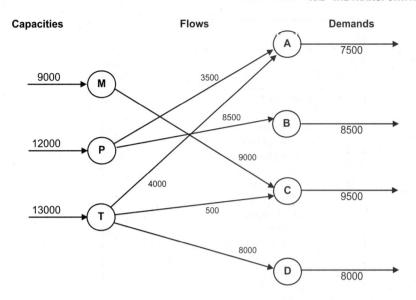

Now let's return to the diagram for our problem and check the figures. This time, we simplify the diagram by ignoring the variables that turned out to be zero, and we include just the nonzero shipments. Figure 10.5 shows the revised version of the network diagram.

At each node, arcs enter and arcs leave. We want to check that the configurations make sense at each location. For example, at node M, there is one outbound flow of 9,000 cartons, which exactly meets capacity. At node P, there are two outbound flows totaling 12,000, also meeting capacity. And at node T, there are three outbound flows totaling 12,500, which is less than capacity. A similar check shows that the inbound flows meet the various demand requirements.

10.2.5 Modifications to the Model

The model layout in Figure 10.4 has another virtue: it is easily expandable. Consider, for example, how to adapt the model to the situation in which Bonner Electronics adds a warehouse facility to its system. In Excel, select column E and then select Insert▶Columns. Figure 10.6 shows the result: both arrays (unit costs and decision variables) are expanded. The following steps are required to update the worksheet:

- Enter the location of the new warehouse in cells E4 and E11.
- Enter the inbound costs to the new warehouse in cells E5:E7.

FIGURE 10.6 Expanded Version of the Bonner Electronics Model

	A	B	C	D	E	F	G	H
1	**Transportation Model**							
2								
3	**Parameters**							
4		*From/To*	Atl	Bos		Chi	Den	*Capacity*
5		Minn	0.60	0.56		0.22	0.40	9000
6		Pitt	0.36	0.30		0.28	0.58	12000
7		Tucs	0.65	0.68		0.55	0.42	13000
8		*Required*	7500	8500		9500	8000	
9								
10	**Decisions**							
11			Atl	Bos		Chi	Den	*Sent*
12		Minn	0	0		9000	0	9000
13		Pitt	3500	8500		0	0	12000
14		Tucs	4000	0		500	8000	12500
15		*Received*	7500	8500		9500	8000	
16								
17	**Objective**							
18		Total Cost	$12,025					
19								

10.3 / 10.4 / **10.6**

FIGURE 10.7 Model
Specifications Window
for the Expanded Version
of the Model

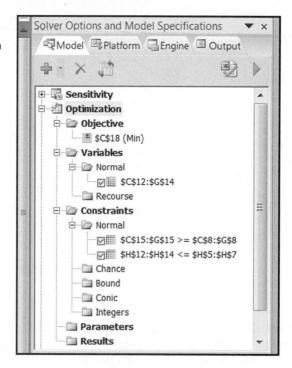

- Enter the demand at the new warehouse in cell E8.
- Copy the formula in cell D15 to E15.

After taking these steps, we click the Refresh icon on the Model tab. The task pane tells us that the model is ready to solve, as shown in Figure 10.7. In other words, the constraint formulas in cells H12:H14 have automatically adapted to the expansion, and so has the objective function formula in cell C18.

One last feature of the transportation model is worth noting: it lends itself readily to the use of range names in Excel. Working with the model of Figure 10.4, we can add range names in the following locations:

- Cell C18 named "Cost"
- Cells C12:F14 named "Shipments"
- Cells G5:G7 named "Capacity"
- Cells G12:G14 named "Sent"
- Cells C8:F8 named "Demands"
- Cells C15:F15 named "Received"

With these names assigned, the specification in the task pane takes the form shown in Figure 10.8. This format communicates the model to the user in a different way. The specification of the model is somewhat self-documenting in this form. The range names would be useful when the model is fully debugged and offered to users who are not comfortable with the cell details that usually appear.

10.2.6 Sensitivity Analysis

The concepts of sensitivity analysis that were introduced in the previous chapter apply here as well. This means that the Optimization Sensitivity tool may be used with network linear programming models with no new considerations. It also means that we can interpret patterns in the optimal solution in terms of economic priorities. Shadow prices in our network example illustrate the concepts involved. (Recall from Chapter 9 that a shadow price is the break-even price at which it would be profitable to acquire more of a scarce resource.)

In the transportation model, we have supply and demand constraints, and the solution to the model provides shadow prices on each. The shadow price on a demand

FIGURE 10.8 Bonner Electronics Model with Range Names Added

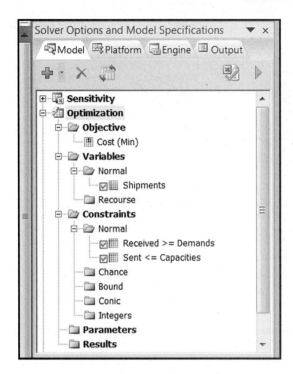

constitent tells us how much it costs to ship the marginal unit to the corresponding location, and sometimes this figure is not obvious without some careful thought.

Consider the demand at the Boston warehouse in the Bonner Electronics example. In the base case, shown in Figures 10.4 and 10.5, Boston demand is 8,500 cartons. This quantity is all supplied from Pittsburgh, incurring a shipping cost of $0.30 per carton. Suppose we vary the demand parameter from 8,200 to 8,800 in steps of 100 and examine the optimal solution. Figure 10.9 shows the resulting output from the Optimization Sensitivity tool. As expected, the optimal total cost increases when Boston demand increases, but from the Change column of the report, we note that the marginal cost of meeting this demand is $0.59.

How do we reconcile the direct cost of $0.30 on the Pittsburgh–Boston route with the marginal cost of $0.59? One way to see the connection involves identifying the qualitative pattern in the problem's solution. In the previous chapter, we introduced the process of discovering a pattern in the optimal solution to a linear programming model. The main idea was to focus on positive variables and binding constraints, and then to identify a priority list that specifies the sequence in which the variables may be calculated. In network models, the steps can be facilitated by using network diagrams.

In this example, there are three supplies and four demands, giving rise to twelve possible shipment routes. However, the solution contains only six nonzero shipments: *MC*, *PA*, *PB*, *TA*, *TC*, and *TD*. The other routes can be ignored when constructing the pattern. This observation allows us to work with the simplified network diagram of Figure 10.5.

As we previously observed, all of the demand constraints are binding. The solution also tells us that two of the supply capacities are binding—in particular, the capacities at Minneapolis and Pittsburgh. The decision variables associated with Tucson are not determined by the capacity at Tucson; instead, as we shall see, they are determined by other constraints in the model.

FIGURE 10.9 Optimization Sensitivity Output for the Bonner Electronics Model

	A	B	C	D	E	F	G	H	I	J	K	L	M	N	O
1	BosDemand	Total Cost	Change	MA	MB	MC	MD	PA	PB	PC	PD	TA	TB	TC	TD
2	8200	$11,848		0	0	9000	0	3800	8200	0	0	3700	0	500	8000
3	8300	$11,907	0.59	0	0	9000	0	3700	8300	0	0	3800	0	500	8000
4	8400	$11,966	0.59	0	0	9000	0	3600	8400	0	0	3900	0	500	8000
5	8500	$12,025	0.59	0	0	9000	0	3500	8500	0	0	4000	0	500	8000
6	8600	$12,084	0.59	0	0	9000	0	3400	8600	0	0	4100	0	500	8000
7	8700	$12,143	0.59	0	0	9000	0	3300	8700	0	0	4200	0	500	8000
8	8800	$12,202	0.59	0	0	9000	0	3200	8800	0	0	4300	0	500	8000
9															

FIGURE 10.10 Diagram for the Reduced Problem

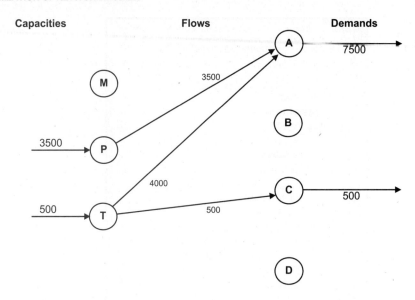

In the optimal solution, some demands are met entirely from a unique source. For example, demand at Boston is all met from Pittsburgh, and demand at Denver is all met from Tucson. In some sense, these are high-priority allocations, and we can think of them as if they were made *first*. There is also a symmetric feature: supply from Minneapolis all goes to Chicago. Dedicating capacity to a unique demand also marks a high-priority allocation. Each of these variables appears alone (with no other positive variables) in a binding constraint.

Once we assign the high-priority allocations, we can ignore the supply at Minneapolis and the demands at Boston and Denver, and we can turn to the problem that remains. Thus, we proceed to a second priority level, where we are left with a reduced problem containing two sources and two destinations, as shown in Figure 10.10. Here *PA* and *TC* are the high-priority allocations in the reduced problem. Setting *PA* = 3,500 consumes the remaining capacity at Pittsburgh; setting *TC* = 500 covers the remaining demand at Chicago.

Having made the second priority assignments, we can ignore the supply at Pittsburgh and the demand at Chicago. We are left with a net demand at Atlanta and unallocated supply at Tucson, as shown in Figure 10.11. Thus, the last step, at the third priority level, is to meet the remaining demand with a shipment along route *TA*. This allocation leaves an excess supply of 500 cartons at the Tucson factory, demonstrating that the utilization of the Tucson supply has been dictated by the supply and demand constraints elsewhere in the problem.

FIGURE 10.11 Diagram for the Last Stage of the Reduced Problem

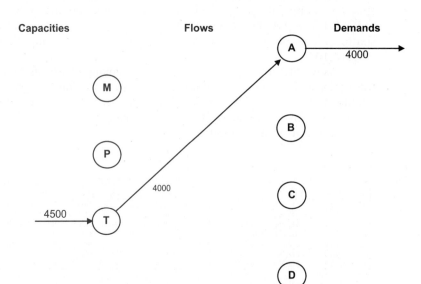

Here is a brief statement of the process, as it applies in general to the solution of a transportation model:

- Identify a high-priority demand—one that is covered by a unique source—and allocate the entire demand to this route. Remove this demand from consideration.
- Identify a high-priority capacity—one that supplies a single destination—and allocate the entire supply to this route. Remove this supply from consideration.
- Repeat the previous two steps using remaining demands and remaining supplies each time, until all shipments are accounted for.

Here is how the process works in the Bonner example:

1. Ship as much as possible on routes *PB*, *TD*, and *MC*.
2. Proceed to the reduced problem at the second priority level and ship as much as possible on routes *PA* and *TC*.
3. Proceed to the reduced problem at the third priority level and ship as much as possible on route *TA*.

At each allocation, "as much as possible" is dictated by the minimum of remaining capacity and remaining demand. Looking back, we can see that this three-stage description characterizes the optimal solution without explicitly using a number. By describing the optimal solution without using the parameters in the problem, we have portrayed a qualitative pattern in the solution and translated it into a list of economic priorities. This retrospective description of the solution is complete and unambiguous. Anyone who constructs a solution using these steps will reach the same result.

This pattern holds not just for the specific problem that we solved but also for similar problems that have some of the parameters slightly altered. For example, suppose that demand at Boston increased by 250 to 8,750. We could verify that the same pattern applies. The revised details of implementing the same pattern are shown in Figure 10.12, where we can see that three of the decision variables have been altered in response to the increased demand at Boston. Furthermore, if we track the cost implications of these changes, we can calculate that the increase in total transportation cost is

$$0.36(3250 - 3500) + 0.30(8750 - 8500) + 0.65(4250 - 4000) = -0.36(250) + 0.30(250)$$
$$+ 0.65(250) = 0.59(250) = \$147.50.$$

Thus, our calculations reveal that the incremental cost of shipment to Boston is $\$147.50/250 = \$0.59$. Although the direct cost is only $\$0.30$, the limited capacity at Pittsburgh forces us to compensate for the additional shipment to Boston by making adjustments elsewhere (while maintaining the optimal pattern). These adjustments lead us to a marginal cost of $\$0.59$.

More generally, we can alter the original problem in several ways at once. Suppose demands at Atlanta, Boston, and Chicago are *each* raised by 100 simultaneously. What will

FIGURE 10.12 Changes in the Diagram for the Altered Problem

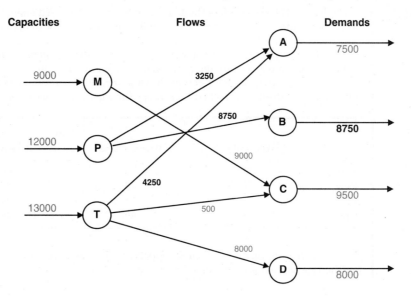

FIGURE 10.13 Changes in the Diagram When Three Demands Change

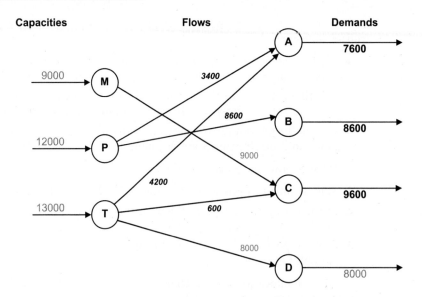

the optimal plan look like? In qualitative terms, we already know. The qualitative pattern of economic priorities allows us to write down the optimal solution to the revised problem without rerunning Solver, but rather by using the pattern's three-stage priority list and adjusting the shipment quantities for the modifications in demands.

Tracing the cost implications, as shown in the diagram of Figure 10.13, we find that the 100-unit increases in the three demands will combine to increase the optimal total cost by

$$0.36(3400 - 3500) + 0.30(8600 - 8500) + 0.65(4200 - 4000) + 0.55(600 - 500)$$
$$= -0.36(100) + 0.30(100) + 0.65(200) + 0.55(100) = 1.79(100) = \$179.$$

On a per-unit basis, this is an increase of $1.79, which corresponds to the sum of the shadow prices on the first three demand constraints.

10.3 ASSIGNMENT MODEL

An important special case of the transportation problem occurs when all capacities and all requirements are equal to one. In addition, total supply equals total demand. This special case is known as the **assignment problem**. The classic assignment model is characterized by a set of people, a set of tasks, and a score for each possible assignment of a person to a task. The problem is to find the best assignment of people to tasks. This model can be applied to the medley relay in swimming.

EXAMPLE
The Buchanan Swim Club

Coach Kemppel is the coach of the Buchanan Swim Club's co-ed team. Her team competes against other swim clubs, and a perennial question for the coach is how to organize the medley relay team. The medley relay requires four swimmers to each swim a different stroke: butterfly, breaststroke, backstroke, and freestyle. The relay is the final event in the competitions, and the outcome of the swim meet often depends on the performance of the relay team.

During practice, Coach Kemppel has asked each of her top four swimmers to try each of the four strokes, and she has tracked their times (in seconds), as shown in the following table:

	Stroke			
	Butterfly	**Breaststroke**	**Backstroke**	**Freestyle**
Todd	38	75	44	27
Betsy	34	76	43	25
Lee	41	71	41	26
Carly	33	80	45	30

With this information, Coach Kemppel is ready to assign swimmers to strokes in the relay race, but she can see that a lot of combinations are possible. ∎

10.3.1 Model Formulation

We can think of an **assignment** as a selection of four numbers from the table of swim times, one from each row and one from each column. (Because the number of swimmers is the same as the number of strokes, we can think of either assigning strokes to swimmers or assigning swimmers to strokes.) The total time associated with such an assignment is the sum of the numbers selected. This is merely another way of saying that the problem is a special transportation problem in which the row "capacities" are each 1 and the column "demands" are also 1. As such, we could easily construct a flow diagram to represent the decision problem in much the same way as we did with the transportation model of Figure 10.2.

For an algebraic statement of our model, we define our decision variables as the possible swimmer-stroke combinations, $T1, T2, \ldots, C4$, where the letter refers to the swimmer's name and the number refers to the stroke (1 for Butterfly, etc.). Our objective function (denoted z) is the total time for an assignment, which can be expressed as the sum of sixteen products. Each term in this sum is a parameter multiplied by a decision variable:

$$\text{Total Time} = z = 38T1 + 75T2 + 44T3 + 27T4 + 34B1 + 76B2 + 43B3 + 25B4$$

$$+ 41L1 + 71L2 + 41L3 + 26L4 + 33C1 + 80C2 + 45C3 + 30C4$$

There are eight constraints, four for the swimmers and four for the strokes. The row constraints, which require that each swimmer be assigned to at most one stroke, are as follows:

$$
\begin{array}{ccccccccc}
T1 & + & T2 & + & T3 & + & T4 & \leq & 1 \\
B1 & + & B2 & + & B3 & + & B4 & \leq & 1 \\
L1 & + & L2 & + & L3 & + & L4 & \leq & 1 \\
C1 & + & C2 & + & C3 & + & C4 & \leq & 1
\end{array}
$$

Meanwhile, the column constraints, which require that each stroke be assigned at least one swimmer, are as follows:

$$
\begin{array}{ccccccccc}
T1 & + & B1 & + & L1 & + & C1 & \geq & 1 \\
T2 & + & B2 & + & L2 & + & C2 & \geq & 1 \\
T3 & + & B3 & + & L3 & + & C3 & \geq & 1 \\
T4 & + & B4 & + & L4 & + & C4 & \geq & 1
\end{array}
$$

All of these constraints could be written as equalities without affecting the problem's solution, but sometimes using the inequalities can avoid confusion.

The assignment problem is to minimize z subject to the eight constraints on the variables. We might wonder whether there should be additional conditions to help us avoid fractional values for the decision variables. For example, if we assigned every variable the value 0.25, we would have a feasible solution to the model, but not one that we could implement in practice. However, we don't need to worry about this problem because the optimal values of the decision variables turn out to be integers in any assignment problem. We elaborate on this point later.

10.3.2 Spreadsheet Model

Figure 10.14 shows a spreadsheet model for the assignment problem. It resembles the spreadsheet for the transportation model introduced in Figure 10.3. The upper portion contains a 4×4 array of assignment costs. The decisions are shown in the lower 4×4 array and highlighted. To the right of each row is the row sum, and below each column is the column sum. As in the transportation model of Figure 10.3, these cells use the SUM function. Finally, in cell C17, we highlight the value of the objective function, or total cost, which is computed as the SUMPRODUCT of the cost array and the decision array.

FIGURE 10.14 Spread-sheet Model for the Buchanan Swim Club Problem

	A	B	C	D	E	F	G
1	**Assignment Model**						
2							
3	**Data**		Butterfly	Breast	Back	Free	
4		Todd	38	75	44	27	
5		Betsy	34	76	43	25	
6		Lee	41	71	41	26	
7		Carly	33	80	45	30	
8							
9							
10	**Decisions**		Butterfly	Breast	Back	Free	Row sum
11		Todd	0	0	1	0	1
12		Betsy	0	0	0	1	1
13		Lee	0	1	0	0	1
14		Carly	1	0	0	0	1
15		Column sum	1	1	1	1	
16							
17	**Objective** Total Time		173				
18							

10.14

Conceptually, there are capacities of 1 for each swimmer and requirements of 1 for each stroke, in analogy to the transportation model. Rather than include these parameters on the spreadsheet itself, they are entered as right-hand-side constants in the constraints. Normally, it is not good practice to enter right-hand-side constants in the Add Constraint window because we prefer to show parameters of the model on the spreadsheet itself, where we might want to explore some what-if questions. However, we make an exception here because the right-hand sides will not change: values of 1 represent the essence of the assignment problem. For the model specification, we enter the following information:

> Variables: C11:F14
> Objective: C17 (minimize)
> Constraints: C15:F15 $\geq$ 1
> G11:G14 $\leq$ 1

The less-than constraints ensure that each swimmer is assigned to at most one stroke, and the greater-than constraints ensure that at least one swimmer is assigned to each stroke. (As mentioned earlier, we could also express all of the constraints as equalities.)

10.3.3 Optimization

Figure 10.14 displays the optimal solution, which achieves a minimum total time of 173 seconds. This optimum is achieved by assigning Todd to the backstroke, Betsy to the freestyle, Lee to the breaststroke, and Carly to the butterfly. By solving this linear programming problem, Coach Kemppel can use her team's talent in the optimal fashion, thus giving them the best chance of winning their medley relay race.

10.3.4 Sensitivity Analysis

As suggested earlier, it is rare that we would want to perform sensitivity analysis with respect to either the supply parameters or the demand parameters in an assignment model. For that reason, we can enter the right-hand constant (1) in the Add Constraints window. However, we may well be interested in sensitivity analysis with respect to the cost parameters. In the medley-relay example, this translates into sensitivity analysis with respect to the swimming times.

Few swimmers can consistently swim the same distance in precisely the same length of time. We might ask, what if one of the swimmers took longer than expected: would we have been better off with an alternative assignment? We focus this example on Todd's time in the backstroke. The following table shows how the optimal solution varies as his time increases from 44 to 46 seconds:

T3 Time	Optimal Relay Time	Todd's Assignment
44	173	Backstroke
45	174	Backstroke
46	174	Breast stroke

In the base case, Todd's time is 44 seconds, and he is optimally assigned to the backstroke even though two other swimmers are faster at that stroke. If his time is 45 seconds, the team's relay time increases from 173 seconds to 174 as a result, but there is no incentive to reallocate swimmers to events. If his time is 46 seconds, however, a reallocation would allow the team to reach a 174-second time. In that reallocation, Todd would be assigned to the breast stroke.

The situation is slightly different for Carly's time in the butterfly, as shown in the following table:

C1 Time	Optimal Relay Time	Carly's Assignment
33	173	Butterfly
34	174	Butterfly
35	175	Butterfly
36	176	Butterfly
37	177	Butterfly
38	177	Breast stroke

In the base case, her time is 33 seconds, fastest on the team. If her time is 34 seconds, the team's relay time increases to 174. If her time is 35 seconds, slower than Betsy's time in the butterfly, it remains optimal to assign Carly to the butterfly, and the team's relay time increases again, to 175. Not until her time rises to 38 seconds is there an incentive to reallocate. At 38 seconds and above, Carly would be assigned to the breaststroke, and the relay time would be 177.

10.4 THE TRANSSHIPMENT MODEL

In the previous section, we saw that the assignment problem is a simplified version of the transportation problem, with unit supplies and demands. By contrast, the **transshipment problem** is a more complex version of the transportation problem, characterized by two stages of flow instead of just one. In the Bonner Electronics diagram of Figure 10.2, there are two levels in the system (plants and warehouses), and all of the flow takes place in one stage, from plants to warehouses. In more complex logistics systems, there are three major levels: plants, distribution centers (DCs) and warehouses, and in such systems, the flow often takes place in two stages.

EXAMPLE
Western Paper Company

The Western Paper Company manufactures paper at two factories (F1 and F2) on the West Coast. Their products are shipped by rail to a pair of depots (D1 and D2), one in the Midwest and one in the South. At the depots, the products are repackaged and sent by truck to three regional warehouses (W1, W2, and W3) around the country, in response to replenishment orders.

Each of the factories has a known monthly production capacity, and the three regional warehouses have placed their demands for next month. The following tables summarize the data that have been collected for this planning problem:

(From) Factory	(To) DC		Capacity
	D1	D2	
F1	$1.28	1.36	2,500
F2	1.33	1.38	2,500
F3	1.68	1.55	2,500

(From) DC	(To) Warehouse				
	W1	**W2**	**W3**	**W4**	**W5**
D1	$0.60	0.42	0.32	0.44	0.68
D2	0.57	0.30	0.40	0.38	0.72
Requirement	1,200	1,300	1,400	1,500	1,600

Knowing the costs of transporting goods from factories to DCs and from DCs to warehouses, Western Paper is interested in scheduling its material flow at the minimum possible cost. ∎

10.4.1 Formulation

A good first step in modeling is to build a diagram of the system, as shown in Figure 10.15. The left-hand side of the diagram shows the potential flows from factories to DCs, and the right-hand side shows the potential flows from DCs to warehouses. The DCs are called **transshipment points**, because material arrives at those locations and is then subject to further shipment. At the heart of the transshipment structure is the need to coordinate the two transportation stages at the transshipment points. This coordination is governed by the **conservation law** of flows in networks: The total quantity flowing out of a node must equal the total quantity flowing in.

In order to describe the conservation law algebraically, we introduce some notation for the decision variables. We use x to represent a first-stage flow, from factory to DC, and y to represent a second-stage flow from DC to warehouse. Thus, let x_{21} represent the quantity shipped from F2 to D1, and let y_{23} represent the quantity shipped from D2 to W3. With this notation, we can write the conservation relationship for D1 as follows:

$$(\text{Flow Out}) = (\text{Flow In})$$

or

$$(\text{Flow Out}) - (\text{Flow In}) = 0$$

or

$$(y_{11} + y_{12} + y_{13} + y_{14} + y_{15}) - (x_{11} + x_{21} + x_{31}) = 0$$

FIGURE 10.15 Diagram for Western Paper

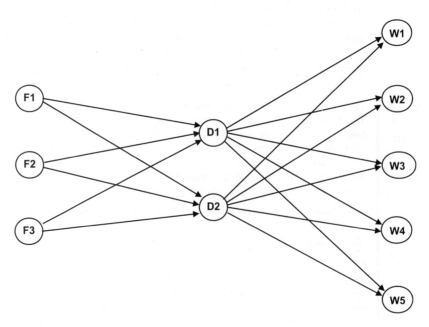

Similarly, for D2, we have:

$$(y_{21} + y_{22} + y_{23} + y_{24} + y_{25}) - (x_{12} + x_{22} + x_{32}) = 0$$

We can see that the conservation law takes the form of an equality constraint for particular nodes in the network. This equality constraint is sometimes called a **balance equation**, because it ensures perfect balance between inputs and outputs.

We can now develop an algebraic statement of the transshipment model, by combining the types of supply and demand constraints we saw in the transportation model with the balance equations introduced here for transshipment nodes. Our model takes the following form:

$$
\begin{aligned}
\text{Minimize } z = {} & 1.28x_{11} + 1.36x_{12} + 1.33x_{21} + 1.38x_{22} + 1.68x_{31} + 1.55x_{32} \\
& + 0.60y_{11} + 0.42y_{12} + 0.32y_{13} + 0.44y_{14} + 0.68y_{15} \\
& + 0.57y_{21} + 0.30y_{22} + 0.40y_{23} + 0.38y_{24} + 0.72y_{25}
\end{aligned}
$$

subject to

$$
\begin{aligned}
x_{11} + x_{12} &\leq 2{,}500 \\
x_{21} + x_{22} &\leq 2{,}500 \\
x_{31} + x_{32} &\leq 2{,}500 \\
y_{11} + y_{21} &\geq 1{,}200 \\
y_{12} + y_{22} &\geq 1{,}300 \\
y_{13} + y_{23} &\geq 1{,}400 \\
y_{14} + y_{24} &\geq 1{,}500 \\
y_{15} + y_{25} &\geq 1{,}600 \\
-x_{11} - x_{21} - x_{31} + y_{11} + y_{12} + y_{13} + y_{14} + y_{15} &= 0 \\
-x_{12} + x_{22} - x_{32} + y_{21} + y_{22} + y_{23} + y_{24} + y_{25} &= 0
\end{aligned}
$$

In our formulation, the balance equations give rise to a set of equality constraints in the model. These constraints could also be expressed in the form of inequalities—that is, the total flow into a DC node must be greater than or equal to the flow out of that node. That version would be consistent with our modeling principle of posing constraints in their most flexible form. However, because of the cost structure, we also know that there is no incentive to ship material to a DC if it is not subsequently brought to a warehouse. Furthermore, by using equality constraints here, we associate a different constraint type (less-than constraint, greater-than constraint, equality constraint) with each of the three different roles (factories, warehouses, and DCs), so that the algebraic structure of the model mirrors the physical structure of the system.

10.4.2 Spreadsheet Model

With a network diagram and an algebraic model in hand, we turn now to the question of spreadsheet layout. The diagram for the Western Paper example depicts two side-by-side transportation problems, and we can lay out a worksheet similarly, showing two stages horizontally on a worksheet, each resembling Figure 10.2 for the transportation model.

In Figure 10.16, we show a worksheet for the Western Paper example, where the left-hand portion corresponds to the first (3×2) stage, and the right-hand portion corresponds to the second (2×5) stage. Cell E15 contains a SUMPRODUCT formula that accounts for the total transportation cost in the first stage. Cell M15 serves the purpose for the second stage. The total cost for the entire system, equal to the sum of the first and second stage costs, is calculated in cell E17.

FIGURE 10.16 Worksheet for the Western Paper Model

		D1	D2	Capacity			W1	W2	W3	W4	W5	
Transshipment Model												
Parameters			**Stage 1**						**Stage 2**			
		D1	D2	Capacity			W1	W2	W3	W4	W5	
	F1	1.28	1.36	2500		D1	0.60	0.42	0.32	0.44	0.68	
	F2	1.33	1.38	2500		D2	0.57	0.30	0.40	0.38	0.72	
	F3	1.68	1.55	2500		Required	1200	1300	1400	1500	1600	
Decisions		D1	D2	Sent			W1	W2	W3	W4	W5	Flow out
	F1	2500	0	2500		D1	1200	0	1400	0	1600	4200
	F2	1700	800	2500		D2	0	1300	0	1500	0	2800
	F3	0	2000	2000		Received	1200	1300	1400	1500	1600	
	Flow in	4200	2800									
Objective		Stage 1 Cost		9665						Stage 2 Cost		3216
		Total Cost		$12,881								

10.4.3 Optimization

For the model specification, we enter the following information:

Variables:	C10:D12, H10:L11
Objective:	E17 (minimize)
Constraints:	C13:D13 = M10:M11
	E10:E12 ≤ E5:E7
	H12:L12 ≥ H7:L7

The formulation contains three less-than constraints (one per factory), five greater-than constraints (one per warehouse), and two equality constraints (one per DC). The optimal solution in this example is shown in Figure 10.16 with a total cost of $12,881. Thus, Western Paper can recognize both stages of its supply chain when it optimizes its distribution costs in one comprehensive model.

Once more, it is a good idea to label the diagram with the values from the optimal solution, to ensure that the solution makes sense. Figure 10.17 shows the optimal flows for the Western Paper example. Again, we drop the arcs with no flow so that we can focus on the feasibility of the decisions. At node D1, we can see that the total inflow is 4,200, and the total outflow is 4,200. At node D2, the total inflow is 2,800, matching the total outflow of 2,800. Thus, we can use the diagram to produce a quick visual check that the decision variables in the optimal solution are consistent with the balance equations for the transshipment points. Then, as in the transportation diagram (Figure 10.5), we can check at the factory nodes and at the warehouse nodes to ensure that total outflow is consistent

FIGURE 10.17 Optimal Solution for Western Paper

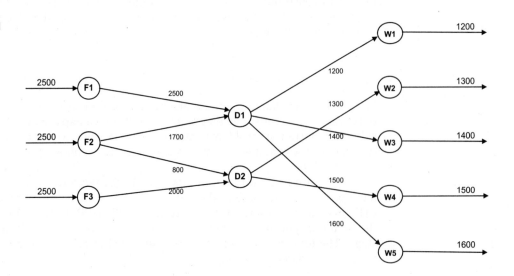

with total inflow. The network diagram serves as a convenient visual check and as a visual aid for communicating the results of the analysis.

10.4.4 Sensitivity Analysis

Examining the optimal solution in Figure 10.16, and focusing on the shipments from the two DCs to the five warehouses, we may be surprised to see that demand at the first warehouse is met from DC1, even though shipments from DC2 would be cheaper per unit. In particular, the optimal solution uses a route that costs $0.60 per unit as part of the solution, in preference to a route that costs $0.57. We might wonder how much cheaper the cost on the latter route would have to be in order to provide an incentive to switch.

To answer this question, we can use the Optimization Sensitivity tool to test the sensitivity of the optimal solution to the cost parameter in cell H6. We find that at a unit cost below $0.55, the optimal solution uses the route from D2 to W1.

10.5 A STANDARD FORM FOR NETWORK MODELS

The transportation, assignment and transshipment problems constitute a special class of network models in linear programming. They all lend themselves easily to the use of a flow diagram, and they all contain a From/To flow structure that suggests a corresponding array layout in a worksheet. When we specify the decision variables in Solver, we do not enter a *row* of adjacent cells, as in the standard format. Instead, we enter an *array*, or, in the case of the transshipment model, a pair of arrays. (This feature could obviously be generalized to cases in which we have three or more stages in the model.) With the array format at the heart of the model, the constraints involve restrictions on totals across a row or down a column, allowing us to use the SUM function, rather than the SUMPRODUCT function that we saw throughout Chapter 9.

One interesting feature of this class of models is that an optimal solution always consists of an integer-valued set of decision variables as long as the right-hand-side parameters arc integers. Recall that the linearity assumption in linear programming allows for divisibility in the values of decision variables. As a result, we may find that some or all of the decision variables in an optimal solution are fractional, and this sometimes makes the result difficult to implement or interpret. However, no such problem arises with these three network models; they will always produce integer-valued solutions as long as the constraint parameters are themselves integers.

Finally, the three network models feature less-than constraints for capacities and greater-than constraints for requirements, along with balance equations in the case of the transshipment model. In the case of the assignment model, we could actually use equality constraints from the outset. However, as we shall discover next, it is possible to formulate any of these problems as linear programs built exclusively on balance equations. Although this approach may not seem as intuitive, it does link the flow diagram and the spreadsheet model more closely, as suggested at the beginning of the chapter, and it allows us to see a more general structure that encompasses other network models as well.

Some network structures do not lend themselves as easily as the transportation model to an array layout for decision variables. For these networks, it is desirable to use the standard linear programming format, with decision variables in a single row and a SUMPRODUCT function in each of the constraints. The distinguishing features of this approach are a flow diagram and the use of material-balance equations.

In a classical network model, each node in the network corresponds to a material-balance equation—the requirement that total outflow must equal total inflow. Figure 10.5 shows the solution to a model in which the total flow into the network (supply capacity) is 34,000 but the total flow out of the network (demand requirements) is only 33,500. To convert this situation to a classical network, we add a "virtual" warehouse to the model—a fifth warehouse (labeled E) with a demand of 500. With this demand quantity, total supply matches total demand.

Next, to make sure that the solution to the original problem is not corrupted, we take the unit transportation costs associated with the virtual warehouse to be zero. Therefore,

FIGURE 10.18 Revised Diagram with a Virtual Destination

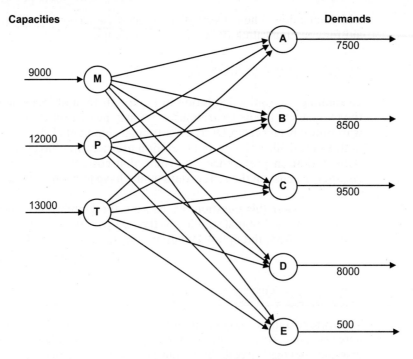

no additional cost is incurred for material shipped to the location E. The revised diagram is shown in Figure 10.18.

Once we have a network diagram for a problem, we can translate it into a linear program by following these simple steps:

- Define a variable for each arc.
- Include supplies as input flows and demands as output flows.
- Construct the balance equation for each node.

In this version of the model, *every* constraint is a balance equation. Thus, the constraints take the following form:

$$
\begin{aligned}
MA + MB + MC + MD + ME - 9{,}000 &= 0 \\
PA + PB + PC + PD + PE - 12{,}000 &= 0 \\
TA + TB + TC + TD + TE - 13{,}000 &= 0 \\
7{,}500 - MA - PA - TA &= 0 \\
8{,}500 - MB - PB - TB &= 0 \\
9{,}500 - MC - PC - TC &= 0 \\
8{,}000 - MD - PD - TD &= 0 \\
500 - ME - PE - TE &= 0
\end{aligned}
$$

One step remains, and that is to rearrange the equations so that the constraint constants appear on the right-hand side. In this step, we still have a choice, and we adopt a sign convention for right-hand-side constants that can provide improved clarity. Under this convention, we write a balance equation with a positive right-hand side when there is flow *into* the network and with a negative right-hand side when there is flow *out of* the network. Thus, the constraint equations take the following form for the purposes of building a spreadsheet model:

$$
\begin{aligned}
MA + MB + MC + MD + ME &= 9{,}000 \\
PA + PB + PC + PD + PE &= 12{,}000 \\
TA + TB + TC + TD + TE &= 13{,}000 \\
-MA - PA - TA &= -7{,}500 \\
-MB - PB - TB &= -8{,}500 \\
-MC - PC - TC &= -9{,}500 \\
-MD - PD - TD &= -8{,}000 \\
-ME - PE - TE &= -500
\end{aligned}
$$

FIGURE 10.19 Worksheet for the Revised Model

Transportation Problem

Decisions

Routes	MA	MB	MC	MD	ME	PA	PB	PC	PD	PE	TA	TB	TC	TD	TE			
	0	0	9000	0	0	3500	8500	0	0	0	4000	0	500	8000	500			

Objective

																	Total cost	
Costs	0.60	0.56	0.22	0.40	0.00	0.36	0.30	0.28	0.58	0.00	0.65	0.68	0.55	0.42	0.00		$12,025	

Constraints

	MA	MB	MC	MD	ME	PA	PB	PC	PD	PE	TA	TB	TC	TD	TE	LHS		RHS
M supply	1	1	1	1	1											9000	=	9000
P supply						1	1	1	1	1						12000	=	12000
T supply											1	1	1	1	1	13000	=	13000
A demand	-1					-1					-1					-7500	=	-7500
B demand		-1					-1					-1				-8500	=	-8500
C demand			-1					-1					-1			-9500	=	-9500
D demand				-1					-1					-1		-8000	=	-8000
E demand					-1					-1					-1	-500	=	-500

The worksheet of Figure 10.19 follows the standard form for linear programs. The 15 variable names are listed in row 4, with their values in the highlighted cells of the next row. The objective function is in the form of a SUMPRODUCT, as is usually the case in standard form. Finally, the constraints are all balance equations, one for each node.

The standard form in Figure 10.19 has features that link it closely to the diagram in Figure 10.18:

- Each variable corresponds to an arc in the diagram (and vice versa).
- Each constraint corresponds to a node in the diagram (and vice versa).
- The right-hand-side constants of the model show up in the network as supplies and demands, with the convention that supply values are positive and demand values negative.
- The coefficients of a given variable in the constraint equations include only two nonzero values, +1 and −1, which occur in constraints corresponding to the tail and head of the corresponding arc, respectively.

The standard form of Figure 10.19 may not be as intuitive as the simpler model in Figure 10.3. Nevertheless, the standard form bears a close relation to the network diagram of Figure 10.18, which provides us with a debugging tool for the spreadsheet model. That is, we can use the diagram as a checklist to make sure that all variables and all constraints are contained in the model. We can also ensure that the supply and demand parameters are properly reflected, and we can even confirm that the (+1) and (−1) coefficients are located correctly.

The virtue of using this standard form is the fact that we can draw on the network diagram as a debugging aid. This may not seem like a large enough benefit to warrant using the standard form when the classical layout of Figure 10.3 is so intuitive. But the concept becomes helpful in models that are more complicated than the transportation model. We present an example in the next section.

10.6 NETWORK MODELS WITH YIELDS

In network diagrams for the transportation, assignment, and transshipment models, arcs carry flow from one node to another. One feature of those models is that the quantity sent out from a source node is precisely the quantity that arrives at the destination node. However, we can extend network models to cases in which this type of conservation requirement need not apply. If the flows of interest are subject to positive or negative yields, we can incorporate that feature as well. Waste in a manufacturing process is an example of a negative yield; interest on a bank balance is an example of a positive yield. Two examples illustrate the role of yields.

10.6.1 Yields as Reductions in Flow

One common type of yield phenomenon involves technologies that produce waste. When wood is cut, shaped, and sanded in a manufacturing process, the amount of usable wood that exits the process is less than the amount that entered. When metal enters a process that involves grinding, drilling, and polishing, the same is true of the amount of metal at the end of the process compared to the amount at the start. This type of reduction in the amount of a flow is called **process yield**.

EXAMPLE
*Planning
Recycling
Operations*

The Ligon Paper Company specializes in paper recycling. The company owns several facilities that obtain paper from commercial or municipal sources, and they produce paper for a variety of markets where customers are looking for recycled content.

Ligon Paper collects three types of input, which they classify as White Paper, Mixed Paper, and Newsprint. Applying various processes, they produce three products: high-quality Office Paper, lower-quality Catalog Paper, and napkin-grade Tan Stock.

One of the processes at Ligon Paper takes White Paper and converts it to Office Paper. For each ton of White Paper input, the process generates 0.85 ton of Office Paper. Alternatively, a ton of White Paper can be converted to Catalog Paper; here the yield is 0.90 ton. Thirdly, White Paper can be converted to Tan Stock, with a yield of 95 percent. For the other types of input, different yields apply, and it is not possible to convert Newsprint to Office Paper. The following table gives a complete set of yield factors, stated as percentages:

	Office	Catalog	Tan Stock
White Paper	85%	90%	95%
Mixed Paper	60%	70%	80%
Newsprint	—	65%	60%

In the coming planning period, Ligon's contracts with suppliers have generated 300 tons of White Paper, 600 tons of Mixed Paper, and 400 tons of Newsprint. In existing markets, Ligon could sell 150 tons of Office Paper at the market price of $25/ton, 750 tons of Catalog Paper at $20/ton, and 550 tons of Tan Stock at $18/ton. The problem is to determine how much of each product to produce. ∎

Except for the effect of yields, the planning problem at Ligon Paper can be represented as a transportation problem. We show the network diagram in Figure 10.20. If there were no yield factors, this diagram would translate into a 3×3 transportation model, and the standard transportation layout would be convenient. However, yield factors make it a little more difficult to use the array-based layout, so we adopt the network layout. In the Ligon Paper example, there is excess demand, so our model contains four supply nodes and three demand nodes. The fourth supply node is a virtual, or fictitious, node that accounts for meeting excess demand. However, because of the yield factors, we cannot calculate the excess demand in advance. Even if we consume the entire supply of 1,300 tons, we can't tell how many tons of product that generates because the amount depends on the specific allocation. Thus, in our diagram, we treat the virtual capacity for meeting excess demand as a variable (X).

Again, there is an intimate relation between the network diagram and the spreadsheet model, which is shown in Figure 10.21. Each arc in the network corresponds to a variable, each node in the network corresponds to a constraint, and all constraints are written as balance equations. The variables are measured in tons of supply; these are the quantities that are *started* into the various processes. To compute the quantities in tons of

FIGURE 10.20 Diagram for Ligon Paper

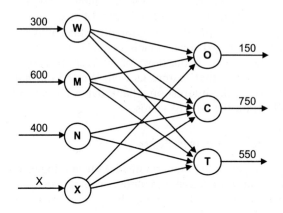

FIGURE 10.21 Worksheet for the Ligon Paper Model

	A	B	C	D	E	F	G	H	I	J	K	L	M	N	O	P	Q	R
1	Recycling Planning																	
2																		
3	Decisions																	
4		Routes	WO	WC	WT	MO	MC	MT	NC	NT	XO	XC	XT	X				
5			176	124	0	0	0	600	400	0	0	379	70	449				
6																		
7		Yields	0.85	0.90	0.95	0.60	0.70	0.80	0.65	0.60	1	1	1					
8	Objective																	
9	Gross	Revenue	25	20	18	25	20	18	20	18	0	0	0	0		Total Revenue		
10	Net	Revenue	21.25	18.00	17.10	15.00	14.00	14.40	13.00	10.80	0	0	0	0		$19,814		
11	Constraints															LHS		RHS
12		W supply	1	1	1											300	=	300
13		M supply				1	1	1								600	=	600
14		N supply							1	1						400	=	400
15		X supply									1	1	1	-1		0	=	0
16		O demand	-0.85			-0.60					-1					-150	=	-150
17		C demand		-0.90			-0.70		-0.65			-1				-750	=	-750
18		T demand			-0.95			-0.80		-0.60			-1			-550	=	-550
19																		

output, we have to apply yield factors. The objective function computes the revenue from the schedule of outputs, as supply costs are fixed for the purposes of this decision. For the model specification, we enter the following information:

> Variables: C5:N5
> Objective: P10 (maximize)
> Constraints: P12:P18 = R12:R18

Figure 10.21 displays the optimal solution to the model, which dictates that White Paper should be processed into Office Paper and Catalog Paper; Mixed Paper should be processed into Tan Stock, and Newsprint should be processed into Catalog Paper. This production plan results in total revenue of $19,814. Thus, the yield-based model provides Ligon Paper with a revenue-maximizing allocation of its capacity.

10.6.2 Yields as Expansions in Flow

In production processes, yields are typically less than one: outputs are smaller than inputs because some waste is generated along the way. However, in other kinds of processes, yields can be greater than one. An example of this feature arises in funds-flow models. The following example is a case in point.

EXAMPLE
Planning for Tuition Expenses

Parents Patti and Russ want to provide for their daughter's college expenses with some of the $100,000 they have recently inherited. They hope to set aside part of the money and establish an account that would cover the needs of their daughter's college education, which begins four years from now, with a one-time investment. Their estimate is that first-year college expenses will come to $24,000 and will increase $2,000 per year during each of the remaining three years of college. The following investment instruments are available:

Investment	Available	Matures	Return at Maturity
A	every year	in 1 year	5%
B	in years 1, 3, 5, 7	in 2 years	11%
C	in years 1, 4	in 3 years	16%
D	in year 1	in 7 years	44%

Faced with this prospect, Patti and Russ wish to set aside the *minimum* amount of money initially that will guarantee that the college expenses will be met. In other words, they seek an investment plan that will cover college financial needs with the smallest possible initial investment. ∎

Investment and funds-flow problems of this sort lend themselves to network modeling. In this type of problem, nodes represent points in time at which funds flows occur. We can imagine tracking a bank account, with funds flowing in and out, depending on our decisions. In this problem, there needs to be a node for Now (the start of year 1) and for the start of years 2 through 8. (Note that the end of year 3 and the start of year 4 are, in effect, the same point in time.) To construct a typical node, we list the potential inflows and outflows that can occur:

Inflows

Initial investment

Appreciation of investment A from one year ago

Appreciation of investment B from two years ago

Appreciation of investment C from three years ago

Appreciation of investment D from seven years ago

Outflows

Expense payment for the coming year

Investment A for the coming year

Investment B for the coming two years

Investment C for the coming three years

Investment D for the coming seven years

Not all of these inflows and outflows apply at every point in time, but if we sketch the eight nodes and the flows that do apply, we come up with a diagram such as the one shown as Figure 10.22. In this diagram, $A1$ represents the amount allocated to investment A at the start of year 1, $A2$ represents the amount allocated to investment A at the start of year 2, and so on. The initial fund in the account is shown as V, and the expense payments are shown as $E5$ through $E8$. The diagram shows the end-of-year nodes as independent elements, which is all we really need; however, Figure 10.23 shows a tidier diagram in which the nodes are connected in a single flow network.

There is no variable $B7$ in the model. A two-year investment starting in year 7 would extend beyond the eight-year horizon, so this option is omitted. However, the variable $A8$ does appear in the model. We can think of $A8$ as representing the final value in the account.

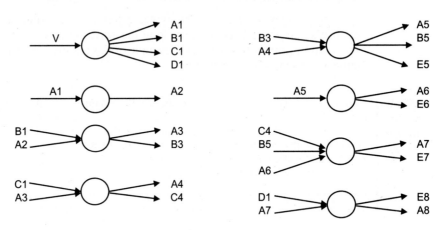

FIGURE 10.22 Diagram for the Tuition Expenses Problem

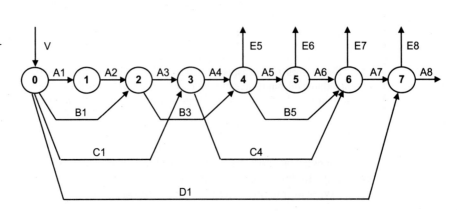

FIGURE 10.23 Alternative Diagram for the Tuition Expenses Problem

Perhaps it is intuitive that, if we are trying to minimize the initial investment, there is no reason to have money left in the account in the end. Still, to verify this intuition, we include $A8$ in the model, anticipating that we will find $A8 = 0$ in the optimal solution.

The next step is to convert the diagram into a linear programming model. For this purpose, the flows on the arcs become decision variables, and each node gives rise to a balance equation, as listed below:

$$
\begin{aligned}
\text{Start of year 1:} \quad & A1 + B1 + C1 + D1 - V && = 0 \\
\text{Start of year 2:} \quad & A2 - 1.05A1 && = 0 \\
\text{Start of year 3:} \quad & A3 + B3 - 1.05A2 - 1.11B1 && = 0 \\
\text{Start of year 4:} \quad & A4 + C4 - 1.05A3 - 1.16C1 && = 0 \\
\text{Start of year 5:} \quad & A5 + B5 - 1.05A4 - 1.11B3 && = -24{,}000 \\
\text{Start of year 6:} \quad & A6 - 1.05A5 && = -26{,}000 \\
\text{Start of year 7:} \quad & A7 - 1.05A6 - 1.11B5 - 1.16C4 && = -28{,}000 \\
\text{Start of year 8:} \quad & A8 - 1.05A7 - 1.44D1 && = -30{,}000
\end{aligned}
$$

The resulting model is shown on the worksheet of Figure 10.24. Notice the systematic pattern formed by the coefficients in the columns of the constraint equations. Each column has two nonzero coefficients: a positive coefficient (of 1), in the row corresponding to the time the investment is made, and a negative coefficient (reflecting the appreciation rate), in the row corresponding to the time the investment matures. The only exceptions are V and $A8$, which represent flows into and out of the network. In other funds-flow models, the column coefficients portray the investment-and-return profile for each of the variables, on a per-unit basis. The right-hand-side constants, following our sign convention, show the profile of planned flows into and out of the system over the various time periods.

The objective function in this example is simply the initial size of the investment account, which is the variable V. Thus, we can depart slightly from the standard format and designate the objective function in cell B7 simply by referencing cell B5.

Once again, there is a close relationship between the network diagram and the spreadsheet model. This relationship allows the diagram to be used as a debugging aid for checking the spreadsheet. After we have checked the spreadsheet for consistency with the diagram, we can proceed with the analysis.

We invoke Solver and specify:

Variables:	B5:P5
Objective:	B7 (minimize)
Constraints:	Q11:Q18 = S11:S18

When we minimize V, Solver provides the optimal solution shown in Figure 10.24, calling for an initial investment of about $80,883.

FIGURE 10.24 Worksheet for the Tuition Expenses Model

	A	B	C	D	E	F	G	H	I	J	K	L	M	N	O	P	Q	R	S
1	Tuition Problem																		
2																			
3	Decisions																		
4		V	A1	A2	A3	A4	A5	A6	A7	A8	B1	B3	B5	C1	C4	D1			
5		80.883	0.00	0.00	0.00	0.00	24.76	0.00	0.00	0.00	60.05	66.66	25.23	0.00	0.00	20.83			
6	Objective																		
7		$80 883																	
8																			
9	Constraints																		
10	Year																		
11	0	-1	1	0	0	0	0	0	0	0	1	0	0	1	0	1	7.11E-15	=	0
12	1	0	-1.05	1	0	0	0	0	0	0	0	0	0	0	0	0	0	=	0
13	2	0	0	-1.05	1	0	0	0	0	0	-1.11	1	0	0	0	0	0	=	0
14	3	0	0	0	-1.05	1	0	0	0	0	0	0	0	-1.16	1	0	0	=	0
15	4	0	0	0	0	-1.05	1	0	0	0	0	-1.11	1	0	0	0	-24	=	-24
16	5	0	0	0	0	0	-1.05	1	0	0	0	0	0	0	0	0	-26	=	-26
17	6	0	0	0	0	0	0	-1.05	1	0	0	0	-1.11	0	-1.16	0	-28	=	-28
18	7	0	0	0	0	0	0	0	-1.05	1	0	0	0	0	0	-1.44	-30	=	-30
19																			

10.24

The optimal value of the objective function in our spreadsheet model appears as 80.883 because we have rescaled our model in thousands of dollars. The rescaling was accomplished by entering the tuition expenses in thousands of dollars on the right-hand side of the last four constraints. In a model such as this one, rescaling is obviously convenient. It allows us to avoid entering a lot of zeros when we type in the model, and it makes the model easier to debug.

SOLVER TIP
Rescaling the Model

Rescaling the parameters of a model—so that they appear in thousands (or millions)—saves us the work of entering lots of zeros. As a consequence, we may avoid some data-entry errors, and the spreadsheet looks a little less crowded than it would with many large numbers on it. However, there is another important practical reason for rescaling. The way that Solver carries out its arithmetic sometimes makes rescaling desirable. As a guideline, the parameters in the objective function and the constraints should not differ from each other, or from the values of the decision variables, by more than a factor of 100,000. A model that tracks cash flows in the millions while also computing percentage returns as decimal fractions violates this rule.

Sometimes, rescaling problems are difficult to avoid when we're trying to keep the model easy to understand. In these cases, we can ask Solver to perform some internal rescaling of the model if we select the value True for the Use Automatic Scaling option on the Engine tab of the task pane. As helpful as the Automatic Scaling option is, however, it is always preferable for the model builder to do the rescaling on the spreadsheet.

Finally, if we need to display our model results in units that are more natural for our audience, we can create a separate presentation worksheet. On that sheet, the numbers can be displayed in any desired format without affecting the optimization process. ∎

10.6.3 Patterns in General Network Models

To reinforce the concept of identifying patterns in optimal solutions, we explore the tuition-planning model in more detail. The optimal solution is shown on the worksheet in Figure 10.24 and on the network diagram in Figure 10.25. In the diagram, we have removed zero variables as the first step in identifying a pattern. (Recall that in searching for a pattern, we normally ignore nonbinding constraints, but in network models, all constraints are balance equations and therefore binding.)

The diagram in Figure 10.25 makes the pattern easy to see. First, with respect to the variables, investment A is seldom used, and investment C is never used. In addition, there is no money left over at the end of the scenario ($A8 = 0$), as we anticipated. Most of the investment is allocated toward instruments B and D. The initial investment B1 is reinvested at year 3 and must appreciate sufficiently to cover the first year of tuition, the investment in $A5$, and the reinvestment in $B5$. Thereafter, $A5$ covers the second year of tuition, $B5$ covers the third, and the initial investment in $D1$ covers the fourth. This is the qualitative pattern in the solution.

When we make a priority list of variables, we must account for the logical sequence in which these variables can be calculated. For this purpose, we start from the end of the problem and work backward. The individual calculation steps are as follows:

1. The expense outflow at node 7 dictates the size of the investment in $D1$. (Specifically, the investment returns 44 percent, so to cover a flow of 30,000, the amount invested must be 30,000/1.44 = 20,833.)

2. The expense at node 6 dictates the size of $B5$ as 28,000/1.11 = 25,225.

FIGURE 10.25 Diagram for the Optimal Decisions in the Tuition Expenses Model

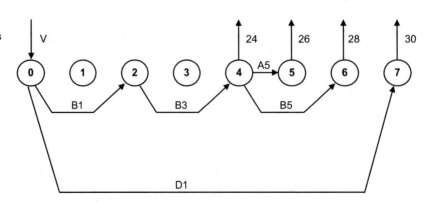

3. The expense at node 5 dictates the size of $A5$ as $26,000/1.05 = 24,762$.

4. The expense at node 4 must be considered in conjunction with the investment outflows for $A5$ and $B5$, which have been determined in steps 2 and 3. Combining the three outflows and dividing by 1.11, we obtain 66,655.

5. The outflow at node 2 dictates the size of $B1$ as $66,655/1.11 = 60,050$.

6. The outflows at node 1 ($B1$ and $D1$) are now determined; we simply sum them to compute the required initial investment of 80,883.

The shadow prices in funds-flow networks are useful as well. Consider the second-year expense of $26,000. Suppose it were to increase by $1. What would the impact be on the objective function? We can answer this question by repeating the calculation steps and including the change:

1. No change in $D1$

2. No change in $B5$

3. Increase $A5$ by $1/1.05 = 0.952$

4. Increase $B3$ by $0.952/1.11 = 0.858$

5. Increase $B1$ as $0.858/1.11 = 0.773$

6. The initial investment must increase by the increment in $B1 = 0.773$

The conclusion is that a dollar's increase in the expense at year 5 can be covered by an increase in the initial investment of $0.773. This amounts to a rate of return of 29.3 percent over the 5-year period, or an average annual return of about 5.28 percent. In financial terms, we can reconstruct this rate as a combination of a 5 percent return (in year 5 from investment A) and a 5.36 percent annual return (in years 1-4, from investment B.) Thus, the shadow price effectively tells us the cost of funds for meeting expenses in any particular year.

10.7 NETWORK MODELS FOR PROCESS TECHNOLOGIES

In the networks we have examined thus far, nodes conform to a conservation law requiring that total outflow equals total inflow. This is the case even in networks where flows are subject to yields. In all of our examples, the material flowing out of a node (money, materials, people, etc.) has been identical to the material flowing into the node. In this section, we consider a generalization in which some nodes represent production operations that actually transform the substance between inflow and outflow. This type of network is particularly suitable for the analysis of production plans in process industries, such as paper, steel, or chemicals. We illustrate with an example from oil refining.

EXAMPLE
Production at Delta Oil

The refining process at Delta Oil Company separates crude oil into components that eventually yield gasoline, heating oil, jet fuel, lubricating oil, and other petroleum products. In particular, gasoline is produced from crude oil by either a distillation process alone or by a distillation process followed by a catalytic-cracking process. The outputs of these processes are subsequently blended to obtain different grades of gasoline.

The distillation tower at Delta's refinery uses 5 barrels of crude oil to produce 3 barrels of distillate and 2 barrels of other "low-end" byproducts. Some distillate is blended into gasoline products; the rest becomes feedstock for the catalytic cracker.

The catalytic-cracking process produces high-quality catalytic gasoline (or catalytic, for short) from the feedstock. Delta's catalytic cracker requires 2.5 barrels of distillate to produce 1.6 barrels of catalytic and 1 barrel of "high-end" byproducts. (The cracking process creates output volume that exceeds input volume.)

Finally, distillate from the distillation tower is blended with catalytic to make regular gasoline and premium gasoline. The blend of distillate and catalytic must be at least 50 percent catalytic to meet the quality requirements of regular and at least 75 percent catalytic to meet the quality requirements of premium. ∎

10.7.1 Formulation

At the Delta Oil Refinery, as in most facilities of this type, it is not hard to find a diagram of the production process. Such a diagram may not have been devised for the purposes of

FIGURE 10.26   Diagram
for Delta Oil

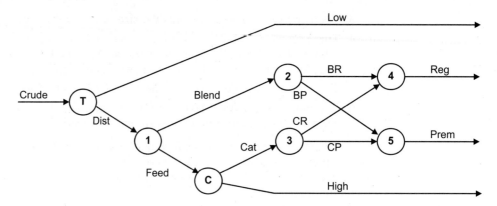

building network models, but it is usually not too different from one that would suit our modeling purposes. Our network model is shown in Figure 10.26. The process has been simplified by aggregating distinct products into such categories as high-end and low-end, but the main process steps are represented.

In the figure, we label each of the arcs in the network, recognizing that these labels will also serve as the names of decision variables in the linear programming model. For convenience, we use some abbreviations, such as *CR*, which represents the amount of catalytic that is combined into regular gasoline. Next, we create node T to represent the tower and node C to represent the cracker. We also add nodes 1, 2 and 3 to represent allocations of flow. At node 1, the distillate must be split into a portion that is directly blended into gasoline and a portion that is used as a feedstock for the cracker. At node 2, the distillate allocated to blending must be split between regular and premium grades of gasoline, and similarly at node 3 for the catalytic produced by the cracker. Finally, nodes 4 and 5 represent the output of the two blending decisions, one for regular and one for premium.

For each node in the diagram, we write a balance equation. Conceptually, however, there is a twist here. Because the nodes represent production processes, the input material may differ from the output material, and there may be multiple input materials and multiple output materials. We then must write a balance equation for each output material. For example, the equations for the tower node (T) take the following form:

$$\text{Flow Out} - \text{Flow In} = 0$$

or

$$Dist - 0.60Crude = 0$$
$$Low - 0.40Crude = 0$$

Thus, there are two balance equations, one each for distillate and low-end byproducts. Each equation contains one input term, for crude. The coefficients of 0.60 and 0.40 correspond to a fractional split of 5 barrels into flows of 3 barrels and 2 barrels, respectively, for the split between distillate (*Dist*) and low-end by-products (*Low*).

A similar pair of equations applies to the cracker node (C):

$$\text{Flow Out} - \text{Flow In} = 0$$

or

$$Cat - 0.64Feed = 0$$
$$High - 0.40Feed = 0$$

The numbered nodes are similar to transshipment nodes in our distribution models, because the inputs and outputs are the same material. At node 1, distillate must be split into either feedstock (*Feed*) or gasoline blending input (*Blend*). The balance equation becomes:

$$Feed + Blend - Dist = 0$$

Nodes 2 and 3 have a similar structure:

$$BP + BR - Blend = 0$$
$$CP + CR - Cat = 0$$

Nodes 4 and 5 are also of this type:

$$Prem - BP - CP = 0$$
$$Reg - BR - CR = 0$$

The system of balance equations and the network flow diagram are different representations of the same model. We can use one form to debug the other by checking for consistency and eliminating structural errors.

In addition to the network flows in this problem, other types of information are needed, including:

- production capacities for each production process
- sales potentials for final products
- blending specifications for gasoline

The first two of these can be stated in appropriate dimensions, such as barrels per day, while the third describes limits on the ratio in which gasoline inputs may be mixed. To illustrate the entire model, suppose the following parametric assumptions apply:

- tower and cracker capacities: 50,000 and 20,000 barrels/day
- sales potential for regular and premium gasoline: 16,000 barrels/day each
- sales potential for byproducts: unlimited
- blending floor for catalytic in regular gasoline: at least 50 percent catalytic
- blending floor for catalytic in premium gasoline: at least 75 percent catalytic

To complete the model, we need the economic factors that make up the objective function. Suppose the following parametric assumptions apply:

- cost of crude oil: $28 per barrel
- cost of operating the tower: $5 per barrel of crude
- cost of operating the cracker: $6 per barrel of feedstock
- revenue for high-end and low-end byproducts: $44 and $36 per barrel, respectively
- revenue for regular and premium gasoline: $50 and $55 per barrel, respectively

10.7.2 Spreadsheet Model

Figure 10.27 shows a spreadsheet model for the entire problem. We see the balance equations in the first portion of the Constraints module, in rows 12–20. The next pair of constraints, in rows 21–22, contains the blending quality requirements for the grades of gasoline. Finally, the four constraints in rows 23–26 contain the ceilings on production capacities and sales volumes. These could alternatively be incorporated as upper bounds on the variables *Crude*, *Prem*, *Reg* and *Prem*.

The objective function is made up of revenue from the sale of outputs, the cost of operations and the cost of input materials. For clarity, we devote a row of the spreadsheet to each of these components of the objective function, recognizing that several of these cells do not apply. In fact, intermediate products such as distillate are not directly associated with either costs or revenues. The value of the objective function, calculated as a SUMPRODUCT, appears in cell O9.

FIGURE 10.27 Worksheet for the Delta Oil Model

	A	B	C	D	E	F	G	H	I	J	K	L	M	N	O	P	Q
1	Refinery Planning Problem																
2																	
3	Decisions	Crude	Dist	Low	Blend	Feed	Cat	High	BR	BP	CR	CP	Reg	Prem			
4	Kbbl.	49.3	29.6	19.7	9.6	20.0	12.8	8.0	8.00	1.60	8.00	4.80	16.0	6.4			
5	Objective																
6	price			36				44					50	55			
7	cost	5				6											
8	cost	28															
9	net	-33	0	36	0	-6	0	44	0	0	0	0	50	55	466.400		
10	Constraints														LHS		RHS
11																	
12	Tower	-0.60	1	0	0	0	0	0	0	0	0	0	0	0	0.0	=	0
13	Tower	0	0	1	0	0	0	0	0	0	0	0	0	0	0.0	=	0
14	Distillate split	0	-1	0	1	1	0	0	0	0	0	0	0	0	0.0	=	0
15	Cracker	0	0	0	0	-0.64	1	0	0	0	0	0	0	0	0.0	=	0
16	Cracker	0	0	0	0	-0.40	0	1	0	0	0	0	0	0	0.0	=	0
17	Blend split	0	0	0	-1	0	0	0	1	1	0	0	0	0	0.0	=	0
18	Catalytic split	0	0	0	0	0	-1	0	0	0	1	1	0	0	0.0	=	0
19	Reg composition	0	0	0	0	0	0	0	-1	0	-1	0	1	0	0.0	=	0
20	Prem composition	0	0	0	0	0	0	0	0	-1	0	-1	0	1	0.0	=	0
21	Reg quality	0	0	0	0	0	0	0	-0.50	0	0.50	0	0	0	0.0	>=	0
22	Prem quality	0	0	0	0	0	0	0	0	-0.75	0	0.25	0	0	0.0	>=	0
23	Tower capacity	1	0	0	0	0	0	0	0	0	0	0	0	0	49.3	<=	50
24	Cracker capacity	0	0	0	0	1	0	0	0	0	0	0	0	0	20.0	<=	20
25	Reg sales	0	0	0	0	0	0	0	0	0	0	0	1	0	16.0	<=	16
26	Prem sales	0	0	0	0	0	0	0	0	0	0	0	0	1	6.4	<=	16
27																	

10.27

10.7.3 Optimization

For the model specification, we enter the following information:

Variables: B4:N4
Objective: O9 (maximize)
Constraints: O12:O20 = Q12:Q20
O21:O22 ≥ Q21:Q22
O23:O26 ≤ Q23:Q26

Figure 10.27 displays the optimal solution to the Delta Oil Company model. In brief, the solution achieves a profit contribution of $466,400. It calls for purchases of 49,300 barrels of crude oil. This quantity leaves the tower with a small amount of excess capacity, but cracker capacity is fully utilized by the optimal allocation of distillate. Sales of regular gasoline are limited by market potential, but this is not the case for premium. Both gasoline products are blended at their minimum quality requirements, suggesting that catalytic is a scarce resource. A brief look at the decision variables reveals that there is flow on every arc in the network diagram.

Viewed as strategic information, the optimal solution provides useful insights into the determinants of profitability at Delta Oil. Of the two main pieces of process equipment, the cracker is currently the more constraining; however, the tower is not far behind. Capacity may have to be raised in both places for Delta to significantly increase its profits. On the output side, profits are also constrained by demand for regular gasoline. If the marketing department could find additional customers for regular gasoline, this could also lead to increased profits. In short, the strategic implications of the Delta Oil model are typical of product mix models; however, the construction of the model itself is driven by the principles of network modeling.

10.8 SUMMARY

Network models, like the allocation, covering, and blending models of the previous chapter, represent a distinct class of linear programs. Network models have special advantages because network diagrams can be used in the modeling process:

- The diagram helps delineate the scope of the model (that is, what to include and what to exclude).
- The diagram defines decision variables by creating arcs.
- The diagram specifies material balance constraints by creating nodes.

- The diagram is relatively easy to understand because it is a visual model.

- The diagram serves as a debugging tool because its elements match up with the elements of an algebraic model or a spreadsheet model.

- The diagram serves as a communication tool, because it conveniently displays system structure, model solution, and even sensitivity analysis.

Transportation, assignment, and transshipment models exhibit a characteristic From/To structure that lends itself readily to spreadsheet display. Rather than laying out decisions along a single row, as in the standard form, this structure allows the model to be built with an array layout for decisions and key objective-function parameters. One additional feature of these models is that they produce integer-valued decisions in the optimal solution.

The balance equations that were first encountered in transshipment nodes are the key constraint format for network models, extending to models in which yield factors apply and even to process models where the inflow and outflow may not be of the same material. The constraints in some network linear programs consist exclusively of balance equations, whereas constraints in more complicated models may include allocation, covering, and blending constraints appended to a central network representation.

Finally, the concepts of sensitivity analysis that were introduced in the previous chapter apply as well to network models. In particular, when it comes to interpreting optimal solutions, the network diagram is a convenient device for constructing patterns. The diagram often provides visual hints that lead to a systematic description of the economic priorities in the solution of a network linear program.

EXERCISES

1. *Transporting Coal.* The Calcio Coal Company produces coal at four mines and ships it to four power plants (P1-P4). The cost per ton of producing coal and the production capacity (in tons) for each mine are known. The number of tons of coal demanded by each customer is also known. The cost (in dollars) of shipping a ton of coal from a mine to each plant is available as well. The following table provides the data:

	P1	P2	P3	P4	Capacity	Cost
Mine 1	9	15	8	10	125	50
Mine 2	7	15	14	12	100	57
Mine 3	5	5	11	12	150	55
Mine 4	3	6	8	11	120	61
Demands	110	115	135	130		

a. Calcio wishes to minimize the cost of transporting coal from its mines to its plants. What is the minimum cost?

b. What is the transportation schedule that achieves the minimum cost in (a)?

2. *Planning Procurement.* An automobile manufacturer wants to award contracts for the supply of five different engine components. Some of the components are used in most models, while other components are specialized to one or two models — therefore, the volumes differ. Five contractors have submitted bids on the components, and the following table summarizes the prices bid per unit. Where no entry appears, the contractor did not bid.

	Component				
	C1	C2	C3	C4	C5
Supplier 1	25	—	55	42	40
Supplier 2	28	78	—	44	41
Supplier 3	30	80	58	40	—
Supplier 4	—	82	57	43	—
Supplier 5	32	88	60	—	42
Demand	40,000	10,000	25,000	10,000	30,000

The manufacturer wants to determine how many units of each component should be awarded to each contractor in order to minimize total cost for the purchases. (For these purposes, fractional solutions in the model are acceptable.)

a. What is the minimum total cost for the manufacturer, if no other conditions are imposed?

b. In fact, Supplier 2 is capacity-constrained and cannot provide more than 25,000 units in total. In addition, the manufacturer does not want more that $2 million allocated to any one of the suppliers. Recognizing these limitations, what is the minimum total cost for the manufacturer?

c. Describe the qualitative pattern (computational scheme) in the solution for (b).

3. *Shipping Carpets.* A manufacturer of nylon carpets produces rolls of carpeting at four factories and ships them to distributors in five locations The following table shows the capacities at the factories and the demands at the distributors for the next quarter, all given in thousands of rolls. Also shown are the unit transportation costs between each factory and each distributor, stated in cost per roll.

To Distributor:	D1	D2	D3	D4	D5	Capacity
From F1	11	16	18	22	15	40
From F2	12	24	20	21	18	50
From F3	18	17	15	15	20	50
From F4	17	22	14	24	21	60
Demand	30	24	42	36	48	

a. What is the minimum-cost distribution plan for the quarter?

b. What is the cost of the distribution plan in part (a)?

c. Suppose instead that demand at D4 increases and demand at D3 decreases, each by 1,000 rolls. What is the new optimal cost, assuming that the schedule can be revised? (Answer this question using the pattern in the optimal solution, not by rerunning the model.)

4. *Distributing Locks.* The Lannon Lock Company manufactures a commercial security lock at plants in Atlanta,

Louisville, Detroit, and Phoenix. The unit cost of production at each plant is $35.50, $37.50, $37.25, and $36.25, respectively; the annual capacities are 18,000, 15,000, 25,000, and 20,000, respectively. The locks are sold through wholesale distributors in seven locations around the country. The unit shipping cost for each plant-distributor combination is shown in the following table, along with the demand forecast from each distributor for the coming year:

	Tacoma	San Diego	Dallas	Denver	St. Louis	Tampa	Balti-more
Atlanta	2.50	2.75	1.75	2.00	2.10	1.80	1.65
Louisville	1.85	1.90	1.50	1.60	1.00	1.90	1.85
Detroit	2.30	2.25	1.85	1.25	1.50	2.25	2.00
Phoenix	1.90	0.90	1.60	1.75	2.00	2.50	2.65
Demand	5,500	11,500	10,500	9,600	15,400	12,500	6,600

a. Determine the least costly way of producing and shipping locks from plants to distributors.

b. Suppose that the unit cost at each plant were $10 higher than the original figure. What change in the optimal distribution plan would result? What general conclusions can you draw for transportation models with nonidentical plant-related costs?

5. *Scheduling Umpires.* Chris Pearson is running a tennis tournament and is in the process of scheduling the umpires for each match in today's rounds. There are five matches to be played today, and there are six umpires available. Every match needs exactly one umpire and no umpire can be assigned to more than one match. The following table shows the number of times (in the past) that each umpire has been scheduled for a match involving one of the competing players in each of the matches. Chris wants to assign umpires to matches in a way that avoids placing umpires with players they have seen many times.

	Previous Pairings				
Umpire	Singles Semifinal 1	Singles Semifinal 2	Doubles Semifinal 1	Doubles Semifinal 1	Junior Final
1	2	1	2	2	2
2	3	0	1	4	1
3	2	2	2	2	0
4	3	2	0	2	3
5	3	3	4	1	0
6	0	1	1	5	1

a. Chris has decided to minimize the sum of the number of times the umpires have previously been paired with the players. What is the optimal assignment of umpires to matches?

b. Suppose Chris were to apply a weighting factor to the assignments, treating the assignments in the three singles matches as if they counted double the other assignments. Does this change the optimal assignments?

6. *Assigning Engineers.* A small engineering firm has 4 senior designers available to work on the firm's 4 current projects over the next 2 weeks. The firm's manager has developed the following table of quality scores, which show each designer's design quality on each type of project, on a scale of 100. Also shown is an estimate of the time (in hours) required for each project.

	Project			
Designer	1	2	3	4
1	90	80	25	50
2	60	70	50	65
3	70	40	80	85
4	65	55	60	75
Time	70	50	85	35

a. Assume that one designer is assigned to each project. What assignment of designers to projects maximizes the sum of the quality scores assigned?

b. Suppose that each designer has 80 hours available over the next two weeks. Assuming that more than one designer can work on a project, what assignment schedule maximizes the sum of quality scores assigned?

7. *Shipping Fruit.* Wollmer Distribution Company collects fruit from several small farms in the region, consolidates its collections, and then ships the fruit to a regional wholesale fruit market by truck. Having made their collections, the company has in stock 57 tons of grapes, 62 tons of peaches, and 81 tons of bananas.

Wollmer owns four trucks that can transport fruit to market. Each truck has its own capacity, and Wollmer has discovered that yield losses occur at different rates depending on which fruit is carried in which truck. The truck suspension system and the efficiency of the refrigeration system seem to account for most of the losses. The following table shows the loss as a percentage:

	Grapes	Peaches	Bananas	Capacity
Truck 1	12%	10%	4%	40 T
Truck 2	12%	14%	5%	50 T
Truck 3	16%	13%	6%	55 T
Truck 4	18%	17%	8%	75 T

The current market prices for the three fruits are as follows:

Fruit	Price/Ton
Grapes	$500
Peaches	1,000
Bananas	1,750

a. As a logical way of loading the trucks, a Wollmer's dispatcher follows a standard rule: take the largest yield from the table of yields and assign as many tons as possible; then go on to the next largest yield available, and so on. For this rule, what is the resulting revenue and how many tons are brought to market?

b. What shipping plan will bring in the most revenue for Wollmer? What is the optimal total revenue?

c. In the optimal solution, how many tons of fruit are delivered to market? What is the maximum possible number of tons brought to market?

8. *Buying and Selling a Commodity.* A small firm buys and sells wheat. They own a warehouse with a capacity of 10,000 bushels, and as of late August, there will be 2,000 bushels in the warehouse. Wheat is delivered to the warehouse during the first week of the month, and it is sold and shipped around the middle of the month. All transactions are on a cash basis because the season is short, and the firm expects to have $20,000 in its accounts at the end of August. This amount is available for making September purchases.

The latest predictions of market prices are shown in the following table:

	Sep 15	Oct 15	Nov 15
Buy	$5.45	$5.75	$6.00
Sell	$6.05	$6.25	$6.30

a. What buy-and-sell schedule will produce the maximum profit for the firm?

b. What is the optimal profit in part (a)?

c. How does the optimal plan change as a function of the firm's account balance? (Consider amounts both above and below the current $20,000.)

9. *Planning Investments.* Your uncle has $90,000 that he wishes to invest now in order to use the accumulation for purchasing a retirement annuity in five years. After consulting with his financial adviser, he has been offered four types of fixed income investments, labeled as investments A, B, C, and D.

Investments A and B are available at the beginning of each of the next five years (call them years 1 to 5). Each dollar invested in A at the beginning of a year returns $1.20 (a profit of $0.20) two years later, in time for immediate reinvestment. Each dollar invested in B at the beginning of a year returns $1.36 three years later.

Investments C and D will each be available at one time in the future. Each dollar invested in C at the beginning of year 2 returns $1.66 at the end of year 5. Each dollar invested in D at the beginning of year 5 returns $1.12 at the end of year 5.

Your uncle is obligated to make a balloon payment on an existing loan, in the amount of $24,000, at the end of year 3. He wants to cover that payment out of these funds as well.

a. Devise an investment plan for your uncle that maximizes the amount of money that can be accumulated at the end of five years. How much money will be available for the annuity in five years?

b. Describe the pattern in the optimal plan.

10. *Financial Planning.* Your sister has just won $300,000 (tax-free) in the state lottery. She's decided to quit her job and devote herself to writing novels for the next ten years, using her lottery winnings to support herself. She figures that she will need $30,000 of income at the start of the coming year, $31,000 at the start of next year, $32,000 for the third year, and so on. In order to meet these expenses, she plans to invest her lottery winnings all at once, in bonds. If she finds that she has extra cash in any year (including the first), she plans to place it in her savings account, which pays 3 percent annual interest, but she does not want to purchase any additional bonds in the future.

At the start of the coming year, bonds with one-, three-, five-, and 10-year maturities will become available on the market. If a bond matures in k years, it pays $100 at the end of each of k years, as well as $1,000 at the end of the kth year. Currently, one-year bonds sell for $1,075, three-year bonds for $1,100, five-year bonds for $1,200, and ten-year bonds for $1,300.

Your sister wants to make sure that the income from her investments will provide for her living expenses year by year. She has asked you to advise her on how many bonds to purchase and has offered to give you any funds left over at the end of the ten-year period.

a. Assume that you wish to maximize the amount of money available to you at the end of ten years. How many of each type of bond should your sister purchase? (Assume that these bonds can be purchased in fractional amounts, as part of an investment pool.)

b. How much money will be available to you at the end of ten years?

c. Suppose you investigate other savings banks and find that interest rates higher than 3 percent are available. What is the minimum interest rate that would alter which of the four types of bonds your sister should buy?

11. *Planning Inventories.* The National Tire Company (NTC) manufactures only one type of tire and wants to plan its production and inventory levels for the next five months. Company policy is to schedule all of its overtime production during one month. The table at the bottom of the page provides the relevant data for each month, where the inventory level requirements refer to the level at the end of each month.

Other relevant information is as follows:

- NTC estimates that it costs $1 to hold one tire in inventory from one month to the next.

- NTC currently has an inventory level of 4,000 tires.

- NTC wants to meet its demand with no backorders; that is, all demand must be met no later than the month in which it occurs.

Month	Unit Demand	Production Cost	Maximum Production Level	Minimum Production Level	Maximum Inventory Level	Minimum Inventory Level
1	12,000	$11.00	18,000	6,000	10,000	2,000
2	18,000	$11.00	18,000	6,000	10,000	2,000
3	24,000	$11.50	30,000	6,000	15,000	2,000
4	20,000	$11.00	18,000	6,000	10,000	2,000
5	22,000	$11.00	18,000	6,000	10,000	2,000

a. Construct a network diagram to represent the NTC scenario. Using the diagram, build a spreadsheet model for the production and inventory plan.

b. What is the minimum total cost, including production and inventory costs, for the five-month period (ignoring the cost of the initial inventory)? What production levels minimize total cost?

12. *Scheduling a Refinery.* Coastal Refining Company operates a refinery with a distillation capacity of 12,000 barrels per day. As a new member of Coastal's management team, you have been given the task of developing a production schedule for the refinery, i.e., determining how much of which products to produce and how.

In simplified form, the refinery process starts with distillation, which feeds crude oil into a *pipestill*, as it is commonly called. Here the crude is heated, and as the temperature rises, different products are given off in vapor form. These products can be collected separately and sold as produced, or blended and sold, or else processed further in a *catalytic cracker*. In the cracker, less profitable products such as heating oil can be converted to more profitable products such as naphtha. Finally, the various products of the pipestill and the cracker are blended and sold on the marketplace.

To streamline the analysis, the lighter distillation products have been grouped under the single category of *naphtha*. Similarly, the lighter streams from the catalytic cracker have been grouped under the single category of *catalytic naphtha*. Based on present operation, a satisfactory gasoline blend can be obtained by combining the straight-run naphtha (directly from the pipestill) and catalytic naphtha in the ratio of at most 5 parts straight run to 4 parts catalytic.

Two crude oil sources are available to the refinery, in quantities up to 10,000 barrels per day for each source of crude. The yields from distillation and the delivered cost of the inputs are as follows:

	Crude 1	Crude 2
Naphtha	0.20	0.15
Diesel Fuel	0.25	0.20
Gasoil	0.40	0.30
Heating Oil	0.10	0.20
Pitch	0.05	0.10
Cost/barrel	$34	$32

The yields for each of the crude oil sources add to less than one because there is always some residue from the process, averaging 10 percent.

Heating oil can be used as feedstock to the catalytic cracker, or alternatively, it can be treated and sold in the form produced by the pipestill. Gasoil can also be fed to the cracker, or, with some blending, it can be sold as equipment fuel. The blending process requires that at least 1 part diesel fuel must be mixed with 4 parts gasoil.

In the catalytic cracking process, the feedstock is recycled through the cracker until fully converted. For example, each barrel of gasoil originally fed into the catalytic cracker uses an average of 4 barrels of capacity when fully cycled. The products of this process will be catalytic naphtha, catalytic heating oil, and pitch. When heating oil is used as feedstock, the possibilities are a bit more complicated. In normal mode, each barrel of heating oil originally fed into the catalytic cracker uses an average of 2.5 barrels of capacity when fully cycled; but there is also a "high-severity" mode of operation, which uses an average of 2.0 barrels of capacity. The capacity of the catalytic cracker is 15,000 barrels of throughput per day and its yields are as follows:

	Heating Oil— Normal	Heating Oil— Hi-severity	Gasoil
Catalytic naphtha	30%	35%	50%
Catalytic heating oil	70%	80%	50%
Pitch	10%	15%	15%

The sums exceed 100 percent because the cracking process reduces the density of the output.

Current prices (in dollars per barrel) for the major final products are as follows: gasoline $42, diesel fuel $38, catalytic heating oil $36, straight-run heating oil $35, equipment fuel $32 and pitch $25. The marketing department has indicated that the company could probably not sell more than 4,000 barrels per day each of diesel fuel and catalytic heating oil, but it could sell as much of the other products as the refinery is able to produce.

A recent internal study has reported that the direct processing cost per barrel of crude oil going into the pipestill is $1.20 and the direct cost for the catalytic cracker is $1.50 per barrel of input, with a 15 percent premium for the high-severity mode of operation.

a. What is the optimal schedule for Coastal Refining?

b. What is the optimal total cost?

c. What are the shadow prices for pipestill capacity and cracker capacity? Over what ranges do these figures hold? What do they tell us about the value of capacity expansion?

11 Integer Optimization

11.1 INTRODUCTION

One of the basic assumptions in linear programming models relates to divisibility of the decision variables: Fractional values of decision variables make sense either literally (12.6 tons of steel can be produced) or as a modeling approximation (in practical terms, 1,776.2 trucks is the same as 1,776). The optimal solution of a linear program may therefore contain fractional decision variables, and this is appropriate—or at least tolerable—in most applications. In some cases, however, it may be necessary to ensure that some or all of the decision variables take on integer values. Accommodating the requirement that variables must be integers is the subject of **integer programming**. In this chapter, we examine the formulation and solution of integer programs.

Before we discuss how to handle the integer requirement with Solver, we review what we have already covered that relates to the subject of fractional values for decision variables. There are, for example, some problem types where the occurrence of fractional decision variables can be avoided entirely. In transportation, assignment, and transshipment models, which were covered in the previous chapter, integer solutions are always produced (provided the supply and demand parameters are integers) without an explicit requirement. As those examples might suggest, there are categories of linear programs that can guarantee integer solutions, but a comprehensive treatment of those special cases is beyond the scope of our coverage.

In some cases, we might be interested mainly in the strategic information that comes with a linear program's solution. That is, we may want to identify the qualitative pattern in the optimal solution, or we may want to find the shadow prices as a guide for strategic initiatives. Neither of these goals is inhibited by a solution that contains fractions. In fact, imposing integer requirements can make it harder to identify certain strategic information. But on some occasions, only an integer solution will do.

Consider the product mix for chairs, desks, and tables discussed in the Veerman Furniture model of Chapter 9. As it turned out, the optimal solution contains no chairs, 275 desks, and 100 tables, so that the decision variables happen to all be integers. Suppose instead that the problem occurs with only 1,800 fabrication hours available, rather than the 1,850 of the base case. As we can see in Figure 11.1, the optimal product mix includes 266.67 desks. Is the fractional number of desks meaningful?

On the surface, it may seem to make no sense to talk about two-thirds of a desk in the product mix. Certainly, if we were interested in the tactical implications of the solution, it would not make sense for us to prescribe the production of two-thirds of a desk to help meet demand. However, there are two interpretations of the fraction that do make sense. For one, we may be willing to round off or truncate fractional values. That is, we might interpret the optimal solution as 266 desks and 100 tables. Although this truncated solution does not use every last hour of capacity, the unused time is about a tenth of one percent of fabrication capacity. The impact on the objective function is equally small. The underlying uncertainty in our knowledge of all the parameters in the model is likely to be much larger than a tenth of one percent. Thus, *any* solution to the model is somewhat approximate. Therefore, rounding is often a perfectly acceptable way of dealing with fractional decision variables.

A second interpretation is also possible. We might want to think of the solution as resulting from a planning model that specifies conditions in a typical week. In that context, when we encounter a figure such as 266.67 in the optimal mix, we could interpret it as prescribing 267 desks for the first two weeks and then 266 desks in the third. That is, we

FIGURE 11.1 Optimal Solution to Linear Version of the Veerman Furniture Model

	A	B	C	D	E	F	G
1	**Allocation: Furniture Production**						
2							
3	**Decision Variables**						
4			C	D	T		
5	Product mix	0	266.667	100			
6							
7	**Objective Function**				*Total*		
8	Profit	15	24	18	$8,200		
9							
10							
11	**Constraints**				*LHS*		*RHS*
12	Fabrication	4	6	2	1800	<=	1800
13	Assembly	3	5	7	2033.333	<=	2400
14	Shipping	3	2	4	933.3333	<=	1500
15	Chair market	1	0	0	0	<=	360
16	Desk market	0	1	0	266.6667	<=	300
17	Table market	0	0	1	100	<=	100
18							

might interpret the solution as the long run average of a repeated activity, where, again, fractions could easily make sense. Thus, rounded-off values and planning averages provide us with two reasons why we might tolerate fractional answers to linear programming problems when they seem impractical in literal terms.

11.2   INTEGER VARIABLES AND THE INTEGER SOLVER

Rounded solutions and planning averages aside, there are still situations where only integers will suffice; for example, when projects must be funded in full or not at all, or when producing a small quantity of large items such as airplanes. In those cases, we must be able to specify that the decision variables be integers.

Solver allows us to directly designate decision variables as integer valued. Adding an integer requirement to a model that is otherwise a nonlinear programming problem or a linear programming problem will give rise to an **integer nonlinear programming problem**, or to an **integer linear programming problem**. In the case of integer linear programs, Solver employs an algorithm that checks all possible assignments of integer values to variables, although some of the assignments may not have to be examined explicitly. This procedure may require the solution of a large number of linear programs, but because Solver can do this quickly and reliably with the simplex algorithm, it will eventually locate a global optimum. In the case of integer nonlinear programs, however, the solution is more challenging because the GRG algorithm cannot distinguish between local optima and global optima. Recognizing that integer nonlinear programs are difficult to solve, we limit our attention in this chapter to linear integer programs.

The use of Solver for integer programming models, once they are formulated, is relatively straightforward. The requirement that a variable must be an integer is treated in Solver much like an additional constraint. Along with the constraint choices of $\leq, \geq$, and $=$, the Solver constraint window also permits the choice of **int** and **bin**. The *int* constraint forces a variable to be *int*eger valued, and the *bin* constraint forces a variable to be either zero or one (*bin*ary valued). As an example, we return to the fractional version of Veerman Furniture from Figure 11.1. Using the Constraints menu in the ribbon, we select Normal Constraint and then the icon for "<=" to obtain the Add Constraint window. Then, we can designate all three variables as integers in the Add Constraint window, as shown in Figure 11.2.

After the model has been built and particular variables have been designated as integer or binary, the next step is to select the Integer Tolerance parameter, which can be found on the Engine tab in the task pane, as shown in Figure 11.3. The default value is normally set at 0, but in earlier versions of the software, the default was 0.05. At 0.05, Solver is guaranteed only to find a solution that is no worse than 5 percent away from the optimal solution. Clearly, we want to find the very best solution, and this calls for setting the Tolerance parameter equal to 0. However, the tighter Tolerance level may require the

FIGURE 11.2 Designating Variables as Integers

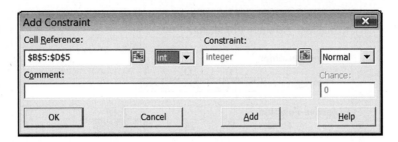

solution procedure to take more time, especially in larger models. Therefore, we sometimes keep the level at 5 percent while we are debugging a large model. If we find that Solver can locate a solution at the 5 percent Tolerance level in a reasonable amount of time, we can experiment by lowering the Tolerance toward the 0 percent level. In our example, which is not a large problem, we set the Tolerance to 0 percent as shown in Figure 11.3. For the model specification, we enter the following information:

$$\begin{array}{rl} \text{Variables:} & \text{B5:D5} \\ \text{Objective:} & \text{E8 (maximize)} \\ \text{Constraints:} & \text{B5:D5} = \text{integer} \\ & \text{E12:E17} \leq \text{G12:G17} \end{array}$$

We obtain the solution shown in Figure 11.4. There are two features of the solution we should anticipate. First, because designating a variable as an integer imposes a constraint that did not originally apply, the objective function cannot get better and will likely get worse. Second, no fractions should occur in the decision variables. This is precisely what we find in the optimal solution: The objective function drops from $8,200 to $8,199, and the optimal mix consists of 1 chair, 266 desks, and 100 tables. This solution is close to the fractional solution, although it is neither a rounded-down solution nor a rounded-off solution. (Of course, Veerman Furniture is unlikely to adopt a plan that calls for just one chair, even if it is optimal for the model.)

FIGURE 11.3 Setting the Tolerance Parameter

FIGURE 11.4 Optimal Solution to the Integer Version of the Veerman Furniture Model

	A	B	C	D	E	F	G
1	Allocation: Furniture Production						
2							
3	Decision Variables						
4			C	D	T		
5	Product mix	1	266	100			
6							
7	Objective Function				Total		
8	Profit	15	24	18	$8,199		
9							
10							
11	Constraints				LHS		RHS
12	Fabrication	4	6	2	1800	<=	1800
13	Assembly	3	5	7	2033	<=	2400
14	Shipping	3	2	4	935	<=	1500
15	Chair market	1	0	0	1	<=	360
16	Desk market	0	1	0	266	<=	300
17	Table market	0	0	1	100	<=	100
18							

As this example suggests, many integer programming models are simply linear programs with certain variables constrained to be integers. To solve these models requires only one or two additional steps beyond those required to solve linear programs. It might appear, therefore, that integer programming is just a minor technical extension of linear programming. However, binary variables allow us to model a number of frequently occurring situations that cannot be modeled using standard linear programming techniques. In the remainder of the chapter, we discuss examples of that class of models.

11.3 BINARY VARIABLES AND BINARY CHOICE MODELS

A binary variable, which takes on the values zero or one, can be used to represent a "go/no-go" decision. We can think in terms of discrete projects, where the decision to accept the project is represented by the value 1, and the decision to reject the project is represented by the value 0. In this section, we examine two problem types that involve **binary choice**.

11.3.1 The Capital Budgeting Problem

Companies, committees, and even households often find themselves facing a problem of allocating a capital budget. As the problem arises in many firms, there is a specified budget for the year, to be invested in multi-year projects. There are also several proposed projects under consideration. Often, a high-level committee is responsible for reviewing the proposals and for deciding which projects to undertake. In modeling terms, the committee's job is to determine how to maximize the value of the projects selected, subject to the limitation on expenditures represented by the capital budget.

In the classic version of the **capital budgeting problem**, each project is described by two values: the expenditure required and the value of the project. As a project is typically a multi-year activity, its value is represented by the net present value (NPV) of its cash flows over the project life. The expenditure, combined with the expenditures of other projects selected, cannot be more than the budget available.

EXAMPLE
The Marr Corporation

Division A of the Marr Corporation has been allocated $160 million for capital projects this year. Managers in Division A have examined various possibilities and have proposed five projects for Marr's capital budgeting committee to consider. The projects cover a variety of activities, as the following list shows:

P1   Implement a new information system.

P2   License a new technology from another firm.

P3   Build a state-of-the-art recycling facility.

P4   Install an automated machining center in production.

P5   Move the receiving department to new facilities on site.

There is just one project of each type. Each project has an estimated NPV and each requires a capital expenditure, which must come out of the budget for capital projects. The following table summarizes the possibilities, with all figures in millions of dollars:

| | Project | | | | |
	P1	P2	P3	P4	P5
NPV	10	17	16	8	14
Expenditure	48	96	80	32	64

The committee would like to maximize the total NPV from projects selected, subject to the budget limit of $160 million. ■

We can formulate this problem as an allocation model with one constraint. To construct an algebraic model, we let

$$y_j = 1 \text{ if project } j \text{ is accepted; and } 0 \text{ otherwise}$$

The decision variables y_j represent binary choice. When $y_j = 1$, project j is selected to be part of the set of projects undertaken; when $y_j = 0$, project j is rejected. Only these two binary values have meaning as decisions. An algebraic statement of the model is the following:

$$\text{Maximize } z = 10y_1 + 17y_2 + 16y_3 + 8y_4 + 14y_5$$

subject to

$$48y_1 + 96y_2 + 80y_3 + 32y_4 + 64y_5 \leq 160$$

The corresponding worksheet is shown in Figure 11.5. (A feasible but suboptimal set of choices is displayed in the model.) Let's first solve this model as a linear programming problem without binary constraints. To run the model, we specify the following information:

Variables:	C5:G5
Objective:	H7 (maximize)
Constraints:	H9 $\leq$ J9

If we optimize this model, the optimal NPV is $40 million, but the solution (see Figure 11.6) would be to select project P4 *five times*. This is because P4 has the lowest cost per dollar of NPV. However, these are one-of-a-kind projects; none can be implemented more than once.

If we were to optimize the model as a linear program with each of the variables constrained to be no more than 1, the NPV would be $35.2 million (see Figure 11.7), and

FIGURE 11.5 Worksheet for the Marr Corporation Model

	A	B	C	D	E	F	G	H	I	J
1	**Capital Budgeting**									
2										
3	**Decisions**									
4			P1	P2	P3	P4	P5			
5		1 for Yes	0	1	0	1	0			
6	**Objective**									
7		NPV	10	17	16	8	14	25.000		
8	**Constraints**									
9		Capital	48	96	80	32	64	128.000	<=	160.000
10										

11.5

FIGURE 11.6 Solution to the Linear Version of the Marr Corporation Model

	A	B	C	D	E	F	G	H	I	J	K
1	**Capital Budgeting**										
2											
3	**Decisions**										
4			P1	P2	P3	P4	P5				
5		1 for Yes	0	0	0	5	0				
6	**Objective**										
7		NPV	10	17	16	8	14	40.000			
8	**Constraints**										
9		Capital	48	96	80	32	64	160	<=	160	
10											

FIGURE 11.7 Solution to the Constrained Linear Version of the Marr Corporation Model

	A	B	C	D	E	F	G	H	I	J
1	**Capital Budgeting**									
2										
3	**Decisions**									
4			P1	P2	P3	P4	P5			
5		1 for Yes	1	0	0.2	1	1			
6	**Objective**									
7		NPV	10	17	16	8	14	35.200		
8	**Constraints**									
9		Capital	48	96	80	32	64	160.000	<=	160.000
10										

the optimal mix of projects would be P1, P4, P5, and 20 percent of P3. However, no fractional projects are possible. We must treat the projects as indivisible: The decision on each one is to either accept it or reject it entirely. Therefore, we must use binary variables, as all-or-nothing variables, for this purpose.

When we add the constraint that each variable is binary, as shown in Figure 11.8, and re-solve the problem, we obtain the maximum NPV of $34 million, by accepting projects P1, P3, and P4 (and consuming the entire $160 million budget). The worksheet containing the optimal solution is shown in Figure 11.9.

FIGURE 11.8 Designating Variables as Binary Integers

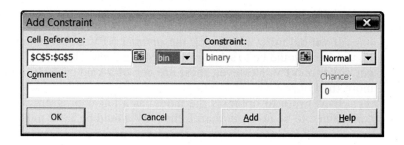

FIGURE 11.9 Optimal Solution to the Marr Corporation Model

	A	B	C	D	E	F	G	H	I	J
1	**Capital Budgeting**									
2										
3	**Decisions**									
4			P1	P2	P3	P4	P5			
5		1 for Yes	1	0	1	1	0			
6	**Objective**									
7		NPV	10	17	16	8	14	34.000		
8	**Constraints**									
9		Capital	48	96	80	32	64	160.000	<=	160.000
10										

11.3.2 The Set Covering Problem

In Chapter 9, we encountered the covering model as one of the basic structures in linear programming. The **set covering problem** is a variation of the covering model in which the variables are all binary. In addition, the parameters in the constraints are all zeroes and ones.

In the classic version of the set covering problem, each project is described by a subset of locations that it "covers." The problem is to cover all locations with a minimal number of projects.

EXAMPLE
Emergency Coverage in Metropolis

The city of Metropolis is in the process of designing a new public emergency system, and their design calls for locating emergency vehicles around the city. The city is divided into nine districts, and seven potential sites have been identified as possible locations for emergency vehicles. Equipment located at each potential site can reach some (but not all) of the districts within the 3-minute time requirement specified by the city. In the following table, an entry of 1 means that the district can be serviced from the corresponding site within the time requirement.

Site	S1	S2	S3	S4	S5	S6	S7
District D1	0	1	0	1	0	0	1
District D2	1	0	0	0	0	1	1
District D3	0	1	0	0	0	1	1
District D4	0	1	1	0	1	1	0
District D5	1	0	1	0	1	0	0
District D6	1	0	0	1	0	1	0
District D7	1	0	0	0	0	0	1
District D8	0	0	1	1	1	0	0
District D9	1	0	0	0	1	0	0

The city wants to provide coverage to all nine districts within the specified time, using the minimum number of sites. ∎

The name *set covering* comes from the fact that each site can be associated with a set of districts that it covers. For example, site S1 is associated with the set {0 1 0 0 1 1 1 0 1} that appears as the first column of the table. If we select S1 to be a site for emergency equipment, then we will have covered districts D2, D5, D6, D7, and D9. For a solution to be feasible, we would have to choose the remaining sites so that they cover D1, D3, D4, and D8.

To formulate a model, we let $y_j = 1$ if site j is selected and 0 otherwise. Then our optimization problem may be stated as follows:

$$\text{Minimize } z = y_1 + y_2 + y_3 + y_4 + y_5 + y_6 + y_7$$

subject to:

$$
\begin{array}{rrrrrrrr}
& y_2 & & +y_4 & & & +y_7 & \geq 1 \\
y_1 & & & & & +y_6 & +y_7 & \geq 1 \\
& y_2 & & & & +y_6 & +y_7 & \geq 1 \\
& y_2 & +y_3 & & +y_5 & +y_6 & & \geq 1 \\
y_1 & & +y_3 & & +y_5 & & & \geq 1 \\
y_1 & & & +y_4 & & +y_6 & & \geq 1 \\
y_1 & & & & & & +y_7 & \geq 1 \\
& & +y_3 & +y_4 & +y_5 & & & \geq 1 \\
y_1 & & & & +y_5 & & & \geq 1 \\
\end{array}
$$

In this algebraic form, all coefficients in the objective function are 1, all constraint coefficients are 0 or 1, and all right-hand side constants are 1. Thus, the model is a specialized covering model, but with the added provision that all variables are binary.

FIGURE 11.10 Work-sheet for the Metropolis Model

	A	B	C	D	E	F	G	H	I	J	K	L
1	Set Covering											
2												
3	Decisions	Site	S1	S2	S3	S4	S5	S6	S7			
4		1=Yes	0	1	1	1	0	1	0			
5												
6	Objective	Sites	1	1	1	1	1	1	1	4		
7												
8	Constraints									cover?		
9		D1	0	1	0	1	0	0	1	2	>=	1
10		D2	1	0	0	0	0	1	1	1	>=	1
11		D3	0	1	0	0	0	1	1	2	>=	1
12		D4	0	1	1	0	1	1	0	3	>=	1
13		D5	1	0	1	0	1	0	0	1	>=	1
14		D6	1	0	0	1	0	1	0	2	>=	1
15		D7	1	0	0	0	0	0	1	0	>=	1
16		D8	0	0	1	1	1	0	0	2	>=	1
17		D9	1	0	0	0	1	0	0	0	>=	1
18												

FIGURE 11.11 Optimal Solution for the Metropolis Model

	A	B	C	D	E	F	G	H	I	J	K	L
1	Set Covering											
2												
3	Decisions	Site	S1	S2	S3	S4	S5	S6	S7			
4		1=Yes	1	0	0	1	0	1	0			
5												
6	Objective	Sites	1	1	1	1	1	1	1	3		
7												
8	Constraints									cover?		
9		D1	0	1	0	1	0	0	1	1	>=	1
10		D2	1	0	0	0	0	1	1	2	>=	1
11		D3	0	1	0	0	0	1	1	1	>=	1
12		D4	0	1	1	0	1	1	0	1	>=	1
13		D5	1	0	1	0	1	0	0	1	>=	1
14		D6	1	0	0	1	0	1	0	3	>=	1
15		D7	1	0	0	0	0	0	1	1	>=	1
16		D8	0	0	1	1	1	0	0	1	>=	1
17		D9	1	0	0	0	1	0	0	1	>=	1
18												

A spreadsheet model for the set covering example is shown in Figure 11.10, although the solution shown is not feasible. If we optimize this model as a linear program, we find that the decision variables turn out fractional, so it is essential to add the binary constraints on the variables. For the model specification, we enter the following information:

$$
\begin{aligned}
\text{Variables:} &\quad \text{C4:I4} \\
\text{Objective:} &\quad \text{J6 (minimize)} \\
\text{Constraints:} &\quad \text{C4:I4} = \text{binary} \\
&\quad \text{J9:J17} \le \text{L9:L17}
\end{aligned}
$$

The optimal solution, shown in Figure 11.11, requires three sites to cover all districts.

In the capital budgeting and set covering examples, we encountered models that resemble linear programming formulations except that the decisions involve binary choice. The use of binary variables was critical because linear programming formulations would not be able to find optimal solutions. In the next section, we study how binary variables can help us accommodate additional information in an otherwise linear model.

11.4 BINARY VARIABLES AND LOGICAL RELATIONSHIPS

We sometimes encounter additional conditions affecting the selection of projects in problems like capital budgeting. These include relationships among projects, fixed costs, and quantity discounts.

11.4.1 Relationships Among Projects

Projects can be related in any number of ways. We cover five types of relationships here:

- At least m projects must be selected.
- At most n projects must be selected.
- Exactly k projects must be selected.
- Some projects are mutually exclusive.
- Some projects have contingency relationships.

To illustrate, we return to the solution of our capital budgeting example, shown in Figure 11.9, where the solution is to adopt projects P1, P3, and P4. Suppose now that projects P2 and P5 are international projects, while the others are domestic. Suppose also that the committee wishes to select *at least one* of its projects from the international arena. We can then add a covering constraint to the base case:

$$y_2 + y_5 \geq 1$$

Because the variables are all binary, this constraint ensures that the combination

$$y_2 = y_5 = 0$$

is not allowed. Therefore, P2, or P5, or both, will be selected, thus satisfying the requirement of one international selection. We can append this covering constraint to the model in row 10 of the worksheet. Of course, the addition of a constraint may make the objective function worse, and in this case, the optimal NPV drops to \$32 million. Figure 11.12 shows that we can achieve this value by accepting projects P1, P4, and P5 (and incurring expenditures of only \$144 million).

This additional constraint illustrates that we can use binary variables to represent structural or policy relationships of the form:

- Select *at least m* of the possible projects.
- Select *at most n* of the possible projects.

Alternatively, management at Marr Corporation may believe that it lacks sufficient personnel to oversee three projects, so it might impose the constraint that exactly two of the projects be chosen. Then we could write:

$$y_1 + y_2 + y_3 + y_4 + y_5 = 2$$

This constraint limits the selection to exactly two projects.

Other relationships that we normally think of as "logical" relationships can also be expressed with binary variables. Suppose that projects P4 and P5 are **mutually exclusive** (for example, they could require some of the same staff resources). Then we could write:

$$y_4 + y_5 \leq 1$$

This constraint prohibits the combination:

$$y_4 = y_5 = 1$$

FIGURE 11.12 Marr Corporation Model with at least One International Project

	A	B	C	D	E	F	G	H	I	J
1	Capital Budgeting									
2										
3	Decisions									
4			P1	P2	P3	P4	P5			
5		1 for Yes	1	0	0	1	1			
6	Objective									
7		NPV	10	17	16	8	14	32.000		
8	Constraints									
9		Capital	48	96	80	32	64	144	<=	160
10				1			1	1	>=	1
11										

FIGURE 11.13 Marr Corporation Model with a Mutually Exclusive Constraint

	A	B	C	D	E	F	G	H	I	J	
1	**Capital Budgeting**										
2											
3	**Decisions**										
4			P1	P2	P3	P4	P5				
5		1 for Yes	0	1	0	0	1				
6	**Objective**										
7		NPV	10	17	16	8	14	31.000			
8	**Constraints**										
9		Capital	48	96	80	32	64	160	<=	160	
10				1			1	2	>=	1	
11						1	1	1	<=	1	
12											

11.12 **11.13**

The mutual exclusivity requirement is just a special case of the *at most n* relationship, but with $n = 1$. Figure 11.13 shows the worksheet for the expanded model, with the mutual exclusivity constraint entered in row 11. As the figure indicates, the new constraint alters the optimal solution, and the best choice is to adopt projects P2 and P5. This solution achieves an optimal NPV of only $31 million, while consuming the entire capital budget.

In addition, we sometimes encounter **contingency** relationships. Suppose that project P5 requires that P3 be selected. In other words, P5 is contingent on P3. To analyze logical requirements of this sort, consider all of the selection combinations for the binary variables. The following table shows that three of the four combinations are consistent with the contingency condition:

y_3	y_5	Consistent?
0	0	Yes
1	0	Yes
0	1	No
1	1	Yes

We can accommodate the three consistent combinations and exclude the one inconsistent combination by adding the following constraint:

$$y_3 - y_5 \geq 0$$

Figure 11.14 shows the result of entering the contingency constraint into row 12 of the worksheet. This time the objective function drops to $30 million, and projects P3 and P5 are selected, consuming $144 million of the budget.

The contingency constraint is an example of how we can include requirements that seem qualitative, or at least nonlinear, in a linear model by employing binary variables. Binary variables provide us with a convenient indicator of a project's status. With binary

FIGURE 11.14 Marr Corporation with a Contingency Constraint

	A	B	C	D	E	F	G	H	I	J	
1	**Capital Budgeting**										
2											
3	**Decisions**										
4			P1	P2	P3	P4	P5				
5		1 for Yes	0	0	1	0	1				
6	**Objective**										
7		NPV	10	17	16	8	14	30.000			
8	**Constraints**										
9		Capital	48	96	80	32	64	144	<=	160	
10				1			1	1	>=	1	
11						1	1	1	<=	1	
12					1		-1	0	>=	0	
13											

11.12 11.13 **11.14**

FIGURE 11.15 Graph of a Cost Function with a Fixed Cost Component

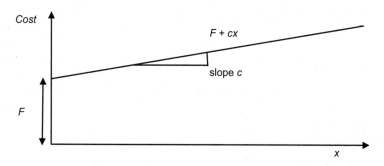

variables, we can represent qualitative or logical information about the set of projects in the model.

11.4.2 Linking Constraints and Fixed Costs

One of the assumptions in linear models is strict proportionality: The cost contributed by an activity is proportional to its activity level. However, we commonly encounter situations in which activity costs are composed of fixed costs and variable costs, with only the variable costs being proportional to activity level. With an integer programming model, we can also integrate the fixed component of cost.

Imagine that we have already built a linear programming model, but one variable (x) has a fixed cost that we want to represent in the objective function. To incorporate this fixed cost into the model, we separate the fixed and variable components of cost. In algebraic terms, we write cost as

$$Cost = Fy + cx,$$

where F represents the fixed cost, and c represents the linear variable cost. The variables x and y are decision variables, where x is a normal (continuous) variable and y is a binary variable. (See Figure 11.15.) Constraints in the linear program involve only the variable portion—that is, they involve only the variable x, not the variable y. In this situation, we also want to make sure that the variables x and y work together consistently. In particular, we want to have $y = 1$ (so that we incur the fixed cost) when $x > 0$, and we want to have $y = 0$ (so that we avoid the fixed cost) when $x = 0$. To achieve consistent linking of the two variables, we add the following generic **linking constraint** to the model:

$$x \leq My,$$

where the number M represents an upper bound on the variable x. In other words, M is at least as large as any value we can feasibly choose for x.

Why does the linking constraint work? As seen by Solver, this is just another feasibility condition to be satisfied. When $y = 0$ (and therefore no fixed cost is incurred), the right-hand side becomes zero, and Solver interprets the constraint as $x \leq 0$. Since we also require $x \geq 0$, these two constraints together force x to be zero. Thus, when $y = 0$, it will be consistent to avoid the fixed cost. On the other hand, when $y = 1$, the right-hand side will be so large that Solver does not need to restrict x at all, permitting its value to be positive while we incur the fixed cost. Thus, when $y = 1$, it will be consistent to incur the fixed cost. Of course, because we are optimizing, Solver will never produce a solution with the combination of $y = 1$ and $x = 0$, because it would always be preferable to set $y = 0$.

The following example illustrates the use of linking constraints for modeling fixed costs.

EXAMPLE
Mayhugh Manufacturing Company

Mayhugh Manufacturing, a medium-size job shop, has been producing and selling three product families. Each product family requires production hours in each of three departments. In addition, each product family requires its own sales force, which must be supported no matter how large or small the sales volume happens to be. The parameters describing the situation are summarized in the following table:

	Product Family			Hours Available
	F1	F2	F3	
Profit per unit	$1.20	$1.80	$2.20	
	Hours Required Per Thousand Units			Hours
Department A	3	4	8	2,000
Department B	3	5	6	2,000
Department C	2	3	9	2,000
Sales cost ($000)	60	200	100	
Demand (000)	400	300	50	

∎

At the heart of this situation lies a product-mix problem. The linear programming representation of the product-mix problem (with no fixed costs) is shown in Figure 11.16. By defining the x-values in thousands, we scale the model so that the objective function is in thousands of dollars. The optimal product mix calls for producing all three families, with F1 at 400,000, F2 at 100,000 and F3 at 50,000. This product mix creates $770,000 in variable profits. If we subtract the total fixed costs of $360,000, we are left with a net profit of $410,000, as calculated in cell F19 of the worksheet.

The linear programming solution might represent the situation for a firm that has introduced and supported various new products over the years and that now finds itself carrying out activities in three product markets. The linear programming framework suggests how to allocate capacity, provided that all three product families are active. However, there is no basis for determining whether any one of the families should be dropped, because fixed cost considerations are not within the scope of the linear programming analysis.

To formulate the full problem as an integer programming model, we make two changes. First, we write the objective function with separate terms for variable profit and fixed cost:

$$NetProfit = 1.20x_1 - 60y_1 + 1.80x_2 - 200y_2 + 2.20x_3 - 100y_3$$

where x_j represents the volume for family j, in thousands. Here, y_j is a binary variable that must take either the value 1 when x_j is positive (and the fixed cost is incurred) or the value 0 when x_j is zero (and the fixed cost is avoided). Next, we add three linking constraints to

FIGURE 11.16 Worksheet for a Product-Mix Version of the Mayhugh Example

	A	B	C	D	E	F	G	H
1	Product Mix (Kernel)							
2	Linear Programming Analysis							
3	Decisions							
4			F1	F2	F3			
5			400	100	50	K-units		
6								
7	Objective							
8		Variable profit	1.20	1.80	2.20	770		
9	Constraints							
10		X	3	4	8	2000	<=	2000
11		Y	3	5	6	2000	<=	2000
12		Z	2	3	9	1550	<=	2000
13			1			400	<=	400
14				1		100	<=	300
15					1	50	<=	50
16								
17		Fixed costs	60	200	100	360		
18								
19		Net Profit				410		
20								

11.16

assure consistency between the *x-y* pairs:

$$x_1 - My_1 \leq 0$$
$$x_2 - My_2 \leq 0$$
$$x_3 - My_3 \leq 0$$

Now we need to identify a large number to play the role of M. Essentially, we need a number large enough so that it will not limit the choice of these variables in any of the other (demand and supply) constraints. For example, a value of 400 (thousand) would work, since that represents the largest demand ceiling, and none of the volumes could ever be larger.

Thus, when $y_2 = 1$, the linking constraint for product family F2 becomes $x_2 \leq 400$; and when $y_2 = 0$, the constraint becomes $x_2 \leq 0$. Similar interpretations apply to families F1 and F3. These are valid linking constraints, but we can streamline the model slightly. Instead of retaining separate constraints to represent the demand ceilings and the linking constraints, we can let the linking constraint do "double duty" if we choose a different value of M for each family and set it equal to the demand ceiling. For example, the value of M selected for the F2 constraint could be 300 instead of 400. Then, when $y_2 = 1$, the constraint on product family F2 becomes $x_2 \leq 300$, which also serves as a demand-ceiling constraint. When $y_2 = 0$, the constraint becomes $x_2 \leq 0$, and the choice of M does not matter. The streamlined model becomes:

$$\text{Maximize } 1.20x_1 - 60y_1 + 1.80x_2 - 200y_2 + 2.20x_3 - 100y_3$$

subject to

$$
\begin{array}{rcrcrccccc}
3x_1 & + & 4x_2 & + & 8x_3 & & & & \leq & 2{,}000 \\
3x_1 & + & 5x_2 & + & 6x_3 & & & & \leq & 2{,}000 \\
2x_1 & + & 3x_2 & + & 9x_3 & & & & \leq & 2{,}000 \\
x_1 & & & & & -400y_1 & & & \leq & 0 \\
& & x_2 & & & & -300y_2 & & \leq & 0 \\
& & & & x_3 & & & -50y_3 & \leq & 0
\end{array}
$$

Our spreadsheet model, shown in Figure 11.17, uses just three columns (one for each product family), where the corresponding pairs of x and y variables appear in the same column. In this spreadsheet, the left-hand side of the linking constraint for each $x-y$ pair appears in the corresponding column. For example, the formula in cell C16 is $=\text{C5} - \text{C15*C6}$,

FIGURE 11.17 Optimal Solution for the Mayhugh Model

	A	B	C	D	E	F	G	H
1	**Product Mix with Fixed Costs**							
2								
3	**Decisions**							
4			F1	F2	F3			
5			400	160	0	K-units		
6			1	1	0	binary		
7	**Objective**							
8		Variable profit	1.20	1.80	2.20			
9		Fixed cost	60	200	100	508	K$	
10	**Constraints**							
11		X	3	4	8	1840	<=	2000
12		Y	3	5	6	2000	<=	2000
13		Z	2	3	9	1280	<=	2000
14								
15		demand	400	300	50	K-units		
16		linking	0	-140	0			
17								

and this value is constrained to be negative or zero. We invoke Solver and specify:

Variables:	C5:E6
Objective:	F9 (maximize)
Constraints:	C16:E16 $\leq$ 0
	C6:E6 = binary
	F11:F13 $\leq$ H11:H13

The optimal solution achieves a net profit of $508,000. In order to attain this level of profits, the company must produce family F1 up to its ceiling, produce family F2 at the level of 160,000, and eliminate production of product family F3. In other words, the integer programming model detects that family F3 does not cover its fixed cost, and the company would be better off not producing and selling that family at all.

Solver Tip
Logical Functions and Integer Programming

In setting up integer programming models, an experienced Excel programmer might be tempted to use the logical functions in Excel (IF, AND, OR, etc.) to express certain relationships among decision variables. A direct means of linking a continuous variable x to its fixed costs would be to substitute the formula =IF(x>0,1,0) in the cell containing the binary variable. For example, in the model of Figure 11.17, we would use the following formula in cell C6.

$$= \text{IF}(C5 > 0, 1, 0)$$

We could then copy this formula into cells D6 and E6. The resulting model has no binary variables and only the three decision variables in C5:E5. It also contains no linking constraints (see Figure 11.18). For the model specification, we enter the following information:

Variables:	C5:E5
Objective:	F9 (maximize)
Constraints:	C5:E5 $\leq$ C15:E15
	F11:F13 $\leq$ H11:H13

Although this approach is logically sound, when we run Solver we encounter the error message reproduced in Figure 11.19, informing us that the model is not linear. We cannot run the linear solver because the IF function is nonlinear. Unfortunately, the linear solver does not always detect the nonlinearity caused by the use of logical functions, so it is important to remember *never* to use an IF function in a model built for the linear solver.[1]

FIGURE 11.18 Using Logical Functions to Represent Fixed Costs

	A	B	C	D	E	F	G	H
1	**Product Mix with Fixed Costs**							
2								
3	**Decisions**							
4			F1	F2	F3			
5			400	100	50	K-units		
6			1	1	1	logical		
7	**Objective**							
8		Variable profit	1.20	1.80	2.20			
9		Fixed cost	60	200	100	410	K$	
10	**Constraints**							
11		X	3	4	8	2000	<=	2000
12		Y	3	5	6	2000	<=	2000
13		Z	2	3	9	1550	<=	2000
14								
15		demand	400	300	50	K-units		
16								
17								

11.16 11.17 **11.18**

[1] In fact, Analytic Solver Platform has the capability to translate IF statements and certain other functions into linear structures by automating some of the techniques described in this chapter. But we prefer to encourage the user to implement the necessary information directly into the model.

FIGURE 11.19 The Non-linearity Message from Solver

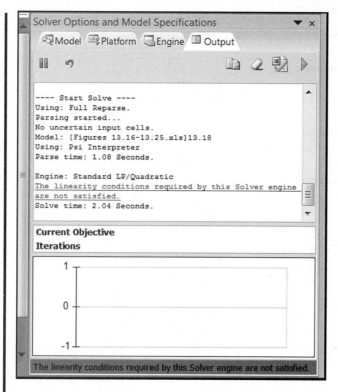

What if we use the nonlinear solver instead? The answer is that our results depend on our initial solution. An initial solution of all zeros cannot be improved by the nonlinear solver; an initial solution of all 50s leads to a solution worth $410,000. Neither, as we already know, is optimal. The presence of the IF function tends to make the nonlinear solver stop its search at a local optimum. For these reasons, we want to avoid using the IF function and the other logical functions in optimization models. ∎

11.4.3 Threshold Levels and Quantity Discounts

Sometimes we encounter cost schedules that require us to participate at a specified minimum level. For example, in purchasing, we might be able to qualify for a discounted price if we buy in quantity. As another example, in manufacturing, a setup is sufficiently disruptive that the line would be set up to assemble a batch of motors only if we're making at least a dozen of them, not merely one or two. These examples illustrate a **threshold-level requirement**: a decision variable is either at least as large as a specified minimum, or else it is zero.

The existence of a threshold level does not directly affect the objective function of a model, and it can be represented in the constraints with the help of binary variables. Suppose we have a variable x that is subject to a threshold requirement. Let m denote the minimum feasible value of x if it is nonzero. Then we can capture this structure in an integer programming model by including the following *pair* of constraints:

$$x - my \geq 0$$
$$x - My \leq 0$$

where, as before, M is a large number that is greater than or equal to any value x could feasibly take. To see how these two requirements work, consider the two possibilities for the binary variable. When $y = 1$, the constraints reduce to $m \leq x \leq M$, so that x is forced to be at or above the threshold level. When $y = 0$, the constraints reduce to $x = 0$. Thus, the pair x and y will behave consistently.

FIGURE 11.20 Mayhugh Model with a Constraint on the Minimum Volume in Family 2

	A	B	C	D	E	F	G	H
1	**Product Mix with Fixed Costs**							
2								
3	**Decisions**							
4			F1	F2	F3			
5			250	250	0	K-units		
6			1	1	0	binary		
7	**Objective**							
8		Variable profit	1.20	1.80	2.20			
9		Fixed cost	60	200	100	490	K$	
10	**Constraints**							
11		X	3	4	8	1750	<=	2000
12		Y	3	5	6	2000	<=	2000
13		Z	2	3	9	1250	<=	2000
14								
15		demand	400	300	50	K-units		
16		linking	-150	-50	0			
17								
18		minimum		250				
19				0				
20								

11.17 / 11.18 / **11.20**

For instance, in the Mayhugh example, we might want to require that product family F2 have a production level of at least 250,000 if it is to have a sales force. Since the model already includes the linking constraint $x_2 - 300y_2 \leq 0$, we need only to add the threshold constraint $x_2 - 250y_2 \geq 0$, and the search for an F2 level will be restricted to production values between 250 and 300, or zero. Figure 11.20 shows the amended model, with the threshold constraint entered in cell D19. Because we are adding a constraint that eliminates our former optimal product mix, we can expect that the optimal profit must drop. We invoke Solver and specify:

$$
\begin{array}{ll}
\text{Variables:} & \text{C5:E6} \\
\text{Objective:} & \text{F9 (maximize)} \\
\text{Constraints:} & \text{C16:E16} \leq 0 \\
& \text{C6:E6} = \text{binary} \\
& \text{D19} \geq 0 \\
& \text{F11:F13} \leq \text{H11:H13}
\end{array}
$$

Figure 11.20 displays the optimal solution, where the threshold constraint is binding, and we achieve a maximum profit of $490,000.

11.5 THE FACILITY LOCATION MODEL

The transportation model, discussed in Chapter 10, is typically used to find optimal shipping schedules in supply chains and logistics systems. The applications of the model can be viewed as tactical problems, in the sense that the time interval of interest is usually short, say a week or a month. Over that time period, the supply capacities and locations are unlikely to change at all, and the demands can be predicted with reasonable precision. Given such information, the model represents shipment patterns as decisions and finds their optimal configuration.

Over a longer time frame, a strategic version of the problem arises. In this setting, the decisions relate to the selection of supply locations as well as the shipment schedule. These decisions are strategic in the sense that, once determined, they influence the system for a relatively long time interval. The basic model for choosing supply locations is called the **facility location model**.

EXAMPLE
Levinson Foods Company

Levinson Foods is in the process of expanding its distribution system. After some planned acquisitions, the company will have ten distribution centers, with monthly volumes (in cartons) as listed below. Six of these sites will be able to support warehouses, in terms of the infrastructure available, and are designated by (W).

Center	Volume	Center	Volume
Albuquerque (W)	3,200	Oklahoma City	3,500
Boise	2,500	Phoenix (W)	5,000
Dallas (W)	6,800	Salt Lake City	1,800
Denver (W)	4,000	San Antonio (W)	7,400
Houston (W)	9,600	Wichita	2,700

Because the properties have been acquired under different circumstances, they would have different characteristics if Levinson Foods were to open warehouses at the sites. Their potential capacities (in cartons) and monthly operating costs are summarized in the following table:

Warehouse	Capacity	Cost
Albuquerque	16,000	$140,000
Dallas	20,000	150,000
Denver	10,000	100,000
Houston	10,000	110,000
Phoenix	12,000	125,000
San Antonio	10,000	120,000

Information has been compiled showing the cost per carton of shipping from each warehouse to any distribution center in the system. Levinson could open warehouses at any of the designated locations, but its criterion is to minimize total cost, including fixed operating costs and variable shipment costs. ∎

11.5.1 The Capacitated Problem

Conceptually, we can think of this problem as having two stages. In the first stage, decisions must be made about how many warehouses to open and where they should be. Then, once we know where the warehouses are, we can construct a transportation model to optimize the actual shipments. The costs involved are also of two types: fixed costs associated with keeping a warehouse open and variable transportation costs associated with shipments from the open warehouses.

Imagine that we have built the 6×10 transportation model for this problem, using the following variables:

$$x_{ij} = \text{quantity shipped from warehouse } i \text{ to center } j$$

Now we want to add considerations for the warehouses. Let

$$y_i = 1 \text{ if warehouse } i \text{ is open, and } 0 \text{ otherwise}$$

We associate these binary variables with the fixed costs, and so we add the following cost expression to the transportation model:

$$\text{Total Fixed Cost} = 140y_1 + 150y_2 + 100y_3 + 110y_4 + 125y_5 + 120y_6$$

In addition, we want to link the binary variables to the corresponding continuous variables, so we add linking constraints of the form:

$$x_{ij} - My_i \leq 0$$

for every combination of i and j. As usual, the linking constraints ensure consistency between the shipment quantities x_{ij} and the binary variables that signify whether a warehouse is open.

FIGURE 11.21 Optimal Solution to the Levinson Foods Model

	A	B	C	D	E	F	G	H	I	J	K	L	M
1	Warehouse Location												
2													
3		Fixed Cost	Alb	Boise	Dall	Denv	Hous	Okla	Phoe	Salt	SanA	Wich	Capacity
4	Albuquerque	140,000	0.00	47.00	32.00	22.00	42.50	27.00	23.00	30.00	36.50	29.50	16,000
5	Dallas	150,000	32.00	79.50	0.00	39.00	12.50	10.50	50.00	63.00	13.50	17.00	20,000
6	Denver	100,000	21.00	42.00	39.00	51.50	31.50	40.50	24.00	47.50	26.00	10,000	
7	Houston	110,000	42.50	91.00	12.50	51.50	0.00	23.00	58.00	72.00	10.00	31.00	10,000
8	Phoenix	125,000	23.00	49.00	50.00	40.50	58.00	49.00	0.00	32.50	50.00	52.00	12,000
9	San Antonio	120,000	36.50	83.50	13.50	47.50	10.00	24.00	50.00	66.50	0.00	32.00	12,000
10	Volume		3200	2500	6800	4000	9600	3500	5000	1800	7400	2700	80,000
11		884,550											
12													
13		Open?					Shipments						Sent
14	Albuquerque	0	0	0	0	0	0	0	0	0	0	0	0
15	Dallas	1	0	0	6800	0	0	3500	0	0	7000	2700	20,000
16	Denver	1	1700	2500	0	4000	0	0	0	1800	0	0	10,000
17	Houston	1	0	0	0	0	9600	0	0	0	400	0	10,000
18	Phoenix	1	1500	0	0	0	0	0	5000	0	0	0	6,500
19	San Antonio	0	0	0	0	0	0	0	0	0	0	0	0
20		Received	3200	2500	6800	4000	9600	3500	5000	1800	7400	2700	46,500
21													
22		Linking	0	0	0	0	0	0	0	0	0	0	
23			-80,000	-80,000	-73,200	-80,000	-80,000	-76,500	-80,000	-80,000	-73,000	-77,300	
24			-78,300	-77,500	-80,000	-76,000	-80,000	-80,000	-80,000	-78,200	-80,000	-80,000	
25			-80,000	-80,000	-80,000	-80,000	-70,400	-80,000	-80,000	-80,000	-79,600	-80,000	
26			-78,500	-80,000	-80,000	-80,000	-80,000	-80,000	-75,000	-80,000	-80,000	-80,000	
27			0	0	0	0	0	0	0	0	0	0	
28													

11.21

The resulting model is shown in Figure 11.21, using a format similar to the transportation model of Chapter 10:

- Capacities are entered in cells M4:M9 (with their total in M10).
- Demands are entered in cells C10:L10.
- Unit costs are entered in cells C4:L9.
- Shipment decisions are entered in C14:L19, with row and column totals labeled *Sent* and *Received*.

In addition to the transportation model that lies at the heart of this formulation, the worksheet contains fixed costs in cells B4:B9 and binary variables in B14:B19. With these additions, the objective function (cell B11) can be expressed as the sum of two SUM-PRODUCT calculations:

Total Fixed Cost	=	SUMPRODUCT(B14:B19,B4:B9)
Total Variable Cost	=	SUMPRODUCT(C14:L19,C4:L9)
Objective function	=	*Total Fixed Cost + Total Variable Cost*

When we turn to constraints, we start with the supply and demand constraints of the transportation model (*Sent ≤ Capacity* and *Received ≥ Demand*); then we must add the linking constraints. These are set up in the array C22:L27. Each entry is of the form $x_{ij} - My_i$. For simplicity, we use the total capacity (80,000) as the value for M, although smaller values would also work. We invoke Solver and specify:

Variables:	B14:L19
Objective:	B11 (minimize)
Constraints:	B14:B19 = binary
	C20:L20 = C10:L10
	C22:L27 ≤ 0
	M14:M19 ≤ M4:M9

One modification has been made in the usual statement of constraints. The demand constraints, normally posed as inequalities, are entered here as equations. This modification is made here because the problem contains some unit costs of zero, so there is no disincentive for shipping more than the demand requirement from some warehouse to a center at its own location. (If a small handling cost were added to all of the unit costs, this

FIGURE 11.22 Streamlined Worksheet for the Levinson Foods Model

		Fixed Cost	Alb	Boise	Dall	Denv	Hous	Okla	Phoe	Salt	SanA	Wich	Capacity	
1	Warehouse Location													
4	Albuquerque	140,000	0.00	47.00	32.00	22.00	42.50	27.00	23.00	30.00	36.50	29.50	16,000	
5	Dallas	150,000	32.00	79.50	0.00	39.00	12.50	10.50	50.00	63.00	13.50	17.00	20,000	
6	Denver	100,000	21.00	42.00	39.00	0.00	51.50	31.50	40.50	24.00	47.50	26.00	10,000	
7	Houston	110,000	42.50	91.00	12.50	51.50	0.00	23.00	58.00	72.00	10.00	31.00	10,000	
8	Phoenix	125,000	23.00	49.00	50.00	40.50	58.00	49.00	0.00	32.50	50.00	52.00	12,000	
9	San Antonio	120,000	36.50	83.50	13.50	47.50	10.00	24.00	50.00	66.50	0.00	32.00	12,000	
10	Volume		3200	2500	6800	4000	9600	3500	5000	1800	7400	2700	80,000	
11	884,550													

		Open?					Shipments						Sent	Linking
14	Albuquerque	0	0	0	0	0	0	0	0	0	0	0	0	0
15	Dallas	1	0	0	6800	0	0	3500	0	0	7000	2700	20,000	0
16	Denver	1	1700	2500	0	4000	0	0	0	1800	0	0	10,000	0
17	Houston	1	0	0	0	0	9600	0	0	0	400	0	10,000	0
18	Phoenix	1	1500	0	0	0	0	0	5000	0	0	0	6,500	-5,500
19	San Antonio	0	0	0	0	0	0	0	0	0	0	0	0	0
20	Received	3200	2500	6800	4000	9600	3500	5000	1800	7400	2700		46,500	

would not be an issue.) When we run the model, Solver produces the optimal solution shown in Figure 11.21, which achieves a minimum total cost of $884,550. Four of the six warehouse possibilities are selected, incurring $485,000 in fixed costs and the remainder in variable distribution costs.

An alternative formulation exists which is sometimes more convenient to use. In this alternative model, we substitute for the linking constraints. Instead of one linking constraint for each distribution variable, we use one linking constraint for each warehouse. For example, for the first warehouse:

$$x_{11} + x_{12} + x_{13} + \cdots + x_{1,10} - My_1 \leq 0$$

and similarly for the other five warehouses. This type of constraint ensures consistency between the binary variable y_i and the set of shipment variables emanating from warehouse i. If any shipment is positive, y_i must be 1; if y_i is zero, then no shipments from the corresponding warehouse are possible. Instead of 60 linking constraints, we need only six. These appear in Figure 11.22, in cells N14:N19. In fact, we can streamline the model a bit further by choosing M values in each of these constraints so that they do "double duty." Thus, the formula in cell N14 reads =M14 – M4*B14. The reference to M4 means that the capacity of the first warehouse plays the role of M, so that when $y_1 = 1$, the linking constraint functions as a capacity constraint. This approach allows us to simplify the specification, which reads as follows:

> Variables: B14:L19
> Objective: B11 (minimize)
> Constraints: B14:B19 = binary
> C20:L20 = C10:L10
> N14:N19 $\leq$ 0

A run of this model reproduces the optimal solution, as shown in the figure.

11.5.2 The Uncapacitated Problem

Once we solve the facility location problem with capacities given, it is not difficult to adapt the model to the uncapacitated case. Obviously, we could choose a virtual capacity for each warehouse that is as large as total demand, so that capacity would never interfere with the optimization. We show this approach in Figure 11.23, where we modify the previous worksheet by taking all capacities to be 46,500, which is the total demand in the problem. As the figure shows, removing the capacity constraints allows us to reach a lower cost, but the improvement is only about 3 percent.

An alternative formulation of the uncapacitated facility location model is sometimes useful. It is based on a simple insight about the nature of an optimal shipment pattern in the uncapacitated case. Notice that, in the optimal solution of Figure 11.23, each center is supplied by a unique warehouse. In particular, supply comes from the cheapest of the open

FIGURE 11.23 Worksheet for the Uncapacitated Version of the Levinson Foods Model

warehouses. That form must always hold in an optimal solution, and this fact permits us to use a slightly different representation of the model.

In the uncapacitated model, we know that if warehouse i provides supply to center j, then the corresponding cost must be the demand at center j multiplied by the unit cost on the route from i to j. In Figure 11.24, we compute these costs in advance, in cells C14:L19. Then we can use decision variables of zero or one to indicate whether a given warehouse-center combination is selected as part of the solution. The "indicator" variables appear in the array C22:L27. A solution is feasible whenever the sum of the indicator variables in every column is equal to 1.

For convenience, we place the fixed costs in rows 14–19, so that the objective function can be expressed with the formula =SUMPRODUCT(B14:L19,B22:L27). Next, we revise the linking constraints by using $M = 10$, which is the number of centers. Thus, in cell N22, the formula reads =M22 − $M$4∗B22, where the number of centers has been entered in cell M4. Thus, we specify the problem as follows:

Variables:	B22:L27
Objective:	B11 (minimize)
Constraints:	B22:B27 = binary
	C28:L28 = 1
	N22:N27 ≤ 0

As Figure 11.24 confirms, this formulation produces the optimal solution as well. The advantage of this form of the model relates to the indicator variables. They are

FIGURE 11.24 Alternative Version of the Uncapacitated Levinson Foods Model

allowed to be fractional, but they behave like binary variables—that is, they are never fractional in the optimal solution. This means that logical conditions (contingency, mutual exclusivity, etc.) can be added to the model, using indicator variables in the role of binary variables.

11.5.3 The Assortment Model

The facility location model, with or without capacity constraints, clearly has direct application to the design of supply chains and the choice of locations from a discrete set of alternatives. But the model can actually be used in other types of problems because it captures the essential trade-off between fixed costs and variable costs. An example from the field of Marketing is the **assortment problem**, which asks which items in a product line should be carried when customers are willing to substitute.

EXAMPLE
*Togawa Steel
Company*

Togawa Steel Company (TSC) manufactures structural beams of a standard length. The strength of a beam depends on its weight, and industry standards specify eight beam weights ranging from 50 pounds to 750 pounds. If a customer requests a given strength, then TSC may meet the demand by substituting a beam of greater strength. In this case, TSC incurs the material cost of providing the heavier beam. For every substitution, the incremental material cost is the difference in weight between the beam demanded and the beam supplied, multiplied by the variable cost of $2 per pound. If TSC decides to manufacture a particular weight, then it incurs a setup cost of $120,000.

The beam weights and their demand requirements for the coming month are tabulated as follows:

Category	1	2	3	4	5	6	7	8
Weight	50	100	150	200	250	400	500	750
Demand	1,000	2,000	400	800	1,000	500	200	100

TSC intends to meet all demand and wants to determine an optimal assortment of strengths to manufacture. ∎

Although the scenario at Togawa Steel appears to have little in common with locating warehouses, there is a key structural similarity: TSC faces the problem of trading off the fixed setup costs associated with greater variety in its product line with the variable substitution costs of meeting demand with heavier beams than necessary. In fact, this trade-off is structurally identical to trading off the fixed costs of operating warehouses with the variable costs of distributing from those warehouses.

Each beam weight that Togawa Steel produces incurs a fixed setup cost. Demands for beam weights that TSC does not produce represent substitution costs. We can imagine an array that contains the unit cost of substituting beam weight i for beam weight j. Figure 11.25 shows this array in cells D8:K15, where the cost entries are in thousands. For example, cell J10 contains the cost of substituting 400-pound beams for 100-pound beams. The cost per beam is $2(400 - 100) = \$600$, which appears in the worksheet as 0.600 due to rescaling.

The diagonal elements are zero because no substitution is involved. Entries below the diagonal would correspond to the substitution of lighter beams than the size demanded, which is infeasible. Rather than exclude those decisions, we have built the model as if they are permitted, but the model imposes a very large cost on these alternatives to make sure that they are never used in the solution. Here, we use the number 99, partly because it is quite a bit larger than the other unit costs in the model (and therefore discourages the use of the corresponding decision variables) and partly because it is a distinct number that signals an arbitrarily large value whose purpose is to inhibit certain decisions.

With the cost array in place, our decision variables appear in the array C20:K27, with the first column filled with binary decision variables signifying which setup costs TSC incurs. The rest of the array represents production quantities, although we should not expect to see a solution with nonzero entries below the diagonal. The objective

FIGURE 11.25 Optimal Solution to the Togawa Steel Model

Assortment Problem

Data	Weight		750	500	400	250	200	150	100	50	Total	
	Demand		100	200	500	1000	800	400	2000	1000	6000	

	Weight Produced	Line Cost	750	500	400	Weight Demanded 250	200	150	100	50		Material Cost
	750	120	0	0.500	0.700	1.000	1.100	1.200	1.300	1.400		2
	500	120	99	0	0.200	0.500	0.600	0.700	0.800	0.900		
	400	120	99	99	0	0.300	0.400	0.500	0.600	0.700		
	250	120	99	99	99	0	0.100	0.200	0.300	0.400		
	200	120	99	99	99	99	0	0.100	0.200	0.300		
	150	120	99	99	99	99	99	0	0.100	0.200		
	100	120	99	99	99	99	99	99	0	0.100		
	50	120	99	99	99	99	99	99	99	0		

Objective   Total Cost   840

Decisions		Produce									Sum	Linking
	750	1	5800	200	0	0	0	0	0	0	6000	0
	500	0	0	0	0	0	0	0	0	0	0	0
	400	1	0	0	6000	0	0	0	0	0	6000	0
	250	1	0	0	0	6000	0	0	0	0	6000	0
	200	1	0	0	0	0	5600	400	0	0	6000	0
	150	0	0	0	0	0	0	0	0	0	0	0
	100	1	0	0	0	0	0	0	5000	1000	6000	0
	50	0	0	0	0	0	0	0	0	0	0	0
			5800	200	6000	6000	5600	400	5000	1000		

function is calculated in the same way as in the location models, here with the formula =SUMPRODUCT(C8:K15,C20:K27). Our model specification resembles the form of location models:

$$
\begin{array}{rl}
\text{Variables:} & \text{C20:K27} \\
\text{Objective:} & \text{E17 (minimize)} \\
\text{Constraints:} & \text{C20:C27 = binary} \\
& \text{D28:K28} \geq \text{D4:K4} \\
& \text{M20:M27} \leq 0
\end{array}
$$

Figure 11.25 displays the optimal solution, showing that Togawa Steel should produce weights of 750, 400, 250, 200, and 100. Demand for 500-pound beams should be met by supplying 750-pound beams, demand for 150-pound beams should be met by supplying 200-pound beams, and demand for 50-pound beams should be met by supplying 100-pound beams. This production plan costs $840,000, which is the minimum cost achievable in the problem.

11.6   SUMMARY

Integer programming problems are optimization problems in which at least one of the variables is required to be an integer. The drop-down menu on the Engine tab of the task pane does not offer a special solution algorithm for integer programs. Instead, whenever the problem formulation specifies an integer (int) variable or a binary (bin) variable among the decision variables, Solver employs a solution procedure that produces integer values as required.

Solver permits integer or binary variables to be used with the linear solver or the nonlinear solver. However, the use of the nonlinear solver with integer constraints is problematic. Because the nonlinear solver is vulnerable to local optima, its effectiveness

with integer variables is open to question. There are no guarantees that Solver's solution to a nonlinear integer program will be close to optimal. On the other hand, Solver's solutions to linear integer programs are reliable: a global optimal solution always occurs as long as the Integer Tolerance parameter has been set to zero.

In this chapter, we examined several examples of linear integer programming problems. The new formulation lessons occurred in conjunction with the use of binary variables. Binary variables can represent all-or-nothing decisions that allow only accept/reject alternatives. Binary variables can also be instrumental in capturing complicated logic in linear form so that we can harness the linear solver to find solutions. Binary variables make it possible to accommodate problem information on:

- Contingency conditions between projects
- Mutual exclusivity among projects

- Linking constraints for consistency
- Threshold constraints for minimum activity levels

With the capability of formulating these kinds of relationships in optimization problems, our modeling abilities expand well beyond the basic capabilities of the linear and nonlinear solvers.

SUGGESTED READINGS

Some advanced perspectives on integer programming techniques can be found in the following books:

Garfinkel, R. and G. Nemhauser. 1999. *Integer and Combinatorial Optimization*. New York: John Wiley & Sons.

Schrage, L. E. 1997. *Optimization Modeling with LINDO*, 5th ed. Pacific Grove, CA: Duxbury Press.

Williams, H. P. 1999. *Model Building in Mathematical Programming*, 3d ed. Chichester: John Wiley & Sons.

EXERCISES

1. *Selecting Projects.* The Texas Electronics Company (TEC) is contemplating a research and development program encompassing eight major projects. The company is constrained from embarking on all projects by the number of available scientists (40) and the budget available for projects ($300,000).

Following are the resource requirements and the estimated profit for each project:

Project	Expense ($000)	Scientists Required	Profit ($000)
1	60	7	36
2	110	9	82
3	53	8	29
4	147	4	16
5	192	7	56
6	185	6	61
7	173	8	48
8	165	5	41

a. What is the maximum profit, and which projects should be selected?

b. Suppose that management decides that projects 2 and 5 are mutually exclusive. That is, TEC should not undertake both. As a result, what are the revised project portfolio and the revised maximum profit?

c. Suppose that management also decides to undertake at least two of the projects involving consumer products. (These happen to be projects 5–8.) As a result, what are the revised project portfolio and the revised maximum profit?

2. *Buying Equipment.* Oriental Airlines is considering a capital expansion in which it will purchase new aircraft for its Pacific runs. Oriental is looking at the purchase of Boeing B797s, Airbus A450s, and Lockheed L120s. The budget for new purchases is $750 million. Boeing B797s cost $42 million, Airbus A450s cost $30 million, and Lockheed L120s cost $27.5 million. On the average, these planes are expected to generate annual profits of $3.5 million, $2.8 million, and $3.0 million, respectively. In an effort to achieve some uniformity with respect to spare parts and maintenance procedures, airline executives have specified that they will not buy fewer than 10 airplanes of any type. Their objective is to maximize total annual profit. Oriental has allocated up to $10 million for additional personnel to support the operation of the new aircraft. Each B797 requires $200,000 in new hires; each A450 requires $180,000; and each L120 requires $190,000.

Currently, the available maintenance facilities allow 800 days of maintenance per year for new purchases. Each B797 requires 45 days of annual maintenance; each A450 requires 38 days; and each L120 requires 42 days. It is possible, however, to increase the available annual maintenance to 1,250 days. To accomplish this, the maintenance facilities would have to be expanded at a capital cost of $16 million, which would come out of the budget for new purchases. In addition, the expansion would augment operating costs by $18 million annually, an expense that would reduce annual profits.

a. What is the optimal purchasing plan, and what is the corresponding annual profit for Oriental?

b. Suppose the maintenance expansion were to augment operating cost to $24 million instead of $18 million. Then, what would be the optimal purchasing plan?

c. Suppose that, in addition to the augmented operating cost of $24 million, the uniformity policy required a minimum of only 8 airplanes of the same type rather than 10 as at present. What would be the optimal purchasing plan under these assumptions?

3. *Make or Buy.* A sudden increase in the demand for smoke detectors has left Acme Alarms with insufficient capacity to meet demand. The company has seen monthly demand from its retailers for its electronic and battery-operated detectors rise to 20,000 and 10,000, respectively. Acme's production process involves three departments: fabrication, assembly, and shipping. The relevant quantitative data on production and prices are summarized as follows:

Department	Monthly Hours Available	Hours/Unit (Electronic)	Hours/Unit (Battery)
Fabrication	2,000	0.15	0.10
Assembly	4,200	0.20	0.20
Shipping	2,500	0.10	0.15
Variable cost/unit		$18.80	$16.00
Retail price		$29.50	$28.00

The company also has the option to obtain additional units from a subcontractor, who has offered to supply up to 20,000 units per month in any combination of electric and battery-operated models, at a charge of $21.50 per unit. For this price, the subcontractor will test and ship its models directly to the retailers without using Acme's production process.

a. What are the maximum profit and the corresponding make/buy levels? (Fractional decisions are acceptable.)

b. Suppose that Acme requires that the solution provided by the model be implementable without any rounding off. That is, the solution must contain integer decisions. What are the optimal make/buy levels?

c. Is the solution in part (b) a rounded-off version of the fractional solution in part (a)?

4. *Investment Choice.* Perry Enterprises is considering a number of investment possibilities. Specifically, each investment under consideration will draw on the capital account during each of its first three years, but in the long run, each is predicted to achieve a positive net present value (NPV). Listed here are the investment alternatives, their net present values, and their capital requirements, and all figures are in thousands of dollars. In addition, the amount of capital available to the investments in each of the next three years is predicted to be $9.5 million, $7.5 million, and $8.8 million, respectively.

	Project					
	One-Phase Expansion	Two-Phase Expansion	Test Market	Advertising Campaign	Basic Research	Purchase Equipment
NPV	4,200	6,800	9,600	4,400	8,700	3,500
Year 1 Capital	3,000	2,500	6,000	2,000	5,000	1,000
Year 2 Capital	1,000	3,500	4,000	1,500	1,000	500
Year 3 Capital	4,000	3,500	5,000	1,800	4,000	900

a. Assuming that any combination of the investments is permitted, which ones should Perry make to maximize NPV?

b. What is the optimal NPV in the combination chosen in part (a)?

c. Suppose that the expansion investments are mutually exclusive and only one of them can be made. How does this alter the solution in part (a)?

d. Suppose that the test market cannot be carried out unless the advertising campaign is also adopted. How does this contingency alter the solution in (a)?

5. *Cutting Stock.* Poly Products sells packaging tape to industrial customers. All tape is sold in 100-foot rolls that are cut in various widths from a master roll, which is 15 inches wide. The product line consists of the following widths: 2″, 3″, 5″, 7″, and 11″. These can be cut in different combinations. For example, one combination might consist of three cuts of 5″ each. Another combination might consist of two 2″ cuts and an 11″ cut. Both of these configurations use the entire 15-inch roll without any waste, but other configurations are also possible. For example, another combination might consist of two 7″ cuts. This combination creates 1 inch of waste for every roll cut this way. Each week, Poly Products collects demands from its customers and distributors and must figure out how to configure the cuts in the master rolls. To do so, the production manager lists all possible combinations of cuts and tries to fit them together so that waste is minimized while demand is met. (In particular, demand must be met exactly, because Poly

Products does not keep inventories of its tape.) This week's demands are shown in the following table:

Size	2″	3″	5″	7″	11″
Demand	60	50	40	30	20

a. How many configurations can be cut from a 15-inch master roll so that there is less than 2 inches of waste (i.e., the smallest quantity that can be sold) left on the roll?

b. What is the minimum amount of waste that can be created if all demand is met exactly?

6. *Optimizing Product Mix.* California Products Company has the capability of producing and selling three products. Each product has an annual demand potential (at current pricing and promotion levels), a variable contribution, and an annual fixed cost. The fixed cost can be avoided if the product is not produced at all. This information is summarized as follows:

Product	Demand	Contribution	Fixed Cost
I	290,000	$1.20	$60,000
J	200,000	1.80	200,000
K	50,000	2.30	55,000

Each product requires work on three machines. The standard productivities and capacities are as follows:

Machine	Hours per 1,000 Units			Hours Available
	Product I	Product J	Product K	
A	3.205	3.846	7.692	1,900
B	2.747	4.808	6.410	1,900
C	1.923	3.205	9.615	1,900

a. Determine which products should be produced, and how much of each should be produced, in order to maximize profit contribution from these operations.

b. Suppose the demand potential for product K were doubled. What would be the maximum profit contribution?

7. *Purchasing with Price Breaks.* Universal Technologies, Inc. has identified two qualified vendors with the capability to supply certain of its electronic components. For the coming year, Universal has estimated its volume requirements for these components and has obtained price-break schedules from each vendor. (These are summarized as "all-units" price discounts in the table at the bottom of p. 313.) Universal's engineers have also estimated each vendor's maximum capacity for producing these components, on the basis of available information about equipment in use and labor policies in effect. Finally, because of its limited history with vendor A, Universal has adopted a policy that permits no more than 60 percent of its total unit purchases on these components to come from vendor A.

a. What is the minimum total cost for Universal's purchases?

b. In the optimal solution to part (a), which purchases are made at discounted prices?

8. *Purchasing with an Incremental Quantity Discount.* In the previous problem, suppose that vendor A provides a new price-discount schedule for component 3. This one is an "incremental" discount, as opposed to an "all-units" discount, as follows:

Unit price = $60 on all units up to 1,000
Unit price = $56 on the next 1,000 units
Unit price = $51 on the next 500 units

a. What is the minimum total cost for Universal's purchases?

b. In the optimal solution to part (a), which purchases are made at discounted prices?

9. *Establishing a Product Line.* National Metals Company (NMC) manufactures titanium shafts. Its equipment is capable of producing shafts in 10 lengths, reflecting settings on its machinery. These lengths are essentially 32 cm to 50 cm in steps of 2 cm. Setting up the machinery to produce one of these lengths (which is done once a week) costs $250. As a result, NMC has decided to make only a selected number of lengths. When a customer requests a given length, NMC may supply it from stock, if it happens to match one of the lengths in the production schedule. Otherwise, NMC trims a longer length to meet the order. The variable cost for producing the shafts is $20 per cm, and NMC receives revenue of $40 per cm. Trim waste can be sold to a recycler for $15 per cm.

The demand requirements for the coming week are tabulated as follows; all demand must be satisfied:

Length	32	34	36	38	40	42	44	46	48	50
Demand	12	4	7	8	16	7	12	5	8	3

a. What is an optimal assortment of lengths for NMC to manufacture?

b. What is the optimal profit in the coming week?

10. *Plant Location.* The Spencer Shoe Company manufacturers a line of inexpensive shoes in one plant in Pontiac and distributes to five main distribution centers (Milwaukee, Dayton, Cincinnati, Buffalo, and Atlanta) from which the shoes are shipped to retail shoe stores. Distribution costs include freight, handling, and warehousing costs. To meet increased demand, the company has decided to build at least one new plant with a capacity of 40,000 pairs per week. Surveys have narrowed the choice to three locations: Cincinnati, Dayton, and Atlanta. As expected, production costs would be low in the Atlanta plant, but distribution costs are relatively high compared to those of the other two locations. Other data are as follows:

Distribution Costs per Pair					
To		**From**			**Demand**
Distribution Centers	**Pontiac**	**Cincinnati**	**Dayton**	**Atlanta**	**(pairs/wk)**
Milwaukee	$0.42	$0.46	$0.44	$0.48	10,000
Dayton	0.36	0.37	0.30	0.45	15,000
Cincinnati	0.41	0.30	0.37	0.43	16,000
Buffalo	0.39	0.42	0.38	0.46	19,000
Atlanta	0.50	0.43	0.45	0.27	12,000
Capacity (pairs/wk.)	27,000	40,000	40,000	40,000	
Production cost/pair	$2.70	$2.64	$2.69	$2.62	
Fixed cost/wk.	$7,000	$4,000	$6,000	$7,000	

a. Assume that the Pontiac plant has no resale value and must remain open. What are the plant locations that will minimize total costs, including production, distribution, and fixed costs? What is the optimal total cost?

b. Assume that the Pontiac plant could be closed at zero net cost. What are the optimal locations? What is the optimal total cost?

11. *Designing a Supply Chain.* The Van Horne Company manufactures air conditioners that are sold to five large

Product	Requirement	Vendor A		Vendor B	
		Unit Price	**Volume Required**	**Unit Price**	**Volume Required**
1	500	$225	0–250	$224	0–300
		$220	250–500	$214	300–500
2	1,000	$124	0–600	$120	0–1,000
		$115	600–1,000	(no discount)	
3	2,500	$60	0–1,000	$54	0–1,500
		$56*	1,000–2,000	$52	1,500–2,500
		$510	2,000–2,500		
Total Capacity (Units)			2,800		2,400

*For example, if 1,400 units are purchased from Vendor A, they cost $56 each, for a total of $78,400.

retail customers around the country. Van Horne is evaluating its manufacturing and logistics strategy to ensure that it is operating as efficiently as possible. The company can produce air conditioners at six plants and stock these units in any of four different warehouses. The cost of manufacturing and shipping a unit between each plant and warehouse is summarized in the following table along with the fixed operating cost and monthly capacity for operating each plant:

	WH 1	WH 2	WH 3	WH 4	Fixed Cost	Plant Capacity
Plant 1	$700	$1,000	$900	$1,200	$55,000	300
Plant 2	800	500	600	700	40,000	200
Plant 3	850	600	700	500	45,000	300
Plant 4	600	800	500	600	50,000	250
Plant 5	500	600	450	700	42,000	350
Plant 6	700	600	750	500	40,000	400

Similarly, the per-unit cost of shipping units from each warehouse to each customer is given in the following table, along with the monthly fixed cost of operating each warehouse:

	Cust1	Cust2	Cust3	Cust4	Cust5	Fixed Cost
WH 1	$40	$80	$60	$90	$50	$40,000
WH 2	60	50	75	40	35	50,000
WH 3	55	40	65	60	80	35,000
WH 4	80	30	80	50	60	60,000

The monthly demand from each customer is summarized as follows:

	Cust1	Cust2	Cust3	Cust4	Cust5
Demand	200	300	200	150	250

a. Considering all of the costs and demands tabulated above, what is the minimum monthly operating cost for Van Horne's supply chain?

b. Which plants and warehouses should Van Horne operate to meet demand in the most cost-effective manner?

12. *Project Team Assignment.* A project-based course assigns students to project teams at the start of the term. For this purpose, each student is asked to examine the set of projects available and to identify three of the alternatives as preferred assignments. A preference of 3 indicates the most preferred project. When these preferences are collected, the instructor assigns the students to project teams, aiming for an optimal assignment of students to teams. The criterion for the assignment is to maximize the total of the preferences assigned.

This year, there are 10 available projects and 16 students enrolled. There is a maximum team size between 2 and 4 on each project, according to the nature of the work to be done. It is not permissible for a student to work alone on a project (that is, in a team of size 1). The table below shows the student preferences and the limits for the team sizes.

a. What is the best value of the criterion—that is, the maximum sum of assigned preferences?

b. In the solution of part (a), how many students are assigned to their first choice? What is the maximum number of students who could be assigned to their first choice, if that were the only criterion?

	S1	S2	S3	S4	S5	S6	S7	S8	S9	S10	S11	S12	S13	S14	S15	S16	Limit
P1	0	3	0	3	0	3	0	3	0	0	0	0	0	0	2	0	3
P2	0	0	3	0	0	0	3	2	0	3	0	0	0	2	0	0	3
P3	2	2	0	0	0	2	0	0	0	0	0	2	2	0	0	0	3
P4	0	0	0	1	2	0	2	0	3	0	0	0	0	0	3	0	4
P5	0	1	0	0	0	1	0	0	0	2	0	1	3	3	0	0	4
P6	1	0	0	0	0	0	1	0	0	0	0	0	0	0	1	2	3
P7	0	0	2	0	3	0	0	0	2	0	3	3	0	0	0	3	3
P8	3	0	0	0	0	0	0	1	0	1	1	0	1	0	0	0	2
P9	0	0	1	2	0	0	0	0	0	0	2	0	0	0	0	0	2
P10	0	0	0	0	1	0	0	0	1	0	0	0	0	1	0	1	2

12 Optimization of Nonsmooth Models

12.1 INTRODUCTION

The previous four chapters cover various types of optimization problems and the Solver algorithms that apply. A central theme of those chapters is that success in finding an optimal solution for a particular type of problem often requires both careful model building and choice of a solution algorithm. Furthermore, the choice of an algorithm has important implications for the degree of confidence we can have that the solution is a global optimum.

For example, in Chapter 8, we learned that in solving smooth optimization problems we must avoid the use of nonsmooth functions in our models and the solution provided by the nonlinear solver may be only a local optimum. In Chapter 9, we learned that in solving linear optimization problems we must also avoid the use of nonsmooth functions in our models, but the solution provided by the linear solver is guaranteed to be a global optimum. In this chapter, we introduce the evolutionary solver, which can be effective on models that cannot be optimized in any other way.

The evolutionary solver, as implemented in Analytic Solver Platform, actually consists of two alternative algorithms, each of which has several variations. For simplicity we refer to it as if it were a single procedure. The evolutionary solver is quite different from the other Analytic Solver Platform solvers in both its design and its application. It can be applied to some of the most difficult optimization problems, but there is a price to pay for this power: the evolutionary solver does not produce guaranteed optimal solutions. It sometimes falls short of producing an optimal solution and we can seldom tell whether it has done so.

The evolutionary solver is particularly suited to models containing **nonsmooth** functions in the objective or in the constraints. Such models are unsuitable for the nonlinear solver discussed in Chapter 8 and for the linear solver discussed in Chapters 9–11. A nonsmooth objective function, for example, exhibits gaps or sharp corners when displayed as a graph. These features create several local optima and often render the nonlinear solver ineffective at finding a global optimum. A solution procedure that is suitable for nonsmooth functions provides us with more flexibility in modeling than the linear and nonlinear solvers permit. In particular, we can use IF functions as well as other nonsmooth functions such as absolute value (ABS), minimum (MIN), maximum (MAX), and table lookup (LOOKUP).

As we have mentioned, the modeling flexibility that the evolutionary solver offers us comes at a price. Because the evolutionary solver makes virtually no assumptions about the nature of the objective function, it is not able to identify an optimal solution. Essentially, this approach conducts a systematic search with random elements, comparing the solutions encountered along the way and retaining the better ones. Eventually it stops when it senses that it is not making progress at finding improved solutions. The best solution it finds may not be optimal, although it may be a very good solution. This type of procedure is called a **heuristic procedure**, meaning that it is a systematic procedure for identifying good solutions, but not guaranteed optimal solutions.

12.2 FEATURES OF THE EVOLUTIONARY SOLVER

In Analytic Solver Platform, we invoke the evolutionary solver on the Engine tab by selecting the Standard Evolutionary Engine. The two algorithms that are available within this solver are the **Genetic Algorithm** and **Scatter Search**. The choice between these two

FIGURE 12.1 The Engine
Tab for the Evolutionary
Solver

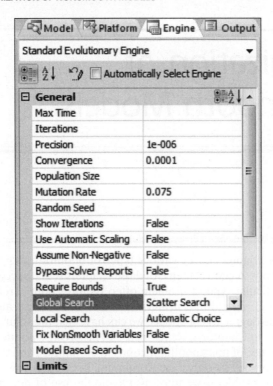

algorithms is made in the General section of the Engine tab, under the Global Search option. (See Figure 12.1.)

The Genetic Algorithm is designed to mimic the process of biological evolution in certain ways. In particular, the algorithm proceeds through a series of stages, which are analogous to **generations** in a biological population. In each generation the approach considers not a single solution, but a **population** of perhaps 25 or 50 solutions. New members are introduced to this population through a process that mimics mating, in that **offspring** solutions combine the traits or **genes** of their **parent** solutions. In addition, occasional **mutations** occur in the form of offspring solutions with some random characteristics that do not come from their parents. The "fitness" of each member of the population is determined by the value of its objective function. Members of the population that are less fit (have a relatively worse value of the objective function) are removed from the population by a process that mimics natural **selection**. This process of selection propels the population toward better levels of fitness (better values of the objective function). The procedure stops when there is evidence that the population is no longer improving or when one of the user-designated stopping conditions is met. When it stops, the procedure displays the best member of the final population as the solution.

Scatter Search also works on a population of solutions rather than a single solution. It generates new solutions by combining old ones in a variety of ways. It also uses methods from artificial intelligence to ensure the algorithm does not reconsider old solutions that have been abandoned, to maintain diversity among the population of solutions, and to move away from locally optimal solutions toward globally optimal ones.

Scatter Search is the default choice within the Standard Evolutionary Engine. The developers of Analytic Solver Platform have found that Scatter Search often works better than the Genetic Algorithm, but they advise users to try both options.

The inner workings of both algorithms are beyond our coverage here. For our purposes, we treat each algorithm as a black box and focus on the information that the user needs to know in order to apply the evolutionary solver effectively. The main point to keep in mind is that the evolutionary solver is not handicapped by the presence of nonsmooth functions, as would be the case for the linear and nonlinear solvers, because it does not rely on the model's mathematical structure to search for better solutions. Rather, it generates new solutions by combining and/or modifying previous solutions. However, it offers no guarantee of a global optimum.

In this chapter, we examine a series of examples with nonsmooth objective functions to illustrate how the evolutionary solver works. In some cases, we revisit problems that we tackled with other solution procedures in earlier chapters, mainly to provide a contrast in optimization approaches. The variety of examples should provide a working knowledge of the evolutionary solver, but—perhaps more than with the other solvers we have covered—this one requires practice and experience in order to use it effectively.

12.3 CURVE FITTING (REVISITED)

As our first example, we look at a curve-fitting problem in which the relationship between two variables is nonlinear and the criterion is the sum of absolute deviations. As discussed in Chapter 8, the most appropriate tool for curve-fitting problems is the nonlinear solver when the criterion is the sum of *squared* deviations. But when the criterion is the sum of *absolute* deviations, there can be several local optima, and the nonlinear solver may not find the best fit. The evolutionary solver is often well suited to such problems.

We revisit the problem facing Van Winkle's Pharmacy, which led to the curve-fitting model discussed in Chapter 8.

EXAMPLE
Van Winkle's Pharmacy

Van Winkle's Pharmacy, a chain of drugstores, owns pharmacies in different types of locations, such as shopping malls, grocery stores, and independent storefronts. Stores in different types of locations are open for different hours, and the company can therefore study a natural experiment to see how revenue varies with store hours. For a sample of 10 stores, the following data show the number of hours the store is open each week and the average revenue.

Store	Hours	Revenue
1	40	5,958
2	44	6,662
3	48	6,004
4	48	6,011
5	60	7,250
6	70	8,632
7	72	6,964
8	90	11,097
9	100	9,107
10	168	11,498

Here, the relationship between the pharmacy's revenue and the number of hours the pharmacy operates is hypothesized to be as follows:

$$Revenue = a \times Hours^b$$

∎

The revenue model appears in cells D5:D14 of Figure 12.2*, where we have assigned the decision variables arbitrary values ($a = 1000$ and $b = 0.5$) as a starting point. The absolute deviations between this model and the actual observations appear in cells F5:F14, and the sum of these deviations appears as the objective function in cell F2. As before, the

FIGURE 12.2 Worksheet for Van Winkle's Pharmacy

	A	B	C	D	E	F	G	H
1	**Pharmacy Hours**		a	1000		*Sum of Absolute Differences*		
2			b	0.5		8486		
3								
4	**Data**	Hours	Revenue	Model	Difference	Abs. Diff.		
5		40	5958	6325	-367	367		
6		44	6662	6633	29	29		
7		48	6004	6928	-924	924		
8		48	6011	6928	-917	917		
9		60	7250	7746	-496	496		
10		70	8632	8367	265	265		
11		72	6964	8485	-1521	1521		
12		90	11097	9487	1610	1610		
13		100	9107	10000	-893	893		
14		168	11498	12961	-1463	1463		
15								

12.2

* To download spreadsheets for this chapter, go to the Student Companion Site at www.wiley.com/college/powell.

optimization problem is specified for Solver as follows:

$$
\begin{aligned}
\text{Variables:} \quad & \text{D1:D2} \\
\text{Objective:} \quad & \text{F2 (minimize)} \\
\text{Constraints:} \quad & \text{None}
\end{aligned}
$$

We can now select the Standard Evolutionary Engine, and our main choice is whether to use the legacy Genetic Algorithm or the newer Scatter Search algorithm. In either case, it's convenient, on the Engine tab, to delete any entries for the Maximum Subproblems option and the Maximum Feasible Solutions option. It's also a good idea, for either algorithm, to use bounds on the variables, even if they are relatively loose, so we set the Require Bounds option to True. Then we enter constraints to set the upper bound on *a* to be 2000 and the upper bound on *b* to be 1.0. We can take the lower bound on both variables to be zero by setting the Assume Non-Negative option to True.

One additional setting is important. On the Platform tab, the first option in the Transformation section is Nonsmooth Model Transformation. This option should be set to Never when either the Genetic Algorithm or Scatter Search is used. Other settings may undermine the efficiency of the algorithm.

To implement Scatter Search, we specify two of the options: Global Search is set to Scatter Search and Model Based Search is set to CPU based, both from drop-down menus. (The CPU based option employs some parallelism and tends to run faster than if the option None is selected.) These settings allow us to run Scatter Search several times in succession.

For exploratory purposes, we set the Max Time option to 10, which limits the search to ten seconds. When we run the algorithm, it is likely that this time limit will interrupt the algorithm, allowing us to stop at the ten-second time limit. (We always have the option to rerun from that point.) When we make a ten-second run for the model of Figure 12.2, the algorithm stops with an objective function value of 5,711. This value is already as good as the values produced by several runs discussed in Chapter 8, but we can run again from this point. Another ten-second run produces no improvement, so our objective function stands at 5,711. A brief run of the evolutionary solver was thus sufficient to match the best run among several that we made with different starting points in Chapter 8, and the existence of several local optima did not present an obstacle in the evolutionary solver's search for a solution.

FIGURE 12.3 Advertising Budget Model with Unit Cost Table

	A	B	C	D	E	F	G	H	I	J
1	**Advertising Budget Model**									
2	SGP/KRB								Cost Table	
3	1/1/2013									
4									Units	Cost
5	PARAMETERS								1	$36.00
6				Q1	Q2	Q3	Q4		1,000	33.00
7		Price	$40.00						2,000	30.00
8		Cost	$25.00						3,000	27.50
9		Seasonal		0.9	1.1	0.8	1.2		4,000	25.00
10		OHD rate	0.15						5,000	22.50
11		Sales Parameters							6,000	21.00
12			35						7,000	20.00
13			3000						8,000	18.00
14		Sales Expense		8000	8000	9000	9000		9,000	17.50
15		Ad Budget	$40,000						10,000	17.00
16										
17	DECISIONS							Total		
18		Ad Expenditures		$10,000	$10,000	$10,000	$10,000	$40,000		
19										
20	OUTPUTS									
21		Profit	$52,702		Base case	$52,702				
22										
23	CALCULATIONS									
24		Quarter		Q1	Q2	Q3	Q4	Total		
25		Seasonal		0.9	1.1	0.8	1.2			
26										
27		Units Sold		3592	4390	3192	4789	15962		
28		Revenue		143662	175587	127700	191549	638498		
29		Cost of Goods		98768	109742	87794	119718	416022		
30		Gross Margin		44894	65845	39906	71831	222477		
31										

12.3

12.4   THE ADVERTISING BUDGET PROBLEM (REVISITED)

The next example illustrates how a seemingly minor change to a model can alter the approach required for optimization. We introduced the Advertising Budget problem in Chapter 3 and optimized it in Chapter 8. The decision variables in this problem are the quarterly expenditures on advertising. The objective function is nonlinear but smooth, because of diminishing returns to advertising (specifically, the number of units sold in a given quarter is a square-root function of the advertising level in that quarter). The nonlinear solver found a global optimum in in which advertising was highest in the two quarters with the highest seasonal sales factors.

EXAMPLE
*Advertising
with Quantity
Discounts*

In previous versions of this problem, the unit cost to manufacture the product was assumed to be $25, regardless of the volume of production. We have recently learned that this figure was based on a limited cost-accounting study and that the unit cost actually depends on the production volume. A broader accounting study has revealed that the unit cost could be as high as $36 when volume is low, but the cost can be as low as $17 when volume is high. The following table gives the complete schedule of unit costs as a function of quarterly production, in the form of a step function that drops at each quantity listed:

Production Quantity	Unit Cost
1	$36.00
1,000	33.00
2,000	30.00
3,000	27.50
4,000	25.00
5,000	22.50
6,000	21.00
7,000	20.00
8,000	18.00
9,000	17.50
10,000	17.00

In light of this new information how should we allocate the $40,000 advertising budget over the four quarters to maximize profit? ■

Our model for this version of the problem is shown in Figure 12.3. The cost table is located in columns I and J. The only change from earlier versions of the model occurs in row 29, where we calculate Cost of Goods using the function

$$=\text{VLOOKUP}(D27,\$I\$5:\$J\$15,2)^*D27$$

This function identifies the appropriate unit cost in the second column of the table in cells I5:J15, based on the quarterly volume in row 27.

We should not expect the nonlinear solver to work well on this problem because the VLOOKUP function is not smooth. However, we can provide a point of comparison by running the nonlinear solver from a starting point at which all four decision variables are $10,000. We invoke Solver and specify:

Variables:	D18:G18
Objective:	C21 (maximize)
Constraints:	H18 ≤ C15

The nonlinear solver converges to a feasible solution with a profit of $68,834 as shown in Figure 12.4. The values for advertising are higher in Quarters 2 and 4, which have the higher seasonal factors, but the variation across quarters is relatively modest. The nonlinear solver identifies a budget allocation that improves profits by about 30 percent over the base case.

FIGURE 12.4 Optimal Allocation from the Nonlinear Solver

	A	B	C	D	E	F	G	H	I	J
1	Advertising Budget Model									
2	SGP/KRB								Cost Table	
3	1/1/2013									
4									Units	Cost
5	PARAMETERS								1	$36.00
6				Q1	Q2	Q3	Q4		1,000	33.00
7		Price	$40.00						2,000	30.00
8		Cost	$25.00						3,000	27.50
9		Seasonal		0.9	1.1	0.8	1.2		4,000	25.00
10		OHD rate	0.15						5,000	22.50
11		Sales Parameters							6,000	21.00
12			35						7,000	20.00
13			3000						8,000	18.00
14		Sales Expense		8000	8000	9000	9000		9,000	17.50
15		Ad Budget	$40,000						10,000	17.00
16										
17	DECISIONS							Total		
18		Ad Expenditures		$6,070	$11,965	$9,017	$12,948	$40,000		
19										
20	OUTPUTS									
21		Profit	$68,834		Base case	$52,702				
22										
23	CALCULATIONS									
24		Quarter		Q1	Q2	Q3	Q4	Total		
25		Seasonal		0.9	1.1	0.8	1.2			
26										
27		Units Sold		3000	4710	3069	5304	16083		
28		Revenue		120000	188391	122777	212157	643325		
29		Cost of Goods		82500	117744	84409	119339	403992		
30		Gross Margin		37500	70646	38368	92819	239333		
31										

The evolutionary solver is not limited by the presence of nonsmooth functions such as VLOOKUP. However, it is generally a good idea to impose bounds on all the decision variables when using the evolutionary solver. In our model, we can insert bounds by imposing a ceiling of $40,000 on each one. Obviously, this is not really a limitation on the search procedure because that is the size of the entire budget. Our specification becomes the following:

$$
\begin{aligned}
\text{Variables:} \quad & \text{C18:F18} \\
\text{Objective:} \quad & \text{C21 (maximize)} \\
\text{Constraints:} \quad & \text{H18} \leq \text{C15} \\
& \text{C18:F18} \leq \text{C15}
\end{aligned}
$$

We run Scatter Search with the CPU-based option, as suggested in the previous section, and a time limit of 10 seconds. The algorithm finds a solution with a profit of $85,763, which is 63 percent higher than the base case and 25 percent higher than the solution found by the nonlinear solver. The advertising expenditures in this solution focus on the fourth quarter. Repeated runs of Scatter Search fail to improve on this solution.

We can also try the Genetic Algorithm on this same problem. For the Genetic Algorithm, the Model-based search option is not relevant, but some other options are important, and we can specify several parameters that affect the implementation of the algorithm. Some of the elements on the Engine tab (see Figure 12.1) are specialized for the Genetic Algorithm, while others are used in conjunction with the linear solver and the nonlinear solver as well. For example, the Max Time parameter limits the amount of time Solver spends searching for a solution before stopping. For the Genetic Algorithm, we use this setting in a secondary role because we have other mechanisms available. The Max Time parameter should be set long enough for other options to have an opportunity to take effect, and it should reflect the length of time we are willing to allow the procedure to run without intervening. For large and complicated problems, that could mean a long wait, but we often choose a short time limit so that we can get feedback quickly. When we are debugging a model, or exploring performance on a given instance, we might set this option to 30 seconds.

The Random Seed parameter is blank by default, so that the random elements within the Genetic Algorithm remain unpredictable. If we run the algorithm twice in succession with the same starting variables, we may get different results. On the other hand, if we specify a number for the seed, such as 999, then two successive runs will yield identical results.

The Population Size parameter determines the number of members in each evolutionary generation. It should be large enough to ensure that the population is sufficiently diverse. The population size must be between 10 and 200, but 25 is often adequate for even very difficult problems. If the user leaves this entry blank, Solver sets this parameter equal to a value ten times the number of decision variables.

The Genetic Algorithm will stop (with a convergence message) when 99 percent or more of the population has objective function values whose relative differences are less than the Convergence parameter (which is specified just above the Population Size parameter).

The Mutation Rate parameter affects the level of randomness in generating new members of the population. A low rate would create few mutations, whereas a high rate would produce greater diversity. The default value is 7.5 percent, and we might raise this value if we find evidence that the evolutionary solver stalls due to lack of diversity.

Further down the list is the Require Bounds setting. Its default setting is True, and it is good practice to leave this option unchanged because the Genetic Algorithm tends to work more efficiently when the decision variables are bounded. With this setting, the model must contain simple bounds on the decision variables, entered as constraints. One of the bounds may well be a non-negativity requirement, which is most conveniently implemented by changing the Assume Non-Negative setting to True. Alternatively, if we are using binary variables, the usual binary specification implicitly provides the required bounds.

The next pair of parameters, Tolerance and Max Time without Improvement, work together. If we set Tolerance to 0.05 percent and Max Time without Improvement to 10 seconds, the search will stop if an improvement of at least 0.05 percent has not been found in the last 10 seconds. It often makes sense to set the Tolerance to zero and to increase the Max Time without Improvement whenever this combination causes the Genetic Algorithm to stop. The message `Solver cannot improve the current solution` indicates that this stopping condition was encountered.

The following table describes particular settings that would be appropriate in the initial stages of using the Genetic Algorithm. Some of these are default values, while others are entered by the user, in some cases overriding the default values.

Suggested Parameter Values for the Genetic Algorithm	
Max Time: 30 (sec)	Maximum Subproblems: blank
Convergence: 0.0001	Maximum Feasible Solutions: blank
Population Size: 25	Tolerance: 0.05 (percent)
Mutation rate: 0.075	Max Time without Improvement: 10 (sec)

Returning to our example, we run the Genetic Algorithm with the recommended settings. (Because of the randomness in the algorithm, the results we report may not be perfectly reproducible, but they illustrate how the algorithm works.) Our first run achieves an objective function value of $87,122. The stopping condition is the convergence message `Solver has converged to the current solutions, all constraints are satis-`fied. For our next run, then, it makes sense to create greater diversity. We raise the population size to 50 and the mutation rate to 10 percent. This time the objective function reaches $87,713, as shown in Figure 12.5, and the Max Time parameter dictates the stopping condition. Further runs do not find an improvement. Thus, in this example, the Genetic Algorithm outperforms the Scatter Search algorithm, ultimately achieving a solution that is 66 percent above the base case. Again, the algorithms cannot detect optimality, but we know from empirical research that these algorithms often produce very good solutions for models containing nonsmooth functions.

The software developers recommend the use of both algorithms in the evolutionary solver, as we illustrated in this example. Although Scatter Search appears as the default, detailed research on the better choice has not yet been done, and we can guess that the answer might depend on the type of problem we have at hand. Moreover, because the Genetic Algorithm has random elements, it does not hurt to rerun it a few times in the hope that a desirable set of random outcomes will produce a better solution than could be obtained with Scatter Search. Having illustrated the use of the two algorithms in tandem, the rest of the chapter simply reports on the results from Scatter Search, with the understanding that improvements might well be possible if we also run the Genetic Algorithm (and run it more than once).

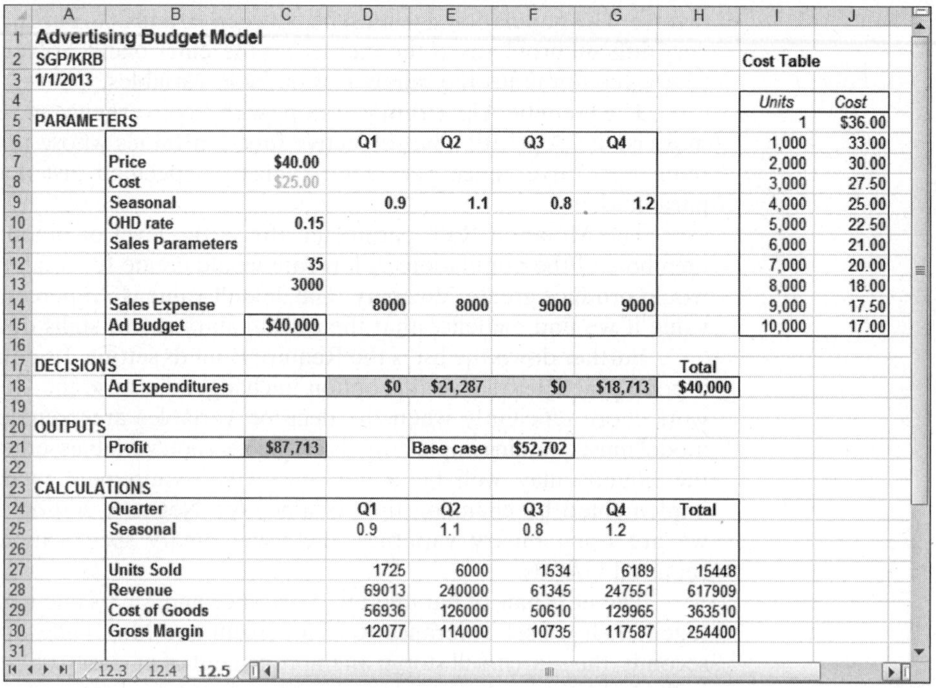

FIGURE 12.5 Optimal
Allocation from the
Evolutionary Solver

	A	B	C	D	E	F	G	H	I	J
1	Advertising Budget Model									
2	SGP/KRB								Cost Table	
3	1/1/2013									
4									Units	Cost
5	PARAMETERS								1	$36.00
6				Q1	Q2	Q3	Q4		1,000	33.00
7		Price	$40.00						2,000	30.00
8		Cost	$25.00						3,000	27.50
9		Seasonal		0.9	1.1	0.8	1.2		4,000	25.00
10		OHD rate	0.15						5,000	22.50
11		Sales Parameters							6,000	21.00
12			35						7,000	20.00
13			3000						8,000	18.00
14		Sales Expense		8000	8000	9000	9000		9,000	17.50
15		Ad Budget	$40,000						10,000	17.00
16										
17	DECISIONS							Total		
18		Ad Expenditures		$0	$21,287	$0	$18,713	$40,000		
19										
20	OUTPUTS									
21		Profit	$87,713		Base case	$52,702				
22										
23	CALCULATIONS									
24		Quarter		Q1	Q2	Q3	Q4	Total		
25		Seasonal		0.9	1.1	0.8	1.2			
26										
27		Units Sold		1725	6000	1534	6189	15448		
28		Revenue		69013	240000	61345	247551	617909		
29		Cost of Goods		56936	126000	50610	129965	363510		
30		Gross Margin		12077	114000	10735	117587	254400		
31										

12.3 / 12.4 / **12.5**

Looking at the larger picture, this example demonstrates that even a modest alteration to one function in a model (here, the product's cost) can fundamentally change the approach required for optimization. The lesson for model building is to recognize that the choice of Excel functions may affect the most suitable optimization algorithms to use and the results that can be achieved.

12.5 THE CAPITAL BUDGETING PROBLEM (REVISITED)

In the capital budgeting problem, our goal is to maximize the value of the projects we select, while respecting a budget limit on capital expenditures. In the Marr Corporation example introduced in Chapter 11, our budget limit was $160 million, and we had five projects that were candidates for selection.

EXAMPLE
The Marr Corporation

Division A of the Marr Corporation has been allocated $160 million for capital projects this year. Managers in Division A have examined various possibilities and have proposed five projects for Marr's capital budgeting committee to consider. The projects cover a variety of activities, as listed below:

P1   Implement a new information system.

P2   License a new technology from another firm.

P3   Build a state-of-the-art recycling facility.

P4   Install an automated machining center in production.

P5   Move the receiving department to new facilities on site.

There is just one project of each type. Each project has an estimated NPV and each requires a capital expenditure, which must come out of the budget for capital projects. The following table summarizes the possibilities, with all figures in millions of dollars:

	Project				
	P1	P2	P3	P4	P5
NPV	10	17	16	8	14
Expenditure	48	96	80	32	64

The committee would like to maximize the total NPV from projects selected, subject to the budget limit of $160 million. ∎

For the base case, we can use the same model we built for integer programming, changing only the engine selected in Solver, along with the relevant options for the evolutionary solver. For the model specification, we retain the following information:

$$
\begin{aligned}
\text{Variables:} \quad & \text{C5:G5} \\
\text{Objective:} \quad & \text{H7 (maximize)} \\
\text{Constraints:} \quad & \text{C5:G5} = \text{binary} \\
& \text{H9} \leq \text{J9}
\end{aligned}
$$

The initial run of the evolutionary solver finds the solution of $34 million, using the entire capital budget. We know from solving the problem with an integer programming approach that this solution is optimal.

Now we consider an additional condition in this basic capital-budgeting scenario. Specifically, licensing a new technology (P2) influences the installation of a new machining center (P4). As a result, savings are possible if the two projects are selected. In particular, some $17 million could be saved with simultaneous adoption. A logical way to amend the spreadsheet model to reflect this condition is as follows. In place of the capital requirement for P2, which is $96 million in cell D9, we can substitute the Excel function

$$= \text{IF}(\text{F5} = 1, 79, 96)$$

Thus, if P4 is selected (equivalently, F5 = 1), then the cost of P2 becomes $79 million; otherwise, it remains at $96 million.

With this modification, the model becomes inappropriate for the linear solver because it contains the nonsmooth IF function in cell D9. However, the presence of the IF function is not an obstacle for the evolutionary solver. On the Engine tab of the task pane, we can select the evolutionary solver and set its main parameters as suggested in the previous section. In addition, we can initialize the model by setting all variables to zero. This is an arbitrary starting point, but it is at least a feasible solution.

One additional change is desirable. Although the evolutionary solver can work with constraints, it is often less efficient when constraints are present, and performance tends to deteriorate as the number of constraints increases. For the purposes of using the evolutionary solver, an alternative exists. Instead of imposing an explicit constraint, we add a term to the objective function that penalizes the solution for violations of a constraint. To illustrate this technique in the Marr Corporation example, we add a calculation to cell J7, inserting the formula

$$= \text{IF}(\text{H9} > \text{J9}, 99, 0)$$

Then if the constraint in row 9 is violated by some choice of decision variables, this cell takes the value 99; otherwise, the value is zero. The next step is to subtract this value from the objective function. Thus, the objective function formula becomes

$$= \text{SUMPRODUCT}(\text{C5:G5}, \text{C7:G7})\text{-J7}$$

The model is shown in Figure 12.6, with the penalty calculated in cell J7.

The value 99 is arbitrary, but it serves two purposes. First, it is an unusual number and provides a symbol for violation of a constraint. Thus, for any set of values in the decision

FIGURE 12.6 Worksheet for the Modified Marr Corporation Example

	A	B	C	D	E	F	G	H	I	J
1	Capital Budgeting									
2										
3	Decisions									
4			P1	P2	P3	P4	P5			
5		1 for Yes	1	0	0	1	0			
6	Objective									Penalty
7		NPV	10	17	16	8	14	18.000		0
8	Constraints									Budget
9		Capital	48	79	80	32	64	80.000	<=	160.000
10										

cells, we can simply observe the value in cell J7 to determine whether the budget constraint is met. Second, the value is large enough to represent a substantial disincentive in the objective function for allowing a constraint to be violated. The specification of the problem now takes the following form:

Variables: C5:G5
Objective: H7 (maximize)
Constraints: C5:G5 = binary

No explicit constraints appear in this formulation, except for the binary designation of the variables. The budget constraint is implicit, appearing in the objective function in the form of a penalty. When a penalty is used in this way, it is important to give the model initial values for the decision variables that form a feasible solution. The evolutionary solver is then unlikely to include many solutions in the population that violate the constraints, and its search for a good, feasible value is enhanced.

When we run the evolutionary solver on this model, we obtain a solution of $35 million, which is better than the optimum in the base case. However, we don't know whether this is an optimal value for the modified problem, so we should run the model using both algorithms. In the case of the Genetic Algorithm, if a run stops because of convergence, we should expand the population size. If it stops because improvement is impossible, then the Max time without Improvement parameter should be increased or the Tolerance parameter should be reduced to zero. If this stopping condition persists, then it is a good idea to start the search with a different set of decision variables. Finally, if we simply run into the time limit, then the maximum time parameter should be increased to 60 seconds (and beyond, if we have the time). In this example, however, it appears that an objective function of $35 million is the best we can achieve.

12.6   THE FIXED COST PROBLEM (REVISITED)

In Chapter 11 we discussed the use of linking constraints as a mechanism for including fixed costs in integer programming models, and we extended the concept to the use of minimum batch-size constraints. Here, for the purposes of illustration, we demonstrate the evolutionary solver approach to a modified version of the Mayhugh Manufacturing example from Chapter 11.

EXAMPLE
Mayhugh
Manufacturing
Company

Mayhugh Manufacturing, a medium-size job shop, has been producing and selling three product families. Each product family requires production hours in each of three departments. In addition, each product family requires its own sales force, which must be supported no matter how large or small the sales volume happens to be. The parameters describing the situation are summarized in the following table:

	Product Family			Hours
	F1	F2	F3	Available
Profit per unit	$1.20	$1.80	$2.20	
	Hours Required per Thousand Units			Hours
Department A	3	4	8	2,000
Department B	3	5	6	2,000
Department C	2	3	9	2,000
Sales cost ($000)	60	200	100	
Demand (000)	400	300	50	

In considering the possibility of curtailing production to improve profitability, management has adopted the policy that product family F2 may not be produced, but if it is produced, then its volume must be at least 250,000. ∎

Figure 12.7 provides a model for the Mayhugh Manufacturing example with the minimum batch-size requirement for family F2. The formula in cell D8 takes on the value

FIGURE 12.7 Worksheet for the Mayhugh Example

	A	B	C	D	E	F	G	H
1	Product Mix with Fixed Costs							
2								
3	Decisions							
4			F1	F2	F3			
5			250	250	0	K-units		
6			1	1	0	binary		
7		Demands	400	300	50			
8		Minimum		250				
9	Objective							
10		Variable profit	1.20	1.80	2.20			
11		Fixed cost	60	200	100	490	K$	
12	Constraints							RHS
13		X	3	4	8	1750	<=	2000
14		Y	3	5	6	2000	<=	2000
15		Z	2	3	9	1250	<=	2000
16								

250 if F2 is produced and the value zero, otherwise. The formula in cell D8 is thus =IF (D6=1,250,0). Similarly, the indicators in cells C6:E6 take on the value 1 if production occurs for the corresponding family and zero if it does not. The demand constraints appear in row 7, and these can be incorporated as upper bounds on the production decision variables. Finally, the capacity constraints on the three departments appear in their usual form, although they could be represented with the use of penalties. The specification of the problem takes the following form:

$$
\begin{aligned}
\text{Variables:} \quad & \text{C5:E5} \\
\text{Objective:} \quad & \text{F11 (maximize)} \\
\text{Constraints:} \quad & \text{C5:E5} \leq \text{C7:E7} \\
& \text{D5} \geq \text{D8} \\
& \text{F13:F15} \leq \text{H13:}H\text{15} \\
& \text{C5:E5} = \text{integer}
\end{aligned}
$$

As mentioned earlier, it is desirable to start the evolutionary solver with values of the decision variables that are feasible and do not produce penalties. With this guideline in mind, we can initialize the model with all three decision variables at zero. Figure 12.7 shows the solution produced by one run of the evolutionary solver, yielding an objective function of $490,000. The solution shown in Figure 12.7 illustrates how fixed costs and minimum batch size constraints can be represented in a natural fashion (with IF statements), leading to the use of the evolutionary solver to produce a solution.

12.7 THE MACHINE-SEQUENCING PROBLEM

In the machine-sequencing problem, a set of jobs waits for processing on a machine. The machine is capable of handling only one job at a time, so the jobs must be processed in sequence. The problem is to find the best sequence. Integer programming approaches to this type of problem are possible, although they are somewhat complicated and often computationally inefficient. An alternative approach is to use the evolutionary solver.

EXAMPLE
Miles Manufacturing Company

Miles Manufacturing Company is a regionally focused production shop that fabricates metal components for auto companies. Its scheduling efforts are centered on a flexible machining center that handles a variety of operations, such as drilling, trimming, polishing, and mechanical testing. Jobs arrive at the machine—each job corresponding to a customer order—and the information system provides data on the size of the order, how long it will take to process and when it is due (the due dates having been previously negotiated with customers.) These due dates, which apply within the production scheduling system, have been adjusted for the delivery time needed to place the order in the customer's hands. When several orders are waiting to be processed, the supervisor looks for guidance on how the jobs should be sequenced. The ideal schedule would allow all jobs to be completed on or before their due dates.

This morning's workload consists of six jobs, as described in the following table. The problem is to sequence the jobs, thereby determining the machine schedule for the next few days.

Job Number	1	2	3	4	5	6
Processing time (hours)	5	7	9	11	13	15
Due date (hours from now)	28	35	24	32	30	40

With 60 total hours of work to schedule, and a latest due date of 40, it is obvious that the jobs cannot all be finished on time, even in the best schedule.

Each job will be either on time or late, as a function of the sequence chosen. If it is late, the amount of time by which it misses its due date is called its **tardiness**. There is no tardiness when a job completes prior to its due date. The objective is to minimize the total tardiness in the schedule.■

Figure 12.8 displays a spreadsheet model for this problem. The first module contains the tabulated data describing the specific problem to be solved. The next module contains a row of decision variables corresponding to the job sequence. Each position in sequence is assigned a job number (from 1 to 6). Since the sequence does not necessarily match the numbered sequence in which the data appear, we use the INDEX function to access the processing times and due dates that match the job in each sequence position. For example, the formula in cell C11, for the processing time of the first job, is

$$= \text{INDEX}(\text{C4} : \text{H6}, 2, \text{C10})$$

The INDEX function references the element in the second row of the data, in the column corresponding to the number in C10. A similar function in cell C13 references the third row of the data, obtaining the due date with the formula

$$= \text{INDEX}(\text{C4} : \text{H6}, 3, \text{C10})$$

The processing times and due dates thus appear in rows 11 and 13. From the processing times, the completion times can be computed directly, as shown in row 12. In row 14, we compute tardiness values, working from the completion time and due date in the two rows directly above. The tardiness values are summed in cell C16; this total represents the value of the objective function.

If someone were to give us a particular job sequence and ask us to compute the corresponding tardiness, we would likely make the calculations in a table that closely resembles Figure 12.8. In other words, we've built a model using the same logic we'd use if we were computing the results by hand. Viewed another way, we've built a model that permits Excel to say, "If you tell me the job sequence, then I'll calculate the measure of performance." In fact, building a model that responds to the "If you tell me . . . " invitation is a logical way to build models for the evolutionary solver.

FIGURE 12.8 Worksheet for the Miles Example

	A	B	C	D	E	F	G	H	I
1	**Sequencing Model**								
2		*Single-Machine Tardiness*							
3	**Data**								
4		Job	1	2	3	4	5	6	Total
5		Process time	5	7	9	11	13	15	60
6		Due date	28	35	24	32	30	40	
7									
8	**Decisions**								
9		Position	1	2	3	4	5	6	
10		Job	6	5	4	3	2	1	
11		Process time	15	13	11	9	7	5	
12		Completion	15	28	39	48	55	60	
13		Due date	40	30	32	24	35	28	
14		Tardiness	0	0	7	24	20	32	
15	**Objective**								
16		Total Tardiness	83						
17									

FIGURE 12.9 The Alldifferent Constraint

In the cells corresponding to decision variables, we want to choose integers between 1 and 6. Therefore, our first instinct might be to add constraints that restrict the decision variables to integers no less than 1 and no greater than 6. However, these constraints permit the choice of some job more than once. We would have to add a module that tests for duplication and penalizes solutions that choose any job multiple times. This procedure can be very inefficient, because it may generate many infeasible solutions. Since only feasible solutions are relevant to our search, a large fraction of the computational effort could be devoted to generating solutions that ultimately do not help in the search. It would be convenient if we could eliminate this inefficient filtering device and generate only solutions for which the integers in the decision cells contain no duplicates.

The capability we seek is usually called an **alldifferent constraint**: it ensures that the values of the decision variables form a set of integers with no duplicates. To implement the alldifferent constraint, we enter the range as the left-hand side and then use the pull-down menu of constraint types to select *dif*, as shown in Figure 12.9. The alldifferent constraint fills the designated range of cells with the integers from 1 to *n* in some order, where *n* is the number of cells in the range.

Because the objective function relies on the INDEX function and on the MAX function, it is nonsmooth and thus suitable for evolutionary solver. For the model specification, we enter the following information:

$$
\begin{aligned}
\text{Variables:} \quad & \text{C10:H10} \\
\text{Objective:} \quad & \text{C16 (minimize)} \\
\text{Constraints:} \quad & \text{C10:H10} = \text{alldifferent}
\end{aligned}
$$

We run the evolutionary solver, starting with the arbitrary solution 6-5-4-3-2-1 and using the default options. The procedure terminates quickly, producing the solution shown in Figure 12.10, with an objective function value of 33. This solution is optimal, as we could verify using integer programming or other, more elaborate techniques. There is no guarantee that runs of the very same model with the Genetic Algorithm will terminate with this solution; however repeated testing suggests that the evolutionary solver performs quite well on sequencing problems. In fact, if the number of variables governed by the alldifferent constraint is as large as 20, the evolutionary solver appears to be likely to find an optimum. On the other hand, when the number of variables is larger than, say, about 25, the performance of the evolutionary solver at finding an optimal solution appears to deteriorate.

FIGURE 12.10 Solution to the Miles Example

▲	A	B	C	D	E	F	G	H	I	
1	**Sequencing Model**									
2		*Single-Machine Tardiness*								
3	**Data**									
4		Job	1	2	3	4	5	6	Total	
5		Process time	5	7	9	11	13	15	60	
6		Due date	28	35	24	32	30	40		
7										
8	**Decisions**									
9		Position	1	2	3	4	5	6		
10		Job	1	3	5	2	4	6		
11		Process time	5	9	13	7	11	15		
12		Completion	5	14	27	34	45	60		
13		Due date	28	24	30	35	32	40		
14		Tardiness	0	0	0	0	13	20		
15	**Objective**									
16		Total Tardiness	33							
17										

12.8   12.10

12.8   THE TRAVELING SALESPERSON PROBLEM

The **traveling salesperson problem** refers to a general class of problems that share a common mathematical structure. In one version of the problem, a sales rep has several customers to visit, each in a separate city. The sales rep knows the distances between pairs of cities and must plan a trip that visits each of the cities once and returns home. This type of trip is called a **tour**. The sales rep would like to plan a tour that is as short as possible — that is, a tour with the minimum total distance. In another version of the problem, a manufacturer must schedule a painting operation that involves different colors for different parts. In this application the colors used for painting parts on the production line play the same role as cities, and the cleaning times between colors play the same role as distances between cities. The manufacturer would like to plan a tour (of the colors) that consumes the minimum total cleaning time. Mathematically, the sales rep and the manufacturer face the same type of problem.

The given information in any traveling salesperson problem is the array of "distances" between "cities." In the sales rep's version of the problem described above, the distances are symmetric — that is, the distance from city A to city B is the same as the distance from city B to city A. However, in the manufacturer's version, involving the painting operation, the cleaning times may not be symmetric. If two successive parts use the same color of paint, then no cleaning is required. But if the items require different colors, then there is a need to clean out the painting equipment. The time required depends on the paint color of the product just painted and on the color of the product to be painted next. The "distance" between colors i and j represents the time required to clean the equipment between color i and color j, and it need not be the same as the cleaning time between colors j and i. In a complete cycle through the parts, with one batch for each color, the *painting* time is fixed, but the length of the schedule is minimized when the total *cleaning* time is minimized. Total cleaning time, in turn, is the total length of a tour in the array of cleaning times.

EXAMPLE
The Douglas Electric Cart Company

The Douglas Electric Cart Company assembles small electric vehicles that are sold for use on golf courses, at university campuses, and in sports stadiums. In these markets, customers like a variety of colors, so Douglas offers several choices. As a result, its manufacturing operations include a sophisticated painting operation, which is scheduled separately from other manufacturing operations.

In today's schedule, there are six colors (C1 through C6) with cleaning times as shown in the following table:

	C1	C2	C3	C4	C5	C6
C1	–	16	63	21	20	6
C2	57	–	40	46	69	42
C3	23	11	–	55	53	47
C4	71	53	58	–	47	5
C5	27	79	53	35	–	30
C6	57	47	51	17	24	–

The entry in row i and column j of the table gives the cleaning time required between batches of color C_i and batches of color C_j. Each production run consists of a cycle through the full set of colors, and the operations manager wishes to sequence the colors so that the total cleaning time in a cycle is minimized. ∎

Returning to the traveling salesperson terminology, we refer to the colors in a production cycle as cities on a tour, and we refer to the cleaning time objective as the total distance. For example, if the painting schedule calls for the color sequence given by the cycle

$$1\text{-}2\text{-}3\text{-}4\text{-}5\text{-}6\text{-}1,$$

then the total distance (cleaning time in the cycle) is

$$16 + 40 + 55 + 47 + 30 + 57 = 245.$$

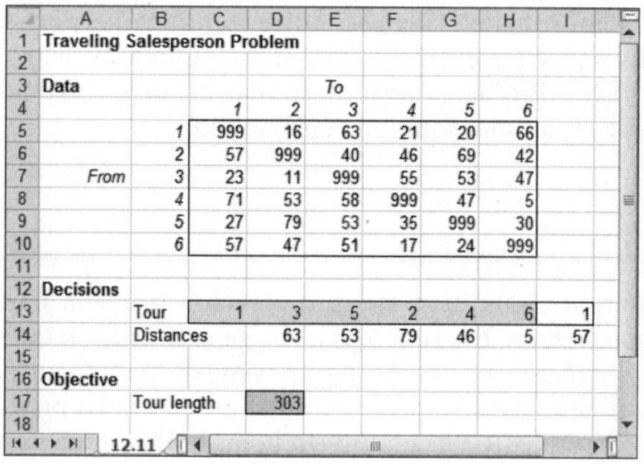

	A	B	C	D	E	F	G	H	I
1	Traveling Salesperson Problem								
2									
3	Data				To				
4			1	2	3	4	5	6	
5		1	999	16	63	21	20	66	
6		2	57	999	40	46	69	42	
7	From	3	23	11	999	55	53	47	
8		4	71	53	58	999	47	5	
9		5	27	79	53	35	999	30	
10		6	57	47	51	17	24	999	
11									
12	Decisions								
13		Tour	1	3	5	2	4	6	1
14		Distances		63	53	79	46	5	57
15									
16	Objective								
17		Tour length		303					
18									

12.11

FIGURE 12.11 Worksheet for the Douglas Example

We would like to know whether we can improve on this value, using a solution approach that relies on the evolutionary solver.

Figure 12.11 displays a spreadsheet model for the six-city example. The first module contains the distance array, which serves as the given data for the problem. The decision variables are listed in row 13, comprising the sequence of cities in the tour. For an n-city problem, this simply means a single row listing the integers from 1 to n, in some order. Since, by definition, a tour must return to its starting point, we repeat the starting city in cell I13. (This cell is not a decision variable; it is simply a reference to cell C13.)

Directly below the cells of the tour, we capture the distances between pairs of cities on the tour, as shown in Figure 12.11. We can use the INDEX function for this purpose. For example, the distance corresponding to the pair in cells C13 and D13 is isolated in cell D14 with the formula

```
= INDEX(C5:H10,C13,D13)
```

In cell D17 we compute the sum of the pairwise distances calculated in row 14. This sum represents the total tour length.

Because we use the INDEX function as a component in the objective function, this is a nonsmooth model, and it is not appropriate for either the linear solver or the nonlinear solver, but it is appropriate for evolutionary solver. For the model specification, we enter the following information:

Variables: C13:H13
Objective: D17 (minimize)
Constraints: C13:H13 = alldifferent

With the default settings, the first run of the evolutionary solver usually delivers a solution of 167, which turns out to be optimal, as shown in Figure 12.12. (More than one optimal tour exists.) Is the evolutionary solver always capable of finding an optimum with such

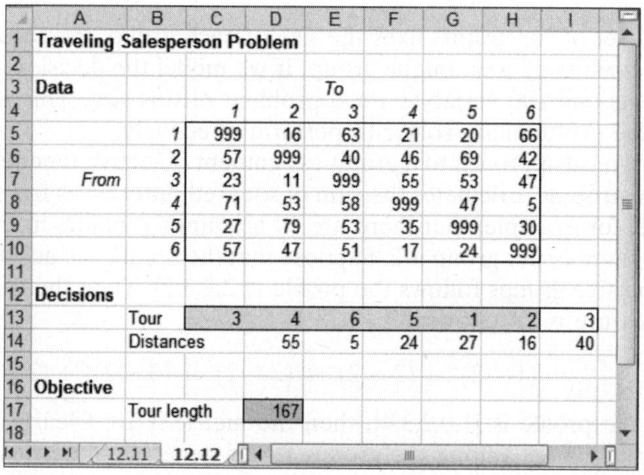

	A	B	C	D	E	F	G	H	I
1	Traveling Salesperson Problem								
2									
3	Data				To				
4			1	2	3	4	5	6	
5		1	999	16	63	21	20	66	
6		2	57	999	40	46	69	42	
7	From	3	23	11	999	55	53	47	
8		4	71	53	58	999	47	5	
9		5	27	79	53	35	999	30	
10		6	57	47	51	17	24	999	
11									
12	Decisions								
13		Tour	3	4	6	5	1	2	3
14		Distances		55	5	24	27	16	40
15									
16	Objective								
17		Tour length		167					
18									

12.11 12.12

FIGURE 12.12 Solution to the Douglas Example

limited effort? Unfortunately, it's not. As we mentioned earlier, sequencing problems with 10 to 20 tasks can frequently be solved to optimality with modest effort using the evolutionary solver. Problems with more than 20 tasks take additional effort, but they, too, seem to reach optimal solutions fairly often.

12.9 GROUP ASSIGNMENT

In several different application areas, a common problem involves the organization of items into groups. Often, the goal is to place similar items in the same group, as in cellular manufacturing—where we try to group similar manufactured parts together—or in market-positioning analysis—where we try to group similar products together. Sometimes, the goal is the opposite: to place *different* items in the same group. A familiar example in educational programs involves the formation of diverse student teams—where we try to form groups of students with dissimilar backgrounds when they are carrying out a particular group task. Business applications of the same type of model arise when consultants are assigned to different project teams or trainees are assigned to discussion groups. The following example involves forming student groups for course projects.

EXAMPLE
Oxbridge College's Accounting Department

Each term, the Accounting Department at Oxbridge assigns students to teams for the purposes of a simulated audit engagement. In this problem, we are given a description of each student on various dimensions, expressed with a set of 0s and 1s. In particular, the Department has recorded the following information for each student:

- Majored in accounting as an undergraduate (1 = yes, 0 = no).
- Previously worked for an accounting firm (1 = yes, 0 = no).
- Gender (1 = male, 0 = female).
- International background (1 = yes, 0 = no).

This term, 20 students will be participating in the exercise, and there will be five 4-person teams. For this exercise, the Department's goal is to achieve diversity in its assignment of students to teams. ∎

In this situation each student can be described by a string of four binary digits. For example, a male student from the U.S. who had not majored in accounting but had worked for an accounting firm would be represented by the string $\{0, 1, 1, 0\}$. A natural definition of decision variables for this problem is the following:

$$x_{jk} = 1 \text{ if student } j \text{ is assigned to group } k, \text{ and } 0 \text{ otherwise}$$

Suppose now that we want to form five teams of four students each. The essential constraints in the problem are as follows:

$$\sum_j x_{jk} = 4 \quad \text{for} \quad k = 1 \text{ to } 5$$
$$\sum_k x_{jk} = 1 \quad \text{for} \quad j = 1 \text{ to } 20$$

The first set of constraints fixes the size of each group; the second set ensures that each student is assigned to a unique group. If we model the decisions in this way, there are 25 constraints and 100 variables for a problem of this size. This is too large a problem to expect the evolutionary solver to perform effectively.

A typical approach to a group-assignment objective function builds on a metric that, for each attribute, calculates the sum of squared differences from the population average. Suppose, for example, that there are 10 accounting majors in the group of 20. Then the average number per group is 2. Suppose that the number of accounting majors assigned to the respective groups follows the profile $\{1,2,2,3,2\}$. Then the calculation of the performance measure is as follows:

$$(1 - 2)^2 + (2 - 2)^2 + (2 - 2)^2 + (3 - 2)^2 + (2 - 2)^2 = 2$$

If the profile is $\{1,0,2,3,4\}$, then the metric is 10. Clearly, the ideal distribution of accounting majors among the groups would generate a metric of zero. For an objective

FIGURE 12.13 Worksheet for the Oxbridge Example

Student	Major	Firm	Gender	Int		Objective Metric	Team	Position	Student	Major	Firm	Gender	Int		Maj	Firm	Gen	Int
Team Formation																		
Data						**Objective**			**Decisions**						**Calculations**			
Student	**Major**	**Firm**	**Gender**	**Int**		**Metric**	**Team**	**Position**	**Student**	**Major**	**Firm**	**Gender**	**Int**		**Maj**	**Firm**	**Gen**	**Int**
1	0	0	0	0		8	1	1	1	0	0	0	0					
2	0	1	1	0			1	2	2	0	1	1	0					
3	1	0	1	1			1	3	3	1	0	1	1					
4	1	0	0	0			1	4	4	1	0	0	0		0	0.2	0	0.4
5	0	1	1	0			2	1	5	0	1	1	0					
6	1	0	1	1			2	2	6	1	0	1	1					
7	1	0	0	1			2	3	7	1	0	0	1					
8	0	0	1	1			2	4	8	0	0	1	1		0	0.2	0.6	2
9	0	1	0	1			3	1	9	0	1	0	1					
10	1	1	0	0			3	2	10	1	1	0	0					
11	0	0	1	1			3	3	11	0	0	1	1					
12	1	0	0	0			3	4	12	1	0	0	0		0	0.4	1.4	0.2
13	0	0	1	0			4	1	13	0	0	1	0					
14	0	0	1	1			4	2	14	0	0	1	1					
15	0	1	0	0			4	3	15	0	1	0	0					
16	1	1	1	0			4	4	16	1	1	1	0		0.6	0.4	0.6	0.4
17	0	0	1	0			5	1	17	0	0	1	0					
18	1	0	0	1			5	2	18	1	0	0	1					
19	1	0	1	0		**Groups**	5	3	19	1	0	1	0					
20	0	1	0	0		5	5	4	20	0	1	0	0		0	0.2	0	0.4
Total	9	7	11	8														
Avg.	1.80	1.40	2.20	1.60														

12.13

function, we can calculate the metric for each attribute and then sum over the four attributes. This objective function can thus be expressed as a nonlinear function of the decision variables x_{jk}.

Although this is a natural formulation of the problem, it creates difficulties for two types of solution approaches. First, a direct formulation as an optimization problem leads to a nonlinear programming model with integer variables. As we pointed out in Chapter 11, this class of problems is poorly suited to the nonlinear solver. Instead, it makes sense to tackle the problem with the evolutionary solver. However, the natural formulation is also poorly suited to the evolutionary solver because it has too many constraints and variables.

An alternative formulation of the problem can take advantage of the alldifferent constraint. Here, we let

$$y_i = \text{student number assigned to position } i,$$

where there are 20 positions: four corresponding to the first group, four for the second group, and so on. The assignment of students to positions is equivalent to an assignment of students to groups. In our example, the y_i values need to satisfy the alldifferent constraint for the integers from 1 to 20. Based on this idea, we can build a spreadsheet model that is well suited to the evolutionary solver. Figure 12.13 shows the model. The data occupy columns A–E, with a four-element string for each student. The solution is described in columns I–K, where the decision cells in column K give the assignment of student numbers to groups and positions. In columns L–O we use the INDEX function to select the appropriate attribute values from columns B–E. The squared differences between each group's attribute count and the population mean are calculated in columns P-S, and their total appears in cell G5 as the objective function. Although this may seem to be a complicated way of computing the objective, it is nevertheless suitable for the evolutionary solver. For the model specification, we enter the following information:

> Variables: K5:K24
> Objective: G5 (minimize)
> Constraints: K5:K24 = alldifferent

The alldifferent constraint is sufficient to capture the constraints of the model, given the layout of our spreadsheet. Starting with different assignments, the evolutionary solver takes us in most cases to a solution with an objective value of 4 quite quickly (see Figure 12.14), suggesting, perhaps, that this is likely to be the optimal value. Alternative starting points and modifications of the options do not seem to produce any improvement. This is stronger evidence that we might have found the optimum, although the evidence is not conclusive. By using the evolutionary solver, administrators at the Accounting Department can achieve their assignment goals where other methods, such as nonlinear integer programming, would likely have failed.

The group assignment problem illustrates one instance in which creative use of the alldifferent constraint helps us to formulate a model that can be solved efficiently.

FIGURE 12.14 Solution
to the Oxbridge Example

	A	B	C	D	E		G		I	J	K	L	M	N	O	P	Q	R	S
1	Team Formation																		
2																			
3	Data						Objective				Decisions						Calculations		
4	Student	Major	Firm	Gender	Int		Metric		Team	Position	Student	Major	Firm	Gender	Int	Maj	Firm	Gen	Int
5	1	0	0	0	0		4		1	1	6	1	0	1	1				
6	2	0	1	1	0				1	2	10	1	1	0	0				
7	3	1	0	1	1				1	3	1	0	0	0	0				
8	4	1	0	0	0				1	4	8	0	0	1	1	0	0.2	0	0.2
9	5	0	1	1	0				2	1	15	0	1	0	0				
10	6	1	0	1	1				2	2	4	1	0	0	0				
11	7	1	0	0	1				2	3	11	0	0	1	1				
12	8	0	0	1	1				2	4	16	1	1	0	0	0	0.4	0	0.4
13	9	0	1	0	1				3	1	7	1	0	0	1				
14	10	1	1	0	0				3	2	2	0	1	1	0				
15	11	0	0	1	1				3	3	12	1	0	0	0				
16	12	1	0	0	0				3	4	13	0	0	1	0	0	0.2	0	0.4
17	13	0	0	1	0				4	1	19	1	0	1	0				
18	14	0	0	1	1				4	2	14	0	0	1	1				
19	15	0	1	0	0				4	3	20	0	1	0	0				
20	16	1	1	1	0				4	4	3	1	0	1	1	0	0.2	0.6	0.2
21	17	0	0	1	0				5	1	9	0	1	0	1				
22	18	1	0	0	1				5	2	5	0	1	1	0				
23	19	1	0	1	0		Groups		5	3	17	0	0	1	0				
24	20	0	1	0	0		5		5	4	18	1	0	0	1	0.6	0.4	0	0.2
25	Total	9	7	11	8														
26	Avg.	1.80	1.40	2.20	1.60														
27																			

H ◄ ► H / 12.13 / 12.14 / ◄

12.10 SUMMARY

The evolutionary solver complements the nonlinear solver (Chapter 8), the linear solver (Chapters 9 and 10), and the integer solver (Chapter 11). Unlike those algorithms, it does not explicitly seek a global optimum or even a local optimum. Nevertheless, it can often find good, near-optimal solutions to very difficult problems, and it may be the only effective procedure when a nonsmooth function appears in the model.

The evolutionary solver works with a user-selected set of options on the Engine tab. For Scatter Search, these do not need to be updated, although we might want to rerun the algorithm if we reach the Max Time limit. We might also try altering the initial values of the decision variables and running again. For the Genetic Algorithm, things are more complicated. Although we have offered suggestions for setting its options, the suggestions are merely a starting point. Different choices might be suitable for different problem types. In addition, we typically use one set of choices at the start of our analysis and other settings in subsequent runs, as we look to improve the solution. Intelligent selection of these parameters can enhance the performance of the Genetic Algorithm considerably. Aside from the guidelines given here, practice and experience are the key ingredients in effective choice of options.

The evolutionary solver is not likely to be trapped by local optima, as is the case with the nonlinear solver. This trait is advantageous in searching for good solutions to problems containing nonsmooth functions, especially nonlinear problems with integer variables. On the other hand, we must realize that the search procedure is both random (subject to probabilistic variation) and heuristic (not guaranteed to find an optimum). For that reason, we usually reserve the use of the evolutionary solver for only the most difficult problems, when the other solvers would fail or when we cannot build a suitable model with a smooth objective function.

One of the most challenging types of problems we address involves optimization of a model that contains probabilistic outcomes. In this setting, the evolutionary solver may be the only practical technique we can apply because the linear, nonlinear, and integer solvers for the most part do not accommodate probabilities. We discuss optimization of probabilistic models in Chapter 15.

EXERCISES

1. *Machine Sequencing.* A set of ten jobs must be scheduled at an integrated machining center that performs a number of metal-cutting operations on components for complex assemblies. These jobs and their processing times (expressed in hours) are described in the following table. In addition, each job has a corresponding due date that has been calculated by the production-control system. As a result of the sequence chosen, each job will either be on time or else it will be late. If it is late, the amount of time by which it misses its due date is called its *tardiness*. The objective is to minimize the total tardiness in the schedule.

Job	1	2	3	4	5	6	7	8	9	10
Processing time	6	1	2	5	9	8	12	3	9	7
Due date	17	5	25	15	20	8	44	24	50	20

What is the minimum total tardiness and a sequence that achieves it?

2. *Machine Sequencing.* A set of ten jobs must be scheduled at an integrated machining center that performs a number of metal-cutting operations on components for complex assemblies. These jobs and their processing times (expressed in hours) are described in the following table. In addition, each job has a corresponding due date that has been calculated by the production control system. As a result of the sequence chosen, each job will either be on time or else it will be late. If it is late, the amount of time by which it misses its due date is called its *tardiness*. The objective is to minimize the number of tardy jobs in the schedule.

Job	1	2	3	4	5	6	7	8	9	10
Processing time	6	1	2	5	9	8	12	3	9	7
Due date	17	5	25	15	20	8	44	24	50	20

What is the minimum number of tardy jobs and a sequence that achieves it?

3. *Scheduling a Production Shop.* Midwest Parts Supply (MPS) is a fabricator of small steel parts that are sold as components to manufacturers of electronic appliances and medical equipment. In the MPS fabrication department, steel sheets are subjected to a series of three main operations— cutting, trimming, and polishing—which must be completed in this order. Each machine processes the jobs in the same order, so it is sufficient to specify a single job sequence in order to describe a schedule. No machine can process more than one job at a time.

This morning, ten jobs have been released to the shop by the ERP system, and the production manager is interested in minimizing the time it takes to complete the entire schedule, usually referred to as the schedule *makespan*. The following table gives the number of hours required for each operation.

Job	1	2	3	4	5	6	7	8	9	10
Cutting time	1	5	7	8	3	7	9	8	6	3
Trimming time	2	9	6	9	2	10	7	9	1	1
Polishing time	9	7	8	9	3	4	7	4	3	1

What sequence achieves the minimum makespan and what is the minimum length of a schedule?

4. *Scheduling with Sequence-Dependent Setups.* A painting operation is scheduled in blocks, where each block involves painting products with a particular color. Cleaning time is required in between each pair of blocks so that the equipment can be prepared for the new color. In each cycle there is one block of each color, and the total painting time is determined by the volume of orders. However, the actual schedule length is determined by the sequence in which the blocks are scheduled, since the cleaning time depends on the color in the previous block and the color in the next block. The following table gives the number of minutes required to clean the equipment, according to the color pair.

From Color	To Color					
	1	2	3	4	5	6
1	–	4	8	6	8	2
2	5	–	7	11	13	4
3	11	6	–	8	4	3
4	5	7	2	–	2	5
5	10	9	7	5	–	2
6	8	4	3	6	5	–

What block sequence minimizes the amount of time spent in cleaning during a full cycle? What is the minimum number of minutes devoted to cleaning?

5. *Sales Response.* Crawford Labs has increased its profitability dramatically by using models to allocate its sales force among the company's major drugs. To guide that effort, a nonlinear sales-response curve is estimated for each drug.

A sales-response curve relates the sale of a product to the effort expended to sell it, which in this case is measured by the number of calls made by the sales force. For low levels of effort, sales rise rapidly with increased effort, but eventually the sales response levels out. Two elements are needed to develop a sales-response curve for a particular product: (1) some data or managerial judgments on the sales at various levels of effort, and (2) a family of S-shaped curves to fit the data.

A suitable family of curves for Crawford is given by the function

$$S = a + \frac{(b - a)E^c}{(d - E^c)}$$

where S = Sales; E = effort; and $a, b, c,$ and d are parameters that determine the shape and location of the curve.

At Crawford Labs, sales of the drug Flecavil were around 200 cases with a sales effort of 500 calls. Management was then asked to estimate sales at other levels of effort. Their estimates are given in the following table:

Effort	Estimated Sales
0% of current	50% of current
25%	53%
50%	55%
75%	75%
100%	100%
125%	120%
150%	127%
175%	132%
200%	135%

a. Fit a sales-response curve to the Crawford data, using a least-squares criterion. (Use percentages relative to the base case for the Effort and Sales measures.) What are the best values of the parameters a, b, c, and d?

b. What sales does the model in (a) predict for an effort of 115 percent?

6. *Planning a Tour.* Recent graduate and world traveler Alastair Bor is planning a European trip. He is influenced by his curiosity about urban culture in the EU and by his study of international relations while he was in school. Accordingly, he has decided to make one stop in each of twelve European capitals in the time he has available. The distances between the capitals are shown below:

From City	To City											
	Ams	**Ath**	**Ber**	**Bru**	**Cop**	**Dub**	**Lis**	**Lon**	**Lux**	**Mad**	**Par**	**Rom**
Amsterdam	—	2166	577	175	622	712	1889	339	319	1462	430	1297
Athens	2166	—	1806	2092	2132	2817	2899	2377	1905	2313	2100	1053
Berlin	577	1806	—	653	348	1273	2345	912	598	1836	878	1184
Brussels	175	2092	653	—	768	732	1738	300	190	1293	262	1173
Copenhagen	622	2132	348	768	—	1203	2505	942	797	2046	1027	1527
Dublin	712	2817	1273	732	1203	—	1656	440	914	1452	743	1849
Lisbon	1889	2899	2345	1738	2505	1656	—	1616	1747	600	1482	1907
London	339	2377	912	300	942	440	1616	—	475	1259	331	1419
Luxembourg	319	1905	598	190	797	914	1747	475	—	1254	293	987
Madrid	1462	2313	1836	1293	2046	1452	600	1259	1254	—	1033	1308
Paris	430	2100	878	262	1027	743	1482	331	293	1033	—	1108
Rome	1297	1053	1184	1173	1527	1849	1907	1419	987	1308	1108	—

a. What sequence achieves a minimum-distance tour of the cities, starting and ending in Brussels? What is the length of the minimum-distance tour?

b. Suppose that Alastair need not return to Brussels but can finish the tour in any of the cities. What sequence achieves a minimum-distance path through all the cities, starting in Brussels?

7. *Cutting Stock.* Poly Products sells packaging tape to industrial customers. All tape is sold in 100-foot rolls that are cut in various widths from a master roll, which is 15 inches wide. The product line consists of the following widths: 3″, 5″, and 7″. These can be cut in different combinations from a 15-inch master roll. For example, one combination might consist of three cuts of 5″ each. Another combination might consist of one 3″ cut, one 5″ cut, and one 7″ cut. Both of these combinations use the entire 15-inch roll without any waste, but other configurations are also possible. For example, another combination might consist of two 5″ cuts and a 3″ cut. This combination creates two inches of waste for every roll cut this way.

Each week, Poly Products collects demands from its customers and distributors and must figure out how to configure the cuts in its master rolls. To do so, the production manager lists all possible combinations of cuts and tries to fit them together so that waste is minimized while demand is met. (In particular, demand must be met exactly, because Poly Products does not keep inventories of its tape.) This week's demands are for 50 3″ rolls, 40 5″ rolls, and 30 7″ rolls.

a. List the combinations that can be cut from a 15-inch master roll so that there is less than three inches of waste (i.e., the smallest quantity that can be sold) left on the roll.

b. Find a set of combinations that meets demand exactly and generates the minimum amount of waste. Stated another way, the requirement is to meet or exceed demand for each size, but excess cuts must be counted as waste.

8. *Locating Warehouses.* Southeastern Foods has hired you to analyze their distribution-system design. The company has 11 distribution centers, with monthly volumes as listed below. Seven of these sites can support warehouses, in terms of the infrastructure available, and are designated by (W).

Center	Volume	Center	Volume
Atlanta (W)	5,000	Memphis (W)	7,800
Birmingham (W)	3,000	Miami	4,400
Columbia (W)	1,400	Nashville (W)	6,800
Jackson	2,200	New Orleans	5,800
Jacksonville	8,800	Orlando (W)	2,200
Louisville (W)	3,000		

The monthly fixed cost for operating one of these warehouses is estimated at $3,600, although there is no capacity limit in their design. Southeastern could build warehouses at any of the designated locations, but its criterion is to minimize the total of fixed operating costs and variable shipment costs. The following table shows the cost per carton of shipping from any potential warehouse location to any distribution center.

From City	To City										
	Atl	**Bir**	**Col**	**Jac**	**Jvl**	**Lvl**	**Mem**	**Mia**	**Nash**	**NewO**	**Orl**
Atlanta	0.00	0.15	0.21	0.40	0.31	0.42	0.38	0.66	0.25	0.48	0.43
Birmingham	0.15	0.00	0.36	0.25	0.46	0.36	0.26	0.75	0.19	0.35	0.55
Columbia	0.21	0.36	0.00	0.60	0.30	0.50	0.62	0.64	0.44	0.69	0.44
Louisville	0.42	0.36	0.50	0.59	0.73	0.00	0.38	1.09	0.17	0.70	0.86
Memphis	0.38	0.26	0.62	0.21	0.69	0.38	0.00	1.00	0.21	0.41	0.78
Nashville	0.25	0.19	0.44	0.41	0.56	0.17	0.21	0.91	0.00	0.53	0.69
Orlando	0.43	0.55	0.44	0.70	0.14	0.86	0.78	0.23	0.69	0.65	0.00

Using the evolutionary solver, find the minimum monthly cost for Southeastern Foods.

9. *Making Car Assignments.* You are organizing rides for a group of campers going on an all-day, off-site trip. You have lined up some drivers, and your problem is to assign campers to drivers. The drivers and the capacities of their cars are provided in the table below.

Driver	Capacity
Saul	5
Chris	4
Rob	3
Erick	5
Anna	6
Jim	5

The campers represent different age groups. Each age group is to be delivered to a different location. Thus, if a car holds campers of different ages, then the driver will have to drive to different destinations. An ideal solution would require each driver to go to just one location. However, such a solution is unattainable. The campers and their age groups are listed in the table below.

Group	Camper	Group	Camper
Age 7	George	**Age 9**	Eric
	Marcia		Scott
	Steve		Sarah
	Andrew		Gretchen
	Brian		Jamie
	Suzanne		Liz
Age 8	Lisa	**Age 10**	Patty
	Ben		Francesca
	Tommy		Adrian
	Vanessa		Ali
	Alberto		Cliff
	Jason		Mickey
	Sean		Matt

a. Although we know what an "ideal" solution would look like, we need a metric for evaluating less-than-ideal solutions. Devise a metric to serve as a measure of performance for the assignment.

b. Find the best assignment for the metric developed in part (a).

10. *Scheduling Power.* During the next 8 months, Metropolis Power Company forecasts the demands shown in the table below (measured in thousands of kwh):

Month	1	2	3	4	5	6	7	8
Demand	96	154	148	77	84	92	119	126

Power will be supplied from the four generating facilities, GF1-GF4. The facilities are each characterized by a generating capacity, a monthly operating cost, a startup cost, and a shutdown cost. These are each shown in thousands in the table below. When a generator is in operation, it provides service at its full capacity, even if that exceeds demand. No operating cost is saved by partial (rather than full) use of a generator's capacity. At the beginning of each month, it is possible to shut down any of the facilities that have been operating or to start up any of the facilities that have been idle.

Facility	Capacity	Cost	Startup	Shutdown
GF1	70	8	4	3
GF2	60	7	3	2
GF3	50	6	3	2
GF4	40	5	2	3

At the start of month 1, facilities GF1 and GF2 are in operation. What is the minimum total cost of providing the power demanded?

11. *Choosing an Assortment.* National Metals Company (NMC) manufactures titanium shafts. Its equipment is capable of producing shafts in ten lengths, reflecting different settings on its machinery. These lengths are 32 cm to 50 cm in steps of 2 cm. Setting up the machinery to produce one of these lengths (which is done once a week) costs $250. As a result, NMC has decided to make only a selected number of lengths. When a customer requests a given length, NMC may supply it from stock if it happens to match one of the lengths in the production schedule. Otherwise, NMC trims a longer length to meet the order. The variable cost for producing the shafts is $20 per cm, and NMC receives revenue of $40 per cm. Trim waste can be sold to a recycler for $15 per cm.

The demand requirements for the coming week are tabulated as follows—all demand must be satisfied:

Length (cm)	32	34	36	38	40	42	44	46	48	50
Demand	12	4	7	8	16	7	12	5	8	3

What is an optimal assortment of lengths for NMC to manufacture?

13 Decision Analysis

13.1 INTRODUCTION

In previous chapters, we have generally assumed that all the information we need for our models is known with certainty. When we recognized uncertainty at all, we addressed it using sensitivity analysis (as in Chapter 4). In the chapters on optimization, we tended to ignore uncertainty because Solver requires us to assume that the parameters in our models are fixed. But many business problems contain uncertain elements that are impossible to ignore without losing the essence of the situation. In this chapter, we introduce some basic methods for analyzing decisions affected by uncertainty.

In the typical spreadsheet model, there are two kinds of inputs: decisions and parameters. Decisions are subject to the control of the decision maker, whereas parameters are beyond the control of the decision maker. Whether based on judgment or derived from empirical data, parameters are usually treated as fixed—known in advance with certainty. Now, we broaden our viewpoint to include **uncertain inputs**—that is, parameter values that are subject to uncertainty. Uncertain parameters become known only after a decision is made.

When a parameter is uncertain, we treat it as if it could take on two or more values, depending on influences beyond our control. These influences are called **states of nature**, or more simply, **states**. In many instances, we can list the possible states, and, for each one, the corresponding value of the parameter. Finally, we can assign probabilities to each of the states so that the parameter outcomes form a probability distribution.

EXAMPLE
Wertz Game and Toy Company

Wertz Game and Toy (WGT) Company has developed an electronic toy for preschoolers that promises to be fun to play while it provides a sophisticated learning experience. WGT believes that its design is innovative enough that it can capture sales in this year's toy market before competitors can copy the major features and bring competing products to market. Nevertheless, WGT also has some doubts about how appealing its design will be. Because the toy is more sophisticated than the mechanical toys traditionally sold to this age group, the market could be very enthusiastic or it could be indifferent.

As WGT's Marketing Manager, we have some choices about how to bring this new toy to market. A conservative approach would be to introduce a single version of the toy and see how it fares. This option would keep the costs down in case the market response is unenthusiastic. A bold approach would be to bring out two versions of the game—basic and advanced—along with a line of accessories based on the original toy. This option would be quite profitable if the market response is positive but unprofitable if the response is indifferent. Finally, there is a compromise option, which involves bringing out two versions but none of the accessories.

Reviewing introductions of other products, our staff believes that it's possible to classify market responses to a new product into three categories: Good, Fair, and Poor. Taking these one at a time, they have estimated the costs and revenues associated with each option, for each possible category of market response. Their economic analysis is summarized in the following table of profit figures (given in thousands):

		Market Response		
		Good	Fair	Poor
	Single Version	100	60	−10
Decisions	Two Versions	200	50	−40
	Full Line	300	40	−100

■

The entries in the table represent estimated profits for the next year for every combination of action and state. We ignore profits beyond next year because it is likely this product will have a very short lifetime. Although detailed analyses were required to produce each of these profit estimates, all we need here is the profit estimate itself.

At WGT, we face a situation in which uncertainty plays an important role, and we must choose a decision by selecting from among the three actions available. Which action is best? We consider several ways of addressing this question.

13.2   PAYOFF TABLES AND DECISION CRITERIA

The table of profits in the WGT example is sometimes called a **payoff table**. The rows correspond to alternative actions and the columns to possible states. For each action-state combination, the entry in the table is a measure of the economic result. Typically, the payoffs are measured in monetary terms, but they need not be profit figures. They could be costs or revenues in other applications, so we use the more general term *payoff*.

The question we face in the WGT example would be much easier to answer if each action had only one payoff value associated with it. Then we could simply identify the best payoff (e.g., the largest profit) and select the corresponding action. But as we can see in the table, each action has not one but *three* payoff values associated with it. In a sense, the complication in this type of problem is that there is more information available than we are used to processing when it comes to selecting a course of action. We'd like to condense the information in the table and produce one value for each action, thus simplifying the choice.

13.2.1   Benchmark Criteria

There are some simple ways to condense the information in each row of the table into one summary value for each action. For example, suppose we focus on the largest profit potential for each action and compute the maximum payoff in each row as a summary value. This approach corresponds to taking an optimistic view of the possible outcomes: We look only at the best case and ignore the others. In the WGT example, the most profitable outcome happens to occur with the Good market response for each of the decisions, yielding the following choices:

	States			Max Payoff
	Good	Fair	Poor	
Single Version	100	60	−10	**100**
Two Versions	200	50	−40	**200**
Full Line	300	40	−100	**300**

Now that we've condensed the information into one value for each action, we can make a straightforward choice. We are led to the Full Line as the best decision. This approach is called the **maximax payoff criterion** because it seeks the largest of the maximum payoffs among the actions.

An obvious alternative is to be pessimistic. We could instead take as the summary value the smallest payoff in each row. These happen to occur with the Poor market response, yielding the following choices:

	States			Min Payoff
	Good	Fair	Poor	
Single Version	100	60	−10	**−10**
Two Versions	200	50	−40	**−40**
Full Line	300	40	−100	**−100**

Again, we have a single value for each action, but here the Single Version is the best decision. This approach is called the **maximin payoff criterion** because it seeks the largest of the minimum payoffs among the actions. As the example illustrates, optimistic and pessimistic perspectives can lead to different choices. The broader point is that the choice of a criterion is critical: Depending on what we choose as a criterion, a different action may turn out to be the best decision.

Although optimistic and pessimistic possibilities would appear to represent the two extremes of choice, there is actually another way to implement conservative thinking. Instead of using the nominal profit values, let's interpret them in relative terms. Suppose, for example, that the Good market state occurs. If we had chosen the Single Version action, then the profit of $100,000 does not convey our feeling about the choice. Sure, a profit of $100,000 is nice, but we would still be aware that, had we chosen the Full Line, we could have been better off by $200,000. In other words, it's the fact that we *could* have done better that influences how we feel about the result. To formalize this approach, we define a measure called the **regret**. For any state and any specific action, the regret is the monetary difference between the best possible payoff for that state and the payoff for the specific action.

In the case of WGT, for the Good state, the Single Version generates regret of $200,000 $(= 300,000 - 100,000)$; Two Versions generates a regret of $100,000 $(= 300,000 - 200,000)$, and the Full Line generates a regret of zero $(= 300,000 - 300,000)$. The table below shows the complete set of regrets, in the same format as our original decision table:

	States		
	Good	Fair	Poor
Single Version	200	0	0
Two Versions	100	10	30
Full Line	0	20	90

To condense the information into a summary value for each action, we again assume that the worst (state) will happen, and we ignore the other outcomes. Thus, we compute the maximum regret in each row, giving rise to the following summary values:

	States			Max
	Good	Fair	Poor	Regret
Single Version	200	0	0	**200**
Two Versions	100	10	30	**100**
Full Line	0	20	90	**90**

Having condensed the information down to one value for each action, the choice is straightforward. Keep in mind that when we use a regret measure, we want to achieve as *small* a value as possible, so we would choose the Full Line as the best decision. This approach is called the **minimax regret criterion** because it seeks the smallest of the maximum regrets among the actions. As the example shows, the minimax regret criterion and the maximin payoff criterion can lead to different decisions, although they both represent pessimistic approaches.

13.2.2 Incorporating Probabilities

The three criteria introduced in the previous section are benchmarks in the following sense. Each one ignores some of the given information as a means of condensing the data down to one value for each action. By focusing on just one extremely optimistic or one extremely pessimistic outcome, we would be ignoring information that could be quite relevant. To develop a more persuasive method for making a decision, we would like to incorporate all the information given.

The three criteria from the previous section also ignore information that we may have about the relative likelihoods of the possible states of nature. If we know something about the probabilities of the various states, our decision will generally improve if we take that information into account.

At WGT, for example, we might come up with the following assessment of the probabilities for different market responses:

	States		
	Good	**Fair**	**Poor**
Probability	0.2	0.5	0.3

Here, we think of the events Good, Fair, and Poor as three mutually exclusive and exhaustive outcomes. We can immediately translate this information into probability distributions for the payoffs corresponding to each of the potential actions. For the Single Version, we have the following distribution of profit:

Profit ($000)	100	60	−10
Probability	0.2	0.5	0.3

Previously, we had three possible (profit) outcomes for each state; now, we have three outcomes along with three probabilities. That's six pieces of information, but our task is still to condense this information into one number for each action so that we can make a straightforward choice.

Given that we have a probability distribution, a standard way to summarize it numerically is to compute its **mean** or **expected value** (see Appendix 3 for more information). The expected value is the weighted average outcome, where the weights are the probabilities of each state. For the Single Version, the calculation of expected profit takes the following form:

$$EP(\text{Single Version}) = (0.2)(100{,}000) + (0.5)(60{,}000) + (0.3)(-10{,}000) = 47{,}000$$

We use the notation EP to represent an expected payoff—in this case, the expected profit. Note that the expected payoff calculation ignores *no* information: all outcomes and probabilities are incorporated into the result. Using the expected payoff as a summary measure, our comparison reduces to the following:

	States			
	Good	**Fair**	**Poor**	**EP**
Probability	0.2	0.5	0.3	
Single Version	100	60	−10	**47**
Two Versions	200	50	−40	**53**
Full Line	300	40	−100	**50**

Thus, with the **expected payoff criterion**, the best choice is Two Versions, which has an expected payoff of $53,000.

To justify the use of expected payoff as a criterion, we might imagine hypothetically that we face a large number of independent opportunities to repeat this same decision (or at least a decision very much like it). Each time, one of the states will occur, and in the long run, the Good state, the Fair state, or the Poor state will occur with frequencies that match their probabilities. Then the action that achieves the maximum profit in the long run would be Two Versions. It would generate a long-run average of $53,000 per opportunity, which would be larger than the long-run average of either of the other two options. In general, the long-run profit would be maximized by the action that achieves the largest expected value at each opportunity.

The analysis of payoff tables captures the main principles of decision making with uncertain outcomes. Furthermore, the necessary calculations could easily be made in a spreadsheet, but we have avoided showing spreadsheet models for these calculations because the table format can sometimes become unwieldy. Decision trees offer a more flexible modeling format, especially when a set of decisions must be made in series. Decision trees are the topic of the next section. Subsequent sections introduce software for drawing and analyzing trees in spreadsheets.

13.3 USING TREES TO MODEL DECISIONS

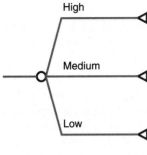

FIGURE 13.1 Simple Probability Tree

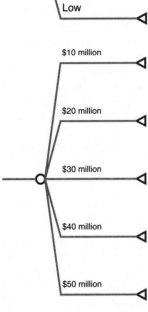

FIGURE 13.2 Probability Tree with Five States

A **probability tree** depicts one or more random factors. For example, if we believe that demand for our product is uncertain, we might model that uncertainty using the probability tree in Figure 13.1. In this simple tree, we assume that demand may take on one of the three alternative values: High, Medium, or Low. The node from which the branches emanate is called a **chance node**, and each branch represents one of the possible states that could occur. Each state, therefore, is a possible resolution of the uncertainty represented by the chance node. Eventually, we'll specify probabilities for each of the states and create a probability distribution to describe uncertainty at the chance node.

In other circumstances, we might want to show greater detail than just three qualitative states for demand, so we might use a tree with more branches, perhaps quantifying the states as $10 million, $20 million, $30 million, $40 million, and $50 million, as shown in Figure 13.2. Again, the tree is meant to show that demand is uncertain and that just one of the alternative states will actually occur. When we specify the probabilities for each of these five states, we create a probability distribution for the dollar value of demand.

Probability trees can accommodate more than one source of uncertainty. In addition to the demand uncertainty in Figure 13.1, suppose we face uncertainty in both the number of competing products and the competitive effectiveness of our advertising. We can draw a tree with three chance nodes. The first chance node represents demand states, characterized as High, Medium, or Low. For each demand state, one of several possible numbers of competitors will occur. Likewise, for each combination of demand and number of competitors, one of several levels of advertising effectiveness will occur. We can depict this situation either in a telegraphic form (Figure 13.3), in which only one chance node of each type is displayed, or in

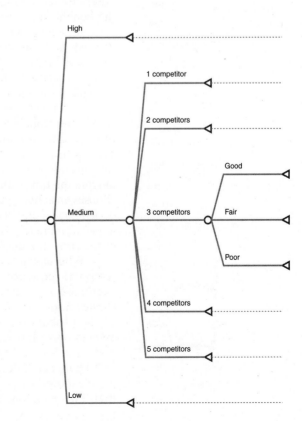

FIGURE 13.3 Three Chance Nodes in Telegraphic Form

FIGURE 13.4 Three
Chance Nodes in
Exhaustive Form

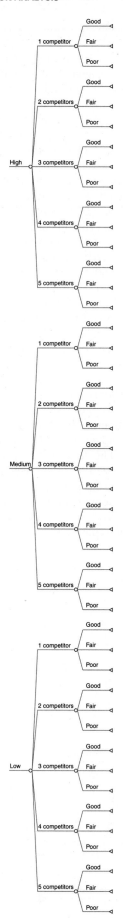

exhaustive form (Figure 13.4), where all possible combinations are displayed. In either case, the tree conveys the idea that there are 45 possible states, corresponding to the following calculation:

$$\text{States} = (\text{demand levels}) \times (\text{number of competitors})$$
$$\times (\text{levels of advertising effectiveness})$$
$$\text{States} = 3 \times 5 \times 3 = 45$$

Once we realize this fact, we could equivalently represent the outcomes with one chance node and 45 states. To perform the steps in analyzing the tree, we would need to examine the details for each of these states. For that purpose, the telegraphic form is not sufficiently detailed, and we would instead need to represent the entire set of 45 alternatives, as in Figure 13.4.

Although probability trees are helpful for displaying chance events and their outcomes, they can quickly become complex when there are several sources of uncertainty, as our 45-state example suggests. At an early stage in building a tree, however, it is not necessary to be precise in specifying the number of alternatives at a chance node. It is more important to recognize which outcomes are uncertain and how to represent them logically.

13.3.1 Decision Trees

Decision-tree models offer a visual tool that can represent the key elements in a model for decision making under uncertainty and help organize those elements by distinguishing between decisions (controllable variables) and random events (uncontrollable variables). In a **decision tree**, we describe the choices and uncertainties facing a single decision-making agent. This usually means a single decision maker, but it could also mean a decision-making group or a company. In our example, we may think of ourselves in the role of the marketing manager, who is also the decision-making agent. Alternatively, we may prefer to think of WGT as the agent because the benefits and costs belong to the firm.

In a decision tree, we represent decisions as square nodes (boxes), and for each decision, the alternative choices are represented as branches emanating from the decision node. These are potential actions that are available to the decision maker. In addition, for each uncertain event, the possible alternative states are represented as branches emanating from a chance node, labeled with their respective probabilities. For the WGT example, the tree contains three possible actions, and each action is associated with a random event with three possible states, as shown in Figure 13.5. The layout, showing the actions on the left and the uncertain events to their right, mirrors the time sequence in which the elements occur: WGT *first* chooses an action, and *then* the uncertain event takes place. Finally, depending on the action chosen and the uncertain event that follows, a specific monetary payoff occurs, shown on the diagram to the right of the corresponding branch.

Whereas we *build* the tree left to right, to reflect the temporal sequence in which a decision is followed by a chance event, we *evaluate* the tree in the reverse direction. At each chance node, we can calculate the expected payoff represented by the probability distribution at the node. This value becomes associated with the corresponding action branch of the decision node. (In Figure 13.6, the three expected values are 47, 53, and 50.) Then, at the decision node, we calculate the largest expected payoff to determine the best action. These calculations confirm that Two Versions is the best decision and that the expected

FIGURE 13.5 Decision Tree for Wertz Game and Toy

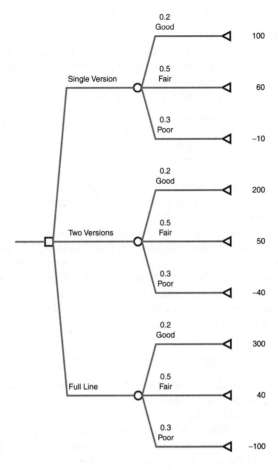

FIGURE 13.6 Analysis of the Tree for Wertz Game and Toy

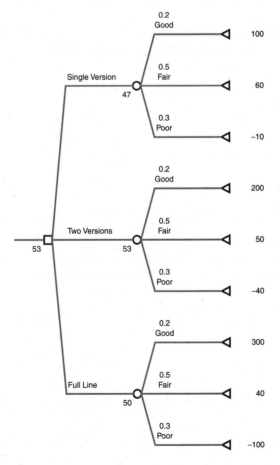

profit for that decision is $53,000. This process of making the calculations is usually referred to as **rolling back** the tree.

After we identify the optimal decision, it is usually a good idea to examine the probability distribution that describes payoffs in the optimal case. For the WGT example, this task is straightforward because the outcomes for the Two Versions decision have been treated explicitly. The distribution is the following:

Profit ($000)	200	50	−40
Probability	0.2	0.5	0.3

The distribution associated with a particular action is called its **risk profile**. The risk profile shows all the possible economic outcomes and provides the probability of each: It is a probability distribution for the principal output of the model. This form reinforces the notion that, when some of the input parameters are described in probabilistic terms, we should examine the outputs in probabilistic terms. In the WGT example, uncertainty about market response means that we need probability models to describe the profits for alternative decisions. After we determine the optimal decision, we can use a probability model to describe the profit outcome. In particular, examining the distribution in the table above, we can confirm that the expected payoff is $53,000, and we can see that there is a 30 percent chance of negative profits with this decision.

13.3.2 Decision Trees for a Series of Decisions

Decision trees are especially useful in situations where there are multiple sources of uncertainty and a sequence of decisions to make. For example, suppose that we are introducing a new product and that the first decision determines which channel to use during test-marketing. When this decision is implemented, and we make an initial commitment to a marketing channel, we can begin to develop estimates of demand based on our test. At the end of the test period, we might reconsider our channel choice, especially if the demand has been low, and we may decide to switch to another channel. Then, in the full-scale introduction, we attain a level of profit that depends, at least in part, on the channel we chose initially. In Figure 13.7, we have depicted (in telegraphic form) a situation in which we choose our channel initially, observe the test market, reconsider our choice of a channel, and finally observe the demand during full-scale introduction.

FIGURE 13.7 Decision Tree with Sequential Decisions

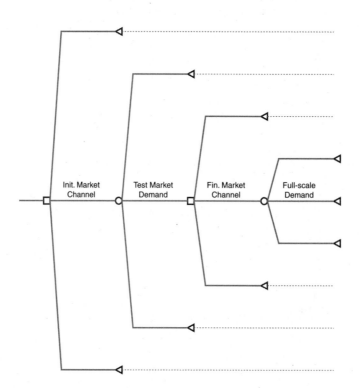

To illustrate the use of a decision tree containing decisions in a serial structure, we analyze the course of a lawsuit.

EXAMPLE
A Patent-Infringement Suit

One of our corporate competitors is threatening us with a lawsuit for patent infringement. The competitor is already in court in a similar lawsuit against another firm, and our legal staff estimates that there is a 50 percent chance that our competitor will prevail. One option open to us is to settle out of court now; the alternative is to wait until the current case is resolved before taking action. If our competitor loses the other suit, it will not pursue an action against us. On the other hand, if the competitor wins, it is likely to sue us. Our legal staff estimates that likelihood at 80 percent. They further estimate that the suit would be brought for $10 million.

If the competitor sues us, we can negotiate a settlement, go to trial and contest the patent-infringement claim, or go to trial and concede the patent infringement but fight the settlement amount. In either case, of course, the trial will dictate the monetary outcome. Our legal staff estimates that a negotiated settlement would cost us roughly $8 million. If we contest the patent, we have a 30 percent chance of winning the suit. If we concede the patent and contest the settlement amount, then the only question would be the size of that amount. Our legal staff envisions two possibilities: High, at $15 million, with a 60 percent probability, and Low, at $5 million, with a 40 percent probability. ∎

Figure 13.8 shows a decision tree for this case, with a display of payoffs and probabilities. The first decision is whether to settle now or wait for the outcome of the competitor's current suit. At this stage, we know very little about what the settlement amount could be, so we have simply labeled it X. If we wait and if the current suit fails, then we will not be sued, and there will be no monetary consequences. However, if the competitor prevails, we show a chance node with an 80 percent probability that our competitor will sue us. If there is no suit, there are again no monetary consequences. If our opponent sues, we have the three choices shown as branches on the tree. First, we could choose to settle. We represent that branch with the estimated cost of $8 million. Next, the outcome of each of the trial branches is shown as random. If we contest the patent, then the outcome is represented with win/lose outcomes, and a 30 percent chance of winning the suit. If we concede the patent and contest the settlement amount, then we represent the outcomes with the settlement amounts and probabilities indicated by our legal staff.

This example illustrates a case in which two sets of decisions must be made and shows how the decisions available to us later on depend on choices made earlier, as well as on chance events. The result is an asymmetric tree, with chance events interspersed among decision opportunities. One important feature of legal proceedings is that both parties have a series of options, and at least as a first cut, we can represent the outcomes of the other party's choices (such as whether to sue) as random events, just like the outcomes of trials.

FIGURE 13.8 Decision Tree for the Patent Infringement Example

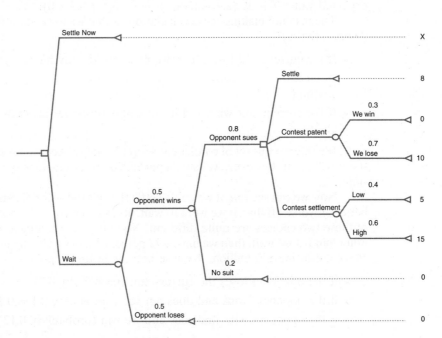

FIGURE 13.9 Analysis of
the Patent Infringement
Example

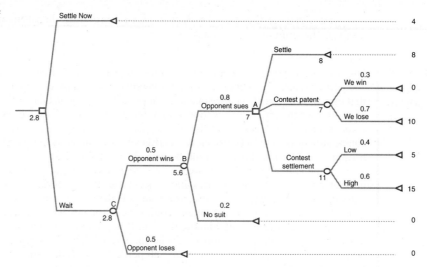

The objective of a quantitative analysis in this case is not simply to determine the optimal decision but also to choose an appropriate value for settling the suit now. For this purpose, we can assign an arbitrary but large amount as the settlement figure so that we can evaluate the expected outcome if we choose to wait. In Figure 13.8, we have denoted this amount as X, and we have included the necessary probabilities and outcome values elsewhere. Note that the outcomes are all costs, so our objective is to minimize expected cost.

We roll back the tree from right to left, calculating expected values at chance nodes and minimizing costs at decision nodes, as shown in Figure 13.9. In the figure, we have arbitrarily set the settlement amount at $4 million. If the opponent wins the current suit and sues us, we have three choices (at node A):

- Settle

- Go to Trial/Contest Patent

- Go to Trial/Concede Patent and Contest Settlement

The expected values for the last two options are $7 million and $11 million, respectively. Because settling at this stage would cost us $8 million, the lowest-cost choice is to contest the patent.

At node B, we will either be sued and lose $7 million in expected value, or we will not be sued and lose nothing. Given that the probability of a suit is 0.8, the expected value at node B is $5.6 million ($= 0.8 \times 7 + 0.2 \times 0$). At node C, we have a 50 percent chance of losing an expected value of $5.6 million and a 50 percent chance of losing nothing. The expected value here is $2.8 million ($= 0.5 \times 5.6 + 0.5 \times 0$).

The result of making these calculations is that we have identified an optimal *decision strategy*, that is:

- If the current suit loses, then we need not do anything.

- If the current suit wins and if our competitor does not sue us, then we need not do anything.

- If the current suit wins and if our competitor sues us, then we should contest the patent.

We refer to this set of contingencies as a strategy because we cannot be certain which states will occur; however, we have determined our best course of action for each possible state.

Now we can see that if we could settle the suit today for $2.8 million, we would be no better or worse off than if we were to wait, at least in terms of expected costs. But the risks of these two choices are quite different. No uncertainties attach to settling now. On the other hand, if we wait, then we have a 72 percent chance of losing nothing and a 28 percent chance of losing $10 million. We lose nothing in three cases:

- if the opponent loses the current suit (probability 0.5)

- if the opponent wins and does not sue (probability $0.1 = 0.5 \times 0.2$)

- if the opponent wins and sues and we win (probability $0.12 = 0.5 \times 0.8 \times 0.3$)

The probabilities of these outcomes sum to 0.72, but the complement, 0.28, represents the probability of a substantial loss. The following simple table represents the risk profile under the optimal strategy:

Cost ($Million)	0	10
Probability	0.72	0.28

Given the 28 percent chance of an outcome we'd like to avoid, we might even decide that it's preferable to offer somewhat more than $2.8 million to settle immediately.

Suppose we consider offering $4 million now to avoid a suit entirely. We can then compare two risk profiles. One risk profile is the two-outcome table shown above, with potential losses of $0 and $10 million. The other risk profile is a one-outcome table corresponding to the settlement amount. The decision boils down to whether we prefer the payment of $4 million to ensure that we will avoid the possible cost of $10 million. It is our preference for one of these risk profiles that will be expressed as a decision. Thus, the decision tree provides some useful quantitative guidance for a possible settlement decision that might otherwise seem entirely subjective.

As this example demonstrates, when there are other players or agents in the scenario, their actions can be depicted as chance nodes, although this may be an oversimplification. If we were to sue a competitor for patent infringement, it is unlikely that they would toss a coin to decide whether to settle or go to court against us. More likely, they would act as we would in that situation—that is, they would study the situation and make a decision aimed at reaching the best outcome for *them*. The analysis of the interrelated decisions of two (or more) actors is quite difficult, and we will not discuss it at length except to mention that representing a competitor's actions as random probably overstates the value we can extract from the situation.

13.3.3 Principles for Building and Analyzing Decision Trees

Decision trees can be built using a fairly standard procedure. Judgment is required, however, in determining which decisions and uncertainties are critical to the situation and therefore must be captured in the tree, as well as in selecting the specific choices and states to recognize. Beginners tend to draw overly complex trees. The more experienced analyst starts with a small number of nodes and a small number of outcomes and expands only when the results suggest that more detail is required. Here is a general procedure for constructing trees:

1. Determine the essential decisions and uncertainties.
2. Place the decisions and uncertainties in the appropriate temporal sequence.
3. Start the tree with a decision node representing the first decision.
4. Select a representative (but not necessarily exhaustive) number of possible choices for the decision node.
5. For each choice, draw a chance node representing the first uncertain event that follows the initial decision.
6. Select a representative (but not necessarily exhaustive) number of possible states for the chance node.
7. Continue to expand the tree with additional decision nodes and chance nodes until the overall outcome can be evaluated.

Decision trees can be used to develop a purely qualitative understanding of a situation, although they are usually used for quantitative analysis as well. This quantitative analysis can identify which decisions are best and can construct the probability distribution of results. To carry out this analysis, we need two types of information: the probability for each possible state and the overall value of arriving at the end of the tree along a particular path. Here is the rollback procedure for analyzing trees:

1. Start from the last set of nodes—those leading to the ends of the paths.
2. For each chance node, calculate the expected payoff as a probability-weighted average of the values corresponding to its branches.
3. Replace each chance node by its expected value.

4. For each decision node, find the best expected value (maximum benefit or minimum cost) among the choices corresponding to its branches.

5. Replace each decision node by the best value, and note which choice is best.

6. Continue evaluating chance nodes and decision nodes, backward in sequence, until the optimal outcome at the first node is determined.

7. Construct its risk profile.

In the rollback procedure, any chance node, or any decision node, can be evaluated once the nodes connected to its emanating branches have been evaluated. In that way, the calculations move from the end of the tree toward the beginning, ultimately identifying the optimal choice at the initial decision node.

13.3.4 The Cost of Uncertainty

In the decision trees we have considered so far, a decision node precedes a chance node. Indeed, the crux of the problem is that an action must be chosen *before* learning how an uncertain event will unfold. The situation would be much more manageable if we could learn about the uncertain event first and *then* choose an action. Reversing the sequence in this way may not be feasible in practice, but it can provide us with some useful insight.

In the WGT example, suppose we could wait to decide on an action until after learning how the market will respond. It's as if we had a crystal ball and could see into the future. Peering into the crystal ball, we could learn one of three things:

- The market will be Good.
- The market will be Fair.
- The market will be Poor.

Each of these conditions places us in a specific column of the original payoff table. If the Good market prevails, then our best choice is the Full Line. The corresponding profit is $300,000. If the Fair market prevails, then our best choice is the Single Version (profit: $60,000). And if the Poor market prevails, then our best choice is again the Single Version (net loss: $10,000).

Of course, we can't know beforehand which state we'll see in the crystal ball, but we already know the probabilities of the three outcomes. These probabilities correspond to the original probability estimates. When we initially quantified the elements of the problem, we took the probability of the Good market response to be 0.2, and therefore, the probability that we will see the Good market response when we peer into the crystal ball is also 0.2. Similarly, the probability that we will see the Fair market response is 0.5, and the probability that we will see the Poor market response is 0.3. Thus, we have three profit outcomes and a probability for each. The probability distribution of profit outcomes then takes the following form:

Profits ($000)	300	60	−10
Probability	0.2	0.5	0.3

The mean of this distribution is $87,000. This value represents the *EP* when we can determine the state first and then choose the most appropriate action. We call this quantity the Expected Payoff with Perfect Information (*EPPI*). In the original decision problem, when the choice had to be made in advance of knowing the state, the expected profit was only $53,000. The difference between these two expected values, equal to $34,000, measures the economic benefit of being able to reverse the order of decision and state. In short, this is the cost of uncertainty: having to make a decision before the uncertainty is resolved leaves us worse off by $34,000 (on average) compared to what we could gain if uncertainty could be resolved before making the decision.

The $34,000 quantity we computed for the WGT example is called the **expected value of perfect information**, abbreviated *EVPI*. Here, the term "perfect" refers to the resolution of uncertainty. When we have to make a decision before uncertainty is resolved, we are operating with imperfect information (uncertain knowledge) about the state of nature. When we can make a decision after uncertainty is resolved, we can respond to

FIGURE 13.10 Decision
Tree for the EVPI
Calculation

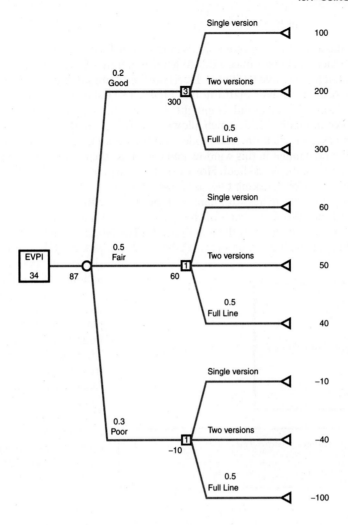

perfect information about the state of nature. Our probability assessments of event outcomes remain unchanged, and we are still dealing with expected values.

To review, the two expected values in the comparison are:

- the expected payoff from following the optimal policy (in the original problem)
- the expected payoff from being able to choose an action with perfect information

In this comparison, the expected payoff with perfect information must always be at least as good as the expected payoff from following the optimal policy in the original problem, and it will usually be better. The *EVPI* measures the difference, or the gain due to perfect information.

The calculation of *EVPI* can also be represented with a tree structure, where we reverse the sequence of decision and chance events in the tree diagram, just as we did in the calculations. Figure 13.10 shows how the diagram would be redrawn for the WGT example and how the *EVPI* is calculated.

13.4 USING DECISION TREE SOFTWARE

As our examples demonstrate, the calculations required to roll back a decision tree are not sophisticated—they require multiplications and additions, and they require finding the maximum or minimum of several numbers. The calculations themselves can be done quite readily in a spreadsheet. However, it is often difficult to create for the calculations a layout that is tailored to the features of a particular example. For that reason, it makes sense to take advantage of software that has been designed expressly for representing decision trees in Excel. Here, we illustrate the use of **Decision Tree**, a tool contained in Analytic Solver Platform for constructing and analyzing decision trees.

13.4.1 Solving a Simple Example with Decision Tree

To illustrate the basic commands in Decision Tree, we apply it in the WGT example. First, we place the cursor in cell B2 (to leave a margin of one row at the top and one column on the left for possible later use). Decision Tree commands can be found in the Tools group on the Analytic Solver Platform tab. Figure 13.11 shows the main menu, containing options for Node, Branch, and Highlight. Holding the cursor over Node reveals the submenu shown in Figure 13.12, which allows us to Add, Change, Delete, Copy, or Paste a node. In this case, we click on Add Node, and the default window in Figure 13.13 appears. If we make no change in this window and click OK, the default diagram shown in Figure 13.14* appears on the worksheet. However, it is convenient to make changes in the Decision Tree window before clicking OK, as shown in Figure 13.15. Here, we have added a branch and labeled the branches with names of the three actions, Single Version, Two Versions, and Full Line. We leave each of the corresponding Value entries at zero because no payoff occurs as a function of the action itself. (The Node name serves as a label that appears in the task pane but not on the worksheet.) When we click OK, the worksheet takes the form shown in Figure 13.16, displaying the actions but not the states.

To add a chance node (or *event*, in the terminology of Decision Tree), we place the cursor on the first terminal node (cell G4) and return to the Decision Tree menu. Again, we click on Add Node from the Node submenu. This time, in the Decision Tree window, we select the button for Event/Chance rather than Decision. Although the default window for an event node lists two outcomes, we can enter a third outcome, as shown in Figure 13.17. We can then add values (scaled in thousands of dollars) and probabilities for each branch, as well as a label for the node. When we click OK, the worksheet is updated, as shown in Figure 13.18. The profit value of 100 that we entered in the Decision Tree window appears under the first event branch, in cell I5. Cells L4 and J5 contain formulas that rely on the payoff value. Although we don't need to use these formulas in an example as straightforward as WGT, these supplementary computations are sometimes helpful in analyzing other decision trees.

At this stage, we can add the second event from scratch, adapting the procedure we just followed. Alternatively, we can copy the first event node and then edit it as needed. To do so, we place the cursor on the first event node (now in cell G9). Then we return to the Node submenu and click on Copy Node. Placing our cursor on the terminal node G19, we return to the submenu and click on Paste Node. We then edit the profit values in cells I20, I25, and I30 as appropriate, leading to the diagram shown in Figure 13.19.

For the third event, we can again copy, paste, and edit, leading to the diagram for the full tree that appears in

FIGURE 13.11 Decision Tree Menu

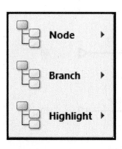

FIGURE 13.12 Node Submenu

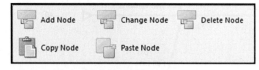

FIGURE 13.13 Node Window for the First Decision

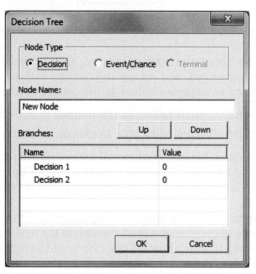

FIGURE 13.14 Default Initial Tree Produced by Decision Tree

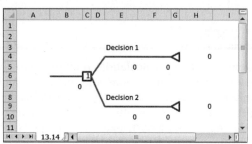

---

*To download spreadsheets for this chapter, go to the Student Companion Site at www.wiley.com/college/powell.

FIGURE 13.15   Details for
the First Decision Node

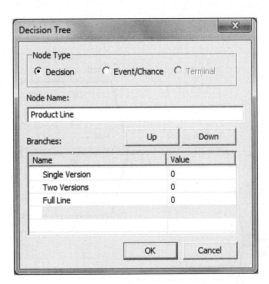

FIGURE 13.16   Expanded
Initial Tree Diagram

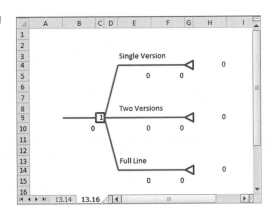

FIGURE 13.17   Node
Window for the First
Event Node

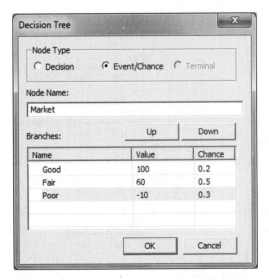

Figure 13.20 (with some labeling added in the first row and the first column). This display also contains some automated calculations. For example, in cells F10, F25, and F40, we find the expected profit at each nearby event node. By examining the Excel formula in one of these cells, we can confirm the calculation for an expected value.

Another automated calculation appears in cell B25. This formula identifies the maximum expected profit among the values corresponding to each of the actions. This value is $53,000, associated with the Two Versions action. The decision node (cell C24) contains the number of the action (2) that produces the maximum expected profit. Thus, Decision Tree performs the rollback calculations automatically, including the identification of the best action. The best action can be reinforced graphically by returning to the Decision Tree menu and following the Highlight menu to the Highlight Best selection on the submenu. This command simply highlights in color the portion of the tree corresponding to the optimal decision.

If we compare Figure 13.20 with the diagram in Figure 13.5, we can see that the software produces a layout for the tree that carries two numbers along any branch. The left-hand entry is the direct payoff associated with that branch. The right-hand entry is a single number summarizing the outcomes of any node on the right that occurs later. If the branch leads to a chance node, then the summary number is an expected value (calculated as the sum of probabilities multiplied by payoff outcomes), and if the branch leads to a decision node, then the summary number is the maximum (or minimum) of the expected payoff outcomes that are available.

13.4.2 Sensitivity Analysis with Decision Tree

A decision-tree analysis, such as we see in Figure 13.20, retains the properties of a spreadsheet model. That is, the worksheet produced by Decision Tree contains inputs, formulas, and outputs, just as in any well-designed model. Therefore, we can perform sensitivity analyses in the usual ways.

As an example, we explore the sensitivity of the optimal solution to the profit of $200,000 that represents the payoff for the Two Versions action when the Good market state occurs. This parameter is located in cell I20 of the worksheet. To trace the effects of other profit values for this action-state combination, we use the Parametric Sensitivity tool. Suppose we wish to vary the profit from a lower value of zero to an upper value of $300,000 in steps of $25,000. First, we designate a cell outside of the tree diagram, such as N24, to

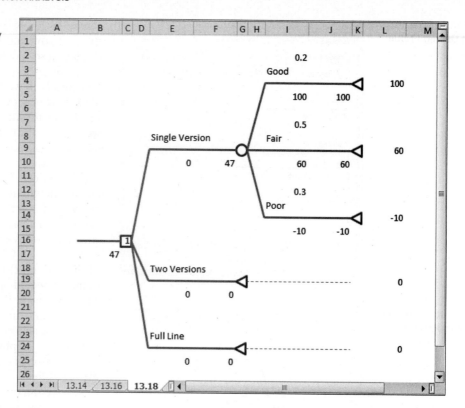

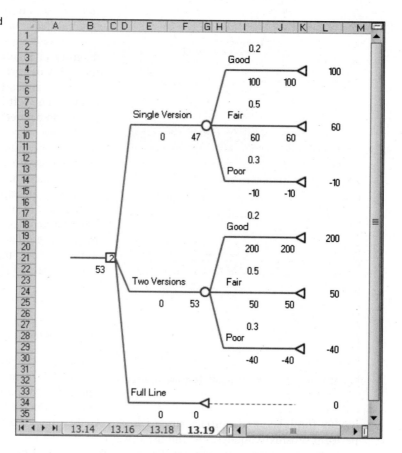

hold the sensitivity information. In that cell, we enter the sensitivity function
=PsiSenParam(0, 300). In cell I20 we then enter a reference to cell N24. (Both cells
display 150, which is the midrange of the lower and upper values.) Next, we place the
cursor on cell C24 and select Analytic Solver Platform▶Parameters▶Parameters▶Monitor
Value and then select cell N25. This step enables the sensitivity analysis to track the effect

FIGURE 13.20 Full
Diagram for the Wertz
Game and Toy Example

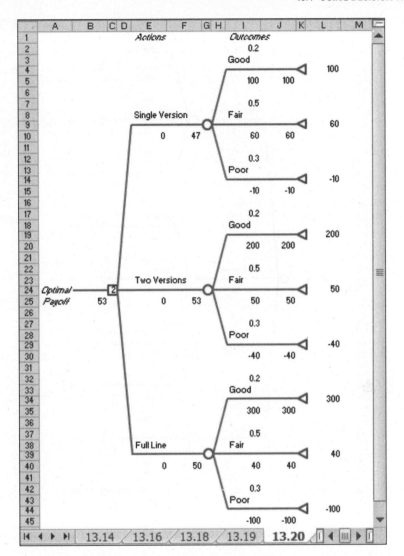

on the optimal decision. Similarly, after placing the cursor on cell B25, we select Analytic Solver Platform▶Parameters▶Parameters▶Monitor Value and then select cell N26. This step enables tracking of the optimal profit. Finally, we run parametric sensitivity (as described in Chapter 4), specifying 13 `major axis points`. The output table is shown in Figure 13.21 after pasting it (with some reformatting) to the right of the Decision Tree model.

As the table in Figure 13.21 shows, the Full Line is the optimal decision (and $50,000 is the optimal *EP*) when the profit figure we're varying ranges from zero up to $175,000; but at $200,000 and above, the optimal decision switches to Two Versions, and the optimal *EP* rises with the parameter being varied. This type of analysis is thus carried out with the usual Parametric Sensitivity tool, once the model has been set up with Decision Tree.

13.4.3 Minimizing Expected Cost with Decision Tree

We introduced Decision Tree by showing how it could be used to analyze a decision-tree problem in which the criterion is expected profit. We could just as easily apply the software to a problem involving the criterion of expected costs by treating all costs as negative profits and finding the maximum expected profit. However, Decision Tree can accommodate costs in a more direct fashion and simply minimize expected cost. To do so, we enter the task pane on the Model tab, select the root node (Decision Tree) in the main window, and in the table below, find the Decision Node parameter and use its pull-down menu (Figure 13.22) to switch from `Maximize` to `Minimize`.

To illustrate the Minimize option, we show a Decision Tree model for the patent-infringement example that we covered earlier in this chapter. In that scenario, all payoffs were in the form of costs, and our objective was to minimize expected total cost.

FIGURE 13.21 Sensitivity Analysis for the Example Model

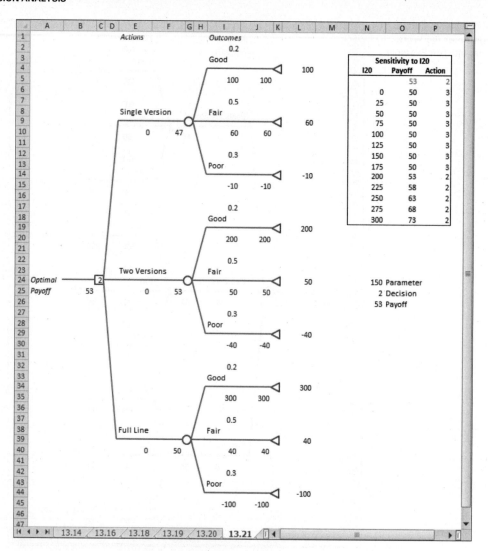

FIGURE 13.22 Location of the Maximization Setting on the Task Pane

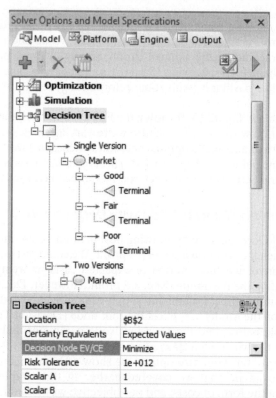

FIGURE 13.23 Decision Tree Model for the Patent Infringement Example

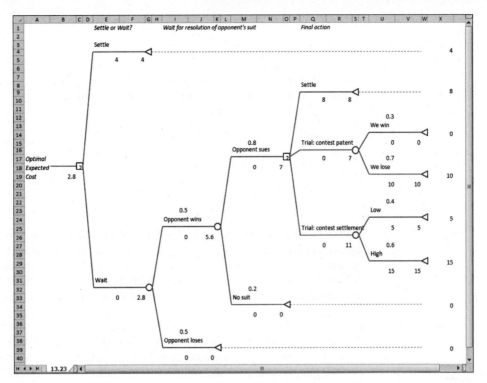

Figure 13.23 shows how the Decision Tree model looks on the worksheet when the Minimize option has been selected.

13.5* MAXIMIZING EXPECTED UTILITY WITH DECISION TREE

Early in this chapter, we introduced three benchmark criteria for decision making with uncertain outcomes. In particular, the maximin payoff criterion and the minimax regret criterion represented two conservative ways of choosing an action. One rationale for this type of conservatism is that by focusing on worst-case outcomes, the analysis tries to capture a decision maker's concern for the risk inherent in uncertain situations. By *risk*, we refer to the possibility of an undesirable outcome. Our main criticism of the benchmark criteria is that they ignore relevant information, including the probabilities of the various states. When we proceeded to examine the expected value criterion, we set aside considerations of risk and focused only on the mean outcome. If a decision maker is not concerned about the riskiness of a particular decision, then the expected payoff is the criterion of choice.

What if we wish to incorporate some aversion to risk in our decision making? A comprehensive treatment of this topic is beyond our coverage, but we can suggest one mechanism that is both theoretically sound and supported by Decision Tree. Suppose that we could evaluate payoffs in some risk-adjusted manner—that is, with a measure that combines notions of monetary value along with the risk of an undesired outcome. To contrast this measure with the measure of pure dollars unadjusted for risk, we'll adopt the name *utils* for this new scale. Using this scale, the decision maker can compute the value of a particular action in utils and select as the optimal decision the action with the largest such value. The value of an action, measured in utils, incorporates both outcomes and probabilities, just as expected value does, but it also reflects risk. We say that a decision maker who is behaving in this way seeks to maximize **expected utility**.

Our task in evaluating a decision tree remains that of condensing the information about the consequences of an action into one summary measure, but now we'll do the math in utility units, not dollars. Although there are many ways of converting dollars to utils, one straightforward method uses an **exponential utility function**:

$$U = a - b \exp(-D/R) \tag{13.1}$$

where D is the value of the outcome in dollars; U is the utility value, or the value of an outcome in utils; and a, b, and R represent parameters. Parameters a and b are essentially

FIGURE 13.24 Example
Graph of Utility Function

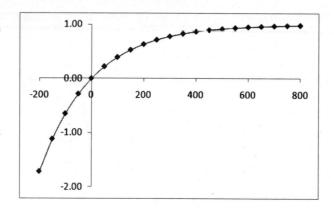

scaling parameters; R influences the shape of the curve and is known as the **risk tolerance**. To carry out the analysis, we use this function to convert each monetary outcome from dollars to utils, and then we determine the action that achieves the maximum expected utility. Although Decision Tree allows the flexibility of setting three different parameters, a standard approach takes $a = b = 1$. This choice ensures that the function in (13.1) passes through the origin, so that our remaining task is to find a value of R that captures the decision maker's preferences. A quick way to approximate R is to offer the decision maker an opportunity to bet $x/2$ dollars with a 50/50 chance of losing it all or winning x dollars. The largest value of x at which the decision maker would be willing to make that bet approximates R.

To appreciate how the utility transformation works, consider a graph of the utility function in (13.1), shown in Figure 13.24 for the case of $R = 500$. The monetary value of an outcome is represented on the horizontal axis, and the utility value is represented on the vertical axis. We can see immediately that the graph is concave. In other words, there are diminishing marginal returns to wealth, when we work in utility units. In addition, gaining and losing money have different implications for the decision maker. On the right-hand side of the graph, the shape indicates that large gains are less than proportionately rewarding (when measured in utils) compared to small gains. On the left-hand side of the graph, the shape indicates that large losses are more than proportionately painful compared to small losses. Working in utils, then, a decision maker tends to prefer an action that leads to outcomes near the middle of the graph to an action that leads to outcomes at the extremes, if the probabilities are roughly the same. In that context, we can understand that a risk-averse decision maker might prefer to avoid an action that is equally likely to gain $2 million or lose $1 million, even though the corresponding expected value is positive. With appropriate parameters in (13.1), an exponential utility function can capture this kind of decision-making criterion.

FIGURE 13.25 Location
of the Risk Tolerance
Parameter on the Task
Pane

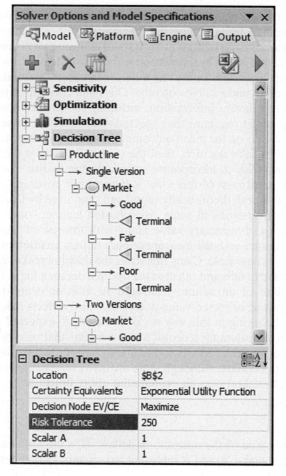

In Decision Tree, it is necessary to specify the three parameters in the exponential utility function. These three values must be entered in the task pane on the Model tab, along with designating the value for Certainty Equivalents to be the Exponential Utility Function. Figure 13.25 shows where these specifications

FIGURE 13.26 Modification of the WGT Model for Exponential Utilities

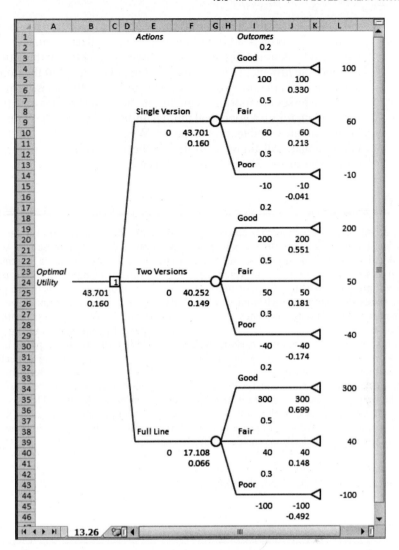

appear. In Figure 13.26, we show the impact of the utility function approach on the WGT analysis, using a value of $R = 250$. After the user designates the use of Exponential Utility Function, Decision Tree displays additional calculations in columns B, F, and J. Immediately below the monetary payoffs, which existed in the original Decision Tree model of Figure 13.20, the display shows the same figures converted to utils. Thus, for example, the profit of $100,000 in cell J5 is transformed as follows:

$$U = a - b\exp(-D/R) = 1 - \exp(-100/250) = 0.330$$

This value is calculated from the formula in cell J6, and similar calculations appear elsewhere in the column. Then, when expected values are calculated at the chance nodes in column F, these are probability-weighted utility values. For the Single Version action, the calculation of expected utility appears in cell F11 as follows.

$$EU = 0.2(0.330) + 0.5(0.213) + 0.3(-0.041) = 0.160$$

Just above this formula, in cell F10, the expected utility is converted back to a dollar value, using the inverse of the formula in (13.1). The dollar value that results ($43,701 in this case) is called the **certainty equivalent**. The certainty equivalent gives the dollar value that a risk-averse decision maker would accept without any uncertainty as being equivalent to the value of the given dollar-value outcomes and their respective probabilities.

Finally, the optimal decision corresponds to the action that achieves the largest certainty equivalent. (The same action would be selected if the choice were based on the maximum expected utility.) In the example shown, the optimal action for expected utility is the Single Version, with a certainty equivalent of $43,701. As this set of calculations indicates, a decision maker with an aversion to risk (as expressed by the risk tolerance value of 250) prefers a different action than the decision maker who focuses on expected payoff. Why does the Single Version choice look better in this situation? When the market is Good, the firm makes a healthy profit in either case, but the doubled amount in the Two Versions case does not provide twice the utility for the decision maker. When the market is Poor, the losses are four times greater in the Two Versions case than in the Single Version case and therefore a good deal more painful. Moreover, the Poor market response is more likely than the Good market response. When the market is Fair, the profits are positive but fairly similar. All things considered, the risk-averse decision maker prefers the set of outcomes for the Single Version choice.

13.6 SUMMARY

A decision tree is a specialized model for recognizing the role of uncertainties in a decision-making situation. Trees help us distinguish between decisions and random events, and more importantly, they help us sort out the sequence in which they occur. Probability trees provide us with an opportunity to consider the possible states in a random environment when there are several sources of uncertainty, and they become components of decision trees.

The key elements of decision trees are decisions and chance events. A decision is the selection of a particular action from a given list of possibilities. A chance event gives rise to a set of possible states, and each action-state pair results in an economic payoff. In the simplest cases, these relationships can be displayed in a payoff table, but in complex situations, a decision tree tends to be a more flexible way to represent the relationships and consequences of decisions made under uncertainty.

The choice of a criterion is a critical step in solving a decision problem when uncertainty is involved. We saw that there are benchmark criteria for optimistic and pessimistic decision making, but these are somewhat extreme criteria. They ignore some available information, including probabilities, in order to simplify the task of choosing a decision. The more common approach is to use probability assessments and then to take the criterion to be maximizing the expected payoff, which in the business context translates into maximizing expected profit or minimizing expected cost.

Using the rollback procedure, we can identify those decisions that optimize the expected value of our criterion. Furthermore, we can produce information in the form of a probability distribution to help assess the risk associated with any decision in the tree. Decision Tree is a straightforward spreadsheet program that assists in the structuring of decision trees and in the calculations required for a quantitative analysis.

SUGGESTED READINGS

Some related material can be found in the following books:

Clemen, R. T. and T. Reilly. 2004. *Making Hard Decisions*. Mason OH: Cengage Learning.

Golub, A. L. 1997. *Decision Analysis: An Integrated Approach*. New York: John Wiley & Sons.

Kammen, D. M. and D.M. Hassenzahl. 2001. *Should We Risk It?: Exploring Environmental, Health, and Technological Problem Solving*. Princeton, NJ: Princeton University Press.

EXERCISES

1. Construct a spreadsheet that makes the calculations required to analyze the decision in the WGT example. Include in the spreadsheet the calculation of the expected profit for each action and the calculation of the expected regret for each action. As a check, confirm that these two expected values match the values mentioned in the chapter.

a. Does the expected regret equal the *EVPI* for this example? Why is this true in general?

b. The probability of a Fair market response is 0.5 under the initial set of assumptions. Suppose this value were to change by an amount p (where $-0.5 \leq p \leq 0.5$). For what values of p does the Two Versions choice represent the optimal decision?

2. Gamma Construction Company has been asked to bid on the construction of 20 lighted tennis courts for State University. Each court will cost $20,000 in construction costs, and, in addition, there will be a fixed expense of $10,000 to cover the preparation and submittal of the bid. Gamma is considering five different bid levels. Each level involves a different profit margin, calculated as a percentage above total construction cost (TCC). Fixed expenses are excluded from this calculation, but they are relevant for profitability. Based on previous experience, Gamma's management is able to estimate the probability that it will win the bid at each level being considered. The bids and the probabilities are summarized in the following table:

Bid Number	Amount of Bid	Probability of Winning
1	TCC + 5%	0.80
2	TCC + 10%	0.70
3	TCC + 15%	0.50
4	TCC + 20%	0.30
5	TCC + 25%	0.20

Gamma's objective is to select the bid that maximizes its expected profit.

a. What is the optimal bid for Gamma to make?

b. What is the expected profit associated with the optimal bid in part (a)?

c. What is the risk profile for the optimal bid in part (a)?

d. Consider the probability of winning the optimal bid. If this parameter were allowed to vary, while all other parameters were kept unchanged, what values could it take without altering the optimal selection?

3. JR Davidson recently started a practice in Landscape Design and is considering the purchase of an automated drafting system. JR can purchase a system with three possible drafting capacities. The payoffs for having any of these systems depend on the demand for drafting services over the next few years. The costs for each system are shown as follows along with JR's assessment of the probabilities that demand will match the capacity of each one:

	Total Cost	Probability
Small system	$10,000	0.4
Medium system	$14,000	0.3
Large system	$20,000	0.3

Working at capacity, each system would generate net cash flow at a yearly rate of 50 percent of its total cost. If a system is chosen that is smaller than demand, it would work at capacity. If a system is chosen that is larger than demand, revenue from the system would be limited by demand. For convenience, JR has initially decided to count cash flow for three years, without discounting. For example, if JR chooses the Medium system and demand is Small, then the profit is calculated as follows:

$$\text{Profit} = 3(0.5 \times 10,000) - 14,000 = \$1,000$$

a. What is the best decision under the maximax criterion?

b. What is the best decision under the maximin criterion?

c. What is the best decision under the minimax regret criterion?

d. What is the best decision under the expected payoff criterion?

e. Reviewing the analysis, JR decides that the assumption of a 3-year horizon is too restrictive. Instead, it makes more sense to treat the horizon as uncertain, with the following probability distribution:

Two years of cash flow has 0.4 probability.
Three years of cash flow has 0.4 probability.
Four years of cash flow has 0.2 probability.

Now, what is the best decision under the expected payoff criterion?

4. You are contemplating an investment project that has two phases. As currently planned, the first phase of the project requires an investment of $100,000 today. One year from now, the project will deliver either $120,000 or $80,000, with equal probabilities. When these Phase I payouts occur, you will be able to invest an additional $100,000 in Phase II. One year later, Phase II will pay out either 20 percent more than Phase I actually delivered, or else 20 percent less, again with equal probabilities.

You may commit to both phases at the start, or you may commit to Phase I (and postpone a decision on Phase II), or

you may invest in neither. If you commit to both phases at the start, there is really no reason to delay. Suppose that you can choose, in that case, to implement both phases virtually simultaneously, so that both investments are made today, and all payouts occur one year from now. (Note, however, that the size of the Phase II payout still depends on the size of the Phase I payout. Conceptually, you can think of the Phase II payouts as occurring immediately after the Phase I payouts.)

a. Using an expected payoff criterion, and discounting at 10 percent, which of the alternatives (First, Both, or Neither) is the optimal decision?

b. What is the breakeven discount rate at which Neither is a better decision than First?

c. Suppose you have access to an additional, similar investment that resembles the original but is more volatile: for the same initial investment, it delivers a Phase I return of ±40 percent (that is, either $140,000 or $60,000) with equal probabilities. Similarly, it delivers a Phase II return of ±40 percent of the Phase I payouts, again with equal probabilities. Show that this new investment is preferable to the original, with a discount rate of 10 percent.

d. Evidently, the higher volatility of the investment (±40 percent as opposed to ±20 percent) makes the potential cash flows attractive. With the discount rate at 10 percent, what levels of volatility would lead to an expected value above zero?

5. Copy Makers Inc. (CMI) has just received a credit request from a new customer who wants to purchase a copying machine. As input to its decision of whether to grant credit, CMI has made the following estimates and assumptions:

- If CMI denies the customer credit, there is a 20 percent chance that the customer will buy the copying machine with cash anyway.

- If CMI grants credit, there is a 70 percent chance the customer will be a good credit risk.

- If CMI grants credit and the customer is a good credit risk, CMI will collect 100 percent of the purchase price.

- If CMI grants credit and the customer is a bad credit risk, CMI has two options. Under the first option, CMI would continue to send the customer a bill and hope it is eventually paid. Under this option, CMI will collect 100 percent, 50 percent, or 0 percent of the amount owed, with probabilities 0.1, 0.2, and 0.7, respectively. Under the second option, CMI would vigorously pursue the collection of the amount owed. To do so would cost CMI 25 percent of the amount owed, regardless of the amount eventually collected. Under this second option, CMI will again collect 100 percent, 50 percent, or 0 percent of the amount owed, with probabilities 0.3, 0.5, and 0.2, respectively.

- The copy machine sells for $8,000 and costs CMI $5,000. Nonvigorous enforcement has no cost, while vigorous enforcement costs $2,000.

a. What is the complete, optimal decision strategy for CMI?

b. What is the optimal expected value?

6. TCS Corporation has recently decided to manufacture a product in its own facilities rather than outsource to Asian manufacturers. Its new plant will last about ten years. TCS is considering two options: build a large plant now that will have sufficient capacity to handle demand into the foreseeable future, or build a small plant that can be expanded two years later, after demand is better known. TCS will not expand the small plant unless demand in the first two years exceeds a threshold level.

TCS assumes that the level of demand in subsequent years will be the same as in the first two years (e.g., if demand is high in the first two years, it will continue to be high in the next eight years).

What additional data are needed to determine the optimal decision?

7. A small manufacturer uses an industrial boiler in its production process. A new boiler can be purchased for $10,000. As the boiler gets older, its maintenance expenses increase while its resale value declines. Since the boiler will be exposed to heavy use, the probability of a breakdown increases every year. Assume that when a boiler breaks down, it can be used through the end of the year, after which it must be replaced with a new one. Also, assume that a broken-down boiler has no resale value.

Some basic data are given in the following table:

Year of Operation	Expenses	Resale Value	Breakdown Probability
1	1,500	7,000	0.1
2	2,000	5,000	0.2
3	3,000	4,000	0.4
4	4,500	2,000	0.5
5	6,000	500	0.8

a. At what year of operation should the boiler be replaced?

b. What is the expected cost per year for the boiler, under the optimal replacement strategy?

8. Delta Electric Service is an electrical-utility company serving parts of several states. It is considering replacing some of its equipment at generating substations and is trying to decide whether it should replace an older, existing PCB transformer. (PCB is a toxic chemical known formally as polychlorinated biphenyl.) Although the PCB generator meets all current regulations, if an incident such as a fire were to occur, and PCB contamination caused harm either to neighboring businesses or farms, or to the environment, the company would be liable for damages. Recent court cases have shown that simply meeting regulations does not relieve a utility of liability if an incident causes harm to others. In addition, courts have been awarding very large damages to individuals and businesses harmed by incidents involving hazardous material.

If Delta replaces the PCB transformer, no PCB incidents will occur, and the only cost will be the cost of the new transformer, estimated to be $85,000. Alternatively, if the company elects to keep the existing PCB transformer in operation, then, according to their consultants, there is a 50/50 chance that there will be a high likelihood of an incident or a low likelihood of an incident. For the case of a high likelihood of an incident, there is also a 0.004 probability that a fire will occur sometime during the remaining life of the transformer, and a 0.996 probability that no fire will occur. If a fire occurs, there is a 20 percent chance that it will be severe and the utility will incur a very high cost, whereas there is an 80 percent chance that it will be minor and the utility will incur a low cost.

The high- and low-cost amounts, including both cleanup and damages, are estimated to be $100 million and $10 million, respectively, based on results from other incidents in the industry. For the case of a low likelihood of an incident, there is a 0.001 probability of a fire during the remaining life of the transformer, and a 0.999 probability of no fire. If a fire does occur, then the same probabilities exist for the severe and minor outcomes as in the previous case. In both cases, there will be no cost if no fire occurs.

a. Should Delta replace its old transformers?

b. What is the expected cost per transformer, under the optimal replacement strategy?

9. In the early 1980s, New England Electric System (NEES) was deciding how much to bid for the salvage rights to a grounded ship, the SS *Kuniang*. If the bid were successful, the ship could be repaired and outfitted to haul coal for the company's power-generation stations. But the value of doing so depended on the outcome of a U.S. Coast Guard judgment about the salvage value of the ship. The Coast Guard's judgment involved an obscure law regarding domestic shipping in coastal waters. If the judgment were to indicate a low salvage value (an outcome with an estimated 30 percent chance of occurring), and if NEES submitted the winning bid, then NEES would be able to use the ship for its shipping needs without additional costs. If the judgment were high, the cost to NEES would run $4 million higher than if the judgment were low. The Coast Guard's judgment would not be known until after the winning bid was chosen, so there was considerable risk associated with submitting a bid. If the bid were to fail, NEES could purchase either a new ship or a tug/barge combination, both of which were relatively expensive alternatives. Analysts at NEES estimated that purchasing a new ship for these purposes would lead to profits of $3.2 million (calculated as a net present value over 20 years of shipping). Purchasing a tug/barge combination would lead to profits of only $1.6 million. By comparison, if NEES could acquire the Kuniang at the low salvage value, it could achieve profits of $15.5 million, exclusive of its bid. One of the major issues was that the higher the bid, the more likely NEES would be to win. NEES judged that a bid of $2 million would definitely not win, whereas a bid of $12 million definitely would win. As a first cut, we can represent three bids:

- A bid of $2 million would certainly not win.
- A bid of $8 million would have a 60 percent chance of winning.
- A bid of $12 million would certainly win.

The goal for NEES was to maximize its profits from supplying coal to its plants.[1]

a. What is the best of the three bids for NEES? What is the optimal expected profit?

b. Consider the estimate of $4 million difference between the cost with a low salvage value and the cost with a high salvage value. For what range of values in this figure does the optimal bid in part (a) remain unchanged?

c. Enrich the bidding submodel as follows. For a bid of x (in millions of dollars), the probability of winning is $W(x)$, where $W(x)$ is a linear function between $x = 2$ and $x = 12$. What is the best value of x?

[1]D. E. Bell, "Bidding for the *S.S. Kuniang*," *Interfaces* 14 (1984): 17–23.

10. In early 1984, Pennzoil and Getty Oil agreed to the terms of a merger. Before any formal documents could be signed, however, Texaco offered Getty Oil a substantially better price, so Gordon Getty, who controlled most of the Getty stock, reneged on the Pennzoil deal and sold to Texaco. Naturally, Pennzoil felt as if it had been dealt with unfairly and filed a lawsuit against Texaco alleging that Texaco had interfered illegally in the Pennzoil-Getty negotiations. Pennzoil won the case; in late 1985, it was awarded $11.1 billion, the largest judgment ever in the United States. A Texas appeals court reduced the judgment by $2 billion, but interest and penalties drove the total back up to $10.3 billion. James Kinnear, Texaco's chief executive officer, had said that Texaco would file for bankruptcy if Pennzoil obtained court permission to secure the judgment by filing liens against Texaco's assets. Furthermore, Kinnear had promised to fight the case all the way to the U.S. Supreme Court if necessary, arguing in part that Pennzoil had not followed the Security and Exchange Commission's regulations in its negotiations with Getty. In April 1987, just before Pennzoil began to file the liens, Texaco offered to pay Pennzoil $2 billion to settle the entire case. Hugh Liedtke, chairman of Pennzoil, faced the choice of whether to accept the Texaco offer. His advisors were telling him that a settlement of between $3 and $5 billion would be fair, so one of his options was to make a counteroffer of $5 billion. If Liedtke were to counteroffer, assume Texaco would be twice as likely to refuse as accept the $5 billion counteroffer. If Texaco would refuse, the case would go to court, where the judge would award Pennzoil $10.3 billion, or reduce the award to $5 billion, or award Pennzoil nothing. The probability that the judge would award Pennzoil nothing is about 50 percent, while the other outcomes were thought to be equally likely (25 percent probability).[2]

a. What is the best decision for Liedtke, and what is his expected payoff?

b. What is the expected payoff if Pennzoil counteroffers and Texaco refuses? Why is the expected payoff to the counteroffer higher than this?

c. Consider the probability that the judge would award Pennzoil nothing. How high would this probability have to go before the best decision would be to accept the $2 billion offer? (Assume that the probabilities of the other two outcomes are always equal.)

11. (Continuation of the previous problem) Liedtke's advisors suggest that Texaco has more options in the face of Pennzoil's $5 billion counteroffer than simply to refuse or accept. In particular, they might counteroffer, probably with an amount near $4 billion.

Modify your analysis to take this new possibility into account. Assume that Pennzoil will either accept or refuse Texaco's counteroffer of $4 billion. If it refuses, the case will go to court and the same outcomes and probabilities apply as in the previous exercise. The probabilities that Texaco accepts, refuses, or counteroffers can be assumed to be 1/3.

a. Now what is the best decision for Liedtke, and what payoff can he expect to receive from it? Why does the expected value change in this case?

b. How sensitive is the overall expected value of this decision to the probability that Texaco counteroffers $4 billion? (Assume the probabilities of Texaco accepting or refusing are equal.) Construct a graph to relate the expected value of the decision to this probability.

c. How would your results change if you added a possible counteroffer of $3 billion?

12. The Taiwanese government recently announced that they would begin construction of a high-speed rail system linking the northernmost city of Taipei to the southernmost city, Tai-Nan. This high-speed train will alleviate the significant traffic problems that the country is experiencing. This is a highly lucrative construction project with many international companies involved in the bidding. However, it is clear that companies who have local negotiators possess a clear advantage in the bidding process.

A construction company from Thailand has asked you to work for them in the hope that your connections will successfully help to secure a portion of the high-speed rail contract. You have given serious thought to the proposal and are now sitting in a meeting with the CEO. As the meeting progresses, the CEO brings up the subject of compensation. You listen intently and are surprised when he discusses the terms.

The CEO proposes the following terms: you can take $20,000 per month for a period of two years regardless of whether or not you secure the high-speed rail contract, or you can gamble any portion of your salary you wish. He agrees that if you successfully acquire the contract for the company, he will double the portion of the salary that you decided to gamble. But if you do not secure the contract, you do not receive any bonus and will be paid only the amount you did not gamble. This deal applies to the entire amount that would have been gambled for the two-year contract no matter when the contract is obtained.

Additionally, if you happen to secure a second, unrelated contract while you are there, the CEO agrees to redouble your entire gambled amount for the two-year period (in effect giving you four times the gambled amount). This deal applies no matter when the second contract is obtained so long as it happens within the two-year period.

The high-speed rail system is going to be built and it will be divided between several companies. Based upon your previous work and investigation into the contract, you feel that there is a 60 percent chance that you can get the contract. However, since you have done little preparation for any other projects, the likelihood of a second contract is probably only 20 percent.

You are debating whether to quit your current job, which pays $122,500 a year, to take on this opportunity. Furthermore, if you decide to take this offer, you will have to face the question of how much to gamble if any.

a. If you were not able to gamble any money what should you do based upon an expected payoff analysis?

b. Suppose that you can gamble part of your salary, what amount would you gamble to be neutral to either decision?

c. Now suppose that you gamble $50,000 and have a risk aversion that can be captured in the exponential utility function $U(x) = 1 - \exp(-x/R)$. Your degree of risk aversion is $100,000. What is your decision based upon utility and what are the utilities of each decision to four significant digits?

d. Suppose the decision with the highest utility was to stay with your current job. How much would the Thai company have to offer as the base salary, to the nearest $100, to get you to change your mind? (Use a gamble amount of $50,000 and $R = \$100,000$.)

---

[2]Clemen, Robert T. and Terence Reilly, 2004. *Making Hard Decisions*. Mason, OH: Cengage Learning.

14 Monte Carlo Simulation

14.1 INTRODUCTION

Change and uncertainty are ubiquitous features of the business world. The effective business analyst and model builder, whose work always involves planning for an uncertain future, must therefore have tools for dealing with these aspects of business life. In earlier chapters, we generally assumed that the parameters and relationships in our models were known with certainty. We did not entirely ignore uncertainty, but we dealt with it as a secondary feature of the situation, perhaps using what-if analysis or scenario analysis to explore how our model results would change if our assumptions changed. In Chapter 13, we began to look at decision problems in which uncertainty is a central, unavoidable feature of the problem, so that if we ignore it, our analysis is sure to be flawed. In this chapter, we present **Monte Carlo simulation**, an important and flexible technique for modeling situations in which uncertainty is a key factor.

Analytic Solver Platform provides the capability to implement Monte Carlo simulation in spreadsheet models. We assume in this chapter that the reader is familiar with the basic concepts of probability, because these are essential to analyzing situations involving uncertainty. The relevant concepts are reviewed in Appendix 3 (Basic Probability Concepts).

In a nutshell, simulation can describe not only what the *outcomes* of a given decision could be, but also the *probabilities* with which these outcomes will occur. In fact, the result of a simulation is the entire **probability distribution** of outcomes. In a sense, simulation is an advanced form of sensitivity analysis in which we attach a probability to each possible outcome.

We are often concerned with the **average** outcome, which is one way of summarizing the distribution of all possible outcomes and perhaps the most prominent measure of performance when outcomes are uncertain. In addition, we often wish to determine the probability of a particular set of outcomes. Such "tail probabilities" are often suitable measures of the risk associated with a decision.

Decision trees provide a simple means for analyzing decisions with uncertainty and risk. In Chapter 13 we discussed how to construct decision trees and how to determine the expected outcome and the probability distribution of outcomes given a choice of actions. Simulation provides a more general approach to similar problems. Simulation is the tool of choice when the model contains a large number of uncertainties, especially when these are represented by continuous distributions. Simulation is also a practical method when the underlying model is complex, as we illustrate later. However, it is important to realize that, just as with decision trees, the result of a simulation is a probability distribution for each outcome. Analyzing these distributions and extracting managerial insights are important parts of the art of simulation.

We begin this chapter with a simple demonstration of Monte Carlo simulation, using the Advertising Budget example we have analyzed in earlier chapters. We follow this with another example, Butson Stores, in which we illustrate the steps in a complete simulation analysis. We then analyze two common business applications in detail: valuing a corporation and pricing a financial option. In the remainder of the chapter, we systematically treat each of the steps in a simulation study.

14.2 A SIMPLE ILLUSTRATION

In this section, we provide a first look at simulation analysis, using the Advertising Budget example. The goal is to develop an intuitive understanding of the inputs and outputs of a simulation analysis; we leave the details of how to use Analytic Solver Platform for simulation to a later section.

When we introduced the Advertising Budget example in Chapter 3, we took it for granted that the price would be $40 and the cost $25. In Chapter 8, we determined that by allocating the advertising budget in the best possible way, we could attain a profit of $71,447. Of course, this result assumes that these and other input parameters are accurate forecasts of next year's values. Now, we consider the more realistic case in which next year's price and cost are both subject to considerable uncertainty. Assume that the most likely value of the price is $45, but it could turn out to be as low as $30 or as high as $50. Similarly, the most likely value for cost is $20, but it could be as low as $10 or as high as $35. Given this uncertainty in the price and cost, we naturally want to know the implications for annual profit. Simulation will answer this question for us by developing the probability distribution for profit, that is, a picture of all the possible outcomes for profit along with their probabilities of occurring.

Because we already have a working model and have determined which of the input parameters are uncertain (price and cost), our first step is to choose a means for representing uncertainty in the input parameters. One way to incorporate the assumption that price can range from $30 to $50 with a most likely value of $45 is to use a triangular probability distribution, as in Figure 14.1. This distribution reflects the assumption that not all values between $30 and $50 are equally likely, but that in fact, high values are somewhat more likely than low values. We can also use a triangular distribution to represent the uncertainty in cost as in Figure 14.2, which shows a distribution in which low values are somewhat more likely than high ones.

Having chosen probability distributions for the two uncertain input parameters, it is a relatively simple process to determine the probability distribution for profit. Essentially, we draw random samples from the distributions of the inputs (using the probability distributions we have chosen) and for each pair of sample values for price and cost,

FIGURE 14.1 Probability Distribution for Price

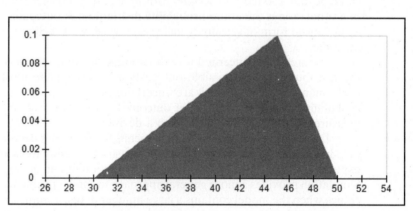

FIGURE 14.2 Probability Distribution for Cost

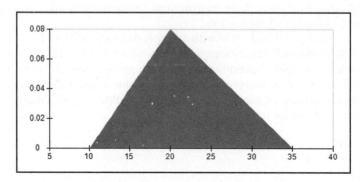

FIGURE 14.3 Advertising Budget Model with One Random Outcome

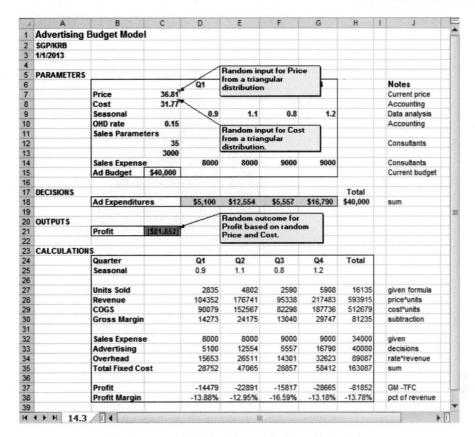

	A	B	C	D	E	F	G	H	I	J
1	**Advertising Budget Model**									
2	SGP/KRB									
3	1/1/2013									
4										
5	PARAMETERS									Notes
6				Q1						Current price
7		Price	36.81							Accounting
8		Cost	31.77							Data analysis
9		Seasonal		0.9	1.1	0.8	1.2			Accounting
10		OHD rate	0.15							
11		Sales Parameters								
12			35							Consultants
13			3000							
14		Sales Expense		8000	8000	9000	9000			Consultants
15		Ad Budget	$40,000							Current budget
16										
17	DECISIONS							Total		
18		Ad Expenditures		$5,100	$12,554	$5,557	$16,790	$40,000		sum
19										
20	OUTPUTS									
21		Profit	($81,852)							
22										
23	CALCULATIONS									
24		Quarter		Q1	Q2	Q3	Q4	Total		
25		Seasonal		0.9	1.1	0.8	1.2			
26										
27		Units Sold		2835	4802	2590	5908	16135		given formula
28		Revenue		104352	176741	95338	217483	593915		price*units
29		COGS		90079	152567	82298	187736	512679		cost*units
30		Gross Margin		14273	24175	13040	29747	81235		subtraction
31										
32		Sales Expense		8000	8000	9000	9000	34000		given
33		Advertising		5100	12554	5557	16790	40000		decisions
34		Overhead		15653	26511	14301	32623	89087		rate*revenue
35		Total Fixed Cost		28752	47065	28857	58412	163087		sum
36										
37		Profit		-14479	-22891	-15817	-28665	-81852		GM -TFC
38		Profit Margin		-13.88%	-12.95%	-16.59%	-13.18%	-13.78%		pct of revenue
39										

Random input for Price from a triangular distribution

Random input for Cost from a triangular distribution.

Random outcome for Profit based on random Price and Cost.

14.3

FIGURE 14.4 Distribution of Profit

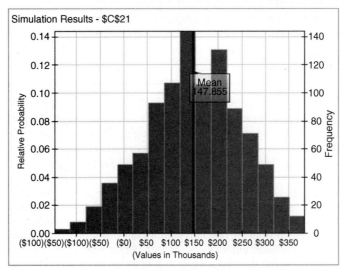

Simulation Results - $C$21

Mean 147.855

Relative Probability / Frequency — (Values in Thousands)

calculate the resulting value for profit. Figure 14.3* shows the Advertising Budget model for one such outcome: Price is $36.81, cost is $31.77, and the resulting profit is –$81,852. Of course, a single random value for profit is not by itself very meaningful. The only way to develop a realistic picture of the range of possible outcomes and their likelihoods is to repeat this process many times. Analytic Solver Platform makes this easy. The results for 1,000 repetitions are summarized in Figure 14.4.

This picture is a **histogram** of 1,000 repetitions of the sampling process described above. We can interpret it as the probability distribution for profit. From the histogram, we can see that profit ranges from less than –$100,000 to more than $350,000. The mean, or **expected value**, is $147,855 (the simple average of all 1,000 outcomes, since each is equally likely). Finally, we can determine the likelihood of making a positive profit by calculating

---

*To download spreadsheets for this chapter, go to the Student Companion Site at www.wiley.com/college/powell. Readers can reproduce the simulation results in the text by setting the Simulation options in Analytic Solver Platform. Choose 1,000 Trials per Simulation, 999 for Sim. Random Seed, and Latin Hypercube for Sampling Method.

FIGURE 14.5 Distribution of Profit Showing Tail Probability

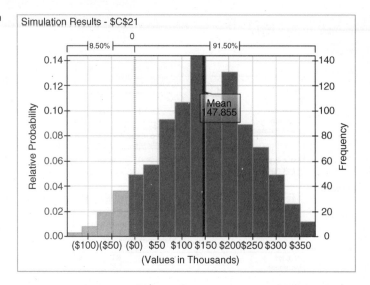

the percentage of positive outcomes among the 1,000 repetitions. Figure 14.5 shows the results: in 91.5 percent of the cases, the profit exceeds zero.

This example illustrates all the essential steps in a simulation:

1. Start with a base-case model and determine which of the input parameters to represent as uncertain.
2. Develop probability distributions for those inputs.
3. Take random samples from those inputs and calculate the resulting output, repeating the process until a clear picture of the output distribution emerges.
4. Create a histogram of the outcomes and interpret it.

Simulation provides two essential pieces of information: mean values (also called expected values) and tail probabilities (in this case, the probability of a positive profit).

14.3   THE SIMULATION PROCESS

In this section we present an example in detail, explaining how to apply the main concepts of simulation and how to use some of the basic features of Analytic Solver Platform for simulation. The reader should work through this example carefully, reproducing the major results we derive here. The most important Analytic Solver Platform features are summarized for future reference in Analytic Solver Tips.

EXAMPLE
Butson Stores

Butson Stores faces a problem in maintaining sufficient cash balances for operations over the first six months of the year. Each month, they must pay certain fixed costs and taxes (see the following table), as well as materials costs that run about 80 percent of the current month's sales. Monthly cash receipts consist of revenues from the previous month's sales, as well as 0.5 percent interest on short-term cash balances. The company enters the six-month period with a cash balance of $250,000 and wishes to maintain at least that balance each month in order to cover cash needs. December sales of $1.54 million have just been recorded. If Butson finishes a month with less than $250,000 in cash, the company can take out a one-month loan at 1 percent interest. The principal and interest are repaid in the following month. Butson's marketing department has made estimates (in thousands) for the mean and standard deviation of sales in each of the next six months (see the following table). Given the uncertainty in sales, Butson would like to know how large their *maximum* monthly loan is likely to be, and how likely they are to exceed their current credit limit of $750,000. Finally, the company would like to know how much on average they will have to pay in interest costs for loans.

Month	Fixed Costs and Taxes (000)
January	250
February	250
March	400
April	250
May	250
June	350

Month	Mean Sales (000)	Standard Deviation of Sales (000)
January	1,800	80
February	1,500	80
March	1,900	100
April	2,600	125
May	2,400	120
June	1,900	90

■

14.3.1 Base-Case Model

Our initial spreadsheet model for this problem is shown in Figure 14.6, where all dollar amounts are shown in thousands.

Parameters

Row 6: Sales for December are known. Mean sales for January through June are forecasts from Marketing.

Row 7: The standard deviations of sales for January through June are forecasts from Marketing. We do not use these parameters in the base-case model but record them for future use.

Row 8: Fixed costs and taxes are given.

Cells C9-C14: Given parameters.

Model

Row 18: In the base-case model, we assume that sales each month is the same as *mean* sales (row 6).

Row 20: The beginning cash balance in January is given. The beginning cash balance in February through June is the final cash balance from the previous month (row 30).

Row 21: The interest on cash is the interest return on cash times the beginning cash balance (row 20).

Row 22: Cash receipts are actual sales from the previous month (row 18).

FIGURE 14.6 Base-Case Model for Butson Stores

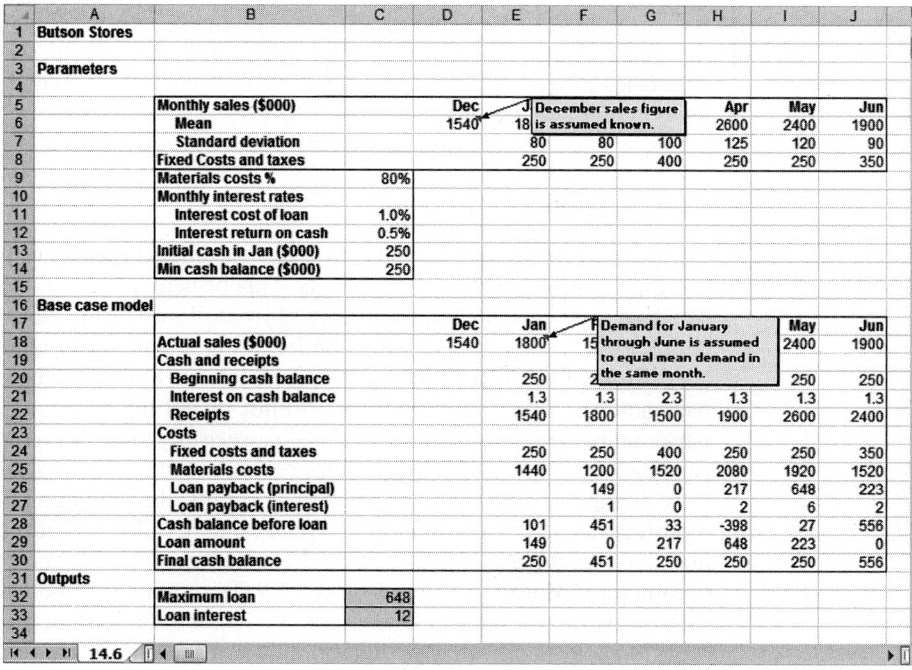

	A	B	C	D	E	F	G	H	I	J
1	Butson Stores									
2										
3	Parameters									
4										
5		Monthly sales ($000)		Dec	J			Apr	May	Jun
6		Mean		1540	18			2600	2400	1900
7		Standard deviation			80	80	100	125	120	90
8		Fixed Costs and taxes			250	250	400	250	250	350
9		Materials costs %	80%							
10		Monthly interest rates								
11		Interest cost of loan	1.0%							
12		Interest return on cash	0.5%							
13		Initial cash in Jan ($000)	250							
14		Min cash balance ($000)	250							
15										
16	Base case model									
17				Dec	Jan	F			May	Jun
18		Actual sales ($000)		1540	1800	15			2400	1900
19		Cash and receipts								
20		Beginning cash balance			250	2			250	250
21		Interest on cash balance			1.3	1.3	2.3	1.3	1.3	1.3
22		Receipts			1540	1800	1500	1900	2600	2400
23		Costs								
24		Fixed costs and taxes			250	250	400	250	250	350
25		Materials costs			1440	1200	1520	2080	1920	1520
26		Loan payback (principal)				149	0	217	648	223
27		Loan payback (interest)				1	0	2	6	2
28		Cash balance before loan			101	451	33	-398	27	556
29		Loan amount			149	0	217	648	223	0
30		Final cash balance			250	451	250	250	250	556
31	Outputs									
32		Maximum loan	648							
33		Loan interest	12							
34										

Row 24: Fixed costs and taxes are given data (row 8).

Row 25: Materials cost is the materials cost percentage times actual sales (row 18).

Row 26: The loan principal payback is the loan amount from the previous month (row 29).

Row 27: The interest on the loan is the loan amount from the previous month (row 29) times the interest cost of the loan.

Row 28: The cash balance before the loan is the sum of the beginning cash balance, interest on the cash balance, and receipts less the sum of fixed costs and taxes, materials cost, loan principal, and loan interest.

Row 29: To calculate the size of the loan, we compare the cash balance before the loan to the minimum cash balance (cell C14). If the cash balance before the loan is less than the minimum, the loan equals the difference. If the cash balance exceeds the minimum, the loan amount is zero. This logic is implemented by the formula =MAX($C$14-E28,0).

Row 30: The final cash balance is the sum of the cash balance before the loan and the loan amount.

Outputs

Cell C32: We calculate the largest loan taken out over the six-month horizon by calculating the maximum loan in row 29.

Cell C33: We calculate the total interest paid on loans by summing the loan interest in row 27.

Our base-case model, in which we assume no uncertainty in sales, shows that the maximum loan will be taken out in April and, at $648,000, will not exceed the credit limit of $750,000. The total interest paid on loans will be $12,000.

MODELING TIP
Creating Simulation Models

Beginners to simulation modeling often find it difficult to build an initial spreadsheet model. This may be because a simulation model must correctly evaluate a large number of combinations of different random inputs.

One useful trick is to *fix the random inputs* at some arbitrary value and build a spreadsheet model to evaluate those inputs. We did this in the Butson example when we fixed sales for January through June at their mean values. This step allowed us to build and debug a spreadsheet with no uncertainty, which is a simpler task than debugging a simulation model. Only after we have debugged this first model will we introduce uncertainty in sales.

However, care must be taken when building a model around a set of fixed inputs. In a simulation model, the model logic must be correct for all possible values of the random inputs. In the Butson example, we calculate the size of the loan in row 29, recognizing that randomness in sales will sometimes result in the cash balance falling below the minimum and sometimes not. Both cases must be handled correctly by the model so that when we simulate 1,000 different sets of monthly demands the results are always correct. ∎

14.3.2 Sensitivity Analysis

Throughout this book, we have stressed the importance of sensitivity analysis in understanding a model and its implications. This principle holds as well for simulation models: The base-case model should be thoroughly explored, using parametric sensitivity, tornado charts, or other methods, before undertaking a simulation analysis.

Most of the sensitivity analysis methods we have presented involve varying a single parameter at a time, and therefore do not reveal the behavior of the model when many parameters vary simultaneously. This is precisely what simulation does, which is why we can think of it as a sophisticated approach to sensitivity analysis.

In the Butson model, we have two outputs: the maximum loan taken out over the six month period, and the total interest paid on loans. The tornado chart in Figure 14.7 shows how the various input parameters affect the maximum loan. By far the most important parameter is Materials Costs % in cell C9. Two other parameters are of some importance: sales in April and sales in December. The maximum loan in the base case is taken out in April, so any change in sales that month will affect the size of the loan directly through the

FIGURE 14.7 Tornado
Chart for Maximum Profit

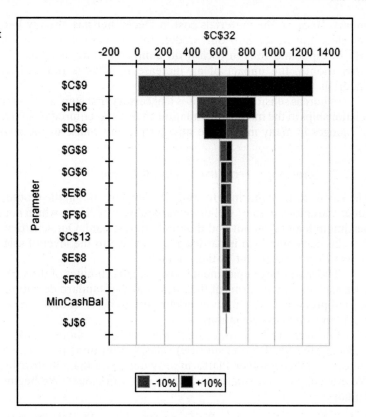

materials cost. Similarly, sales in December will influence receipts in January and therefore the size of the loan taken out in that month. All other parameters have a much smaller relative impact on the maximum loan taken out.

Figure 14.8 shows the tornado chart for total interest paid. Here again, Materials Costs % is the most important parameter, but sales in December also have a significant

FIGURE 14.8 Tornado
Chart for Total Interest
Paid

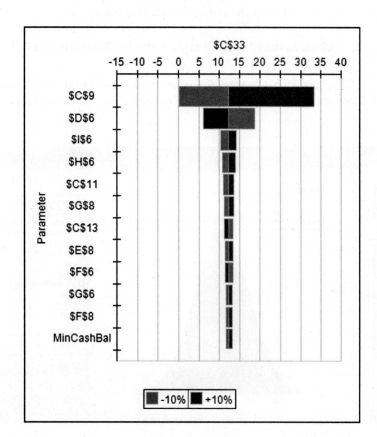

impact. Because the materials cost in December has already been paid (in December) and does not figure into our model, any increase in sales in December goes directly into receipts and thus into cash on hand, reducing any loan dollar-for-dollar. In any other month, the impact of an increase in sales is reduced by the amount due for materials cost.

Whereas sensitivity analysis is a necessary first step, and can often reveal unexpected relationships in the model, a simulation analysis is required to analyze the combined effects of changes in many inputs. We now turn to this phase of the analysis.

14.3.3 Specifying Probability Distributions

The key uncertainty facing Butson is the level of sales in the months from January through June. Variations in sales will drive variations in receipts, which could ultimately affect the maximum loan taken out and the total interest paid. Our sensitivity analysis has revealed that the maximum loan is particularly sensitive to the level of sales in April, because the largest loan is taken out in that month.

The marketing department has provided estimates of the variability to be expected in sales each month, in terms of the mean and the standard deviation. We will assume that a normal probability distribution is appropriate here, since it can be defined in terms of its mean and standard deviation.

Our first task is to convert the base-case model into a simulation model by replacing the fixed (deterministic) sales assumptions in row 18 with probability distributions. Analytic Solver Platform provides more than 30 distributions for this purpose. We first copy the base-case model to a new worksheet. We begin with cell E18, sales for January:

1. Select Analytic Solver Platform▶Simulation Model▶Distributions▶Common▶ Normal. This opens the window shown in Figure 14.9. The window displays a normal distribution, with a mean of 0 and standard deviation of 1, and provides a task pane (on the right) for changing the parameters and changing the display.

2. Enter the cell address for mean sales in January, E6, under `Parameters` next to `mean`.

3. Enter the cell address for the standard deviation of sales in January, E7, under `Parameters` next to `stdev`. Notice that the display changes to reflect the numerical values in these cells.

4. Click on Save and check that the formula `=PsiNormal(E6,E7)` has been entered in cell E18.

The next step is to enter the same formula for the months February to June, cells F18: J18. Since the PsiNormal function behaves like any other function in Excel, we can copy it

FIGURE 14.9 Entering the Normal Distribution

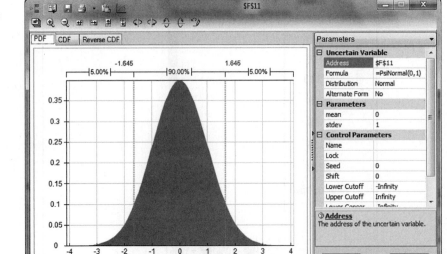

to these cells from E18. Because we have used relative cell references in defining cell E18, the distributions for cells F18:J18 each reference the appropriate mean and standard deviation for the given month.

14.3.4 Specifying Outputs

The second step in setting up a simulation model is to define the model outputs so that Analytic Solver Platform can save these values during a simulation run. In the Butson model, we have two outputs, the maximum loan and the total loan interest, so we will specify cells C32 and C33 as output cells:

1. Place the cursor on cell C32.
2. Select Analytic Solver Platform▶Simulation Model▶Results▶Output▶In Cell. This selection adds the function PsiOutput() to the formula already in the cell, MAX(Loans). This is how the user communicates to Analytic Solver Platform that a particular cell will be an output cell.
3. Place the cursor on cell C33.
4. Enter + PsiOutput() after the existing formula in this cell, SUM(F27:J27). (We can enter the PsiOutput formula either by typing it into a cell or through the command sequence in step 2 above.)

Figure 14.10 shows the Butson model fully set up for simulation.

14.3.5 Setting Simulation Parameters

Analytic Solver Platform allows the user to configure a simulation model by choosing values for a number of parameters. The simulation options can be displayed by selecting the Options icon and choosing the Simulation tab (Figure 14.11). Most of these options can safely be left at their default settings. We will set just one parameter here: the number of **Trials per Simulation**. The number of trials in Analytic Solver Platform is the number of times model outputs are calculated for different random values of the inputs. Enter the value 1,000 under Trials per Simulation.

14.3.6 Analyzing Simulation Outputs

Analytic Solver Platform can perform simulations in either a manual or an automatic mode. In the manual mode, we run a single simulation by selecting Analytic Solver

FIGURE 14.10 Simulation Model for Butson Stores

	A	B	C	D	E	F	G	H	I	J
1	Butson Stores									
2										
3	Parameters									
4										
5		Monthly sales ($000)		Dec	Jan	Feb	Mar	Apr	May	Jun
6		Mean		1540	1800	1500	1900	2600	2400	1900
7		Standard deviation			80	80	100	125	120	90
8		Fixed Costs and taxes			250	250	400	250	250	350
9		Materials costs %	80%							
10		Monthly interest rates								
11		Interest cost of loan	1.0%							
12		Interest return on cash	0.5%						Normal distribution	
13		Initial cash in Jan ($000)	250						using cells J6 and J7	
14		Min cash balance ($000)	250							
15										
16	Simulation model									
17				Dec	Jan	Feb	Mar	Apr	May	Jun
18		Actual sales ($000)		1540	1673.94	1516.47	1995.46	2639.02	2372.78	1986.36
19		Cash and receipts								
20		Beginning cash balance			250	250	414	250	250	250
21		Interest on cash balance			1.3	1.3	2.1	1.3	1.3	1.3
22		Receipts			1540	1674	1516	1995	2639	2373
23		Costs								
24		Fixed costs and taxes			250	250	400	250	250	350
25		Materials costs			1339	1213	1596	2111	1898	1589
26		Loan payback (principal)				48	0	314	682	197
27		Loan payback (interest)				0	0	3	7	2
28		Cash balance before loan			202	414	-64	-432	53	486
29		Loan amount	PsiOutput		48	0	314	682	197	0
30		Final cash balance			250	414	250	250	250	486
31	Outputs									
32		Maximum loan	682	PsiOutput						
33		Loan interest	12.41							
34										

14.6 14.10

FIGURE 14.11 Simula-
tion Options

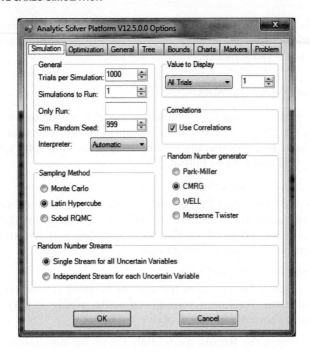

Platform►Solve Action►Simulate►Run Once. This will cause Analytic Solver Platform to
sample from each of the input probability distributions, calculate the resulting values for
the output cell or cells, and repeat for the number of trials. In this mode, Analytic Solver
Platform will *not* run a simulation when we enter a parameter or take any other action
that results in the spreadsheet being recalculated (including pressing F9). In the
automatic mode, however, a simulation will be conducted whenever the spreadsheet
is recalculated. To choose this mode, select Analytic Solver Platform►Solve
Action►Simulate►Interactive. The lightbulb icon will turn yellow, signifying automatic
simulation is on.

Analytic Solver Platform stores simulation results for each output cell in the cell
itself. By double-clicking on an output cell we can display the results in various formats.
Figure 14.12 shows the frequency distribution or histogram for the maximum loan in cell
C32. We can see that the mean or average value is around $650,000, but the maximum loan
could be as low as $300,000 or as high as $1,000,000. More significantly, we can see that
there is a 16 percent chance that the maximum loan amount will exceed the credit limit of
$750,000. (To determine this tail probability, enter the value $750,000 in the task pane
under Chart – Statistics - Upper Cutoff. The desired probability then appears next to

FIGURE 14.12 Distribu-
tion of the Maximum
Loan

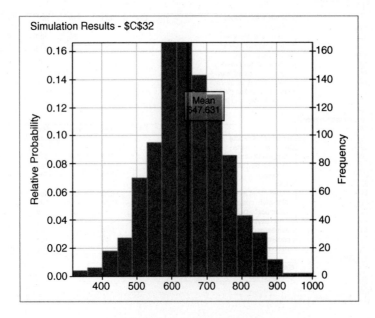

FIGURE 14.13 Distribution of the Maximum Loan with Tail Probability

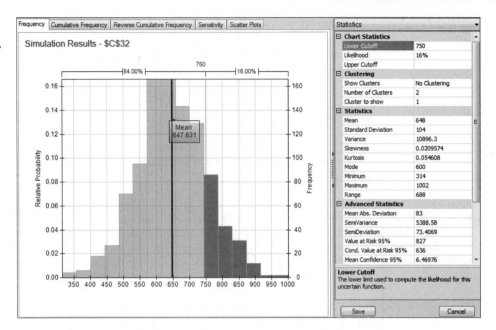

Likelihood and the chart shows the probabilities of being above or below this value. See Figure 14.13.) The distribution of loan interest is shown in Figure 14.14. The mean value is $12,370, but the range is from $8,000 to about $17,000.

What have we learned by simulating values of sales for the six months from January to June for Butson Stores? Our base-case model, which was based on mean sales forecasts, showed that the maximum loan would be $648,000 and that we would pay $12,000 in loan interest. Once we take the uncertainty in sales into account, we can see the ways in which these results are accurate and the ways they are misleading. In this particular model, we find that the *mean values* of the outputs do not change significantly when we take uncertainty into account. However, we also see that the range of possible values for each of the outputs is very wide. Most importantly, there is a significant chance that we will exceed our credit limit. There is no more practical way than simulation to estimate this critical value.

We now recapitulate the simulation process and provide recipes in capsule form for the most commonly repeated processes in Analytic Solver Platform.

1. Selecting uncertain parameters

The first step in any simulation (after building an appropriate spreadsheet and performing sensitivity analysis) is to select parameters to treat as uncertain. Each of these parameters requires its own probability distribution. Because it takes time and effort to find an appropriate distribution, some economy is called for in selecting uncertain parameters. As we saw in Chapter 4, large changes in some parameters may generate only modest changes in the outcomes. These parameters probably do not warrant treatment as uncertain. Therefore, we recommend performing an initial sensitivity analysis to select those parameters that have the most influence on the results. A tornado chart is a natural tool in this

FIGURE 14.14 Distribution of Loan Interest

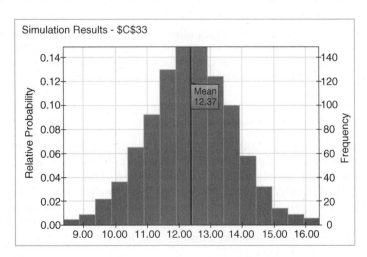

selection process. Among the most influential inputs, some may be decision variables: These should *never* be considered uncertain, because they are under our control. Only the most influential and uncertain parameters should be replaced with probability distributions. In a later section, we describe in more detail how to select uncertain parameters.

2. Selecting probability distributions

Once we have decided that a particular input parameter should be treated as uncertain, we must develop a probability distribution for it. In most cases, this step involves a mixture of data analysis and judgment. A small set of probability distributions is commonly used in business analysis. We describe these in a later section and indicate when each is appropriate.

ANALYTIC SOLVER TIP
Entering Distributions

1. Highlight the target cell.
2. Select Analytic Solver Platform▶Simulation Model▶Distributions. This sequence displays six categories of distributions: Common, Advanced, Exotic, Discrete, Custom, and Certified. Highlight any category and the specific distributions in that category are displayed graphically. A total of 46 distributions is available. A Distribution Wizard is also available that guides the user through these choices.
3. Select a particular distribution and a probability distribution window such as Figure 14.9 opens.
4. Each probability distribution window depicts the distribution in the form of a PDF (probability distribution function), a CDF (cumulative distribution function), or a Reverse CDF. It also allows the user to input the parameters of the distribution, such as the mean and standard deviation, either as numbers or as cell references.
5. Click on Save to enter the distribution in the target cell. (Probability distributions can also be entered into cells by typing the relevant formulas directly.) ∎

3. Selecting output(s)

Every simulation produces a probability distribution for one or more outputs. Generally the output cell represents the single most important aspect of the model. But in simulation, we are not confined to considering only one output variable. In fact, one of the powerful aspects of simulation is that any cell in the spreadsheet can be considered an output cell. We might, for example, be interested not only in the profit we generate, but also in the NPV, the ratio of cost to revenues, and so on. Any variable we can represent in a single cell can be treated as an output.

ANALYTIC SOLVER TIP
Defining Output Cells

1. Highlight the target cell.
2. Select Analytic Solver Platform▶Simulation Model▶Results▶Output▶In Cell. This sequence adds the function `PsiOutput()` to the formula in the target cell. Any cell with this function will contain the probability distribution for the cell value once a simulation is run. (Alternatively, simply type +PsiOutput() after the formula in the cell.)
3. To create a separate cell with the distribution of the target cell, highlight the target cell and select Analytic Solver Platform▶Simulation Model▶Results▶Output▶Referred Cell. Then move the cursor to the desired cell location and click once. This will enter the PsiOutput function in the given cell with a cell reference to the target cell.
4. Analytic Solver Platform also allows the user to record various aspects of the distribution of a cell on the spreadsheet. For example, to record the mean of cell C16 in cell C17, highlight cell C16, select Analytic Solver Platform▶Simulation Model▶Results▶Statistics▶Mean, and click on cell C17. Alternatively, enter the formula =PsiMean(C16) in cell C17. ∎

4. Running a simulation

Executing a simulation consists of sampling from the input distributions and storing the results of the outputs. Analytic Solver Platform provides a number of options for tailoring the simulation run to the situation. The simulation options are available by selecting Analytic Solver Platform▶Options▶Options▶All Options and choosing the Simulation tab. A key choice is the sample size—or, in simulation language, the number of *trials*. Whether we are interested in the mean profit or the probability of a loss, the larger our sample size, the more precise our estimates become. We elaborate later on how to select an appropriate level of precision and how to choose other Analytic Solver Platform settings.

5. Analyzing outputs

The result of running a simulation is a histogram, which we interpret as a probability distribution, for each of the output cells. How we analyze this distribution depends on the problem. Often, we are concerned simply with the expected value, or mean outcome. Many other useful aspects of the distribution, such as the minimum outcome or the Value at Risk, are calculated by Analytic Solver Platform.

ANALYTIC SOLVER TIP
Analyzing Outputs

1. If we double-click on the output cell, we open the output window, which contains five tabs: Frequency, Cumulative Frequency, Reverse Cumulative Frequency, Sensitivity, and Scatter Plots. The first three tabs show different views of the histogram of outputs. The Sensitivity tab shows the correlations between input distributions and the output. The Scatter Plots tab shows scatter plots of each input distribution against the output. The panel to the right of the histogram displays 23 statistics for the output, starting with the mean. By using the pull-down arrow to the right of the Statistics we can also display the percentiles of the histogram (and modify the chart itself in a variety of ways).

2. We can avoid opening the output window and searching for specific statistical results by capturing them directly in cells on the spreadsheet. For example, to capture the 95th percentile of the output cell C16 in cell C17, highlight cell C16 and select Analytic Solver Platform▶Simulation Model▶Results▶Range▶Percentile, and click on cell C17. Alternatively, enter the formula =PsiPercentile(C16, 0.95) in cell C17. ∎

14.4 CORPORATE VALUATION USING SIMULATION

In this section, we illustrate how simulation can be applied to the valuation of a company. Although valuation is often carried out with deterministic models, it is a very suitable application for Monte Carlo simulation, especially in the case of valuing a startup company.

NETSCAPE COMMUNI-CATIONS*

The initial public offering (IPO) of Netscape Communications Corporation on August 9, 1995, is thought to have signaled the beginning of the Internet boom. The underwriters of the IPO planned to offer five million shares at $28 per share, thereby raising $140 million. Up to that point, about $27 million had been invested in Netscape, and the company had yet to show a profit. At $28 per share, Netscape's market value would be more than $1 billion, despite a book value of just $16 million.

The IPO underwriters calculated the value of the firm by adding the present value of the free cash flows through 2005 to the present value of the firm after 2005. This latter value, known as the **terminal value**, was calculated under the assumption that the free cash flows after 2005 would grow forever at a constant rate.

The underwriters' valuation was based on an annual revenue growth rate of 65 percent. Also, the terminal-value growth rate was set at 4 percent, and the tax rate was assumed to be 34 percent. Some of the other assumptions included:

Cost of sales	10.4% of revenues
R&D	34.6% of revenues
Depreciation	5.5% of revenues
Other operating expenses	80% of revenues in 1996, decreasing to 20% by 2002 and level thereafter
Capital expenses	45% of revenues in 1996, decreasing to 10% by 2000 and level thereafter
Beta	1.50
Riskless rate	6.71%
Market-risk premium	7.50%

With these assumptions, a discounted cash-flow model for Netscape gave a valuation of $28 per share, supporting the underwriters' plans. ∎

*This example is based on the work of Professor Anant Sundarum.

14.4.1 Base-Case Model

Our deterministic model for this problem is shown in Figure 14.15, where all dollar amounts are shown in thousands. As usual, we have isolated the parameters in one location and grouped the calculations separately. The model includes actual values for 1995 in column B and builds the forecasts for the years 1996–2005 using recursive formulas along with growth rates and ratios given in the Assumptions section.

The free cash flows shown in row 33 are negative until 1999, but turn positive in 2000 and grow dramatically thereafter. The terminal value of the firm, which is an estimate of its value after 2005, is calculated in cell B34. Here, we take the 2005 free cash flows and project them forward one year using the terminal-value growth rate; then we divide by the difference between the cost of equity and the terminal-value growth rate. This calculation gives the present value in 2006 of an endless stream of cash flows growing at the terminal-value growth rate.

One interesting feature of this model is that we can measure four or five different aspects of the value of Netscape (see cells B40:B44). The single most important measure of the value of the firm is the total net present value (cell B40), which adds the present value of free cash flows from 1995–2005 to the present value of the terminal value. Another interesting measure is the ratio of the terminal value to the total present value (cell B41), which reflects how much of the overall value comes after 2005. A third measure is the year in which cash flows first turn positive (cell B42), which is 2002 in the base case. Another measure that relates to financing is the cumulative loss (cell B43), or the cumulative negative free cash flow during the initial years before the cash flow turns positive. Because this is the amount that must be financed, it can indicate whether the current IPO will raise sufficient funds. Finally, we calculate the price per share (cell B44), by apportioning the total net present value of the firm to the 38,000 shares that will be outstanding after the IPO. A detailed description of the model follows:

Assumptions

Cells B4:B15: Given data.

Row 9: Other operating expenses decline from 80 percent in 1996 to 20 percent by 2002 and remain level thereafter.

Row 10: Capital expenditures decline from 45 percent in 1996 to 10 percent by 2000 and remain level thereafter.

Cell B16: Under the assumptions of the Capital Asset Pricing Model, the cost of equity for Netscape is equal to the riskless rate (cell B14) plus the product of its beta (cell B13) and market-risk premium (cell B15).

Cell B17: Given data.

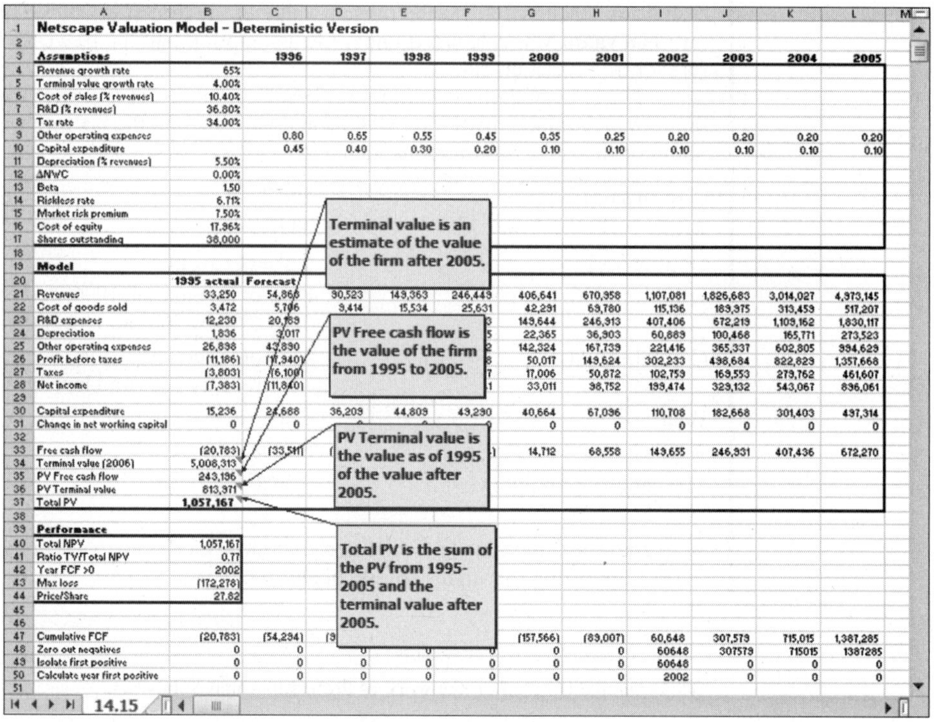

	A	B	C	D	E	F	G	H	I	J	K	L
1	**Netscape Valuation Model – Deterministic Version**											
2												
3	**Assumptions**		1996	1997	1998	1999	2000	2001	2002	2003	2004	2005
4	Revenue growth rate	65%										
5	Terminal value growth rate	4.00%										
6	Cost of sales (% revenues)	10.40%										
7	R&D (% revenues)	36.80%										
8	Tax rate	34.00%										
9	Other operating expenses		0.80	0.65	0.55	0.45	0.35	0.25	0.20	0.20	0.20	0.20
10	Capital expenditure		0.45	0.40	0.30	0.20	0.10	0.10	0.10	0.10	0.10	0.10
11	Depreciation (% revenues)	5.50%										
12	ΔNWC	0.00%										
13	Beta	1.50										
14	Riskless rate	6.71%										
15	Market risk premium	7.50%										
16	Cost of equity	17.96%										
17	Shares outstanding	38,000										
18												
19	**Model**											
20		**1995 actual**	**Forecast**									
21	Revenues	33,250	54,863	90,523	149,363	246,449	406,641	670,958	1,107,081	1,826,683	3,014,027	4,973,145
22	Cost of goods sold	3,472	5,706	9,414	15,534	25,631	42,291	69,780	115,136	189,975	313,459	517,207
23	R&D expenses	12,230	20,189			3	149,644	246,913	407,406	672,219	1,109,162	1,830,117
24	Depreciation	1,836	3,017			5	22,365	36,903	60,889	100,468	165,771	273,523
25	Other operating expenses	26,898	43,890			2	142,324	167,739	221,416	365,337	602,805	994,629
26	Profit before taxes	(11,186)	(17,940)			8	50,017	149,624	302,233	498,684	822,829	1,357,668
27	Taxes	(3,803)	(6,100)			7	17,006	50,872	102,759	169,553	279,762	461,607
28	Net income	(7,383)	(11,840)			1	33,011	98,752	199,474	329,132	543,067	896,061
29												
30	Capital expenditure	15,236	24,688	36,209	44,809	49,290	40,664	67,096	110,708	182,668	301,403	497,314
31	Change in net working capital	0	0				0	0	0	0	0	0
32												
33	Free cash flow	(20,783)	(33,511)	(		)	14,712	68,558	149,655	246,931	407,436	672,270
34	Terminal value (2006)	5,008,313										
35	PV Free cash flow	243,196										
36	PV Terminal value	813,971										
37	Total PV	**1,057,167**										
38												
39	**Performance**											
40	Total NPV	1,057,167										
41	Ratio TV/Total NPV	0.77										
42	Year FCF >0	2002										
43	Max loss	(172,278)										
44	Price/Share	27.82										
45												
46												
47	Cumulative FCF	(20,783)	(54,294)	(9			(157,566)	(89,007)	60,648	307,579	715,015	1,387,285
48	Zero out negatives	0	0				0	0	60648	307579	715015	1387285
49	Isolate first positive	0	0	0	0	0	0	0	60648	0	0	0
50	Calculate year first positive	0	0	0	0	0	0	0	2002	0	0	0
51												

FIGURE 14.15 Deterministic Spreadsheet for Netscape

Model

Row 21: Data for 1995 is actual. Revenues grow at the given growth rate (cell B4) from 1996 through 2005.

Row 22: Cost of goods sold for 1996 through 2005 is revenue (row 21) times the cost-of-goods-sold percentage (cell B6).

Row 23: R&D expense for 1996 through 2005 is revenue (row 21) times the R&D percentage (cell B7).

Row 24: Depreciation for 1996 through 2005 is revenue (row 21) times the depreciation percentage (cell B11).

Row 25: Other operating expenses for 1996 through 2005 is revenue (row 21) times other operating-expense percentage (row 9).

Row 26: Profit before taxes is revenues (row 21) less cost of goods sold (row 22) less R&D expenses (row 23) less depreciation (row 24) less other operating expenses (row 25).

Row 27: Taxes are profit before taxes (row 26) times the tax rate (cell B8).

Row 28: Net income is profit before taxes (row 26) less taxes (row 27).

Row 30: Capital expenditures are revenues (row 21) times the capital-expenditure percentage (row 10).

Row 31: The change in net working capital is assumed to be zero throughout.

Row 33: Free cash flow is net income (row 28) plus depreciation (row 24) less capital expenditures (row 30) less change in net working capital (row 31).

Cell B34: The terminal value is calculated by taking the free cash flow in 2005 (cell L33) and multiplying it by one plus the terminal-value growth rate (cell B5). This is an estimate of the free cash flow in 2006. We then assume this value grows at the terminal-value growth rate forever. The present value of these cash flows in 2006 is calculated by discounting at the cost of equity (cell B16).

Cell B35: The present value of the free cash flows from 1995 to 2005 is the sum of the value in 1995 (cell B33) plus the net present value from 1996–2005 (cells C33:L33).

Cell B36: The present value of the terminal value in 2006 is the terminal value (cell B34) discounted 11 years at the cost of equity (cell B16).

Cell B37: The total present value of Netscape is the sum of the present value of free cash flows to 2005 (cell B35) and the present value of the terminal value (cell B36).

Performance

Cell B40: Total NPV is taken directly from the model (cell B37).

Cell B41: The ratio of the terminal value to the total NPV is the ratio of the terminal value (cell B36) to the total NPV (cell B37).

Cell B42: The year the free cash flow first turns positive is calculated using the intermediate calculations in rows 47 to 50. In row 47, we calculate the cumulative free cash flow by adding successive terms in row 33. In row 48, we use an IF statement to replace any negative cumulative free cash flows with zero. In row 49, we isolate the first positive free cash flow by using an AND statement to identify the cell in which free cash flow turns from negative to positive, and an IF statement to replace all other cells with zero. In row 50, we use an IF statement to determine the *year* in which the free cash flow first becomes positive. Finally, in cell B42, we add all the values across row 50, only one of which contains the year the free cash flow turns positive, all others being zero.

Cell B43: The cumulative loss is the minimum value of the cumulative free cash flows in row 47.

Cell B44: The price per share is the total present value (cell B37) divided by the number of shares outstanding (cell B17).

Our deterministic model gives us some interesting insights. The total present value of Netscape comes to more than $1 billion under this set of assumptions, apparently justifying the IPO share price. Netscape's cumulative free cash flows are expected to turn positive by

2002, but the maximum loss is more than $170 million, indicating that the proceeds from the IPO may not be sufficient to cover the investment Netscape needs to fuel its growth. Finally, the terminal value of more than $800 million makes up more than three-quarters of the total value of $1 billion. This suggests that the valuation is heavily dependent on assumptions that affect the terminal value.

14.4.2 Sensitivity Analysis

Before we incorporate uncertainty, we should undertake some sensitivity analysis with the deterministic model. Since we know that the terminal value makes up about 77 percent of the total present value, it is natural to ask how sensitive the terminal value (cell B36) is to its driving variables: the terminal-value growth rate and the market risk premium. The two-way parametric sensitivity table shown in Figure 14.16 illustrates how small changes in either the terminal-value growth rate or the market-risk premium have significant effects on the terminal value of Netscape and hence on the total valuation. With the market-risk premium at 7.5 percent, the terminal value ranges from about $650 million to $1.5 billion for terminal-value growth rates between 1 percent and 10 percent. Similarly, when we vary the market-risk premium from 5 percent to 10 percent with the terminal-value growth rate at 4 percent, the terminal value ranges from $1.6 billion to $450 million.

Since we have a large number of input parameters in this model, it is also useful to create a tornado chart to evaluate which parameters most affect the valuation. The tornado chart in Figure 14.17 is based on the assumption that each parameter in the range from B4 to B15 varies up and down by the same percentage (10 percent) of its base-case value. The

FIGURE 14.16 Two-Way Sensitivity for Netscape

	A	B	C	D	E	F	G	H	I	J	K	L
1	PV Terminal Value											
2												
3												
4	TV Growth Rate	Market Risk Premium										
5		5.00%	5.50%	6.00%	6.50%	7.00%	7.50%	8.00%	8.50%	9.00%	9.50%	10.00%
6	0.00%	1096993	969611	859582	764133	681007	608352	544640	488600	439168	395451	356693
7	1.00%	1191836	1049458	927198	821695	730248	650664	581147	520218	466650	419416	377656
8	2.00%	1302215	1141627	1004677	887219	785965	698278	622024	555459	497150	445909	400745
9	3.00%	1432286	1249209	1094348	962479	849523	752258	668104	594981	531194	475351	426303
10	4.00%	1587836	1376423	1199334	1049818	922705	813971	720450	639617	569439	508266	454747
11	5.00%	1777165	1529182	1323925	1152401	1007873	885208	780432	690426	612713	545306	486595
12	6.00%	2012615	1716039	1474179	1274598	1108237	968358	8498 Base Case:				522498
13	7.00%	2313378	1949844	1658935	1422629	1228260	1066680	9311 TV Growth Rate = 4%				563282
14	8.00%	2711005	2250835	1891616	1605655	1374347	1184747	10275 Market Risk Premium = 7.5%				610016
15	9.00%	3261271	2652830	2193652	1837751	1556021	1329167	1143906	990811	863014	755404	664103
16	10.00%	4072946	3216920	2601479	2141702	1788091	1509874	1286938	1105599	956233	831890	727429
17												

14.15 14.16

FIGURE 14.17 Tornado Chart for Netscape

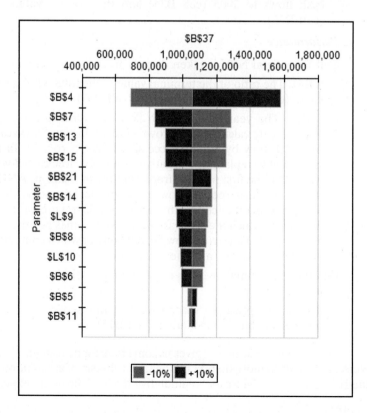

results suggest that the valuation is most dependent on four parameters: revenue growth rate, R&D as a percentage of revenues, beta, and the market-risk premium. Since the value of beta can be estimated with reasonable accuracy from the performance of comparable companies, our uncertainty analysis focuses on the other three parameters.

14.4.3 Selecting Probability Distributions

Having built a deterministic model and having carried out various sensitivity analyses, we are now ready to undertake a risk analysis using simulation. We have identified three parameters that have a particularly strong impact on the valuation: the revenue growth rate, the R&D percentage, and the market-risk premium. Based on what was known at the time about the uncertainties governing each of these parameters, we adopt the following probability distributions:

Revenue growth rate: Normal, with a mean of 65 percent and a standard deviation of 5 percent.

R&D as a percentage of revenues: Triangular, with a minimum of 32 percent, most likely value of 37 percent, and a maximum of 42 percent.

Market-risk premium: Uniform, with a minimum of 5 percent and a maximum of 10 percent.

The questions before us now are:

- How does the uncertainty in these parameters affect the valuation of Netscape?
- Was the IPO valuation justified in light of these uncertainties?

14.4.4 Simulation Analysis

Our second model for this problem, shown in Figure 14.18, includes the appropriate probability distributions for the revenue growth rate, R&D as a percentage of revenues,

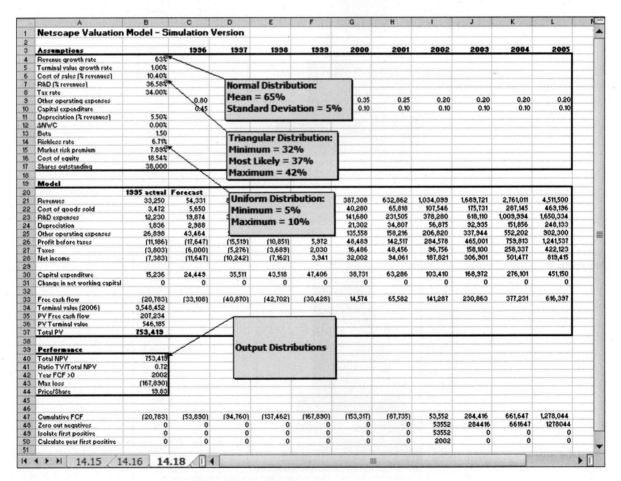

FIGURE 14.18 Simulation Model for Netscape

and the market-risk premium. Output cells are cells B40:B44. We run 1,000 trials to generate histograms for each of the five outcome measures we have described (see Figures 19–23). Analysis of these histograms sheds light on the nature of the uncertainties facing the Netscape IPO.

Figure 14.19 shows that, while the mean valuation (cell B40) remains around $1 billion ($964 million), the present value can be as low as $200 million or as high as $3.0 billion. There is a 10 percent chance that the value will be less than half a billion, a far cry from the deterministic valuation of $1 billion. Thus, simulation analysis allows us to quantify the extreme uncertainty in the overall value for this IPO.

Figure 14.20 shows that the terminal value (B41) is at least 66 percent of the total valuation and can be as high as 93 percent. As in the deterministic case, the great majority of the total value of this firm appears to come after ten years' time.

Figure 14.21 shows that the cumulative loss (B43) averages $173 million, but can be as large as $215 million. More significantly, if the current IPO raises $140 million, there is less than a 1 percent chance that this amount will be sufficient to fund the entire future development of the company.

Figure 14.22 shows that cumulative free cash flows turn positive (B42) either in 2002 or 2003. There is relatively little variation in the turning point.

Figure 14.23 shows that the stock price (B44) ranges from a low of about $5 to a high of $80, with a mean value of about $25. Although the stock price is closely related to the total value of the firm, this outcome measure may be more valuable to a potential investor. This result shows that stock purchased at $28 today may actually be worth as little as $5; nevertheless, it has a 11 percent chance of being worth more than $40.

FIGURE 14.19 Distribution of Total Value for Netscape

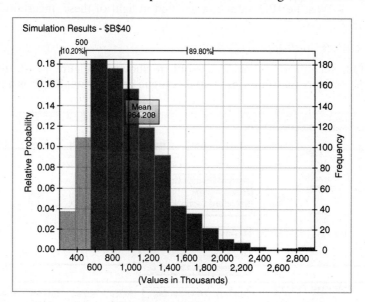

FIGURE 14.20 Distribution of Ratio of Terminal Value to Total Value for Netscape

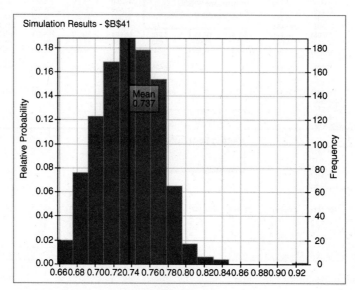

FIGURE 14.21 Distribution of Cumulative Loss for Netscape

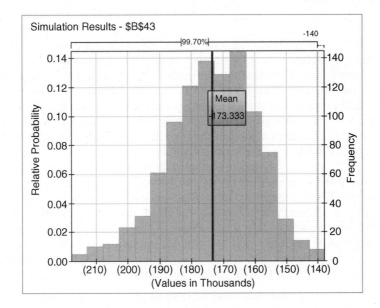

FIGURE 14.22 Distribution of Year that Cash Flows Turn Positive for Netscape

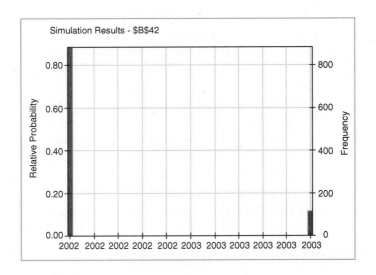

FIGURE 14.23 Distribution of Stock Price for Netscape

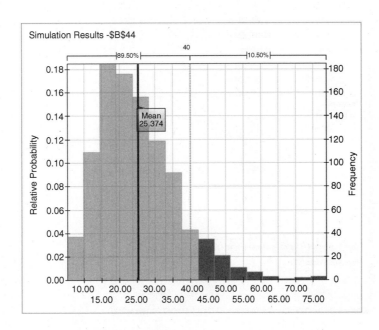

14.4.5 Simulation Sensitivity

The foregoing simulation analysis has allowed us to quantify uncertainty in the future value of Netscape along a number of different dimensions. It suggests that we should be somewhat skeptical that the company's future value really supports a share price of $28. Questions remain, however. We might ask, for example, how our simulation estimates would vary if one of the underlying parameters were to change. We pointed out above that the terminal-value growth rate strongly influences the terminal value of the firm, which in this case accounts for most of the overall value. Thus, it is natural to ask how sensitive the expected NPV is to the terminal-value growth rate.

To answer this and similar sensitivity questions with a simulation model, we need to run a simulation in Analytic Solver Platform once for each value of the parameter we wish to test. This is done in two steps. First we define the range of values for the input parameter using a PsiSimParam function, akin to the PsiSenParam function for deterministic sensitivity analysis. Then we create a table (Report) or chart of values for specific statistics of an output cell by running simulations for each value of the input.

As an illustration, we run a simulation on the Netscape model, varying the terminal-value growth rate from 1 percent to 10 percent in increments of 1 percent.

1. Enter the function =PsiSimParam(1%,10%) in a convenient unused cell, such as D40. This function provides inputs for the simulation sensitivity analysis.

2. Enter a reference to D40 in cell B5.

3. Place the cursor on the Total NPV output cell, B40.

4. Select Analytic Solver Platform▶Analysis▶Reports▶Simulation▶Parameter Analysis. This sequence opens the Multiple Simulations Report window (Figure 14.24).

5. Select the output cell B40 from among the options in the pull-down menu at the top of the window.

6. Select the output statistics Minimum, Maximum, and Mean by checking the corresponding boxes.

7. Select the parameter D40 containing the input range.

8. Select Vary All Sensitivity Parameters one at a Time from the pull-down menu near the bottom of the window.

9. Specify 10 Major Axis Points.

10. Click on OK. These steps create a new sheet named Sim Analysis Report.

FIGURE 14.24 Multiple Simulations Report Window

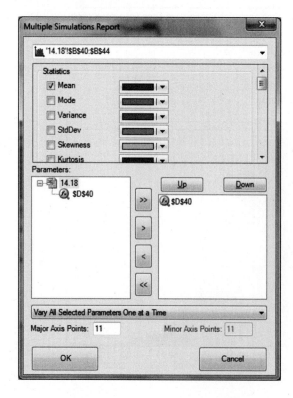

FIGURE 14.25 Total NPV as a Function of the Terminal-Value Growth Rate

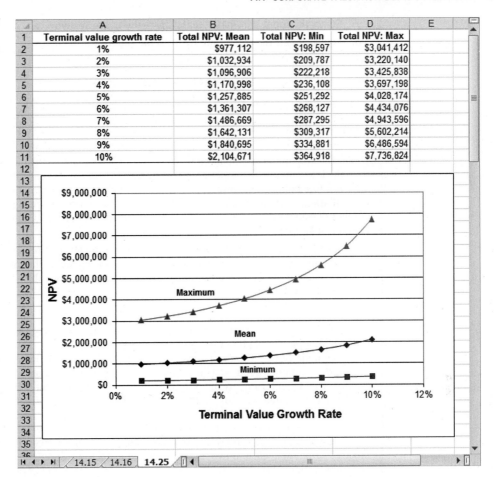

Terminal value growth rate	Total NPV: Mean	Total NPV: Min	Total NPV: Max
1%	$977,112	$198,597	$3,041,412
2%	$1,032,934	$209,787	$3,220,140
3%	$1,096,906	$222,218	$3,425,838
4%	$1,170,998	$236,108	$3,697,198
5%	$1,257,885	$251,292	$4,028,174
6%	$1,361,307	$268,127	$4,434,076
7%	$1,486,669	$287,295	$4,943,596
8%	$1,642,131	$309,317	$5,602,214
9%	$1,840,695	$334,881	$6,486,594
10%	$2,104,671	$364,918	$7,736,824

The resulting values for the three statistics of the distribution of Total NPV are shown in Figure 14.25. The table is the output of Analytic Solver Platform; the graph was created from the table. We see that as the terminal-value growth rate varies from 1 percent to 10 percent, the mean Total NPV varies from about $1 billion to $2 billion. The minimum value varies little over this range, from about $0.2 billion to $0.4 billion. However, the maximum value increases from $3 billion to more than $7 billion, indicating that the likelihood of extremely high valuations increases rapidly with the terminal-value growth rate.

The Netscape example illustrates an approach to valuing a company that is used throughout the finance industry. One weakness of this approach is that a single growth rate is used for revenues over a period as long as ten years, with no detailed modeling to explain the sources for this growth. Another weakness is that the terminal value often dominates the overall value of the firm, and as we have seen, the terminal value is highly sensitive to the assumptions on which it is based. Without simulation, no insights into the effects of uncertainty would be possible, and the evaluation could easily be optimistic. Simulation reveals the range of uncertainty in the valuation itself, as well as in other important aspects of the firm's future, such as the adequacy of funding.

ANALYTIC SOLVER TIP
Simulation Sensitivity

1. Create and run a simulation model with at least one output cell.
2. Define the sensitivity range for the input parameter(s) by referencing the function `PsiSimParam(lower limit, upper limit)`.
3. Place the cursor on the Output cell(s).
4. Select Analytic Solver Platform▶Analysis▶Reports▶Simulation▶Parameter Analysis. This sequence opens the Multiple Simulations Report window.
5. Choose the output cell(s) from the drop-down list at the top of the window.
6. Select one or more statistics of the output cell(s) by placing check marks appropriately.

7. Select the input parameter cell(s) from the list provided.

8. Select one of the three options from the pull-down menu:

`Vary All Selected Parameters Simultaneously`

`Vary All Selected Parameters One at a Time`

`Vary Two Selected Parameters Independently`

Under the first option, a simulation will be run for each value specified in the PsiSimParam functions from the lower limit to the upper limit. The number of values is given by the number of `Major Axis Points` (see below). Under the second option, separate sets of simulations will be run, one for each PsiSimParam function. Finally, the third option creates a two-dimensional table of results, with the number of values on one axis specified by the number of `Major Axis Points` and the other by the number of `Minor Axis Points`.

9. Specify the number of `Major Axis Points` (and `Minor Axis Points` if necessary for a two-dimensional table). Analytic Solver Platform will divide the range for the input parameter specified in the PsiSimParam function into the number of values specified here, and run one simulation for each of these values.

10. Click on OK.

A three-dimensional chart can be created using the same steps, starting with Analysis▶ Charts▶Multiple Simulations▶Parameter Analysis.

Analytic Solver Platform runs each of these simulations using the number of trials and the random number seed specified under All Options. It is good practice to fix the random number seed by entering any integer other than 0 (999 is a common choice) under `Sim`. Random Seed on the Simulation tab in the Options window (the reasons for this are explained in Section 14.8).

Just as we can perform a two-way sensitivity analysis on a deterministic model, we can perform a two-way simulation sensitivity analysis. This requires entering PsiSimParam functions to define the range of variation in each of two inputs. Then in the Multiple Simulations Report window, we select both inputs under `Parameters` and specify the appropriate number of `Major Axis Points` and `Minor Axis Points`. The result is a two-way table of simulation results for each of the statistics that we checked in Step 6. If we choose more than one statistic for the output cell, Analytic Solver Platform will generate a two-way table for each statistic. ∎

14.5 OPTION PRICING USING SIMULATION

An **option** is the right to buy or sell an asset, without the corresponding obligation. For example, we might negotiate an option to purchase an office building at any time in the coming year for a set price. If the economy does well and the value of the building increases, we might decide to exercise the option and make the purchase, but if the economy does poorly, we are not obligated to buy.

Financial options, which include the right to buy or sell stocks, have become central to modern finance and investment. Financial options have value primarily because they allow the holder to hedge against changes in the value of the underlying financial asset. Billions of dollars' worth of options are traded each year. Every buyer or seller of an option has a stake in determining a fair price for the option. The theory behind option pricing is based on rather advanced mathematics, but the principles involved can be readily understood. In this example, we develop the basic concepts behind pricing options, and we use simulation to make those concepts concrete.

EXAMPLE
Pricing a European Call Option

A **European call option** on a stock gives the owner the right to purchase the stock at a specified price on a given date. The specified purchase price is called the **strike price**, and the given date is called the **expiration date**. Imagine that we had a call option with a strike price of $40 and an expiration date six months away. If the stock price on the expiration date turns out to be $45, we could make a profit of $5 by exercising the option to purchase the stock for $40 and then selling it for $45. If the stock price on the expiration date turns out to be $30, we would lose $10 if we exercised the option to buy at $40, so we would not exercise the option. If the stock is currently selling at $35, what would be a fair market price for this option? ∎

14.5.1 The Logic of Options

As the example shows, the value of an option depends on the actual price of the underlying stock at the expiration date. The higher the actual price is *above* the strike price, the higher our profit; but no matter how far the actual price is *below* the strike price, nothing is lost except the cost of acquiring the option. Future stock prices, of course, are not easily predicted, so it is natural to develop a probability distribution for the stock price at the expiration date. We first illustrate the concepts behind option pricing by using a simple but unrealistic distribution. Then, we develop a more realistic model for the evolution of stock prices over time, and we use it to determine option prices.

For the moment, assume there is a 50 percent chance that the stock price at expiration will be $45.00 and a 50 percent chance the stock price will be $35.00. If the price is $45.00, we can exercise the option and gain a profit of $5.00. If it is $35.00, we will not exercise, and we will lose nothing. The value of the option at the expiration date is called its **intrinsic value**. The intrinsic value is $5.00 when the price is $45.00; it is $0.00 when the price is $35.00.

Since we are considering buying the option today, we have to adjust for the time difference between now and the expiration date. The present value of the possible $5.00 gain, assuming a 7 percent annual discount rate, is $4.83 $(= 5/(1 + 0.07/2))$. The present value of the $0.00 gain if the price falls is obviously $0.00. The *expected value* of the option would be $2.42 $(= 0.5 \times 4.83 + 0.5 \times 0)$. Financial theory and practice both confirm that this expected value is an appropriate market price for the option.

14.5.2 Modeling Stock Prices

Now let's return to the question of what is a realistic probability distribution for stock prices. Studies of the actual behavior of stock prices over time indicate that stocks are subject to small random changes every day, with a small upward trend. In other words, although daily prices vary, stocks show an average gain in price over longer periods. The evidence also suggests that stock prices at any date in the future tend to follow an asymmetric distribution, with a maximum value farther above the mean than the minimum is below it. Figure 14.26 shows a lognormal distribution, a family of distributions that is generally accepted as fitting actual stock prices quite well.

A realistic model that reproduces these aspects of actual stock prices takes the form

$$P_t = P_0 e^N \tag{14.1}$$

where P_t is the price at some future time t, P_0 is the price today, and the exponential term e^N gives the appropriate growth factor. The parameter N, which is a sample from a normal distribution, represents the return on the stock.

For readers who haven't studied Finance, we provide some background on the measurement of stock returns. When we speak of returns, we usually refer to a stock price increasing by x percent or dropping by y percent. Let's take a closer look at the mathematics involved, assuming at the outset that no randomness occurs. Suppose we own a stock worth $100. When we track its price over the next two months, we find that it gains 10 percent in the first month and then loses 10 percent in the second month. Is its value back to $100 after two months? The answer is no. After one month, its value went up by 10 percent to $110, but a month later, it dropped by 10 percent to $99. The lesson: when we add percentage changes in price, we get a misleading result. Here, adding +10 percent and −10 percent would give us 0 percent, but the stock return was not 0 percent after two months.

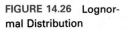

FIGURE 14.26 Lognormal Distribution

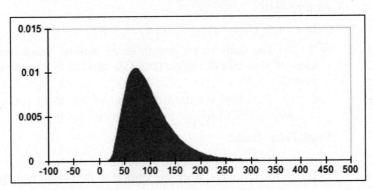

If adding percentage returns can mislead us, how should we do the math? One convenient answer is that we can multiply *relative* prices. In our example, the relative gain in price after month 1 is $P_1/P_0 = 1.1$, and the relative gain after month 2 is $P_2/P_1 = 0.9$. Multiplying the two relative gains, we get $1.1 \times 0.9 = 0.99$. Indeed, $P_2/P_0 = 0.99$, and multiplying relative gains gives us the correct value.

An equivalent approach to multiplying is to add logarithms. Consider that $\ln(1.1) = 0.09531$ and $\ln(0.9) = -0.10536$. When we add these two logarithms, we obtain -0.01005. To invert this logarithm, we use it as the argument for the exponential function and obtain the value $e^{-0.01005} = 0.99$. Thus, adding the logarithms of individual relative returns, and then inverting, gives us the correct value for the aggregate return. The reason we often prefer to use logarithms is that we are not restricted to discrete periods (such as months), and we can work with the flexibility of viewing time as continuous. Thus, we define **return** from time zero to time t as the logarithm of the relative gain in price, or $\ln(P_t/P_0)$. Similarly, in a continuous-time world, a return of 10 percent means that the relative gain is $e^{0.10}$. Mathematically, this expression corresponds to 1.1052, or a gain of 10.52 percent. That's slightly more than the nominal 10 percent gain, but we can interpret the value as the result of continuous compounding at a 10 percent rate.

Where does randomness enter the picture? In the mathematics of Finance, stock returns over a period of length t are assumed to follow a normal distribution with mean μt and variance $\sigma^2 t$. In other words, the logarithm of the relative gain in price is represented by a normal random variable. When this is the case, the stock price (relative to a starting value P_0) follows a lognormal distribution, for which the mean is equal to $\mu t + 0.5\sigma^2 t$. Historical data on the stock's performance are used to estimate the mean μt and the standard deviation $\sigma\sqrt{t}$ of the annual distribution of returns.

In summary, stock returns are measured as the logarithm of the ratio of prices—that is, as $\ln(P_t/P_0)$, as represented in (14.1). Because of continuous compounding, the mean for the distribution of N is $(\mu - \sigma^2/2)$, and the standard deviation is σ. Thus, the final model takes the form:

$$P_t = P_0 e^{N\left(\mu - \frac{\sigma^2}{2}, \sigma\right)} \tag{14.2}$$

We need to convert the annual values for the parameters (μt and $\sigma^2 t$) to daily equivalents, in order to track movements over shorter time periods. For this purpose, we assume that $t = 250$ trading days in a year, so that one day represents 0.004 years. Suppose the return of a particular stock is 12 percent with an annual standard deviation of 30 percent. This means that $E[P_t/P_0] = 0.12$, or $\mu t + 0.5\,\sigma^2 t = 0.12$. Equivalently, the daily mean is:

$$\mu = 0.12(0.004) - 0.5(0.3)^2(0.004) = 0.0003.$$

The daily standard deviation is

$$0.3(0.004)^{0.5} = 0.01897$$

Our model for projecting stock prices is shown in Figure 14.27. The key to simulating daily stock prices is generating random samples from a normal distribution with the given daily mean return and daily standard deviation. For this purpose, we use the Excel formula, `=EXP(PsiNormal($C$11,$C$12))`.

The Analytic Solver Platform function in this formula, `PsiNormal(mean, standard deviation)`, takes a sample from the appropriate normal distribution. This value becomes the argument for the Excel function `EXP()`.

Assumptions

Cells C4:C9: Given data.

Cell C11: The daily mean growth is the annual mean (cell C7) less one-half the squared standard deviation (cell C8) divided by the number of trading days in a year (cell C6).

Cell C12: The daily standard deviation of the stock price is the annual standard deviation (cell C8) divided by the square root of the number of trading days (cell C6).

Stock Price Model

Cells B16:B141: We model the evolution of the stock price from its initial value on Day 0 for 125 days, since the option to be priced is a six-month option.

FIGURE 14.27 Stock Price Model

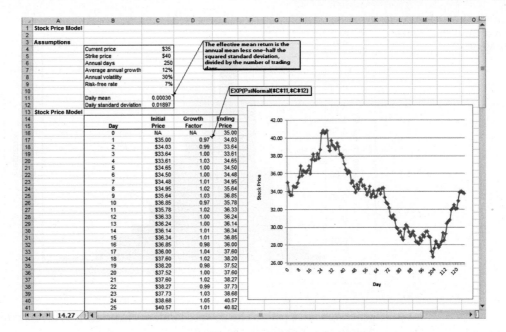

Cells C17:C141: The initial price each day is the ending price from the previous day (column E).

Cells D17:D141: To determine the growth in the stock price each day, we first take a random sample from a normal distribution with the daily mean return (cell C11) and the daily standard deviation (cell C12), using the Analytic Solver Platform function `PsiNormal($C$11,$C$12)`. Then we take the exponential function (EXP()) of this quantity as specified in the model for stock price growth.

Cells E16:E141: The ending price on Day 0 is given. The ending price each subsequent day is the initial price (column C) times the growth factor for that day (column D).

One projected price path over the six-month period is shown graphically in Figure 14.27. By running several simulations and observing the graph, we can get a visual sense of the price paths this model generates. Figure 14.28 shows five of these randomly

FIGURE 14.28 Five Paths for Stock Prices

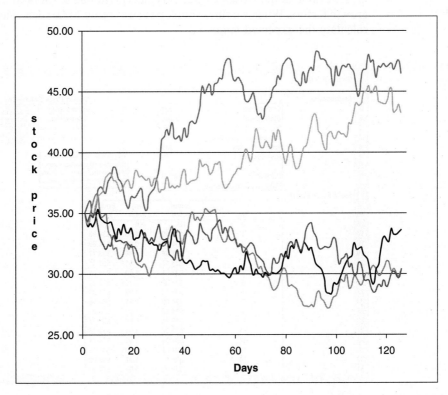

FIGURE 14.29 Distribution of Stock Prices After Six Months

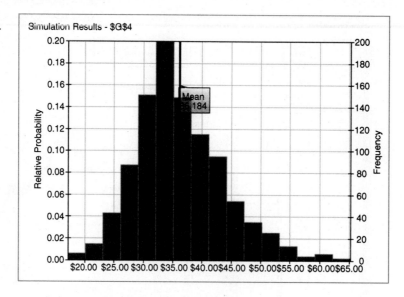

generated price paths. The upward tendency in prices is evident in this graph, as is the large degree of variability in the price.

We can determine the distribution of prices at the end of the 125-day period by designating the final price (cell E141) as an output cell. Figure 14.29 shows the distribution of prices in a simulation of 1,000 trials. The mean price is $36.18. The distribution also has the asymmetric shape that actual stock prices show, with a minimum value of about $15.00, or roughly half the mean, and a maximum above $70.00, more than twice the mean.

14.5.3 Pricing an Option

Now that we have a realistic model for the evolution of stock prices over time, we can return to the question of pricing the option. In the spreadsheet of Figure 14.30, we calculate the present value of the option for every randomly generated stock price. The price of an option can be calculated as the *expected value* of the *present value* of the *intrinsic value* of the option, which is its value at the terminal date. In this spreadsheet, we calculate the present value of the intrinsic value (in cell G7) for one set of random outcomes of the daily growth factors. When we run a simulation, we create 1,000 such values and average them to calculate the expected value.

FIGURE 14.30   Option Pricing Model

	A	B	C	D	E	F	G	H	I
1	Option Pricing								
2									
3	Assumptions					Option Price Calculation		Output: Price at expiration	
4		Current price	$35			Stock price	$29.39		
5		Strike price	$40			Strike Price	$40.00		
6		Expiration (days)	250			Intrinsic value	$0.00	Output: Intrinsic value	
7		Average annual growth	12%			Present value	$0.00		
8		Annual volatility	30%						
9		Risk-free rate	7%		To price an option, use the		Output: Option price	
10					risk-free rate rather than			
11		Daily mean	0.00010		the average annual growth			
12		Daily standard deviation	0.01897		rate as the effective mean.			
13	Stock Price Model								
14			Initial	Growth	Ending				
15		Day	Price	Factor	Price				
16		0	NA	NA	$35.00				
17		1	$35.00	1.00	$34.98				
18		2	$34.98	0.99	$34.69				
19		3	$34.69	0.96	$33.17				
20		4	$33.17	1.01	$33.51				
21		5	$33.51	1.02	$34.02				
22		6	$34.02	0.99	$33.82				
23		7	$33.82	1.03	$34.89				
24		8	$34.89	0.98	$34.28				
25		9	$34.28	1.03	$35.24				
26		10	$35.24	0.96	$33.97				
27		11	$33.97	1.01	$34.35				
28		12	$34.35	0.99	$34.14				
29		13	$34.14	1.03	$35.11				
30		14	$35.11	1.02	$35.92				
31		15	$35.92	0.97	$34.95				

The model in Figure 14.30 is a modified version of the stock price model in Figure 14.27. First, to calculate an option price that is consistent with the risk-neutral valuation principle of Finance theory[*], we must assume that the annual growth rate is equal to the annual *risk-free* rate (C9). Then in cell C11 we can enter the formula for the daily rate μ as calculated earlier:

$$0.07(0.004) - (0.5(0.3)^2)(0.004) = 0.00010.$$

The second modification creates cells in column G for the ending stock price, the strike price, the intrinsic value, and the present value:

Cell G4: The stock price at the end of six months, when the option comes due, is calculated in cell E141 and copied here.

Cell G5: The strike price, which is the value for which the stock can be sold at the expiration date, is given data (cell C5).

Cell G6: The intrinsic value of the option is calculated using the formula MAX(0,G4 - G5).

Cell G7: The present value is the intrinsic value discounted to the present at the risk-free rate.

When we use Analytic Solver Platform to generate 1,000 trials, we obtain 1,000 values for the stock price as well as 1,000 corresponding values for the present value of the intrinsic value of the option (cell G7). The average of these 1,000 values becomes our estimate of the fair market value for this option.

Figure 14.31 shows the distribution of option prices over the simulation trials. Here, we observe that the option has no value about 70 percent of the time. In these cases, the price of the stock has not risen above the strike price ($40.00) at the end of six months, so the option is not exercised. In the other 30 percent of the cases, the stock price is above the strike price, and the option does have value. In the extreme case, the price rises to about $70.00, giving an intrinsic value of about $30.00. On average, in our sample of 1,000, the discounted value is $1.59, which is an estimate of the fair market value for this option. Note the extreme asymmetry of the distribution of option prices. As we mentioned, options are used to hedge risk. In our example, however, roughly 70 percent of the time, the option has no value. But when the stock price rises sharply, an owner of this option can make significant profits. At the extreme, for an investment of $1.59, the owner can make a profit of $30.00 in just six months' time. No wonder many investors are tempted to invest in options!

FIGURE 14.31 Distribution of Option Prices

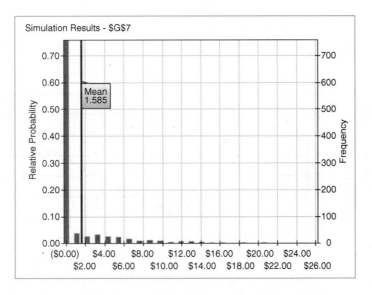

[*]For details, see D. L. McLeish, *Monte Carlo Simulation and Finance* (2005) Wiley, p. 109.

14.5.4 Sensitivity to Volatility

We can get some additional insight into the forces behind the value of options by considering the impact of variability in the stock price. We assumed that the underlying stock has an annual standard deviation of 30 percent. Would the option be worth more or less if the stock price were more volatile? To answer this question in the abstract, recall our two-price model for price uncertainty, where prices could go up to $45.00 or down to $35.00 with equal probabilities. We found that the option under these assumptions had a value of $2.42. But what if the stock price was more variable and could be $50.00 or $30.00 with equal probabilities? When the price is low, we still make nothing, but when the price is high, we make $10.00 at the terminal date instead of $5.00. In this case, the option is worth much more than in the original case: Its value is $9.66 (= 10/1.035). In general, increasing the variability of a stock price increases the value of an option, because the gains increase while the losses never go below zero.

Figure 14.32 shows the results of varying the standard deviation in our option-price model from 10 percent to 90 percent. Once again, we use the Simulation Sensitivity tool to carry out this set of simulations. We can see that an option is worth very little when the underlying stock has low volatility, but can be worth a great deal when the stock is highly volatile. Of course, the exact value is also influenced by the strike price and the time to expiration.

14.5.5 Simulation Precision

We mentioned previously that our option prices were estimates, based on a simulation of 1,000 stock prices six months out. How precise are these estimates? One simple way to answer this question is to take repeated samples of 1,000 prices and compare estimates of the mean values. (To do so we must set the Simulation Random Seed in the Analytic Solver Platform Options to 0.) The following table shows the results of ten simulations, each with 1,000 trials:

Run	Option Price
1	$1.69
2	$1.73
3	$1.66
4	$1.72
5	$1.59
6	$1.68
7	$1.67
8	$1.65
9	$1.57
10	$1.50

FIGURE 14.32 Sensitivity of Option Price to Volatility

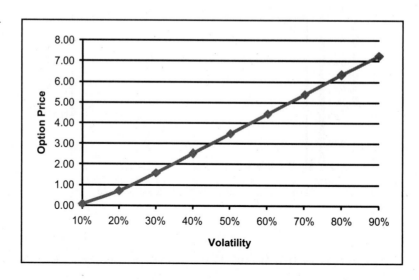

Our original estimate of $1.58 is certainly in the right ballpark, but these estimates range from a low of $1.50 to a high of $1.73. We would have to take a much larger sample than 1,000 trials if we needed to determine the option price to within $0.05 or $0.01. Later, we discuss more formal methods of achieving acceptable levels of precision with simulation estimates.

14.6 SELECTING UNCERTAIN PARAMETERS

With few exceptions, some degree of uncertainty surrounds the true value of *every* parameter in a model. Nevertheless, it would be a mistake to treat every parameter as uncertain in a simulation analysis. As we know from our discussion of sensitivity analysis in Chapter 4, variations in many parameters have little effect on the outcomes. Therefore, it is likely that randomness in these parameters will generate negligible randomness in the outcomes. It takes time and effort to develop an appropriate probability distribution for a parameter; this time and effort can be better used elsewhere if that parameter has little impact on the outcome.

Selecting which parameters to treat as uncertain is more an art than a science. However, some guidelines are useful. First, it is essential to carry out a deterministic analysis with the model *before* considering simulation. This involves establishing a base-case set of inputs and calculating the base-case outputs. Some thought should be given, even at this early stage, to where the base-case inputs lie within their ranges of uncertainty. In the Advertising Budget example, if we assume that the price next year is $40, we should ask whether this is the *average* price or the *minimum* price.

The next step is to perform sensitivity analysis, not only to test the model and learn about the range of possible outcomes, but also to get a sense of whether simulation is needed. In the Advertising Budget example, we might test prices as low as $30 and as high as $50. If profit does not vary significantly within this range, we have a good indication that uncertainty in price is not a central concern. (We can think of the range from $30 to $50 as a crude first attempt at defining a probability distribution for the price. In this context, we should test values at or near the extremes rather than values near the mean.)

A tornado chart is a useful way to determine which parameters have a significant impact on the outcome. In Chapter 4, we illustrated the use of tornado charts in the Advertising Budget example. We varied each of thirteen input parameters within ±10 percent of its base-case value. The results suggested that only four of the thirteen parameters have a significant impact on profits (price, cost, sales parameter, and overhead rate; see Figure 14.33). For the remaining nine parameters, the impact was negligible.

FIGURE 14.33 Tornado Chart with 10 Percent Ranges

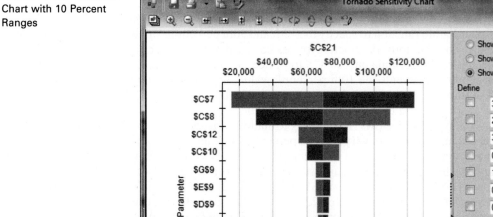

At this point, we could conclude that none of those nine parameters needs to be modeled as random, unless its true range of variability is much larger than ±10 percent, and we could concentrate on the top four parameters.

We also pointed out in Chapter 4 that using a common and symmetric uncertainty range for all the parameters could lead to erroneous conclusions. A ±10 percent range may be realistic for one parameter, while ±20 percent is realistic for another, and a third parameter might range above the base case by 5 percent and below by 25 percent. The critical factor is the size of the forecast error above and below the base case for each parameter. If these ranges are significantly different, we should assign different ranges to different inputs.

To this point in our sensitivity analysis, we have not associated probabilities with any of the variations we have considered. We have assigned ranges to each input, but we have not addressed the likelihood that the parameter will take on specific values within this range. Of course, if we ultimately decide to perform a simulation, we have to assign a specific probability distribution to each uncertain input. Creating these distributions can be time consuming. Therefore, it is useful to have the option to perform a deterministic sensitivity analysis, but with parameter variations that carry probabilistic interpretations.

One effective approach is to use readily determined **percentiles** of the distribution for each uncertain parameter as the endpoints of a parametric sensitivity analysis. Although any percentiles could be used, we illustrate this approach using the 10th and 90th percentiles. The 10th percentile is the number *below* which the parameter falls with probability 10 percent; the 90th percentile is the number *above* which it falls with probability 10 percent. Of course the 10th and 90th percentiles are not restricted to being symmetric about the base-case value. For example, when we specified a 5 percent range for price (around the $40 base-case value), we allowed it to vary from $38 to $42. This might represent a rough estimate of one standard deviation about the base-case value. But the 10th percentile value could be $33, and the 90th percentile $52, if we believe that extremely high values are more likely than extremely low ones.

We assume the following values for the critical four parameters:

Parameter	10th Percentile	Base Case	90th Percentile
Price	33	40	52
Cost	19	25	31
Sales Parameter	30	35	40
Overhead Percentage	0.12	0.15	0.19

To generate the appropriate tornado chart we use the Analytic Solver Platform PsiSenParam function to specify the 10th and 90th percentile values as the lower and upper limits for the four parameters price, cost, sales parameter, and overhead rate. For example, the formula in cell C7 for price is =PsiSenParam(33, 52, 40). The first argument represents the 10th percentile value; the second argument the 90th percentile. The third argument in this function specifies the base-case value. This is the value that will be displayed and used for ordinary calculations in the spreadsheet.

Figure 14.34 shows the resulting tornado chart. (After the top four parameters, all the remaining parameters vary by ±10 percent.) Price and cost continue to appear to be the most sensitive inputs, but this analysis provides additional insights over the earlier approaches. Figure 14.34 suggests that the uncertainty in cost can lead to a profit as low as −$25,000 and as high as $160,000. But the uncertainty in price leads to even more asymmetry, from −$25,000 to $225,000. The upside potential caused by the likelihood of an extremely high price (or low cost) is an important factor that can be uncovered by using this method of analysis.

To summarize, uncertain parameters should be selected only after a thorough sensitivity analysis. The purpose of this sensitivity testing should be to identify parameters that have a significant impact on the results and the likely range of uncertainty for each parameter. The process begins with simple what-if testing of high and low values. Parametric sensitivity can also be used to test a range of inputs and to determine whether the model is linear in the given parameter. Tornado charts can then be used to test the impact of entire sets of parameters. The easiest approach, although perhaps not the most revealing, is to vary each parameter by the same percentage. More information is required to assign a separate range

FIGURE 14.34 Tornado Chart with Percentile Ranges

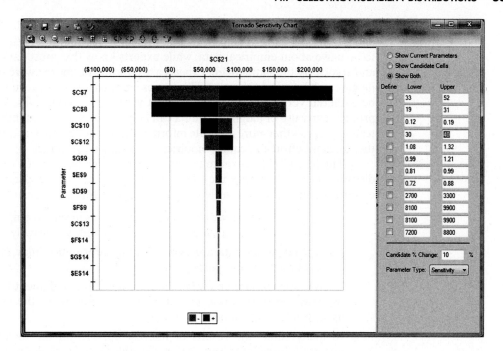

of variation to each parameter, but the results are likely to be more meaningful. One approach is to use the 10th and 90th percentiles of the distribution of a parameter, to show how extreme (and possibly asymmetric) inputs affect the outputs. Although neither of these methods requires us to develop a complete probability distribution, the percentiles approach does require us to think carefully about uncertainty.

14.7 SELECTING PROBABILITY DISTRIBUTIONS

Once we have selected a set of uncertain parameters, the next step is to choose a probability distribution for each one. But which type of distribution should we choose: discrete, uniform, normal, triangular, or perhaps something else? And once we have chosen a type of distribution, how do we choose its specific parameters (such as the mean and standard deviation for the normal distribution)? While Analytic Solver Platform provides dozens of types of distributions, most business analysts use only a handful.

14.7.1 Empirical Data and Judgmental Data

In considering how to choose probability distributions, it is important to distinguish between **empirical data** and **judgmental data**. Empirical data consists of numerical observations from experience, such as monthly sales for the past four years or daily stock returns over the previous year. It is often assumed, especially in textbooks, that empirical data are available and are directly relevant to the problem at hand. That is often not the case in problems encountered by the business analyst. Where, for example, could we hope to get relevant empirical data on the sales of an entirely new kind of product or service, such as the sales of an Internet company a year or two after its founding?

There is, however, another source of highly relevant data for the business analyst—one that is often overlooked or devalued. This is judgmental data, such as estimates made by experts in the field or by the decision makers most closely involved in the analysis. While the marketing department may not have empirical data on new product sales, its senior members probably have many years of experience in marketing new products. This experience is legitimate knowledge, and when a group of experts such as these are carefully queried for their judgment on a particular question, that judgment should be taken seriously. With a little prior training, we can learn to ask decision makers for probability estimates such as the mean, the minimum, or the 10th and 90th percentiles needed for tornado-chart analysis. As we discuss, some probability distributions are especially suited for fitting to judgmental data, because their parameters correspond to probability questions that business experts find relatively easy to answer.

In Chapter 1, we noted that expert modelers focus more on the structure of the model, and less on collection of empirical data, while novices do the reverse. Novice modelers tend to be naive about empirical data, while experts know that most data contain hidden biases and errors. By the same token, experts are typically far more aware of the benefits of using judgmental data, and are more willing to use it, than are novices. Judgmental data can often be gathered very quickly, sometimes just with a few phone calls. Within the prototyping process, early use of judgmental data can help test and debug an initial model. If sensitivity testing suggests that more accurate information is needed about a particular parameter, then the time and effort to acquire empirical data may be justified.

The traditional answer to the question of which distribution to choose is to select the distribution that provides the "best fit to the data," where the reference is usually to empirical data. However, at least four aspects of this advice can be misleading:

- In most cases, unless we are doing scientific research, no empirical data at all will be available. (Judgmental data, on the other hand, are usually available.)

- Even if empirical data are available, the information may be biased or otherwise inappropriate for the purposes at hand.

- Even if appropriate empirical data are available, judgment is needed to determine whether the distribution that provides the best fit to the given empirical data is appropriate in the model.

- In many cases, the results of interest depend on the mean and variance of an uncertain parameter, but not on the specific form of the probability distribution.

For all these reasons, we believe that empirical data alone are seldom sufficient. Even when empirical data are available, it takes careful judgment to decide whether some or all of that data should be used. Often, we also have some judgmental data at hand, if only the opinions of the decision makers, and these data should be combined with the empirical data when choosing a probability distribution. Using data effectively always requires good judgment, not merely good statistical technique.

14.7.2 Six Essential Distributions

While Analytic Solver Platform provides dozens of types of probability distributions, many of these are specialized and rarely used. In business analysis, six families of distributions are used most heavily. Three of these are discrete distributions, which appear on the Distributions menu in the Discrete category: the Bernoulli, integer uniform, and binomial. Three others are continuous distributions, which appear on the Distributions menu in the Common Category: the continuous uniform, triangular, and normal.

The **Bernoulli** distribution is used in situations where an uncertain parameter can take on one of only two possible values. For example, a competitor can either enter the market next year or not. This uncertain event can be described by a Bernoulli distribution having the outcome 1 (for entry) and 0 (for no entry), with suitable probabilities. Figure 14.35 shows a Bernoulli distribution with a probability of the outcome 1 of 0.8.

We often wish to model a random outcome that takes on a small number of discrete values with equal probabilities. For example, the lifetime of a customer might be random between 1 and 10 years, with fractional values having no meaning. In this case, the **integer uniform** distribution can be used, as shown in Figure 14.36. For another example, we might represent future market share as being in the High, Medium, or Low state with equal probabilities. If we used the number 3 for High, 2 for Medium, and 1 for Low, the states would be numerically valued. A discrete uniform distribution from 1 to 3 would represent this situation well. On the other hand, if we assumed the probability of High share were 0.25, Medium share 0.50, and Low share 0.25, then we would use the **discrete custom** distribution instead (because the probabilities would not be equal), as shown in Figure 14.37. This distribution type appears on the Distributions menu in the Custom category.

The **binomial** distribution is used for the number of outcomes on repeated trials. For example, if a drug is successful in treating a disease in an individual 70 percent of the time and it is tested on 10 patients, the binomial distribution describes the number of successful treatments. The binomial distribution is specified by two parameters: the number of trials, and the probability of success on each trial. In our example these parameters are 10 and 0.7. Figure 14.38 shows the binomial distribution for the number of successes in 10 trials where the probability of success on each trial is 70 percent.

FIGURE 14.35 A Bernoulli Distribution

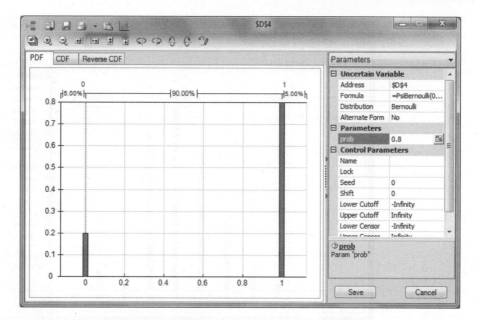

FIGURE 14.36 An Integer Uniform Distribution

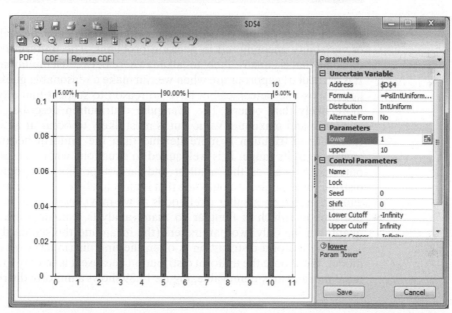

FIGURE 14.37 A Discrete Custom Distribution

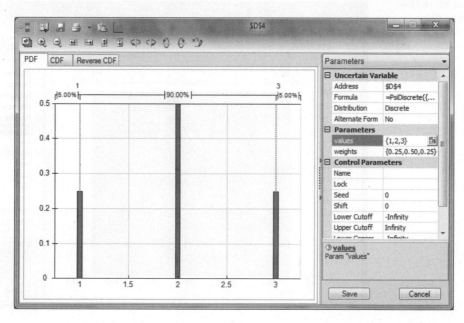

FIGURE 14.38 A Binomial Distribution

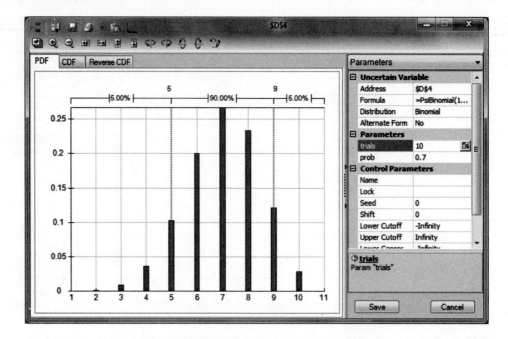

Three continuous distributions provide a good deal of flexibility in capturing the kind of variability encountered in decision problems. The **uniform** distribution describes an outcome that is equally likely to fall anywhere between a minimum and a maximum value. It is particularly appropriate when we can make a reasonable guess about the smallest and largest possible outcomes but have no reason to suspect that any values in between are more likely than others. The **triangular** distribution describes an outcome that has a minimum and maximum value but is most likely to occur at an intermediate point. The triangular distribution is more flexible than the uniform because it can have a peak anywhere in its range. It is well suited to situations where we can identify a *most likely* outcome as well as the smallest and largest possible outcomes. Finally, the **normal** distribution describes an outcome that is most likely to be in the middle of the distribution, with progressively smaller likelihoods as we move away from its most likely value. This distribution, which is familiar to many analysts, can describe a symmetric uncertain quantity using only two parameters (the mean and the standard deviation).

The uniform distribution is often the first distribution we use when prototyping a model. We choose the uniform distribution because it is so easy to specify, requiring only a minimum and maximum value. Figure 14.39 shows a uniform distribution whose outcomes

FIGURE 14.39 A Uniform Distribution

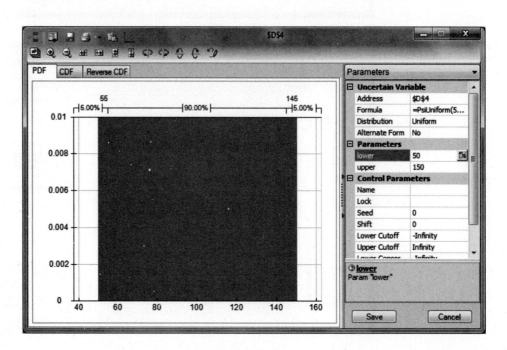

FIGURE 14.40 A Triangular Distribution

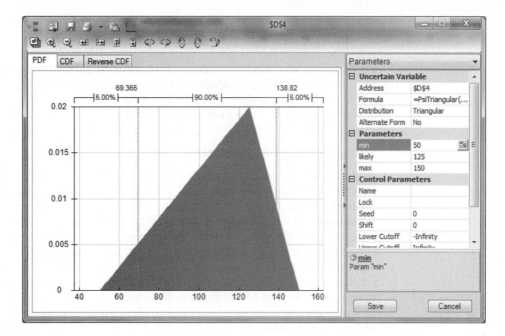

lie between 50 and 150. The mean for a uniform distribution is midway between the minimum and maximum values (100 in this case). The critical property that defines the uniform distribution is that every outcome between the minimum and the maximum is equally likely. Often, this is a reasonable assumption, especially when first testing the effects of uncertainty in a model and when no empirical data or other kinds of information are available to suggest different likelihoods.

The triangular distribution is a more flexible family of continuous distributions. These distributions are specified by three parameters: the minimum, maximum, and most likely values. Figure 14.40 shows a triangular distribution between 50 and 150, with a most likely value of 125. Triangular distributions are particularly useful for representing judgmental estimates. Very few managers can specify offhand a probability distribution for an uncertain quantity, but most can give reasonable estimates for the minimum, maximum, and most likely values.

The normal distribution is a symmetric distribution, usually specified by its mean and standard deviation. The normal distribution shown in Figure 14.41 has a mean of 100 and a standard deviation of 25. The normal is often appropriate for representing uncertain quantities that are influenced by a large number of independent factors, such as the heights

FIGURE 14.41 A Normal Distribution

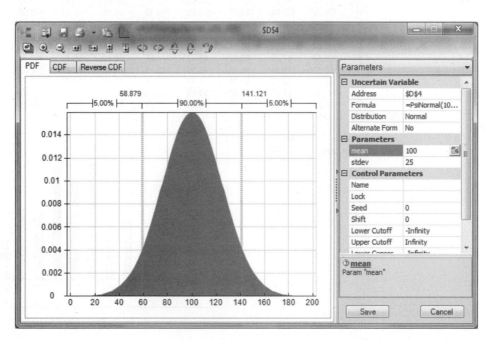

of a group of people or the physical measurements of a manufactured product. But the normal is often overused, perhaps because it is prominent in statistics, where it plays a central role. The normal should not be used unless there is reason to believe the distribution is symmetric. It also has the sometimes problematic property that negative outcomes are possible, especially if the standard deviation is large relative to the mean. Thus, the normal would not be an appropriate probability model for demand or price, unless the standard deviation is small relative to the mean (say, 25 percent of the mean or less).

14.7.3 Fitting Distributions to Data

Although it is important to understand the limitations of empirical data, it is also important to know how to utilize empirical data when they are available. Assume we have appropriate data on a given parameter, and we wish to choose a probability distribution for simulation purposes. For example, Figure 14.42 gives 50 observations on sales of a particular product. The first step is to create a histogram of the data and calculate the mean and standard deviation, as shown in the figure. In our example, the mean is a little over 100, and the standard deviation is about 24. The histogram suggests that values close to the mean are more likely than values at the extremes, but the histogram does not strongly suggest any one type of distribution. If we were to select a normal distribution, we would probably choose a mean of 100 and a standard deviation somewhat higher than that observed in the data, say 30 or 35. If we were to select a triangular distribution, we might pick a minimum of 40 (somewhat below the lowest value observed), a maximum of 170 (somewhat higher than observed), and a most likely value of 110 or 120. When choosing a distribution based on empirical data, it is generally advisable to widen the range because actual results tend to underestimate the extremes. By contrast, the sample average is usually an accurate estimate of the population mean, and there is no built-in bias, even with a small sample.

Analytic Solver Platform provides a tool for fitting continuous or discrete distributions to sample data. As an illustration, we apply the tool using the data in Figure 14.42. Highlight the data and select Analytic Solver Platform▶Tools▶Fit. This sequence brings up the Fit Options window shown in Figure 14.43. In this window we have specified the location of the data and chosen to fit continuous distributions to the data. (Three test statistics are available for ranking the goodness-of-fit; the default is the Kolmogorov-Smirnov statistic, which is appropriate for most situations.) When we press the Fit button,

FIGURE 14.42 Using Data to Choose a Distribution

	A	B	C	D	E	F	G	H	I	J
1	Empirical Data									
2										
3	73.69	96.29	102.80	102.03	101.82	102.42	116.94	99.93	116.02	109.76
4	126.76	103.84	103.70	102.06	136.12	86.32	83.47	158.99	89.27	102.87
5	82.51	86.97	49.91	67.52	129.75	99.12	100.50	68.51	107.81	148.51
6	109.19	125.51	45.05	128.18	102.52	85.75	49.57	116.48	121.10	83.45
7	84.54	119.96	80.47	117.68	109.15	82.36	94.29	92.60	68.17	126.53
8	107.69	67.30	63.22	89.43	151.96	78.71	99.89	108.78	95.48	64.64
9	97.53	119.94	79.98	93.90	116.62	142.01	79.03	132.63	100.91	131.22
10	132.90	62.78	97.81	84.48	79.44	83.70	84.94	128.79	90.24	91.61
11	141.86	61.63	135.33	89.41	96.30	111.07	120.18	88.82	80.00	144.28
12	131.01	110.21	99.34	94.64	115.54	87.55	88.35	122.25	64.92	120.13
13										
14										
15	Mean	100.59								
16	St. Dev.	23.80								

FIGURE 14.43 Fit
Options Window

Analytic Solver Platform fits each of the continuous distributions in turn to this data set and presents them in order of goodness-of-fit. Figure 14.44 shows that the best-fitting distribution here is the logistic distribution. When we close the window, Analytic Solver Platform offers the option of entering this distribution in a cell of our choosing.

In reality, we created the data in this example by simulating 100 independent trials from a *normal* distribution with a mean of 100 and a standard deviation of 25. The sample data clearly reflect the distribution that created them: the sample mean is 100.59, the sample standard deviation is 23.80, and the histogram looks approximately normal. However, the normal distribution was not the closest fitting distribution and many other distributions fit nearly as well. The lesson is that if there is this much difference between a data sample and the distribution that generated it, we should be very skeptical that actual empirical data accurately reveal the *shape* of the underlying probability distribution. Judgment in this matter, as always, is required.

Summarizing this section, we recommend tackling the problem of choosing probability distributions with a liberal amount of judgment, supported by judicious use of data analysis. In our experience, it is often the mere recognition of variability in the critical parameters that gives rise to the vital business insights, not the specific form of the probability distributions chosen to represent that variability. For example, it would be a rare case in which the essential results of an analysis would change if we replaced a triangular distribution with a similar normal distribution. This can happen, but it is unusual unless there are major benefits or costs corresponding to outcomes in the tails of the probability distribution. Thus, time spent trying to identify the best probability distribution for a parameter is probably not time well spent.

FIGURE 14.44 Fit
Results

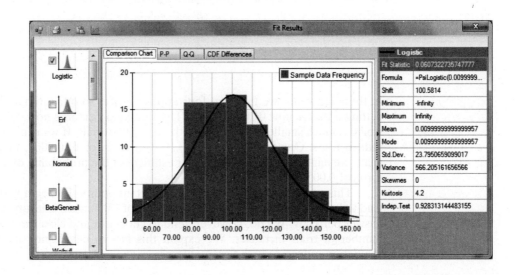

14.8   ENSURING PRECISION IN OUTPUTS

Every time we run a simulation, we are performing an experiment. The purpose of this experiment is to estimate some quantity, such as the expected value of profit or the probability of a loss. With any simulation result, there is some difference, or error, between our estimate and the true value we are after. Thus, our estimate of the mean profit and the true value of the mean profit differ by some amount of **simulation error**. As with any good experiment, a well-planned simulation study requires effort to measure this error. More specifically, we must ensure that whatever conclusions we draw from the simulation study are not seriously compromised by simulation error.

Simulation error is not the only source of error in our modeling efforts. It may not even be the most important source of error. All models are abstractions of the real situation they mimic, and for that reason, they differ in their behavior from the real thing. We can use the term **model error** to refer to this divergence between the behavior of the model and the behavior of the real thing. The essence of modeling is to abstract the essential features of the problem and then to interpret the model results in order to gain useful insights about the behavior of the real system. In most practical situations, model error is a much larger problem than simulation error. Nonetheless, simulation error itself can cause problems in interpreting model results, and for that reason, it should be measured and controlled.

14.8.1   Illustrations of Simulation Error

We begin with the simplest possible illustration, one in which we know the answer in advance. We can simulate one roll of a fair die by entering an integer uniform distribution in Analytic Solver Platform, with the outcomes 1 through 6 all having probability 1/6. We know that the probability of getting, say, a four on one roll is 1/6 or 0.1667; how well does simulation work at finding this result?

Each time we take a sample from this distribution, we get one outcome of rolling the die. Imagine we take one sample and get the value three. Based on this information alone, we would have to conclude the probability of getting a four is zero. The difference between the true value of 0.1667 and the estimated value of zero is very large: 0.1667. This is the error in our simulation at this point. Imagine we run a second trial and get a one. Still, the probability of a four is 0 (= 0/2), and still the error is high.

When we run ten samples, we might get these results:

Trial	Result for Die
1	3
2	1
3	5
4	4
5	3
6	2
7	5
8	5
9	4
10	3

In these ten trials, we find that four appears twice, so our estimate of the probability of getting a four is now 0.20 (= 2/10). The simulation error is now 0.0333 (= 0.2 − 0.1667), which is much smaller than it was with one or two trials. If we run 100 trials, we might get sixteen fours. Our estimate now is 0.16 with an error of 0.0067. Finally, if we run 1,000 trials, we might get 161 fours, and our estimate of the probability of a four is 0.161 with an error of 0.0057.

This example illustrates several important points. To begin with, small samples can lead to large errors. However, even a sample of 1,000 trials is insufficient to determine the answer perfectly. We do, however, tend to get closer and closer to the right answer as the number of trials increases. We exploit this fact in developing methods for estimating simulation outcomes with acceptable precision.

Let's take a closer look at simulation error in a realistic application before we suggest strategies for dealing with it. Refer again to the Advertising Budget example. We know that profit is $71,447 when the price is $40 for certain. The mean profit remains $71,447 even when price is uniformly distributed between $30 and $50. Now let's see how the number of trials of a simulation affects our estimate of the mean profit.

For dramatic effect, we start with one trial. In our run, we found that price is $42.05 and profit is $99,617. (In other trials, we would get different results.) Since we have only one sample for profit, it becomes our best estimate for the mean, but the simulation error is huge: $99,617 − $71,447 = $28,170 (or 39 percent above the true mean). Of course, no one would seriously suggest taking only a single sample in a simulation. How much closer to the true value would we get if we took, say, ten samples and averaged them?

The following table shows typical results:

Trial	Result for Profit
1	$99,617
2	−2,246
3	84,813
4	189,680
5	−206
6	10,663
7	66,730
8	185,044
9	83,019
10	201,057

The average of these ten trials is $78,579, with a simulation error of $7,132 (10 percent). This is still a significant error, but we see that the larger sample has brought us considerably closer to the true mean of $71,447. Would 100 samples be good enough? When we run 100 trials, we get an average of $73,911, or an error of only $2,464 (3 percent). Now we're getting close. With 1,000 trials, we get an average of $71,444, which is indistinguishable from the true mean profit.

What have we learned? Clearly, a sample of one or even ten is not nearly enough in this situation. But a sample of size 1,000 is probably close enough for most situations. In fact, 1,000 trials may be overkill for practical purposes. As we should expect, the precision of any simulation estimate increases as the run length increases.

14.8.2 Precision versus Accuracy

Before we address simulation error from a technical point of view, some specialized terminology is helpful. We assume a probability distribution exists for the outcome of interest—profit in our example—although we do not know the distribution. Our interest lies in particular aspects of this distribution, such as the expected value or the probability of a particular range of profit outcomes. Because our model is complex, we cannot determine these quantities exactly but must resort to simulation. Using simulation, we create a set of sample outcomes for profit from which we can estimate features of the probability distribution for profit. If our goal is to determine the expected value of profit, we compute the average of all the simulation outcomes. For clarity, we refer to this average as the **sample average**, to distinguish it from the true mean profit.

The sample average is an estimate of the true mean. (The sample average of the ten trials for the Advertising Budget example in the previous section was $78,579.) Likewise, if we wish to determine the probability of a loss in our simulation, we compute the percentage of outcomes in which a loss occurs. This percentage is the **sample proportion**, an estimate of the true probability of a loss. Whether we are interested in a mean value or a tail probability, our simulation produces an estimate of the true quantity. Our goal here is to understand and control the error in this estimate.

It is important to distinguish between *precision* and *accuracy*. A single sample gives us a perfectly accurate estimate of the true mean profit, as long as there is no bias in the process. Technically, we are saying that the expected outcome of a sample of size one is the true mean. In this sense, a sample average from a large sample is no more *accurate* than a sample average from a small sample. But an estimate based on the larger sample is more *precise* than an estimate based on the smaller sample because the *variance* of the sample average declines with sample size. In other words, a second sample of size one will most likely be very different from the first, whereas a second sample of size 1,000 will most likely *not* be very different from the first, at least for the purposes of estimating the true mean. Repeated batches of samples are more like each other (that is, they show less variability) as the sample size increases, and they are therefore more precise.

While it is important to ensure an appropriate level of precision in our results, there is a trade-off between the *precision* of the results and the *time* it takes to get them. We know that time is valuable for practical modelers, and time spent doing simulation runs may come at the expense of time spent formulating the model, testing, collecting data, or carrying out some other aspect of the modeling process. Thus, an effective modeler does not undertake long simulation runs unless the additional precision has more value than the next best use of that time.

On a contemporary desktop computer, it takes less than a second to run 100,000 trials for the Advertising Budget model. This suggests that we can easily afford the time for the precision we get at 1,000 trials, and we might even think about increasing the run length if more precision is valuable. But this is a very simple simulation model, so the trade-off between time and precision favors precision. However, it is not difficult to construct a complex spreadsheet model for which 1,000 trials would take quite a long time. In such a case, it is worthwhile to investigate more carefully how much precision is really needed and to choose a run length that provides sufficient precision without taking too much time.

14.8.3 An Experimental Method

The simplest approach to determining the precision of a simulation estimate is to experiment with multiple independent runs. To do this, we must ensure that different random numbers are used each time we run a simulation. In Analytic Solver Platform, we select Analytic Solver Platform▶Options▶All Options, select the Simulation tab, and enter 0 in the Sim. Random Seed field. Now we pick an initial sample size—say, 100. We perform 5 to 10 simulations using this run length and compare the estimates of the output. Are they close to each other or far apart? If they are too far apart for our purposes, we have not achieved sufficient precision in our estimates, and so we cannot rely on any single run at the current run length. We therefore increase the run length, possibly to 500 or 1,000. We make another 5 or 10 runs at this new run length and again compare the results. When the set of results has a sufficiently small range, we have an appropriate sample size.

We can illustrate this procedure with the Advertising Budget model (under the assumptions of Section 14.2). We set the run length to 10 trials and carry out five runs. The five successive estimates of profit are given in the following table:

Trial	Profit
1	$150,344
2	156,385
3	149,749
4	146,782
5	155,231

Based on these results it seems justified to conclude that the true profit is around $150,000, but the range is at least $\pm$ $5,000. If we feel these results are too imprecise we can increase the run length to 100 trials and run five more times, with the following results:

Trial	Profit
1	$148,424
2	148,387
3	148,201
4	148,336
5	148,058

At this run length it is clear the mean profit is about $148,000, although there is still a range from lowest to highest of $366. For more precision we can perform five runs at 1,000 trials. Here, the results range from $148,205 to $148,228, a difference of only $23. The range of results on independent runs gets narrower as the number of trials increases.

14.8.4 Precision Using the MSE

A more sophisticated approach to measuring the precision in a simulation estimate relies on the **mean standard error** (MSE), also known as the standard error of the mean, or simply the standard error. In a simulation experiment, we are essentially estimating the mean value of a population, and a confidence interval describes the precision associated with our estimate. A confidence interval is constructed around the estimated mean value by adding and subtracting a multiple of the MSE. The larger the multiple, the wider the confidence interval and the higher the probability that the true mean value will lie within the confidence interval.

For example, if we add and subtract the MSE of the estimated mean, we form a 68 percent confidence interval. If we add and subtract *twice* the MSE on either side of the estimated mean, we form an approximate 95 percent confidence interval. (More precisely, a 95 percent confidence interval for the true mean extends to 1.96 MSEs on either side of the sample mean.)

In the Advertising Budget simulation model, for example, a run length of 1,000 trials generates an MSE of 3,275. This is reported as the Standard Error in the Simulation Results window under `Statistics – Advanced Statistics`. (Results may vary slightly due to simulation error when this experiment is repeated.) Thus, a 68 percent confidence interval for the mean is $147,730 \pm 3,275$, or from 144,455 to 151,005. In other words, in repeated experiments, the true mean falls within this interval 68 percent of the time.

If we want a confidence level higher than 68 percent, we have to widen the range. For example, a 95 percent confidence level corresponds to $147,730 \pm 1.96(3,275)$, or from 141,311 to 154,149. In repeated experiments, the true mean falls within this interval 95 percent of the time. (Analytic Solver Platform reports the 95-percent confidence interval as `Mean Confidence 95%` under `Advanced Statistics`.)

With a smaller sample size, we would expect the simulation error, and therefore the MSE, to be larger. For an experiment consisting of 100 trials, the sample average is $151,831, and the MSE is 10,848, or about 7 percent of the mean. Thus, we would expect the true mean to lie within the range from 140,983 to 162,679 about 68 percent of the time. Note that a range of one MSE on either side of the sample average may *not* include the true mean. This should be sobering, if not startling. There is, after all, no *guarantee* that a range of even 1.96 MSEs around the sample mean contains the true mean. All we can say is that the probability of this outcome is 95 percent in repeated experiments.

The MSE declines roughly with the square root of the number of trials, so as we increase the number of trials, we increase the precision of our estimates, but not in a linear fashion. In fact, if we want to cut the MSE in half, we have to *quadruple* the number of trials, due to the square-root relationship. More trials are always better, but additional trials contribute less and less additional precision.

A good way to use the MSE is to determine the acceptable error before running a simulation. In the Advertising Budget model, we might be willing to accept an MSE that is roughly 5 percent of the mean, or about 7,385. Suppose we run 100 trials and find that the MSE is about 15 percent of the mean. We could then increase the sample size by trial-and-error until the MSE is sufficiently small. Or, drawing on the square-root relationship in the formula, we could increase the sample size by a factor of about 9. This approach always requires us to run at least a small simulation experiment, in order to estimate the MSE.

14.8.5 Simulation Error in a Decision Context

Sometimes, when analysts lose sight of the broader context, they devote excessive effort to ensuring that individual simulation runs are highly precise. But the ultimate goal of a simulation study is usually not to estimate a single number. The broader goal is to provide help in making a decision. The ultimate test of our efforts is whether we have made a good *decision*, not whether our simulation results are highly precise. True, simulation error can lead to bad decisions, but it is only one source of error. As we have pointed out, modeling itself introduces errors by the very nature of the abstraction process; the model is not the real world. So the model we use to represent the world itself contains errors, and increasing the simulation run length cannot in any way reduce those errors. In addition, extreme precision may not be necessary if our goal is to make the best decision. (We return to this issue in the next chapter, when we discuss optimization in simulation.)

For example, imagine we are estimating the NPV of a single project in which the choices are simply to accept the project or reject it. Our decision criterion is to accept the project if the expected NPV is positive and otherwise to reject it. Our simulation model, using a run length of 100, shows an NPV of $12.7 million and repeated runs range from $9 to $15 million. Now this is not a very precise estimate of the NPV. But the chances are slim that the expected NPV is *negative*, so the decision to accept the project is pretty clear. In this case, a run length of 100 trials seems fully justified. However, if we were choosing *between* two projects, this level of precision might not be sufficient. If the competing project were to show an estimated expected NPV of $13.9 million and a range from $10 to $14 million in repeated runs, we could not be confident that the second project was actually better than the first. In this case, a longer run length would be needed to correctly identify which of these two projects has the higher expected NPV.

14.9   INTERPRETING SIMULATION OUTCOMES

When we run a simulation with, say, 1,000 trials, the raw result is simply a collection of 1,000 values for each outcome cell. Fortunately, we rarely have to work with the raw data directly. Instead, we use Analytic Solver Platform to display and summarize the results for us. Most often, that summary takes the form of a histogram, or frequency chart, but there are other ways of summarizing output data. We first discuss how to use the Simulation Results window and how to capture results directly on the spreadsheet.

14.9.1   Simulation Results

In the Advertising Budget example, our output cell is Profit in C21. When we double-click on this cell after running a simulation, the Simulation Results window opens (Figure 14.45). This figure shows a histogram that displays the frequency of all the simulation results for this cell within a certain number of ranges, or bins. In this example, we have set the number of bins to 20 and we can see that the highest-frequency outcomes occur around a profit of $200,000. (We set the number of bins by clicking on the vertical bar at the right-hand edge of the window to display the task pane, and enter 20 in the Bins textbox under Chart Type.)

FIGURE 14.45 The Simulation Results Window

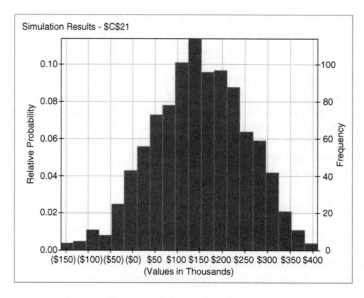

FIGURE 14.46 The Simulation Results Window Showing the Mean and a Tail Probability

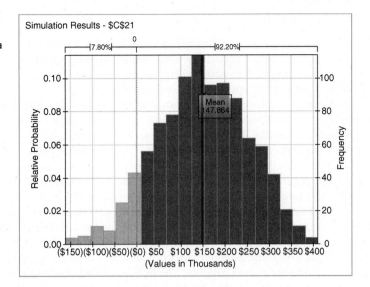

We can show the mean value for the simulation outcomes on the histogram by selecting Markers in the task pane. We then click on the double-plus icon, select Mean under Type, and enter Mean in the Description window. In addition, we can calculate and display a tail probability by entering a lower or upper cut-off value under Statistics – Chart Statistics. In Figure 14.46, we have entered 0 as the minimum value and the display shows that there is about an 8 percent chance that profit will be negative.

The Simulation Results window provides additional tabs in which the output cell results are displayed in alternative ways. The Cumulative Frequency tab shows the results in the form of a cumulative distribution, which gives the probability of an outcome less than or equal to a given value. The Reverse Cumulative Frequency tab gives the probability of an outcome greater than a given value. The Sensitivity tab reports the correlations between each of the input probability distributions and the output cell. The same information is conveyed in the form of a chart in the Scatter Plots window. In Figure 14.47, for example, we see that there is a strong positive correlation between the random price (cell C7) and profit, and a strong negative correlation between the random cost (cell C8) and profit. If we return to the Sensitivity tab we see that these correlations are 0.6 and −0.8, respectively. Statistical information on the frequency distribution, such as the mean, minimum, maximum, standard deviation, and various percentiles is reported under Statistics and Percentiles.

FIGURE 14.47 The Scatter Plots Tab in the Simulation Results Window

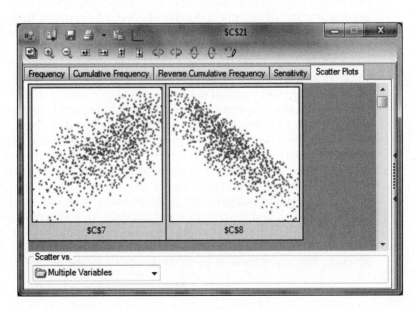

14.9.2 Displaying Results on the Spreadsheet

In most cases, we refer to the Simulation Results window to analyze the results of a simulation. Sometimes, especially when we must run a simulation many times, it is more convenient to record the results directly on the spreadsheet. Analytic Solver Platform provides a number of special functions for this purpose.

The most commonly used measure of the results of a simulation is the mean. Rather than open the Simulation Results window to find the mean, we can display it directly on the spreadsheet using the PsiMean() function. For example, if the output cell is D19, we can display the mean of the output cell by entering =PsiMean(D19) in any other cell. We can also do this using the Analytic Solver Platform tab. Place the cursor on the output cell and then select Analytic Solver Platform▶Simulation Model▶Results▶Statistics▶Mean. Then click on the target cell and the PsiMean() formula will be entered as desired.

Other statistics can be captured on the spreadsheet in a similar manner. Some of the most common statistics are the mean and standard deviation (select Analytic Solver Platform▶Simulation Model▶Results▶Statistics), the Value at Risk and the conditional value at risk (Analytic Solver Platform▶Simulation Model▶Results▶Measures), and the minimum and maximum (Analytic Solver Platform▶Simulation Model▶Results▶Range).

In some circumstances, such as when we want to develop custom graphs of the results, it is useful to work directly with the simulation data itself. One way to capture the results of an output cell is to use the PsiData() function, which is an array formula that contains the results of a specified output cell for all the simulation trials. If the output cell is D19, then PsiData(D19,1) records the value of the output cell on the first trial. Thus a column of 1,000 such function values, from PsiData(D19,1) to PsiData(D19,1000), will capture all 1,000 trials for cell D19.

While most of this discussion has been devoted to the details of finding specific summary measures for simulation results, there is more to the art of interpreting simulations. First, we must take care in defining outcome variables. Unless we capture the essential aspects of the model, our interpretations will be handicapped. Having done that, we must then ensure that our estimates are sufficiently precise to support meaningful interpretation. Finally, we come to the results themselves. In most simulations, we are interested in both the expected outcome and the variability in outcomes. These two aspects of the situation are captured in the mean value, in the variance (or standard deviation), and in tail probabilities. Often, the value of simulation comes from providing insight into the trade-off between the expected outcome and the associated risks. This trade-off is illustrated well in the Netscape IPO example discussed earlier, where a deterministic analysis supported a high value for the company, whereas the simulation analysis revealed some extreme risks associated with the IPO.

14.10 WHEN TO SIMULATE AND WHEN NOT TO SIMULATE

Sometimes it is *not* necessary to carry out a simulation in order to understand the effects of uncertainty. Recall that the optimal profit in the Advertising Budget example was $71,447 when we assumed no uncertainty and a price of $40. If we now assume that price is the only uncertain input and that it has a uniform distribution between $30 and $50, we find that the mean profit (with 1,000 trials) is $71,444, only 0.004 percent different from the original value. In fact, if we were to increase the number of trials we would eventually find that the simulated mean was identical to the deterministic mean. In other words, replacing an input with a distribution *can* leave the expected result essentially unchanged. There is a general principle at work here that is important to understand.

The impact that uncertainty in an input parameter (such as price) has on the output (such as profit) depends on the form of the relationship between the two. If that relationship is *linear*, then the expected value of the output is related by the same linear relationship to the expected value of the input. Thus, if we replace an input by a distribution without changing the expected value, then the expected value of the output does not change, and simulation is not needed. An analogous relationship holds for tail probabilities when the relationship between input and output is linear.

As a simple example, consider a firm's profit as affected by uncertainty about sales revenue. We might think of profit as described by the equation:

$$Profit = Margin \times Revenue - Fixed\ cost$$

where *Margin* is stated as a proportion. For example:

$$Profit = 0.4 \times Revenue - 100$$

This equation takes the linear form $Z = aX + b$, with Z in the role of *Profit* and X in the role of *Revenue*. Clearly, *Profit* becomes uncertain when we treat *Revenue* as uncertain. We might want to estimate the expected value of *Profit*, or perhaps the probability that *Profit* is positive. Because the relationship is linear, it follows that:

$$Expected\ Profit = Margin \times (Expected\ Revenue) - Fixed\ cost$$

Also:

$$\begin{aligned} P(Profit > 0) &= P(Margin \times Revenue - Fixed\ cost > 0) \\ &= P(Revenue > Fixed\ cost / Margin) \end{aligned}$$

In the Advertising Budget case, the uniform distribution for *Price* translates directly into a comparable distribution for *Profit* due to the linear relation between *Profit* and *Price*. In algebraic terms, we have the following equation for *Profit*:

$$Profit = Sales \times (1 - Overhead\ Rate) \times Price - Unit\ cost \times Sales - Fixed\ Cost$$

This expression is linear in *Price*, so that we can write:

$$\begin{aligned} Expected\ Profit =\ &Sales \times (1 - Overhead\ Rate) \times (Expected\ Price) \\ &- Unit\ cost \times Sales - Fixed\ cost \end{aligned}$$

$$Expected\ Profit = 16,160 \times (1 - 0.15) \times 40 - 478,019$$

$$Expected\ Profit = 71,447$$

Similarly, with respect to the probability of breaking even:

$$P(Profit > 0) = P(13,737 \times Price - 478,019 > 0) = P(Price > 34.8) = 0.24$$

Inputs and outputs are not always related in a linear fashion. To illustrate, we examine the impact of uncertainty on another parameter in this model. Cell C13 contains the parameter from the sales-response function that determines the base level of sales when advertising is zero. In the original analysis, this parameter took on the value 3,000. To illustrate the effect of uncertainty in this parameter, we replace this single value with a uniform distribution having the same mean value but a minimum of $-5,000$ and a maximum of 11,000. (To make the comparison clearer, we also assume for the moment that price is $40 for sure.) When we run a simulation under these assumptions, we see that uncertainty *reduces* mean profit, from $71,447 in the no-uncertainty case to $68,438 under uncertainty (Figure 14.48). We also see that the shape of the profit distribution is no longer uniform. In fact, values toward the upper end of the range are more likely than lower ones. Because the relationship here is not linear, the expected profit is not linear in the expected value of the input parameter.

FIGURE 14.48 Distribution of Profit with Random Sales Parameter

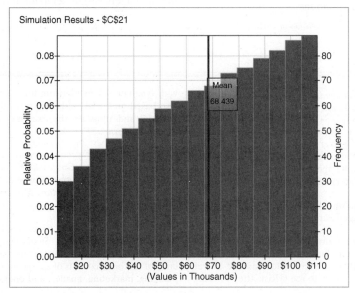

To summarize these two cases: uncertainty in *price* gives us no new information about the expected profit or about the probability of breaking even, but uncertainty in the *sales parameter* shifts the mean profit and changes the shape of the profit distribution. Why are these two cases different? The explanation lies in the relationship between the outcome variable and the uncertain parameters: profit is linear in price but nonlinear in the sales parameter. (Recall that, in this model, sales are related to the square root of the product of advertising and the sales parameter.)

There are other cases in which it is possible to determine the expected value of the output without using simulation. Occasionally we may go to the trouble of conducting a simulation only to discover that the effort could have been avoided. However, in complex models with many uncertain parameters, it is often difficult to determine whether simulation can be avoided. Moreover, we do not often know in advance exactly which outputs we want to analyze. Thus, unless our model is particularly simple and we suspect that linearity holds, simulation remains our general-purpose tool for analyzing uncertain situations.

14.11 SUMMARY

We introduced simulation in Chapter 4 as one phase in a general analytic procedure for spreadsheet models. Simulation answers the question, "What are the risks?" It shows us how uncertainty in the inputs influences the outputs of our analysis. Like optimization, simulation can be seen as a sophisticated form of sensitivity analysis.

In Excel, simulation can be carried out conveniently using Analytic Solver Platform, which provides all the probability models needed to express the uncertainties in our assumptions, and automates the repetitive process of sampling from these distributions. Finally, it provides extensive methods for displaying and analyzing the results.

Simulation is a powerful tool when used appropriately, but it should never be performed *before* an appropriate sensitivity analysis is carried out on a deterministic version of the model. What-if analysis, involving use of parametric sensitivity and tornado charts, uncovers those input parameters that have the biggest impact on the outcomes. These should be the focus of any uncertainty analysis. The tornado chart tool supports a sequence of analyses that can help focus the simulation analysis on the critical parameters.

Every simulation analysis involves four major activities:

- selecting uncertain parameters
- selecting probability distributions
- ensuring precision in the outcomes
- interpreting outcome distributions

The parameters that are treated as uncertain in a simulation analysis should be those that are subject to substantial uncertainty and have a significant impact on the outcome. Selecting uncertain parameters is a natural outgrowth of sensitivity analysis. Although many probability models are available, only a few are used routinely by business analysts. We have described these models (the Bernoulli, binomial, uniform, triangular, normal, and custom distributions), and we have indicated the most appropriate applications for each. Ensuring that simulation results are sufficiently precise is primarily a matter of choosing a suitable run length. However, we have stressed the importance of determining how much precision is really needed in a given analysis before making this decision. Finally, simulations produce probability distributions as outcomes, which are by their nature complex. We have emphasized the importance of summarizing and simplifying these results, in order to make them useful to managers.

Although simulation is more sophisticated than simple spreadsheet modeling, it is one of the most widely used of the advanced management science tools. It is relatively easy for business analysts to learn, and it provides a means for expressing and understanding the uncertainty that is so prevalent in business. It does require some familiarity with probability, the language of uncertainty, but many analysts have this familiarity, and most can acquire what they need. Often, the bigger challenge with simulation is translating the results into a form that managers can understand and act upon.

SUGGESTED READINGS

Evans, J. R., and D.L. Olson. 2002. *Introduction to Simulation and Risk Analysis*. 2d ed. Upper Saddle River, NJ: Prentice Hall.

This full-length text is devoted to simulation using Crystal Ball, a software alternative to Analytic Solver Platform. The coverage of Crystal Ball is somewhat less detailed than the coverage of Analytic Solver Platform in this chapter, but there are many examples and applications. Discrete event simulation using ProModel is also covered.

Seila, A. F., V. Ceric, and P. Tadikamalla. 2003. *Applied Simulation Modeling*. Mason, OH: Cengage Learning.

This book covers simulation from the business and engineering points of view. It uses @Risk and the discrete event simulation language Arena. @Risk is another alternative to Analytic Solver Platform. It is not difficult to learn how to use @Risk after working with Analytic Solver Platform for a while. The following books are also based on @Risk, although it would not be difficult to read the material and translate the exercises and examples into Analytic Solver Platform.

Winston, W. 2008. *Financial Models using Simulation and Optimization: A Step-By-Step Guide with Excel and Palisade's Decision Tools Software* (Third Edition). Newfield, NY: Palisade.
Winston, W. 2001. *Simulation Modeling with @Risk*. Mason, OH: Cengage Learning.

Financial Models contains 63 examples of simulation applications, most with a financial flavor. *Simulation Modeling* is more like a textbook, with some introductory chapters on simulation in general. The body of this book consists of a large number of worked examples from planning, marketing, finance, and operations.

EXERCISES

1. *Profit Analysis*. A consumer electronics firm produces a line of battery rechargers for cell phones. The following distributions apply:

Unit price	triangular with a minimum of $18.95, most likely value of $24.95, and maximum of $26.95
Unit cost	uniform with a minimum of $12.00 and a maximum of $15.00
Quantity sold	$10,000 - 250 \times$ Unit price, plus a random term given by a normal distribution with a mean of 0 and a standard deviation of 10
Fixed costs	normal with a mean of $30,000 and a standard deviation of $5,000

a. What is the expected profit?

b. What is the probability of a loss?

c. What is the maximum loss?

2. *R&D Planning*. A firm is in the process of assessing the economic prospects for a new bottling machine it is developing. Future research and development expenses could range from $4 to $9 million, with a most likely value around $7 million. The life of the product will be anywhere from 3 to 10 years. Yearly unit sales will range from 100 to 500, with a most likely value around 300. The machines will sell for between $20,000 and $25,000 each. The production cost of the machine is expected to be $13,000 but could be as low as $11,000 or as high as $15,000. The firm's discount rate is 10 percent.

a. What is the expected NPV for this new machine over ten years?

b. What is the probability of a positive NPV?

3. *Door-to-Door Marketing*. A small nonprofit organization is planning a door-to-door marketing campaign to sell Christmas wrapping and gifts. They plan to visit 100 homes. Consultants have estimated that they should expect to find someone home 80 percent of the time. When someone is home, 65 percent of the time it is a female. Thirty percent of females make a purchase, and when they do so the dollar value of their purchase is normally distributed with a mean of $22 and a standard deviation of $5. Males purchase 20 percent of the time, and the dollar value of their purchase is normally distributed with a mean of $28 and a standard deviation of $3.

a. What is the total amount they can expect to generate in revenues from these 100 visits?

b. What is the standard deviation of total revenues over 100 visits?

c. What is the probability they will make more than $750?

4. *Facility Design*. A firm operates a docking facility for container ships in Singapore. At present, the facility consists of two identical docks. Ships typically arrive during the night. The number of ships that arrive during a single night varies from night to night, as given in the distribution below. Each dock can unload one ship during the day. Ships unable to unload must wait until the following day. The cost of delaying a ship (called a *demurrage* charge) is $10,000 per day. A new dock will cost $5 million a year, including amortized construction costs, maintenance, and operating costs.

Nightly Arrivals	Frequency
0	0.30
1	0.30
2	0.20
3	0.10
4	0.05
5	0.05

a. With the current system, what is the average demurrage charge *per year*?

b. Can you justify adding one or more additional docks?

c. How sensitive are your results to the assumption you make about the number of ships waiting at the beginning of the simulation?

5. *Retirement Planning*. A recent MBA would like your assistance in determining how much to save for retirement. He is planning to invest $3,000 in a tax-sheltered retirement fund at the end of each year (i.e., appreciation of the fund is not taxed). The rate of return each year can be modeled as a normally distributed random variable with a mean of 12 percent and a standard deviation of 2 percent.

a. If he is 30 years old now, how much money should he expect to have in his retirement fund at age 60?

b. What is the probability that he will have more than $1 million in his retirement fund when he reaches age 60?

c. How much should he invest each year if he wants the mean value of his portfolio to be at least $1 million at age 60?

d. How much should he invest each year if he wants there to be a 90 percent chance of having at least $1 million in his retirement fund at age 60?

6. *Health Claims*. A large manufacturing company self-insures its employee health insurance claims. That is, it collects a fixed amount each month from every employee for health care costs and then it pays the entire claim amounts using its own funds to make up the difference. It would like to estimate its total health care payments for the coming year.

The total number of employees at the start of the year is 11,124. The firm expects the number of employees to change each month over the coming year by a percentage that is uniformly distributed between −2 percent and 5 percent. Employees contribute $125 each per month toward their health care costs, while the average claim is $250 per month. The average claim itself is expected to grow by an amount given by a normal distribution with a mean of 1 percent and a standard deviation of 2 percent.

a. What is the expected cost to the company of covering employee health care costs in the coming year?

b. What is the maximum cost to the company of covering employee health care costs in the coming year?

c. What is the probability that costs will not exceed $20 million?

7. *New Product Forecasting*. Kardjian Brothers, Inc. has invented a fundamentally new way to control the photolithography process used in manufacturing computer chips. Before they sell or license this technological breakthrough, they would like to have some idea of how rapidly it might gain market share. Their analysis is based on the Bass diffusion model, which rests on three assumptions:

There is a fixed population of potential users, all of whom will eventually adopt.

Adoptions from *innovators* are proportional to the current number of potential adopters.

Adoptions from *imitators* are proportional to the product of the current number of adopters and the remaining potential adopters.

While there are many interpretations of this general model, it is common to attribute the innovation effect to marketing efforts such as advertising, which convert some percentage of potential adopters every time period. The imitation effect is thought to operate through word of mouth, in which every contact between an adopter and a potential adopter results in a new adoption with some probability.

The following model is consistent with these assumptions:

$$n(t) = pN_0 + (q - p) \times N(t) - (q/N_0) \times N(t)^2$$

where

$n(t)$ = customers adopting at time t
N_0 = total number of potential adopters
$N(t)$ = cumulative adopters at time t
p = propensity to innovate (percentage of potentials per time period)
q = propensity to imitate (percentage of potentials times adopters per time period)

Assume an initial population of 1,000 and parameter values of 0.03 for p and 0.38 for q. (These are the average values found over dozens of new products and technologies ranging from toasters to CT scanners.)

a. Build a deterministic model for the number of adopters over time. In what year will the cumulative numbers of adopters *first* exceed half the original population?

b. Build a simulation model for the number of adopters over time, assuming the following uniform distributions for the parameters: p lies between 0 and 0.5; q lies between 0.28 and 0.48. What is the average number of *years* it takes for the cumulative number of adopters to reach 50 percent of the initial population?

c. What is the probability that it will take more than 10 years for the cumulative number of adopters to reach 50 percent of the initial population?

8. *Drug Development.* A pharmaceutical company has a new drug under development and would like to know how much profit it might expect to make. The drug has to be tested to pass FDA approval. One hundred subjects will be tested and the company estimates that the probability that each subject will pass the test is 25 percent. The FDA will approve the drug if at least 20 out of the 100 subjects pass. Future R&D costs will be between $3 and $5 million (uniformly distributed). Advertising costs will run between $12 and $18 million, with $16 million the most likely amount. The total population of potential users of the drug is 40 million. The company expects to gain 8 percent of this market if its drug is successful. (Assume a normal distribution for market share with a standard deviation of 2 percent.) There is a one-in-four chance of a competitor entering this market, and if it does, the monopoly share will be reduced by 5 to 15 percent (uniformly distributed). The profit per customer is expected to be $12.

a. What is the mean profit?

b. What is the probability the company makes no profit at all?

c. What is the maximum profit they can make?

9. *IPO Valuation.* A small, private company is contemplating an initial public offering (IPO) in which they will sell 40,000 shares of stock. The price of the stock at the IPO is uncertain, with the following distribution:

Price	Probability
10	0.10
11	0.20
12	0.30
13	0.20
14	0.10
15	0.10

In each of the next five years there is a 30 percent chance the company will fail. If it does not fail, its stock value will increase by an amount given by a lognormal distribution with a mean of 1.5 percent and a standard deviation of 0.5 percent.

a. What is the mean value of the stock at the end of five years, assuming the company does not fail in the interim?

b. What is the probability the company will still be in existence after 5 years?

10. *New Product Profitability.* A new product will sell for $8. The company expects to sell around 900,000 units. (Use a normal distribution with a mean of 900,000 and a standard deviation of 300,000.) Fixed costs are normally distributed with a mean of $700,000 and a standard deviation of $50,000. Unit variable costs are also normally distributed with a mean of $3 and a standard deviation of $0.25. Selling expenses are lognormally distributed with a mean of $900,000 and a standard deviation of $50,000.

a. What is the expected value of profit for this product?

b. What is the probability that profit will exceed $3 million?

11. *Software System Evaluation.* A new software system will cost $2 million initially and take around 2 years to install (the actual time to complete installation will be lognormally distributed with a mean of 2 years and a standard deviation of 0.5 years). Development costs each year will be normally distributed with a mean of $1 million and a standard deviation of $0.25 million. (Each year is an independent sample.) The system will cost $5 million per year to operate in the first year. Thereafter, the growth rate will be normally distributed with a mean of 10 percent and a standard deviation of 3 percent.

The system will generate benefits in the first year given by a normal distribution with a mean of $6 million and a standard deviation of $0.5 million. (Benefits start accruing only after the system is complete.) After the first year, benefits will increase at a rate given by a normal distribution with a mean and standard deviation of 30 percent.

Determine the present value of net benefits for this software over the next five years at a discount rate of 10 percent.

a. What is the expected present value of net benefits over a five-year period?

b. What is the probability that net benefits will be positive?

12. *NPV Analysis.* You have been asked to evaluate the following investment opportunity. A small firm is available for purchase at an initial cost of $150,000, to be paid to the current owner in equal installments over the next five years. The firm has been generating annual revenues of $100,000. Operating costs are 65 percent of revenues. For tax purposes, the firm's earnings would appear on your personal income tax return, and the applicable tax rate would be about 36 percent. Your investment would be deductible when calculating taxes. Under these assumptions, the NPV (at a discount rate of 10 percent) for this project is $12,131.

In light of the fact that most of your information about this firm comes from the current owner, you are concerned that some of your assumptions may be inaccurate. After some research, you have determined the following about the key inputs to this problem:

- Actual revenues could be as low as $60,000 or as high as $125,000. The most likely amount is $100,000. Revenues in successive years are independent.

- Operating costs could be as low as 55 percent of revenues or as high as 75 percent, with any value in between being equally likely. Costs in successive years are independent.

- The tax rate in any year will be 36 percent with probability 0.4 and 40 percent with probability 0.6, depending on factors outside your control and independent from year to year.

- In the case of negative taxable income, you will have other income, so the tax effects represented in the model will still hold.

a. What probability distributions are appropriate for the three uncertain quantities in this analysis?

b. What is the mean NPV under the assumptions given above?

c. What is the probability that the NPV will be negative?

d. What is the probability that the cash flow will be positive in all five years?

13. *Value of a Customer.* As the manager of credit card services at Bank of Hanover (BOH), you're aware that the average profitability of a credit card customer grows with the number of years they have used the credit card. Two probabilistic factors affect actual profitability. The mean profitability function is given in the table below, which has been gathered from data on BOH customers. The actual profit in a given year follows a normal distribution, with a standard deviation equal to 25 percent of the mean profit.

In addition, there is a probability less than one that a customer will continue to use the card during year *t*. This probability is sometimes called the *retention rate*. For instance, an 80 percent retention rate means that, during any year, there is a 20 percent chance the customer will cancel their credit card. Assume that if a customer cancels during year *t*, then the cancellation occurs at the end of the year, and BOH still gets profits from year *t*. The current retention rate has been estimated at 80 percent.

BOH uses a discount rate of 10 percent for calculating net present values.

Year	Mean Profit	Year	Mean Profit
1	−40	11	111
2	66	12	116
3	72	13	120
4	79	14	124
5	87	15	130
6	92	16	137
7	96	17	142
8	99	18	148
9	103	19	155
10	106	20	161

a. When the retention rate is 80 percent, what is the average NPV from a customer?

b. When the retention rate is 80 percent, what is the probability that the NPV for a given customer will exceed $100?

c. Determine the average NPV from a customer when the retention rate is 85 percent, 90 percent and 95 percent. Sketch a graph that describes how the average NPV varies with the retention rate, for retention rates above 75 percent; then, interpret the sketch.

14. *Production Scheduling.* A simple model is sometimes used in order to illustrate the production-scheduling maxim, "balance flow, not capacity." Consider a factory that consists of three workstations where each customer order must proceed through the workstations in sequence. Next, suppose that the workloads are balanced, which means that, *on average*, each order requires equal amounts of work at each of the three stations. Assume that the average operation time is 60 minutes.

Now suppose that six orders are to be scheduled tomorrow. Using average times, we would expect that completion times would look like the following:

Order	1	2	3	4	5	6
Complete Station 1	60	120	180	240	300	360
Complete Station 2	120	180	240	300	360	420
Complete Station 3	180	240	300	360	420	480

and we would expect that the schedule length would be 480 minutes.

Suppose that actual operation times are random and follow a triangular distribution with a minimum of 30 minutes and a maximum of 90 minutes. Note: no order can start at a station until the previous order has finished.

a. What is the mean schedule length?

b. What is the probability that the schedule length will exceed 480 minutes?

c. Change the range of the distribution from 60 to 40 and to 20, and then repeat (a) and (b). What is the mean schedule length in each case? What do you conclude from these observations?

15. *Competitive Bidding*. Two partners have decided to sell the manufacturing business they have been running. They have lined up five prospective buyers and have hired a consultant to help them with the bidding and the sale. The consultant, an expert in assessments of this sort, has told the partners that the business is worth $10 million.

The consultant has obtained indications that the prospective buyers would be willing to participate in a sealed-bid auction to determine who will buy the business and at what price. Under the rules of the auction, the sale price would be the highest bid.

Due to their limited information about the business, the bidders may overestimate or underestimate what the business is actually worth. After listening to some of their preliminary thoughts, the consultant concludes that limited information will lead each of them to value the business at a minimum of $8 million and a maximum of $15 million. Their most likely value is $10 million. (We interpret this to mean that a suitable model for an individual value will be a triangular distribution.) The bidders, however, have an instinct about the Winner's Curse, and they each plan to bid only 75 percent of their estimated value for the business.

(The Winner's Curse is a phenomenon in competitive bidding where the winner is generally the one that most overestimates the value of the prize.)

a. What is the expected price that the partners will receive for their business?

b. What is the probability that the partners will receive more than $10 million for the business?

c. Suppose the consultant asks for a fee in order to identify five more bidders to participate in the auction. How large a fee should the partners be willing to pay for this service?

16. *Equilibrium in Competitive Bidding*. A sealed-bid auction is going to be held in the near future for Medex Pharmaceuticals. You represent one of two companies expected to enter bids. The basic data available to your firm consist of an estimate of the value of Medex and some information on the uncertainty surrounding that value. Your task is to prepare a quantitative bidding strategy for this auction. The attached letter from your boss explains his thinking about the problem and offers some suggestions for your approach.

MEMO

TO: Susan Morganstern
FROM: Vaughn Newman
RE: Bidding for Medex

As promised, I am following up our conversation of a few days ago with more information. You mentioned that your staff group might be able to help us prepare our bid for Medex Pharmaceuticals. Here are some of the details you asked about.

First of all, I don't want you to get the impression that our primary objective is simply to win the bid. We'd like to own Medex, of course, but only if the net effect is to increase our shareholder value. One of my big concerns is that we might win the bid but overestimate the value of Medex. That would not be a success.

Second, I'm confident that my Valuation Committee is doing its best to determine how much Medex is worth, but, as you said, we have to recognize the uncertainty we're dealing with. Medex might be worth a lot more or a lot less than our estimate—it really depends on how their R&D division does and on what happens to the market for the new drug they just got approved. I looked back at some of our previous work, and it looks like we've been high or low in our assessment by as much as 50 percent.

That's a lot of uncertainty, but it just seems to be the nature of the situations we've been in.

Third, I am pretty sure that the only other bidder for Medex will be National, in which case we'll have only one rival to worry about. Somehow, this ought to make things simpler than if there were several bidders out there.

Finally, as a corporation, National resembles us closely, and whichever one of us gets Medex should be able to extract the same value from the assets. National's access to information is about the same as ours, so their level of uncertainty should be the same. In addition, National has had some experience in this sort of bidding, and they're not naive about bidding strategy. Judging from their track record, they'll want to avoid overbidding, too. In essence, I guess I'm saying that they are likely to analyze the deal pretty much the way we are.

Any insight you could give us on how we should approach the bidding would be appreciated. The sealed bid is due at Morgan Stanley next Friday.

Here are some guidelines for your analysis:

Your boss has provided an estimate, based on his past experience, of the range of errors that are likely to be made in valuing companies such as Medex. Errors up to 50 percent above and below the true value are possible. If we assume that the true value is $100 million, we could represent the

range of possible estimates by a uniform probability distribution with a minimum value of $50 million and a maximum value of $150 million. Other probability models would also be plausible.

We know that our competitor, National, is similar to our company in all important ways. Thus, we may assume that their probability distribution for the value of Medex is the same as ours.

Bidding theory suggests that we should bid less than our estimated value in a common-value auction such as this. Formulate your strategy in terms of a *bid level*, which is the percentage of our estimated value we will bid.

We clearly cannot know for certain what bid level National will choose. But we can determine what our bid level *should* be for any given bid level they might choose.

Although your boss has specified the problem rather precisely, you should explore the sensitivity of your results to your assumptions, including the range of uncertainty, the form of the probability distribution, and the number of bidders.

17. *Pricing Exotic Options.* A given stock is currently priced at $100. Historically, its annual return has been 12 percent with a standard deviation of 15 percent. Build a spreadsheet simulation model for the stock price, using the option pricing model described in the text. Build the model to simulate the stock price over 126 days. Assume that the risk-free rate of return is 6 percent.

a. A particular European call option gives the owner the right to purchase this stock after six months at a strike price of $105. What is the price of the option?

b. Create a graph of the option price as a function of the strike price, for strike prices from $100 to $110 in increments of $1.

c. A particular European put option gives the owner the right to sell this stock after six months at a strike price of $95. What is the price of the put?

d. A lookback call option on this stock has an exercise price given by the minimum price observed over its six-month term. What is the price of the lookback option?

e. An Asian option on this stock has a strike price set by the average value of the stock during its term. What is the price of the Asian option?

f. A knockout call option on this stock terminates if the stock price reaches or exceeds $125 (that is, the option cannot be exercised). Otherwise, it has the same structure as the normal call. What is the price of the knockout option?

15 Optimization in Simulation

15.1 INTRODUCTION

In the simplest terms, simulation is a method for describing the probability distribution of an outcome variable, given a set of input variables. Sometimes those input variables include one or more decision variables, and the ultimate goal is to determine the best values for those inputs. But simulation, by itself, offers no assistance in identifying an *optimal*, or even good, set of decisions.

Ideally, we would like to marry optimization's power to identify the best decision variables with simulation's power to describe outcome distributions. Unfortunately, the optimization approaches that we covered in Chapters 8–12 are based on the premise that the objective function can be measured deterministically. But in simulation models the objective function is not deterministic; instead, it is the expected value or some other function of a random variable. In many cases, Analytic Solver Platform can optimize these models as well. However, in the context of simulation models, a number of issues arise that do not arise when optimizing deterministic models.

We begin with a simple but common example of a simulation problem containing a single decision variable, and we illustrate how to optimize such models using simulation sensitivity. We use the same example to introduce the optimization capabilities in Analytic Solver Platform as they apply to simulation models. We then show how to use Solver in more complex problems involving more than one or two decision variables. We organize this discussion around three types of models: expected-value models, in which the objective function and constraints use expected values based on simulation; chance-constrained models, in which some constraints must be satisfied a certain percentage of the time; and two-stage models with recourse, in which some decisions can be postponed until after uncertainty is resolved.

15.2 OPTIMIZATION WITH ONE OR TWO DECISION VARIABLES

We begin our study of optimization in simulation models with an example that involves choosing a supply quantity before demand is known for certain.

EXAMPLE
Hastings Sportswear

In November, Jeff Hastings of the fashion skiwear manufacturer Hastings Sportswear, Inc., faces the task of committing to specific production quantities for each skiwear item the company will offer in the coming year's line. Commitments are needed immediately in order to reserve space in production facilities located throughout Asia. Actual demand for these products will not become known for at least six months.

Production costs for a typical parka run about 75 percent of the wholesale price, which in this case is $110. Unsold parkas can be sold at salvage for around 8 percent of the wholesale price.

Jeff has asked six of his most knowledgeable people to make forecasts of demand for the various models of parkas. Forecasts for one product are given in the following table, along with the average and standard deviation of the forecasts. (Experience suggests that the actual standard deviation in demand is roughly twice that of the standard deviation in the forecasts.) Based on this information, Jeff must decide on an order quantity for this model of parka.

Forecaster 1	900 units
Forecaster 2	1,000
Forecaster 3	900
Forecaster 4	1,300
Forecaster 5	800
Forecaster 6	1,200
Average	1,017
Standard deviation	194

15.2.1 Base-case Model

Our first model for this situation is shown in Figure 15.1*. This model has one decision variable, the number of parkas ordered. We have arbitrarily set it equal to the mean demand of 1,017 (cell C13). We have also assumed a normal distribution for demand, with a mean of 1,017 units and a standard deviation of 388, or twice the standard deviation of the six forecasts. Random samples from this distribution are created in cell C16 using the Analytic Solver Platform formula =PsiNormal(C8,C10*C9). However, a normal distribution with a standard deviation nearly 40 percent of the mean can produce negative results, so we truncate the normal sample with the MAX function to ensure that demand is nonnegative. The effects on the actual mean and standard deviation of demand in the model are negligible. A complete description of the model follows:

Data

Cells C4:C9: Given data.

Cell C10: A parameter representing the amount by which we inflate the standard deviation of the demand estimates. The problem statement suggests the value 2.

FIGURE 15.1 Hastings Sportswear Spreadsheet

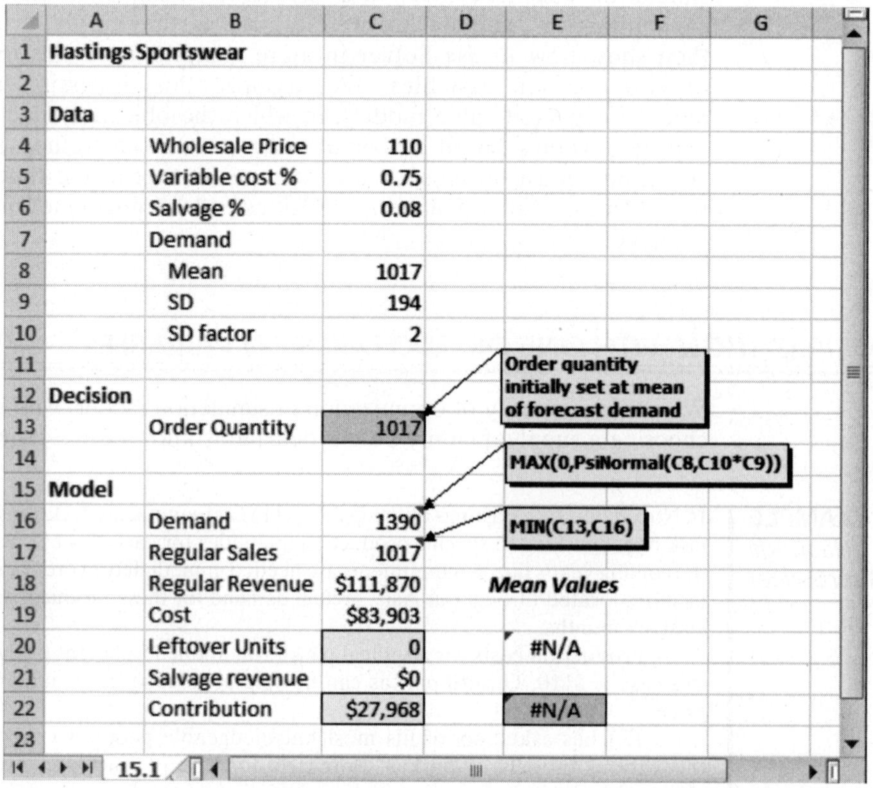

* To download spreadsheets for this chapter, go to the Student Companion Site at www.wiley.com/college/powell. Users may find their results differ slightly from those shown here due to the effects of random sampling.

Decision

Cell C13: The order quantity.

Model

Cell C16: The actual demand is calculated using a normal distribution with mean given in cell C8 and standard deviation given by the standard deviation of the forecasts (cell C9) multiplied by the SD factor (cell C10), truncated to be nonnegative.

Cell C17: Regular sales is calculated as the smaller of demand (C16) and the quantity ordered (C13).

Cell C18: Regular revenue is regular sales (C17) times the wholesale price (C4).

Cell C19: The cost is the number of units ordered (C13) times the wholesale price (C4) times the variable cost percent (C5).

Cell C20: Leftover units are calculated as the difference between the order quantity and demand, or zero if demand exceeds the order quantity.

Cell C21: Salvage revenue is leftover units (C20) times wholesale price (C4) times the salvage percent (C6).

Cell C22: Profit contribution is the sum of regular revenue (C18) and salvage revenue (C21), less cost (C19).

Two outcomes of this model are of particular interest: the profit contribution and the number of leftover units. Accordingly, we have designated two output cells: Contribution in cell C22 and Leftover Units in cell C20. By double-clicking on either of these cells after the simulation run, we can view the histogram of their values. In the same window, we can also find the mean, maximum, minimum, and several other summary statistics obtained from the simulation run. In addition, because the mean values of these two output cells are of particular interest, we place those values in column E. To record the mean contribution on the spreadsheet, place the cursor on cell C22. Then select Analytic Solver Platform▶Simulation Model▶Results▶Statistics▶Mean, and select cell E22. This places the formula =PsiMean(C22) in cell E22. We could also simply enter this formula directly into the cell. The mean number of leftovers can similarly be recorded in cell E20 using the function =PsiMean(C20).

Although both outcomes are important, we take the maximization of mean contribution as our primary objective. Our approach is to maximize mean contribution subject to secondary consideration for the mean number of leftover units. The results of running this simulation using 1,000 trials are shown in Figure 15.2 and Figure 15.3. Figure 15.2 shows that the average contribution from this product is about $12,358 if we order 1,017. In the simulation, the contribution values ranged from a low of –$74,953 to a high of $27,968. Evidently, there is considerable financial risk associated with this decision, in addition to the risk of having leftover units. The upper limit on the contribution ($27,968) is determined by the order quantity. Because we cannot sell more than we order, revenues

FIGURE 15.2 Distribution of Profit Contribution for Hastings Sportswear

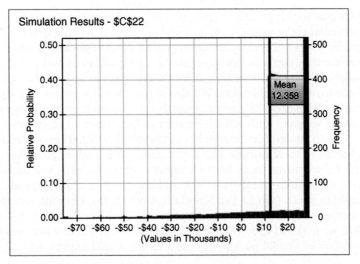

FIGURE 15.3 Distribution of Leftover Units for Hastings Sportswear

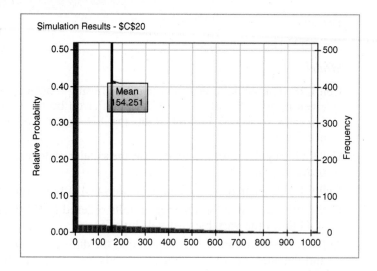

cannot exceed the value of the wholesale price times the order quantity. Whenever demand exceeds the order quantity, we sell exactly what we ordered, and the contribution is $27,968. According to Figure 15.2, this occurs about 50 percent of the time. One of the interesting aspects of this case is how the symmetrical normal distribution for demand is transformed by the structure of the model into the highly asymmetrical distribution of profit contribution shown in Figure 15.2.

Figure 15.3 shows the distribution of leftover units associated with ordering 1,017 parkas. On average, we can expect to have 154 units left over, but this amount could range from zero to 1,017. In about half the cases simulated, demand exceeds supply, so no units are left over. But there is also a small chance that demand will be zero, and then the entire stock will be left over.

We remarked earlier that simulation should be used only in situations where uncertainty is an essential feature of the problem. This is one of those situations. If there were no uncertainty in demand, and we knew demand would be exactly 1,017, we would simply order 1,017 and be guaranteed to make $27,968 with no units left over. Without uncertainty, the decision is obvious, and the results are entirely predictable. But if we ignore uncertainty, we miss the essential challenge of the problem—that when demand is uncertain, we must strike a balance between two kinds of risks. In one direction, we risk ordering too many and having costly leftovers; in the other, we risk ordering too few and having unmet demand. With uncertainty, moreover, our expected profit is only $12,358, far short of the maximum value of $27,968.

Simulation analysis allows us to measure the risks associated with setting the order quantity equal to mean demand, but to this point, it does not suggest an optimal order quantity. The next question is: Can we improve on our initial decision to order 1,017 parkas?

15.2.2 Grid Search

Our goal in this problem is not merely to estimate the contribution we would receive for a particular order quantity, but to determine the best order quantity. The term "best" implies the largest possible expected contribution, but it might also involve ensuring that the risk of a low contribution is not too great and that the number of parkas left over is acceptable. At this stage of our analysis, we have determined only that we would make $12,358 on average if we were to order 1,017 parkas. We also observed that we would have an average surplus of 154 parkas. These results might suggest that we consider ordering fewer than 1,017 parkas, since having so many units left over seems to be a waste of resources.

It is straightforward to change the number of parkas ordered (cell C13) and rerun the simulation to determine a new expected contribution. However, we want to ensure that the comparisons focus on the impact of differences in the decision and not differences due to random numbers in the simulation. For that purpose, we specify the random number seed. (Go to the Simulation tab in the Options window and enter a positive number such as 999 for Sim. Random Seed.) The results are as follows: when we order 900, we make $14,351 on average, which is better than when we order 1,017. The average number of unsold parkas declines, as we would expect, to 103. If we reduce the order quantity still further, to 800, average contribution rises to $14,979, and the average number unsold drops to 69. If we order 700, we make $14,722 with an average of 45 unsold; at 600, we make $13,721 with an average of 27 unsold. It appears that, up to a point, ordering fewer parkas than mean demand can increase average contribution while also decreasing the leftover stock.

It is worthwhile to pause and think through the implications of these results. Parkas sell for $110 and cost Hastings Sportswear $82.50 ($= 0.75 \times 110$). Ordering one parka fewer than demand results in one lost sale. The forgone profit is $27.50 ($= 110 - 82.5$). But ordering one too many results in $82.50 of excess production cost, of which only $8.80 (8 percent of 110) is recouped in salvage revenue. The surplus cost is $73.70 ($= 82.5 - 8.8$). Thus, there is a basic asymmetry in the costs of ordering one too many ($73.70) or one too few ($27.50). The economics favor ordering fewer than mean demand, because the incremental cost of ordering too few is only one-third the incremental cost of ordering too many.

This conclusion is true only within the model world. One implication of ordering fewer than demand is that it will result in more unsatisfied customers—people who wanted our product but found it out of stock. This result can have serious consequences in the long run for our company, if unsatisfied customers tend to drift away to competitors. Such costs are not captured in our model. If they were, we would probably recommend a somewhat higher order level.

The procedure we have illustrated here is a form of **grid search**. In a grid search, we select a series of values we wish to test for a decision variable, and we run the simulation at each of these values. Our grid in this case consisted of the order levels 600, 700, 800, and 900. We show the results of an expanded grid search in the following table:

Parkas Ordered	Expected Contribution	Expected Leftovers
600	$13,721	27
650	14,305	35
700	14,722	45
750	14,953	56
800	14,979	69
850	14,783	85
900	14,351	103
950	13,669	123
1,000	12,732	146
1,050	11,536	171
1,100	10,080	199
1,150	8,371	230
1,200	6,417	263

These results suggest that contribution is highest in the vicinity of 800 units, with an average of about 69 units unsold. (For more precision in our estimate of the best order quantity, we could refine the grid search by using a step size smaller than the 50 used in this table.) The summary table shown here can be produced by re-running the simulation for the 13 different order quantities, each time recording the mean value of contribution and the mean value of leftovers, from cells E22 and E20, respectively. Alternatively, the calculations can be automated, using the Parameter Sensitivity tool described in Chapter 4, and designating cells E22 and E20 as Result Cells. However, for simulation models, greater flexibility in sensitivity analysis is available if we use the Simulation Sensitivity tool, which we discuss next.

15.2.3 Optimizing using Simulation Sensitivity

Simulation sensitivity, which we introduced in Chapter 14, can also be used for optimization when we have one or two decision variables. We illustrate this approach using the Hastings Sportswear model (Figure 15.1). We first plot the mean contribution over a range of order quantities, then display the minimum and maximum along with the mean.

To prepare for sensitivity analysis, we create a simulation sensitivity cell in C14 with the formula =PsiSimParam(500,1300). Then we replace the number in cell C13 with the formula =C14. Using a separate cell for sensitivity values in this way allows us to document the sensitivity analysis conditions while still allowing the model to be used for

FIGURE 15.4 Multiple Simulations Chart Window

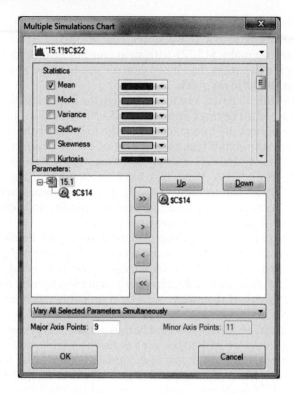

evaluating specific order quantities. The PsiSimParam function normally displays the Lower parameter, or 500 in this example.

To plot the mean contribution over the range of order quantities from 500 to 1,300, we select Analytic Solver Platform▶Analysis▶Charts▶Multiple Simulations▶Parameter Analysis. Select the output cell C22 from the drop-down list at the top of the window, check the box for the Mean output, select C14 as the Parameter, select Vary All Selected Parameters Simultaneously, and specify 9 Major Axis Points (Figure 15.4). Analytic Solver Platform then runs 9 simulations for order quantities between 500 and 1,300 and displays the mean contribution as a function of order quantity, as shown in Figure 15.5.

Figure 15.5 shows clearly that the optimal order quantity for maximizing mean contribution is around 800. We can easily add the minimum and maximum values in each of the nine simulations to the chart by repeating the charting procedure and checking two additional boxes in Figure 15.4, one for Minimum and one for Maximum, along with the box for Mean. The result is shown in Figure 15.6. The chart shows that the maximum contribution increases linearly with the order quantity, and the minimum contribution decreases linearly. The chart reveals that the range of outcomes (from minimum to maximum contribution)

FIGURE 15.5 Sensitivity of Mean Contribution to Order Quantity

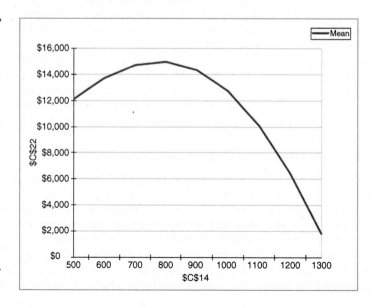

FIGURE 15.6 **Sensitivity of Mean, Minimum and Maximum Contribution to Order Quantity**

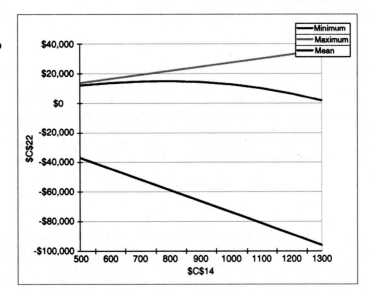

FIGURE 15.6 **Sensitivity of Mean, Minimum and Maximum Contribution to Order Quantity**

increases as we increase the order quantity, so it might be advantageous to order fewer than 800 if we want to limit the downside risk. For example, if we wish to limit our worst-case result to a loss of about $50,000, we should order around 700 units.

In this model, the only decision variable is the number of parkas ordered, cell C13. We would like to optimize this variable, but we might also like to know how sensitive the results are to the cost of parkas (cell C5). Using simulation sensitivity, we can run a simulation and record the expected contribution for each combination of input values for order quantity and unit cost. First we designate a second cell for sensitivity values, say C12, and enter the formula =PsiSimParam(0.7,0.9). Then we enter the formula =C12 in C5. (We plan to vary the relative cost from 0.7 to 0.9 in steps of 0.05.) As before, the formula in cell C14 allows us to vary the order quantity from 500 to 1,300 in steps of 100. We then select Analytic Solver Platform▶Analysis▶Reports▶Simulation▶Parameter Analysis. Select the output cell C22 at the top of the Multiple Simulations Report window (Figure 15.7), check the box for the Mean output, select cells C12 and C14 as the

FIGURE 15.7 **Multiple Simulations Report Window**

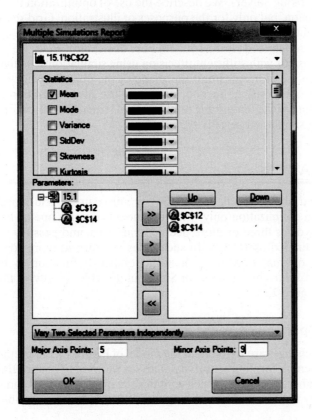

FIGURE 15.8 Sensitivity of Contribution to Order Quantity and Price

	A	B	C	D	E	F	G	H	I	J
1	Mean : $C$12 by $C$14									
2										
3										
4	$C$12	$C$14								
5		500	600	700	800	900	1000	1100	1200	1300
6	0.70	$14,884	$17,021	$18,572	**$19,379**	$19,301	$18,232	$16,130	$13,017	$8,976
7	0.75	$12,134	$13,721	$14,722	**$14,979**	$14,351	$12,732	$10,080	$6,417	$1,826
8	0.80	$9,384	$10,421	**$10,872**	$10,579	$9,401	$7,232	$4,030	-$183	-$5,324
9	0.85	$6,634	**$7,121**	$7,022	$6,179	$4,451	$1,732	-$2,020	-$6,783	-$12,474
10	0.90	**$3,884**	$3,821	$3,172	$1,779	-$499	-$3,768	-$8,070	-$13,383	-$19,624
11										

15.1 / 15.2 / 15.3 / 15.4 / 15.5 / 15.6 / 15.7 / **15.8**

Parameters, check Vary Two Selected Parameters Independently, and specify 5 Major Axis Points and 9 Minor Axis Points. Finally, we set the random seed to some nonzero number (such as 999) to ensure that the differences produced in the simulations are due to the different parameter values, not due to different random samples. For these settings, Analytic Solver Platform runs forty-five simulations (nine values for the order quantity times five values for costs) and builds the table shown in Figure 15.8. For a fixed order quantity, we can see how sensitive the mean contribution is to the cost by reading down the columns. For a given cost, we can determine how sensitive the mean contribution is to the order quantity by reading across the rows. The optimal expected contribution for each value of the cost parameter is highlighted in bold. One interesting message emerging from this table is that the optimal number of parkas drops from about 800 to 500 as costs increase from 70 percent to 90 percent.

15.2.4 Optimizing Using Solver

For the Hastings Sportswear model, Figure 15.5 suggests that the optimal choice for the order quantity is around 800. However, this graph is the result of a coarse grid search, in which we test only order quantities that are multiples of 100. If we want to determine the optimal order quantity with more precision, we have two options: either refine the grid (using simulation sensitivity with a larger number of Axis Points) or use optimization directly (invoking Solver). We describe the use of optimization for Hastings Sportswear in the next section, but only for the purposes of illustration. Grid search is usually the better choice when the model contains just one or two decision variables, unless a high degree of precision is required. Two reasons support this choice. First, we can usually identify the optimal decisions with sufficient precision using simulation sensitivity, and in doing so, we may acquire useful insights into the shape of the objective function that we cannot gain from direct optimization. Second, successful use of optimization algorithms requires an understanding of the underlying mathematical structure of the model that is not necessary when using simulation sensitivity.

15.3 STOCHASTIC OPTIMIZATION

As discussed above, simulation sensitivity automates a grid search, but it is a practical approach to optimization only when the model contains one or two variables. When the problem involves three or more decision variables, and possibly constraints as well, grid search has limited usefulness. In such cases, we turn to more sophisticated methods for identifying optimal decisions when the objective function is based on probabilistic outcomes. To introduce the use of Solver in this role, we revisit the Hastings Sportswear model in Figure 15.1.

15.3.1 Optimization of the Base-Case Model

Only a few changes are required to the model of Figure 15.1 to prepare it for Solver. First, if we have been performing sensitivity analyses we want to restore the original model, so we enter a number in cell C13 (which contains the order quantity) and remove any references to sensitivity functions. Then we designate C13 as a decision variable using Analytic Solver

Platform►Optimization Model►Decisions►Normal. Next, we designate E22 as the objective using Analytic Solver Platform►Optimization Model►Objective►Max►Normal. Because the model is being used to compare simulation outcomes, we again set the random number seed to an arbitrary value such as 999. This step ensures that the differences produced in the optimization are due to different choices of decision variables, not due to different random samples.

We specify the model as follows:

Variables:	C13
Objective:	E22 (maximize)
Constraints:	None

With this specification, we can select the Standard LSGRG Nonlinear Engine, reflecting what we learned when we created Figure 15.5; that is, the expected contribution is a smooth, nonlinear function of the order quantity. Upon running Solver, we find that the optimal order quantity is about 781 units, corresponding to a mean contribution of $14,995. This result confirms the conclusions that we drew earlier from simulation sensitivity, but this time we have identified the optimum with higher precision.

In terms of applying Solver, the main lesson from this solution of the Hastings problem is that when we specify an expected value using the PsiMean function, we can treat the function as a Normal objective function. However, Solver offers us an alternative to using the PsiMean function. We can designate the output cell C22 as the objective. This output cell contains a distribution, so we must tell Solver which aspect of the distribution we wish to maximize or minimize. With the cursor on cell C22, we select Analytic Solver Platform►Optimization Model►Objective►Max►Expected. (In other circumstances, we could choose a different summary measure of the distribution.) Then, in the task pane, the model's objective is identified as `Expected($C$22)` `(Max)`. The model specification is now slightly different.

Variables:	C13
Objective:	C22 [Expected] (maximize)
Constraints:	None

We can maximize the expected profit, and thus find the optimal order quantity, using either of the two specifications. Using the PsiMean function is more direct and preserves the similarity to the optimization of deterministic models. On the other hand, designating the distribution cell as an objective permits Solver to try approximation techniques, which we discuss later.

Analytic Solver Platform offers various options that can potentially provide more help in the optimization steps we have just described. In the Optimization Model section of the Platform tab, set Interpreter to `Automatic`, Solve Mode to `Solve Complete Problem`, and `Solve Uncertain Models` to `Automatic`. Under `Simulation Model`, set `Interpreter` to `Automatic`, and under `Transformation`, set `Nonsmooth Model Transformation` to `Never` and `Stochastic Transformation` to `Automatic`. These are default selections (see Figure 15.9), and together they represent the most suitable starting point in using optimization with simulation.

In anticipation of employing the evolutionary solver later, we enter an upper bound on the decision variable (for instance, C13 ≤ 1,500) and confirm that the Assume Non-Negative option is set to `True` on the Engine tab. (With these additions, the model is suited to either the evolutionary solver or the nonlinear solver.) Next, we access the Engine tab and check the box for `Automatically Select Engine`. Then we run the optimization by clicking on the green triangle on the Model tab or the Output tab.

After the optimization run completes, the Output tab contains documentation for the run in the form of a log. In particular, it reports that Stochastic transformation did not succeed and that Solver reverted to Simulation/Optimization. It also reports that the model was diagnosed as Stochastic NSP (Non-Smooth Problem), after which it reports choosing the evolutionary solver. In other words, the presence of simulated data in the model left Solver unable to recognize that the model could be treated as a smooth nonlinear optimization problem, so its best alternative was to use the evolutionary solver.

In the Hastings example, however, we know from the chart in Figure 15.5 that the objective function behaves like a smooth nonlinear curve. Therefore, we can override the

FIGURE 15.9 **Platform Tab with Default Options**

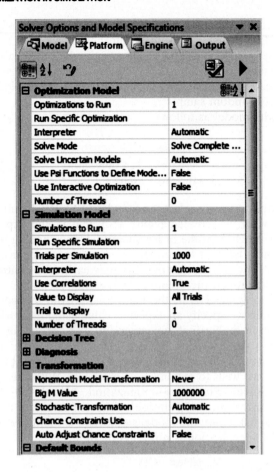

automatic selection of an algorithm by unchecking the box for `Automatically Select Engine` and selecting the `Standard LSGRG Nonlinear Engine`, as we routinely do for nonlinear optimization. When we check the log in the Output window after the optimization run, we find much of the same information, except for the engine selected. (Depending on the performance of the evolutionary solver, the nonlinear solver may well produce a slightly better value for the objective function.)

Thus, we can rely on Analytic Solver Platform by allowing it to "automatically" choose the algorithm, or we can specify the choice. We return later to diagnosing the problem type and attempting a transformation. Both of these procedures tend to work best when the default options on the task pane are in place, as described above. (The same options can also be found on the Simulation and Optimization tabs in the Options window: Analytic Solver Platform▶Options▶Options.)

To demonstrate how to accommodate constraints in this situation, observe that in the optimal solution produced above, the mean number of leftover units is about 64. Suppose instead we wish to limit this value to 50. The model specification becomes the following:

$$\text{Variables:} \quad C13$$
$$\text{Objective:} \quad E22 \text{ (maximize)}$$
$$\text{Constraints:} \quad E20 \le 50$$

In this specification, cell E20 contains a mean value, using the formula `=PsiMean (C20)`, and the constraint is entered using Analytic Solver Platform▶Optimization Model▶Constraints▶Normal Constraints▶<=. Thus, our model contains an expected value in a constraint as well as in the objective function, but the use of the PsiMean function allows Solver to proceed with a Normal constraint and a Normal objective function value, even though the model is not deterministic.

Invoking the nonlinear solver again, we find that the optimal order quantity is about 724, achieving a mean contribution of $14,859, but with the mean number of leftovers equal to 50. Compared to the unconstrained solution, we were able to reduce the mean number of leftovers by about 14 units (about 22 percent), at a sacrifice of only $136 (1 percent) in expected contribution.

15.3.2 A Portfolio Optimization Problem

In Chapter 8, we introduced the problem of determining the best allocation of a pool of money to a set of investments. Each investment vehicle has its own characteristics for return and risk. Some, such as government bonds, tend to have low returns and low risk. Others, such as technology stocks, tend to have high returns and high risk. The investing objective is to build a portfolio that has an attractive overall return with an acceptable level of risk. In general, however, these goals conflict because a high return is usually associated with a high risk.

Risk and return can be defined in alternative ways in the context of investments. Return is usually defined as the mean or expected return on an individual asset or on a portfolio of assets. Risk is usually measured by the variability of the asset or portfolio. The most common measure of variability is the standard deviation of returns, so we initially focus on finding a portfolio that has a high mean return and a low standard deviation. However, other measures of risk exist for a portfolio, and we subsequently explore an alternative.

EXAMPLE
A Four-Stock Portfolio

We have recently received $100,000 and have decided to invest in four stocks: Microsoft (MSFT), Ford (FORD), Dow Chemical (DOW), and AT&T (T). The table below gives the average returns on these investments as well as the standard deviation of returns. (For simplicity in this hypothetical example, we assume that returns among these assets are uncorrelated.) We want to determine how much to invest in each stock to maximize the overall average return, while keeping risk at an acceptable level. We also want to explore the sensitivity of our solution to risk.

Stock	Mean	St. Dev.
MSFT	0.40	0.28
FORD	0.16	0.22
DOW	0.20	0.24
T	0.30	0.18

■

Our spreadsheet model for this problem is shown in Figure 15.10. The given data consist of the mean and standard deviation of the return for each stock, and we assume that stock returns follow Normal distributions with those parameters. The four decision variables represent the percentage of the portfolio invested in each stock. The Total amount is calculated by adding the four decision variables, and we require this sum to be 100 percent. The return on the portfolio, which is the basis for our objective function, is the

FIGURE 15.10 Portfolio Model

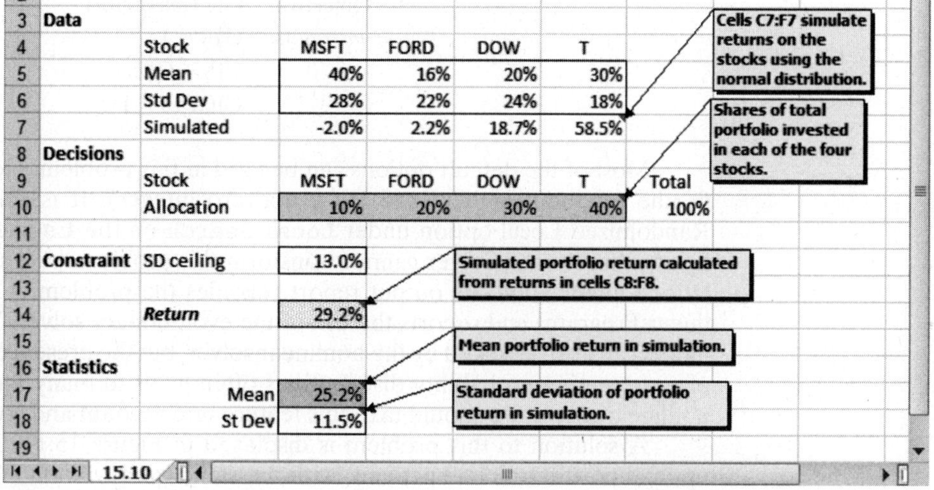

	A	B	C	D	E	F	G
1	Portfolio Optimization						
2							
3	Data						
4		Stock	MSFT	FORD	DOW	T	
5		Mean	40%	16%	20%	30%	
6		Std Dev	28%	22%	24%	18%	
7		Simulated	-2.0%	2.2%	18.7%	58.5%	
8	Decisions						
9		Stock	MSFT	FORD	DOW	T	Total
10		Allocation	10%	20%	30%	40%	100%
11							
12	Constraint	SD ceiling	13.0%				
13							
14		*Return*	29.2%				
15							
16	Statistics						
17		Mean	25.2%				
18		St Dev	11.5%				
19							

weighted average of the returns generated by the four stocks. A detailed description of the model follows.

Returns Data

Cells C5:F5: Mean annual stock returns.

Cells C6:F6: Standard deviation of annual stock returns.

Cells C7:F7: Simulated stock returns, using the Normal distribution

Decisions

Cells C10:F10: Percentages allocated to each stock.

Constraints

Cell G10: The total of the percentages must be 100 percent.

Cell C12: The maximum desired standard deviation for the portfolio.

Results

Cell C14: The return for the portfolio. This value is calculated as the weighted average of the simulated stock returns (C7:F7), with the percentages (C10:F10) as weights, using =SUMPRODUCT(C7:F7,C10:F10).

Cell C17: The mean return for the portfolio. This value is calculated as the mean of the distribution in cell C14, using =PsiMean(C14).

Cell C18: The standard deviation of the return for the portfolio. This value is calculated as the standard deviation of the distribution in cell C14, using =PsiStdDev(C14).

Our primary objective is to make the mean return on the portfolio as large as possible. This objective could be achieved by investing the entire portfolio in Microsoft, because it has the highest mean return of the four stocks. However, the portfolio would have a very high risk, as measured by the standard deviation of 28 percent. One way to control the risk is to maximize the mean return subject to a constraint on the portfolio standard deviation. This optimization task can be accomplished using Solver.

The final constraints are bounds on the decision variables, included in anticipation of using the evolutionary solver.

The steps in constructing the optimization model are as follows:

1. Designate cells C10:F10 as decision variables using Analytic Solver Platform ▶Optimization Model▶Decisions▶Normal.

2. Place the cursor on the output cell C17 and designate it as the objective using Analytic Solver Platform▶Optimization Model▶Objective▶Max▶Normal.

3. Designate the constraints using Analytic Solver Platform▶Optimization Model▶Constraints▶Normal Constraint, completing the information as needed.

We specify the model as follows:

Variables:	C10:F10
Objective:	C17 (maximize)
Constraints:	G10 = 1
	C18 ≤ C12
	C10:F10 ≤ 1

Most of the default options can be used in this problem. However, it is important to fix the random number seed (to a nonzero integer). It is also helpful to choose the Randomized Local option under Local Search on the Engine tab. As in the Hastings Sportswear model, Solver cannot transform this problem successfully and chooses Simulation/Optimization. Its output report classifies the problem as a Stochastic NLP (Nonlinear Program) and reports the use of the evolutionary solver. We may suspect that this model can also be solved by the nonlinear solver, but the presence of simulation as a means of representing probability distributions often leads to many local optima. If we use the nonlinear solver, we should take this feature into account and try multiple starting points.

A solution to this problem is displayed in Figure 15.11. The mean return for the optimal portfolio is 30.9 percent, with the standard deviation at its ceiling of 13 percent.

FIGURE 15.11   Solution to the Portfolio Model

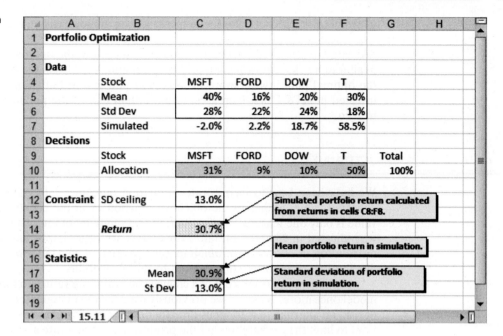

	A	B	C	D	E	F	G	H
1	**Portfolio Optimization**							
2								
3	**Data**							
4		Stock	MSFT	FORD	DOW	T		
5		Mean	40%	16%	20%	30%		
6		Std Dev	28%	22%	24%	18%		
7		Simulated	-2.0%	2.2%	18.7%	58.5%		
8	**Decisions**							
9		Stock	MSFT	FORD	DOW	T	Total	
10		Allocation	31%	9%	10%	50%	100%	
11								
12	**Constraint**	SD ceiling	13.0%					
13								
14		**Return**	30.7%					
15								
16	**Statistics**							
17		Mean	30.9%					
18		St Dev	13.0%					
19								

Simulated portfolio return calculated from returns in cells C8:F8.

Mean portfolio return in simulation.

Standard deviation of portfolio return in simulation.

Optimal weights are 31 percent for Microsoft, 9 percent for Ford, 10 percent for Dow, and 50 percent for AT&T. (The results of successive runs with the evolutionary solver may differ slightly.) This portfolio achieves the highest possible mean return while limiting risk—as measured by the standard deviation—to an acceptable level.

We can gain additional insight into this solution by varying the tolerance for risk, as expressed by the ceiling on the standard deviation of the portfolio return. Figure 15.12 shows the results of using optimization sensitivity on this model for values of the standard deviation target from 12 percent to 30 percent. (No feasible portfolios have lower levels of risk.) Several observations can be made based on these results. As we increase the

FIGURE 15.12   Sensitivity Analysis in the Portfolio Model

	A	B	C	D	E	F
1	St.Dev	Return	MSFT	FORD	DOW	T
2	0.12	29.2%	25.6%	14%	14%	47%
3	0.14	32.2%	33.8%	3%	7%	56%
4	0.16	34.5%	45.3%	0%	0%	55%
5	0.18	35.9%	58.8%	0%	0%	41%
6	0.20	36.9%	68.7%	0%	0%	31%
7	0.22	37.7%	77.4%	0%	0%	23%
8	0.24	38.5%	85.3%	0%	0%	15%
9	0.26	39.3%	92.8%	0%	0%	7%
10	0.28	40.0%	100.0%	0%	0%	0%
11	0.30	40.0%	100.0%	0%	0%	0%
12						

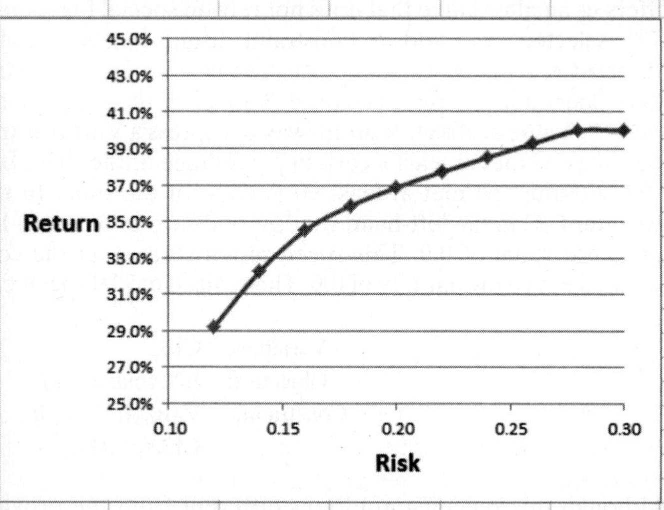

Return vs Risk chart (rows 13-33):

Return (vertical axis: 25.0% to 45.0%) plotted against Risk (horizontal axis: 0.10 to 0.30).

15.11   15.12

allowable risk, the portfolio mean increases but at a decreasing rate. When the allowable risk reaches 28 percent, no improvement is possible because the entire portfolio is dedicated to Microsoft. When the allowable risk is low, the optimal plan involves investing in all four stocks—most heavily in Microsoft and AT&T. As the allowable risk increases, the optimal plan invests more in Microsoft and less in both Ford and Dow. The share invested in AT&T first increases, to more than half of the portfolio, and then decreases to zero.

15.4 CHANCE CONSTRAINTS

We have seen how to incorporate simulation outcomes into optimization models using expected values, either in the objective function or in the constraints. But the expected value is only one feature of a distribution that might be of interest to a decision maker. As we indicated in Chapter 14, tail probabilities are often important measures describing a distribution. A *chance constraint* imposes a restriction on a tail probability in the simulated distribution, or on a function related to that probability.

To illustrate the concept of a chance constraint, we return to the Hastings Sportswear model once more. Whereas we previously used the mean number of leftovers as a measure of risk, an alternative is to focus directly on poor profit outcomes. In particular, we might want to limit the probability that the product fails to generate a profit. We can write such a constraint as follows:

$$P(C22 \leq 0) \leq 0.1$$

In words, the probability of failing to achieve a positive contribution is less than or equal to 0.1.

We can enter a chance constraint into a Solver model in one of two ways. The more direct way is to create a cell to represent the 10th percentile of the distribution. Thus, in cell F22 we enter the formula =PsiPercentile(C22,0.1). This formula calculates the 10th percentile of the distribution in C22. If the 10th percentile is negative, then more than 10 percent of the distribution falls below zero—that is, the probability of a loss is greater than 10 percent. To meet our desired constraint, we can require that cell F22 be at least zero. The revised model specification becomes the following.

Variables:	C13
Objective:	E22 (maximize)
Constraints:	F22 $\geq$ 0
	C13 $\leq$ 1,500

Solver finds the constrained optimum of about 715 units, with a 10th percentile at zero and an expected contribution of $14,810.

Instead of using the PsiPercentile function to constrain the tail probability, Solver offers us an alternative that does not rely on special functions on the worksheet. With cell C22 selected, we add a constraint using Analytic Solver Platform▶Optimization Model▶Constraints▶Chance Constraint▶>=. This selection brings up the familiar Add Constraint dialog. Instead of Normal in the right-hand window, the display shows VaR (for **Value at Risk**). A useful way to express a VaR constraint is to describe a condition that must be met at least a certain percentage of the time. In this example, the condition C22 $\geq$ 0 must be met at least 90 percent of the time. In the Add Constraint window, we enter C22 in the left-hand window and zero in the right-hand window. Then we enter a Chance value of 0.9. This specification states that the constraint (C22 $\geq$ 0) must be satisfied with a probability of 0.9. The revised model specification becomes the following:

Variables:	C13
Objective:	E22 (maximize)
Constraints:	$VaR_{0.9}(C22) \geq 0$
	C13 $\leq$ 1,500

Although this specification looks different from the previous one, it is equivalent for the purposes of optimization, and the Solver runs are essentially the same. Direct entry

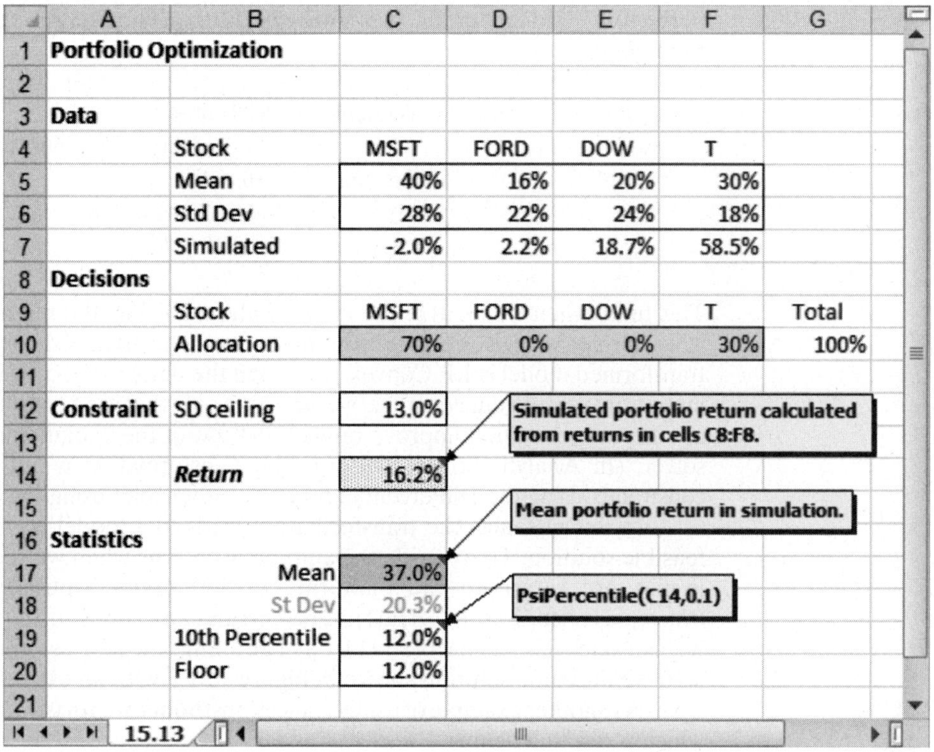

FIGURE 15.13 Portfolio Model with a Chance Constraint

	A	B	C	D	E	F	G
1	**Portfolio Optimization**						
2							
3	**Data**						
4		Stock	MSFT	FORD	DOW	T	
5		Mean	40%	16%	20%	30%	
6		Std Dev	28%	22%	24%	18%	
7		Simulated	-2.0%	2.2%	18.7%	58.5%	
8	**Decisions**						
9		Stock	MSFT	FORD	DOW	T	Total
10		Allocation	70%	0%	0%	30%	100%
11							
12	**Constraint**	SD ceiling	13.0%		Simulated portfolio return calculated from returns in cells C8:F8.		
13							
14		*Return*	16.2%				
15					Mean portfolio return in simulation.		
16	**Statistics**						
17		Mean	37.0%				
18		St Dev	20.3%		PsiPercentile(C14,0.1)		
19		10th Percentile	12.0%				
20		Floor	12.0%				
21							

15.13

of a chance constraint using the VaR specification has the advantage that it uses cells already on the worksheet. Its disadvantage is that to confirm whether the constraint is binding in the optimal solution, we have to examine the details of the distribution cell. As we saw above, the use of the PsiPercentile function requires an additional cell but allows us to determine whether the constraint is binding directly from the worksheet.

We can apply the concept of a chance constraint in our portfolio model as well. In particular, we might want to find a portfolio in which risk is measured not by the standard deviation but rather by the probability the total return falls below a target level. In our example from the previous section, suppose we require that the probability of a portfolio return less than 12 percent is at most 0.1. Again, we have two alternatives for specifying this information in the optimization model.

In Figure 15.13, we show the portfolio model with the 10th percentile of the portfolio return entered in cell C19 with the formula =PsiPercentile(C14, 0.1). In place of a ceiling on the standard deviation, we place a lower bound on the 10th percentile and enter it in cell C20. In this case, the 10th percentile must be no less than 12 percent. The model specification becomes the following:

$$
\begin{aligned}
\text{Variables:} &\quad \text{C10:F10} \\
\text{Objective:} &\quad \text{C17 (maximize)} \\
\text{Constraints:} &\quad \text{G10} = 1 \\
&\quad \text{C19} \geq \text{C20} \\
&\quad \text{C10:F10} \leq 1
\end{aligned}
$$

Before attempting a solution, we can ask Solver to analyze the problem without solving by selecting Analytic Solver Platform▶Solve Action▶Optimize▶Analyze Without Solving. From the report on the Output tab, we learn that the stochastic transformation did not succeed and that Solver reverts to Simulation/Optimization. We can expect the automatic selection of an engine to choose the evolutionary solver, but we can also specify the nonlinear solver to get a solution. We find that the optimal expected return is 37 percent, with the 10th percentile exactly at its ceiling of 12 percent.

Suppose that we adopt the alternative specification, in which we use the PsiOutput cell as the objective. Instead of relying on the Normal constraint involving the 10th percentile, we can enter the VaR condition. The model specification becomes the following:

$$
\begin{aligned}
\text{Variables:} \quad & \text{C10:F10} \\
\text{Objective:} \quad & \text{C14 [Expected] (maximize)} \\
\text{Constraints:} \quad & \text{G10} = 1 \\
& \text{VaR}_{0.9}(\text{C14}) \geq \text{C20} \\
& \text{C10:F10} \leq 1
\end{aligned}
$$

This time, when we analyze the model without solving, the report states that Stochastic Transformation succeeded using Robust Counterpart with D Norm and that the transformed model is LP Convex. Although the details of the Robust Counterpart transformation are beyond our coverage, we note here only that it is a conservative approximation, and one that we can often improve on with the use of the evolutionary solver or the nonlinear solver. (In Analytic Solver Platform, the transformation is not available if we formulate constraints using the PsiPercentile function rather than using the VaR form.)

In this instance, the transformation leads to a model in which Solver cannot find a feasible solution. To override the automatic choices when we see the Robust Counterpart in use, we return to the Platform tab and under Optimization Model, set Solve Uncertain Models to Simulation Optimization. Furthermore, on the Engine tab we can uncheck Automatically Select Engine and use the nonlinear solver, which leads to the same solution shown in Figure 15.13, with an expected return of 37.0 percent.

As another example of using chance constraints, we revisit an example from Chapter 10, which is restated below.

EXAMPLE
Planning for Tuition Expenses

Parents Patti and Russ want to provide for their daughter's college expenses with some of the $100,000 they have recently inherited. They hope to set aside part of the money and establish an account that will cover the needs of their daughter's college education, which begins four years from now, with a one-time investment. They estimate that first-year college expenses will come to $24,000 and will increase $2,000 per year during each of the remaining three years of college. The following investment instruments are available:

Investment Available	Matures	Return at Maturity	
A	every year	in 1 year	5%
B	in years 1,3,5,7	in 2 years	11%
C	in years 1,4	in 3 years	16%
D	in year 1	in 7 years	44%

Faced with this prospect, Patti and Russ wish to set aside the minimum amount of money that will guarantee they will be able to meet tuition expenses.   ∎

Taking a deterministic view of the situation, as we did in Chapter 10, this scenario gives rise to a linear programming model. Our analysis showed that the minimum initial investment is $80,833, and that the optimal investment plan relies on investments B1, D1, B3, A5, and B5. But perhaps it is more realistic to think of future college tuition as uncertain. For our present purposes, we assume that the predicted tuition amounts are mean values and that the actual amounts follow Normal distributions, each with a standard deviation of $4,000. One further condition appears in our model: tuition never drops from one year to the next.

First, we show a detailed breakout of the relevant cash flows in Figure 15.14. This worksheet contains no probabilistic elements, so the calculations are equivalent to those in Figure 10.24. The figure shows the optimal solution, obtained from a run of the linear solver. A detailed description of the model follows:

Data

Cells C4:F4: Parameters consisting of returns for each investment type.

Decisions

Cells B7:O7: Investments in the various investment possibilities, in thousands.

FIGURE 15.14 Deterministic Tuition-Planning Model

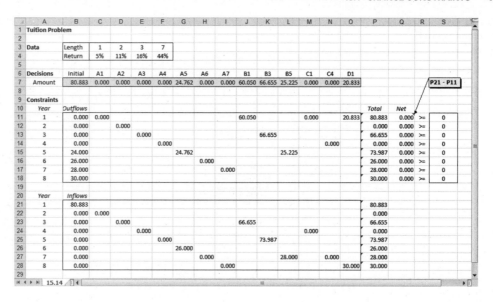

Calculations

Cells C11:O18: The investment decisions of row 7 are shown as outflows in the year that they occur.

Cells C22:O28: The values of the investments in C11:O18 are shown at maturity in the year that they occur.

Cells B11:B18: The required net outflows, shown for each year.

Cells P11:P18: The sum of the outflows, shown for each year.

Cells Q11:Q18: The net inflows, calculated for each year as the difference between total inflows and total outflows.

Cell B21: The initial investment becomes the only inflow in year 1.

Cells B21:B28: The inflows reference net flows from the previous year.

Cells P21:P28: The sum of the inflows, shown for each year.

Constraints

The net outflows in Q11:Q18 must be nonnegative.

Results

Cell B7: The initial investment serves as the objective function.

Next, we add probabilistic elements to the model. The entries in cells B15:B18 are replaced by distributions. For example, the formula in cell B16 yields a sample from a Normal distribution, constrained to be no smaller than the value in cell B15. The formula is `=MAX(B15,PsiNormal(26,4))`.

Now we have an opportunity to use chance constraints. Suppose that Patti and Russ would like to know that their investments will cover the tuition requirements with a high probability. Specifically, they want to meet cash needs year by year with a probability of 0.9, allowing for a 10 percent chance that they might have to cover any unanticipated shortfall from their checking account. Of course, chance constraints are unnecessary for the first four years because no uncertainty occurs until later. Therefore, we can simply require that net cash balances in the first four years (Q11:Q14) never go negative. These appear in the model as Normal constraints. In years 5 through 8 (Q15:Q18), the net cash flows become probabilistic outputs. In cells R15:R18, we enter percentiles of the corresponding values in column Q. For example, in cell R15, we enter the formula `=PsiPercentile(Q15,0.1)` and copy the formula to the three cells immediately below. In each year, these values must be at least zero; that ensures no more than a 10 percent chance that the net investment returns will be insufficient to cover tuition. The revised model is shown in Figure 15.15.

FIGURE 15.15 Stochastic Tuition-Planning Model

	A	B	C	D	E	F	G	H	I	J	K	L	M	N	O	P	Q	R
1	Tuition Problem																	
2																		
3	Data	Length	1	2	3	7												
4		Return	5%	11%	16%	44%												
5																		
6	Decisions	Initial	A1	A2	A3	A4	A5	A6	A7	B1	B3	B5	C1	C4	D1			
7	Amount	93.559	0.000	0.000	0.000	0.000	28.930	0.000	0.000	70.599	78.365	28.936	0.000	0.000	22.960			
8																		
9	Constraints																	
10	Year	Outflows														Total	Net	Percentiles
11	1	0.000	0.000							70.599				0.000	22.960	93.559	0.000	
12	2	0.000		0.000												0.000	0.000	
13	3	0.000			0.000						78.365					78.365	0.000	
14	4	0.000				0.000								0.000		0.000	0.000	
15	5	17.996					28.930					28.936				75.862	11.123	0.00
16	6	23.494						0.000								23.494	18.006	0.00
17	7	27.781							0.000							27.781	22.344	0.00
18	8	36.330														36.330	19.076	0.00
19																		
20	Year	Inflows														Total		
21	1	93.559														93.559		
22	2	0.000	0.000													0.000		
23	3	0.000		0.000						78.365						78.365		
24	4	0.000			0.000								0.000			0.000		
25	5	0.000				0.000					86.985					86.985		
26	6	11.123					30.376									41.499		
27	7	18.006						0.000				32.119		0.000		50.125		
28	8	22.344							0.000						33.063	55.407		

Callouts: =P21 - P11; =P25-P15 + PsiOutput(); 1st tuition payment: =PsiNormal(24,4); 2nd tuition payment: =MAX(B15,PsiNormal(26,4)); PsiPercentile(Q15,0.1)

We specify the model as follows:

> Variables: B7:O7
> Objective: B7 (minimize)
> Constraints: Q11:Q14 ≥ 0
> R15:R18 ≥ 0
> B7:O7 ≤ 150

The upper bounds of 150 on the variables anticipate the use of the evolutionary solver.

A few runs of the evolutionary solver generate solutions similar to the one shown in Figure 15.15. (The nonlinear solver can also run on this model.) We find a minimum investment of $93,559, which is somewhat larger than the optimal value in the deterministic model. But this result makes sense: we need extra funds if we want to protect cash flows from the higher tuition levels that could occur in the probabilistic case. At the same time, the specific instruments used in the optimal solution match those in the deterministic solution: B1, D1, B3, A5, and B5.

Thus the basic form of a chance constraint places a restriction on the tail of a particular output distribution. Although we can most easily specify the information using the PsiPercentile function, the VaR form is essentially equivalent. The drawback of this type of constraint is that although we can limit the *probability* of a constraint violation—an undesirable outcome—we cannot limit the *extent* of the violation. In the tuition example, we can limit the probability that Patti and Russ will have to use their checkbook, but that specification does not necessarily limit how large a check they may have to write. An alternative to the VaR form of the constraint helps meets this need. It is called the CVaR form, for **Conditional Value at Risk**. CVaR is the expected value of a distribution, taking into account only those values at or below a given percentile. In the Add Constraint dialog window, Solver provides the option of entering a CVaR constraint, using the drop-down menu on the right.

In the tuition example, suppose that Patti and Russ prefer a constraint that limits the mean size of the shortfall to $1,000 in the 10 percent of occasions when a shortfall exists. This means that the mean shortfall at the 10th percentile should be no greater than $1,000 (or equivalently, the net cash position should not fall below –$1,000 on average). In cell R15 we enter the formula =PsiCVaR(Q15,0.1) and copy it to the three cells below. Then we add Normal constraints requiring these four values to each be at least as large as the cells S15:S18, in which we enter –1,000. Now the model is specified as follows:

> Variables: B7:O7
> Objective: B7 (minimize)
> Constraints: Q11:Q14 ≥ 0
> R15:R18 ≥ S15:S18
> B7:O7 ≤ 150

FIGURE 15.16 Stochastic Tuition-Planning Model with CVaR Considerations

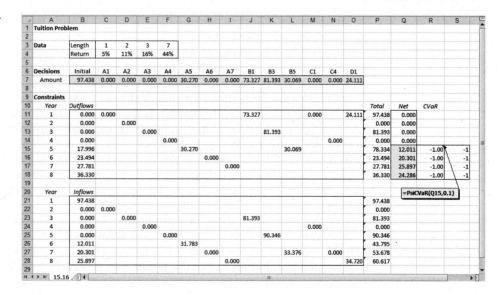

The Transformation does not succeed in this model (at least partly due to the presence of the PsiCVaR functions). We can proceed with Simulation/Optimization and use either the evolutionary solver or the nonlinear solver. With a sufficiently long run, Solver produces the solution shown in Figure 15.16. The expected shortfall requirements are binding in the solution, and the initial investment is $97,438. Thus, posing the risk constraint in terms of CVaR leads Patti and Russ to invest a larger amount than in the earlier stochastic formulation. The investments of choice remain as before: B1, D1, B3, A5, and B5.

15.5 TWO-STAGE PROBLEMS WITH RECOURSE

In a typical application of simulation, decisions must be made *before* the uncertain outcomes become known. In the Advertising Budget example, next year's price and cost are uncertain at budgeting time when we commit to our advertising plan for the entire coming year. But it's possible that certain decisions can be made *after* some uncertainties have been resolved. For example, we might be able to accurately forecast next year's price by the time the third quarter begins. In that case, we could choose our advertising expenditures for the third and fourth quarters based on that knowledge.

When decisions can be made after uncertainties are resolved, we are better off if we take those results into account. If we ignore the option to act later with more complete knowledge, we must make our decisions based on all the uncertainties. On the other hand, if we can make our decision after we know the outcome of an uncertain event or parameter, we can match our decision more closely to that outcome and eliminate some of the risks. In the Hastings Sportswear example, if we must make our production decision before we know demand, we have to balance the risks of producing too many or too few. However, if we already know demand when we decide on production, we can eliminate both risks by simply producing to demand.

A somewhat more complex example involves a decision to purchase several types of production machinery, each of which has the flexibility to produce different products. Today, we face the initial decision of how much production capacity of each type to purchase. Future demand for each product is uncertain. In future years, we will know demand for that year fairly accurately, and we will be able to allocate machine capacity to specific products so as to minimize cost. Each year in the future, this choice of an optimal production plan will be constrained by the capacity choices we make today. To model this problem realistically, we first need to represent the uncertainty in demand. Then, we need to formulate the optimization problem of allocating production capacity to minimize cost, when demand is given. Finally, knowing how we would react optimally to each possible demand outcome, we can evaluate total costs for the initial capacity choices. More specifically, we can find the minimum total expected cost, where the expected value is calculated across all the different uncertain outcomes.

Problems of this type, where some decisions are made after uncertainty has been resolved, are known as **two-stage problems with recourse decisions**. The two stages refer to the two sets of decisions, one of which arises before uncertainty is revealed and the other after. Recourse decisions are those decisions made *after* the uncertainty is resolved.

Analytic Solver Platform can solve problems of this type when the objective function and constraints are both linear. The major change from one-stage stochastic optimization problems, such as those covered earlier, is the introduction of recourse decision variables. However, the results also require careful interpretation because the optimal values for the recourse decisions are not unique. Since they are optimized after uncertainties are resolved, one set of recourse variables corresponds to every simulation trial.

In a typical recourse decision problem we make long-term, strategic commitments before uncertainty is resolved, and we make short-term, tactical decisions after the uncertainty is resolved. In the following example, the long-term decisions involve how much capacity to build at various production facilities. The uncertainties involve the demands for multiple products. The short-term decisions involve where to produce products and what routes to use for delivery. These tactical decisions are made after demand is known, but also after the production capacities have been determined.

EXAMPLE
Capacity Planning at Bagby Chemical Company

Bagby Chemical Company, a producer of industrial chemicals, has three manufacturing plants from which it ships its products to four regions of the country. The company must decide how much capacity to dedicate at each plant for production of a relatively new product whose market size is just beginning to level off. Because distribution costs are substantial, the profit margin on each unit sold depends on the delivery route. That is, the unit profit depends on the location of manufacture and the region where the sale takes place. Since industrial chemicals are sold on annual contracts, demand is quite predictable at the start of each year. Thus, we can choose the optimal production and distribution plan once we know demand. However, at the time capacity decisions must be made, demand is uncertain.

Marketing analysts have predicted that annual demand for the product can be modeled by using normal distributions with stable parameters. Distribution costs are known in advance, and from that information Bagby Chemical can anticipate its profit margins throughout the distribution network. Finally, the costs associated with establishing capacities at the three plants have been determined based on construction bids. ∎

Bagby Chemical faces a two-stage problem with recourse decisions because the amounts to produce and the distribution schedule can be determined after sales contracts are finalized and demand is revealed. However, plant capacities have to be chosen very soon, before demands can be known. To model this sequence of decisions and random outcomes, we simulate demand and then optimize production and shipment decisions based on the simulated outcomes. Every set of simulated demands leads to a corresponding set of optimal short-term decisions and resulting profit. To determine the optimal long-term decisions, we must take into account the impact of capacities on this set of short-term outcomes.

Our spreadsheet model is shown in Figure 15.17. The product is manufactured at three plants located in California, Michigan, and South Carolina and shipped to regional warehouses in Bagby Chemical's four market regions: South, East, Central, and West. The model contains 18 decision variables in all: three long-term capacity decisions (one for each plant location) and 15 short-term shipment quantities (one from each plant to each region). The objective is to maximize profit, which is calculated by subtracting annual fixed costs on total capacity from the total margin on units sold. Two sets of constraints apply: the amount sold in each region cannot exceed regional demand, and the amount produced at each plant cannot exceed its capacity. A detailed description of the model follows.

Parameters

Cells C4:F4: Mean demand in each region.

Cells C5:F5: Standard deviation of demand in each region.

Data

Cells C8:F10: Unit profit for each combination of plant and region.

Cells C11:F11: Demand in each region.

Cell H8: Fixed cost per unit of capacity.

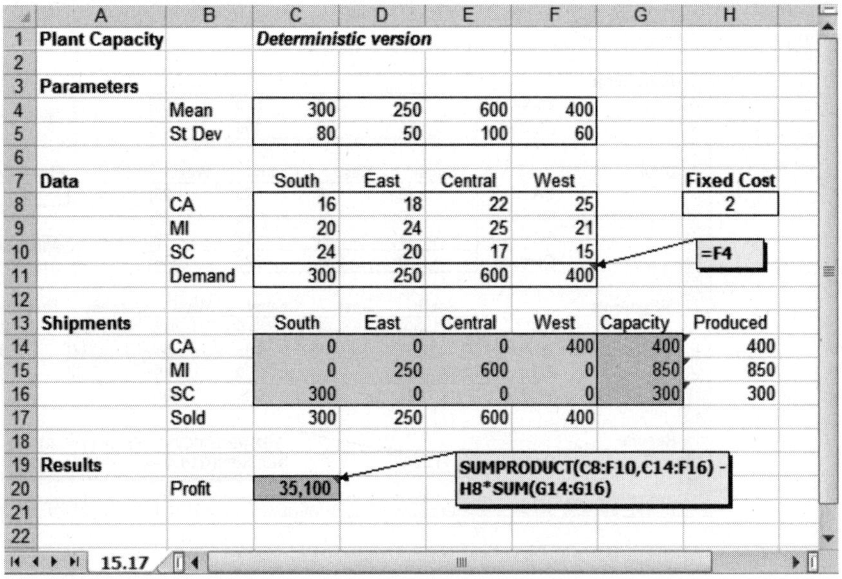

FIGURE 15.17 Deterministic Capacity-Planning Model

Decisions

Cells C14:F16: Shipment quantity for each combination of plant and region.

Cells G14:G16: Capacity level at each plant.

Constraints

Cells H14:H16: Total produced at each plant must be no greater than capacity.

Cells C17:F17: Quantity sold at each plant must be no greater than demand.

Results

Cell C20: Net Profit: profit from shipping less fixed capacity cost.

As a first step in our analysis, we can set up a deterministic, one-stage version of this model that includes both long-term and short-term decisions. Taking demands at their mean values, we can create the model shown in Figure 15.17. This is not a stochastic optimization problem because we have suppressed randomness entirely and substituted mean values for uncertain demands. As a result, the model is a linear program, and the optimal solution, with profit of $35,100, is displayed in the figure. The details of the solution are not surprising: the optimal total capacity exactly matches total demand, and each demand is met along the most profitable shipping route.

The stochastic version of this model differs in only a few ways from the deterministic version. The capacities in cells G14:G16 are still Normal (first-stage) decision variables. The constraints still require that production at each plant cannot exceed capacity and that shipments to each region cannot exceed demand. The demands in cells C11:F11 are now simulated from the respective demand distributions, and therefore Net Profit, which depends on these outcomes, is also a simulated output (Figure 15.18).

One new feature of this model is the designation of shipment decision variables in cells C14:F16 as Recourse decisions. This designation ensures that these variables are chosen optimally *after* each realization of simulated demands.

We specify the model as follows:

Variables:	G14:G16 (Normal)
	C14:F16 (Recourse)
Objective:	C20 (Expected)
Constraints:	C17:F17 $\leq$ C11:F11
	H14:H16 $\leq$ G14:G16

FIGURE 15.18 Stochastic Capacity-Planning Model

	A	B	C	D	E	F	G	H	I
1	Plant Capacity								
2									
3	Parameters								
4		Mean	300	250	600	400			
5		St Dev	80	50	100	60			
6									
7	Data		South	East	Central	West		Fixed Cost	
8		CA	16	18	22	25		2	
9		MI	20	24	25	21			
10		SC	24	20	17	15		=PsiNormal(F4,F5)	
11		Demand	360	286	636	266			
12									
13	Shipments		South	East	Central	West	Capacity	Produced	
14		CA	0	0	0	463	463	463	
15		MI	54	244	605	21	934	923	
16		SC	375	0	0	0	375	375	
17		Sold	429	244	605	484			
18									
19	Results								
20		Profit	39,524			SUMPRODUCT(C8:F10,C14:F16) − H8*SUM(G14:G16) + PsiOutput()			
21									

In the two-stage model, Solver recognizes that each set of simulated demands gives rise to an optimization problem of finding the most profitable shipping plan. Given a choice of capacity levels, this optimization problem involves 12 variables and 7 constraints. For each set of demands, this model is incorporated into the original problem (involving decisions about capacity), thereby creating one large (deterministic) linear program to solve.

Before attempting a solution, we can ask Solver to analyze the problem without solving by selecting Analytic Solver Platform▶Solve Action▶Optimize▶Analyze Without Solving. (A simpler method is to click on the corresponding icon on the Output tab of the task pane.) Solver's report indicates that Stochastic Transformation succeeded using Deterministic Equivalent. The transformed model is LP Convex, meaning that it can be solved by a linear solver or a nonlinear solver. However, the report also states that the Transformed model is too large to solve with the selected engine. The report proceeds to another transformation.

The transformed model is too large to solve when the total number of decision variables or constraints exceeds the limits of the software. In this problem, for each demand realization we incorporate 12 variables and 7 constraints into the overall model. Thus, if we have a simulation sample size of 1,000, then the model will have 12,000 variables (plus three more for the capacity decisions) and 7,000 constraints (plus one more for the objective function.) For the typical educational version of the software, this problem size outstrips the software's limits. However, we can adjust our model size by reducing the number of simulation trials. For example, suppose our software has limits of 2,000 variables and constraints. Then a sample size of 100 will give rise to a model containing $100 \times 12 + 3 = 1,203$ variables and $100 \times 7 + 1 = 701$ constraints, well within the limits. The smaller number of simulation trials may not provide quite as much precision as 1,000, but it is still a good representation of uncertainty in the problem.

The appropriate options for a two-stage problem with recourse decisions, if it can be formulated as a linear problem, are the following:

> Optimization Model group: Solve Uncertain Models = Stochastic Transformation
> Transformation group: Stochastic Transformation = Deterministic Equivalent

With these settings and the smaller sample size, Solver produces an optimal solution. The optimal solution chooses capacity levels that maximize expected profit over all simulated outcomes for the second-stage problem. In the optimal solution shown in Figure 15.18, the solution for capacity levels is 463 at the CA plant, 934 at MI, and 375 at SC. The values for the recourse decisions shown in the figure are appropriate only for the simulation trial that is displayed. In fact, Solver compiled 100 distinct sets of optimal recourse decisions, one for each simulation trial. These cases can be examined individually by clicking on the left and right arrows on the Tools tab on the Analytic Solver Platform ribbon. Alternatively, we can go to the drop-down menu between the two arrows and select Sample Mean. This step places the optimal value of the objective function (that is, the expected profit) in the objective cell, C20, as shown in Figure 15.18.

Since this method uses simulation to generate 100 outcomes for demand and then solves for the optimal recourse decisions for each simulation trial, we should expect different results on successive runs if we change the random seed. To test the extent to which the optimal capacities vary from run to run, we repeated the two-stage optimization five additional times. The following table summarizes the results:

Plant	CA	MI	SC	Total
Deterministic case (Fig. 15.17)	400	850	300	1,550
Stochastic case (Fig. 15.18)	**463**	**934**	**375**	**1,772**
Run 1	455	926	362	1,742
Run 2	459	938	375	1,772
Run 3	461	940	376	1,777
Run 4	465	950	378	1,793
Run 5	460	950	377	1,787
Average	460	941	373	1,774

The results in the table reveal that the optimal capacities show little variation among the runs. The three capacities found in Figure 15.18 are all within the range from the minimum to the maximum in the other five runs.

If we compare the optimal capacities in the two-stage problem to those in the deterministic problem, we find optimal capacity in the two-stage problem is about 14 percent larger. What explains the difference? In the deterministic solution, the optimal capacities are identical to the demands from the region(s) they serve: there is never too much capacity or too little. But when there is randomness in demand, we face the trade-off of too much capacity (and unnecessary fixed costs) versus too little capacity (and lost profits). Given the relative scale of those two opportunity costs, it's not surprising that the optimal capacities are larger in the probabilistic case than in the deterministic case.

If we cycle through the solutions to the recourse problem (by clicking the left and right arrows on the Tools tab on the ribbon), we see that in many cases the pattern of shipments is identical to that in the deterministic case. Occasionally CA supplies a portion of demand from the Central region and SC supplies a portion from the East. MI usually supplies two regions but sometimes three or even four.

Another important feature of this problem that distinguishes it from the deterministic case is that the profit we can expect to attain under the optimal solution is itself random because it depends on the demands. For every random sample drawn from the demand distributions, there is a unique set of optimal production and shipment recourse variables and a corresponding realized profit. The distribution of profit can also be viewed by cycling through the solutions to the recourse problem and recording the corresponding value of profit in cell C20. In our run, the distribution of profit ranged from a low of $25,977 to a high of $40,146. Thus, even when we can optimize our production decisions after demand is known, profits can still vary over quite a large range. Finally, the mean profit over the one hundred trials is $34,457, as can be verified by selecting Sample Mean from the drop-down menu between the arrows on the Tools menu. Interestingly, this figure is greater than the optimal solution to the deterministic version of the problem, indicating that the ability to take advantage of the timing in recourse decisions can lead to greater profit. The distribution of profits gives a far more realistic picture of the true uncertainties facing Bagby Chemical than does the deterministic solution.

15.6 SUMMARY

Simulation is primarily a way to describe uncertainty in the results of a model. It does not automatically provide insight into which decision variables lead to the best possible value of the objective. Thus, optimizing within a simulation analysis is not routine. The tools of deterministic optimization—the various algorithms in Solver—do not directly apply because in a simulation model the objective function is a probability distribution. Nevertheless, several effective approaches exist if we want to optimize within simulation, ranging from simple grid search to sophisticated uses of Solver.

Simulation models with one or two variables can be optimized using a variety of techniques. Grid search is the general name for a procedure that evaluates the objective over a pre-specified set of values of the decision variables. Grid search can be automated easily using simulation sensitivity.

To optimize simulation models with three or more decision variables requires the use of Solver. In the most general approach, we rely on the evolutionary solver to find solutions when the objective is an expected value or when the expected value of an output cell is subject to constraints. Sometimes a tail probability, rather than an expected value, is the key statistic in an objective or a constraint. When constraints can be violated a specified percentage of the time, Solver offers the Value at Risk option to represent the constraints. Value at Risk can also be recognized in the

objective. When the concern is mainly with the size of a violation, rather than its frequency, Solver offers the Conditional Value at Risk option.

Two-stage problems with recourse are characterized by a three-step sequence consisting of: (1) determining the value of strategic decision variables, (2) observing random outcomes, and (3) determining the values of tactical decision variables. In these problems, we first make decisions for the long run, then we learn how random occurrences are resolved, and finally, we make short-run decisions within the limitations imposed by our previous long-run decisions. Solver enables us to handle linear problems of this type by identifying recourse decision variables and exploiting a transformation that uses a larger, deterministic-equivalent model.

SUGGESTED READINGS

Winston, W. 1999. *Decision Making under Uncertainty with RISK Optimizer.* Newfield, NY: Palisade.

This handbook contains thirty-four worked examples for optimization in simulation. It uses @Risk and RISKOptimizer, but the examples can be converted to Analytic Solver Platform quite easily.

EXERCISES

SIMULATION SENSITIVITY PROBLEMS

1. *Airline Revenue Management.* Alpha Airlines has ordered a new fleet of DC-717s. At this stage of the contract, Alpha's operations manager must specify the seating configuration on the aircraft that will be used on the Boston-Atlanta-Chicago-Boston circuit. Alpha flies this route once each day.

The configuration decision involves specifying how many rows will be allocated for first class and how many for tourist class. If the aircraft were configured entirely of tourist rows (containing six seats each), there would be forty rows. First-class seats are wider and afford more legroom, so that, in order to make room for one first-class row (containing four seats), two tourist rows must be removed. Thus, conversion from tourist to first-class seating involves the loss of some seats, but the conversion may be appealing because the revenues are higher for first-class passengers than for tourist passengers (see Exhibit 1).

A perfect match between the configuration and the demand for seats is seldom possible. Historical data suggest a probability distribution of demand for seats on each leg (as detailed in Exhibit 2). There is another distribution for the fraction of demand that corresponds to first-class seats (Exhibit 3), which seems to apply on all legs, although the fraction that occurs in one market on any day is independent of the fraction in the other markets. Finally, there is some chance that all seats in either seating category will be booked on a given leg when demand for that category occurs. Under present management policies, such demand is simply lost to competitors.

EXHIBIT 1 **Revenue per Seat**

	First-class	Tourist
Boston-Atlanta	$400	$175
Atlanta-Chicago	$400	$150
Chicago-Boston	$450	$200

EXHIBIT 2 **Distribution of Total Demand for Seats**

	minimum	most likely	maximum
Boston-Atlanta	160	180	220
Atlanta-Chicago	140	200	240
Chicago-Boston	150	200	225

EXHIBIT 3 **Distribution of Fraction First Class**

Fraction	5%	12%	15%
Probability	0.2	0.5	0.3

The fixed cost of operating the full circuit is $100,000 per day. Alpha Airlines is seeking a profit-maximizing configuration.

a. What is the expected profit per day for a configuration of three first-class rows and thirty-four tourist rows? For convenience, you may allow fractional values of demand in your model.

b. With the suggested configuration, what proportion of the days will Alpha at least break even on the Boston–Atlanta–Chicago–Boston circuit?

c. For the demand that Alpha faces, what is the maximum expected profit, and what is the seat configuration that achieves it?

2. *Inventory Planning.* Rowers North, Inc. (RNI) would like to develop an inventory policy that will minimize the total cost associated with the company's inventory of rowing machines, while ensuring that few customers are unable to purchase a machine the day they walk in the store.

The type of inventory policy they prefer involves a fixed reorder point and order quantity. The *reorder point* is the level of inventory at which an order is sent to the supplier. The *order quantity* is the amount ordered each time. These are decision variables, but once chosen, they will not be changed.

Inventory planning at RNI is complicated by several factors. One is uncertainty in demand. Weekly demand can range from zero to five machines. Data covering the past year is given in Exhibit 4. A further complication is that the time it takes for an order to arrive from the manufacturer is variable. This lead time has been as long as four weeks. Exhibit 5 gives the actual lead times for the twenty most recent orders. (Once an order has been placed, the lead time is determined by the supplier and communicated to RNI.)

Some of the relevant cost data are known. For example, it costs $1 per week to hold a rowing machine in inventory, and it costs $50 to place an order (regardless of its size).

One of the central issues for RNI is the cost of being out of stock. Since there are a number of competing retailers in the area, it is common for a customer who doesn't find the preferred machine in stock to leave and look for it elsewhere. Some customers may be loyal enough to wait until the product is back in stock, but even those customers may be displeased by the service they receive. The VP of marketing has suggested that the cost of an unsatisfied customer is simply the forgone margin on the lost sale (roughly $50 per machine). Others in the company argue that the cost is less, perhaps much less.

Note that if RNI places an order in every week in which final inventory falls below the reorder point, it may find itself with multiple, redundant orders arriving in subsequent weeks. To control this, firms typically track their *order backlog* (i.e., the quantity of units ordered but not yet received). They then take the backlog into account when deciding whether to order in a given week.

a. Estimate the total cost for a reorder point of 1 and a reorder quantity of 5.

b. Determine an optimal reorder point and order quantity.

c. How sensitive is the optimal solution to the cost of an unsatisfied customer (in the range from $25 to $75)?

EXHIBIT 4

Week	Demand	Week	Demand	Week	Demand
1	3	21	4	41	1
2	0	22	1	42	0
3	1	23	1	43	1
4	1	24	2	44	0
5	0	25	0	45	1
6	1	26	1	46	4
7	5	27	1	47	1
8	1	28	0	48	1
9	1	29	1	49	1
10	1	30	5	50	1
11	1	31	0	51	0
12	0	32	1	52	2
13	1	33	1		
14	2	34	1		
15	2	35	1		
16	4	36	3		
17	2	37	1		
18	1	38	5		
19	3	39	0		
20	1	40	1		

EXHIBIT 5

Order	Lead Time (wks.)
1	3
2	1
3	2
4	3
5	1
6	4
7	3
8	3
9	2
10	1
11	4
12	2
13	3
14	3
15	2
16	3
17	3
18	3
19	3
20	2

3. *Valuing a Real Option.* You have been hired to estimate the value of the startup company Garcia, Ltd. Garcia has one product, which is expected to sell in the first year for $100. The price will grow in subsequent years by an amount given by a normal distribution with a mean of 5 percent and a standard deviation of 3 percent. Initial sales will be 5,000 units, expected to grow at 5 percent. The unit cost initially will be $75, and this will grow at a rate given by a normal distribution with a mean of 10 percent and a standard deviation of 3 percent. The valuation will be based on a time horizon of ten years. The discount rate is 10 percent.

Garcia wants to investigate an option to decide in year 6 whether to continue in business or go out of business. (This is what is known as a *real option*, as opposed to the *financial options* discussed in the text.) Specifically, management intends to execute the option to go out of business at the end of year 6 if the year 6 contribution is less than some cutoff value. If they opt to go out of business, they will receive zero contribution in years 7–10.

a. Estimate the expected NPV of the business *without* the option to go out of business.

b. What is the *optimal* cutoff value? That is, what cutoff value should Garcia use in year 6 to maximize the expected NPV of the company from the start?

c. The value of this option is the *difference* between the expected NPV *with* the option from part (b) and the expected NPV *without* the option from part (a). What is the value of this option?

4. *Production Planning with Returns.* A computer manufacturer sells its laptop model through a web-based distributor, who buys at a unit cost of $200 and sells at a unit price of $500. The product life cycle is so short that the distributor is given only one opportunity to order stock before the technology becomes obsolete and a new model becomes available. At the beginning of the cycle, the distributor orders a stock level in the face of uncertain retail demand. Based on similar experiences in the past, the distributor believes that a reasonable demand model is a uniform distribution with a minimum of 1,000 and a maximum of 8,000 laptops. The items originally stocked are ultimately sold, returned, or scrapped. Customers place orders on the Web, and the distributor tries to satisfy their orders from stock. If there is a stockout, demands are lost.

The computer manufacturer offers the distributor a returns policy of the following form: It will pay $100 for each returned unit at the end of the product life cycle, but only up to a maximum of 20 percent of the original number of units ordered. Excess stock that cannot be returned to the manufacturer is picked up as scrap material by an electronics recycling center, with no cost or revenue involved. The decision facing the distributor is to choose an appropriate stock level.

a. Suppose there is no ceiling on the return of excess laptops. How many laptops should the distributor stock in order to maximize its expected profit?

b. With the returns ceiling in place, how many laptops should the distributor stock?

c. In part (b), what would be the maximum expected profit for the distributor?

d. What would be the corresponding expected profit for the *manufacturer* if the manufacturing cost is $125 per laptop, and the distributor uses the policy in part (b)?

5. *Overbooking in the Hospitality Industry.* A small hotel has 50 rooms that rent for $105 per night and cost $45 to clean and prepare each night they are used. All rentals are by reservation and there is a 10 percent chance that an individual reservation will not show up. If a customer arrives at the hotel with a reservation and there is no room available due to overbooking, the hotel will rebate the cost of the room and pay on average $150 to put the customer up at another hotel. The hotel would like to determine its *overbooking limit*: the number of rooms to accept reservations for each night in excess of capacity. Its objective is to maximize expected profits.

a. What is the expected profit with an overbooking limit of 50?

b. What is the optimal overbooking limit?

c. Using the optimal overbooking limit, what is the expected number of customers turned away?

d. How sensitive is the optimal overbooking limit to rental prices in the range from $90 to $125 per night?

6. *New Technology.* A firm is trying to decide whether to enter a highly uncertain market now or to wait to decide two years from now, when the size of the market will be less uncertain. If it enters now it must invest $3 billion, while if it waits to invest two years from now the costs will rise to $4 billion. The market size in units this year will be normally distributed with a mean of 5 million and a standard deviation of 1 million. The growth rate in subsequent years will be normally distributed with a mean of 10 percent and a standard deviation of 5 percent (whatever the growth rate turns out to be, it will be the same in all future years). Unit margins each year are normally distributed with a mean of $50 and a standard deviation of $10. The discount rate is 15 percent and the analysis should cover 15 years.

a. What is the expected NPV if the firm invests now?

b. What is the expected NPV if the firm invests in two years?

c. Modify your model to implement a policy in which the firm will invest after two years only if the market size in year 2 exceeds a cutoff value. What is the optimal cutoff and the resulting expected NPV?

STOCHASTIC OPTIMIZATION PROBLEMS

7. *Capacity Planning.* Lang Drug needs to determine the proper capacity level for a new drug, Niagara. Its goal is to maximize the expected NPV earned from the drug during years 0–14, assuming a discount rate of 10 percent per year. It costs $10 to build enough capacity to produce one unit of drug per year. All construction cost is incurred during year 0. It costs $1 per year to maintain a unit of annual production capacity. In year 1, demand will be for 160,000 units of Niagara. The mean annual percentage growth of demand for Niagara is equally likely to assume any value between 10 percent and 20 percent. The actual growth rate of demand during any year is normally distributed with the given mean and a standard deviation of 6 percent. During year 1, each unit of Niagara sells for $8. The price of Niagara will almost surely grow at 5 percent per year. Unit variable cost is known to be 40 percent of the sales price.

Suppose that Lang Drug has the additional opportunity to review demand during year 5 and, if desired, build additional capacity. This means that Lang Drug may not need to build as much capacity during year 1, because they can wait and see whether demand will be high. If demand is high, they can ramp up capacity during year 5 for future years; if not, they can stick with their year 1 capacity. To model this situation, assume that after observing year 5 demand, Lang Drug proceeds as follows: If the ratio of year 5 demand to capacity exceeds some cutoff point C, then Lang Drug will add capacity. If capacity is added, then Lang Drug will add enough capacity to bring total capacity to a multiple M of year 5 demand. We assume it costs $12 to build one unit of capacity at the end of year 5. Thus, Lang Drug's capacity strategy is defined by three decisions:

- initial capacity (year 1)
- the cutoff value C, which determines whether capacity is added after year 5 (assume that capacity arrives in time for year 6)
- the multiple M that defines how much capacity is added.

a. Assuming Lang Drug *cannot* build additional capacity in year 5, what capacity level will maximize expected discounted profit? Assume that all building costs are incurred during year 0 and that all cash flows occur at the beginning of the year.

b. With the additional opportunity to review demand and add capacity in year 5, what values would you recommend for the initial capacity, for C, and for M? What is the maximum expected discounted profit when these parameters are optimized?

8. *The Secretary Problem.* You have been asked to interview candidates for an open secretarial position. Each candidate's qualifications for the job can be modeled with a lognormal distribution with a mean of 10 and a standard deviation of 5. Unfortunately, you must decide whether to offer the job to each candidate in turn before being able to interview additional candidates. In other words, you will interview candidate 1 and decide to make an offer or not. If you do not make an offer to candidate 1 you will interview candidate 2 and again make an offer or not. If you pass on candidate 2 you will go on to candidate 3, and so on. If you get to the 10th candidate without having made an offer, you will be forced to accept that candidate regardless of his or her qualifications. Assume all offers are accepted.

Your objective is to hire the candidate with the highest possible qualifications. To achieve this you plan to set minimum acceptable scores (MAS) at each interview. For example, you might decide to accept the first candidate with a score over 8. Then your MAS would be 8 at each interview. An alternative policy would be to accept over 8 on the first interview, over 7 on the second, and so on. In general, you have 9 decision variables: one MAS for each interview.

a. What are the expected qualifications of the candidate hired if all MAS are set at 5?

b. What is the best choice for the MAS if you use the same MAS for all interviews?

c. Using Solver and 9 decision variables, determine the best policy. What are the optimal values for the 9 MAS and the resulting expected qualifications?

d. Using simulation sensitivity, determine which of the nine MAS have the biggest impact on the expected qualifications of the candidate hired.

e. Assume that a linear relationship applies among the 9 MAS. In other words, parameterize the decisions using the linear equation *MAS(stage t)* = $a + bt$, where t ranges from 1 for the first interview to 9 for the last. What is the optimal policy under this assumption and what are the resulting expected qualifications?

9. *Pricing Surplus Inventory.* A large retailer of kitchen appliances has asked you for advice on how much to stock and how to price leftovers of its products.

Here's a typical situation: Demand for espresso machines in the northeast region runs about 2,000 per year (with a standard deviation of 500). They cost the retailer $20 and sell for $40. Since the models change yearly, unsold machines can be hard to sell at the end of the year. Steep markdowns are usually offered, but no real effort has gone into determining what price to set for unsold stock, since the relationship between the price and sales has not been well understood. Management has estimated the following relationship between the price they set for leftovers and demand. Note: this represents *mean* demand; actual demand may vary around this mean by a standard deviation of 20 percent of the mean.

Price for leftover stock	Mean demand for leftovers
$0	1000
$10	600
$15	450
$20	300
$25	150
$30	10

For intermediate values, use linear interpolation. For example, demand at a price of $16 is $450 - (16 - 15)/(20 - 15) \times (450 - 300) = 420$.

The retailer needs to know how many machines to order originally, as well as how to set prices on leftover stock. Since the number of units left over is unpredictable, it needs to select recommended price points for its various outlets that will apply regardless of the situation. A typical price schedule is as follows:

Quantity left	Recommended price
0	$30
10	$25
150	$20
300	$18
450	$16
600	$14
1000	$12

Again, to determine the recommended price for intermediate values, use linear interpolation.

a. What is the expected profit for an order quantity of 2,000, given that they price all leftovers at a price of $25 regardless of the quantity left?

b. Based on the assumptions in a), show how expected profit varies for order quantities between 1,000 and 3,000 (with a step size of 100). Also, determine the probability that profits are negative, and show how this varies across the same range of order quantities.

c. Determine the optimal values for the order quantity and the seven recommended price points (as in the second table above).

10. *Call Center Staffing.* A high-volume call center must determine how many customer service representatives (CSRs) to schedule each day of the week to cover the call volume. CSRs work a five-day week with two days off but can start their week on any day. For example, CSRs who start their week on Wednesday work Wednesday through Sunday with Monday and Tuesday off. Average call volumes (in units of CSRs) are given in the following table (actual call volume is normally distributed, with a standard deviation given by 10 percent of the mean.)

Day	Call volume
Sunday	22
Monday	45
Tuesday	37
Wednesday	33
Thursday	34
Friday	40
Saturday	29

The regular daily wage for a CSR is $400. However, if on a given day volume is such that the regular staff is inadequate, the call center will bring in extra CSRs for all or part of a day. The wage for this emergency work is equivalent to $800 per day. (In other words, if 0.5 CSR units of work are needed on an emergency basis, the cost is $400.)

a. If the call center's objective is to minimize the total cost, including emergency staffing cost, what is the optimal number of CSRs to hire each day and what is the resulting cost?

b. How much emergency staffing will be required under the optimal plan?

c. How would the staffing plan and the minimum cost change if overtime costs were either $600 or $1,000?

d. Working on weekends is unpopular, which leads to higher than normal absenteeism on Saturdays and Sundays. Would it be advantageous for the call center to pay a $100 bonus (a daily wage of $500) for work on Saturdays and Sundays?

11. *Capacity Planning* (Source: Winston, *Decision Making Under Uncertainty*, pp. 123–128.) An electric utility currently operates ten plants. The following table gives the fixed costs, variable costs, and capacities of each of these plants. Daily demand is highly uncertain, given by a normal distribution with a mean of 200,000 kwh and a standard deviation of 40,000 kwh. The utility produces power using the cheapest plants it has to meet the demand each day. If demand exceeds its total capacity, it buys power on the open market at $15/kwh. The utility needs to determine which plants to keep open in the long term, given that it will choose the cost-minimizing plants to use to produce power each day.

Plant	Fixed cost ($000)	Variable cost ($/kwh)	Capacity (000 kwh)
1	122	4.3	25
2	185	5.6	34
3	95	6.7	19
4	118	7.8	23
5	121	12.0	14
6	135	4.1	16
7	103	4.9	20
8	188	6.2	21
9	119	5.6	33
10	156	6.9	12

a. If all ten plants are kept open, what is the total expected cost of meeting demand?

b. If the utility is allowed to close some plants, which ones should it close and what will be the resulting minimum cost?

12. *Project Planning*. An architectural design firm is faced with a decision as to which projects to bid on for the coming year. Ten projects are available for which they are qualified. The following table lists the profit they can expect to make from each project, as well as the initial investment they will have to make and the design time required. They cannot afford to invest more than $55,000 or use more than a total of 1,000 hours of design time. Their objective is to choose those projects that will maximize their expected profit.

Project	Profit ($000)	Investment ($000)	Design time (hours)
1	55	6.2	123
2	75	8.8	145
3	98	8.4	164
4	67	5.9	135
5	78	6.9	153
6	82	8.9	122
7	51	6.7	87
8	90	9.2	145
9	76	6.1	137
10	69	6.0	143

a. Assuming *no uncertainty* in profits, investment, or design time, what is the maximum profit the firm can achieve, and which projects should it select? Note: this solution must not use more investment capital or design time than is available.

b. Represent the uncertainty in profits, investment, and design time using normal distributions, with standard deviations of 5 percent of the mean for profit, 10 percent for the initial investment, and 15 percent for design time. Determine the maximum expected profit the firm can achieve under these assumptions, and which projects it should select. Note: this solution must be such that the investment and design time constraints are violated no more than 5 percent of the time.

Modeling Cases

RETIREMENT PLANNING

Bob Davidson is a 46-year-old tenured professor of marketing at a small New England business school. He has a daughter, Sue, age 6, and a wife, Margaret, age 40. Margaret is a potter, a vocation from which she earns no appreciable income. Before she was married and for the first few years of her marriage to Bob (she was married once previously), she worked at a variety of jobs, mostly involving software programming and customer support.

Bob's grandfather died at age 42; Bob's father died in 1980 at the age of 58. Both died from cancer, although unrelated instances of that disease. Bob's health has been excellent; he is an active runner and skier. There are no inherited diseases in the family with the exception of glaucoma. Bob's most recent serum cholesterol count was 190.

Bob's salary from the school where he works consists of a nine-month salary (currently $95,000), on which the school pays an additional 10 percent into a retirement fund. He also regularly receives support for his research, which consists of an additional two-ninths of his regular salary, although the college does not pay retirement benefits on that portion of his income. (Research support is additional income; it is not intended to cover the costs of research.) Over the 12 years he has been at the college his salary has increased by 4 to 15 percent per year, although faculty salaries are subject to severe compression, so he does not expect to receive such generous increases into the future. In addition to his salary, Bob typically earns $10,000 to 20,000 per year from consulting, executive education, and other activities.

In addition to the 10 percent regular contribution the school makes to Bob's retirement savings, Bob also contributes a substantial amount. He is currently setting aside $7,500 per year (before taxes). The maximum tax-deferred amount he can contribute is currently $10,000; this limit rises with inflation. If he were to increase his savings toward retirement above the limit, he would have to invest after-tax dollars. All of Bob's retirement savings are invested with TIAA–CREF (Teachers Insurance and Annuity Association-College Retirement Equities Fund; home page: www.tiaa-cref.org), which provides various retirement, investment, and insurance services to university professors and researchers. Bob has contributed to Social Security for many years as required by law, but in light of the problems with the Social Security trust fund he is uncertain as to the level of benefits that he will actually receive upon retirement. (The Social Security Administration's website is www.ssa.gov.)

Bob's TIAA-CREF holdings currently amount to $137,000. These are invested in the TIAA long-term bond fund (20 percent) and the Global Equity Fund (80 percent). The Global Equity Fund is invested roughly 40 percent in U.S. equities and 60 percent in non-U.S. equities. New contributions are also allocated in these same proportions.

In addition to his retirement assets, Bob's net worth consists of his home (purchase price $140,000 in 1987; Bob's current equity is $40,000); $50,000 in a rainy-day fund (invested in a short-term money market mutual fund with Fidelity Investments); and $24,000 in a Fidelity Growth and Income Fund for his daughter's college tuition. He has a term life insurance policy with a value of $580,000; this policy has no asset value but pays its face value (plus inflation) as long as Bob continues to pay the premiums. He has no outstanding debts in addition to his mortgage, other than monthly credit-card charges.

Should Bob die while insured, the proceeds on his life insurance are tax free to his wife. Similarly, if he dies before retirement, his retirement assets go to his wife tax free. Either one of them can convert retirement assets into annuities without any immediate taxation; the monthly income from the annuities is then taxed as ordinary income.

Bob's mother is 72 and in good health. She is retired and living in a co-op apartment in Manhattan. Her net worth is on the order of $300,000. His mother-in-law, who is 70, lives with her second husband. Her husband is 87 and has sufficient assets to pay for nursing home care, if needed, for his likely remaining lifetime. Upon her husband's death, Bob's mother-in-law will receive ownership of their house in Newton, Massachusetts, as well as one-third of his estate (the remaining two-thirds will go to his two children). Her net worth at that point is expected to be in the $300,000–400,000 range.

Bob's goal is to work until he is 60 or 65. He would like to save enough to pay for his daughter's college expenses, but not for her expenses beyond that point. He and his wife would like to travel, and do so now as much as his job and their family responsibilities permit. Upon retirement he would like to be able to travel extensively, although he would be able to live quite modestly otherwise. He does not foresee moving from the small town where he now lives.

Bob has a number of questions about how he should plan for his retirement. Will the amount he is accumulating at his current rate of savings be adequate? How much *should* he be setting aside each year? How much will he have to live on when he retires? How long after retirement will he be able to live comfortably? What are the risks he faces, and how should his retirement planning take these risks into account?

DRAFT TV COMMERCIALS[*]

Your client directs TV advertising for a large corporation that currently relies on a single outside advertising agency. For years, ads have been created using the same plan: The agency creates a draft commercial and, after getting your client's approval, completes production and arranges for it to be aired.

Your client's budget is divided between creating and airing commercials. Typically, about 5 percent of the budget is devoted to creating commercials and 95 percent to airing them. Lately the client has become dissatisfied with the quality of the ads being created. Along with most advertising people, he believes that the ultimate profitability of an advertising campaign is much more strongly influenced by the content of the advertisement than by the level of expenditure on airing or the media utilized (assuming reasonable levels of expenditure). Thus, he is considering increasing the percentage of his budget devoted to the first, "creative" part of the process.

One way to do this is to commission multiple ad agencies to each independently develop a draft commercial. He would then select the one for completion and airing that he determines would be most effective in promoting sales. Of course, since his budget is essentially fixed, the more money he spends on creating draft commercials the less he has to spend on airing commercials. He will have to pay up front for all of the draft commercials before he has a chance to evaluate them.

The standard technique for evaluating a draft commercial involves showing it to a trial audience and asking what they remembered about it later (this is known as "next day recall"). Ads with higher next day recall are generally those with higher effectiveness in the marketplace, but the correlation is far from perfect. A standard method for assessing the effectiveness of a commercial *after* it has been aired is to survey those who watched the show and estimate "retained impressions." Retained impressions are the number of viewers who can recall the essential features of the ad. Ads with higher retained impressions are usually more effective in generating sales, but again the correlation is not perfect. Both the effectiveness of a commercial (the number of retained impressions it creates) and the exposure it receives (the number of times it is aired) will influence sales.

How would you advise your client on the budget split between creating and airing a commercial?

[*]*Source*: O'Conner, G. C., T.R. Willemain, and J. MacLachlau, 1996. "The value of competition among agencies in developing ad compaigns: Revisiting Gross's model." *Journal of Advertising* 25:51–63.

ICEBERGS FOR KUWAIT[*]

The cost of desalinating seawater using conventional technology in the Persian Gulf is high (around 0.1£ per cubic meter) and requires extensive amounts of oil. Some time ago scientists suggested that it could well prove both practically feasible and less expensive to tow icebergs from the Antarctic, a distance of about 9,600 km. Although some of the ice would undoubtedly melt in transit, it was thought that a significant proportion of the iceberg would remain intact upon arrival in the Gulf. Bear in mind that since water expands upon freezing, 1 cubic meter of ice produces only 0.85 cubic meter of water.

A study was carried out to evaluate the practical problems associated with such a proposal and to quantify the factors that were likely to influence the economics of such a venture. One factor was the difference in rental costs and capacities of towing vessels (summarized in Table 1). Note that each vessel has a maximum iceberg it can tow (measured in cubic meters). It was found that the melting rate of the iceberg depends on both the towing speed and the distance from the South Pole (see Table 2). The data in

TABLE 1 Towing Vessel Data

Ship Size	Small	Medium	Large
Daily rental (£)	400	600	800
Maximum load (cu. meter)	500,000	1,000,000	10,000,000

TABLE 2 Melting Rates (meter/day)

	Distance from Pole (km)			
	1,000	2,000	3,000	$\geq$4,000
Speed				
1 km/hr	0.06	0.12	0.18	0.24
3 km/hr	0.08	0.16	0.24	0.32
5 km/hr	0.10	0.20	0.30	0.40

this table represents the rate at which a hypothetical spherical iceberg shrinks *in radius* over a day at the given distance from the Pole and at the given towing speed. Finally, fuel cost was found to depend on the towing speed and the (current) size of the iceberg (see Table 3).

Determine whether it is economically feasible to produce water from icebergs in the Persian Gulf, and if it is, determine the best means to do so.

Source: Cross, M. and A.O. Moscardini, 1985. *Learning the Art of Mathematical Modeling*. Ellis Horward Limited, West Sussex.

TABLE 3 Fuel Costs (£/km)

	Current Volume (cu. meter)		
	100,000	1,000,000	10,000,000
Speed			
1 km/hr	8.4	10.5	12.6
3 km/hr	10.8	13.5	16.2
5 km/hr	13.2	16.5	19.8

THE RACQUETBALL RACKET*

It is early in 2000, and a friend of yours has invented a new manufacturing process for producing racquetballs. The resulting high-quality ball has more bounce, but slightly less durability, than the currently popular high-quality ball, which is manufactured by Woodrow, Ltd. The better the players, the more they tend to prefer a lively ball. The primary advantage of the new ball is that it can be manufactured much more inexpensively than the existing ball. Current estimates are that full variable costs for the new ball are $0.52 per ball as compared to $0.95 for the existing ball. (Variable costs include all costs of production, marketing, and distribution that vary with output. It excludes the cost of plant and equipment, overhead, etc.)

Because the new process is unlike well-known production processes, the only reasonable alternative is to build a manufacturing plant specifically for producing these balls. Your friend has calculated that this would require $4–6 million of initial capital. He figures that if he can make a good case to

the bank, he can borrow the capital at about a 10 percent interest rate and start producing racquetballs in a year.

Your friend has offered to make you a partner in the business and has asked you in return to perform a market analysis for him. He has already hired a well-known market research firm, Market Analysis, Ltd., to do some data gathering and preliminary market analysis. The key elements of their final report are given below.

Your problem is to determine how the new balls should be priced, what the resultant market shares will be, and whether the manufacturing plant is a good investment. Your friend is especially concerned about the risks involved and would like some measures of how solid the investment appears to be. He would like you to make a formal presentation of your analysis.

*Adapted from a class assignment developed by Dick Smallwood and Peter Morris.

RACQUETBALL MARKET ANALYSIS
Market Analysis, Ltd.
January 20, 2000

a. The market for this type of high-quality ball is currently dominated by a single major competitor, Woodrow, Ltd. Woodrow specializes in manufacturing balls for all types of sports. It has been the only seller of high-quality racquetballs since the late 1970s. Its current price to retail outlets is $1.25 per ball (the retail markup is typically 100 percent, so these balls retail around $2.50 each, or $5.00 for the typical pack of two).

b. Historical data on the number of people playing the sport, the average retail price of balls, and the (estimated) total sales of balls is given in the following table:

Year	Number Players (Thousands)	Retail Price (per ball)	Balls Sold (millions)
1985	600	$1.75	5.932
1986	635	$1.75	6.229
1987	655	$1.80	6.506
1988	700	$1.90	6.820
1989	730	$1.90	7.161
1990	762	$1.90	7.895
1991	812	$2.00	7.895
1992	831	$2.20	8.224
1993	877	$2.45	8.584
1994	931	$2.45	9.026
1995	967	$2.60	9.491
1996	1,020	$2.55	9.996
1997	1,077	$2.50	10.465
1998	1,139	$2.50	10.981

c. According to industry trade association projections, the total number of players will grow about 10 percent a year for the next 10 years and then stabilize at a relatively constant level.

d. In order to assess relative preferences in the marketplace, a concept test was performed. In this test, 200 customers were asked to use both balls over a three-month period, and then specify which ball they would buy at various prices. Many customers indicated they would pay a premium for the Woodrow ball, based on their satisfaction with it and its better durability. Nevertheless, about 11 percent of the customers interviewed indicated a preference for the new, bouncier ball at equal prices. The actual observed distribution of price premiums is as follows:

Price Ratio*	Percent Who Would Buy New Ball
0.5	0
1.0	11
1.5	41
2.0	76
2.5	95
3.0	100

*Price of Woodrow ball / Price of new ball.

THE XYZ COMPANY*

The XYZ Company makes widgets and sells to a market that is just about to expand after a period of stability. As the year starts, the widgets are manufactured at a cost of $0.75 and sold at a market price of $1.00. In addition, the firm has 1,000 widgets in finished goods inventory and a cash account of $875 at the beginning of January. During January, sales amount to 1,000 units, which is where they have been in the recent past.

Profitability looks good in January. The 1,000 units of sales provide profits for the month of $250. This amount goes right into the cash account, increasing it to $1,125.

In February, the sales level rises to 1,500 units. For the next several months, it looks like demand will rise by 500 each month, providing a very promising profit outlook.

The XYZ Company keeps an inventory of finished goods on hand. This practice allows it to meet customer demand promptly, without having to worry about delays in the factory. The specific policy is always to hold inventory equal to the previous month's sales level. Thus, the 1,000 units on hand at the start of January are just the right amount to support January demand. When demand rises in February, there is a need to produce for stock as well as for meeting demand, because the policy requires that inventory must rise to 1,500 by March. February production is therefore 2,000 units, providing enough widgets to both meet demand in February and raise inventory to 1,500 by the end of the month.

Your first task is to trace the performance of the XYZ Company on a monthly basis, as demand continues to increase at the rate of 500 units per month. Assume that all revenues are collected in the same month when sales are made, all costs are paid in the same month when production occurs, and profit is equal to the difference between revenues and costs. The cost of producing items for inventory is included in the calculation of monthly profit. Trace profits, inventory, and cash position on a monthly basis, through the month of June. This analysis will give us an initial perspective on the financial health of the XYZ Company. Does the company seem to be successful?

In reality, the XYZ Company behaves like many other firms: it pays its bills promptly, but it collects cash from its customers a little less promptly. In fact, it takes a full month to collect the revenues generated by sales. This means that the firm has receivables every month, which are collected during the following month.

XYZ Company actually starts the year with receivables of $1,000, in addition to inventory worth $750 and a cash account worth $875. (Therefore, its total assets come to $2,625 at the start of the year.) A month later, receivables remain at $1,000, inventory value remains at $750, and cash increases to $1,125 (reflecting receivables of $1,000 collected, less production expenses of $750).

When February sales climb to 1,500 units, XYZ Company produces 2,000 widgets. Of this amount, 1,500 units are produced to meet demand and 500 units are produced to augment inventory. This means that a production bill of $1,500 is paid in February. During February, the January receivables of $1,000 are collected, and at the end of February, there are receivables of $1,500, reflecting sales made on account during the month.

For accounting purposes, XYZ Company calculates its net income by recognizing sales (even though it has not yet collected the corresponding revenues) and by recognizing the cost of producing the items sold. The cost of producing items for inventory does not enter into its calculation of net income. In January, net income is therefore calculated as $250, representing the difference between the revenue from January sales of $1,000 and the cost of producing those 1,000 units, or $750.

Refine your initial analysis to trace the performance of the XYZ Company, again with demand increasing at the rate of 500 units per month. Assume that all revenues are collected in the month following the month when sales occur, but that all costs are paid in the same month when they occur. Trace net income, receivables, inventory, and cash on a monthly basis, through the month of June. This will give us another perspective on the financial health of the XYZ Company. What financial difficulty does the model portray?

*Adapted from a homework exercise developed by Clyde Stickney.

MEDICAL SUPPLIES FOR BANJUL[*]

You are the team leader of a unit of a U.S. nonprofit organization based in Banjul, Gambia (capital city). The nonprofit's mission is to ensure that rural populations worldwide have access to health and sanitation-related supplies. Due to the sudden departure of one of your team leaders, you are taking over responsibility for ordering certain medical supplies for three villages. Each village consists of four groups:

- Senior citizens (those over 65)
- Children (population 12 and under)
- Teens (those aged 13–19)
- The population aged 20–65

The medical supplies required by each village include bandages (types A, B, and C), medical tape, and hearing aids. Children need type A bandages; teens need type B bandages; and adults (i.e., everyone else), need type C bandages. All members of the population use the same kind of medical tape. Only senior citizens require hearing aids. The former team member explained to you that a good rule of thumb is to ensure that at all times a village should keep in stock two bandages per person and hearing aids for 5 percent of the senior citizen population. Cost and packaging information for the products is as follows:

- Type A bandages come in packages of 30. Each package costs $3.00.
- Type B bandages come in packages of 30. Each package costs $5.00.
- Type C bandages come in packages of 30. Each package costs $6.00.

- Medical tape comes in rolls of 2 feet each. You usually use one roll per package of bandages. One roll costs $2.50.
- Hearing aids are sold in single units (1 per package) and are $5.00 each.

Your unit's budget does not enable you to purchase more supplies than you need in a given quarter. At the end of every quarter, one of your team members provides you with the population count by age group for the village and the stocks remaining in each village.

The former team member completed this cumbersome task by hand every quarter. However, owing to your other responsibilities, you will have no more than a few minutes to spend on this task on a quarterly basis—doing it by hand is out of question. In addition, you may be transferred to another post in three to six months, so you may have to pass on the responsibility to a successor before too long.

It is 6:00 a.m. Monday morning. You have three hours left at the city headquarters until you leave to begin two weeks of fieldwork in the villages without computer access. The initial order must be placed by next Friday, so you will have to take care of procuring a check from the finance officer and placing the order before you leave. Other team members are beginning to arrive, but the office is still quiet. Everything else on your plate can wait until you return. Yet, something else could pop up at any moment, so you have to work quickly. You don't have the latest population or stock figures yet, but the team member who has them will arrive at 8:30 a.m.

[*]Contributed by Manisha Shahane.

REID'S RAISIN COMPANY

Located in wine country, Reid's Raisin Company (RRC) is a food-processing firm that purchases surplus grapes from grape growers, dries them into raisins, applies a layer of sugar, and sells the sugar-coated raisins to major cereal and candy companies. At the beginning of the grape-growing season, RRC has two decisions to make. The first involves how many grapes to buy under contract, and the second involves how much to charge for the sugar-coated raisins it sells.

In the spring, RRC typically contracts with a grower who will supply a given amount of grapes in the autumn at a fixed cost of $0.25 per pound. The balance between RRC's grape requirements and those supplied by the grower must be purchased in the autumn, on the open market, at a price that could vary from a historical low of $0.20 per pound to a high of $0.35 per pound. (RRC cannot, however, sell grapes on the open market in the autumn if it has a surplus in inventory, because it has no distribution system for such purposes.)

The other major decision facing RRC is the price to charge for sugar-coated raisins. RRC has several customers who buy RRC's output in price-dependent quantities. RRC negotiates with these processors as a group to arrive at a price for the sugar-coated raisins and the quantity to be bought at that price. The negotiations take place in the spring, long before the open market price of grapes is known.

Based on prior years' experience, Mary Jo Reid, RRC's general manager, believes that if RRC prices the sugar-coated raisins at $2.20 per pound, the processors' orders will total 750,000 pounds of sugar-coated raisins. Furthermore, this total will increase by 15,000 pounds for each penny reduction in sugar-coated raisin price below $2.20. The same relationship holds in the other direction: demand will drop by 15,000 for each penny increase. The price of $2.20 is a tentative starting point in the negotiations.

Sugar-coated raisins are made by washing and drying grapes into raisins, followed by spraying the raisins with a sugar coating that RRC buys for $0.55 per pound. It takes 2.5 pounds of grapes plus 0.05 pound of coating to make one pound of sugar-coated raisins, the balance being water that evaporates during grape drying. In addition to the raw materials cost for the grapes and the coating, RRC's processing plant incurs a variable cost of $0.20 to process one pound of grapes into raisins, up to its capacity of 1,500,000 pounds of grapes. For volumes above 1,500,000 pounds of grapes, RRC outsources grape processing to another food processor, which charges RRC $0.45 per pound. This price includes just the processing cost, as RRC supplies both the grapes and the coating required. RRC also incurs fixed (overhead) costs in its grape-processing plant of $200,000 per year.

Mary Jo has asked you to analyze the situation in order to guide her in the upcoming negotiations. Her goal is to examine the effect of various "What-if?" scenarios on RRC's profits. As a basis for the analysis, she suggests using a contract purchase price of $0.25, with a supply quantity of 1 million pounds from the grower, along with a selling price of $2.20 for sugar-coated raisins. She is primarily interested in evaluating annual pretax profit as a function of the selling price and the open-market grape price. She believes that the open-market grape price is most likely to be $0.30.

THE BIG RIG TRUCK RENTAL COMPANY

The Big Rig Rental Company, which owns and rents out 50 trucks, is for sale for $400,000. Tom Grossman, the company's owner, wants you to develop a five-year economic analysis to assist buyers in evaluating the company.

The market rate for truck rentals is currently $12,000 per year per truck. At this base rate, an average of 62 percent of the trucks will be rented each year. Tom believes that if the rent were lowered by $1,200 per truck per year, utilization would increase by seven percentage points. He also believes that this relationship would apply to additional reductions in the base rate. For example, at a $7,200 rental rate, 90 percent of the trucks would be rented. This relationship would apply to increases in the base rate as well. Over the next five years, the base rental rate should remain stable.

At the end of five years, it is assumed that the buyer will resell the business for cash. Tom estimates that the selling price will be three times the gross revenue in the final year.

The cost of maintaining the fleet runs about $4,800 per truck per year (independent of utilization), which includes inspection fees, licenses, and normal mainte-

nance. Big Rig has fixed office costs of $60,000 per year and pays property taxes of $35,000 per year. Property taxes are expected to grow at a rate of 3 percent per year, and maintenance costs are expected to grow 9 percent per year due to the age of the fleet. However, office costs are predicted to remain level. Profits are subject to a 30 percent income tax. The tax is zero if profit is negative.

Cash flow in the final year would include cash from the sale of the business. Because the trucks have all been fully depreciated, there are no complicating tax effects: Revenue from the sale of the business will effectively be taxed at the 30 percent rate. Investment profit for the buyer is defined to be the Net Present Value of the annual cash flows, computed at a discount rate of 10 percent. (All operating revenues and expenses are in cash.) The calculation of NPV includes the purchase price, incurred at the beginning of year 1, and net income from operations (including the sale price in year 5) over five years (incurred at the end of the year). There would be no purchases or sales of trucks during the five years.

FLEXIBLE INSURANCE COVERAGE

A company health plan offers four alternatives for coverage, from a low-cost plan with a high deductible to a high-cost plan with a low deductible. The details of coverage are given in the following table. The Human Resources Department would like to develop a means to help any employee, whether single or married, small family or large, low medical expenses or high, to compare these plan alternatives.

			Plan Options and Costs		
				Annual Premium	
	Deductible	Co-insurance	1-Person	2-Person	Family
Option 1	$1,500/$2,500	none	$1,825	$3,651	$4,929
Option 2	500/1,000	20%	2,016	4,032	5,444
Option 3	250/500	20%	2,245	4,491	6,063
Option 4	100/200	10%	2,577	5,154	6,959

The deductible amount is paid by the employee. The first figure applies to an individual; the second applies to two-person or family coverage. In the case of Option 1, for example, this means that the insurance coverage takes effect once an individual has paid for $1,500 worth of expenses. (This limit holds for any individual under two-person or family coverage, as well as for an individual with one-person coverage.) In the case of two-person or family coverage, the insurance also takes effect once the household has incurred $2,500 worth of expenses.

The co-insurance is the percentage of expenses that must be paid by the employee when the insurance coverage takes effect. In the case of Option 2, for example, this means that the insurance covers 80 percent of all expenses after the deductible amount has been reached.

The Annual Premium is the cost of the insurance to the employee.

SNOEY SOFTWARE COMPANY

Snoey Software Company is developing a new piece of software that can be tailored to various market segments. At this stage, the developers envision three versions of the software: an Educational version, a Large-Scale version, and a High-Speed version. Each is built around the same basic design, but a number of data-handling and input/output procedures are different in the different versions. By creating these versions, Snoey hopes to extract more value from the marketplace than it could obtain with just one version.

Currently, the developers are close to completing the Educational version, but they have done little more than outline the other two versions. The estimated R&D expenditures required to finish those tasks are $100,000 for the Large-Scale version, and $150,000 for the High-Speed version. The actual variable costs are estimated to be $10 for the Educational version, $20 for the Large-Scale version, and $36 for the High-Speed version.

The marketing director at Snoey Software has identified five market segments that would respond differently to the new software: (1) university students, (2) academic and government laboratories, (3) consultants, (4) small companies, and (5) large companies. The potential sales in each of these markets, together with the cost of advertising in each market, are as follows:

Segment	Market Size	Marketing Costs
Students	400,000	$350,000
Laboratories	1,200	75,000
Consultants	12,000	150,000
Small companies	24,000	200,000
Large companies	6,000	100,000

In a series of surveys and focus groups, the marketing staff has tested the interest of each market segment in the three different versions of the software. The results of the tests have been summarized in a table of values that represent the prices each segment would be willing to pay for each of the versions. This information is shown in the following table.

Segment	Educational	Large-Scale	High-Speed
Students	$25	$40	$75
Laboratories	125	300	1,000
Consultants	100	500	750
Small companies	75	250	500
Large companies	150	1,000	2,500

In order to develop a price structure for the software, the marketing director uses the following logic. For each segment and for each version, the potential customer will calculate the difference between the price and the value. The highest difference will dictate what the customer will purchase. On that basis, it will be possible to estimate the sales volumes of each version in each segment and compute the resulting profits.

You have been hired to build a model that will compute the sales of each version in each market segment and then calculate the resulting profit for Snoey Software. Given the approach they have taken thus far, the company is committed to the Educational version, but it could halt development activities on either or both of the other versions. The question on everybody's mind is: which versions should be brought to market?

COX CABLE AND WIRE COMPANY

Meredith Ceh breathed a sigh of relief. Finally, all the necessary figures seemed to be correctly in place, and her spreadsheet looked complete. She was confident that she could analyze the situation that John Cox had described, but she wondered if there were other concerns she should be addressing in her response.

Mr. Cox, president of Cox Cable and Wire Company, and grandson of the company's founder, had asked Meredith to come up with plans to support the preliminary contract he had worked out with Midwest Telephone Company. The contract called for delivery of 340 reels of cable during the summer. He was leaving the next day to negotiate a final contract with Midwest and wanted to be sure he understood all of the implications.

According to Mr. Cox, he had been looking for a chance to become a supplier to a large company like Midwest, and this seemed to be the right opportunity. Demand from some of Cox Cable's traditional customers had slackened, and as a result there was excess capacity during the summer. Nevertheless, he wanted to be sure that, from the start, his dealings with Midwest would be profitable, and he had told Meredith that he was looking for cash inflows to exceed cash outflows by at least 25 percent. He also wanted her to confirm that there was sufficient capacity to meet the terms of the contract. He had quickly mentioned a number of other items, but those were secondary to profitability and capacity.

Background

The Cox Cable and Wire Company sold a variety of products for the telecommunications industry. At its Indianapolis plant, the company purchased uncoated wire in standard gauges, assembled it into multiwire cables, and then applied various coatings according to customer specification. The plant essentially made products in two basic families—standard plastic and high-quality Teflon. The two coatings came in a variety of colors, but these were changed easily by introducing different dyes into the basic coating liquid.

The production facilities at Indianapolis consisted of two independent process trains (semiautomated production lines), referred to as the General and National trains, after the companies that manufactured them. Both the plastic-coated and the Teflon-coated cable could be produced on either process train; however, Teflon coating was a faster process due to curing requirements. Planning at Cox Cable was usually done on an annual and then a quarterly basis. The labor force was determined by analyzing forecast demand for the coming year, although revisions were possible as the year developed. Then, on a quarterly basis, more specific machine schedules were made up. Each quarter the process trains were usually shut down for planned maintenance, but the maintenance schedules were determined at the last minute, after production plans were in place, and they were often postponed when the schedule was tight.

As a result of recent expansions, there was not much storage space in the plant. Cable could temporarily be stored in the shipping area for the purposes of loading trucks, but there was no space for cable to be stored for future deliveries. Additional inventory space was available at a nearby public warehouse.

Meredith had become familiar with all of this information during her first week as a summer intern. At the end of the week, she had met with Mr. Cox and he had outlined the Midwest contract negotiation.

The Contract

The preliminary contract was straightforward. Midwest had asked for the delivery quantities outlined in Table 1. Prices had also been agreed on, although Mr. Cox had said he wouldn't be surprised to find Midwest seeking to raise the Teflon delivery requirements during the final negotiation.

Meredith had gone first to the production manager, Jeff Knight, for information about capacity. Jeff had provided her with data on production times (Table 2), which he said

TABLE 1   Contract Delivery Schedule and Prices

Month	Plastic	Teflon
June	50	30
July	100	60
August	50	50
Price	$360	$400

TABLE 2   Production Capabilities, in Hours per Reel

Process Train	Plastic	Teflon
General	2.0	1.5
National	2.5	2.0

TABLE 3   Unscheduled Production Hours

Month	General	National
June	140	250
July	60	80
August	150	100

TABLE 4   Accounting Data for Production

Cost Category	General	National
Machine Depreciation	$50.00/hr	$40.00/hr
Direct labor	16.00	16.00
Supervisor	8.00	8.00
Production Overhead	12.00	12.00

were pretty reliable, given the company's extensive experience with the two process trains. He also gave her the existing production commitments for the summer months, showing the available capacity given in Table 3. Not all of these figures were fixed, he said. Apparently, there was a design for a mechanism that could speed up the General process train. Engineers at Cox Cable planned to install this mechanism in September, adding 80 hours per month to capacity. "We could move up our plans, so that the additional 80 hours would be available to the shop in August," he remarked. "But that would probably run about $900 in overtime expenses, and I'm not sure if it would be worth while."

After putting some of this information into her spreadsheet, Meredith spoke with the plant's controller, Donna Malone, who had access to most of the necessary cost data. Meredith learned that the material in the cables cost $160 per reel for the plastic-coated cable and $200 for the Teflon-coated cable. Packaging costs were $40 for either type of cable, and the inventory costs at the public warehouse came to $10 per reel for each month stored. "That's if you can get the space," Donna commented. "It's a good idea to make reservations a few weeks in advance; otherwise we might find they're temporarily out of space." Donna also provided standard accounting data on production costs (Table 4). According to Donna, about half of the production overhead consisted of costs that usually varied with labor charges, while the rest was depreciation for equipment other than the two process trains. The machine depreciation charges on the two process trains were broken out separately, as determined at the time the machinery was purchased. For example, the General process train originally cost $500,000 ten years ago and had an expected life of five years, or about 10,000 hours, hence its depreciation rate of $50 per hour.

The Analysis

Meredith was able to consolidate all of the information she collected into a spreadsheet. Making what she felt were reasonable assumptions about relevant cost factors, she was able to optimize the production plan, and she determined that it should be possible to meet the 25 percent profitability target. Nevertheless, there seemed to be several factors in it that were subject to change—things that had come up in her various conversations, such as maintenance, warehousing, and the possibility of modifying the contract. She expected that Mr. Cox would quiz her about all of these factors, and she knew it would be important for her to be prepared for his questions.

THE BMW COMPANY

Late in the summer of 1989, the government of Germany was seriously considering an innovative policy affecting the treatment of scrapped vehicles. This policy would make auto manufacturers responsible for recycling and disposal of their vehicles at the end of their useful lives. Sometimes referred to as a "Producer Responsibility" policy, this regulation would obligate the manufacturers of automobiles to take back vehicles that were ready to be scrapped.

The auto takeback proposal was actually the first of several initiatives that would also affect the end-of-life (EOL) treatment of such other products as household appliances and consumer electronics. But in 1989, no other industry had faced anything like this new policy. Managers at BMW and other German automakers struggled to understand the implications for their own company. Perhaps the first exercise was to gauge the magnitude of the economic effect. Stated another way, management wanted to know what the cost of the new policy was likely to be, if BMW continued to do business as usual.

Background

A loose network of dismantlers and shredders managed most of the recycling and disposal of German vehicles, accounting for about 95 percent of EOL volume, or roughly 2.1 million vehicles per year. Dismantling was a labor-intensive process that removed auto parts, fluids, and materials that could be re-sold. The hulk that remained was sold to a shredder. Shredding was a capital-intensive business that separated the remaining materials into distinct streams. Ferrous metals were sold to steel producers, nonferrous metals were sold to specialized metal companies, and the remaining material was typically sent to landfills or incinerators. The material headed for disposal was known as Automobile Shredder Residue (ASR) and consisted of plastic, rubber, foam, glass, and dirt. ASR was virtually impossible to separate into portions with any economic value, so shredders paid for its removal and disposal. As of 1989, the annual volume of ASR came to about 400,000 tons. On average, an automobile stayed in service for about 10 years.

Although dismantlers and shredders were unaffiliated, private businesses in 1989, it was conceivable that, under the new government policy, they would be taken over by the auto companies. Even if they remained independently owned businesses, the costs of dismantling and shredding would ultimately be borne by the auto companies, since the policy made them legally responsible for the waste.

Economics of disposal

The costs in this system had been increasing and, in fact, were about to increase more quickly due to two major trends, one involving disposal costs and the other involving material composition. On the material side, automobiles were being designed with less metal each year and more plastics. In the 1960s, a typical car was made up of more than 80 percent metal, but the new models of 1990 were only about 75 percent metal. This meant that more of the vehicle was destined to end up as ASR. Averaged across the market, autos weighed an average of about 1,000 kg each. See Exhibit 1 for some representative figures.

Exhibit 1. Material Trends in Automobile Composition

Material	1965	1985	1995 (est.)
Iron and Steel	76.0%	68.0%	63.0%
Lead, Copper, and Zinc	4.0%	4.0%	3.0%
Aluminum	2.0%	4.5%	6.5%
Plastics	2.0%	9.0%	13.0%
Fabric, Rubber, and Glass	16.0%	14.5%	14.5%

BMW 1989 Models	Weight (kg)	Plastics Content
3 series	1,150	11.3%
5 series	1,400	10.9%
7 series	1,650	10.3%

On the disposal side, a much more significant trend was in progress. As in most of Europe, landfill options were disappearing in Germany. In 1989, about half of the waste stream found its way to landfills, with 35 percent going to waste-to-energy incinerators, and the remaining 15 percent to recycling of some kind. But the number of landfills was declining, and it looked like this trend would continue, so that by 1999 landfill and incineration would handle approximately equal shares. The effects of supply and demand were visible in the costs of disposal at landfills. Exhibit 2 summarizes recent and projected costs.

Exhibit 2. Recent and Projected (*) Landfill Costs

Year	Cost (DM/ton)
1987	30
1988	40
1989	60
1990	120
1991*	200
1993*	500 ± 100
1995*	1200 ± 600

Many landfills were of older designs, and public concern about their environmental risks had grown. Recent environmental regulations were beginning to restrict the materials that could be taken to landfills, and there was a good chance that ASR would be prohibited. Specially designed hazardous waste landfills were an alternative, but they tended to be three or four times as costly as the typical solid-waste landfill.

Meanwhile, the number of incinerators had grown from a handful in the early 1960s to nearly 50 by 1989, with prospects for another 25 or more in the coming decade. However, incinerators were expensive to build, and awareness of their environmental impacts was growing. In particular, the incineration of plastics had come under special scrutiny. The net effect was that incineration was about twice as costly as landfill disposal in 1989, and it was uncertain how the relative cost of incineration would evolve in the years to come.

Trends in the Market

Prior to the 1980s, BMW cars were known for their reliability and quality. Only during the 80s did BMW acquire a reputation for performance and begin to compete in the high-end market. As a result, its domestic market share had risen from about 5.6 percent at the start of the decade to 6.7 percent in 1989. Some details of financial and market performance for BMW are summarized in Exhibits 3 and 4.

In 1989, BMW seemed poised to benefit from its successes over the previous several years, having consolidated its position in the marketplace. Long-range forecasts predicted that the economy would grow by about 2 percent in the coming decade, with inflation at no more than 4 percent. However, the proposed takeback policy raised questions about whether the company's profitability could endure. Assuming that, in the new regulatory regime, automakers bear the cost of disposal, the task is to estimate how much of the firm's net income will be devoted to EOL vehicles 10 years into the future.

Exhibit 3. Selected Companywide Financial Data for BMW

	1989	1988	1987	1986	1985
Net Sales (DM millions)	20,960	19,880	17,660	15,000	14,240
Sales (Vehicles)	511,000	486,600	459,500	446,100	445,233
Production (Vehicles)	511,500	484,100	461,300	446,400	445,200
Net Income (DM millions)	386.0	375.0	375.0	337.5	300.0

Exhibit 4. Selected Market Data for BMW Automobiles

Cases	1989 Sales	1989 Share	1988 Sales	1988 Share
Germany	191,000	6.7%	180,200	6.4%
Europe (rest)	163,200	1.7%	153,100	1.9%
N. America	69,200	6.4%	78,800	6.8%
Other	57,300	1.1%	47,700	1.1%

THE ERP DECISION*

During the 1990s, many large companies began to realize that lack of integration among their information systems was leading to serious operational inefficiencies. Furthermore, these inefficiencies were beginning to cause many companies to lose ground to other, better-organized firms. At the same time, enterprise resource planning (ERP) software, especially SAP R/3 (http://www.sap.com/), was reaching a high state of maturity as its penetration rate among the Fortune 1000 rose. The decision whether to convert to SAP (or a competing product) was a strategic one for many companies at this time, both because of the high costs and risks of cost overruns (many SAP implementations had failed or been far more costly than expected) and because of the high risks of *not* implementing integrated software. This case will allow you to explore the analysis done by one typical company for this decision.

What is ERP software? An ERP system is companywide software that links all operations to a central database. ERP software is organized by module, one for each functional area such as Finance, Accounting, Manufacturing, Payroll, Human Resources, and so on. Each of these modules has a common software design, and it shares information as needed with the central database. While converting old systems to ERP is a massive undertaking, once it is accomplished the firm has one common database, one common definition of business concepts, one central warehouse in which all information resides, and individual modules for each functional area that are compatible but can be upgraded independently.

The Situation at Mega Corporation

Mega Corporation has for many years been a dominant manufacturer in its industry. As a worldwide firm, it has four main manufacturing sites and sales offices spread across the world. Since most of the growth in the firm occurred in the 1970s and 1980s, before integrated firm-wide software was available, few of the company's information systems can communicate with each other. This lack of information integration is becoming an increasing burden on the firm. Each of the manufacturing sites has its own hardware and software, and none are linked electronically. As a consequence, much of the sharing of information that goes on among the manufacturing sites is done by telephone, fax, or memo. Each of the main sales offices has purchased and developed its own information systems, and these do not communicate with each other or with manufacturing. Again, this forces the sales offices to use telephone and faxes to share data. The accounting department is centralized at headquarters, but its software system does not interface with the others. Much of their time is spent manually transferring accounting data from the field into their central system. Purchasing is done by each of the manufacturing sites independently, and since their systems do not communicate, the firm cannot keep track of its purchases from single vendors and thus misses out on many discounts. This is just a sample of the problems that Mega suffers due to a lack of information integration.

As these problems deepened, and the need for some centralized solution became more and more apparent, a conflict arose between the chief information officer (CIO) and the chief financial officer (CFO). The CIO wanted to install an integrated system immediately despite the costs and risks; the CFO wanted to kill any attempt to install this software. Here is a summary of the pros and cons of this decision, as expressed by the two executives.

The Case for ERP

The CIO argued that partial fixes to the company's current information systems were becoming more expensive and less effective every year. The conversion to ERP was inevitable, so why not do it now? Once the system was up and running, the firm could expect to see lower inventories both of finished goods and raw materials. Finished goods inventories would be lower because Marketing and Manufacturing would be able to share common forecasts; raw materials inventories would be lower because Manufacturing would communicate its needs better to Purchasing, which would not have to maintain large stocks of raw materials to cover unexpected orders. In addition, Purchasing would be able to obtain quantity discounts from more vendors by pooling its orders from the various manufacturing sites. Sales would increase because, with better communication between

Marketing and Manufacturing, there would be fewer canceled orders, fewer late shipments, and more satisfied customers. Software maintenance costs would go down because the company would not have to maintain the old, nonintegrated software, much of which existed simply to allow one system to communicate with another. Decision making would also improve with the ERP system, because such basic information as current production costs at the product level would be available for the first time. Finally, once the basic ERP system was in place it would become possible to install more sophisticated software such as a customer-relationship management or CRM system. A CRM system sits on top of the ERP system, using its database to help answer questions such as "Are we making money selling products to our customers in the Northeast?" and "Is our sales force in East Asia fully productive?"

The Case against ERP

The case against ERP was made forcefully by the CFO. ERP hardware and software costs are high and must be paid in full before any benefits come in. ERP systems change almost everyone's job, so the retraining costs are enormous. Some people will even leave the company rather than retrain on the new systems. No one within the company has any experience with ERP, so an expensive group of consultants must be hired over many years. Even after the consultants are gone, the company will have to hire a substantial number of highly trained and highly paid systems people to maintain the ERP system. Improved decision making sounds valuable, but it is hard to quantify, and besides, if the company has as much difficulty as some firms have had implementing ERP, the "benefits" may well be negative!

The only rational way to develop an understanding of the likely costs and benefits of implementing ERP, and perhaps to settle this argument, is to develop a model. You have been asked by the Board to do just that. Your model should be *complete* in that it accounts for all the possible costs and benefits from both an ERP system and from installing a CRM system on top of the ERP system. The model should be *flexible*, so that alternative assumptions can easily be tested. It should be *robust*, in that nonsensical inputs should be rejected. It should also provide *insights*, so that the Board can use it effectively to decide under what circumstances the ERP/CRM project would make sense. Some of the initial assumptions on which the Board would like the model to be built are described next.

Assumptions

First, the model should cover 20 years, from 2005–2024. Second, it should account for changes in sales (and revenues) from the ERP and CRM systems, as well as changes in inventories. Finally, it should include the costs of hardware, software, consultants, permanent employees, training of nonprogramming staff, and maintenance of old systems. Specific numerical assumptions follow:

- Without ERP, sales are expected to hold steady at about $5 million per year over the next 15 years.
- Sales can be expected to grow about 1 percent/year once an ERP system is fully operational, which will take two years.

- If a CRM system is installed, sales growth will become 2 percent/year. (The CRM system would be installed in year 4 and become operational beginning in year 5.)
- The company currently spends $5 million per year maintaining its old systems, and this cost will grow by $100,000 per year. All of this maintenance cost will be avoided if an ERP system is installed.
- ERP hardware will cost $5 million in the first year of installation and $1 million in the second.
- ERP software will cost $10 million in the first year of installation and $1 million in the second.
- CRM hardware and software will each cost $1 million in the year of installation (year 4). The CRM installation cannot occur before three years after the ERP installation is begun.
- Consultants work 225 days per year.
- The accompanying table gives:
  - the number of ERP and CRM consultants required, along with their daily rate
  - the number of additional programmers required, as well as their yearly salary
  - the costs of training nonprogramming staff
- Without ERP, inventory turns over 11 times per year. Thus, the average level of inventory (in dollars) is annual sales divided by 11. With the ERP system, turns are expected to increase to 13. To hold a dollar of finished goods inventory for one year costs $3.50.
- Variable costs (excluding the costs of inventory) are 75 percent of sales revenues.
- The hurdle rates normally used in the company to evaluate capital investments range from 10 to 15 percent. However, an argument has been made that

a significantly higher rate should be used given the risks of this project.
- Efficiency gains from ERP systems have varied widely from firm to firm. Some managers within this firm are optimistic and would estimate these gains at $7 million per year. Others are pessimistic and would see a loss of $5 million per year due to cost overruns and unexpected retraining expenses. Finally, there is a neutral camp that would prefer to assume no efficiency gains or losses from ERP.

Analysis

Using the assumptions already given and whatever additional assumptions you feel are warranted, build a model to project the Net Present Value of the gains from the ERP and CRM decisions. Remember that your model should be complete, flexible, robust, and capable of providing insight.

Establish a base case. Perform what-if analysis. Over what ranges for critical parameters does the project look attractive? Which assumptions appear to be especially critical in determining the gains from ERP? Where are the breakeven values for critical parameters at which the project changes from attractive to unattractive?

Synthesize what you have learned from this analysis into a short PowerPoint presentation to the Board. Your presentation should use graphical means wherever possible to convey your insights. Do not repeat anything the Board already knows—get right to the point.

[*]This case was adapted by Steve Powell and Jeff Camm from "The Mega Corporation's ERP Decision," Case 10 in *Problem-Solving Cases* by J. A. Brady and E. F. Monk, Course Technology, 2003.

Year	Number of ERP Consultants	Number of CRM Consultants	Cost of Consultants/Day	Number of Added Programmers	Cost of Added Programmers/Year	Training Costs
2005	10	0	1,500	10	100,000	3,000,000
2006	8	0	1,515	8	105,000	2,000,000
2007	6	0	1,530	6	110,250	1,000,000
2008	4	2	1,545	4	115,762	500,000
2009	2	1	1,560	2	121,550	200,000
2010	1	1	1,575	1	127,627	100,000
2011	0	0	1,590	1	134,008	0
2012	0	0	1,605	0	140,708	0
2013	0	0	1,621	0	147,708	0
2014	0	0	1,637	0	155,130	0
2015	0	0	1,653	0	162,886	0
2016	0	0	1,669	0	171,030	0
2017	0	0	1,685	0	179,581	0
2018	0	0	1,701	0	188,560	0
2019	0	0	1,717	0	197,254	0
2020	0	0	1,733	0	206,019	0
2021	0	0	1,749	0	214,784	0
2022	0	0	1,765	0	223,549	0
2023	0	0	1,781	0	232,314	0
2024	0	0	1,797	0	241,079	0

NATIONAL LEASING, INC.*

Background

New-vehicle leasing has grown to the point that it represents a major factor in new-car sales. Consumers who would otherwise have purchased a new car every few years are now attracted by monthly lease payments lower than those for financing a new-car purchase. Such consumers can thereby drive a nicer vehicle than they could afford to buy or finance. The most popular leases are for expensive or midrange vehicles and carry a term of 24 or 36 months.

The majority of leases are sold via "captive" leasing companies, run by a vehicle manufacturer. About 40 percent of leases are sold by independent leasing companies, primarily banks and other financial firms. Among the independents, six are major national players, competing against a host of smaller regional companies.

Increasing competition among leasing companies and online pricing information have made vehicle leasing nearly a commodity. Consumers care most about getting the lowest monthly payment, other factors being equal. Online information sources at dealers readily report the lowest lease payments for a given vehicle.

Demand for any one lease is highly unpredictable. However, it is generally accepted that demand is sensitive to the gap between the monthly payments of a given leasing company and the going rate in the market for that car model, which is usually set by the lease with the lowest monthly payments. Other factors, such as the contract residual value, appear to be secondary in the consumer's mind.

The most common form of leasing is the *closed-end lease*, in which the monthly payment is computed based on three factors:

- *Capitalized Cost*: The purchase price for the car, net of trade-ins, fees, discounts, and dealer-installed options.
- *Residual Value*: The value of the vehicle at the end of the lease, specified by the leasing company in the lease contract. The consumer has the right to purchase the vehicle at this price upon lease termination (this is known as the "purchase option").
- *Money Factor, or Rate*: The implicit interest rate the leasing company (the "lessor") charges in the monthly payments.

A typical leasing company gets its money at a very low interest rate and finances the purchase of the cars it will lease. Thus, the leasing company is essentially making a monthly payment to its bank on the full price of the vehicle, while getting a monthly lease payment from its customer based on the difference between the full price and the contract residual price.

For a given vehicle, a lower residual value implies a greater drop in value over the term of the lease, prompting higher monthly payments. Therefore, a leasing company offering the highest residual value usually has the lowest, and most competitive, monthly payment. Such a high residual value, relative to competitors, is likely to sell a lot of leases. However, one need only consider what happens at the end of the lease term to understand how this can be a time bomb. If the *actual* end-of-lease market value is lower than the contract residual value, the consumer is likely to return the car to the lessor. The lessor then typically sells the vehicle, usually at auction, and realizes a "residual loss."

If a leasing company sets a low, "conservative," residual value, then the corresponding monthly payments are higher. This reduces the number of leases sold in this competitive market. And at the end of these leases, if the actual market value is greater than the contract residual, the consumer is more likely to exercise their purchase option. By then selling the vehicle for the prevailing market value, the consumer in essence receives a rebate for the higher monthly payments during the term of the lease. (Of course, the consumer may also decide to keep the car.) When consumers exercise their purchase option, the lessor loses the opportunity to realize "residual gains."

The economically rational thing for the lease owner to do at the end of the lease is to purchase the car when the actual market value exceeds the contract residual (and resell at the higher price) and to leave the car to the leasing company when the actual market value falls below the contract residual. However, not all consumers are rational at the end of the lease. Some percentage will buy the vehicle regardless of the actual market value, presumably because they have become attached to the vehicle or because the transactions costs of acquiring a new vehicle are too high. Some will not purchase even when the actual market value is well above the contract residual. By the same token, some will purchase even when the actual market value is below the contract residual.

The primary challenge, then, for companies offering a closed-end lease, is to intelligently select the contract residual value of the vehicle 24, 36, 48, or even 60 months into the future. Intelligent selection means that the leasing company must offer competitive monthly payments on the front end while not ignoring the risk of being left with residual losses on the back end. To cushion financial performance against this risk, auto lessors set aside a reserve against residual losses in order to report income accurately. This practice is similar to insurance companies' reserves against future claims.

During the period 1990–1995, used car prices rose faster than inflation (5 to 6 percent per year on average in nominal terms). This price rise was driven by the higher quality of used cars (itself a result of higher manufacturing quality standards in new cars), high new-car prices making used vehicles more attractive, and a shift in consumer perceptions making it less unfashionable to own a used vehicle.

In this environment, lessors realized very few residual losses because they were generally conservative in setting residuals, forecasting low used-vehicle prices. They admittedly missed some opportunity to capture the upside "hidden" in residual gains, but this trend caught all players off guard and therefore no single leasing company was able to take advantage of the trend by offering lower monthly payments.

In 1996–1997, used-vehicle prices first leveled off, then dramatically dropped. This shift was driven largely by the oversupply of nearly new used vehicles returned at the end of their leases. The oversupply and attendant price drops were particularly evident for the popular sport-utility vehicles and light trucks. Suddenly, lessors found themselves with mounting residual losses on their books, in some cases as much as $2,500 per vehicle. These losses greatly exceeded reserves.

Company Profile: A Leader in Trouble

National Leasing, Inc. is a major independent provider of auto leases, with $10 billion in vehicle assets on its books. National sold just over 100,000 leases in 1997. Buoyed by the general used-vehicle price strength described above, the company experienced very fast growth and excellent profitability from 1990 to 1994. Competition has driven down share dramatically in the past few years, slowing growth and reducing profitability.

From 1995 to 1997, National Leasing's portfolio became concentrated in less than 20 vehicles, those in which the company offered a competitive (high residual) monthly payment. Six vehicles accounted for about half the total volume. One sport-utility vehicle in particular accounted for nearly 20 percent of total units in the portfolio. These concentrations arose from a "winner's curse" or adverse selection phenomenon, in which National sold large volumes of leases for which it set the highest residual compared to the competition. Such competitive rates were the keys to success in a period of generally rising used-car prices.

But in 1997, when used-car prices dropped 8 percent in the first six months of the year, National was left with significant residual losses. Consequently, the company reported a loss of net income of $400 million in fiscal year 1997, prompting an internal audit. The audit revealed that many of the losses were related to operational errors and inefficiencies, including improper data entry, inadequate information systems, and faulty reporting procedures.

The audit also revealed flaws in the current residual-value forecasting process:

- No explicit consideration is given to the risks of setting residual values too high or too low.
- External market information and expertise are ignored, as estimates are made by a small group of internal analysts.
- Current market residual values are relied upon excessively in setting future contract residual values.

Current Situation

During the first half of 1998, National Leasing revamped its operations, thereby correcting most of the problems related to data entry and information technology. At the same time, the internal residual value forecasting group adopted a very conservative posture, setting residuals for new leases at low levels across the board. Rumors suggested that a new manager would be brought in to run residual setting and that a new process would be developed.

In mid-1998, senior management was divided on the question of what new residual forecasting method to use.

Some believed that National should simply use values in the Auto Lease Guide (ALG), a standard industry reference publication. Others strongly disagreed with this approach, on the grounds that using ALG eliminated National's competitive advantage. This faction further supported their opinion with analysis showing that using ALG would not have avoided the 1997 losses.

Despite a general consensus among industry insiders that most other major lessors experienced similar net income losses in 1997, National's major competitors did not follow its lead in setting lower residuals. The higher monthly payments associated with National's low residual values resulted in a 50 percent drop in sales volume in the first six months of 1998. Used-car prices continued to decline in 1998, apparently driven by flat (or falling) new-car prices. National Leasing's senior management, fearing that the industry was entering a period of sustained used-car price deflation, was therefore reluctant to raise residuals to competitive levels. They thought the competition must be "crazy."

Your Challenge

In recent meetings among the senior management, a number of possible solutions to these problems have been discussed, including improving residual-setting techniques, acquiring competitors, entering the downstream used-car business, and even exiting the new-vehicle leasing business. Your modeling talents and general business savvy have caught the attention of an influential senior manager at National. She believes that a modeling approach might assist National in making better decisions on lease terms on individual vehicles. (She has even hinted that she might be interested in your ideas on how to manage the lease portfolio, that is, the entire book of outstanding leases.) In order to give you a forum in which to promulgate your ideas, she has arranged time for you to make a short presentation to the Board in a week's time. In this presentation, your goal will be to convince the Board that your modeling approach will significantly improve their management of the lease business.

You are being asked to build a prototype model to prove a concept—that is, that modeling can help National management to sell more profitable leases. You are not being asked to find the right answer or build a day-to-day decision-support system, of course, but only to show what you could do with the appropriate time and resources.

In this context, you would not be expected to have the last word on what the relationships or parameters were for your model, but the relationships should be plausible and you should be able to say where you would get the data to refine your parameters (if needed).

The most effective way to impress this client is to show that a prototype model can be used to generate insights she currently does not have. Such insights are not usually dependent on the precise relationships or parameters in a model, but rather reflect underlying structural properties.

---

*This case was developed as a class exercise by Peter Regan, Steve Powell and Jay Goldman.

MEGA PHARMA AND MICRO PHARMA*

Background

Mega Pharma is a large pharmaceutical company with sales in the year 2000 of $5 billion per year (all figures are in constant year 2000 dollars). Mega is developing a drug code-named MegaCardia for a particular variety of cardiovascular disease. MegaCardia was expected to reach the market in 2003. Mega learned that a competitor, Micro Pharma, was developing a similar compound called MicroCardia that was also expected to reach the market around the year 2003. Micro Pharma is a small pharmaceutical company with sales of $1 billion per year. These two compounds are instances of a new class of therapy, and no other companies are thought to be developing competitive products. Patent experts at Mega believe Micro's patent position is quite strong in this area, so it stands a good chance of preventing Mega from marketing its own compound. (*Note*: Micro can only sue Mega for patent infringement if it is successful itself in developing a marketable product.)

Executives at Mega are considering making a deal with Micro that will allow both companies to profit from sale of this new drug without getting tied down in litigation or other costly competitive actions.

Product Development Process

A typical pharmaceutical product goes through a predictable series of development phases, as follows:

Preclinical phase: animal trials focusing on safety (typically lasts 13 weeks)

Phase 1: safety studies conducted on 50 to 100 normal healthy male volunteers (typically lasts from three to six months)

Phase 2: efficacy and safety trials on a diseased target population under controlled medical conditions (typically lasts six to nine months)

Phase 3: efficacy and safety trials on the target population under actual conditions of use (typically lasts six to nine months and may involve thousands of patients)

FDA submission: preparation of a new drug application (NDA), involving extensive statistical analysis and report writing (typically takes six months)

FDA review: FDA evaluation of the NDA based on the preclinical and clinical data, (typically takes 17–24 months)

Both MegaCardia and MicroCardia are currently about to start Phase 2.

Mega's Perspective on Its Compound

Mega believes that its compound has a 50 percent chance of success in Phase 2 and an 80 percent chance of success in Phase 3. The chance of rejection by the health authorities in the major markets (United States, Europe, and Japan) is negligible given successful Phase 3 results. Phase 2 studies will cost $10 million and Phase 3 studies will cost $40 million. Regulatory review support will cost $2 million.

According to Mega's marketing staff, sales of the new therapeutic class represented by MegaCardia and MicroCardia are expected to peak at $500 million worldwide five years after launch. Sales should stay near the peak until patent expiration, which for both compounds will occur in 2013. Profits over the product's lifetime are expected to be 75 percent of sales. Mega believes that its market share of the new therapeutic class worldwide will be 50 percent if MicroCardia is also in the market and virtually 100 percent otherwise. Since the products are almost identical, they will very likely succeed or fail together; clinicians estimate that if one product is successfully brought to market, then there is a 90 percent chance that the other will also be successful.

Patent infringement litigation typically commences when a drug is first marketed. Mega believes that Micro will almost certainly sue and has a 50 percent chance of winning the suit and thereby entirely preventing Mega from marketing its product.

The management at Mega Pharma usually evaluates drug development decisions on the basis of a Net Productivity Index (NPI), which is the ratio of the net profit to the development costs. The reason they do not simply evaluate projects on the basis of NPV is that development funds are limited, so there is an opportunity cost (which is not reflected in the NPV) associated with spending money on one project because it cannot be spent on another. The NPI allows them to compare the net returns from various projects to the net development costs each incurs.

The NPI is calculated by first determining the flow of profits that can be expected from the product after launch, discounting this to the present at an appropriate discount rate, and then by taking an expected value over the different possible future scenarios. Similarly, the net development cost is calculated by determining the pattern of development costs over time, discounting to the present, and taking an expected value. Generally speaking, Mega management would like to see the NPI exceed 5, but there is no specific hurdle rate. (The figure below provides a generic illustration of the calculation of NPI.)

Mega's Perspective on Micro

In thinking about the problem from Micro's perspective, Mega's analysts believe the same success probabilities and cost estimates apply since the compounds are so similar. They also use the same market estimates. The profit received by Micro differs slightly, however, from Mega's case in that Micro does not have the marketing strength to sell its product in Japan or Europe. It will need to find a partner in those markets and will likely receive a 10 percent royalty on sales as opposed to a 75 percent margin. Mega anticipates peak sales in each market of $250 million for the United States, $150 million for Europe, and $100 million for Japan.

Initial Negotiations and Next Steps

Several months ago, Mega decided to offer Micro $50 M for the rights to MicroCardia. When the two companies met to discuss the situation, Micro declined Mega's offer. Mega's executives believe the reason was that Micro expects the new therapeutic class to have greater penetration into traditional treatments. One Micro executive suggested that peak sales for the new treatment market would likely be $900 million (rather than $500 million as estimated by Mega's marketing department).

Mega's executives have asked their internal management science group to do some work on this problem and report back in a week when the executive team meets to prepare for the next round of negotiations with Micro. The following issues are of particular interest to them:

1. Is there a dollar amount that Mega would be willing to pay for the rights to Micro's compound that Micro would be likely to accept? (If Mega buys the rights from Micro, Micro will agree not to develop the drug and not to sue.)

2. Rather than buying the rights to the compound outright, is there a possible deal in which Mega purchases a license from Micro to avoid a patent battle? (Under a license agreement, Mega would pay Micro a set percentage of its revenues if it is successful in the market. Micro can still develop its own drug but cannot sue.) This option would allow both companies to market their compounds separately. If so, how much would Mega be willing to pay and Micro be willing to accept?

3. Mega's CEO is interested in the question of whether a co-development deal could be struck where Mega and Micro form a joint effort to share both development costs and commercial returns. Under such an agreement, both development labs could continue to operate in parallel, or could be combined into a single team. Assuming co-development, at what point should the joint team drop one compound and go forward with only the most promising one?

*This case was developed as a class exercise by Steve Powell and Peter Regan.

Expected Profit

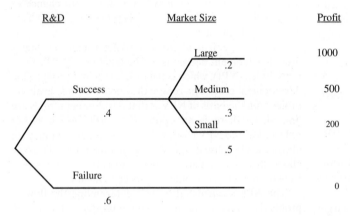

$$EV = 0.4 \times (0.2 \times 1000 + 0.3 \times 500 + 0.5 \times 200) + 0.6 \times 0 = 180$$

Expected Development Costs

Phase 1	Phase 2	Review	Probability	Cost
		Success .9	0.162	10 + 30 + 5
	Success .6			
Success .3		Failure .1	0.018	10 + 30 + 5
	Failure .4		0.120	10 + 30
Failure .7			0.7	10
			1.0	

$$EV = 0.3 \times 0.6 \times 0.9 \times 45 + 0.3 \times 0.6 \times 0.1 \times 45 + 0.3 \times 0.4 \times 40 + 0.7 \times 10 = 8.8$$

NPI

$$NPI = EV \text{ Profit}/EV \text{ Cost} = 180/8.8 = 20.45$$

Appendix 1:
Basic Excel Skills

INTRODUCTION

Excel may be the most versatile software program ever created. It is used daily by millions of people in every conceivable walk of life. Some of its users are simply adding up short columns of numbers, while others are creating sophisticated applications in which Excel is performing complex numerical calculations while interacting with several other software systems. With such a versatile and flexible tool, it is difficult for any user to determine just which of the thousands of features in Excel are really worth knowing. In this appendix, we describe the basic Excel skills we think are important for every business analyst along with some more advanced skills that are useful in several business applications.

This appendix is not intended to serve as a beginner's tutorial on Excel. Those who are new to Excel and need a tutorial should work through a book, CD, or online course. Those who have a working knowledge of Excel will find in this appendix some reminders about familiar tools and perhaps pointers to some new ones as well. We have found that many experienced users have never taken the time to explore Excel systematically, so their skills are deep in some areas but shallow in others. We recommend skimming this appendix for Excel features that are new. A few minutes spent learning how to use Excel more efficiently, even for users with some experience, can pay dividends in the building of spreadsheet models.

EXCEL PREREQUISITES

What are the spreadsheet skills that are prerequisites for an analyst who would like to learn to *model* in Excel? The most basic skill, and one that doesn't show up in the books, is the ability to *learn by trial and error*. Few successful users of software learn primarily from manuals or help facilities. Most have learned to scan the menus and search in a partly random, partly intelligent fashion for the tool they need and to experiment freely, knowing that (almost) nothing they do cannot be undone. In fact, the Undo command is one of the most important features in Excel!

Getting down to Excel itself, the first necessary skill is to be able to navigate around a worksheet and between worksheets in a workbook. This includes moving the cursor, scrolling, using the Home and End keys, and so on. Even the novice modeler needs to enter text and enter data and to choose the format of these entries. It is handy to be able to change the font name, style, and size, to use bold and italics, and to color a cell or its contents. The ability to edit the contents of a cell is important. Other necessary skills include inserting and deleting rows or columns and entire worksheets; cutting, copying and pasting; printing; and drawing charts.

Skillful use of formulas and functions separates the novice spreadsheet user from the advanced user. To create formulas effectively, users must understand both relative cell addressing and absolute cell addressing. Excel has innumerable built-in functions that can drastically simplify calculations. Some of the most useful are SUM, IF, MAX, MIN, AVERAGE, and NPV. The Insert Function window not only lists all the available functions by category, but also specifies the syntax of each function, explaining what inputs each requires and in what order.

Beyond these basic tools, Excel contains literally hundreds of specialized features. Few modelers use more than several dozen of these routinely, and even fewer can

FIGURE A1.1 Office
Building Spreadsheet

	A	B	C	D	E	F	G
1	Office Building						
2							
3	Parameters	Rate of increase	Year 1	Year 2	Year 3	Year 4	Year 5
4	Building cost per sq ft		$80.00				
5	Size of building		180,000				
6	Rent per sq ft	5%	$15.00	15.75	16.54	17.36	18.23
7	Operating expense per sq f	6%	$1.20	1.27	1.35	1.43	1.51
8	Vacancy rate	-4%	30%	0.26	0.22	0.18	0.14
9	Percent financed		85%				
10	Mortgage rate		12%				
11	Sale multiple		12				
12	Cost of capital		10%				
13							
14			Year 1	Year 2	Year 3	Year 4	Year 5
15	Cash Flow						
16		Gross income	1,890,000	2,097,900	2,321,865	2,562,982	2,822,406
17		Operating expense	216,000	228,960	242,698	257,259	272,695
18		Net operating income	1,674,000	1,868,940	2,079,167	2,305,722	2,549,710
19		Interest cost	$1,464,720	$1,464,720	$1,464,720	$1,464,720	$1,464,720
20		Before-tax cash flow	$209,280	$404,220	$614,447	$841,002	$1,084,990
21							
22		Down payment (at time 0)	$2,160,000				
23		Sale price					$30,596,526
24		Mortgage cost					$12,240,000
25		End of year cash flows	$209,280	$404,220	$614,447	$841,002	$19,441,516
26							
27	NPV	$11,472,032					
28							

A1.1

remember all of them between uses. It is *not* necessary to master all of these specialized tools in order to succeed at modeling.

We will use a simple spreadsheet model as an example throughout this appendix. The reader should open this model and use it to test the features described below. The spreadsheet itself is shown in Figure A1.1*.

Example
Office
Building Plans

Potential investors in an office building construction project have asked us to evaluate this opportunity. Our task is to predict the after-tax cash flows resulting from constructing and operating this proposed office building over a five year period. At a planned size of 180,000 square feet, the expected construction cost is $80 per square foot. The investors plan to take out a mortgage for 85 percent of the cost of the building (paying the remainder in cash), and they have been guaranteed a rate of 12 percent for a term of 30 years. The owners must also pay for the cost of operating the building, which includes taxes, insurance, maintenance, and certain utilities. They assume that the average operating cost per square foot will be $1.20. They have also estimated that they can charge a rental rate of $15 per square foot, with an occupancy rate of 70 percent. The cost of capital is 10 percent. Rents in the future are expected to grow 5 percent per year, while operating expenses grow 6 percent and the occupancy rate drops 4 percentage points yearly as the building ages. The owners plan to sell the building at the end of the fifth year for 12 times the final year's net operating income. ∎

THE EXCEL WINDOW

Each Excel file is called a workbook. A workbook consists of a number of individual worksheets. We will use the word "spreadsheet" to refer to both workbooks and worksheets.

The basic spreadsheet layout consists of a grid of rows and columns of cells (see Figure A1.2). The rows are labeled with numbers and the columns are labeled with letters. The maximum number of rows in a single worksheet is 1,048,576; the maximum number of columns is 16,384. The address of a cell corresponds to its column and row label—for example, C3 or AB567.

---

* To download spreadsheets for this appendix, go to the Student Companion Site at www.wiley.com/college/powell.

FIGURE A1.2 Features of the Excel Window

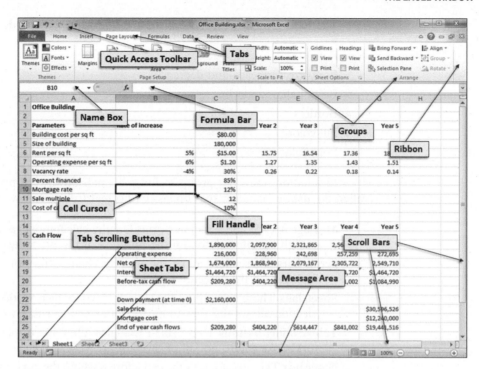

On the computer screen, Excel displays a portion of this grid surrounded by other information. Some of the important features of the Excel window are described below and noted in Figure A1.2.

File Tab The File tab, the leftmost tab on the ribbon, provides access to the most commonly used commands, such as Save, Save As, Open, Close, and Print. It also provides access to Excel's Options.

Quick Access Toolbar In the top left section of the window is the Quick Access Toolbar. This toolbar holds a set of icons for shortcuts to frequently used commands. You can customize this toolbar by selecting the downward pointing arrow to the right of the icons.

Tabs The main Excel commands are organized across the top row into the following tabs:

- File
- Home
- Insert
- Page Layout
- Formulas
- Data
- Review
- View
- Add-ins

Additional tabs may appear at the user's option or when specialized software has been loaded.

Ribbons and Groups Each tab gives access to a ribbon in which commands are organized into groups. For example, the Home tab has the following groups of commands:

- Clipboard
- Font
- Alignment
- Number
- Styles
- Cells
- Editing

The Font group includes icons for the following commands:

- Font
- Font size (increase and decrease)
- Bold, italics, underline
- Borders
- Fill color
- Font color

In addition, the Font group includes a small downward-pointing arrow icon (↘), called the *dialog launcher*, that opens the Format Cells window.

Message area When Excel performs lengthy calculations, a message appears in this area giving information on the progress of the procedure.

Scroll bars These bars allow the user to change the portion of the spreadsheet displayed on the screen.

Sheet tabs These tabs allow the user to select which worksheet is displayed. The selection allows the user to move from sheet to sheet within a workbook.

Tab-scrolling buttons These small triangles allow the display of a different tab, in workbooks where not all of the tabs are visible at once.

Name box This box displays the cell address where the cursor is located, as well as the list of any named ranges. (Named ranges are covered later.)

Formula bar This box displays the contents of the cell where the cursor is located, whether a number, formula, or text. This is usually the area in which the user enters information into a cell.

Cursor The location of the cursor is shown with an open cross symbol.

Cell cursor When a cell has been selected, it is outlined with a dark border. When a range of cells has been selected, it is colored blue and outlined with a dark border.

Fill handle At the lower right-hand corner of the cell border is a cross that can be selected for copying the contents of the cell to adjacent cells. When this cross is selected, the mouse cursor changes to a darkened cross.

CONFIGURING EXCEL

Many users are not aware that they can control the look and behavior of their spreadsheets by setting certain parameters. Select File▶Options and a window appears with ten categories listed in a column on the left (see Figure A1.3). Except where noted below, most of the choices can safely be left at their default values.

General Select an appropriate font and font size.

Formulas In most uses, it is preferable to have the spreadsheet calculate all formula cells each time a change is made to any cell. This updating occurs if `Automatic` is selected under Calculation options. On occasion, it is useful to turn this feature off. To do so, select `Manual`. When the manual calculation option is chosen, the spreadsheet can be recalculated at any time by pressing F9, but it will not recalculate automatically when a cell is changed. The message "Calculate" will appear in the Message area when a cell has been changed but the spreadsheet has not been recalculated.

When a spreadsheet contains simultaneous relationships, calculations cannot be made in the usual manner. This situation typically generates an error message warning of a circular reference. This error message is useful because circular references usually occur when there is a mistake in the logic. However, there are circumstances where a circular reference is sensible (for example, when linking income statement and balance sheet models). In these cases, it is necessary to specify a number of iterations to calculate the desired values. Check the box labeled `Enable iterative calculation` to implement an iterative approach.

FIGURE A1.3   The Excel
Options Window

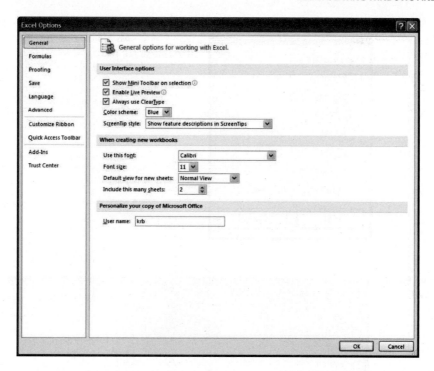

Under Error Checking check the box labeled `Enable background error checking`. Check all nine `Error checking rules`.

Proofing Select the preferred options for the AutoCorrect feature in Excel.

Save Check the box labeled `Save AutoRecovery information` so that Excel will automatically save our spreadsheets as often as specified.

Language Choose language options for dictionaries, grammar checking, and so on.

Advanced Under Editing options check the boxes labeled `Enable fill handle` and `cell drag-and-drop`, and `Allow editing directly in cells`. Under Cut, copy, and paste check the boxes labeled `Show Paste Options buttons` and `Show Insert Options buttons`.

Customize Ribbon Move commands and options from the left-hand window to the desired place listed in the right-hand window.

Quick Access Toolbar Customize the Quick Access Toolbar. Experienced users will recognize that they use some commands quite frequently, so instead of hunting for the commands in the ribbon, they place the corresponding icon in the Quick Access Toolbar for convenience.

Add-ins View and manage add-ins.

Trust Center Information on privacy and security.

MANIPULATING WINDOWS AND SHEETS

Since most workbooks contain far more information than can be displayed on a computer screen, it is important to know how to display the most useful portion of the worksheet. The Zoom level (or magnification) of the worksheet can be set with a slider located in the lower right corner of the Excel window (see Figure A1.2). Alternatively, click on the 100% button to the left of the slider and the Zoom window opens (Figure A1.4). This window allows us to choose a pre-set or custom level of magnification. (The Zoom window can also be opened by selecting View▶Zoom▶Zoom.)

The View▶Window command makes it possible to simultaneously display more than one worksheet on the screen. These sheets may be from the same workbook or from different workbooks. This command can be particularly useful when we are building formulas in one sheet using cells located in another. Select Window▶New Window to add a spreadsheet window; then resize the new window and select the sheets to display, as in Figure A1.5.

FIGURE A1.4 The Zoom Window

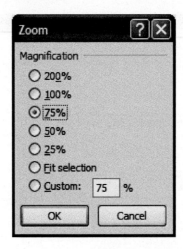

FIGURE A1.5 Two Excel Windows Displayed Simultaneously

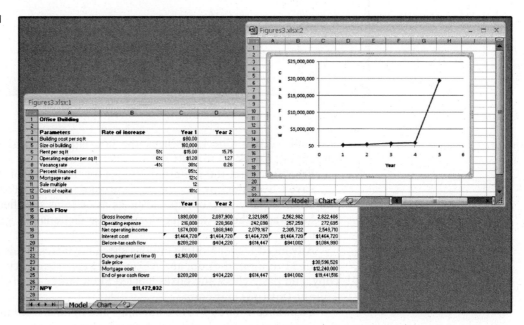

Excel provides an option to split the screen horizontally, vertically, or both, in order to display two sets of rows or columns in the same spreadsheet. If, for example, we wish to enter formulas in row 100 that reference cells in rows 1–10, we highlight row 10 and select View▸Window▸Split. Excel will open a second pane of rows with its own scroll bar, splitting the window horizontally. We can then display row 100 in the bottom pane while displaying rows 1–10 in the upper pane. The window can also be split vertically, by highlighting a column. The window can even be split both horizontally and vertically, by highlighting a cell. Figure A1.6 shows the worksheet split both horizontally and vertically at cell B13. (The screen can also be split by dragging the horizontal or vertical split bars, which are located just above and to the right of the row and column scroll bars, respectively.)

NAVIGATION

There are several ways to move the display from one portion of a spreadsheet to another. The horizontal and vertical scroll bars move the display of the portion of the entire spreadsheet that contains cell entries left and right or up and down, respectively. However, the scroll bars cannot move the display to blank areas. This can be done by clicking on the scroll arrows above and below the vertical scroll bar and to the left and right of the horizontal scroll bar. We can also shift the display by clicking on a cell and highlighting a range that extends outside the display area.

FIGURE A1.6 Splitting the Screen to Fix Row and Column Headings

	A	B	C	D	E	F	G
1	Office Building						
2							
3	Parameters	Rate of increase	Year 1	Year 2	Year 3	Year 4	Year 5
4	Building cost per sq ft		$80.00				
5	Size of building		180,000				
6	Rent per sq ft	5%	$15.00	15.75	16.54	17.36	18.23
7	Operating expense per sq f	6%	$1.20	1.27	1.35	1.43	1.51
8	Vacancy rate	-4%	30%	0.26	0.22	0.18	0.14
9	Percent financed		85%				
10	Mortgage rate		12%				
11	Sale multiple		12				
12	Cost of capital		10%				
13							
14			Year 1	Year 2	Year 3	Year 4	Year 5
15	Cash Flow						
16		Gross income	1,890,000	2,097,900	2,321,865	2,562,982	2,822,406
17		Operating expense	216,000	228,960	242,698	257,259	272,695
18		Net operating income	1,674,000	1,868,940	2,079,167	2,305,722	2,549,710
19		Interest cost	$1,464,720	$1,464,720	$1,464,720	$1,464,720	$1,464,720
20		Before-tax cash flow	$209,280	$404,220	$614,447	$841,002	$1,084,990
21							
22		Down payment (at time 0)	$2,160,000				
23		Sale price					$30,596,526
24		Mortgage cost					$12,240,000
25		End of year cash flows	$209,280	$404,220	$614,447	$841,002	$19,441,516
26							
27	NPV	$11,472,032					

A1.1

The display area also can be moved by using the arrow keys ($\uparrow\downarrow\leftarrow\rightarrow$). If we hold one of these keys down, the cursor moves in the direction indicated until it reaches the limit of the display area, at which point the display shifts to keep the cursor on the screen. The Page Up and Page Down keys also shift the display up or down by a fixed number of rows. These keys are useful for quickly scanning the contents of a spreadsheet.

Another way to navigate around a spreadsheet is to type a cell address into the Name Box (just above column A). When we press the Enter key, the cursor moves to the cell address we have entered and the display shifts to accommodate the change. (If we use Names for cells or ranges of cells, they will appear in this box and we can click on them to move the cursor. Range Names are covered later.) We can also use Home▶Editing▶Find & Select▶Go To to shift the cursor and display within a worksheet or to another worksheet.

SELECTING CELLS

Excel offers many ways to select some or all of the cells in a spreadsheet. Here are the basic ones.

Selecting All Cells in a Worksheet Click on the box immediately to the left of column A and above row 1.

Selecting a Column or a Row Click on a single row label or column label (for example, A or 1). To select several adjacent columns or rows, click on the first label and drag the cursor to the last label.

Selecting Rectangular Ranges Any rectangular range of cells can be selected by selecting one of its four corner cells and dragging the cursor across to the diagonal corner. The same effect can be achieved by selecting a corner, dragging across the columns to the opposite corner and then across the rows to the diagonal corner, or vice versa.

Selecting Noncontiguous Ranges To select two distinct rectangles of cells, select the first range, hold down the Control key, and select the second range. This method can be used to select three or more ranges as well.

ENTERING TEXT AND DATA

The contents of a selected cell appear in two places: in the cell itself and in the formula bar. We can edit the contents either by moving the cursor to the formula bar or by double-clicking on the cell and editing directly in the cell.

FIGURE A1.7 The Series
WIndow

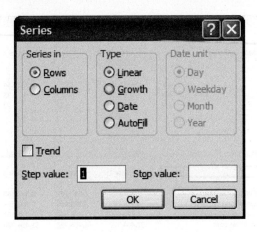

When we type letters into a cell, Excel automatically understands that the contents are text, and it left-justifies the contents in the cell. When we type numbers, it recognizes the contents as numerical and right-justifies the contents.

To copy the contents of one cell to adjacent cells, we can either drag the Fill handle (the solid square at the lower right corner of the selected cell) over the adjacent cells, or else use Home▶Editing▶Fill▶Down (or Right, Up, Left).

We often need to enter a series of numbers or dates. Examples include the numbers of successive customers (1, 2, 3, 4, . . .) or successive quarters in a year (Q1, Q2, Q3, . . .). Excel provides several ways to enter these series quickly. The Home-▶Editing▶Fill▶Series command will enter various kinds of series (see Figure A1.7). The same effect can be accomplished by entering the first two cell entries, highlighting them, and copying to the rest of the range using the Fill handle. Excel can usually guess the pattern correctly. For example, enter 1 and 2 in one column. Highlight the two cells. Fill down to the next eight cells using the Fill handle, and the remainder of the series (3, 4, 5, 6, 7, 8, 9, 10) will appear. To enter the numbers between 10 and 50 in steps of 5, enter 10 and 15 in adjacent cells and fill down until 50 is reached.

EDITING CELLS

Excel offers several ways to edit the information in cells. Here are the most useful alternatives:

Formula Bar The simplest way to edit is to click on the Formula bar. A vertical cursor will appear in the Formula bar, and information can be entered or modified using all the normal Windows typing options. If the selected cell is not empty, its contents will appear in the Formula bar. Clicking on the text there will make the editing cursor appear.

Double-Click A handy alternative approach is to double-click on a cell, or, equivalently, to press the F2 key. This allows editing in the cell itself. If the selected cell is not empty, any cells referred to in the formula will be highlighted in color, a useful debugging device. See Figure A1.8, where we have double-clicked on cell E19 and the formula in the cell is displayed. The four cell references used to calculate the result in cell E19 (C4, C5, C9 and C10) are highlighted in color, and a border with the matching color is drawn around each of those cells. Finally, the function used in the formula (ISPMT) is displayed below the cell, along with its arguments. If we click on the function name, the Help page for that function will appear.

We can modify the cell contents by inserting the vertical cursor where it is needed and typing directly into the cell or by moving the vertical cursor to the formula bar and typing there. Alternatively, we can alter any cell reference in a formula by dragging the highlighted outline to another location. This option provides a visual device for editing, which is convenient when the formula is based on distinctive reference patterns.

FIGURE A1.8 Double-Clicking on a Cell Containing a Formula

	A	B	C	D	E	F	G
1	Office Building						
2							
3	Parameters	Rate of increase	Year 1	Year 2	Year 3	Year 4	Year 5
4	Building cost per sq ft		$80.00				
5	Size of building		180,000				
6	Rent per sq ft	5%	$15.00	15.75	16.54	17.36	18.23
7	Operating expense per sq f	6%	$1.20	1.27	1.35	1.43	1.51
8	Vacancy rate	-4%	30%	0.26	0.22	0.18	0.14
9	Percent financed		85%				
10	Mortgage rate		12%				
11	Sale multiple		12				
12	Cost of capital		10%				
13							
14			Year 1	Year 2	Year 3	Year 4	Year 5
15	Cash Flow						
16		Gross income	1,890,000	2,097,900	2,321,865	2,562,982	2,822,406
17		Operating expense	216,000	228,960	242,698	257,259	272,695
18		Net operating income	1,674,000	1,868,940			
19		Interest cost	$1,464,720	$1,464,720 =-12*ISPMT($C$10/12,1,360,$C$9*$C$4*$C$5)			
20		Before-tax cash flow	$209,280	$404,220			
21							
22		Down payment (at time 0)	$2,160,000				
23		Sale price					$30,596,526
24		Mortgage cost					$12,240,000
25		End of year cash flows	$209,280	$404,220	$614,447	$841,002	$19,441,516
26							
27	NPV		$11,472,032				
28							

A1.1

Insert Function An alternative for editing a formula is Insert Function (the f_x icon to the left of the formula bar). If we click on this icon when the cursor is on a cell that does not contain a function, it will bring up the Insert Function window, which lists all available functions. If a specific function is then selected, it will be entered into the formula, and its own window will appear, which facilitates entering the inputs properly. If we click on the f_x icon when the cursor is on a cell that already contains a function, it will bring up the corresponding function window, allowing the definition of the function to be verified or the arguments of the function to be revised.

Absolute and Relative Cell References A relative reference to cell C3 is simply C3, whereas an absolute reference is $C$3. These types of references are useful primarily to make copying of complex formulas easy and reliable. Rather than typing in the appropriate dollar signs, it can be easier to enter all addresses in relative form (without dollar signs), highlight one or more addresses, and then press F4 repeatedly until the desired combination of absolute and relative references appears. (More information on formulas is covered later.)

FORMATTING

We can change individual column widths and row heights by moving the vertical or horizontal lines between the column and row labels. Widths or heights common to multiple columns or rows can be set using the Home▶Cells▶Format▶Cell Size▶Row Height/Column Width commands after highlighting the appropriate rows or columns. Alternatively, change one column width or one row height after highlighting the appropriate columns or rows.

Any range of cells can be formatted by highlighting the range and then selecting Home▶Cells▶Format▶Format Cells (or by selecting Home▶Font↘). This opens a window with the following six tabs (see Figure A1.9):

Number Choose a type of formatting—for example, Currency or Date—and specify parameters such as the number of decimal places displayed.

Alignment Align text horizontally and vertically, and choose Wrap Text to fit long text labels into cells.

Font Specify font, size, color, and superscript or subscript for the cell contents.

Border Set various borders around a range of cells.

Fill Set a background pattern or a color shade for the cell (but not its contents).

Protection Lock or hide cells for safety.

FIGURE A1.9 The Format Cells Window

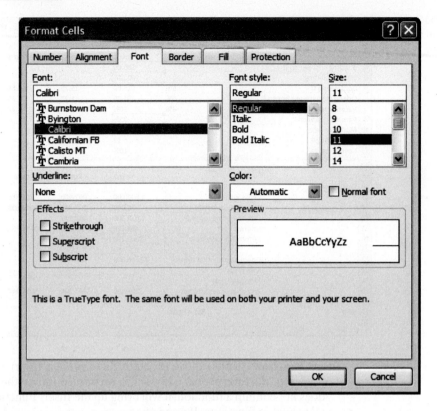

Many of these options are also available on the Home ribbon. The most frequently used icons on this ribbon are Increase Decimal and Decrease Decimal, which change the number of decimals displayed in selected cells by one decimal place each time they are clicked.

BASIC FORMULAS

Formulas in Excel provide the basic mechanism for entering the relationships in a model. In modeling terms, every cell in a spreadsheet that involves a formula is either an output of the model or an intermediate calculation needed to calculate an output.

With very few exceptions, well-written formulas contain no numbers, only cell references. Although it is permissible to use numerical constants in a formula, like the value 24 for the number of hours in a day, it is dangerous to embed parameters that may change in formulas. Because formulas are built up from the values in other cells, they are written in terms of references to the contents of those cells.

Excel uses the following symbols for the basic arithmetic operations:

- addition   +
- subtraction   −
- multiplication   *
- division   /
- raise to a power   ^

Excel formulas start with the equal sign (=) and are evaluated from left to right. However, arithmetic operations will be carried out in a specified order unless parentheses are used to control the calculation order. The basic arithmetic operations are calculated in the following order:

- negation (as in −1)
- exponentiation (^)
- multiplication and division (* and /)
- addition and subtraction (+ and −)

If a formula involves both multiplication and division (or both addition and subtraction) the left-most of these operations is performed first.

Here are some examples that show how the calculation order and the use of parentheses can determine the outcome of a calculation.

- $2+3/10 = 2.3$
- $(2+3)/10 = 0.5$
- $(2+3)/10^2 = 0.05$
- $(2+3)/(10^2) = 0.05$
- $2+3/10^2 = 2.03$

It is generally a good practice to use parentheses to make the meaning of a calculation clear and to ensure that it is calculated correctly.

When a formula is to be entered into just one cell, the references to its inputs can simply specify column and row. For example, (D2+D3)/D5. The cell reference D2 is an example of a **relative reference**. If the formula above was entered in cell E3, then the reference to cell D2 is interpreted by Excel as referring to the cell one column to the left and one row above the current cell. That is, the cell reference is interpreted *relative to the current cell*. Likewise, from cell E3 a reference to J14 is interpreted as a reference to the cell 5 columns to the right and 11 rows down.

Many spreadsheets are built by copying formulas from one cell to a range of cells. For example, row 18 in the Office Building spreadsheet (Net operating income) requires subtracting Operating Income from Gross Income each year. Thus the formula (C16-C17) entered into cell C18 is the same formula we need in the following years, cells D18:G18. We can fill these four cells efficiently by entering the formula once in cell C18 and then copying it to the other cells. Because Excel interprets the cell addresses C16 and C17 relative to the current cell, when we copy the formula it continues to apply correctly.

However, this same procedure will not work for row 17, in which we calculate Operating Expense. The Operating Expense for Year 1 is the size of the building in square feet (C5) times the cost per square foot (C7). Thus we could calculate the correct value in C17 using the formula C5*C7. But the Operating Expense in the next year, Year 2, is not calculated in the same way. The size of the building is fixed for all time in C5, but the cost per square foot grows each year as given in cells D7:G7. So the correct formula in cell D17 is C5*D7. In other words, one of the addresses in the original formula (C5) needs to remain fixed, while the other (D7) needs to shift from year to year. Clearly, we need a way to write a cell address for C5 that Excel can interpret not in a relative fashion but as fixed. This is done using dollar signs before the column letter and row number, as in $C$5. The first dollar sign fixes the column during copying; the second dollar sign fixes the row. So, if we write the original formula in cell C17 as $C$5*C7, which does not change the value in C17, we can then copy it across the row correctly. The reference to the size of the building in C5 will remain fixed and the reference to the cost will change as needed. Addresses with fixed columns or rows are known as **absolute addresses**. Examine all the formulas in the Office Building spreadsheet to see how relative and absolute addresses are used to make copying easy.

BASIC FUNCTIONS

Excel provides hundreds of built-in functions for calculating almost anything. No matter how complex or unusual the calculation we have in mind, Excel almost always has a function (or perhaps several functions) that can accomplish the task. Using Excel functions presents three challenges:

- Identifying the appropriate function or functions
- Using the function correctly
- Testing that the results match what was intended

An efficient way to locate useful functions is to open the Insert Function window by clicking f_x next to the formula bar. (The Insert Function window can also be accessed from the Formulas ribbon.) Figure A1.10 shows the Insert Function window with the category

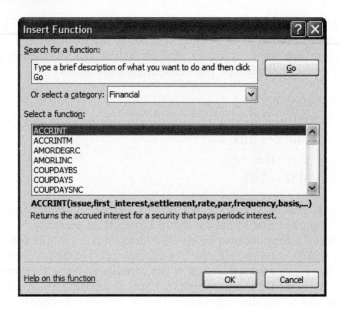

Financial selected. The drop-down menu displays a list of function categories. The major categories are:

- Most Recently Used
- All
- Financial
- Date & Time
- Math & Trig
- Statistical
- Lookup & Reference
- Database
- Text
- Logical
- Information

To find a function, first identify the category it is likely to fall into, and then scan the alphabetical list of functions in this category. Each time a function is highlighted, the Insert Function window displays a brief description of the function and its inputs. For example, in Figure A1.11 we have highlighted the financial function ISPMT. The window displays its

FIGURE A1.11 The
ISPMT Function

Insert Function

Search for a function:

Type a brief description of what you want to do and then click Go

Go

Or select a category: Financial

Select a function:

INTRATE
IPMT
IRR
ISPMT
MDURATION
MIRR
NOMINAL

ISPMT(rate,per,nper,pv)
Returns the interest paid during a specific period of an investment.

Help on this function   OK   Cancel

FIGURE A1.12 The Function Arguments Window for the ISPMT Function

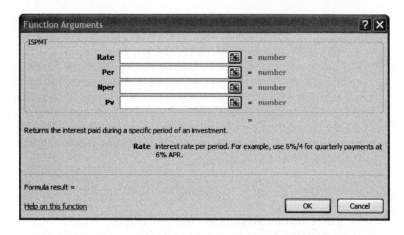

inputs (`rate`, `per`, `nper`, `pv`) and gives a short description: `Returns the interest paid during a specific period of an investment.`

At this point, click on OK and the Function Arguments window opens (Figure A1.12). This window displays a reference box for each of the arguments of the function (four in this case). We can either enter numbers directly in these boxes or (better) enter cell addresses (click on the icon at the right end of the box and identify the inputs by selecting them in the spreadsheet). The Function Arguments window shows the numerical value of each input as it is entered, and when enough inputs are entered, the window shows the value of the function. This allows us to see if we are getting plausible results before entering the function in the spreadsheet. (Help on this specific function is also available directly from the link at the bottom of this window.) Figure A1.13 shows the Function Arguments window with all four inputs entered and the result calculated (−122,060). Click on OK and the function will be entered in the cell we are editing.

Business analysts make heavy use of just a few of the hundreds of functions in Excel. We will describe six of the most important of these functions here. Other, more advanced functions are described later.

The SUM function is used to add a set of numbers. Its arguments can simply be a list of cell references. For example, `SUM(C1,C3,C5)` adds the contents of the three cells listed, where the cell references are set off by commas. Alternatively, `SUM(C1:C5)` adds the contents of the cells in the range C1:C5. The SUM function can also be used to add a list of non-contiguous ranges, for example `SUM(C1:C5,D2:D6,E3:E7)`.

The MAX and MIN functions are used to find the largest and smallest values in a range. Thus `MAX(1,3,5)` yields 5, and `MIN(C1:C5)` calculates the smallest value in the range C1:C5.

The AVERAGE function calculates the average of the values in a range. The range can be in a column, in a row, or in an array (a rectangular range extending over multiple columns and/or rows). If we are averaging a column of data that contains empty cells, does the AVERAGE function include those cells in the calculation? Click on Help in the Function Arguments window and note that the AVERAGE function ignores cells

FIGURE A1.13 The ISPMT Function Evaluated

Function Arguments

ISPMT

Rate	$C$10/12	= 0.01
Per	1	= 1
Nper	360	= 360
Pv	$C$9*$C$4*$C$5	= 12240000

= -122060

Returns the interest paid during a specific period of an investment.

Pv   lump sum amount that a series of future payments is right now.

Formula result =   -$122,060

Help on this function   OK   Cancel

containing text, logical values (TRUE or FALSE), and empty cells, but does include cells containing the value zero.

The NPV function calculates the net present value of a stream of payments at a given discount rate. We illustrate the use of the NPV function in the Office Building spreadsheet. In this example, we make a down payment of $2,160,000 at the present time, the *start* of Year 1 (cell C22). Then we receive cash inflows at the *end* of the next five years (cells C25:G25). To calculate the net present value of this set of payments (cell B27) we discount the cash inflows to the present, using the discount rate given in cell C12, and subtract the down payment. (Because it occurs at the present time, it is not discounted.) The formula is

$$\text{NPV(C12,C25:G25)} - \text{C22}$$

The Function Arguments window (Figure A1.14) shows the cell addresses of the arguments of the NPV function as well as their numerical values. It also shows the resulting value of the NPV calculation ($13,632,032.03), as well as the value of the entire formula ($11,472,032).

It is important to remember that the NPV function discounts the first payment in a stream of payments. Thus in the Office Building example, we discounted the cash inflow in Year 1 because according to the model it comes in at the *end* of the year and the date of the evaluation is the *beginning* of the year. If, instead, the first cash inflow occurred at the beginning of the year, at the same time as the down payment, we would discount with the NPV function starting with Year 2 and add the undiscounted cash inflow from Year 1.

The IF function is used to perform a logical test and calculate one value if the test is true and another if it is false. The syntax for the IF function is

$$\text{IF(logical test,value} - \text{if} - \text{true,value} - \text{if} - \text{false)}$$

The first argument, the logical test, is an expression that Excel can evaluate as TRUE or FALSE. For example, the expression $100 > 0$ evaluates as TRUE, while $100 > 200$ evaluates as FALSE. (For practice, go to the Office Building spreadsheet and in an empty cell enter the formula =C4>0. The result should be TRUE. The formula =E16>5000000 should be FALSE.)

If the logical test in an IF statement is TRUE, the *second* argument (value-if-true) is calculated and placed in the cell. If the logical test is FALSE, the *third* argument (value-if-false) is calculated and placed in the cell. For example, IF(100>0,25,50) evaluates as 25, and IF(100<0,25,50) evaluates as 50. Each of the three arguments in an IF function can be as complex as needed, as long as Excel can evaluate the logical test as TRUE or FALSE. So we could write the following function to choose one of two column sums, depending on the relative values of two other cells:

$$\text{IF(D36} > \text{G76,SUM(A1:A100),SUM(B1:B100))}$$

FIGURE A1.14 The NPV Function

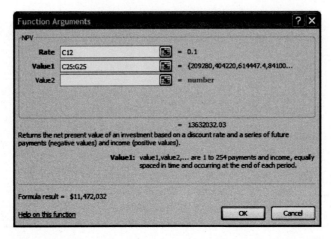

This example illustrates the **nesting of functions**. Nesting involves using one function within another. So in the example above, we have nested two SUM functions within an IF function. Excel imposes no practical limit on the number of functions that can be nested. However, nested functions can become complex and difficult to debug. It is good practice to calculate the components of a complex nested function separately to ensure that the logic is correct before bringing them together. And remember that future users of the model will appreciate documentation of formulas like the following one, whose meaning is not transparent:

$$IF(D345<I87,OFFSET(G118,,MAX(I87:J129)-I86),-H45)$$

CHARTING

Charting is an essential skill for the business analyst, because model results can often best be understood in graphical terms. Excel provides tools that automate much of the detailed work involved in developing a chart. Charts are created by selecting the Insert tab and the Charts group.

The first step in creating a chart is to highlight the relevant data on the spreadsheet. Then select Insert►Charts. Next select the type of chart (Column, Line, Pie, Bar, Area, Scatter, or Other Charts). A window then opens showing a variety of ways to depict that type of chart. Select one of these and Excel will plot the data in that format.

When Excel displays a chart, it adds three Chart Tools tabs to the ribbon (Design, Layout, and Format). These tabs also appear whenever an existing chart is selected. The Design tab includes the following groups:

- Type
- Data
- Chart Layouts
- Chart Styles
- Location

The Type group allows a change in the chart type or saves the current chart as a template. The Data group allows data rows and columns to be swapped or the data range to be modified. Chart Layouts includes a variety of chart layouts for titles, axes, and so on. Chart Styles offers a variety of colors and shades. Finally, the Location group places the chart in the current worksheet or in its own worksheet.

We illustrate two types of frequently used charts: **line charts** and **scatter charts**. The data involve advertising and sales over the past 11 years, as given in the table below. A line chart allows us to see how Advertising and Sales have changed over the past eleven years, while a scatter chart allows us to see whether Advertising and Sales are related to each other.

Year	Advertising	Sales
1995	56	600
1996	56	630
1997	59	662
1998	60	695
1999	61	729
2000	61	766
2001	63	804
2002	65	844
2003	69	886
2004	68	931
2005	67	977

To create a line chart for Advertising and Sales over time, highlight all the data in the spreadsheet (including the column headings) and select Insert►Chart. Choose the Line chart type and the 2D-Line sub-type that shows each data point (Line with Markers), as shown in Figure A1.15. This chart is problematic because the years have been plotted as a

FIGURE A1.15 Initial Line Chart for Advertising and Sales

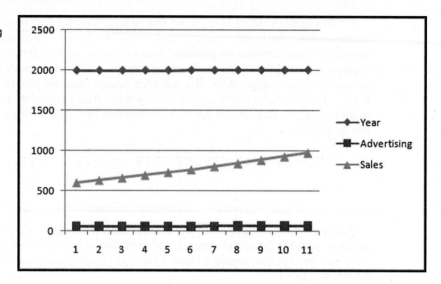

data series rather than as the values on the X-axis. To correct this, and to ensure that Years are on the horizontal axis, select Design▶Data▶Select Data. Under Legend Entries (Series) highlight Year and click on Remove. Also, under Horizontal (Category) Axis Labels click on Edit and enter the range for years: C5:C15. Click on OK and the chart will appear as in Figure A1.16. Clearly, Sales have increased steadily over this period. A close look reveals that the same is true for Advertising.

We can continue to refine this chart, using the options under Chart Layouts and Chart Styles. Our final version, shown in Figure A1.17, has an overall title, a Y-axis label, and a key showing the exact values for each data point. This is just one of 12 pre-defined options under Chart Layout.

FIGURE A1.16 Entering Years as X-Axis Labels

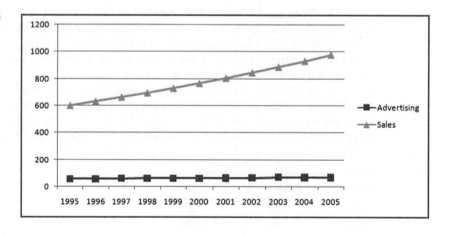

FIGURE A1.17 Final Line Chart for Advertising and Sales

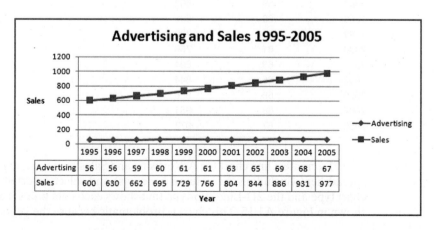

FIGURE A1.18 Initial Scatter Chart for Advertising and Sales

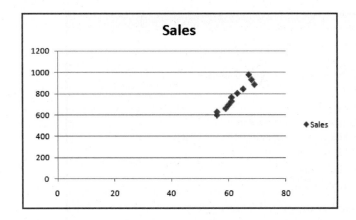

To create a scatter chart (sometimes referred to in Excel as X Y (Scatter)), highlight just the Advertising and Sales data, select Insert▶Chart▶Scatter▶Scatter with only Markers. The result is shown in Figure A1.18. This graph is correct, but it does not display the data in the clearest fashion because the axis scales are inappropriate. We change the horizontal axis scale by right-clicking in the Chart Area, selecting `Format Chart Axis`, and setting the minimum value under `Axis Options` to 50. Repeat this process for the vertical axis, setting the minimum to 500 and the maximum to 1000. The improved chart is shown in Figure A1.19.

This chart conveys a different message from the line chart. Here we see that higher levels of Advertising seem to be associated with higher levels of Sales, which suggests perhaps that Advertising is effective in increasing Sales. But the relationship may be influenced by other factors, since the scatter chart is not a straight line.

PRINTING

Printing in Excel is similar to printing in any Office application, with a few exceptions we discuss here.

First, many spreadsheets contain too much information to print on a single page. Depending on the column width and row height, Excel will select a range of cells to print on each page. Open the Office Building spreadsheet and select File▶Print. Excel displays the spreadsheet as it will look when printed. After printing, the spreadsheet is divided into pages with heavy dotted lines. The first page extends from A1 to E52; the second page from A53 to E104, and so on.

We can select certain cells for printing by highlighting the relevant range and selecting Page Layout▶Page Setup▶Print Area▶Set Print Area.

We display the Page Setup window by selecting Page Layout▶Page Setup. Figure A1.20 shows the Page Setup window, which allows us to control other aspects of the printed page. For example, on the Page tab we can change the orientation of the printed spreadsheet from Portrait to Landscape. We can also change the scaling on this tab.

FIGURE A1.19 Final Scatter Chart for Advertising and Sales

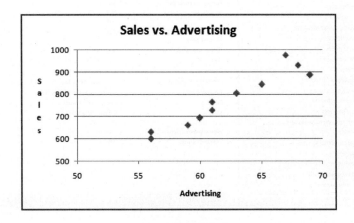

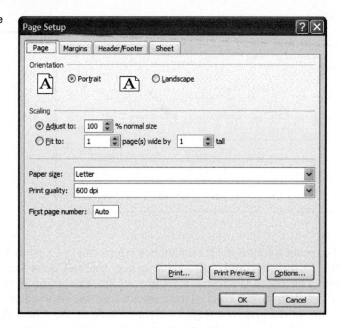

A particularly useful option here is the button that fits a worksheet to a specified number of pages. Quite often, the number of pages is set to 1 for a scaled snapshot of the entire worksheet. On the Margins tab, we can alter the top, bottom, left, and right margins and the location of the contents on the page. Using the Header/Footer tab we can enter text that will appear on every printed page, such as a page number or the name of the author of the workbook. Moreover, on the Sheet tab we can control whether gridlines and row and column headings will appear on the printed spreadsheet.

HELP OPTIONS

A great deal of useful information is available in Excel Help, which is opened either by pressing F1 or clicking on the question mark icon in the upper right corner of the spreadsheet (Figure A1.21).

Excel also offers access to targeted Help topics in a variety of specific situations. For example, some dialog boxes show a question mark at the right-hand end of the title bar.

FIGURE A1.21 The Excel
Help Window

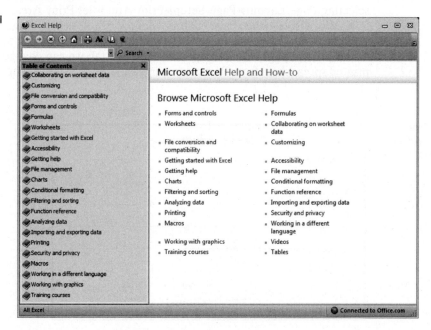

Click on the question mark and Excel opens the Help window for the operation controlled by the window. In other windows, there is a special link to Help. For example, the Insert Function window has a link `Help on this function` which opens the Help window for the function highlighted.

KEYBOARD SHORTCUTS

Most users of Windows are familiar with using the keyboard as an alternative to selecting commands or tools with the mouse. In Word, for example, using only the mouse to copy and paste a portion of text requires highlighting the text, selecting the Copy icon from the Home tab, clicking on the new location for the text, and selecting the Paste icon from the Home tab. Alternatively, and possibly more quickly, we can replace the first selection with the keystroke combination Ctrl + C and the second selection with the keystroke combination Ctrl + V. These keystroke combinations are examples of **keyboard shortcuts**. Since Ctrl + C and Ctrl + V can be executed with two fingers of the left hand, we can keep the right hand on the mouse and use both hands almost simultaneously. (Most keyboard shortcuts are not case sensitive, so upper and lower cases give the same results.)

Excel shares many keyboard shortcuts with other Windows applications. For example, we can use Ctrl + C and Ctrl + V in Excel to copy and paste the contents of individual cells or ranges of cells just as we copy text in Word. Other shortcuts for familiar actions include:

Ctrl + N:	File►New
Ctrl + O:	File ►Open
Ctrl + S:	File ►Save
Ctrl + P:	File ►Print
Ctrl + X:	Home►Clipboard►Cut
Ctrl + F:	Home►Editing►Find & Select►Find
Ctrl + H:	Home►Editing►Find & Select►Replace
Ctrl + G:	Home►Editing►Find & Select►Go To

These familiar shortcuts are only a small sample of the shortcuts available in Excel. Most of these use the special keys labeled F1-F12, Ctrl, Alt, or Shift. Here is a further sample:

Format cells:	Ctrl + 1
Display Help:	F1
Insert new worksheet:	Shift + F11
Move cursor to cell A1:	Ctrl + Home
Display the Find and Replace dialog box:	Shift + F5
Switch to the next nonadjacent selection to the left:	Ctrl + Left Arrow

In Figure A1.22 we list for handy reference some of the most useful of these keyboard shortcuts. (An exhaustive list is available under Help: search on "keyboard shortcuts" and select the topic `Excel shortcut and function keys`.) We recommend scanning this list for shortcuts that may have been forgotten or new ones for operations that have become routine. Whenever we regularly encounter a tedious and slow operation, it makes sense to search for a keyboard shortcut to save time.

CELL COMMENTS

With few exceptions, the spreadsheets we have seen in actual use are poorly documented. Most practicing analysts have experienced the frustration of trying to understand a complex formula or a model design six months after they built it, or two years after someone else built it. But while everyone agrees we should document our spreadsheets, almost no one does it. The reason seems to be that most forms of documentation are too

FIGURE A1.22   Useful
Keyboard Shortcuts

	Moving and scrolling
Home	Move to the beginning of the row
Ctrl + Home	Move to the beginning of the worksheet (A1)
Ctrl + End	Move to the bottom-right corner of the used area of the worksheet
Ctrl + arrow key	Move to the edge of the current data region
PgDn	Move down one screen
PgUp	Move up one screen
Alt + PgDn	Move one screen to the right
Alt + PgUp	Move one screen to the left
	Entering data on a worksheet
Shift + Enter	Complete a cell entry and move up one cell
Tab	Complete a cell entry and move to the right cell
Shift + Tab	Complete a cell entry and move to the left cell
Ctrl + Delete	Delete text to the end of the line
Shift + F2	Edit a cell comment
Ctrl + D	Fill down (a selected column of cells with the content of the first cell)
Ctrl + R	Fill to the right (a selected row of cells with the content of the first cell)
	Working in cells or the formula bar
Ctrl+ ~	Display all formulas
F2	Edit the active cell
F3	Open the Paste Name window
Shift + F3	Open the Insert Function (or Function Arguments) window
F9	Calculate all sheets in all open workbooks
Ctrl + Alt + F9	Calculate all worksheets in the active workbook
Shift + F9	Calculate the active worksheet
Ctrl + Shift + Enter	Enter a formula as an array formula
Ctrl + ;(semicolon)	Enter the current date
Ctrl + Shift + :(colon)	Enter the current time
	Inserting, deleting, and copying selection
Delete	Clear the contents of the selection
Ctrl + - (hyphen)	Delete (dialog box)
Ctrl + Z	Undo the last action
Ctrl + Shift + Plus sign	Insert (dialog box)
	Selecting cells, columns, or rows
Shift + arrow key	Extend the selection by one cell
Ctrl + Shift + arrow key	Extend the selection to the last nonblank cell in the same column or row
Ctrl + space bar	Select the entire column
Ctrl + A	Select the entire worksheet
	Working with macros
Alt + F8	Display the Macro dialog box
Alt + F11	Display the Visual Basic Editor (VBE)
	Note: In most cases, these shortcuts are not case sensitive.

time consuming. Cell comments are one easy way to document the details behind a cell or range of cells.

Inserting Comments To insert a comment in a particular cell, highlight the cell and choose Review▶Comments▶New Comment. This opens a comment window to the side of the cell, linked to the cell by an arrow. The comment contains the user's name as a default. It also places a red triangle in the upper right corner of the cell, which is the indicator that the cell contains a comment.

The location or size of a comment can be changed after it is highlighted (by clicking on its border). It is good practice to size the comment box so that is does not extend beyond the contents, and to place it on the spreadsheet where it will be visible but not cover up other important cells. Figure A1.23 shows a comment entered in cell C12 and sized to fit a blank portion of the spreadsheet.

Displaying Comments All of the comments in a workbook can be displayed by choosing Review▶Comments▶Show All Comments. This command toggles back and forth between showing all of the comments and showing none of them. The command Show/Hide Comment applies only to the selected cell.

FIGURE A1.23 Cell Comment

	A	B	C	D	E	F	G
1	Office Building						
2							
3	Parameters	Rate of increase	2002	2003	2004	2005	2006
4	Building cost per sq ft		$80.00				
5	Size of building		180,000				
6	Rent per sq ft	5%	$15.00	15.75	16.54	17.36	18.23
7	Operating expense per sq	6%	$1.20	1.27	1.35	1.43	1.51
8	Vacancy rate	-4%	30%	0.26	0.22	0.18	0.14
9	Percent financed		85%				
10	Mortgage rate		12%				
11	Sale multiple		12				
12	Cost of capital		10%				
13							
14			2002	2003	2004	2005	2006
15	Cash Flow						
16		Gross income	1,890,000	2,097,900	2,321,865	2,562,982	2,822,406
17		Operating expense	216,000	228,960	242,698	257,259	272,695
18		Net operating income	1,674,000	1,868,940	2,079,167	2,305,722	2,549,710
19		Interest cost	$1,464,720	$1,464,720	$1,464,720	$1,464,720	$1,464,720
20		Before-tax cash flow	$209,280	$404,220	$614,447	$841,002	$1,084,990
21							
22		Down payment (at time 0)	$2,160,000				
23		Sale price					$30,596,526
24		Mortgage cost					$12,240,000
25		End of year cash flows	$209,280	$404,220	$614,447	$841,002	$19,441,516
26							
27	NPV	$11,472,032					
28							

(Comment box on cells D9–F10: "This is the discount rate used on all projects in this class.")

Sheet tab: A1.23

Editing Comments Edit the comment by placing the cursor anywhere within the comment box. All the usual Excel text editing features can be used inside comment boxes.

Deleting Comments To delete a comment, click on Review▶Comments▶Delete. Another way to access these commands is to select a cell with a comment and then right-click. The menu that appears will contain the commands that manage cell comments.

Copying Comments When a cell containing a comment is copied, the contents and the comment are both copied to the new cell. To copy *just* the comment in a cell, copy the source cell, then highlight the destination cell. Next, select Home▶Clipboard▶Paste▶Paste Special, selecting Comments and clicking OK.

Printing Comments Comments on the spreadsheet will be printed just as they appear on the screen. If the comments are extensive, we may want to print them in one place. Print all comments at the end of the worksheet by choosing Page Layout▶Page Setup▶ ↘▶Sheet tab and selecting Comments: At end of sheet.

NAMING CELLS AND RANGES

Individual cells and ranges of cells can be given names, and these names can be used in formulas to make them more readable. Named ranges are also used occasionally in other contexts, such as identifying a database for filtering or specifying input data for a Pivot Table. The use of range names is highly recommended in corporate settings for models that are used by many people. However, for the solo modeler, it is an open question whether the additional complexity of range names justifies their use.

Some examples of the use of range names will make their advantages clear. Here is a typical formula from a financial spreadsheet written in the standard manner, with cell addresses:

$$D20 = D13 + D14 + D15$$

Here is the same formula when written using range names:

$$Total\ Expenses = Cost\_of\_Goods\_Sold + Depreciation + Interest$$

Here are two equivalent formulas for calculating the actual quantity of a product sold depending on whether demand is more or less than the quantity available:

```
D14 = IF(D13 > D10,D10,D13)
Sales = IF(Demand > Qty_Available,Qty_Available,Demand)
```

In both of these cases, the formulas with range names are easy to read and easy to test against the underlying logic of the situation. In other words, when we see that Interest is included in the calculation of Total Expenses, we can mentally check whether this is the correct accounting treatment of interest costs. It is more difficult to do so when we see that D20 includes D15. Similarly, we can read and verify the logic of the IF statement more easily when it is written using range names than when it involves cell references.

However, there are some drawbacks to using range names. The most obvious is that entering range names takes time away from other work. Another drawback is that we must verify that each range name actually points to the correct cell or range. For example, it is not enough to check that Interest is *conceptually* part of Total Expenses; we must also verify that the range name "Interest" actually points to the cell where interest is calculated. Range names introduce an additional layer of complexity in a model, even as they simplify the look of formulas. Perhaps the best argument for their use is that they make a model more understandable for new users. Thus, if a model is expected to have a long lifetime and to be used and modified by a number of other users, range names are probably a worthwhile investment.

The simplest way to define a range name for a single cell is to place the cursor on that cell and note that the address of the cell appears in the Name box above column A. Click in the Name box and enter the name of the cell there. For example, place the cursor on cell C4 in the Office Building workbook, and its cell address appears in the Name box. Type "Building_cost" in the box and press Enter. (Range names cannot contain blanks, so one common approach is to use the underscore character to turn a multiword name into a single word.) Now whenever we highlight cell C4, its range name appears in the Name box. When range names have been entered for all the parameters in cells B4:C12, we can click on the down arrow at the side of the Name box and a list of all range names will appear. Highlight one of those names and the cursor will move to the named cell.

An alternative means for entering range names is to choose Formulas▶Defined Names▶Define Name. This opens the New Name window, as shown in Figure A1.24. The cell address of the cursor appears in the lower portion of the window. In this example, the range name includes the sheet name (followed by an exclamation point) and an absolute reference to the cell location ($C$4). To enter the range name Size for cell B5 place the cursor on cell B5, choose Formulas▶Defined Names▶Define Name, and type Size in the upper box. Now when the cursor is placed on B5, Size will appear in the Name box. In the New Name window, the user has an option to select the scope of the name, determining whether it applies to the workbook or just to the worksheet. The default is workbook scope, which is the most common use because it avoids

FIGURE A1.24 New Name Window

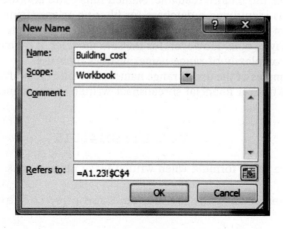

FIGURE A1.25 Documenting Range Names with the Paste List Command

	A	B	C	D	E	F	G
22		Down payment (at time 0)	$2,160,000				
23		Sale price					$30,596,526
24		Mortgage cost					$12,240,000
25		End of year cash flows	$209,280	$404,220	$614,447	$841,002	$19,441,516
26							
27	**NPV**		$11,472,032				
28							
29							
30	**Range Names**	Building_cost	='4.6'!$C$4				
31		Cost_of_Capital	='4.6'!$C$12				
32		Down_payment__at_time_0	='4.6'!$C$22				
33		End_of_year_cash_flows	='4.6'!$C$25:$G$25				
34		Mortgage_rate	='4.6'!$C$10				
35		Operating_expense	='4.6'!$C$7				
36		Operating_expense_growth	='4.6'!$B$7				
37		Percent_financed	='4.6'!$C$9				
38		Rent	='4.6'!$C$6				
39		Rent_growth	='4.6'!$B$6				
40		Sale_multiple	='4.6'!$C$11				
41		Size	='4.6'!$C$5				
42		Vacancy	='4.6'!$C$8				
43		Vacancy_growth	='4.6'!$B$8				
44							

A1.23 **A1.25**

confusion. When names are entered in the Name box, they are automatically assigned workbook scope.

Entering a name for a cell does not automatically change cell references in existing formulas to name references. For example, the original formula in cell D6, $C$6*(1+$B$6), does not change when we later assign range names to cells B6 and C6. We can rewrite this formula, however, using the range names, as Rent*(1+Rent_growth). Similarly, we can rewrite the formula in E6 as D6*(1+Rent_growth) and copy this formula to the two cells to the right. Alternatively, to insert newly-created range names into existing formulas, we can highlight the range D6:G6 and select Formulas▶DefinedNames▶DefineName▶ Apply Names . . . Then we select Rent-growth from the list of range names and click OK. When we look at the formulas in cells D6:G6, we will see that $B$6 has been replaced by its range name.

In the worksheet corresponding to Figure A1.25, we have entered range names for all the input parameters and for many of the formulas. Examine this worksheet carefully to see how range names are used and how they improve the readability of formulas. Note that the formula for NPV in cell B27 reads

NPV(Cost_of_capital,End_of_year_cash_flows)-Down_payment_at_time_0

The range names Cost_of_capital and Down_payment_at_time_0 each refer to a single cell. However, the range name End_of_year_cash_flows refers to the range C25: G25. Range names can refer to ranges of any size and dimension and can be used in formulas and functions as long as the range itself is appropriate.

Range names often need to be edited, deleted, or redefined. All of these operations can be carried out in the Name Manager window. Another useful option within that window tabulates the range names on the spreadsheet. To create the table, move the cursor to an unused area of the spreadsheet. Choose Formulas▶DefinedNames▶Use in formula, then select Paste Names . . . and Paste List. Figure A1.25 shows the range names and their cell addresses pasted into cells B30:C43. This procedure documents range names and makes them easier to check. However, if we redefine the location of a range name, this list will *not* be updated automatically.

Many more options exist for using range names, but a warning is in order: range names are not a panacea for the problems arising from obscure and undocumented formulas. One limitation of range names is that in most cases copying and pasting formulas is easier with a mixture of relative and absolute addresses than with range names. Another limitation is the added complexity and possibilities for error that range names introduce. It is always a good idea to keep individual formulas as simple as possible and to document any formula whose logic is not self-explanatory.

Excel Tip	Advantages:
Advantages and Dis-advantages of Range Names	• Formulas are easier to understand. • Useful in Pivot Table and other applications. Disadvantages: • May reference incorrect cells or ranges. • Adds complexity to spreadsheet. • Requires additional effort. • Complicates copying.

SOME ADVANCED TOOLS

Sophisticated use of formulas and functions is a mark of an expert Excel modeler. Unfortunately, there are so many different ways to use these tools that no book can communicate them all. The exhaustive lists of functions that are commonly provided in Excel manuals are a useful reference, once the user knows what function to look up. But users who don't know the basics of creating complex formulas often cannot use such references effectively. In this section we present some advanced tools for formulas and functions:

- R1C1 references
- Mixed addresses
- Advanced functions

R1C1 Reference Style

Most Excel users are familiar with the column-and-row style of cell references. Thus, D16 and $D$16 are two different ways to refer to the contents of the cell in the fourth column and 16th row. Although familiar, this system has some disadvantages. One is that the columns after column Z are designated AA, AB, and so on; and the columns after column ZZ are designated AAA, AAB, and so on. Another is that when we copy a formula that employs a relative address, the relative cell reference changes in each successive cell. Thus, a formula like $C$6*(1+D6), when copied to the right, becomes $C$6*(1+E6), $C$6* (1+F6), $C$6*(1+G6), and so on, which makes debugging a challenge.

Excel makes available a different way to reference cell addresses that corrects some of these problems. In the **R1C1 style,** the columns are numbered from 1 to 16,384. Absolute cell references simply specify the row and column of the cell, as in R16C4 for D16. Relative references specify the number of rows above or below the current cell and the number of columns left or right of the current cell. For example, the relative address R[1]C[1] refers to the cell one row below the current cell and one column to the right. The address R[−1]C[−1] refers to the cell one row above and one column to the left. To refer to the cell one row above and in the same column, we simply use R[−1]C. To refer to the cell in the same row and one column to the right we use RC[1].

To get an idea of what this style of cell references looks like in practice, open the Office Building model (Figure A1.23). The formula in cell C16, which reads $C$5*C6* (1-C8), involves both absolute and relative addresses. It is constructed to allow copying to cells D16:G16. Now turn on the R1C1 reference style by selecting File▶Options▶ Formulas. Then, under Working with formulas, check the box R1C1 reference style. The same formula now appears this way:

$$R5C3*R[-10]C*(1 - R[-8]C)$$

Instead of the absolute reference $C$5 we have the absolute reference R5C3. Instead of the relative reference C6 we have the relative reference R[−10]C. And instead of the relative reference C8 we have R[−8]C. Note that this formula can also be copied across the row. The biggest difference between these two approaches is that in the R1C1 style *all* the formulas from C16 to G16 are identical. This makes debugging a model much simpler. In fact, all of the formulas in this worksheet that are copied across the columns are identical (see rows 6–9, 16–20, and 25).

Since Excel allows us to switch back and forth from one style of addressing to the other, there is no reason not to use the system that is most convenient at the moment. Some modelers use the R1C1 style when developing their models but switch to the normal style when the model is complete. In this way, they enjoy the benefits of the more logical and more easily debugged R1C1 style without imposing this less well known style on users.

Mixed Addresses

Earlier we discussed using absolute and relative addresses like $C$5 and C5 to make the copy-paste operation easier. We can think of the dollar signs in absolute addresses as fixing the column and the row of the address during copying. Often, we wish to fix both column and row, but there are circumstances in which we want to fix just one. We do this with **mixed addresses**. In a mixed address, either the column is fixed and not the row, as in $C5, or the row is fixed and not the column, as in C$5.

Here is an example of a situation in which mixed addresses are useful. Refer to the workbook in Figure A1.26. In column B, we have input data on sales covering twelve months from January to December. In column C, we want to calculate cumulative sales from January to the current month. Can we enter a formula for cumulative sales in cell C2 that we can copy for the remaining eleven months? Each month we need a formula that sums the cells in column B from January (row 2) down to the current row. This can be accomplished with the formula SUM($B$2:$B2). Note that the absolute address $B$2 fixes the starting value for the sum, and the mixed address $B2 allows the row (but not the column) of the ending value to change as we copy. Enter this formula in cell C2; the result is 145 as expected. Then copy it down to row 13 and verify that it calculates the cumulative sales as required. The formula for December (C13), for example, becomes SUM($B$2:$B13).

Entering the dollar signs in cell addresses can be tedious, especially when using mixed addresses. The function key F4 is a useful hotkey in this situation. When editing a formula, place the cursor on a relative cell reference. Press F4 once and both dollar signs are added; press again, and only the column dollar sign appears; press a third time, and only the row dollar sign appears; press a fourth time and the original relative reference appears (with no dollar signs).

Advanced Functions

AND and OR   The logical functions AND and OR can be used to detect the relationship between values in various cells in a spreadsheet as it changes during analysis. For example, in the Office Building model we can determine whether the building cost is above $100 and the NPV is above $10,000,000 by using

$$AND(C4 > 100, B27 > 10000000)$$

The logical functions take on only two values: TRUE and FALSE. Thus in this spreadsheet

$$AND(C4 > 100, B27 > 10000000) = TRUE$$
$$OR(C4 < 100, B27 < 10000000) = FALSE$$

Logical functions can also be used to set flags, which are cells that warn the user when spreadsheet values are outside normal or acceptable ranges.

FIGURE A1.26 Using Mixed Addresses in Copying

	A	B	C
1	**Month**	**Sales**	**Cumulative**
2	January	145	145
3	February	106	251
4	March	76	327
5	April	89	416
6	May	106	522
7	June	113	635
8	July	96	731
9	August	66	797
10	September	104	901
11	October	73	974
12	November	77	1051
13	December	119	1170
14			

A1.26

Truth tables are helpful for understanding how these logical functions operate. For example, the AND function is only true when *both* conditions are true, as shown in the table below.

Truth Table for AND

| | | Condition 1 | |
		True	False
	True	True	False
Condition 2			
	False	False	False

The OR function, on the other hand, is true if one or the other or both conditions are true, as shown in the following table.

Truth Table for OR

| | | Condition 1 | |
		True	False
	True	True	True
Condition 2			
	False	True	False

Logical functions are particularly useful in combination with the IF function. When the logical test in an IF function depends on two conditions being true, such as D3>10 and D4<5, we could use two IF functions:

IF(D3 > 10, IF(D4 < 5, value_if_true, value – if – false), value – if – false))

Or we can simplify using the AND function:

IF(AND(D3 > 10, D4 < 5), value_if_true, value – if – false)

If the logical condition were true when one or the other or both conditions were true, we would use the OR function:

IF(OR(D3 > 10, D4 < 5), value_if_true, value – if – false)

SUMIF and COUNTIF   Two functions closely related to the IF function are SUMIF and COUNTIF. SUMIF adds all the cells in a range that satisfy a specified condition, while COUNTIF counts all the cells in a range that satisfy a specified condition. (COUNTIF is related to the COUNT function, which counts all the cells in a range that contain numbers.)

For example, if the range from D1 to D5 contains the following values

26
19
33
14
21

then SUMIF(D1:D5, "< 20") = 33 and COUNTIF(D1:D5, "< 22") = 3. (Note that the condition in the SUMIF and COUNTIF functions is enclosed in quotes.)

VLOOKUP and HLOOKUP   The VLOOKUP (and HLOOKUP) functions are useful for capturing relationships based on tables. Suppliers, for example, typically offer discounts for larger order quantities. Here is an example of such a price schedule:

Order at least	Unit price
100	$39.50
200	38.00
300	37.00
400	36.00
500	35.00

We could capture this relationship using IF functions, but it would require nesting five IF functions. A simpler way is to use VLOOKUP, which takes three inputs: Lookup_value, Table_array, and Col_index_number. The Lookup_value is the value in the first column of the table. In this case, it is the order quantity for which we want to determine the price. The Table_array is the range in which the table is located. If the two columns of data in the above table were in cells C4:D8, the Table_array would be C4:D8. Finally, the Col_index_number is the number of the column in the table in which the result lies. In our example this is column 2. So

$$VLOOKUP(100, C4:D8, 2) = 39.50$$

and

$$VLOOKUP(425, C4:D8, 2) = 35.00$$

The values in the first column of the table must be sorted, in either ascending or descending order. When the Lookup_value is not found in the first column, the VLOOKUP function finds the range in which it lies and chooses the next value in the table. Thus, all values above 400 but below 500 are treated as if they were 500. (Other options are available; see the Function Arguments window or Help.)

The HLOOKUP function performs the same function as the VLOOKUP function except that it is designed for horizontal tables.

INDEX, SMALL, and MATCH [*] The following example shows how three specialized functions, INDEX, SMALL, and MATCH, can be used in combination to carry out a sophisticated sequence of calculations. The example arises in power generation, where a large set of power plants must be brought into production in order from lowest cost to highest. Figure A1.27 shows part of the data in a workbook that contains cost and capacity data for 50 plants. The plants are numbered from 1 to 50 in column B. Plant capacities and costs are given in columns C and D, respectively. Our goal is to determine cumulative capacity when we employ only a certain number of plants in order of cost. Thus, we want to know, for example, how much capacity we have if we use the 35 cheapest plants.

The first step is to rank the costs from lowest to highest. We do this in column F using the SMALL function. The SMALL function calculates the kth smallest value in a range. So SMALL($D$6:$D$55,B6) returns the lowest cost; SMALL($D$6:$D$55,B7) the second lowest cost, and so on. Next, we need to find the relative position of a ranked cost in the cost range. For example, the lowest cost is 0.5; which plant has that cost, the 10th lowest, or the 25th lowest? We answer these questions in column G using the MATCH function,

FIGURE A1.27 Using Nested Functions

	Plant	Capacity	Cost		Ranked	Match	Incremental Capacity	Cumulative capacity
Cumulative capacity								
JG/SP/KB								
1/1/2013								
	1	600	15.0		0.5	15	200	200
	2	700	18.0		0.5	16	300	500
	3	750	20.0		0.7	17	400	900
	4	800	25.0		1.0	20	350	1250
	5	1000	28.0		2.0	18		1750
	6	800	45.1		2.1	19		2200
	7	600	46.5		7.0	46		3400
	8	500	42.3		7.5	47	1500	4900
	9	650	43.7		9.0	48	1100	6000
	10	700	49.4		9.5	49		
	11	600	40.9		11.0	50		
	12	650	52.2		15.0	1	600	9500
	13	400	52.9		18.0	2	700	10200
	14	500	53.6		20.0	3		
	15	200	0.5		25.0	4		
	16	300	0.5		28.0	5	1000	12750
	17	400	0.7		40.9	11	600	13350
	18	500	2.0		42.3	8	500	13850
	19	450	2.1		43.7	9	650	14500

Formula:
=SMALL($D$6:$D$55,B6)

Formula:
=MATCH(F6,$D$6:$D$55,0)

Formula:
=INDEX($C$6:$C$55,MATCH(F6,$D$6:$D$55,0))

---

[*] This example is courtesy of Jay Goldman.

which gives the relative position of an item in a range. Thus MATCH(F6, $D$6:$D$55,0) = 15, which says that the lowest cost of 0.5, which appears in cell F6, is associated with the 15th plant. The next step is to determine the capacity of each plant as it appears in cost order. In other words, we know that the lowest cost plant is number 15; what is its capacity? We calculate this value using the INDEX function. The INDEX function gives the value at the intersection of a row and column index in a given range. So INDEX($C$6:$C$55, MATCH(F6, $D$6:$D$55,0)) = 200. This function says, in effect, in the capacity range, find the value of the 15th entry. Column H thus gives the capacities of all the plants as they occur in cost order. Column I completes the calculation by adding up cumulative capacity. (Note that column G was included only for this explanation; it could be omitted from the final spreadsheet.) Also, this procedure will not work properly if two plants have identical costs, since the MATCH function will rank the same plant twice. To correct for this, the MATCH function in cells G7:G55 can be embedded in an IF statement to first test for identical costs and if it finds them to increment the previous value in column G by 1. If no two costs are identical, the MATCH function as written will work properly.

Text and Date Functions   Excel offers a variety of functions for working with text and dates. These functions are often needed when working with information from databases. For example, if the first names of customers are in column A and the last names in column B, we can form their full names using the CONCATENATE function, which joins several text strings into one. Thus CONCATENATE("Sue","Smith") = SueSmith. (To insert a space between the two names, we can use CONCATENATE("Sue","","Smith")). Other useful text functions include EXACT, which compares two test strings, and LEFT, which returns a specified number of characters from the start of a string.

Date and time functions largely convert data from one format to another. Excel uses a date code in which years are numbered from 1900 to 9999. Thus, if we enter the NOW function and format the cell as a date, the result is today's date, which happens to be 8/2/2013. However, if we format it as a number, the result is 41489 in Excel's date code. Similarly, DATE(2013, 8, 2) = 8/2/13 as a date and 41489 as a number.

ROUND, CEILING, FLOOR, and INT   There are several ways to change the precision with which numbers are maintained in a spreadsheet. The CEILING function rounds up, and the FLOOR function rounds down, both to a given significance. The INT function rounds down to the nearest integer, and the ROUND function rounds to the specified number of digits. For example, ROUND(23.346,2) = 23.35. Note that these functions actually *change* the number that is stored in the cell, whereas formatting a cell does not change the number actually used in calculations. So we can format the number 23.346 to two digits and it will appear as 23.35, but any calculations based on this cell will use 23.346. By contrast, if we use ROUND(23.346,2), then both the display and the actual number are 23.35.

RAND and RANDBETWEEN   Random numbers are often useful in modeling simple situations involving uncertainty. The RAND() function returns a uniformly distributed random number between 0 and 1 each time the spreadsheet is calculated. To choose from a list of names randomly, we can create a random number for each student using this function and then sort students from the lowest to the highest value of the random number. The RANDBETWEEN function also returns a random number, in this case between two limits set by the user, with the endpoints included. For example, RANDBETWEEN(50,150) returns uniformly distributed random integers between 50 and 150. Thus, in this case, the function returns one of 101 possible integer outcomes.

Financial Functions   Excel provides dozens of functions for financial calculations, some quite specialized. We have already discussed the NPV function, which is used frequently in evaluating investments. Some closely related functions are PV, which calculates the present value of a constant stream of payments; FV, which calculates the future value of a constant stream of payments; and IRR, which calculates the internal rate of return of a stream of payments. A couple of other functions that simplify complex calculations are PRICE, which calculates the price of a bond for given settlement date, redemption date, redemption value, rate and yield; and SYD, which gives the sum-of-years' digits depreciation for given cost, salvage value, life, and period.

Appendix 2: Macros and VBA

Macros are small computer programs that automate Excel tasks that are performed frequently. Macros are written in a language called Visual Basic for Applications (VBA), so a deep understanding of macros requires knowledge of VBA. Fortunately, Excel provides a mechanism for creating macros simply by recording the steps involved, so many straightforward macros can be created by users who have little or no programming knowledge. In this appendix, we illustrate how to create a macro by recording keystrokes, how to edit a macro using basic concepts from VBA to make it more powerful, and how to turn a macro into a user-defined function.

Any set of steps in Excel that a user repeats frequently is a good candidate for a macro. For example, some organizations require that every spreadsheet has a certain header and footer (containing date, author, and related information) and that the first several columns are formatted in a standard manner. To carry out these tasks manually might require 20–30 separate actions in Excel and take 10–15 minutes every time a new workbook must be created. If these actions can be captured in a macro, the entire sequence can be executed with one key combination that takes only a moment to run. Some firms provide such macros to employees as a way of ensuring compliance with corporate standards for good spreadsheet practice.

Beyond the automation of routine tasks, VBA provides a platform for magnifying the power of Excel. Tasks that might seem too complicated for a spreadsheet can sometimes be managed by a VBA program, thus giving the analyst an even broader set of tools than we normally associate with spreadsheets. The topics we cover represent only an introduction to VBA, but they provide a glimpse of the powerful capabilities that come with Excel.

RECORDING A MACRO

Small businesses often use a standard invoice format to bill customers. An example of a simple invoice is shown in Figure A2.1. This invoice is relatively straightforward to build in Excel, but the task is a bit tedious and, as a result, subject to errors. However, by using Excel's macro recorder, we can simplify the task considerably and automate it in the process.

To record a macro for this process, display a blank worksheet. Then turn on the Macro Recorder, which records every action performed on a workbook until the Recorder is turned off. The Recorder is turned on by selecting Developer▶Code▶Record Macro. (If the Developer tab is not visible initially, select File▶Options▶Customize Ribbon and check the box for Developer in the right-hand window.) This step opens the window shown in Figure A2.2. Give the macro a descriptive name (such as PB_Invoice), assign it an optional shortcut key that is not normally used (for example, use "*a*"), and store it in This Workbook. Click on OK, and notice that the Stop Recording button has replaced the Record Macro button in the Code group. Next, proceed carefully through the steps to create the form shown in Figure A2.1. The order of the steps is not critical; however, it is a good idea to select a particular cell (such as A1) as the first step. Later, it is probably most convenient to de-select the grid lines (in the Show group of the View ribbon) as the last

487

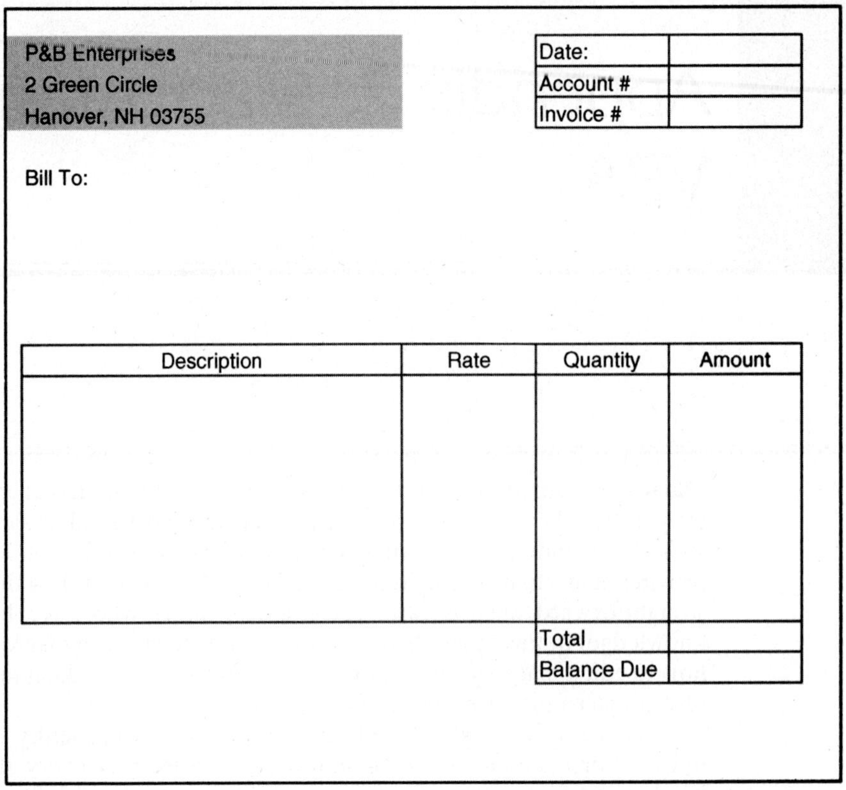

FIGURE A2.1 A Company's Invoice

		Date:	
P&B Enterprises		Account #	
2 Green Circle		Invoice #	
Hanover, NH 03755			

Bill To:

Description	Rate	Quantity	Amount
		Total	
		Balance Due	

main step, followed by placing the cursor in cell A6 (in preparation for entering a customer's name). Then click on the Stop Recording button.

To check that the macro has been recorded, move to a blank worksheet (or add one to the workbook) and press the shortcut key combination (Ctrl+a). The worksheet should then be transformed immediately into the invoice for P&B Enterprises. Thus, a tedious procedure that's subject to typos can be automated and executed with a click of the keyboard. For a small business that might have to generate dozens of these invoices in a day, the macro saves quite a bit of time.

To get a better appreciation of what has taken place, open the **Visual Basic Editor** (VBE) by clicking on the Visual Basic icon in the Developer ribbon or simply pressing the key combination Alt+F11. The VBE displays four windows, as shown in **Figure A2.3**. (If any of these is not displayed, select the View menu in the VBE and choose Project Explorer, Properties Window, Code, or Immediate Window, as needed.). In the upper left,

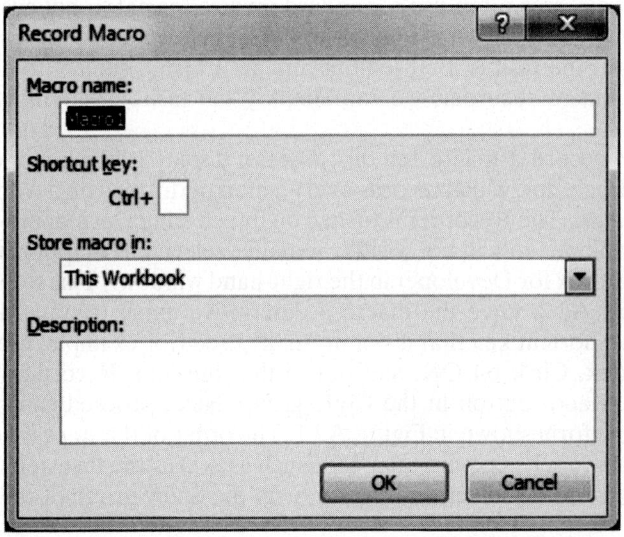

FIGURE A2.2 The Record Macro Window

Record Macro

Macro name:
Macro1

Shortcut key:
Ctrl+

Store macro in:
This Workbook

Description:

OK   Cancel

FIGURE A2.3 A Portion of the Macro Code in the VBE

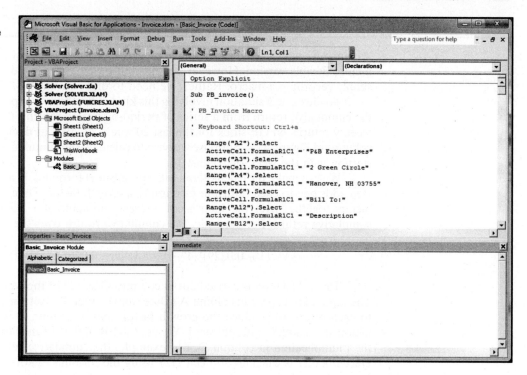

the **Project Explorer window** displays a file hierarchy that contains all open workbooks, including the currently open Excel workbook. Within the workbook, we can see the worksheet(s) of the current workbook, and in this case, an icon for Module 1. The name of the module appears in the lower left, in the **Properties window**, where we could overwrite the module name with something more meaningful (such as Basic_Invoice). In the large pane on the upper right, the **Code window** displays the code that was created when we recorded the macro. Figure A2.3 displays the first portion of the code. Here we see the header Sub PB_Invoice(), which identifies the code as belonging to the macro we previously named. (The last line of the code reads End Sub.) The next five lines each begin with an apostrophe, which identifies them as comments; but if we scroll down through the contents of the Code window, we find that there are more than 250 lines of code. This surely seems like more steps than we executed manually. Indeed, one of the features of recorded macros is that their code is often quite complex and inefficient. To give just one brief example, the first two lines of code to be executed are:

```
Range("A2").Select
ActiveCell.FormulaR1C1 = "P&B Enterprises"
```

The first of these statements selects the upper left-hand cell in the worksheet. Having made that cell active, the second statement enters a text formula. These two lines can be replaced by just one statement using the syntax of VBA:

```
Range("A2").FormulaR1C1 = "P&B Enterprises"
```

Although it seems as if the macro recorder should be able to simplify in this way, remember that it responds to almost any manipulation in the workbook, and it must accurately capture the steps being executed. For that reason, the macro recorder sacrifices efficiency for flexibility and accuracy. Although the simplification shown above may seem almost intuitive, in general we need to be familiar with the VBA language to simplify many other statements in recorded code. (In fact, a reasonable familiarity with VBA allows us to create an equivalent macro containing fewer than 40 statements.)

Suppose now that we'd like to store a copy of this macro in another workbook. We can open the other workbook, at which time it will appear in the Project Explorer window. We can then drag the Module 1 icon (or the Basic_Invoice icon, if we have renamed it) into the other workbook. At that point, the macro resides in both locations, as desired.

EDITING A MACRO

At times, we may want to record a macro with the specific intent of editing it and producing a more flexible version. However, the flexibility we have in mind cannot be delivered by simply recording a macro. Rather, we need to draw on the VBA language.

To illustrate a situation involving this kind of flexibility, suppose we need to calculate the cumulative return from a series of period-by-period returns. Consider specifically the weekly returns on GE stock for the last 20 weeks of 2010, as documented in the first two columns of Figure A2.4. Suppose we wish to calculate the cumulative return for each week, starting with the week of August 16.

We can make the calculations with spreadsheet formulas, in a series of steps. The first step adds one to each return to turn it into a growth factor. Then we multiply the growth factors together over the interval of interest and subtract 1 from the result to get the cumulative return. For example, the cumulative return over the first three weeks is:

$$(1 - 0.0229)^*(1 - 0.0213)^*(1 + 0.0465) - 1 = 0.0008$$

This calculation is carried out in columns C and D of the worksheet in Figure A2.4. The input data appear in column A (Date) and column B (Return). In column C we add 1 to each return to produce the growth factor, and in column D we multiply the growth factors in column C and subtract 1. We use the PRODUCT function to faithfully represent the multiplication in column D. For example, the cumulative return from August 16 to December 27 is calculated in cell D27 using the formula =PRODUCT($C$2:C21)-1.

Although the calculations are routine, one shortcoming is that we have to repeat these steps every time we want to calculate a cumulative return, which could be dozens of times a day. It might be more effective instead to automate the calculations with a macro. As before, we invoke the macro recorder (naming the macro CumReturn) and record the following four steps:

Step 1: In the cell to the right of the first return, enter a formula that adds 1 to the first return (entering =B2+1 into cell C2).

Step 2: Copy this formula down the column to the last time period.

Step 3: In the next column to the right, enter a formula that calculates the cumulative return (entering =PRODUCT($C$2:C2)-1 into cell D2).

FIGURE A2.4 Calculating Cumulative Returns

	A	B	C	D	E	F
1	Date	Return	Growth	CumReturn		
2	8/16/2010	-0.0229	0.9771	-0.0229		
3	8/23/2010	-0.0213	0.9787	-0.0437		
4	8/30/2010	0.0465	1.0465	0.0008		
5	9/7/2010	0.0382	1.0382	0.0390		
6	9/13/2010	0.0268	1.0268	Formula: =PRODUCT($C$2:C2)-1		
7	9/20/2010	0.0228	1.0228			
8	9/27/2010	-0.0178	0.9822	0.0717		
9	10/4/2010	0.0460	1.0460	0.1210		
10	10/11/2010	-0.0477	0.9523	0.0676		
11	10/18/2010	-0.0150	0.9850	0.0515		
12	10/25/2010	-0.0020	0.9980	0.0494		
13	11/1/2010	0.0437	1.0437	0.0953		
14	11/8/2010	-0.0286	0.9714	0.0640		
15	11/15/2010	-0.0020	0.9980	Formula: =PRODUCT($C$2:C21)-1		
16	11/22/2010	-0.0255	0.9745			
17	11/29/2010	0.0618	1.0618	0.0987		
18	12/6/2010	0.0563	1.0563	0.1606		
19	12/13/2010	-0.0012	0.9988	0.1592		
20	12/20/2010	0.0270	1.0270	0.1905		
21	12/27/2010	0.0140	1.0140	0.2071		
22						

A4.4

FIGURE A2.5 Com-
pound Growth Macro as
Recorded

Macro Command	Description
`Range("C2").Select`	Select cell C2
`ActiveCell.FormulaR1C1 = "=RC[-1]+1"`	Enter formula into C2
`Range("C2").Select`	Select cell C2 again
`Selection.Copy`	Copy the selected cell
`Range("C3:C21").Select`	Select the range C3:C21
`ActiveSheet.Paste`	Paste into selected range
`Range("D2").Select`	Select cell D2
`Application.CutCopyMode = False`	Turn off dashed border
`ActiveCell.FormulaR1C1 = "=PRODUCT(R2C3:RC[-1])-1"`	Enter formula into D2
`Selection.Copy`	Copy the selected cell
`Range("D3:D21").Select`	Select the range D3:D21
`ActiveSheet.Paste`	Paste into selected range
`Range("A1").Select`	Reposition the cursor at A1

Step 4: Copy this formula down the column to the last time period.

The recorded code can again be viewed in the VBE, listed as a separate macro in Module 1. The specific lines of code and their explanations are listed in Figure A2.5.

The macro we have created works effectively for calculating cumulative returns as long as the data are located in the range B2:B21 and the calculations can be made in the next adjacent columns. That's because the recorded code is specific about the cells to manipulate. But if we have a different number of returns or if they are located somewhere else in the spreadsheet, the macro will not work correctly. How can we modify the existing macro so that it works more generally?

VBA provides a few ways to answer this question. Here, we illustrate one approach that underscores a major limitation of recorded macros: a recorded macro cannot query the user for input. On the other hand, the VBA language contains syntax for simple input (and output). Returning to the example, suppose we want our code to work with ranges other than B2:B21. In that case, we can begin by asking the user where the data can be found. Then, as before, we enter the appropriate formulas in the two adjacent columns. A set of VBA commands that does so (each accompanied by an explanatory comment) is listed below:

```
' Declare "myData" as a string variable
Dim myData As String
' Capture the user's input as the range variable "myData"
myData = InputBox("Enter range of data")
' In the next column, enter a formula that adds 1.
Range(myData).Offset(0, 1).FormulaR1C1 = "=RC[-1]+1"
' In the next column, enter a formula for the cumulative product.
Range(myData).Offset(0, 2).FormulaR1C1 = "=PRODUCT(R2C3:RC[-1])-1"
'Return the cursor to a neutral position.
Range("A1").Select
```

We can replace the content of our macro with these statements. Alternatively, we can enter them separately in the Code window, as a separate macro. First, however, we must name our program. In the Code window, we enter Sub CumReturn2(), right after the code for the recorded macro. VBA automatically enters the line End Sub just below. Between these two lines of code, we enter the statements listed above. As a result, we'll have two macros (or "subs") in the workbook, both residing in the same module. We refer to the first sub as a recorded macro and the second sub as a VBA procedure. To select which macro to run, we return to the Developer tab, click on the Macros icon, and select the sub we want.

Let's take a closer look at how the new procedure works. In the sub CumReturn2, the first statement introduces a variable called myData and declares it to be a string (a sequence of characters rather than, say, a number). The next statement queries the user for

FIGURE A2.6 A Window
for User Input

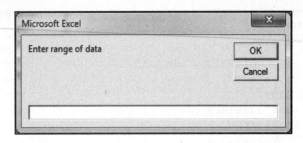

the range where the data are located and captures that information in the variable myData. The form of the query is the standard input box, shown in Figure A2.6.

The user enters an address into the input window. For example, if our spreadsheet contained the table in the first two columns of Figure A2.4, we would enter B2:B21. This step would assign the value "B2:B21" to the variable myData. (Here, the quotation marks identify the content as a character string.) With this value established, the reference to Range(myData) becomes a reference to Range("B2:B21"), which is indeed where the returns appear. In the code, we can then refer to the neighboring cells using the Offset specification, which works like the OFFSET function in Excel—that is, with a base reference, adjusted by a given number of rows and columns. In our case, the formula that adds 1 is assigned to the cells immediately to the right of myData; then the product formula is assigned to the cells immediately to the right of those cells. Finally, the last statement repositions the cursor.

In this example, the command that enters a formula actually does so for all the cells in a range using just one statement, instead of requiring one statement for each formula that appears. For this purpose, the R1C1 reference style (see Appendix 1) is particularly convenient because the formula in each range does not change, as it would if we used conventional Excel notation with relative addresses. Thus, by exploiting a few features of VBA, we simplify the recorded macro and render it more flexible as well, in this case by allowing for user input.

CREATING A USER-DEFINED FUNCTION

In addition to input/output capability, the VBA language has two important features that are unavailable in recorded macros: branching and looping. Branching refers to contingencies—that is, proceeding along one path or an alternative according to conditions encountered during the execution of the program. Branching involves the same logic familiar to us in Excel's IF statement, but with additional flexibility. Looping refers to repeating a basic set of commands but allowing for slightly different conditions each time those commands are repeated. Whereas Excel allows this type of calculation by copying and pasting a formula that involves relative addresses of the variables, VBA extends this capability from a single formula to a collection of commands. We illustrate with an example that builds on the cumulative return calculation of the previous section. Ideally, we'd prefer to have Excel provide a built-in function for calculating cumulative returns. Then we could simply enter this function into any cell where it was needed. Although Excel does not provide such a function, we can create one in VBA.

Our edited code for calculating cumulative returns is flexible with respect to the location (and size) of the input, but it still requires a workspace consisting of two empty columns of cells adjacent to our data. Of course, we could add code to insert two columns for this purpose, but VBA allows us to avoid the resulting "footprint" and the clutter that accompanies it. Instead, we can use a looping strategy and keep track of our calculations within the VBA code, without having to record the results on the spreadsheet.

We can distinguish two kinds of procedures in VBA: Sub procedures and Function procedures. Both perform actions in Excel. The macros we have created so far are examples of Sub procedures. A Function procedure differs from a Sub procedure in that it returns a numerical value. (A Sub procedure need not return any information.) The user-defined function we wish to create would provide the cumulative return (expressed as a numerical value) for a user-specified range of returns data. Figure A2.7 shows such a program written in VBA.

FIGURE A2.7 User-defined Function for Cumulative Return

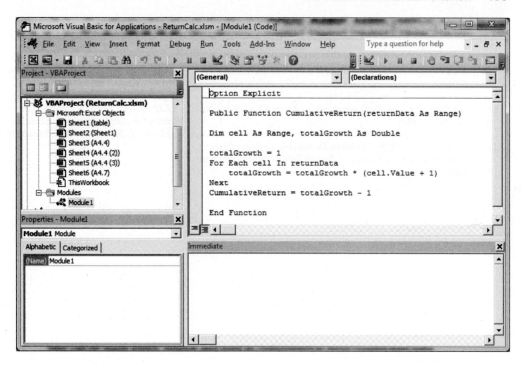

A user-defined function begins with the words Public Function, the function name (in this case, CumulativeReturn), and the type of inputs it accepts. In our example, the only input needed is a range containing the period-by-period return data, and our code refers to this range as the variable returnData.

In the code of Figure A2.7, the Dim statement declares two variables, `cell` (a one-cell range) and `totalGrowth` (the cumulative growth from the first period's return, expressed as a numerical value with extended or "double" precision.) The variable `totalGrowth` is initialized as 1.0 and then multiplied by each successive period's growth factor as we loop through the returns. The loop is bounded by the `For` and `Next` statements in the code, which prescribe a loop for each cell contained in the range specified as the function's argument. This loop takes each cell in the range `returnData`, adds 1, and multiplies by the current value of `totalGrowth`. When we subtract 1 from the final value of `totalGrowth` we have the cumulative return over the range, which is assigned to the function value, `CumulativeReturn`. The entire code can be entered in the Code window, to supplement the subs we discussed previously.

How can this function be used in a spreadsheet? First, we can confirm that the function is available in a given spreadsheet by opening the Insert Function window and selecting the User Defined category. The name `CumulativeReturn` should appear alphabetically on this list. Then we can use the function just as we use any other Excel function. In the worksheet containing the original returns data, we can enter the formula `=CumulativeReturn($B$2:B2)` in any empty cell. Then we can copy that function down the column into the cells below. The resulting values will be identical to those we found using macros.

User-defined functions are preferable to macros in many ways. They are usually easier to understand for the user who is unfamiliar with macros. They can be used to calculate just the needed results without adding extraneous calculations to the spreadsheet. Finally, they can be made highly general and used as components in more complicated procedures.

We have not attempted to give a comprehensive overview of VBA in this appendix, but rather to convey a sense of what can be accomplished using macros and VBA. For those who spend a lot of time creating elaborate spreadsheets and performing highly repetitive spreadsheet tasks, macros and VBA represent the next frontier in power and efficiency.

SUGGESTED READINGS

An interactive Excel tutorial that covers many of the topics in this chapter can be downloaded at a modest cost from www.excelnow-tutorial.com.

There are a number of excellent advanced books on Excel. Here are some of our favorites.

Albright, S. C. 2011. *VBA for Modelers: Developing Decision Support Systems with Microsoft Office Excel, Fourth Edition.* South-Western Publishing, Mason, OH.

Gross, D., F. Akaiwa, and K. Nordquist, 2010. *Succeeding in Business with Microsoft Excel 2010:* A Problem-Solving Approach. Boston, MA: Course Technology.

Sengupta, C. 2010. *Financial Modeling Using Excel and VBA, Second Edition.* Hoboken, NJ: John Wiley & Sons.

Winston, W. 2011. *Microsoft Excel 2010: Data Analysis and Business Modeling.* Redmond, WA: Microsoft Press.

Appendix 3:
Basic Probability Concepts

INTRODUCTION

Probability is the language of risk and uncertainty. Since risk and uncertainty are essential elements of business life, a basic understanding of this language is essential for the business analyst. In this appendix, we present some of the elements of probability as they are used in business modeling. We focus on knowledge that an analyst might want to draw on during a model-building project. We begin by describing probability distributions for uncertain parameters; then we discuss expected values, variances, and tail probabilities, describing why they are generally appropriate measures for decision making. Finally, we describe the elements of sampling theory in order to provide the background for the text's coverage of data analysis and simulation.

PROBABILITY DISTRIBUTIONS

For any parameter in a model, we should give some thought to the precision associated with its value. Very few parameters are known for certain, especially in models that predict the future. In various chapters of the book, we discuss ways to take this uncertainty into account. The simplest approach is sensitivity analysis, in which we vary one or more parameters to determine how sensitive the model results are to changes in the parameter values. For example, we might determine that if sales are high next year (50 percent above this year's level), our profits will be $5 million, whereas if sales are low (25 percent below this year's level), our profits will be only $1 million. With just this kind of information—an optimistic alternative and a pessimistic alternative—we have the beginnings of a probability model for the parameter in question. In Chapter 14, we forge an important link between sensitivity analysis and uncertainty. However, to appreciate this link, we need some basic concepts related to probability distributions.

A **probability distribution** is simply a description of an uncertain event or parameter. A simple and familiar probability distribution is based on tossing two coins and counting the number of heads. The distribution can be described in a table as follows:

Number of Heads	0	1	2
Probability	0.25	0.50	0.25

The same distribution can be described in a chart, as shown in Figure A3.1. Both the table and the chart depict the **outcomes** of the coin toss and the **probabilities** of each outcome. Any probability distribution must describe these two aspects of an uncertain event.

A **random variable** is a numerically valued outcome of an uncertain event. In the case of tossing two coins, we could have described the outcomes qualitatively (with the list HH, HT, TH, and TT), and we could still associate probabilities with those outcomes. However, when we describe the outcome as the *number* of heads, we are using a numerical value to describe the outcome. In this sense, we can look at a numerical parameter in our models as if it were a random variable. Our three-outcome table is thus the probability distribution for the random variable "number of heads."

FIGURE A3.1 Probability
Distribution for Number
of Heads

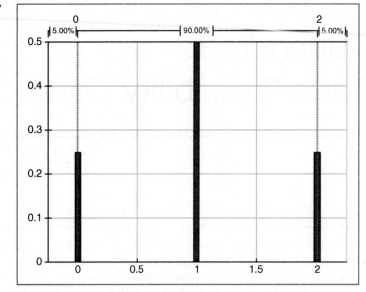

When we can conveniently list the possible outcomes of a random variable or identify them with *integers*, as in the coin-tossing example, we refer to the random variable, and the probability distribution, as **discrete**. We can describe a discrete probability distribution (or, more simply, a discrete distribution) with a table like the one in our example: a list of outcomes together with a list of corresponding probabilities. Since the outcomes are mutually exclusive and exhaustive, the probabilities must sum to 1.

Conceptually, we use a discrete distribution when we are describing a quantity that involves measurement by counting, such as the number of heads, or the number of customers, or the number of defects. A discrete distribution might not be suitable, however, if we were measuring a time interval or the length of an object. When we deal in intervals, especially where the outcomes are real numbers, we refer to the random variable, and its probability distribution, as **continuous**. In such a case, we describe a continuous probability distribution (or, more simply, a continuous distribution) not with a table but rather, with a function—which we often depict in a graph. The function gives the relative likelihood of various outcomes, and, conceptually, there could be an infinite number of outcomes. For example, how long will it take to drive to the airport? The graph of the function in Figure A3.2 shows a continuous distribution for the length of the airport trip. In the graph, *x*-values for which the function is high are more likely to occur than values for which the function is low. In addition, the probability that the length of the trip will lie between two values such as 40 and 70 corresponds to the area under the curve between those values, as shown in the figure. Since probabilities correspond to areas, the area under the entire function must be equal to 1.

FIGURE A3.2 Probability
Distribution for Time to
Airport

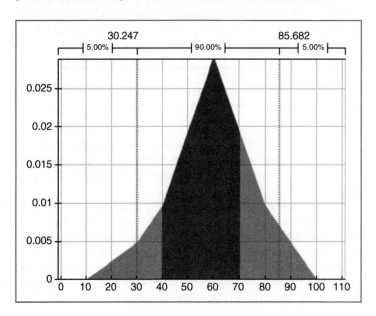

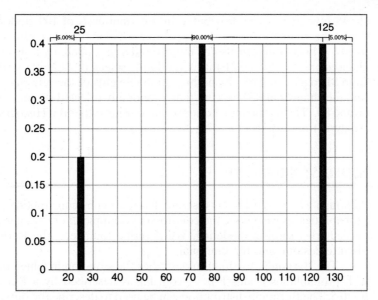

What if we were dealing with an event that has a vast number of discrete outcomes? Suppose we want to model the number of light bulbs that will be sold in our hardware chain next month. Although we could use a discrete distribution and enumerate the individual possibilities for the sales quantity, the list of outcomes could be unmanageably long. It would be more convenient to use a continuous approach, ignoring the fact that fractions are not possible (because we cannot sell a fraction of a light bulb). Thus, a graph resembling Figure A3.2 could represent a continuous distribution used as a model for light bulb sales.

Alternatively, we might describe the outcomes with ranges of values. We might classify next year's sales into three outcome ranges: sales below 50,000, sales between 50,000 and 100,000, and sales between 100,000 and 150,000. One way to simplify the ranges is to substitute their midpoints as a single outcome representing the entire range. Thus, the first outcome would be sales of 25,000; the second outcome, sales of 75,000; and the third outcome, sales of 125,000. Figure A3.3 shows a distribution for these events in which the probability of sales in either the middle or high range is twice that of sales in the low range. This is a discrete distribution with three distinct outcomes and three corresponding probabilities. For some purposes, this model would be a sufficient representation of the possibilities for next year's sales, even though it involves a good deal of simplification.

These two examples show that phenomena in the real world are not intrinsically discrete or continuous. Rather, we can choose to use discrete or continuous models to represent those phenomena. The choice sometimes comes down to what is convenient for modeling purposes and what is plausible for the user.

A frequency distribution, or **histogram**, is a commonly encountered chart that shows how members of a population are distributed according to some criterion. Figure A3.4

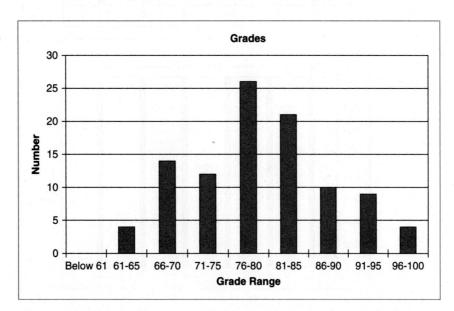

shows how grades are distributed in a certain class of 100 students. Note that the bars depict the number of students whose grades fall in the given ranges (for example, from 86 to 90). A histogram can also be interpreted as a probability distribution. For example, the chances are $21/100 = 0.21$ that a randomly selected student's grade will fall in the range from 81 to 85. Similarly, by adding up the heights of the relevant bars, we can determine that the chances are 52 percent that a randomly selected student's grade will fall between 66 and 80. (Histograms can be constructed using either the Histogram function in the Data Analysis tool in Excel or using XLMiner.)

EXAMPLES OF DISCRETE DISTRIBUTIONS

Although we can specify any discrete distribution by constructing a table of outcomes and probabilities, as we did for the coin-tossing example, there are a few distributions that are particularly useful in modeling. We describe four here: the Bernoulli, integer uniform, discrete custom, and the binomial.

The **Bernoulli** distribution describes the situation in which there are two outcomes, with probabilities p and $1-p$. A coin flip is described by a Bernoulli distribution with $p = 0.5$. The Bernoulli distribution can be used to describe the outcome of making a sale to a customer, when the probability on each sale is 0.7. Figure A3.5a shows a Bernoulli distribution with $p = 0.7$.

The **integer uniform** distribution can be used when the outcomes can be numbered 1 through n, and each outcome occurs with equal probability. The result of rolling a fair die can be described by an integer uniform distribution with six outcomes, as shown in Figure A3.5b.

FIGURE A3.5 Four Discrete Distributions

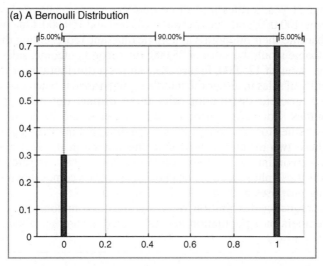

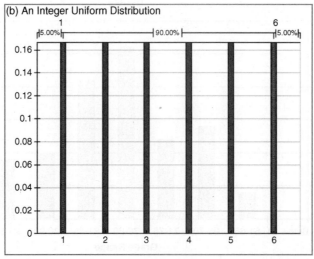

FIGURE A3.5
(*Continued*)

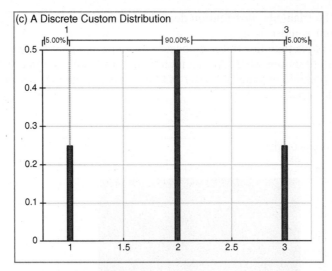

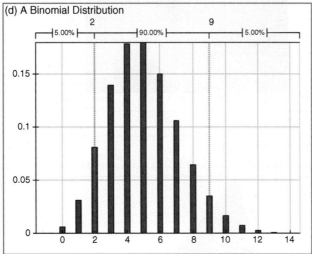

The **discrete custom** distribution is used when we have a small number of outcomes with different probabilities of occurring. Figure A3.5c shows a discrete custom distribution when there are three outcomes with probabilities 0.25, 0.5, and 0.25, respectively.

Another useful distribution is the **binomial distribution,** which describes a random variable that counts the number of successful outcomes in a series of n independent experiments (trials), each with a success probability of p. The possible outcomes are the numbers 0, 1, 2, . . . , n. Suppose we are counting the number of defective chips in a production batch of $n = 100$. (As is often the case in quality control, we can represent a defect as a "success.") If we know that there is a 5 percent chance that an individual chip is defective, then the number of defects in the batch can be modeled as following a binomial distribution with parameters $n = 100$ and $p = 0.05$ (see Figure A3.5d). We need two parameters to specify a binomial distribution—the number of trials and the success rate.

EXAMPLES OF CONTINUOUS DISTRIBUTIONS

As with discrete distributions, there are many types of continuous probability distributions. However, three are particularly useful ones in modeling uncertainty in business situations: the uniform, triangular, and normal distributions. These three provide us with a good deal of flexibility in capturing the kind of variability we usually encounter in decision problems.

The **uniform distribution** describes an outcome that is equally likely to fall anywhere between a prescribed minimum and a prescribed maximum. It is particularly appropriate when we can make a reasonable guess about the smallest and largest possible outcomes but have no reason to suspect that any values in between are more likely than others. Figure A3.6a shows a uniform distribution between 50 and 150.

The **triangular distribution** describes an outcome that has a minimum and maximum value but is most likely to occur at an intermediate point. The triangular distribution is more flexible than the uniform because it can have a peak anywhere in its range. It is well suited to situations where we can identify a most likely outcome as well as the smallest and largest possible outcomes. Figure A3.6b shows a triangular distribution between 100 and 200 with a peak at 125.

FIGURE A3.6 Three Continuous Distributions

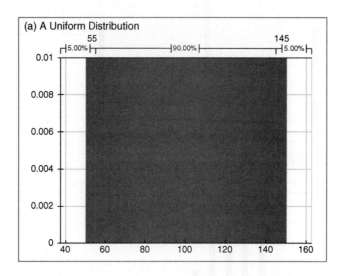

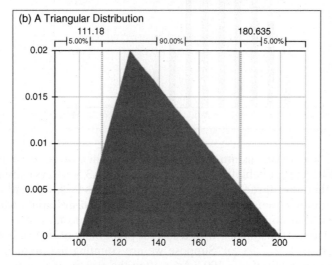

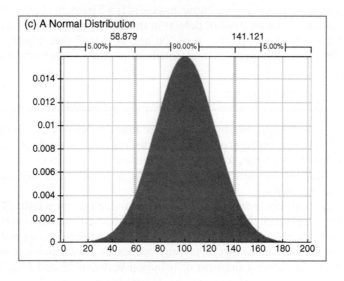

Finally, the **normal distribution** describes an outcome that is most likely to be in the middle of the distribution, with progressively smaller likelihoods as we move away from the most likely value. This distribution, which is familiar to many analysts, can describe a symmetrical uncertain quantity using only two parameters (the mean and standard deviation). Figure A3.6c shows a normal distribution with a mean of 100 and a standard deviation of 25.

EXPECTED VALUES

While probability distributions are important, they are also quite complex. In particular, many decision makers cannot easily understand the implications of a probability distribution for their situation. Therefore, it is important to be able to capture the essential features of a distribution in a single number. Usually, that number is the expected value. Most often the symbol μ is used to represent the expected value of a distribution.

An **expected value** is simply an average, but an average of a somewhat special kind. Recall that Figure A3.4 depicts the grades of 100 students in a class. One way to summarize this chart is with the average grade, which we calculate simply by adding all 100 grades and dividing by 100. But this procedure does not work as well in calculating the average sales in Figure A3.3. Here, the outcomes (sales of 25M, 75M, or 125M) do not occur with equal probabilities—the outcome of 25M is half as likely as the other outcomes. Any estimate of the average outcome should take the probabilities into account. The expected value does so by multiplying each outcome by its probability. Thus, the expected value of sales in this distribution is

$$0.2 \times 25M + 0.4 \times 75M + 0.4 \times 125M = 85M$$

If S represents the sales random variable in this example, then we write its expected value as

$$E[S] = 85M.$$

Note that, as this example illustrates, the expected value is not necessarily one of the actual outcomes of the distribution.

To clarify terminology, we use the terms *expected value* and *mean* interchangeably in this book. However, we reserve the word **average** to refer to the simple (unweighted) average. Thus, we might refer to the expected value of the exam scores in Figure A3.4 as an average, but the expected value of sales in Figure A3.3 would be called a mean.

It is straightforward to calculate the expected value for discrete distributions: We simply multiply each outcome by its probability and add the products. (The calculation can easily be carried out using the SUMPRODUCT function in Excel.) However, in the case of continuous distributions, there is always an infinite number of outcomes, and the procedure for calculating the expected value is more complex. When any distribution is symmetric, however, the expected value lies at the center of the distribution. Thus, the mean for both the uniform and normal distributions is the center of the distribution.

One of the important properties of the expected value is **linearity**. Essentially this means that if an outcome is related in a linear fashion to an uncertain parameter, then the expected value of the outcome is also related in the same linear fashion to the expected value of the parameter. An example will make this clearer. Consider the following simple model for profit:

$$Profit = Margin \times Sales - Fixed\ Cost$$

In this model, we assume that Margin and Fixed Cost are known with certainty. Sales, however, is an uncertain quantity. Consequently, Profit is uncertain. But because the relationship is linear, if we want to find the expected value of Profit, we need to know only the expected value of Sales, that is:

$$E[Profit] = Margin \times E[Sales] - Fixed\ Cost$$

This property of linearity becomes important when we consider the implications of uncertainty in a parameter on the outcomes of a model. We noted earlier that most parameters are uncertain, although we may choose to ignore the fact. Often, the uncertainty present in the situation is not sufficient to justify a full uncertainty analysis. This discussion of linearity points out one such situation: If our model is linear (that is, if the output is related in a linear fashion to uncertain inputs), and if we want to determine the *expected value of the output*, then we can simply use the *expected values of the parameters* as our inputs and not use probability distributions in our evaluation. On the other hand, if either of these requirements is not met, then we will need to take a probabilistic view when analyzing the model.

Why is the expected value of the output a reasonable summary measure of all the possible outcomes? There are several reasons, but the most important one is that the expected value is actually the long-run average outcome if the uncertain situation represented by the model is repeated many times. For example, consider a simple game in which we flip a fair coin and receive $10 for Heads and pay $5 for Tails. Let W represent our winnings when we play the game. The expected winnings can be calculated as a probability-weighted average:

$$E[W] = 0.5 \times 10 - 0.5 \times 5 = 2.5$$

This is not a bad deal, of course: Our *expected* winnings are $2.50 each time we play. If we were to play 1,000 times, we would probably make very close to $2,500, since, in such a large number of repetitions, we would win close to 50 percent of the time. So if we could play this game many times, it would be reasonable to use the expected value of the outcome as a measure of its long-run value. In effect, we can ignore the uncertainty on a single repetition of this game because we are planning to play many times. The general notion here is that a manager facing a series of decisions influenced by uncertainty will maximize profits in the long run by maximizing expected profit on each individual decision.

But what if the outcomes were not in dollars but in *millions* of dollars? The expected outcome is still attractive, at $2.5 million, but we might not be able to ignore the uncertainty we face on each repetition. For example, if we had resources of less than $5 million available, then a loss on the first coin flip would leave us incapable of continuing, and thus incapable of reaching the long run, where our winnings would be great. In this case, the expected value is *not* a sufficient measure of the outcome, even if we can play many times, because it does not recognize the possibility that we could go bankrupt at the first coin flip. Thus, we have to qualify the principle of maximizing long-run profits by acknowledging that the manager can reach the long run only if the firm survives. The risk of an extreme outcome, especially if it jeopardizes the firm's ability to persist, should therefore be considered explicitly.

Throughout this book, we advocate a two-phased approach to summarizing the uncertainty of outcomes. The first phase is almost always to consider the expected value of the outcome. Even in situations where this is not completely sufficient, it is a necessary first step. But as our simple example shows, sometimes the risks associated with a course of action are so high that the expected outcome is not sufficient by itself. In addition to the expected value, we should be looking at the probability of extreme outcomes as well.

CUMULATIVE DISTRIBUTION FUNCTIONS

The cumulative distribution function (or **cdf**) gives, for any specified value, the probability that the random variable will be *less than or equal to* that value. For example, suppose we are using the following distribution for the number of machine breakdowns on a production line in a day. (The mean of this distribution is 2.)

Outcome	0	1	2	3	4	5	6	7	8
Probability	0.135	0.271	0.271	0.180	0.090	0.036	0.012	0.003	0.001

The cdf at a particular value, y, gives the probability that the random variable will be *less than or equal to y*. Thus, the cdf at 0 is 0.135. The cdf at 1 is equal to 0.406, the sum of the probabilities for outcomes 0 and 1. The cdf at 2 is equal to 0.677, the sum of the

FIGURE A3.7 A Cumulative Distribution Function

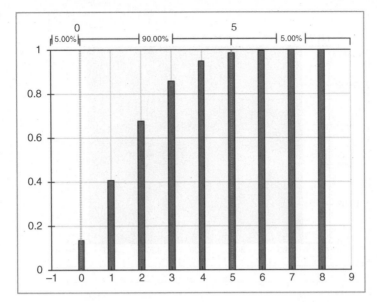

probabilities for outcomes 0, 1, and 2. Simple addition of consecutive values allows us to construct a table of cumulative distribution values:

Outcome	0	1	2	3	4	5	6	7	8
Probability	0.135	0.271	0.271	0.180	0.090	0.036	0.012	0.003	0.001
Cumulative	0.135	0.406	0.677	0.857	0.947	0.983	0.995	0.999	1.000

As we move from low to high outcomes the cdf always increases from 0 to 1.

The cdf is usually written as the function $F(y)$, and, mathematically speaking, it is defined for all possible values of y. For instance, in the example above, it follows from the table that $F(4.3) = 0.947$. A graph of this particular cdf is shown in Figure A3.7.

In the case of continuous random variables, the cumulative distribution function $F(y)$ again represents the probability that the random variable is less than or equal to y. However, in many cases (such as the normal distribution), this function cannot be expressed algebraically. Therefore, it is common to describe the cdf graphically. In Figures A3.8 through A3.10, we show pairs of graphs for the uniform, triangular, and normal distributions, respectively. The first graph of the pair is the probability distribution, and the second graph is the cdf. Mathematically, the cdf $F(y)$ gives the area under the probability distribution graph to the left of y.

TAIL PROBABILITIES

While the expected value is a useful summary of the long-run average value of an uncertain situation, we are sometimes interested in a particular set of outcomes, especially extreme outcomes. An example would be the outcomes that lead to bankruptcy in our coin-flip example discussed earlier. Another example might be related to our probability distribution of machine breakdowns. Suppose our repair department can handle only two breakdowns in a day without exhausting its repair capabilities. What is the probability that the repair capabilities will be sufficient on a given day?

Another way to ask this question is: What is the probability that there will be at most two breakdowns in a day, or what is the probability that the number of breakdowns will be less than or equal to 2? The answer is the sum of probabilities on the left-hand side of the table above, or, in terms of the cdf, we want $F(2)$. Referring to our table of cdf values, we can see that this value is 0.677.

Probabilities relating to a set of outcomes at one side of the distribution are called **tail probabilities**. In some cases, we are interested in the side of the distribution containing the smaller values, in others the larger values. For example, in our machine breakdown

FIGURE A3.8 Probability Distribution and Cumulative Distribution Functions for the Uniform Distribution

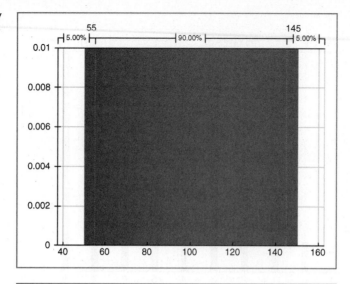

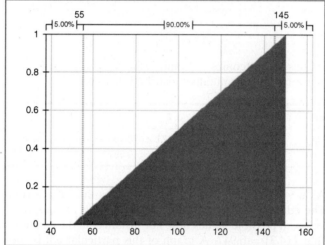

FIGURE A3.8 Probability Distribution and Cumulative Distribution Functions for the Uniform Distribution

example, the risk is that our repair capabilities will be outstripped so we are concerned with the larger numbers of breakdowns. The probability of this event is the probability of an outcome larger than 2, which we may write as the complement of the cdf: $1 - F(2) = 0.323$. The probability represented by a cdf value is a tail probability, or, more precisely, a **left-hand** tail probability, since it involves probabilities of outcomes to the "left" of a given value in the table or distribution. The probability represented by the complement of a cdf value is a **right-hand** tail probability.

In this context, risk is measured as the probability of some undesirable event, such as running out of funds or losing money on an investment. The probability of such events is often easy to describe as a tail probability. Thus, tail probabilities give us a means of quantifying the extent of particular risks.

VARIABILITY

Another sense of the term *risk* relates to the unpredictability of an outcome. In terms of a probability distribution, this means considering the variance. In particular, for a quantity X that is subject to a probability distribution, we define the **variance** as follows:

$$\sigma^2 = E\left[(X - \mu)^2\right]$$

In words, the variance is the expected value of the squared deviation from the mean. In the case of our machine breakdown distribution, we can illustrate the calculation of the variance as follows. Recall that the mean is known to be $\mu = 2$.

FIGURE A3.9 Probability Distribution and Cumulative Distribution Functions for the Triangular Distribution

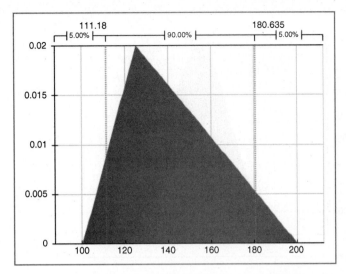

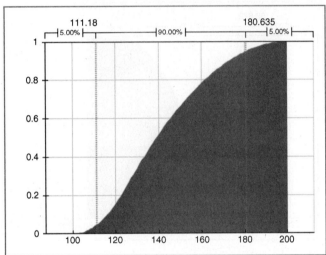

Outcome (X)	0	1	2	3	4	5	6	7	8
Probability	0.135	0.271	0.271	0.180	0.090	0.036	0.012	0.003	0.001
$(X - \mu)$	−2	−1	0	1	2	3	4	5	6
$(X - \mu)^2$	4	1	0	1	4	9	16	25	36

Multiplying the values in the last row by the corresponding probabilities (or using SUMPRODUCT in Excel), we obtain a value for the variance of $\sigma^2 = 1.99$.

In the case of continuous probability distributions, the calculation of a variance is complicated, as in the case of calculating the mean itself, although in some cases relatively simple formulas exist. A normal distribution is usually specified by supplying the mean (μ) and the variance (σ^2), so there is rarely a need to compute the variance if the normal distribution has already been specified.

The variance is an important feature of a probability distribution because it measures dispersion—that is, the extent of the unpredictability in the outcome. In some settings, the extent of unpredictability is a reasonable measure of risk, and therefore the variance is sometimes used to assess the level of risk. The variance and tail probabilities are two types of features associated with probability distributions, but they have special importance in business modeling because of their use as measures of risk.

SAMPLING

Basic probability concepts form the foundation for statistical analysis. One important application involves the average of a random sample from a population whose mean and

FIGURE A3.10 Probability Distribution and Cumulative Distribution Functions for the Normal Distribution

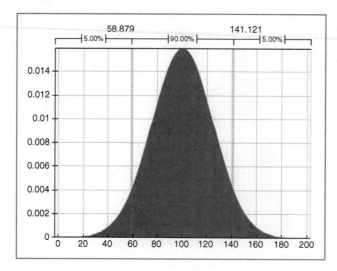

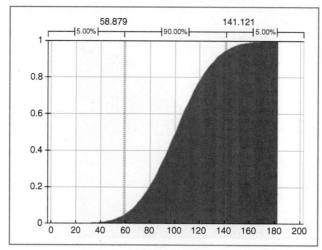

variance are not known. We take a set of n independent numerical observations (or samples) from the population, and then we compute the average of the observations. We are interested in the nature of this computed average.

We refer to the value of the jth observation as X_j, and we treat it as a random variable, with unknown mean μ and unknown variance σ^2. When we compute the average of the sample observations, we use the following standard formula, giving rise to another random variable:

$$M = \sum_j X_j / n$$

When we compute the variance of the sample observations, we use another standard formula, as follows:

$$S = \sum_j (X_j - M)^2 / (n - 1)$$

We wish to know the probability distribution of the sample average M. It turns out that this distribution is approximately normal if n is reasonably large, due to the Central Limit Theorem. Since this result allows us to deal with a normal distribution, we need a mean and variance in order to specify the distribution completely, and for this purpose, we use the observed values of M and S. In particular, the linearity property of expected values leads to the following result:

$$E[M] = \mu$$

This result means that when we treat the sample average as a random variable, its mean value is μ, identical to the mean of the unknown distribution for X_j.

FIGURE A3.11 Distribution of the Sample Average

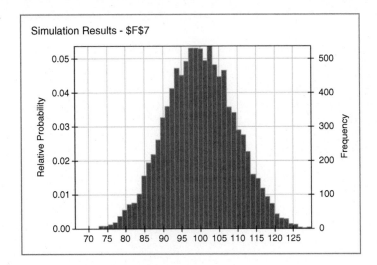

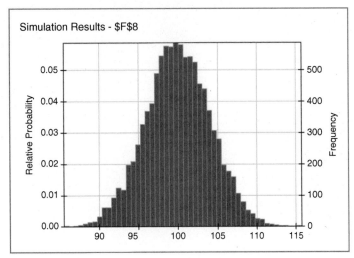

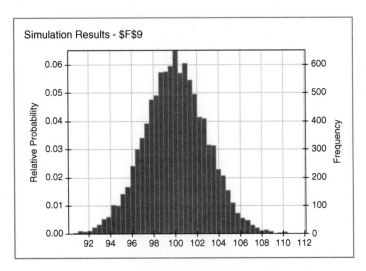

A companion result states that the variance of the random variable M is equal to σ^2/n. Thus, when we treat the sample average as a random variable, its variance is equal to the variance of the unknown distribution for X_j, divided by the sample size. It follows that in a large sample, the variance of M is small. Figure A3.11 illustrates this result by showing the distribution of the sample average when sampling from a uniform distribution with a minimum of 50 and a maximum of 150 for three sample sizes: 10, 50, and 100. The charts show that the variability in the sample average declines as the sample size increases.

Index